PENGUIN BOOKS

OWNING UP

George Melly was born in Liverpool. He has been a professional jazz singer with John Chilton's Feetwarmers since 1974. Between 1965 and 1973 he was a pop music, film and television critic for the *Observer*. For fifteen years George Melly wrote the storylines and balloons for Wally Fawkes's (Trog) comic strip *Flook*. He has written scripts for the films *Smashing Time* (1968) and *Take a Girl Like You* (based on the Kingsley Amis novel, 1970). His books include three volumes of autobiography: *Scouse Mouse* (1984), *Rum, Bum and Concertina* (1977) and *Owning Up* (1965); *Revolt into Style* (1970); *Paris and the Surrealists* (with Michael Woods, 1991) and *Don't Tell Sybil*, a memoir of the Belgian surrealist E. L. T. Mesens.

George Melly

OWNING UP: THE TRILOGY

With a new introduction and afterword
by the author

PENGUIN BOOKS

For Kezzie soon
and
Django eventually

PENGUIN BOOKS

Published by the Penguin Group
Penguin Books Ltd, 27 Wrights Lane, London W8 5TZ, England
Penguin Putnam Inc., 375 Hudson Street, New York, New York 10014, USA
Penguin Books Australia Ltd, Ringwood, Victoria, Australia
Penguin Books Canada Ltd, 10 Alcorn Avenue, Toronto, Ontario, Canada M4V 3B2
Penguin Books India (P) Ltd, 11, Community Centre, Panchsheel Park, New Delhi - 110 017, India
Penguin Books (NZ) Ltd, Private Bag 102902, NSMC, Auckland, New Zealand
Penguin Books (South Africa) (Pty) Ltd, 5 Watkins Street, Denver Ext 4, Johannesburg 2094, South Africa

Owning Up first published by Weidenfeld & Nicolson 1965
Rum, Bum and Concertina first published by Weidenfeld & Nicolson 1977
Scouse Mouse first published by Weidenfeld & Nicolson 1984
Published with a new introduction and afterword as a Classic Penguin
in one volume under the title Owning Up: The Trilogy 2000

3

Copyright © George Melly, 1965, 1977, 1984, 2000
All rights reserved

The moral right of the author has been asserted

Set in 10.5/13 pt PostScript Monotype Sabon
Typeset by Rowland Phototypesetting Ltd, Bury St Edmunds, Suffolk
Printed in Great Britain by CPI UK

CONTENTS

INTRODUCTION

Naturally I was thrilled, opening a dull post one wet February morning, to find a letter from Penguin UK offering to reprint in one volume my three separate autobiographies as part of a new series.

They told me later that the book's title is *Owning Up – The Trilogy*. This seems to me a neat solution. *Owning Up* was in fact the title of my first book, the one describing the jazz world of the fifties, but the title is equally, if not more, applicable to *Rum, Bum and Concertina,* about my naval life in the forties, and indeed it seems to me that almost any autobiography, if free of hypocrisy, cant or special pleading, might be called *Owning Up*. It is surely what a writer in this genre should aim to do.

The less agreeable aspect of the otherwise encouraging letter was that I was expected to write a 1,000-word introduction. I have in the past contributed several prefaces, and have never found it at all intimidating. One's own writing is another matter. To pass a subjective evaluation would force me to strike either self-deprecating or mock-modest Anglo-Saxon attitudes, and to avoid this essentially English predicament – for Celts, the French and, above all, the Americans suffer no such inhibitions – I will remain as objective as possible, leaving any subjective judgement to others. A cop-out!

The three volumes are printed here in chronological order – Liverpool childhood, naval service, the fifties jazz world – and there's no reason not to read them in that order. In fact, though, they were written in reverse: jazz life, bell bottoms, mewling and puking, and with quite long and irregular gaps in between; they took 19 years *in toto*. So, I write slowly, but why in reverse? I'm quite often asked this and tend to fall back on an aphorism I happened on just in time to quote it on the cover of *Scouse Mouse*. It read: 'Life is lived forwards but understood backwards.' I've no idea who wrote it, or where I read it, but it came in handy. Nor can I decide if it makes sense or just sounds as if it did. One thing I do know – it had nothing to do with the order in which I wrote my three books.

At the beginning of the sixties, regularly employed inventing the plots and dialogue for Wally 'Trog' Fawkes' strip cartoon 'Flook' in the *Daily Mail*, and fulfilling other commissions including a lot of work for the BBC, I decided to leave the jazz life and see if I could earn a living through my pen.

This decision more or less coincided with my taking up with my second and indeed current wife Diana, preceding this by only a week or two but somehow proving the certainty of chance. As an envoy to the band wagon I had contributed to *Vogue* an article describing 'A Weekend in the Jazz World' and asked Di if she thought it might expand into a book. Her response was to arrange a lunch with the publisher, her friend George Weidenfeld. George was famous for asking everyone he met to write a book for him but, unlike most of his invitees, I eventually did.

It was much harder than I had thought and I might well have jacked it in if the opening chapters hadn't been very highly recommended by a reader who turned out to be the late Julian Jebb. Thus encouraged, and rattling with Drinamil, I eventually delivered it and it was published as *Owning Up*, with a cover and illustrations by Wally 'Trog' Fawkes.

George was nervous of it. Despite the successful outcome of the Lady Chatterley trial, he worried about the four-letter words and sexual couplings – both minimal by today's standards – and to hedge his bets he didn't offer me one of his lavish launch parties. Diana and I were really pissed off about that.

In the end, apart from a predictably sour dismissal by Philip Larkin, it was well received, and George, emboldened, commissioned a second volume. For a time I couldn't decide on a subject, but then my mother, who was moving to a smaller flat, asked me if I had any use for a large box full of the letters I'd written to her from the Navy. Painfully slowly, I composed *Rum, Bum and Concertina*, this time without chemical aids.

Given the change of climate, and despite its largely homosexual theme, George was this time far less jumpy. The only thing that embarrassed him was the title, a problem he surmounted by running all the words together so that it came out as *Rumbumandconcertina*. This time we got our launch party.

George came back for a third helping and I will always be grateful, despite my affectionate mockery, for his faith in me.

With my mother becoming senile and my father long dead, I decided to go for my childhood. *Scouse Mouse* is indeed my personal favourite and was the easiest to write. I don't know why the events of over sixty years ago should be so much clearer than those of yesterday afternoon, but they are. It is also why Diana insisted that the book should be subtitled 'or I never got over it', and she and my son Tom kept a beady eye open for deeply purple passages. These became known as 'squirrels' bones', a deleted image and the most shaming example.

When first published, all three books were well received, but that was then and this is now. I hope the jokes hold up and the period detail is of some interest.

To avoid hubris I find it effective, Hamlet-like, to stare at the metaphorical skull of a once well-regarded writer. There are plenty of them knocking around the literary graveyard. Hello Angus. How's it going Colin? Well, I'll soon find out, won't I? And that's it then.

SCOUSE MOUSE

I

Place of birth: Liverpool. Year: 1926. I was born a fortnight late during an August heatwave.

This took place neither in hospital, nor in my parents' tiny flat in Linnet Lane, but a mile away in my grandfather's large house, The Grange, on the banks of the Mersey. I was a rickety-looking baby with a wobbling head and didn't take kindly to my mother's milk. It turned my stools bright green and I had to be weaned on Cow & Gate. I survived however and the Mellys were delighted. It seems to me odd that they should set such store on an heir in the direct line. There were no large estates to inherit and the money they left was always divided equally between sons and daughters.

Great-aunts Eva and Florence in their black, floor-length dresses came to view me a day or so later and I was carried out of the bedroom by the midwife for their inspection. My mother called for them to come and see her but they refused. According to their Victorian conventions it would have been improper to visit a woman so soon after an 'interesting event'.

Rather subdued at her breach of etiquette, my mother heard Florence remark to Eva in respect of me: 'What a good thing he's a Melly!'

My great-great-grandfather, André Melly, was born in Switzerland in 1802. He could trace his ancestry back to the early sixteenth century when one Jean Colombe had a son called Matthieu who later, for reasons connected with becoming a burger of Geneva, changed his name to '*Mesley ou Melly*'. Family legend held that Jean Colombe was the son or grandson of a Genoese pedlar, in itself not much of a *cachet* except that he was meant to be a direct descendant of Christopher Columbus. Certainly, to substantiate this rather nebulous claim, the family crest is a pair of doves' wings while the shield depicts a dove in an azure sky hovering above a ship sailing towards the setting sun. The motto, with no especial relevance, maintains that 'A Good Name is Better than a Golden Girdle.'

André Melly seems to have been an amiable young man, if a little solemn. In his youth he was touched by the scepticism of Voltaire, and revolutionary enough to have incurred the displeasure, through some remarks overheard at a café table, of the Neapolitan Government. For several years afterwards, when travelling on the Continent, he was closely watched by secret police and put to some inconvenience. He later regained his faith and became a model of propriety.

In the 1820s he emigrated to England and engaged in business, mostly in Manchester and Liverpool. His probity was such that, during the financial crisis of 1825–6, he was able to ride out the storm supported by considerable loans from friends, secured without interest. He eventually married a Miss Grey, whose father was his partner, and became a naturalised citizen through a special Act of Parliament, as was necessary in those days. He suffered from migraines, played the flute adequately and was a keen entomologist; a collection of beetles he assembled and mounted is still in the museum at Geneva. An engraving reveals a marked resemblance to Schubert: curly hair, small round glasses and a stock.

His business, which was to extend to railways, was at first confined solely to cotton. He had dealings with America, but his principal activity was in Egypt, a country which had always excited his interest and was to prove the place of his death. He became, in the 1820s, the Liverpool agent to the Pasha, Mahomet Ali; a lucrative if anxious connection as it was forbidden for strict Muhammadans to insure their goods or to allow anyone else to do so. He was also commissioned to furnish a palace for the Pasha 'in the English style', a task he knew better than to interpret literally. His choice of ottomans with gold fringes, huge mirrors and extravagant chandeliers was well received.

In 1850 André himself set off for Egypt with his wife, his two sons, and his only daughter on an enterprise unconnected with commerce. It had long been his ambition to attempt to discover the source of the Nile, visiting its antiquities and adding to his collection of beetles *en route*. On their way back, on 1 January 1851, he was struck down by a fever from which, at 6.15pm some five days later, having first established the exact time by the angle of the sun, he died, and was buried in the native cemetery in the village of Gagee. His wife and family, after much difficulty and some danger, sadly returned to Cairo and embarked for Liverpool.

André's daughter, Louisa, never married, but his sons, Charles, the elder, and George, my great-grandfather, both did. Charles, a melancholy philanthropist with an interest in good works in general and an obsessional passion for providing drinking fountains for the working classes, bought a house for his mother and siblings on Mossley Hill, some five miles from the city centre. It was called Riverslea, and the original building was in a restrained and rather charming Regency Gothic, although Charles was to tack on a wing in the heavy Victorian revivalist taste with castellations and a tower. Riverslea stood in its own considerable grounds. Its owner, after increasing bouts of mental illness, eventually took his own life. He left eight children.

When Charles's brother, George, married in the 1850s, he deserted Riverslea and set himself up in a large and solid Georgian house in Chatham Street within walking distance of his place of business. He was of a very different temperament from his earnest father and his gloomy, if worthy, brother. He became, until his financial interests made it impracticable, the Liberal MP for Stoke-upon-Trent; he was a JP, a keen sportsman and a lively writer of amusing, if mildly snobbish, memoirs, privately printed and handsomely bound. He had seven children. His youngest son, Samuel Heywood Melly, was my grandfather.

By the time I was born the family had divided firmly, and not without a certain tart rivalry, into the Riverslea and Chatham Street Mellys; although the latter were in fact the cadet branch, they considered themselves top dogs. Both Riverslea and Chatham Street were still occupied in 1926 and were to remain so until the middle 1940s.

I don't know much about my mother's family. There are no records going back to the fifteenth century. There were rumours, not much aired, of a Polish pedlar, but unlike the Mellys' Genoese hawker this one was rather too recent to be a source of pride, nor was he believed to be descended from a famous explorer. But while the origins of my maternal grandfather, Albert Edward Isaac, may have been obscure, everything I have heard about him suggests an honourable, intelligent and very lovable man.

Teaching the piano didn't make him rich, but it provided a living sufficient to support his wife and three children in modest comfort and to employ a cook and a housemaid. His interests were broad. He was very well read – Dickens was a passion with him – and he delivered several lectures ('The Poetry of Robert Browning', 'The Modern Theatre') to the Liverpool Philomathic Society which were later published as pamphlets. He was also a keen amateur Shakespearean actor, an interest he shared with his wife and more particularly his daughter, and a considerable wit. His photographs show a handsome man with neat but luxuriant moustache. His expression is mild but alert.

My parents married about eighteen months before my birth after facing initial opposition from my father's family. There were three reasons for this. My mother was eight years older than my father. Her mother, a widow since 1912, had very little money; and she was Jewish. I don't know which of these objections was primary. The Chatham Street Mellys were not, so far as I know, particularly anti-Semitic by the standards of the twenties; their tradition was Unitarian and Liberal although, by that time, they had become both Conservative and C. of E. They were on the other hand rich, and the rich tend to favour 'a good match'. I dare say that at thirty-two they felt my mother was rather old to start a family. At all events they did what they could to break it up.

My father was then in shipping. He worked for Lamport & Holt, a firm of which his Uncle George had been Managing Director. The family arranged for him to be sent 'on business' to their office in South America for a year. He wrote to my mother on the voyage out: 'They are playing our tune – "Swanee".'

I asked him later what he remembered of South America. He only recalled, with some horror, an abattoir built like a helter-skelter; the cattle walking up a ramp snaking round the outside, to be slaughtered as they entered through a door at the top and dismembered by stages inside until their carcasses were carried out, ready to be frozen, at the base. As the animals, with their foreboding of death, were reluctant to move, they were sprinkled constantly with water and then touched with an electric prod at the base of the ramp, transmitting a visible blue flash along their wet flanks right up to the top. The shock made them push, panic-stricken, forward and upwards to their doom. Although he enjoyed shooting and fishing, my father detested gratuitous cruelty and the image remained with him always; a glimpse of hell in the otherwise even landscape of his life, for he was still training in 1918 and never saw the trenches.

When he returned to Liverpool from South America he remained obstinate in his determination to marry my mother and eventually his family caved in. His Uncle George gave her a rather fine diamond spray as a peace offering. He said it was 'to bury the hatchet'.

There were no religious objections to their union. My mother's father had been mildly orthodox but he had died, much mourned, when she was nineteen. His widow and younger son, Alan, eventually became Liberal Jews. The elder son Fred gave up religion altogether, but my mother converted, almost instantly, to the Church of England, possibly because she was a passionate dancer and some of the best dances in Liverpool were held on Friday nights.

Although there was money in the background, my father at twenty-six earned very little. My parents took a tiny flat in Linnet Lane and could afford only one cook–housemaid, an almost unheard of privation for the middle classes in 1926. My mother grew enormous during her pregnancy. When she got into bed my father would say: 'The *Dreadnought* is now in dock.'

At the time of his marriage, as my father had shown no aptitude or liking for shipping, my grandfather bought him a partnership in a firm of woolbrokers, founded by his late Uncle Hugh, and registered as 'Seward & Melly'. Here he was his own boss but, although well liked, he never displayed much enthusiasm for business. He told me once that he would have chosen to manage a country estate but that the family wouldn't hear of it. Burdened by expectations – he was to inherit a considerable fortune from his mother only a few years before his own early death in 1961 – he did what was expected of him. His last words to me were: 'Always do what you want to. I never did.'

*

I was in Liverpool recently, singing for two nights at Kirklands, originally an elegant nineteenth-century bakery, now a wine bar with a music room above it. I stayed, as I usually do, with the painter and poet Adrian Henri and his companion, the poet Carol Ann Duffy. Before my second gig, Adrian having left to recite his poems somewhere in Cumbria, I invited Carol Ann to dine with me in a bistro in Lark Lane in the suburb of Sefton Park and as it was a fine evening in late March, I suggested we took a short bus ride to the gates of Prince's Park and walked from there. Carol Ann didn't know this part of Liverpool very well, but I did. It was where I lived until I left to work in London in the late forties.

We caught the bus opposite The Rialto, a 'Moorish' cinema built during the twenties and now a furniture store, and moved smoothly up Prince's Boulevard. There is a statue of a Victorian statesman at each end of the tree-lined yellow gravel walk running up its centre, and I could see the ghosts of the tramlines where the 33 used to rattle and sway from the Pier Head to distant Garston. My maternal grandmother always advised her friends to wait for a 33. It took, in her view, 'a prettier way' than either the 1 or the 45 which ran to the Dingle through slums and dilapidated shops closer to the river.

Prince's Park, an alternative childhood walk to the far larger, almost adjacent Sefton Park, is long and narrow, surrounded by the backs of big houses and mansion blocks, and enclosing a chain of artificial lakes, duck-strewn and the colour of Brown Windsor soup, fenced in by croquet-hoop-like railings. At the entrance to the lakes is a small gravestone commemorating 'Judy, the children's friend', a donkey which died at an advanced age in 1924. My mother, wearing a sailor's blouse and a wide straw hat, had ridden on Judy as a child. On the edge of the largest of the lakes is a disused boathouse in the style of a Swiss chalet; a mode much favoured at the turn of the century for park-keepers' lodges and other small municipal buildings connected with recreation. At the end of the lakes the park, shedding its shrubs and marshalled flower beds, widens out into a bare and scruffy valley with trees on the further slope. Carol Ann and I left the park and, crossing Ullet Road, entered the district of Lark Lane itself.

Ullet Road is, I was always being told, a corruption of Owlet Road and, given that Linnet Lane runs off it at right angles to meet

Lark Lane, I think this is probably the case. At the other end of Ullet Road is the Dingle where the 33, leaving 'the prettier way' behind it, joined up again with the 1 and 45 emerging from the slums to service Aigburth Road. Ahead of us, enclosed within this rectangle, lay my childhood.

Most of the suburb consists of Victorian and Edwardian family houses with quite large gardens, but within it is a smaller, more consistent grid of streets and it was through these we strolled. Built presumably by a firm of speculative architects, the three-storeyed terraces are named after the novels of Sir Walter Scott and display late nineteenth-century romanticism on an absurdly miniature scale. Of red or yellow brick, detailed in local sandstone or ceramic tiling, bulging with bay windows, bristling with useless little towers and pinnacles, they pay homage to the fag-end of the Pre-Raphaelite dream of Medieval England. Crossing Tristram, Waverley and Bertram Roads, walking down Marmion Road, we emerged into Ivanhoe Road where my parents, having given up their flat in Linnet Lane before I had time to become conscious of my surroundings, had rented Number 22.

I pointed it out to Carol Ann, telling her that there used to be a dairy behind the house with its own cows. Born into the age of the great milk combines, she found this hard to believe so we turned the corner. There was the arch into Hogg's Dairy with the name still painted on a fading sign over the entrance and the cowsheds surrounding the small yard. Furthermore, although the cows are long gone, it is still in use as a piggery. We walked inside and the pigs, with their beady eyes, grunted and strained up at us from their odoriferous pens inside the sheds. A man in his thirties came out of the office built into the side of the deep arch. I asked him about Tommy Hogg who smelt sourly of milk and was something of a ladies' man, walking out successively with several of our maids. 'My Uncle Tommy,' he said. 'He died two years ago.'

The cows had lodged there only in the winter. It was one of the signs that summer had arrived to watch them, herded by Tommy and his father, lowing their way down busy Aigburth Road to graze in the fields of a small farm which lay between the river and Aigburth Vale. Despite the 'Picture Houses', trams and shops, little pockets of rural life persisted then at the ends of cobbled 'unadopted' lanes. We said goodbye to Tommy Hogg's nephew.

Repassing our 'entry', the local name for those narrow high-walled alleys skirting the back-yards, we crossed Ivanhoe Road. There was what used to be a fire station on the opposite corner, an elaborate little Ruritanian building. I once dreamt that my mother, screaming silently, gave birth to a child in one of its empty rooms with me present but unable to help. Another thirty yards and we were in Lark Lane itself, the great sandstone gate-posts to Sefton Park visible at the far end.

Lark Lane is a shopping street. Some of the shops I remember are still there, although most have changed their names: a grocer's, a fishmonger's, a florist's, two cake shops, several tobacconists and sweet shops, a saddler's (gone), a wine merchant's, an undertaker's, and a small Gothic police station. Most of the shops delivered. They knew their customers by name, and had pretended to admire them in their prams, and the under-takers measured them up when they died.

As we were still a bit early for dinner, Carol Ann and I went into The Albert, a handsome, château-like public house built in the 1880s with a walled bowling green behind it. My father had used The Albert almost every day of his adult life and twice on Sundays. Inside, some disastrous 'improvements' have been made in recent years. The old smoke room is now a smart cocktail lounge, the engraved mirrors are gone and so are the bronze horses rearing up on the high mantelpiece over a coal fire, but there is still the barley-sugar Corinthian column in the public, the fine mahogany bar, the elaborate plaster-work ceilings, orange with tobacco smoke. We had a couple of drinks and I thought of my father sitting with his circle: Jack and Maisy Forster, 'Boy' Henshaw, Copper and Donald Carmichael, 'the Major'.

Lark Lane had its quota of unfortunates when I was young: an errand boy with so large a goitre bulging from his neck that he had to lean sideways on his heavy bicycle to keep his balance; an old woman whose feet in their surgical boots were turned inwards so that she had to lift one above the other to move forwards; a huge man, the son of a police sergeant, who was simple and had been, so they said, castrated because he had molested children. Despite this he had alarmed my parents by offering to take my younger brother to 'see some chickens', but Bill had sensibly refused and run safely home. There was another simpleton, harmless and much loved. He was small and wore a huge cap. His name was 'Silly Syd' and he would stand up in the local cinemas during the ice-cream interval and shout out: 'Give me a penny, I'm daft.'

Carol Ann told me that Lark Lane was becoming quite fashionable. There was a wine bar nearer the park. The bistro, a word and concept unknown to my parents, stands on a corner with big windows along both sides. It was a junk-shop in the fifties and before that a record shop. I had bought many of my first jazz 78s there in the holidays from Stowe and on leave from the Navy.

You 'come-to' as a child as if from a major operation. Pink blurs loom up, solidify into faces, become recognisable. Objects materialise. Continuity establishes itself.

Early memory is fragmentary: a boxful of unsorted snaps, many of them of people and places whose significance is lost; a few film clips of random lengths shown in no particular order. Nor is it possible to distinguish in retrospect between what you can really remember and what you were told later, and anyway many early memories are false.

I am sitting beside my mother in an open car. She is driving along a seaside promenade festooned with fairy lights at night. Everything is in shades of milky blue: the sea, the pier, the boarding houses. I am very happy. I smile up at my glamorous mother. The only flaw is that my mother never drove a car.

A real one. A maid, a friend of my nanny's, is hanging up sheets in a small garden on the side of a house opposite ours in Ivanhoe Road. A blue sky full of little clouds, blossom on a stunted soot-black tree, the sheets very white, the arms of the maid red from the suds, the whole composition cramped and angular, without depth. Why this image chosen from so many which have been forgotten? Why a white horse galloping across a green hillside in North Wales lit by brilliant sunshine under a dark sky? Early memory has no discrimination. When everything is equal, without associations, without any meaning beyond itself, there is no measure available, no scale. My mother drives her car; the maid hangs up the washing (wooden pegs bought from gypsies who came to the door); the white horse gallops under the dark sky.

I was a discontented baby. My mother, to amuse me later, would recreate her nights in that small bedroom in the flat in Linnet Lane. A whimper leading to a prolonged wail. Her leap from the bed before my father could wake up. Her walking the floor, rocking me in her arms, crooning one of two songs: Paul Robeson's 'Curly-headed babby' or Harrow's 'Forty Years On'. My subsidence into silence and careful replacement in my cot. Her return to bed. The approach of sleep. A whimper leading to a prolonged wail . . .

On my afternoon walk I would scream in my pram and could only be quietened by her drawing an umbrella along the railings. By the time we moved to Ivanhoe Road my parents could afford and had room for a nanny, and anyway I was beyond the screaming stage.

We spent my early summer holidays in Llandudno or Colwyn Bay, those adjacent Victorian seaside resorts on the coast of North Wales. My maternal grandmother was often with us. My nanny, Bella, always. My father would spend a fortnight there and commute at weekends for the rest of the month. Sometimes his parents visited us in their chauffeur-driven car. Still an only child I exercised an iron will, insisting on a rigid and rather extravagant routine: a visit to the pier to feed the seagulls, to watch them banking down out of the salt air, beady-eyed and sharp-billed, to grab the biscuits. The biscuits came from a special kiosk. There was a notice in its window: 'the biscuits the birds like'. The birds were selective in their tastes; the biscuits they liked were rather expensive. Soon it was time for Punch and Judy, for which I early developed a passion which has never left me.

The Professor was called Codman. He was a Liverpudlian who during the winter months performed on the steps of St George's Hall in the city centre, and in consequence Punch and his victims all affected a strong, if squeaky, Liverpool accent and always will have in my ears. I soon knew most of the script by heart, deriving deep satisfaction from the thwack of Punch's stick, and his raucous pleasure in his own wickedness. I didn't mind the crocodile, accepting that Punch could believe, until the very moment his nose was between its jaws, that it was a domestic cat, but when the ghost appeared to drag him gibbering down to hell, I demanded, panic-stricken, to be taken away.

The afternoons, while less crippling financially, were given over to equally obsessional activities. My projects were either the removal of innumerable stones from one part of the beach to another or the filling of a bucket from a rock pool and emptying it at a given point above the tideline. The first exercise was called 'Stones', the second 'Bucket-a-boat'. I was prepared to spend several hours alone engrossed in these monotonous tasks, but preferred to enlist an adult working under my direction. Few were amenable for long with the exception of my patient, if rarely available, grandfather dressed, as always, in a grey homberg hat the same colour as his full moustache and wearing a three-piece dark suit of antique cut with a watch-chain across the waistcoat, and a starched butterfly collar – his bare feet and rolled up trousers the only concession he was prepared to make to the sartorial licence of the seaside. While we worked he would whistle tunelessly through his false teeth, an habitual mannerism which used to drive my mother mad with irritation. He smelt, deliciously, of Turkish cigarettes.

There were other entertainments. The pier itself with its salt-corroded penny-in-the-slot machines. There was 'The Haunted House' and 'The Execution of Mary Queen of Scots'. Of these I preferred the latter: two doors slowly opening on the façade of a castle, the executioner bringing down his axe, the Queen's head tumbling into the basket, the doors banging shut. I was mystified as to how the head rejoined the trunk in time for the next penny. There was also a 'What the Butler Saw' machine. I enjoyed turning the handle very fast so that the fly-stained sepia image of a massive-thighed Edwardian lady was forced to remove her voluminous clothing at breakneck speed.

There was a concert party which, until I was old enough to understand the jokes, my parents enjoyed rather more than I did. What they liked was it being so hopeless. There was a sketch one year, an exchange between the 'light' and 'low' comedians about a family called 'The Biggers'. It described how the little Bigger had grown bigger than the bigger Bigger and so on. 'I see', said the 'low' comedian at the conclusion of this rigmarole, 'there's been a bit of bother at the Biggers.' My parents laughed so much at this that a young man, sitting alone in a deck chair in the row ahead of them, turned indignantly round and told them it wasn't kind to laugh at him just because he had red hair.

Sometimes I was put on a donkey but I didn't enjoy it much especially when the donkey man would run with it jogging me up and down on its fat, yet bony, back. Nor did I appreciate being taught to feed a pony in a small enclosed field in front of our boarding house. My maternal grandmother, who was fond of animals, insisted I did this, balancing the lump of sugar on the palm of my hand, bending back my fingers to avoid them being nibbled. I can still feel the pony's wet, warm, snuffling breath and see its dilating hairy nostrils. Often I would drop the sugar and she'd make me start again. She believed, unlike my mother, in discipline or at any rate didn't lack the courage to apply it. My mother feared unpopularity, however short-lived, even from a child. 'When did you last punish George?' my grandmother asked her once. She couldn't remember.

They were happy holidays. I was the centre of attention, my every word repeated later to others in my hearing as though a miracle of wit or perception, every pose recorded by my mother's Brownie: the birds were fed on the biscuits they preferred, the stones were shifted, the water transported, and Punch was dragged squeaking and whacking his way along the road to perdition on the pebbly beach against the grey horizon.

As to why Llandudno comes back to me in such sharp focus from a time when Liverpool still seems fragmentary and vague I have, although it is apparently a common experience, no explanation. Perhaps the frame of the holiday, its yearly repetition clarified by growing terms of reference, developed and printed it in the dark-room of memory.

2

Number 22 Ivanhoe Road – a three-storey terrace house with steep
front steps set back in a tiny front garden with a low wall. Behind
its ornate brickwork and sash windows I spent most of the first
nine years of my life. There were six of us living there to start
with. My mother and father, my nanny Bella, a cook and a house
parlour-maid. Later there was also my brother and, for a short
time, my sister.

Opening the façade as if it were a doll's house; thinking of it as
a setting for a play described by the dramatist before the maid
enters to answer the telephone; this is how it was arranged.

Behind the front door, to the right, a small pram-room with just
enough space for the pram and later tricycles or fairy cycles. The
pram an imposing object, its rubbery smell, deriving presumably
from its concertina hood and clip-on cover, scented the room. After
the war, unless very grand, it was rather 'common' to own a big
pram; push-chairs, as battered as possible, became fashionable,
but in the thirties the middle classes subscribed to these imposing
objects, the insides of which could be adjusted later to accommodate
sitting toddlers. Dark and highly polished, the pram, with its large
spoked wheels, remained closer to a horse-drawn carriage than a
motor car.

Facing the pram-room was the lounge. It was called that as a sign
of modernity, implying gin before dinner instead of sherry, and the
use of lipstick. My grandparents and great-uncles and aunts had
drawing-rooms. There was a great deal of furniture in that small
lounge: a 'baby grand' piano which my mother used to tell visitors
was 'off a ship', its top covered with framed and signed photographs
of actors and actresses she knew; a rather 'good' bookcase, glass-
fronted shelves above, a cupboard below in which my father stored

several cartons of Black Cat cigarettes in their tin boxes from which to fill his case. There were easy chairs and a sofa before the fireplace and, in front of the sofa, a long low oak stool with a webbed leather top with the *Radio Times* on it. In winter there was a coal fire in the modern grate, protected when the room was empty by a winged brass-netted guard, and the coal was kept in a beaten brass scuttle. There were two standard lamps, their bases in twenties black lacquer with gold dragons climbing up them and parchment shades.

In the space beyond was my mother's desk with its reproduction Chippendale chair and, within reach on a little round-topped table, the flower-like, long-stemmed telephone. Opposite the desk, between the tail of the piano and the windows, was a wireless set (eventually to be replaced by a radiogram), with its heavy acid-filled batteries and its fretwork cloth-backed front. There was a built-in window seat. The carpet wasn't fitted, the surrounding floorboards were stained a shiny black. The colour scheme, in keeping with calling it the lounge, was rather 'daring': cream wallpaper, oatmeal loose covers, and burnt orange curtains and cushions. There were no pictures in the room.

Next to the lounge, facing the bottom of the stairs, was the dining-room. It looked out over the back-yard, a scruffy little square of grass with an outside lavatory for the maids smelling strongly of Jeyes fluid, and a shed of the kind much-advertised in the back pages of the *Radio Times* against the far wall, next to a back door leading into the entry. You couldn't see the back-yard from the dining-room because there were net curtains covering the bottom half of the window.

The dining-room, unlike the lounge, was entirely traditional except for its hemp carpet. There was a polished table with two leaves, Georgian chairs, a small glass-topped carving table, a corner cupboard and a square piano, bought for five pounds in an auction and wrongly believed to be a spinet. On the square piano, leaning against the wall, was a tray – a wedding present, with a collage of different kinds of Brussels lace arranged symmetrically behind its glass surface. There was a grandfather clock in the corner by the window with a phoenix painted on the face. My father wound it up on Sunday mornings after lunch. It gave me great pleasure to watch the heavy weights ascending on their chains as he did so, and to see the adjustable pendulum swinging to and fro through the narrow open door in the case. In the corner cupboard were heavy cut-glass tumblers, engraved burgundy glasses in beautiful glowing colours, claret glasses and liqueur glasses. Yet my parents, unlike my grandfather's generation, never drank wine; indeed, my mother never drank at all.

On the walls were early nineteenth-century hunting and shooting prints: 'The View', 'Gone to Ground', 'The Kill' and gentlemen in frock coats and top coats bringing down partridges, snipe, and pheasants. The dining-room was warmed by a gas fire with fragile clay elements which slotted in over the jets. Gas fires then tended to bang loudly when you lit them, and sometimes when you switched them off. I imagine some early experience of this must have alarmed me deeply as I still have a phobia about lighting gas appliances, allied to a reluctance to open – although not to drink – champagne.

The only other door off the hall was at the back and covered with a fringed brown curtain on a brass rail to show that it led to the kitchen. This was far from streamlined. The solid wooden cupboards and drawers had big wooden handles, primitively carved curly bits at the corners and were painted white. There was a big, old-fashioned gas-stove and two battered wicker chairs in front of the grate, a scrubbed wooden table with kitchen chairs, a clothes pulley which squeaked when you raised or lowered it and, hanging from the light bulb, a sticky fly-paper textured with the corpses of many a summer's bluebottle, plump on the manure of Hogg's cows. There was no fridge, but in the back kitchen, with its sink and draining-board, was a wooden wire-meshed meat safe. Bread, flour and rice were kept in big round enamel tins, raisins, tapioca and sultanas in smaller editions of the same, and most of the shelves were covered in gingham-patterned oil-cloth for 'easier cleaning'.

The hall itself had comparatively little in it. There was an oak 'footman's chair', rather out of scale, and below the stairs a chest dated 1694 in which my father kept his rods and guns. On the chest was a little brass pestle and mortar and a small brass crinoline lady that was really a bell. Above it was a beautiful plate of the twenties, another wedding present. In brilliant blues, greens and gold, it represented some elves crossing a bridge in a landscape dominated by mushrooms. My mother, when I asked her later, could neither remember it nor imagine what had become of it. I expect it was broken in a move, and much regret it. It was the most magic object in the house. There was also a barometer you tapped to find out if it was going to rain and a useless and nasty little brass warming-pan.

On the first floor, up the dog-legged staircase with its carpet rods and a gate fixed across the top to stop us falling down, there was a different pattern of rooms. In the front were the nursery and the night-nursery. The night-nursery, where our nanny slept with us when we were still young, has become vague, but the nursery is as clear as if I had just left it. The floor was of dark green cork, the walls white, the furniture apple-green. There was a gas fire with a tall fender guard and in front of it a grubby, faded white rug with animals on it. There was a big toy cupboard, a table with cane-bottomed chairs, a child's table, round with four legs, and two little chairs; one curved with arms, the other with a rush seat like Van Gogh's. There was a shelf of books, mostly tattered copies of Beatrix Potter, a small sand tray with tin animals, and a big chest, once my father's tuck-box, containing a large number of wooden building blocks. There was a wind-up gramophone and a few old records, a framed print of Margaret Tarrant's sugary 'All Things Bright and Beautiful'. There were dark green blinds instead of curtains, and an ottoman in front of the windows.

Behind the nursery was my parents' bedroom, which overlooked the back-yard and the roof of Hogg's dairy. The general effect was blue largely because of the shiny blue eiderdowns on the twin beds with their dark polished headboards rounded at the corners. Twin beds for married couples, like calling the drawing-room 'the lounge', were a further proof of being 'modern'. My grandparents' generation still slept in a double bed which my parents believed to be unhygienic. Between the beds was a cupboard with a chamber-pot in it and a small drawer below containing medicines; a far from hygienic arrangement I should have thought. Although the bath-room was next door to them, my mother and father always used the pot, though my mother, as a further proof of her modernity, emptied it herself every morning instead of leaving it to the maids as my grandparents did. Over the beds were two nineteenth-century lithographs: sly Pandora and her box, and Lady Hamilton looking rather distraught. The originals were perhaps by Reynolds or Gainsborough. My mother believed them to be valuable because they were wedding presents from a rich woman. Over the gas fire was a water-colour, a gift of a local artist and 'rather modern'. It represented barges on the Seine. There was a tall mahogany wardrobe with mirrors, a quite good chest of drawers and a dressing-table in the window with silver hair brushes and a cut-glass scent spray with a bulb. My mother's jewel case had very little in it: a few rings, some art-deco clips, some earrings, a string of pearls, and Uncle George's 'peace offering'. There was a Coty powder box which was round and had a pattern of little black and orange powder puffs on it. This pattern was very important to me, but it wasn't until I saw one recently in an antique shop (£5), that I realised what the black and orange shapes represented.

The bathroom, with the only indoor lavatory, was pretty functional. My father used a heavy safety razor with a one-edged blade which he honed on a special leather strap. There was a loofah, a sponge and a pumice-stone on the wooden rack over the claw-footed bath. No bathroom was then complete without these objects.

My father's dressing-room built out over the back kitchen was tiny, although later I was to sleep in it in a child's wooden bed of Swiss origin that had been handed down from my great-grandfather. Before this it had little in it except a wardrobe and a chest of drawers with a mirror above. On the chest was a cedar-wood Chinese 'mess-box' full of collar-studs, stiffeners, golf-tees and, as I discovered later, a solitary French letter, surely by that time unreliable, which once I had learnt its function I used to show my giggling and impressed school friends. There were also some racing binoculars in a leather case, his crested hair brushes and a bottle of Bay Rum, a lotion he was later to blame for his bald patch. His use of Bay Rum with its spicy smell was untypical, imposed by a legacy of several crates left to him by a deceased acquaintance. He never used aftershaves or deodorants even after they became acceptable. He rated them on a level with carrying a pocket comb, one of his few serious taboos. There was a single picture in his dressing-room. It contained three stages of a cock fight, the cocks a collage of real feathers with only their beaks and claws drawn in. Along the walls of the bedroom floor were spidery etchings of harbours and shipping.

The top floor, under the fanciful eaves, contained the two maids' bedrooms, mysterious, seldom visited territory with fluff under the iron bedsteads and worn parquet-patterned linoleum. There was a washbasin but no bath so I presume they used the one downstairs, but when and how often I could not say. The curtains were thin, the wallpaper dingy.

I can seldom remember fresh flowers in the house. Owing to the Depression, my parents felt increasingly badly off, but in the hall there was an earthenware jug with Cape Gooseberries and Honesty.

It would be absurd not to admit to the obsessive spirit in my remembering so minutely the contents and decoration of an unre-markable terrace house some fifty years ago, but I have always tended to understand people initially through the objects they accumulate and the manner in which they display or conceal them.

My father's discretion is for me implicit in the way he stored his rods and guns – the proof of his frustrated desire for a country life – in the chest in the hall, while the French letter he concealed in his 'mess-box' was indicative of his low sexual drive. Similarly my mother's thwarted theatrical ambitions, only partially alleviated by her involvement in amateur dramatics, were more openly expressed by the display of the signed photographs of past and present members of the Liverpool rep on the top of the piano 'off a ship', but these conclusions are of course retrospective.

It is impossible for an adult to paint with the naivety of a child; the huge parents with their great heads and stick-like limbs, the neat formalised house, far too small to contain them, the grinning sun smiling down. It is equally beyond me to recreate how I saw my parents when I was very young, but there are two tableaux which do so for me.

The nursery at breakfast time: Bella and I seated in front of a different dish every day: fish cakes, grilled tomatoes on fried bread, kedgeree, eggs in various forms. My father liked to eat with me before he left for the office, standing in front of the window with a bowl of Grapenuts, and staring abstractedly into Ivanhoe Road. He usually said little but some mornings there would be the sound of intermittent muffled hooting from the tugs on the Mersey a mile or so away. His response to this was always identical. Joining the words together he would observe, 'It's foggy on the river.'

I have the impression that this response was not his originally, but something he remembered from his own Edwardian childhood. His life was much ruled by such formal responses. Many snatches of verse, the choruses of music-hall and popular songs, repetitive physical gestures (rubbing the skin between the base of the left thumb and forefinger with the thumb of the opposite hand), seemed to act as runes against the dangerous chaos of life. Potentially clever, it was as if he had deliberately trained himself to aim low. It made him an easy companion. His lack of competitiveness prevented any tension between us as I grew older. He was genuinely pleased at anything his children achieved but, on the negative side, offered us no incentive. 'As long as they're happy' was his reaction to whatever we did or didn't do. Good-looking, and with an easy charm and a quiet wit, he was ruled by lethargy. My mother used to say, and he didn't contradict her: 'Tom's motto is never do today what you can put off until tomorrow week.'

She on the contrary was intensely ambitious and, I believe, very highly sexed. In neither direction was she fulfilled. Her ambitions were displaced; it was her children to whom she looked in order to realise them. Her sexuality was inhibited by her fear of the opinion of others. Only once, she told me later, was she nearly unfaithful to my father. In Chester at a dance (Tom must have been away fishing) a young man tried to persuade her to spend the night in an hotel. She was tempted to accept but finally refused on the grounds that she would have been forced to return home next morning in her evening dress. She sublimated her libido by a series of what she called 'affairs' with young homosexuals, revelling in their confidences and delighting in their company. This suited my father very well as there were comparatively few plays, and certainly no ballets, that he wished to see.

Every evening when my father was at The Albert I would be taken down to spend an hour with my mother in the lounge. She would put on a very elaborate performance for my benefit, reading a certain amount, *The Jungle Books* were my favourite, imitating music-hall and cabaret artistes, and speaking of her early life in a rather indiscreet and grown-up way which widened its scope rapidly as I grew older and proved myself a precocious pupil at her knee.

I especially liked her to 'do' accents. Her Liverpool was perfect, her cockney adequate, if stagey, and she could manage a fair approximation of Welsh, Lancashire, Scottish and Irish. It amused her to imitate a woman called Alice Delysia, who performed monologues in English with a French accent, but what impressed me most was when she recreated an American colonel she had met during the war. 'Lady,' she'd say with a broad twang, 'do you mind if I spit in the fire?' and she would then swing round to face the grate and pretend to expectorate. For a long time afterwards I was convinced that all Americans indulged in this inexplicable custom.

In fact, despite her ear for accents, my mother had never been abroad except once, as a child, to the Isle of Man. She claimed, although a strong swimmer, to be afraid of the sea, but I believe it was more a question of insularity.

'Everyone says I'd adore New York,' she told me, 'and that New York would adore me, but . . .' Everyone in this case was a few of her more cosmopolitan friends. She did however go to London once a year and, on her return, loaded with toys from Hamleys, would paint it in glowing colours. 'I did five shows in four days,' she'd tell us, 'and had supper twice at the Savoy with Rex Evans.' Rex Evans was a night-club owner of the period, a plump and bespectacled man who performed sophisticated songs at the piano. He stood high in her pantheon. My father was delighted that Rex Evans should take my mother to the Savoy. He himself was rather intimidated by London and would never go there if he could avoid it. As to the Savoy, he would have considered that a waste of money, as in some ways, and especially when it came to eating out, he was almost comically mean.

There was another aspect of those evenings I spent with my mother about which I had mixed feelings, and that was her recitation of several late-Victorian poems recalled from her childhood which she would send up in such a way that I soon realized that I was meant to be amused by their pathos, but which nevertheless moved me to furtive tears. One told of a cockney orphan girl returning to her sick little brother with some flowers presented her by 'a bang-up lady' who had learnt of his plight. 'Flowers in 'eaven? I suppose so,' she replies in answer to his loaded question. Predictably, in the final verse, he is in a position to find out the answer to this theological conundrum.

Starving waifs watching a banquet; 'naughty little Briar Rose' who saved a village from flooding at the cost of her own, until then worthless, life; and a criminal 'Burglar Bill' who breaks into a doll's house at the request of a winsome tot; were others who figured in her repertoire. I dare say she knew she upset me with these mawkish poems, but was unable to resist so receptive an audience. As a child, she told me, she had once recited a poem about the Boer War, then in progress, at a benefit concert. She had no idea what it meant but had even so reduced many of her audience to tears.

'You've seen them dragging the guns along at the Agricultural Hall,' she'd lisped, 'But nobody saw them at Ladysmith when the shells began to fall'; and as the widows and mothers who had lost husbands and sons 'in far Natal' sobbed into their black-edged handkerchiefs, she experienced a glow of pride.

While not beautiful or even pretty, my mother was both animated and vivacious. She should have been an actress, but her mother wouldn't have it. Once, and it was typical of my grandmother, she had taken my mother aged sixteen to an audition held by a Shakespearian actor–manager who was so impressed that he offered her an immediate position in his company. 'I wouldn't dream of allowing Maud to go on the stage,' said my grandmother; 'I just wanted to find out how good she was.'

My mother told this as a kind of joke at her mother's expense, but I believe it had upset her profoundly. She also maintained she wouldn't have liked acting anyway as she had too jealous and envious a temperament, but I didn't believe her, even then.

When my father came home from The Albert, he and my mother would go up and change for dinner and Bella took me away to be given Horlicks and ginger biscuits and got ready for bed. My parents always came in to hear my prayers and kiss me goodnight, and I fell asleep thinking of the dying boy with flowers and the drowning Briar Rose and the American colonel spitting in the fire.

Although my parents employed a series of house parlour-maids wearing black uniforms, aprons and caps, I can recall none of them during my early childhood. The people I remember clearly were my nanny Bella and the cook, Minnie Roberts, partly no doubt because they came and went several times throughout my childhood, sometimes on a temporary, sometimes on a more permanent basis, and remained in contact with the family throughout.

Bella had red hair and was given to what my mother called 'moods'. Nevertheless she was admitted to be 'superior', that is to say, quiet rather than raucous, and with a minimal Liverpool accent, although she did say 'buke' and 'luke' instead of 'book' and 'look', and was so convinced this was correct that she tried to teach me to do the same. She was firm but fair and had a strong sense of humour although when she was amused she would compress her lips and shake with silent laughter as though reluctant to display her teeth. She was a strong believer in routine insisting, before I was old enough to use the lavatory, that I sat on my pot until I'd been a 'good boy' or, if nothing was forthcoming, dosing me on syrup of figs. Every morning she cleaned out my earholes with a twist of cotton wool, its tip coated in vaseline, and examined my tongue. She tried to make me eat everything up, and put me reluctantly to rest every afternoon for precisely one hour.

My father, who was also fond of her, called her 'Mrs Spilsbury', after the eminent forensic expert Sir Bernard Spilsbury whose close examination of the corpses of murder victims had sent several poisoners to the gallows. The reason for this nickname was that Bella was always bringing him food to sniff in order to confirm her opinion that it had 'gone off'. She was a strong swimmer and had once entered a contest which entailed battling against treacherous currents around the Great Orme in Llandudno. It transpired later that the other two entries were professionals and in consequence Bella came in very much last, but nevertheless finished the gruelling course. Bella stayed with us initially for at least five years, before she left to marry a long-distance lorry-driver called Jack, a gentle giant of a man who adored his small wife. Eventually they had a daughter called Beryl, who was very pretty and adept at tap-dancing in the manner of Shirley Temple. Unfortunately, Jack didn't live very long and it was then that Bella returned to us.

One afternoon, when Jack and Bella were still courting and I was about three, instead of walking in Prince's or Sefton Park, she pushed my pram down Aigburth Road as far as the rather run-down district of Garston and off into a maze of streets which led eventually to the yard somewhere near the Mersey where Jack's employer housed his lorries. They loomed up all around me like elephants and Jack lifted me high into one of the driving compartments and allowed me to pretend to steer with the great wheel. The yard was paved with cinders and had its own petrol pump. It was a hot summer's day, the sky was bright blue, the river sparkled and beyond it the Welsh mountains, some fifty miles away, appeared surprisingly close. That visit to Jack's yard remains loaded with inexplicable significance. I felt a party to their happiness, almost a conspirator.

Minnie Roberts and Bella were very close. Minnie was a lively woman with springy dark hair, strong glasses, and the rapid high-pitched cadences of her native North Wales. She was adept at creating a sense of excitement at the thought of treats to come, in particular of the promise of 'the beano' when my parents and Bella should chance to be absent at the same time. This didn't take place for several years, although she mentioned it frequently enough to keep me in constant anticipation. When 'the beano' eventually materialised, it turned out to be a very literal event encompassing baked beans on toast and staying up half-an-hour later than usual. 'Don't tell on me now,' said Minnie Roberts, but her conspiratorial manner and frantic gaiety were sufficient to dispel any sense of anti-climax. She encouraged me, and eventually my brother and sister, to call her 'Auntie Min'.

Auntie Min was married to an almost silent man called Tom who worked on the railways. Although Auntie Min lived in, they owned their own small house the other side of Sefton Park. The parlour was very clean and full of bric-à-brac, and had that mildly disquieting atmosphere of a room used for séances or psychic consultations although, despite her Celtic blood, Auntie Min was in no way 'gifted' in that direction. She was what was called 'a good plain cook', which suited my father who disliked elaborate dishes. Otherwise, apart from his insistence on finishing every meal with a savoury, he was not at all fussy. My mother on the other hand had a very sweet tooth. 'I put sugar on everything,' she'd say as though it were somehow a proof of her worldliness, 'even salad, and I love

Chicken Maryland – that's a *banana* with *fried* chicken.' In fact however she was perfectly satisfied with Auntie Min's roasts, stews and over-cooked vegetables.

Apart from the anonymous housemaids, there was only one other creature in the house: a fat neuter tabby cat called Joey who lived entirely in the kitchen. My mother felt a cat to be necessary to discourage the mice, but she couldn't bear him anywhere near her. She put this down to a dream she'd had as a child in which she'd found herself lying on a bed of partly squashed kittens scratching and biting in their death-throes. Her mother had thought this phobia ridiculous and insisted on having her daughter, aged ten, photographed stroking, with a look of agonised repulsion, a kitten seated on a velvet cushion.

When I was three my brother Bill was born. Unlike me with my reluctance to leave the womb, he was minimally ahead of schedule. My mother's waters broke on the lavatory and I was rushed round by Bella to my maternal grandmother's flat a quarter of a mile away. Again, whereas I had been underweight and fractious, Bill was plump and contented, but it was not for a year or two that I recognised in him a distinct threat to my position. With his blue eyes, curls and sturdy body, he was an infinitely more attractive child. His nature too was sunny and his manner easy and agreeable but worse, from my point of view, he was adept at learning necessary skills. He could do up his shoelaces long before I could and whereas I was seven before I could read, he could manage it at four and a half. His socks stayed up where mine fell down. He enjoyed physical exertion where I detested it. Admittedly there was a tendency to smugness in his reiterated cry, 'I can do it easily', but then he usually could.

Nemesis paid him out in one direction only. We both ran through the gamut of what were known as 'childish ailments': German and common-or-garden measles, scarlet fever, chicken-pox, mumps and whooping-cough but, although I nearly died of influenza when I was about six, Bill was continuously plagued by recurrent and painful attacks of toothache and earache. Huge water blisters like army pill boxes erupted on his fair skin (they had to be pricked with a sterilized needle and the empty carapace removed with tweezers, an operation which gave me enormous satisfaction). He had a hard time, frequently toddling into my parents' bedroom in the small hours sobbing: 'Why do I get everything?' Otherwise I suffered from the comparison, not from Bella or Auntie Min, although the former could sometimes become exasperated by my ham-fisted obstinacy in contrast to Bill's adeptness, and certainly not from my parents. My eagerness to show off appealed to my mother; my rebellious streak struck a suppressed chord in my father's nature. But most relations and certainly other children's nannies and their employers favoured Bill. I, who had been king of the castle, the centre of attention, the repository of lineal hopes, was entirely overshadowed by this golden child to such an extent that my mother felt obliged as some visitor lavished attention on him to cry out in defence of her less-favoured first-born: 'George has his fans too.'

My revenge lay in my discovery that Bill was a highly conventional little boy. On our walks, for instance, if he refused to agree to some whim of mine, I would threaten to pretend to have a fit approaching strangers and would have my way. If I wanted some of his dinner I would tell him, while Bella was out, that the source of the meat was a dead tortoise which had ended its life writhing with maggots and, as he had a queasy stomach, we would rapidly change plates. Although I was sometimes caught out and reprimanded severely for tormenting him, he never sneaked on me, partly because he had from his earliest years an understanding of the correct code, and perhaps also because he suspected, quite accurately, that I would invent other and worse revenges if he were to do so. We quarrelled continuously as children, but later got on much better. My mother chose to date this from his emergency operation for a ruptured appendix during which, for a whole night, his life hung in the balance – a typically dramatic explanation on her part. My own view is that our improving relationship was more gradual and due to my realisation that our potentials were so different that we were not really in competition.

3

My mother and her brothers, Fred and Alan, usually called their mother 'Griff' when speaking to her directly and 'the Griff' when referring to her in the third person. This nickname was an invention of my Uncle Fred who had once introduced her, assuming the accent of a fairground barker or circus ringmaster, as 'The only Griff in captivity'. He was adept at such nonsense. When my grandmother and I played duets together at the upright piano, she inevitably and rightly critical of my lack of concentration, he would announce us as 'those famous virtuosi of the keyboard, Mr Umpty-Plum and Mrs Oochamacootch'.

'The Griff' suited my grandmother. It seemed to encapsulate her neat fastidiousness, her small but upright stature, her horn-rimmed glasses, her feet, permanently set at 'quarter to four' (another observation of Uncle Fred's), the result of a broken ankle sustained while playing golf. We children called her 'Gaga', presumably due to my early inability to pronounce 'Granny'. With its implication of senility she never liked this and was always trying to get us to amend it to 'Gargie', but we never did.

My mother and the Griff didn't get on all that well. Many women of the Griff's generation deliberately prevented their daughters from marrying so as to have the use of an unpaid companion and dogsbody. There were many such elderly and embittered spinsters in our neighbourhood whom we would meet while shopping and whose entire conversation centred nervously around 'Mother'. The Great War had helped to reinforce their ranks. They had lost sweethearts or fiancés in the trenches, and afterwards found themselves 'on the shelf'. The Griff hadn't succeeded here, nor in fairness had she wanted to, although my mother's comparatively late marriage at the age of thirty-four must have made it seem a distinct possibility. Nevertheless she tended to treat Maud as though her main duty was to be at her beck and call.

She was also a skilful tease and my mother took teasing badly. The Griff's main weapon here was the assertion that 'Maud isn't a sport'. This gibe encompassed not only my mother's refusal to play golf and bridge, both of which the Griff did, although extremely badly, but also her neither smoking nor drinking, her refusal to go abroad; and even her inability to drive a car. The Griff had once been to Knocke le Zoute in Belgium to play golf; had been 'finished' in Germany; and drove a Morris Minor very dangerously right into her early eighties. She would also ignore my mother's advice especially when she had asked for it. It wasn't beyond her to make my mother go round to her flat, some ten minutes away from Ivanhoe Road, to help her decide between two hats, only to settle inevitably on the one my mother had rejected. Furthermore when she was on holiday she would encourage my father, who needed little persuading, to linger at the golf-club bar so as to make them late for lunch, one of my mother's phobias which the Griff dismissed with a wave of her Gold Flake, although she herself expected punctuality from anyone lunching with her. Nor should one forget earlier traumas; the audition with the actor–manager, the photograph of Maud stroking the kitten. And of course, much as I loved her, it was not without some ambivalent feelings of pleasure that I would watch my mother rising to my grandmother's teasing, turning red with irritation, clenching her fists, leaving the room to conceal her repressed anger, especially as the Griff would enlist us children as conspirators.

I suspect however that at the bottom of their antipathy was my mother's grief at the early death of her beloved father and her resentment that during her childhood she had watched him treat my grandmother as though she were a precious piece of Dresden china, appearing to believe that she had done him an immense favour by marrying him. The Griff was, it's true, very spoilt. As the youngest of her family she had been pampered as a child and she had been equally indulged by her husband. Both her sons lived at home for most of her life and my mother was never far away. She had a maid and a cook who adored her despite her imperiousness. She would ring the bell and tell Mary, the quiet and pretty Irish parlour maid: 'You may poke the fire.' 'Suppose,' said my mother, 'she said "I don't want to."' As to why the Griff and my mother were on speaking terms, the reason was Maud's terror of rows, of being thought badly of, whatever the provocation. What's more in some ways, and with good reason, she admired her.

The Griff had indeed many admirable qualities: generosity, a sense of fun, self-respect. Her chests of drawers and clothes cupboards were in apple-pie order, her household accounts correct to the ha'penny, and she had never been overdrawn in her life, even after my grandfather's early death had left her for a time in comparative poverty. My mother used to say, with a certain wistfulness, 'She has a very strong character.'

With children, while firm, she showed great empathy. Her toy drawer, as orderly as the rest, was full of treasures which she would get out one at a time rather than allow us to rummage; a technique which made playtime with her very special by removing the unsettling element of choice. She had scrap-books, a top which threw out multi-coloured sparks, games of snap and animal grab, spillikins, and a kind of bingo called Housie Housie. She would buy transfers where we damped a piece of paper bearing the faint imprint of an image, pressed it on the page of an exercise book and then peeled it back to reveal a brilliantly coloured butterfly or rose. Teatime was always a treat. She would roll chocolate finger biscuits in thin bread and butter, or sculpt an apple to form a chicken with its drumsticks, peas and potatoes. She could also peel an apple so that the skin remained an unbroken spiral. She read to us well and patiently: the Blue and Red fairy tales, *The Wallypug of Wye*, *The Cuckoo Clock* and particularly the *Golliwog* books, large illustrated adventures, naturally in immaculate condition, in which the manly and ingenious Golly and some rather soppy wooden dolls emerged unscathed from terrible adventures. I still have a clear and anxious-making vision of them nearly drowning when the sea destroyed a dyke in Holland. Finally, and to the great embarrassment of my mother and our delight, she would sing and dance the favourites of her childhood: 'You should see me dance the polka', 'Tommy make room for your uncle, there's a little dear', and especially a rather frisky number called 'Now then, young men'. This went as follows:

> Now then young men don't be melancholy.
> It's my duty just to make you jolly.
> Whenever things go wrong with me I never cry or pout.

At this point she would stick out her lip and rub the corners of her eyes, and then, after a pause, she would conclude with great emphasis:

> For I *always* am, and I *mean* to be
> The jolliest girl that's out.

During the last two lines she would raise an arm above her head and jig round on one leg.

And jolly she was most of the time, but the Griff was occasionally prey to bouts of deep depression lasting for several weeks or even months. She was then convinced that she had neither friends nor money. Her conversation excluded all other themes. No friends. No money. Round and round like a pet mouse on a wheel. This was not a recent development. She had apparently always suffered from these dark visitations known to her family as 'doing herself'. During the thirties it was suggested that she might benefit from psychological help and she was persuaded, much against her will, to visit several specialists. All they accomplished was to arouse her resentful contempt. She called them 'talking fools'.

One of her obsessions when she was 'doing herself' was that all she was fit for was to work as an attendant in a station lavatory. Her eldest brother, Frederick Harvey-Samuel, a distinguished London barrister, was apprised of this by my mother who was sent to stay with him several times before the Great War, presumably in the hope of making 'a catch'. Sweeping up the ends of his luxuriant moustache, a court-room mannerism he had carried into his private life, he passed judgement.

'It would have to be Lime Street,' he said thoughtfully. 'I couldn't afford to have a sister of mine working at Edge Hill. It might have a damaging effect on my practice if it became known that Edith was employed in this capacity at a goods station.' Frederick Harvey-Samuel died before I was born, but the Griff continued to maintain that working in a station lavatory was the only resort open to her in her friendless and penniless state.

After her depressions had run their course, she would wake up one morning in the best of spirits. Life was agreeable once more. There was golf, bridge, 'runs' in the car, my mother to tease and badger, a gin and orange before lunch and a Gold Flake cigarette after it. The only lavatory she felt the need to resort to was her own. Her bathroom window was of particular dimpled glass and the same glass was let into the upper panels of the flat's front door. I have come upon this glass since, but it is only comparatively recently that I have recognised it as the source of an instant evocation of my grandmother. Despite her maid, she chose to answer the door herself, and would cry: 'Wait a minute!' (her entire conversation was punctuated by this phrase) as her blurred and faceted image materialised behind the panes. This same glass still produces a certain anxiety: Are my nails clean? My knee-length socks with their concealed elastic garters pulled up? My rebellious 'cow's lick' of hair combed back? She was very critical of such details. 'George is quite frightened of the Griff,' said my mother. And so I was, but I was very fond of her too.

I was not, however, at all frightened by the hysterical barking of her current dog as she came to open the door, although I am in general as wary of dogs as of lighting gas appliances or opening champagne. I have no idea why this should be so. My father had a spaniel when I was a baby. He had bought it for when he was invited to shoot by his uncles but it turned out to be gun-shy and given to biting people so it had to be put down. It never bit me, however, and indeed I was told later that I was extremely fond of it and pulled its ears and tail with impunity. Nor, as far as I know, was I ever bitten or menaced by any other dog. Nevertheless for as long as I can remember I have felt apprehensive of them, and my brother Bill's only, but extremely effective, riposte to my teasing during our childhood walks was to threaten to pat strange dogs, a ploy which reduced me instantly to placatory behaviour.

The Griff's dogs aroused no such atavistic anxieties because although nervous barkers – 'good house dogs' is how she described them – they were without any aggression or indeed character. What they were was indistinguishably wet with brown sentimental eyes and perpetually wagging tails. As one died, it was replaced by another which, although temporarily appealing as a puppy ('Isn't it an Uncle Wuff,' said the Griff, an expression she used for anything sweet or cuddly), soon grew up to become indistinguishable from its predecessor. They were all rather basic animals of no known breed and yet lacking the grotesque collage effect of dogs conceived on vacant lots. They might have posed for the 'D is for Dog' entry in a rather unimaginative alphabet book, yet if anyone tried to please my grandmother by offering the cliché that 'mongrels are more intelligent' she would respond firmly by insisting they were cross breeds. They were given names as banal as themselves: Jock was followed by Zip who was replaced by Peter. Jock was the first I can remember. Peter was 'put to sleep' during the war because the bombing made him hysterical. None of them resembled or grew to resemble the Griff in either appearance or character.

The 'cross-breed' syndrome was typical of her. It tied in with her insistence that people coming to see her took the 33 tram instead of the 1 or '45. She also told everybody that the few mediocre Victorian prints she possessed were 'artist's proofs', although I doubt she had any idea what an artist's proof was. Her family came from Birmingham, but she would never admit it. She always maintained that she was born in Warwickshire.

The Griff's flat was in a three-storeyed Edwardian block called York Mansions in a street of the same period called Sandringham Drive. The building was of red brick with 'Tudor' eaves. There were six flats in all; hers was on the first floor to the right of the slightly pompous entrance. A caretaker and his family, the Polands, lived in the basement below the level of the square back garden with its large tree in the centre of the sparse lawn. The stairs of York Mansions were of uncarpeted granite which Mrs Poland mopped down every morning, polishing the tenants' brass bells and knockers en route. She was a pale thin woman who sighed resignedly when you had to pass her at her task. Mr Poland, equally lugubrious, did the garden under my grandmother's directions. She would point at the weeds in an imperious manner. She was an accomplished pointer at things for other people to do; my mother gave an excellent imitation of this trait. If a workman came to the flat she would stand over him and point at what needed doing until he'd finished. 'Then,' she would tell my mother, 'I gave him a cigarette.' She'd say this with the magnanimous and gracious air of one who had awarded a major and much sought-after honour.

The Polands had a rather large, plump, moon-faced, almost silent son called Billy. We would play with him sometimes in the garden, but he was as conscientious and melancholy as his parents. We felt he had been told he had to play with us whether he wanted to or not. It went with his parents' job, like the stairs and the weeding.

The rooms in my grandmother's flat led off a very dark dog's leg passage. The rooms at the front (the dining-room, the lounge and 'the little room' for guests), and at the back (my grandmother's bedroom, the bathroom and the maid's bedroom) were well-lit, while those at the sides (the kitchen, and the 'boys' room') faced the walls of the adjoining houses and were almost as dark as the passage.

The Griff's furniture was solidly Edwardian and rather out of scale: great wardrobes, massive dining-room table and chairs of an unpleasing orange wood, 'nests' of occasional tables, but the lounge – and it was typical of her wish to be 'up to date' that she called it that – had a bright magenta carpet, white textured wallpaper and sea-green curtains. Her bedroom was more conventional – faded pink chintz – while on her dressing-table were silver-backed hair-brushes and pretty little tortoiseshell boxes for hair pins and other necessities. She always took, even during her depressions, what my mother called 'a pride in herself'.

In the front hall by the coat stand was something rather odd: a cigarette machine into which she and her sons put money for their packets of Gold Flake. It was filled once a fortnight by one of those men to whom my grandmother, appropriately enough in this case, 'gave a cigarette'. On the chest which faced the hat stand were some comparatively large wooden carvings of two dappled horses with detachable huntsmen and a small pack of hounds. She had bought these on a holiday in the New Forest. On the wall behind them hung two rather busy etchings. One celebrated the great events of Queen Victoria's reign. In the centre of it sat the old Queen on the occasion of her Golden Jubilee while around her soldiers slaughtered natives, great ships were launched, and the Crystal Palace glittered in Hyde Park. The other was devoted to the events of the same year, and contained an image which both fascinated and appalled me. In a menagerie or zoo a roaring lion reared up, the bars of its cage snapping like matchsticks, the bustled and top-hatted crowd recoiling in confused panic. Perhaps my fondness for zoos stems from this corner of a small etching. I have always enjoyed being alarmed. The only other picture I can recall was a misty drawing of the young, long-haired Paderewski over the upright piano in the lounge, presumably a sign of my piano-teaching grandfather's admiration for that virtuoso. My grandmother was uninterested in the arts although she very much disliked modernism. She referred to all modern works of art of whatever tendency as 'futurist'.

Her two sons, Fred and Alan, lived with her; Fred until he married in the forties, Alan until she died a decade later. They were not at all alike, as different in their temperaments as Bill and I. When a child, Fred had employed similar tactics to my own to get his way. On cold nights he would force his younger brother to warm up his bed before allowing him to climb into his own. If Alan showed reluctance Fred would begin to recite 'Wolsey's farewell', a speech which always reduced Alan to hysterical tears, and rather than hear it through, he would submit to his role as a human warming-pan.

They had both been sent to Clifton, the only public school with a Jewish house. The housemaster, a Mr Pollack, was a cousin of my grandfather's and both his son and grandson were to become housemasters in their turn. When my grandfather died there was not enough money for his sons to stay on there and they had to leave and go into business. Alan accepted this without rancour, but it made Fred both bitter and resentful and, witty and charming as he could be, there remained a mistrustful streak in Fred's nature which emerged strongly when he had taken drink. Alan was a much sweeter character and showed no rancour at Fred's teasing, which continued into their middle age. Alan for instance read very little while Fred was, like his father, a devoted Dickensian. During the thirties, in my hearing, someone asked Alan if he had read a particular book, I believe it was *Rebecca*. Fred put his head abruptly on one side, always a sign he was about to make a joke. 'I shouldn't think so,' he said, 'he hasn't finished *The Wouldbegoods* yet.'

Physically too there was little resemblance between them. Fred was quite short and plump with the face of a clownish baby;

Alan rather tall with more defined and sensitive features, more conventional on the surface, and given to describing every detail of his daily life as if the late departure or early arrival of a train at Lime Street Station, or the menu provided at an annual dinner, concealed some essential clue to the meaning of the universe. It was almost as if he were bent on establishing an alibi to satisfy a particularly suspicious detective-inspector.

I believe that Fred, like my mother, would have chosen to go on the stage. He could play the ukelele, dance nimbly, sing adequately, and time jokes brilliantly. When very young I was taken to see him in an amateur production of a musical comedy called *Victoria and her Hussar* and remember the audience becoming hysterical with laughter at his performance. During the Great War, throughout which he remained, mysteriously for a public schoolboy, a private soldier, he had spent most of his time in a concert party, and I believe he had the talent to succeed if he had decided to turn professional. The need to help support his mother probably made him decide against it and perhaps reinforced his sense of grievance. The 'failure' of having to leave Clifton early gave him an obsessive determination to succeed.

He went into oil, a firm called Samuel Banner, starting as a commercial traveller; it was a period of his life about which he could be extremely funny, but which I suspect he resented strongly. He rose to become a director alongside his boyhood friend Cyril Banner who, as heir to the company, had no need to struggle as Fred did to achieve this position. He also, in middle age, became Captain of Formby Golf Club. Formby, one of the several clubs strung out along the sandy coast between Liverpool and Southport, was considered the smartest. To become Captain at all was an honour but for Fred, as a Jew, it was a formidable achievement. Golf clubs tended to be anti-Semitic. During the late fifties, dining with my father and Uncle Fred, I had raised the question. Was Formby anti-Semitic? My father, who was also a member, denied it. He hadn't an atom of racial prejudice in him; a quality he had proved in marrying my mother in the face of familial opposition. Not so Fred. 'They've got their own club,' he said. 'They don't know how to behave. They drink lemonade and bring out wads of money to pay for it. They discuss business.'

My father was rather shocked, and yet the anti-Semitic Jew is not uncommon, and usually Fred concealed his prejudice behind a defensive humour. He told me once that he had been involved in a slight car accident with a Jewish man who, in a state of high excitement, had demanded his name. 'Isaac,' said Uncle Fred. 'This is no time for joking,' screamed his adversary. 'Vat's your real name?'

Fred had never kept up with Clifton but Alan, who had been removed even younger, had always done so and regularly attended the Pollack House old boys' dinner in London. One year he persuaded Fred to join him, putting him on his honour to behave. The dinner was held in an hotel in Park Lane. While the old boys were drinking their cocktails asking each other what had happened to Cohen minor who had been such a promising full-back, or whether J.R.Goldberg was still in Bangkok, a page boy opened the door in search of a guest for whom he had a message.

'Mr Smith please,' he shouted. 'Mr Smith please.'

Uncle Fred was unable to resist the opening. He hunched his shoulders and spread the palms of his hands upwards: 'Vat initial?' he demanded.

My mother's attitude was more ambivalent. She would often claim to be 'proud of her Jewish blood', but with her awareness of anti-Semitism, was very disturbed by any overt Jewish characteristics or any scandal involving Jews. She would express relief if a financier accused of fraud had an obviously Christian name and deplored, during the war, Jewish women wearing expensive fur coats in queues or talking too loudly to each other. Like Jonathan Miller in the *Beyond the Fringe* sketch, she felt she was Jewish rather than a Jew.

I don't think the Griff gave it much thought. She would occasionally serve gefilte fish, but otherwise her cuisine was in no way kosher. From time to time she would invite the Reverend Frampton to lunch. He was a rabbi, a man of great culture and charm, but very anglicised. He dressed like a clergyman of the Church of England, and I was disappointed the first time I met him to discover he had no beard or high-crowned hat. The Griff's main dilemma apropos her race lay in relation to her burial. Her husband was buried in the Orthodox Cemetery at Broad Green and she wanted to lie next to him. This however would involve being shaved and anointed with oil, and vain to the last, she disliked the idea of not 'looking her best' even in the coffin. In the end she had decided that the proximity of her much-loved Albert Isaac was more important than her invisible final bow. My mother used to say that the Griff's main regret in relation to her funeral was the thought of being unable to see who turned up.

What with Fred's resentment, my mother's nervousness, and the Griff's indifference, it was Alan alone who involved himself in the Jewish community, especially devoting himself to Harold House, a Jewish Boys' Club, and to the Jewish Lads' Brigade of which he became Colonel. When we were small we were sometimes taken to watch the Brigade move down Prince's Boulevard with Alan, extremely smart in his uniform with its Sam Browne belt, marching at its head. It always seemed to be a clear grey winter's day on these occasions. I can hear the drums and bugles drawing closer and I felt proud of my Uncle Alan, so serious and precise, as they swung past. Yet this didn't stop me laughing when Alan had fallen asleep one Sunday after lunch and was snoring and Fred suggested that the noise he was making was 'ooorghh-cadetzzz'.

Alan had been a Lieutenant in the 1914–18 war and a casualty too. While demonstrating the use of poisonous gas the wind had changed and, as a result, throughout the twenties and thirties he was in and out of a nursing home for major operations on his intestines. The scars on his stomach were as complicated as a railway junction but he never complained. The nursing home was in Gambia Terrace and overlooked a rather romantic graveyard in a steep valley of sandstone with the Anglican Cathedral rising slowly on the other side. Gambia Terrace was, like much of inner Liverpool, respectable Georgian architecture and, like the whole district, had already begun to 'go down'. In the late fifties John Lennon had a chaotic flat there. It was close to the Art School which was itself round the corner from the Liverpool Institute where Paul McCartney did less and less work as the two became involved with Rock and Roll. The Cathedral, of which my father had seen the foundation stone laid by Edward VII, was completed only very recently.

Between operations Alan worked on the Cotton Exchange and later for a large store called Owen Owens, but it was not until middle age that he was fit enough for long enough to pursue a steady career. He joined a firm that manufactured children's clothes for Marks & Spencer and eventually became a director. He was also involved in managing the Basnett Bar, a seafood restaurant near the Liverpool Playhouse much used by the theatrical profession and the slightly raffish set which included Brian Epstein. When the Basnett Bar was pulled down he became a partner in a restaurant in Chester and still goes there most days at lunchtime to welcome guests and check that everything is 'as it should be'. Alan has always been a meticulous believer in things being done correctly.

His other great passion was and remains The Ramblers, an amateur football club for Liverpudlian public and grammar school-boys founded over one hundred years ago. He, as the longest serving member, was elected honorary President for the centenary year at the age of eighty-four and had to make a speech at the dinner, a task which occupied and obsessed him for three years before the event. He was especially worried that he might leave someone out from those who had to be thanked. But on the night it was a triumph, and he was much moved by the warmth of the applause. He was given a record of his speech on cassette but, while he was on holiday in the Isle of Man, it was stolen by a burglar. Happily, it was not the only copy and could be replaced. I believe that the Ramblers' centenary dinner was the high spot of Alan's life, all of it spent, with the exception of the 1914–18 war, holidays and trips abroad, within a quarter of a square mile.

Fred would never have spent three years worrying about a speech. He was a brilliant public speaker, much in demand for golf-club dinners. He never improvised, however, but would rehearse and time himself until he sounded entirely spontaneous. He had an equal talent for composing verses set to popular tunes for special occasions, which he and Alan would perform together accompanied by Fred's ukelele. At my parents' wedding reception they scored a great hit with Fred's version of 'It ain't gonna rain no more':

> This afternoon at three o'clock
> Our hearts were beating fast.
> My brother turned to me and said
> 'We've got her off at last.'

It was Fred who had been instrumental in my parents' meeting.
He had invited Tom home to tea after a rugger match and Tom
had fallen in love with my mother immediately. It was not Maud's
first engagement. Just after the war she had almost married a rich
man called Jack Eliot Cohen, but had broken it off because he had
no sense of humour. The Eliot Cohens were the reverse of upset at
this: not in this instance because of my mother's race – their name
alone would dispel this as grounds for disapproval – but because
she had no dowry.

When Maud eventually became engaged to my father she
received, as was then the custom, many congratulatory flowers.
Reading out the accompanying cards to the Griff she came to Mrs
Eliot Cohen's contribution: 'We are delighted and relieved', she
read. The Griff exploded with indignation until Maud told her that
she had added the 'and relieved'.

She was adept at teasing the Griff by such means. It never failed.
On another occasion she was reading out a pamphlet in connection
with an appeal for the Liverpool Foot Hospital, an organisation on
whose committee she served. 'And thanks are due to Mrs Tom
Melly,' she improvised, 'for allowing her feet to be photographed.'
'You didn't!' shouted the Griff indignantly. My mother's feet had
always been a disaster area of twisted joints and bunions.

Serving on charitable committees was very much an obligation
for the middle classes between the wars. My father, despite his
indolence, was chairman of the Foot Hospital committee, although
probably only to please my mother; his own feet were rather elegant.
My mother did several days' voluntary work a week for 'The
Personal Service', a forerunner of the Citizens' Advice Bureau, in
which Tom was also involved, and Alan, as I said, was very active in
this direction. Fred however did very little – his cynicism dismissed
charity as beside the point – but he did join the Masons. I was very
curious about the Masons even when I was quite young. He showed
me his trowel and apron, but refused to tell me what they actually
got up to, although sometimes I heard him in the 'boys' room'
reciting the ritual for his next step up the Masonic ladder.

My curiosity was intensified to an unhealthy degree after I had
bought a pamphlet on the subject from a rosy-cheeked, beshawled
old Catholic woman who came to the door. The cover showed

some hooded figures about to commit a ritual murder; the whole text accused the organisation of every kind of wickedness and blasphemy. With an early taste for Gothic horrors, I was even more fascinated. Was it possible that Uncle Fred with his jokes and ukelele was involved in such things? I did not dare ask him, but I showed the pamphlet to my father. He dismissed it out of hand but added that he found the Masons both ridiculous and dubious in their support for each other in business.

Fred tried to interest Alan in the Masons but I don't think he succeeded. I should guess Alan would have been discouraged by the amount of learning by heart involved.

That Alan and Fred, both over thirty by the time I was born, should share and continue to share the same bedroom for many years, may seem odd today. It was less so then. Alan was a bachelor, but Fred, on the contrary, was a great one for the girls. My mother frequently told me that she could remember him and his friend Cyril Banner, while still in their teens, going out to parade along the prom at Llandudno in the hope of picking up 'a bit of fluff'. Fred was, I discovered later, highly sexed and perfectly prepared to indulge himself, but he had no intention of marrying until he was good and ready, and living at home was no doubt a useful alibi. I suspect he was mostly drawn to shopgirls, barmaids and waitresses although once, during the thirties, he had had a serious mistress, a rather glamorous blonde divorcée with a child, who gave my grandmother some alarm. It didn't last, however, and he returned to more casual promiscuity. During the late fifties his sexual philosophy led to us quarrelling so severely that he cut me out of his will. Separated from my first wife, I resisted his instructions to divorce her before she 'takes every penny you've got'. 'Always wriggle,' he told me, 'that's what kept me out of trouble. I always wriggled.'

Despite what I feel to be dubious in his character, I much regret we never made it up. Apart from the laughter he gave me, he was extremely kind and generous to me during my childhood. He was the first to take Bill and me to restaurants; my father considered it an absurd extravagance. We went to The State, a grand establishment by Liverpool standards with art nouveau stained-glass windows, a string quartet and the rich smell of roasts and stews. The speciality was 'chicken on the griller', a delicacy I misinterpreted, genuinely the first time, as 'chicken on the gorilla', a sinister form of cuisine that I was eager to sample. Having scored a hit with this notion, I didn't hesitate to repeat it on every possible occasion. This I believe to be a universal vice in children and an extremely tiresome one. My subsequent malapropism, 'suggestive biscuits' for 'Digestive biscuits', was equally successful and I was guilty of looking on any lunch table as an excuse for reviving it long after I was aware of its inaccuracy.

If Fred was a bachelor from choice and the need to support his mother, Alan remained one from temperament. Several girls, according to my mother, were 'keen' on him but eventually turned elsewhere for lack of encouragement. There was one in particular who probably remained a spinster her whole life for Alan's sake. She was one of the 'Mother' brigade, but a woman of spirit and dry wit, usually encountered riding a large bicycle down Lark Lane with a shopping basket on the front and a back pedal brake. Her devotion to Alan was so obvious as to arouse Fred's mockery. He maintained every Christmas that she was crocheting a little net bag to support Alan's 'arrangements'.

'Arrangements' was the Griff's word for the sexual organs. I was first aware of it when she took me, as quite a small boy, to the Walker Art Gallery. We stopped in front of a Cranach. She looked at it with some distaste. 'You can't tell me, George,' she said, 'that ladies' and gentlemen's arrangements are pretty.' I had, at that time, no firm view on the subject, but at least I was more aware than most of my contemporaries as to what adult arrangements looked like.

This was because Maud and Tom had somewhere absorbed the theory that it was healthier for children to be exposed to their parents' nakedness from the start. This was comparatively unusual thinking for the time and was especially odd in that they were not particularly 'advanced' in any other direction. Nevertheless we were encouraged to accompany them to the bathroom to watch my father shave and my mother in the bath, or my father in the bath and my mother on the lavatory. I am unable to analyse the effect of this on my sexual development, nor to decide what they imagined it might be. All it gave me during my childhood was something, like the

French letter in my father's 'mess-box', to swank about to my school friends.

As the Griff was one of twelve children she must have had a lot of relations and so, though on a lesser scale, had her husband. Nevertheless, although it is always said to be a Jewish characteristic, neither she nor my mother and uncles were at all obsessed by the structure of the family, and those I met or heard about existed in familial isolation. I didn't even know in most cases from which side they came. It was on the contrary the Mellys who were concerned with who was whose second cousin twice removed.

Of the Griff's childhood I knew nothing except that she had developed a precocious taste for wine, and that whenever she had asked hopefully what there was to drink for luncheon, her mother had always answered: 'Water, Edith.' Of her finishing school in Germany she was equally vague. She would sometimes recite a piece of doggerel about a miller's three sons, all she retained of what was once presumably a fair knowledge of the language, and the only other thing she chose to remember was a visit to a famous sculpture, the nude torso of Venus, which was exhibited revolving slowly on a podium under a flesh-coloured spotlight in a dark room hung with black velvet.

I remained in ignorance as to how she came to meet my grandfather or the setting for their courtship. Of their early days together in Ivanhoe Road she told me only that she had 'draped her own mantelpiece', an accomplishment apparently denied to the majority of her contemporaries, but that was all.

Of her eleven siblings I met only one, her sister Lily, who was married and lived in Monte Carlo. She was a small, vivacious woman who always referred to herself as 'Naughty Little Auntie Lily', wore strong scent and seemed to me, on the one occasion she visited Liverpool during my childhood, the epitome of Continental sophistication. I suspect I first heard of her from my mother whilst walking past a particular house in Alexandra Drive, a long curving street of large late-Victorian houses which links Sandringham Drive to Ivanhoe Road with its more modest terraces. The house was of cream stucco in the style of an Italianate villa and with a glass porch supported on slender but ornate iron columns. The words

'Monte Carlo' have always projected this house like a magic-lantern slide on my mind's eye, while similar architecture – in the Holland Park area of London for example – has the same effect in reverse.

During the German breakthrough in 1940 Lily and her husband were trapped in Vichy France. Her husband too was Jewish and they were by then quite old. We heard after the war that they had died of malnutrition.

Lily, who loved comfort, had stayed at the Adelphi during her visit. The Griff put up very few people as the only route to her spare-room was through the 'boys' room' with its distinctive smell of cleaning fluid and shoe polish. Both Fred and Alan were very particular about their appearance. Nevertheless there was an annual visit from her middle-aged niece, Cis Pollack, who was married to one of the Clifton Pollacks and whose son Phil was to become housemaster there in his turn. No one could call Cis beautiful; she resembled an elderly Harpo Marx. But she was one of those rare people whose inner qualities are immediately discernible. Children were drawn to her as to a toyshop window. She had a great sense of fun and adored teasing my grandmother whom she always called 'Auntie'. She was involved with a charity for East End Jewish girls and was constantly being asked to their weddings. At one of these, she told us, the father-in-law of her erstwhile protégée stood up and asked: 'Who'll swap a bitta fat for a roast potater?' Cis lived to a great age, dying at her son's house in Clifton; a move she effected with some reluctance as she was devoted to her own little house in Cricklewood. When I was doing a gig in Bristol during the seventies I visited her only a week or two before she died. She was in bed, very frail, and wandering in her mind, but the sweetness, almost saint-like in its charisma, was as powerful as ever.

The Griff's only other regular guest was another niece, Lulu Davis, who lived with her sister Emmy in Birmingham, or Warwick-shire as the Griff would have it. Lulu was my godmother and allegedly well off. I thought of her as rather dashing, but this may have been connected with her name. One of Uncle Fred's pieces on the ukelele was a song of the twenties called 'Don't bring Lulu'. It was about a man who is giving a party. His friends are welcome to turn up with any companion of their choice – 'Rose with the turned-up nose', 'Peg with the wooden leg' – but the eponymous heroine is barred. She 'knocks things off the shelf'. She 'always wants to do just what we don't want her to' and generally creates havoc. Lulu Davis certainly appeared conventional enough in her behaviour, but for a child a song is as real as a person. After all, if Uncle Fred could take part in ritual Masonic murders, there was no reason why Lulu, back in Birmingham, mightn't revert to knocking things off the shelf.

But this was only speculation. What I knew for a fact was that Lulu was extremely mean. She would give us sixpence where other relatives would hand over half-a-crown and, considering I was her godson, her birthday presents were so meagre that I was even more reluctant than usual to write her a thank-you letter. My mother, rather beadily, told me that it was 'worth keeping in her good books' as I might well be mentioned in her will. I eventually blew it on my nineteenth birthday when she sent me a packet of Gold Flake. I was stationed in Malvern in a naval camp, and I wrote to her a postcard pointing out that as Malvern was quite near Birmingham she could have hitch-hiked over and saved herself the stamp. Naturally enough I never heard from her again and, when she died, no lawyer wrote to advise me to get in touch if I wished to hear something to my advantage.

My mother was a little more forthcoming about her relations, but only when they had amused her in some way.

There were three Jewish Irish cousins, elderly women as poor as synagogue mice who lived in London, and whom she liked to imitate. When she visited them, one of them would always press a pound in her hand and cut short protestations by saying: 'Now don't annoy me', in her strong Dublin brogue. They were upset when she failed to marry Jack Eliot Cohen, a match they supported on the grounds that 'it will please your Uncle Lou'. Uncle Lou was another, Liverpool-based, brother of the Griff's but I learnt nothing more about him, except that he had been married to a lady called Auntie Reb who had provided enormous Edwardian teas for Maud and her brothers, and was always worried that there wasn't enough to satisfy 'the de-ah children'.

When Maud became engaged to my father they went to London, and she took him to visit the Irish cousins. They had forgiven her

for failing to please her Uncle Lou, but feigned indignation on
Tom's behalf for having to meet them.

'What will your fiancé think of you?' they cried. 'Bringing him to
meet all your relations!'

There was also a rich first cousin of Maud's, a girl called Joan
Harvey-Samuel who later married a military man and who spent
her entire life complaining about everything. She had her own lady's
maid whose shortcomings were a constant irritant to her. She would
begin most of the conversations she had with my mother in their
teens with the phrase 'that dreadful maid Rose!'

With all these I became, at one remove, familiar. They would figure
briefly in my mother's entertainments for me in the lounge at Ivanhoe
Road after tea. They would pop up like characters in a radio comedy
series, recognised and loved for their catchphrases: 'Now don't annoy
me', 'the de-ah children', 'that dreadful maid Rose'.

More substantial were her tales of her Uncle Fred Harvey-Samuel,
the barrister who had lived in Wimpole Street and who was so
concerned that the Griff, if she was determined to work in a station
lavatory, should only be employed at a main-line terminus. Even
the Griff occasionally mentioned him because he had 'passed out
first in all England', a feat which put him on a level with the signed
artist's proofs. He sounded an impressive, if somewhat intimidating,
figure offering Maud, a nervous young provincial girl with her hair
only just up, a temporary glimpse into the great world of London
with liveried servants and a carriage at the door.

Maud told me of smart dinner parties where the sweets were
enormous architectural confections which, despite her sweet tooth,
she felt obliged to refuse in favour of milk pudding in case the
insertion of an ill-judged spoon should cause the whole trembling
edifice to topple off the plate and on to the carpet. She was, I
gathered, in some awe of her Uncle Fred as he could be witheringly
sarcastic.

He was a keen bridge player and one evening, when the only
guests were another couple eager for a few rubbers, regretted her
inability to make up a four. Maud was able to tell him that since
her last visit she had in fact learnt to play, as the Griff had told her
it was selfish not to. She and her uncle were partners. The stakes
were high, and partly from nerves, partly from lack of ability, she

played extremely badly. When the beaming guests had departed with their winnings, her uncle poured himself a stiff brandy and soda. After sweeping up his moustache, he turned to her and remarked mildly: 'Did Edith say it was selfish of you not to learn bridge?' She blushed crimson and burst into tears.

Yet she was fond of him and regretted, following his early death, that the life he'd shown her was no longer open to her, the door closed. On the rare occasions when she and Tom were in London together, and inevitably got lost, she would always say: 'I think we're somewhere near Uncle Fred's.' For the rest of his life, whether on a North Wales by-pass or the outskirts of Nottingham, if ever my father wasn't sure of the way, he would repeat this sentence to himself.

In Liverpool, by the time I was old enough to take in people, there were very few relations of my mother's living there. Off Lark Lane, in a small flat facing Sefton Park, was a sad, freckled cousin called Dodo, a middle-aged spinster whose only companion was a small and harmless dog of puggish origins called Terror. Poor Dodo, like her aunt the Griff, suffered from deep depressions only, in her case, with no one close to turn to. In the middle thirties, shortly after it had become necessary to put down the blind and incontinent Terror, poor Dodo gassed herself.

Maud's other Liverpudlian cousins were two unmarried sisters, Winnie and Ethel Mussons. They both had sallow complexions, and high mournful voices tinged by the sing-song Liverpool accent. Ethel, in particular, had been Maud's great friend and confidante before the war. They had gone to dances together, and always met next morning at Sissons tea-rooms for what my mother called 'a thorough committee'. They discussed, with appalled relish, the outrages of one 'Racer' Marsh, so named because she was considered 'fast'.

'Did you see?' Ethel remarked at one 'committee' after a dance at the Wellington Rooms. 'Racer Marsh had *shaved* under her *arms*!'

Sometimes Ethel would ring up my mother, breathless to transmit some piece of scandalous intelligence. When Maud asked her who on earth had told her, Ethel, after a pause, would usually reply, 'Now I come to think it over – you did.'

Ethel and Maud went ice-skating together, played lawn-tennis at the Mersey Bowman in Sefton Park, and discussed men endlessly, if innocently; Maud believed until well into her teens that you conceived a baby by kissing, a theory which gave her many moments of anxiety. They were both 'keen' on a man called Jimmy Duncan who, for some reason, was considered unsuitable. I asked Uncle Alan why this should have been so. He thought for some time. 'I can't imagine,' he told me eventually, 'he always struck me as a thoroughly decent feller.' Perhaps it was simply because he wasn't Jewish and my grandfather was still alive.

Maud told me that Jimmy Duncan, when he had friends with him, would sometimes ring her up at home to get her to belch 'God Save the King' down the telephone, an unladylike accomplishment of hers which occasionally featured at my request in her after-tea divertissements.

After the war and her eventual marriage, my mother and Ethel became less close. Towards the end of the thirties, presumably for financial reasons, the Mussons opened a cake shop in Lark Lane. It was called Sugar and Spice and was in competition with the long-established Miss Stephenson's a few doors up. My mother felt obliged to patronise Sugar and Spice but would furtively slink into Miss Stephenson's as well. Miss Stephenson herself, a formidable old lady with a striking resemblance to Queen Victoria, was noted for her brandy snaps for which Maud had conceived an almost indecent passion. Ethel's cakes, while pure and wholesome, had a somewhat amateur look to them.

The Griff, who unlike Maud didn't care what people thought of her, remained completely faithful to Miss Stephenson despite her family ties with the rival establishment. Her imperious behaviour in local shops was a continuous embarrassment to my mother. Once, in Irwin's, the grocers, when a plain assistant hurried forward to attend to her, she announced that she 'wished to be served by the pretty young lady'.

4

A first cousin of my father's, a plump, bespectacled, kindly, noisy, mildly pompous man called Willie Bert Rawdon Smith, devoted his later years, following his retirement to Coniston Water, to writing a small pamphlet called 'The George Mellys'. His object, given in the preface, was 'to enlighten the next generation about the last, who either never knew them, or only knew them when children and therefore more for what they had in their pockets than for what they were'. The main body of the work does indeed deal with the Chatham Street Mellys, but there is a section on the Riversleas, and notes on those servants who remained with the family over a long period. I must admit that from my point of view it's a very useful crib.

Willie Bert's mother was a Melly, but I believe his obsession with the family was not merely due to a desire to be associated with a more unusual name than his own. Of his mother Beatrice, he writes:

In 1881 she married Francis Rawdon Smith (1851–1930), a member of a Liverpool family then living in Shropshire. He was an only child and thoroughly spoilt. The marriage ended by her leaving her husband in 1891. A deed of separation was drawn up giving her the custody of the four children . . . Owing to what was then an invidious position she did not go into Society much.

Could it have been this which made him so much more obsessive about his connection with the Mellys than most of those who bore the name? Certainly my father, the direct male heir, showed no great interest in the minutiae of his family history. Nor was he beyond teasing Willie Bert on the subject.

When my Great-Uncle Bill died in the forties, leaving 90 Chatham Street to the University and the drawing-room furniture to the museum, there was one object which Willie Bert felt merited special consideration. This was a massive and enormous book supported on an elaborate if spindly brass lectern. It had been presented to my great-great-grandfather, George Melly, by the electorate of Stoke-upon-Trent after business reasons had forced him to retire as their MP. The tortoiseshell front was decorated with oval china plaques representing the crests of the Five Towns, and inside were stiff board pages, tile-like designs by local art students, much influenced by the Arts and Crafts movement, with affixed sepia photographs of the town halls and other places of interest. With its Gothic hinges and gilt edges, it was a grotesque monument to Victorian decorative excess. The museum, perhaps wrongly, was not interested in it.

Willie Bert wrote earnestly to my father soliciting his views as to what should be done with it. My father, who was in the navy stationed at Troon, replied on a postcard: 'I feel it should be returned to Stoke-on-Trent so that the sins of the fathers should be visited on the sons.'

Willie Bert was not amused and perhaps this accounts for his note on Tom in 'The George Mellys': 'He had an acute vein of humour.' There are several such concealed barbs in his pamphlet. Of his Uncle George, the son of the MP, he wrote '. . . he did not suffer fools gladly.' Had he perhaps been put in his place by George for his neurotic determination to insist endlessly on his close connection with the family?

Concerning my grandfather, Samuel Heywood Melly (1871–1937), there are no hidden gibes. The tone on the contrary is a shade patronising. He describes him as: '. . . a very small man standing at 5 feet 3 inches but very neatly made'. He remarks that 'His interests were the Territorial Army, fishing and shooting especially the former', but then adds: 'He never had a chance to make as much of a mark as he might have done in business being completely overshadowed by his more brilliant brother George.' He hints, too, at a psychological explanation: 'He also suffered from having five mothers in his babyhood; his three sisters who were from seventeen to thirteen years old when he was born, his own mother, and Libby the nurse.' He notes that he married my grandmother, Edith Matilda Court, in 1898.

To children all grown-ups are about the same height, and I never thought of my grandfather as a very small man nor, as my mother maintained, decidedly plain. There was, however, no doubt that my father's good looks came from his mother, who remained exceptionally beautiful to the end of her life. She was also the dominant partner, keeping an especially beady eye on my grandfather's drinking habits. He was forbidden whisky but allowed sherry and sometimes, my father told me later, would secretly empty the sherry decanter and replace it with scotch. At the end of lunch or dinner he would walk purposefully towards the sideboard and pour himself a large Kummel, which his wife believed, incorrectly, to be comparatively harmless. To help defuse this moment he would make the same joke or, to be more precise, repeat the same ritual. No joke delivered twice a day can hope to retain that element of surprise which is the essence of humour. Between chair and sideboard he would ask a question.

'What was the name of that Turkish General?'

Nobody was expected to answer this enquiry, and my grandmother would stare at the table with an expression in which exasperation and resignation fought for supremacy. Then, as he helped himself to a generous measure, my grandfather would answer his own conundrum.

'Mustapha Kummel!'

I never saw my grandfather noticeably drunk but I dare say, like many of his generation, he was usually mildly fuddled.

Although he would occasionally visit the commercial district of Liverpool, he had retired from business in 1924 at the age of forty-nine. He had been Passenger Superintendent at Lamport & Holt, the shipping firm to which my father had been temporarily and reluctantly attached. My grandfather's older brother George was joint Managing Director but had resigned following a row with Lord Kylsant who had taken over the company. My grandfather had left as a sign of solidarity, overshadowed, even here, by his 'more brilliant' sibling. No great sacrifice was involved. He had some money of his own and in 1927 George had died leaving what was, in those days, an enormous fortune to be divided among his brothers and sisters. From then on, apart from some charity work, my grandfather resigned himself happily to doing very little.

Nobody ever called him by his first name, Samuel. Although his middle name was held in common by most members of the Chatham Street Mellys, he alone chose to be known as Heywood. His wife often made it sound like a call to heel. To his older brothers and sisters he had apparently been known as 'Pup', but I never heard any of those still living refer to him by this affectionate diminutive. My father called him 'Guv'nor'.

Collectively my grandparents were nicknamed 'Mumbo' and 'Jumbo'. As neither of them was in the least elephantine, I suppose this to have derived from the parents of the hero of the then popular but now taboo children's book, *Little Black Sambo*. Bill and I called them 'Gangie' and 'Gampa', obviously a childish mispronunciation of Grannie and Grandpa. The Griff was irritated that we should call my other grandmother 'Gangie' ás, unlike 'Gaga', it carried no suggestion of senile feeble-mindedness, but she was in general jealously competitive of Gangie, a failing we were well able to exploit.

When speaking of him to servants and tradesmen Gangie referred to her husband as 'the Colonel', and his correspondence was addressed to 'Colonel Heywood Melly'. He had indeed followed the family tradition of commanding the 4th West Lancashire Brigade, but in his case only from 1914 to 1916. He had led the regiment to France in 1915, but the following year was invalided out on account of acute dysentery. He was awarded the Territorial Decoration. It was hardly a glittering military career but he, or perhaps his wife, chose to retain the courtesy title.

On the eve of leaving for France, the 4th West Lancashire Brigade held a day of manoeuvres on a plain outside Liverpool. A tea-tent was erected on a nearby hill so that the Colonel's lady and the wives and families of his brother officers could watch their husbands charging about below; a picture which bore little relation to the filthy, lice-ridden trenches which were their destination. Due to the hostilities the regiment had trebled its size and among the men were many volunteers from the Liverpool docks, a class far removed from the clerkly respectability of pre-war days.

Among the lieutenants was a very young man called Tom Todd who had never been exposed before to six hours of strong language on such an insistent level. During the tea interval, seeing my grandfather in conversation with his wife and without a cup, he hurried over to make good this deficiency. 'Have a cup of fucking tea, Colonel,' he proposed politely. The effect was that of an animated H. M. Bateman cartoon. This was a favourite after-dinner story of my grandfather's, and my father would sometimes repeat the invitation as he poured himself out a cup from the dumb waiter between returning from the office and leaving for The Albert.

Until I was about five Gangie and Gampa lived in the large house where I was born. It was called The Grange and was built on the banks of the Mersey in the Parish of St Michael's, a small pocket of *rus in urbe* which lay unexpectedly concealed behind the bustle of Aigburth Road with its small shops and noisy trams.

Even then I was charmed by the abrupt transition. You turned off Aigburth Road down the side of the Rivoli Cinema and walked along one of those two-up two-down terraced streets built of yellow brick with lace curtains and holy-stoned steps. This eventually petered out, and there were perhaps six semis of the early twenties, speculative building on a decidedly unambitious scale, and traversed by a very small street along the side of two of the houses but of great interest and pride to me in that it was called Melly Road. I imagined then that this was due to the proximity of my grandfather, but realise now it was probably named after the family. If so it was a very modest acknowledgement of a century of public service and commercial acumen.

Beyond the semis was the entrance to a lane, its surface unmacadamed, partially cobbled, dusty in summer, muddy in winter. It was, according to its street sign 'unadopted', which meant that it was not the responsibility of the Liverpool Corporation. It was darkened by great Arthur Rackham-like trees and there were fields behind its tangled hedges and sandstone walls. At the end was a tiny lodge which served the four or five houses which surrounded it. The lodge keeper was a gnomish, startlingly white-haired Welshman called Mr Griffiths, who would emerge suddenly from his pointed nail-studded door to identify visitors, cackling high-pitched forelock-tugging greetings at those he recognised.

The Grange, shielded from its neighbours by tall shrubberies, was a long, low grey house of restrained early-Victorian Gothic. It had a large walled garden which ran down to the river. There were old fruit trees and little twisted walks. I found it enchanting if a shade sinister. The rooms of The Grange seemed, in contrast to Ivanhoe Road, enormous. My mother always maintained that 'Mrs Melly has no taste', by which I suppose she meant that she made no concessions to modernity. There were several good pieces of eighteenth-century furniture, polished floors with faded Turkish carpets and old glazed chintzes. It's true the pictures weren't up to much – mediocre water-colours in wide gold mounts and engravings of Arabs around an oasis – but my parents didn't collect master-pieces either. There was one engraving I really liked. It showed an elderly but robust gentleman in eighteenth-century clothes toasting his beaming white-haired wife at the other end of a dining-room table. On the wall above the fireplace hung two oval portraits of them in their youth. I believed, despite their wig and lace-cap, that it represented my grandparents. Gangie, apart from her sternness over drink and frequent irritation at my grandfather's unwavering devotion to the habit, was extremely fond of him. He for his part worshipped her; her very strictness compensating no doubt for the loss of his 'five mothers'. He wasn't wholly in awe of her however. He would occasionally stand behind her chair while she criticised some aspect of our behaviour, making his false teeth pop in and out of his mouth – a course which, much to her uninformed surprise, reduced us to instant hysterics. I, for my part, was much less intimidated by Gangie than by the Griff. She was more easily diverted from course, less severe in her standards.

There were only two indoor servants at The Grange, both of whom were there before I was born and who remained with my grandmother, heavily exploited and frequently abused, until her death in 1959. Her maid was called Marjorie, a large, rosy-cheeked, heavy-breathing woman who retained the slow rural burr of her native Shropshire. She had caught my grandmother's feudal fan-tasies and whenever I went to call on Gangie at however short an interval, would greet me with a cry of 'Welcome home, Master George', as if I were the young lord returning to his great estates after completing the Grand Tour. When I was small this seemed merely peculiar. I knew that my real home was 22 Ivanhoe Road. It was later that I found it absurd, and especially after my grand-parents had left The Grange, which at least resembled a modest manor house, and moved into a semi-detached facing Aigburth Boulevard. After my grandfather's death Gangie rented a flat, but even this didn't modify Marjorie's ritual. Dressed during the war as a temporary post-woman, she would still evoke wide parklands and rolling acres.

Over the years she had developed several eccentricities which Gangie either failed or affected not to notice. When serving vegetables, if anyone, even for a moment, was slow to notice Marjorie's heavy-breathing presence at their side, she would nudge them quite sharply with her elbow. Her obsession was tree-felling or, failing the opportunity for that, the illegal collection of firewood from public places, an activity she pursued with Freudian intensity. Once, on discovering my father cutting down a small tree, she warned him in words which seemed loaded beyond their overt meaning: 'You be careful, Mr Tom,' she said, 'or you'll do yourself a bad injury.'

In the late 1950s, when Gangie was senile and almost speechless, Marjorie used to wheel her from her flat into adjacent Sefton Park in an invalid chair. My mother, meeting them by chance one windy afternoon, noticed that my grandmother seemed to be perched unnaturally high beneath her rugs. Marjorie had been thrusting all available branches and logs under her charge, jacking her up several inches.

Marjorie's greatest friend was the cook, Annie. They had been engaged the same week and were to share a flat together after my grandmother's death some thirty years later. Annie was almost a midget and badly crippled. She had a sweet face, always smiling, and rolled about her duties on her bowed legs with cheerful vigour. She was also an excellent and consistent cook which in no way deflected Gangie from cursing her roundly for any minor short-coming or misunderstanding, referring to her on such occasions as 'Silly Little Annie'. Annie was especially skilled at soups for which Gampa had a particular liking, sucking them up with noisy appreciation from the side of one of the large crested spoons, a habit which set my mother's nerves on edge but had no effect on my grandmother beyond impelling her to raise her voice. For Bill and me, however, it was Silly Little Annie's puddings that won our enthusiasm, and in particular a creamy combination of rice and jam known as 'Freddie's Delight'.

The Griff, aggravated by our constant and maliciously appreciative references to Freddie's Delight, badgered Gangie for the recipe,
a word she always pronounced 'receipt'. Gangie wasn't having any.
It was 'her' pudding. They were on very formal terms anyway,
never progressing beyond 'Mrs Melly' and 'Mrs Isaac'. Rather than
admit defeat the Griff ordered her cook to try and create Freddie's
Delight from our description alone. Week after week we were faced
by variations of rice pudding, some so congealed as to form a
mould, others so runny that they were almost a drink, but none of
them even approximating to the delicious original. Eventually, and
to our relief, for we had in effect been penalised by our own
mischief, the Griff gave up.

With two dailies, Marjorie, Silly Little Annie and a gardener five
days a week, The Grange might have been considered adequately
staffed, but my grandfather also employed a uniformed chauffeur.
It was not that he went in for very grand cars. His Chatham Street
brothers, his cousin, the shipping heiress Emma Holt, owned huge
old-fashioned Daimlers with the chauffeur like a stuffed animal in
a glass case taking his orders through a flexible speaking tube, freesia
in little vases and sal volatile and smelling salts in silver-topped glass
bottles slotted into the upholstery, but Gampa preferred a more
modern if solid motor car, a maroon Armstrong-Siddeley. It was
also his habit to sit by his chauffeur, with whom he chose to
establish an officer-and-batman relationship, a military illusion
reinforced by his being addressed as 'Colonel' and the obvious
pleasure he derived from casually but inevitably returning the
obligatory salute of passing AA men on their three-wheeled motor-
cycles.

There were three chauffeurs during my childhood. The first,
whom I can only just remember, was called Burscoe, a name that
in itself sounded like the noise of an old-fashioned motor-horn. He
was a small, thickset man like a sturdy little bull and apparently
extremely randy. My father told me, although it may have been
apocryphal, that Gampa once discovered Burscoe in the kitchen of
a country house in Yorkshire where they were staying, rogering
the cook from behind while she continued, impassively, to peel
potatoes; a tableau which could well have come from 'My Secret
Life', and formed part of my grandfather's stock of mildly indecent

after-dinner stories when the ladies had left the room. Burscoe was
not dismissed for this peccadillo. Like Tom, Gampa had apparently
a tolerant view of sexual behaviour.

After Burscoe retired he was replaced by Kane, a big ebullient
man with an open mobile face as innocent as Tommy Cooper. He
was married to a small woman with unfashionably long hair and
the looks of a beautiful gypsy. Kane was marvellous at amusing us
on long journeys. He would recite a string of gibberish which he
pretended to be the Chinese alphabet. He told us that RAC stood
for Running After Chickens. He kept us in such stitches that I even
forgot to feel car-sick.

Kane was succeeded by Jenkins, a friendly but silent Welshman
and perhaps rather more to the liking of adult passengers, who
knew what RAC really stood for and felt less need of continuous
distraction. When Gampa was dying he sent for Marjorie, Annie
and Jenkins and asked them to 'look after the Missus', a request
they felt, in the circumstances, unable to refuse. Jenkins continued
therefore to drive my grandmother about until the last few months
of her life.

Gampa, like my father, died of a perforated ulcer in his sixties.
Gangie, like the Griff, lived on well into her eighties. She was a
practical-minded woman with nothing sentimental in her character
but with a strong imaginative streak. Her childhood was odd. She
had been brought up by her grandmother, although from which
side of her family I never discovered, in a dark old house called
Denham on the Cheshire marshes near the mouth of the Welsh Dee;
a bleak landscape criss-crossed by deep and treacherous irrigation
ditches, and within sight of those fatal sands where the doomed
Mary was sent to call the cattle home. As my grandmother was
born in the 1870s, her grandmother must have grown up during the
Regency and Gangie, in consequence, used several expressions of
a vigour and directness denied to her Victorian contemporaries.
Moments of exasperation would be met by a cry of 'Dash m'wig!'
People who bored her were 'dull dogs'. Those who annoyed her she
would threaten to shake until their noses bled.

She had a varied repertoire of old songs and snatches. Her
speciality was a mysterious ballad called 'Marjorie sat on the bowling green'. She was unaware of its origin. Her grandmother used to

recite it to her on stormy winter nights, and afterwards she would be very reluctant to take her candle and go up alone to bed along the creaking corridors of Denham. My father had excited my interest in this poem when I was very young, but Gangie refused to recite it to me until I was about eight, and even then in broad daylight. I didn't think I'd be frightened. For one thing I found myself imagining Marjorie to be my grandmother's maid, and for another the only bowling green I had seen was in Sefton Park where, on summer evenings, the old men in their waistcoats frequently accused each other of cheating, angrily demanding that someone 'fetch the string' to settle a dispute. The idea of lugubrious heavy-breathing Marjorie in her cap and apron seated on the turf of the Sefton Park bowling-green was an absurd rather than a sinister image.

My grandmother sat me on her footstool, fixed me with her fine dark eyes and began. The ballad was set to a lugubrious chant in the minor key and went like this:

Marjorie sat on the bowling green, the trees grew all around.
'Twas in the middle of the night she heard a frightful sound.

(and here, after a long pause, Gangie gave vent to two long low groans)

'Is that my father dead, or is it my Uncle John,
Or is it Willie, my long lost love, who from the sea has come?'

(two more groans)

'It is not your father dead, nor is it your Uncle John,
But it is Willie your long lost love who from the sea has come'

(two further groans)

'And have you brought me any fine clothes, or any fine things to put
    on?'
'No but I've brought a long winding sheet to wrap your dead bones
    in.'

And at this point my grandmother, who had appeared to be in a trance, leapt out of her chair, flung her arms wide, and gave a sudden piercing scream. I almost fell off the footstool with terror.

The low chant, the repeated groans, the lulling effect of the tune all of course contributed to the shock of the finale, but it's quite a chilling little piece even on the page. I remembered every word instantly and could hardly wait to get home and recite it to Bill. I did so that very evening in the dark nursery with a candle on the little table between us. It gave him frightful nightmares.

Gangie was fond of acting in general, keen on organising charades and dumb crambo. Her party piece at family gatherings was one of 'Mrs Caudle's Curtain Lectures', drawn from a popular Victorian book of that name, which she performed with my grandfather on a bed improvised from armchairs or a sofa. Mrs Caudle nags her husband non-stop about his shortcomings during the day without allowing him any defence; a role that suited Gampa very well as he remained entirely silent throughout and yet was able to engage the sympathy of the audience. His own speciality was a recitation of 'The Village Blacksmith' as performed by a man with an articulated wooden arm and hand which he appeared to manipulate to illustrate the imagery of the poem. I never saw Gangie act in a stage play but my mother, who was not altogether fond of her, said that her idea of acting was running about a great deal and flapping her arms.

My mother's antipathy towards her was based in part on Gangie's habit of saying exactly what came into her head but more especially on her insinuation that Tom wasn't looked after properly. That she should refer to him more often than not as 'poor dear Thomas' was a constant irritant. She implied too that 'poor dear Thomas' was primarily her son rather than Maud's husband and that we were her grandchildren rather than Maud's children. In fact she applied this proprietorial attitude to everything she was connected with. In her later years she became completely hooked on *Mrs Dale's Diary* and was always furious if interrupted while listening to what she called 'My Dales'.

She came from an old Cheshire family and told me that her grandfather had fallen in love with her grandmother when he had seen her, from his horse, swinging on a gate. The Courts had once been considerable landowners but most of the estates had been lost by some profligate over the gaming tables, and all that remained was an old manor farm near Nantwich. Gangie's younger brother Percy, after several years in Canada as an engineer, had returned to manage this, but he was a very unlucky farmer, and Gampa had felt obliged to lend him several fairly substantial sums over the years to help him out. In the large hall of the farm hung a reminder of former prosperity; an enormous picture in very bad repair showing a park with a substantial hall in the background. In the foreground were several men in tall top hats and tight breeches, women in *directoire* dresses, children bowling hoops or mounted on hobby horses and a toddler in a donkey cart.

Whatever its financial shortcomings, for us children the farm was a magic domain. There was a large duckpond in front of it, still referred to as 'the moat'. There was a priest's hole in the huge chimney. The building, with its exposed beams and yellow-washed walls, stood in gentle rolling country under wide skies. Uncle Percy, who was also known as 'Pip', although given to occasional unconvincing explosions of exasperation, was a courteous and charming man, physically remarkably like my father. His wife Isobel was not a beauty – she resembled Flora Robson – but she had startling blue eyes and a fascinating voice like a dove cooing. She had been a suffragette.

While specialising in Friesian cows, it was very much a general farm. There were rather intimidating geese and a few turkeys as well as scratching hens, several pig-sties, and a great bull in a dark dung-scented shed rattling its chain and rolling its baleful eyes. The bull had been awkward to start with until Percy realised it was lonely, and from then on spent several hours a week talking to it. The cows were milked by hand and sometimes, if he spotted us watching from the entrance of the shippon, the farmhand would aim a jet of warm milk at Bill or me with ribald accuracy. He also took us ferreting, although most of the time was spent digging out the mean-faced snake-like albino creatures from deep in the warren and there were few rabbits to show for it.

Sometimes we went down for the day in Gampa's Armstrong-Siddeley. The ride itself was a great treat as it involved crossing the muddy Mersey on the Runcorn Transporter Bridge, a huge nineteenth-century structure big enough to carry across many cars and lorries on each journey. Sometimes we would stay for a few days, being met at Crewe by Uncle Percy in an old van smelling of meal. We fell asleep in the attics listening to the owls hooting, and were woken by the rooks in the great elms. We helped Aunt Isobel

feed the poultry, watched Percy and the hands getting in the hay
and visited the animals. Once there was a litter of pigs who had lost
their mother and had to be fed by hand. Bill and I discovered a cruel
but irresistible trick. If you picked up one of the squealing piglets
and squeezed it immediately after it had been fed, it would shoot
out a stream of milk at one end and piss at the other. They soon
got wise to us and whenever we entered the outhouse would run
hysterically under a pot-bellied stove called 'the cheerio'.

The interior of the farmhouse, while rather run down, was very
beautiful in its simplicity. Isobel had a charming faded drawing-
room looking on to a walled garden full of cottage flowers. There
was a great linen press on the landing and old brass beds. The
Courts ate extremely well. On one early visit with Gangie and
Gampa we had lunch on a wooden table which stood outside the
main door in front of the moat. There was a goose and a very rich
chocolate pudding and I was disastrously car-sick on the way back.
There was home-made bread and unsalted butter churned in the
dairy. Bill and I called this 'country butter'. We always took some
home with us.

They were still there during the fifties. I once took Mick Mulligan
to tea when we were playing that evening at the Nantwich Civic
Hall. We ate at the same table in front of the house, much intrigued
by a sinuous little brown creature leaping and weaving on the other
side of the moat. Suddenly there was a loud explosion. Percy had
fired both barrels of a shotgun over our heads from his office
window. 'A damn weasel after the water hens,' he explained mildly
as he rejoined us.

When Isobel died, Percy sold the farm and went to live with his
son Peter and daughter-in-law Dot in a small house outside Leicester
where Peter practised as a vet. I visited him there once. He seemed
to have shrunk and looked out of context in that modern setting,
but his smile was as warm as ever, his manner as gentle and
old-fashioned. The sale of the farm had been sufficient to repay my
grandfather's estate with interest. Dot later wrote to me to say that
the new owner had pulled it down and built a new house on the
site.

Percy was still active enough to come to Gangie's funeral. But at
the graveside it was noticed he was missing. He had fallen asleep in

the back of Peter's car outside my grandmother's flat and been forgotten in the confusion of deciding the protocol of the limousines. He was still there and still asleep when they got back from the cemetery.

Gangie herself would have been amused by this absurd incident. She took a robust view of death due, I suspect, to her unquestioning belief in a personal afterlife. She was a steady church-goer, a keen if garish arranger of altar flowers and heaper-up of vegetable produce at Harvest Festivals, and on Good Fridays spent the three hours of the Passion on her knees in Christ Church, Linnet Lane. Unlike the Mellys, with their Unitarian background, she was drawn towards lace and incense, and keen on entertaining the odd canon.

When Gangie's sister-in-law Florence Melly died in 1928 my mother, who had been fond of her, arrived at 90 Chatham Street for the post-funeral baked meats wearing a rather tearful expression which she felt appropriate. The first member of the family she encountered was her mother-in-law in high spirits. 'Come in! Come in!' cried Gangie. 'The party's just getting going.' Maud was very shocked by this, and brought it up quite frequently over the years as a proof of Gangie's insensitivity.

A dedicated if apparently rather bossy committee woman, Gangie served for many years on the Ladies' Committee of the Liverpool Hospital for Women. When I was about seven, the hospital moved into a large new building in 'bankers' Georgian' style, and one morning Gangie took Bill and me over it. On a trolley in an ante-room was a shrouded object. Gangie strode briskly towards it. 'Look at our corpse!' she cried, whisking back the sheet. We nearly fainted with horror, but it turned out to be no more than an articulated life-size model on which student nurses practised their splints and bandaging.

When Gampa died so unexpectedly in 1937, Gangie came back that evening from the nursing home with 'poor dear Thomas' to Ivanhoe Road, and sat in the nursery looking a little dazed. Bill and I, who had not been told yet, were building a Roman Coliseum out of the wooden building blocks which were kept in my father's old tuck-box. The point of doing this was in order to push it over when it was finished and my mother, assuming what we were later on to call her 'church voice', asked us not to because Gangie was 'feeling rather upset'. But Gangie would have none of it. 'Don't mind at all,' she said. 'Push it over. Knock it down!'

Next morning my father told Bill and me; my sister Andrée at five was considered too young to understand. We both howled and sobbed, and I had the sensation, as always at moments of emotion, of watching myself as if on film. Gampa was the first person near to us to die. It seemed dreadful that I would never hear him drink soup again, or whistle through his teeth, or imitate a man with a wooden arm reciting 'The Village Blacksmith'.

Gampa had filled in the pools almost from their beginnings, but had never won a dividend. When Gangie got back to Dunmail (they had moved there from The Grange some years before) there was an envelope from Littlewoods. Inside was a postal order for half-a-crown.

I suppose they left The Grange because it had become too big, but their choice of Dunmail was curious. It was a substantial, half-timbered semi-detached house built during the twenties and facing Aigburth Boulevard. This was a continuation of Aigburth Road, admittedly more residential and lined with Japanese cherry trees, and with the trams partially concealed behind low hedges but, even so, ill-fitted to Gangie's mild delusions of grandeur. There was a dark little morning-room on the ground floor the previous owner had hung with hideous embossed leather. Gampa spent most of his day there, coughing over his Turkish cigarettes, snoozing, and reading large leather-bound illustrated volumes with titles like *Through Africa with Rod and Gun*. Otherwise the rooms were arranged very like The Grange except that, because they were far smaller, the furniture looked rather cramped. In the hall was a big dinner-gong suspended from a yoke supported by two elaborately carved Indian deities. When it was time for lunch or dinner Marjorie, as had been her custom at The Grange, would strike this several times – with deafening effect in so confined a space.

The only advantage of Dunmail was that it was a few hundred yards from The Dell where the Leathers lived. Dorothy Leather was Gangie's only living daughter. We called her 'Auntie Golly'. She was a kind, pretty, rather nervous person with a talent for water-colours and writing sketches some of which were printed in *The Lady*. She suffered terribly from migraines. Her husband, Ronald

Fishwick Leather, was an energetic forthright man, who went bald early and wore a black moustache. He was very practical and used to make elaborate mechanised table-centre decorations every Christmas. The year Disney's *Snow White* came out, he designed one in which the seven dwarfs emerged from their mine, crossed a bridge over a looking-glass stream and vanished into a wood, returning, concealed and upside down, to repeat the exercise. It was powered by a small electric motor.

Uncle Ronnie was a keen business man, and became Executive Manager of Pilkingtons, the glass manufacturers, in nearby St Helens. Unlike my father, who was only mildly Conservative, Ronnie was extremely right-wing with a deep loathing for the trade unions. He was rather short-tempered but good company. The Dell, like The Grange, was built at the end of another unadopted lane leading down to the Mersey. It had a large steep garden, which gave it its name, in which Ronnie worked fanatically. He was an obsessive perfectionist.

The Leathers had two children, John and Gillian. John was a few years older than me. He had a lopsided grin and had inherited his father's biting wit; a kind of Noel Coward of the nursery. I was in some awe of him. Gillian was my brother's contemporary and mad on horses. She pronounced her name with a hard 'G'. They had a strict, rather handsome nanny called Cadwallader. In their nursery was an old glass-fronted music-box with huge flexible metal discs for different tunes. There was also a small wall-cupboard with a leering wizard painted on it mixing a spell from bottles and phials of poisonous coloured liquids. It was an image I found disturbing.

Bill and I once went to the pictures with my mother and the programme included a 'short' featuring Wilson, Keppel and Betty, a well-known variety act. Wilson and Keppel performed a lugubrious sand-dance dressed as unlikely looking Arabs. Betty just wiggled a bit wearing a yashmak. Bill and I became hysterical at this performance, not only because of its innate absurdity, but also because Wilson and Keppel bore a strong resemblance to Uncle Ronnie. When they next appeared at a local music-hall we were taken to see them in the flesh. From then on we always referred to Wilson and Keppel as 'The Uncle Ronnies'.

*

When I went with Gangie to put flowers on Gampa's grave, I discovered for the first time that Tom and Dorothy hadn't been her only children. On the stone, under my grandfather's newly-chisled name, I read that he lay next to Mary Melly, a daughter who was born and died on the same day in 1914. I found this inexplicably sad.

A mystery I never solved was why Gangie was brought up by her grandmother. Not only had she a mother then, but she was still alive in my childhood. She was known as 'Tiny Granny', a very pretty little person like a Beatrix Potter mouse and in full command of her faculties in spite of her great age. She had a flat just round the corner from Christ Church, Linnet Lane, and we used to be taken to call on her after 'Children's Service'. Tiny Granny lived with my grandmother's younger sister, my Great-Aunt Gwen, her husband Guy Watts and their eighteen-year-old son Newton.

Gwen, who had pince-nez and dyed red hair piled up into a kind of mad bird's nest, was considered something of a caution. When she was driven anywhere in my Grandfather's Armstrong-Siddeley she would imperiously order the chauffeur to drive faster or slower, to raise and lower the windows as if the car were hers. 'You devil Burscoe!' she used to shout, much to my father's amusement. Guy, a large, rather boisterous man, had been very rich at one time but was more or less ruined in the Depression. Their son Newton was incredibly spoilt. He was usually still in bed when we arrived about eleven o'clock, reading a risqué magazine of the thirties called *Razzle* which had a striking front cover in art deco lettering. My father maintained that Guy had indulged Newton ridiculously during his childhood, allowing him to take school friends to the Adelphi and sign the bill. No wonder he lay in bed and read *Razzle*. Later on Newton was always getting into scrapes. He had a mistress and a child, which everyone thought very shocking, but when Guy and Gwen were old and poor it was Newton's mistress who went and looked after them.

I only discovered this much later when she turned up and introduced herself and her daughter at a club we were playing near St Asaph, North Wales, during the middle seventies. She had long left Newton. There was a question I was longing to ask her. Tom and I had once discussed fetishism, or at least I'd brought the subject up and he'd asked what it was. I'd mentioned rubber, fur, boots and shoes.

'I wonder if that explains your Great Uncle Guy,' he said. I asked him if what explained my Great Uncle Guy.

'He was always buying Gwen kid boots,' he told me, 'and he used to clean them all on Sunday afternoons. She didn't even have particularly pretty feet.'

I said it sounded like it, but he wasn't entirely convinced. Fifteen years after my father's death I asked Newton's mistress.

'Was he not!' she said, 'and right up to the end. A perfect old nuisance. I used to have to sit on my feet when I was reading to him!' I wish I could have told Tom.

Newton, of course, was one of those people that Gangie wanted to shake until their noses bled.

5

One afternoon, above the yards with pigeon-lofts and the tall garden walls that faced the shops in Aigburth Road, I watched a small aeroplane sky-writing the word 'Rinso', a form of advertising quite common in the thirties. The wind had blurred the letter R before the o was completed. As I still couldn't read, I asked my mother what it said. She told me. I knew Rinso was the name on the soap-flake carton by the sink in the back kitchen but the concept of writing it across the sky as a commercial exercise was beyond me. I believed that what the aeroplane was doing related to our packet, a private message to me alone. When we got home, before even taking off my galoshes, I ran into the back-kitchen to look at it. I was surprised not to find the letter R blurred.

I demanded constant explanations. 'Why? Why? Why?' I nagged, tugging at my mother for attention, but her answers often confused me further. There was a middle-aged woman we sometimes met when we were out walking or shopping. She was usually on the corner of Ivanhoe and Parkfield Road, where a brick wall, banked high on the other side with earth, bulged dangerously outwards and a brass plate, screwed to the front gate, announced the practice of a certain Dr Mary B. Lee. The woman wore a purple hat with cloth violets hanging from it. Her face was heavily painted and she talked in an excitable and disconnected way. I usually got very bored when my mother stopped to talk to people in the streets and shops, but I was fascinated by this lady and didn't, as was usual, pull insistently at my mother's coat to get her to come along. On the contrary, it was she who appeared eager to break away. Once, after an especially long and disjointed monologue, I asked my mother why the lady seemed so different from everyone else. She told me that she drank. This made no sense to me at all. Everybody drank but they didn't all wear purple hats and talk with smeared red mouths and lipstick on their teeth.

Rather precocious in some ways, I was incredibly backward in others. Anything which didn't interest me I ignored. Why bother to learn to read boring stories with short words when grown-ups could be wheedled or bullied into reading to me about Mowgli carried off through the jungle by the Bandar-log, or Peter and Benjamin crouching terrified in the bone-littered darkness outside Mr Todd's kitchen? I was seven before I could read at all but then, almost overnight, I could read everything. I couldn't add up, however; I simply shut off when anyone tried to teach me. I developed like one of those crabs with a tiny body and one huge claw.

I worried sometimes that when I grew up I would have to make a living, presumably by going into business. The only thing was that I couldn't understand what 'business' meant. I knew it was how my father and uncles 'made money' and that it took place in offices in the city, but even after visiting them I was none the wiser. My father's office was quite small. It was high up in a tall narrow building near the pier-head. The hall was dark and had a board on the wall saying who was on each floor. There was a lift with open iron-work and a man in uniform with one arm pulled it up and down with a rope. The names 'Seward & Melly' were painted on the glass door of my father's office. Inside sat a lady typing. The office smelt damp and pungent. This was because there was a little back room with big brown paper parcels with dirty black and yellow-grey wool bursting out of them. Did he sell the wool? No. They were what were called 'samples'. My father was a wool-broker. What he tried to do, he told me, was to buy wool, which he never saw, when it was cheap and sell it to people when the price went up. I stopped trying to understand although I pretended I did. The lady, whom he called his secretary, gave me biscuits and let me bang away on the big old-fashioned typewriter.

Then my father took me to have my hair cut in a brightly-lit basement under a shop. It had tiles on the walls and lots of mirrors. If you stood in the right place where one mirror faced another you could see yourself over and over again getting smaller and smaller. The barber's chair went up and down on a foot-pedal and tipped backwards like the chair at the dentist's. There were lots of pretty bottles of hair oil on the shelves with names like 'Honey and Flowers'. A respectful but cheerful man in a white coat cut my hair. When he'd finished he brushed the back of my neck with a soft brush which felt nice, but some little hairs from the clippers always got down the back of my neck and tickled. It was easy to understand what barbers did, but not wool-brokers.

Uncle Fred's office at Samuel Banner was even more mysterious. It was round the corner from my father's but in a much grander building. There were lots of offices in Samuel Banner and several secretaries. Uncle Fred had an office of his own with wooden panelling and photographs of ships. He sat behind a big desk. There was no room at the back with samples, only a little carved mahogany rack on his desk with test tubes in it each containing an oil of a different viscosity. Uncle Fred took me out to lunch. I was introduced to lots of big noisy men as his nephew, or 'Tom's boy'. He was always very funny in the restaurant. Afterwards my mother, who had been doing her voluntary work at The Personal Service, picked me up and we went home on a tram.

Would I really have to be a business man when I grew up? I'd rather have been a shopkeeper because I could understand what they did, but then all the shopkeepers had Liverpool accents. When Mr Arnold rang up every day to ask what meat we wanted he said: 'Arnold the butt-cher'. There were other jobs people did. There were policemen, soldiers, park-keepers, tram-drivers and conductors, carpenters, decorators, ice-cream men, waiters, watchmakers, but all my relations, except for Uncle Percy and George Rawdon Smith who was a doctor, seemed to be in business and so did all my father's friends. Later on I found there were other things I might do. I could become a barrister like my mother's Uncle Fred, or an architect or a vicar, but all these meant years of study. I wanted to be something you could become at once. Above all I wanted to be famous.

Some of my mother's friends were famous. Most of them were actors and actresses who appeared at the Playhouse. Their photographs were outside, taken by Burrell and Hardman in Bold Street which my mother called 'the Bond Street of Liverpool'. The photographs were very dramatically lit with velvety backgrounds. One actor, wearing a soft hat, was pretending to light a pipe. The

actresses all held their heads at funny angles like the ducks on Sefton
Park Lake. They were the same photographs we had on the piano.
I knew all their names because my mother said them so often in a
special kind of casual throw-away voice: Bobby Flemyng, Geoffrey
Edwards, Ruth Lodge, Harry Andrews, Michael Redgrave, Mar-
jorie Fielding, Ena Burrill. There was also the producer William
Armstrong. I thought he must be even more famous because my
mother mentioned him most of all. She always called him 'Dear
William Armstrong'. He was bald and funny and had a high-pitched
Scottish accent.

I met all these people when I was very young because I was
allowed to stay up and see them when they came to supper on
Sunday nights. A bit later I saw them on the stage too, at first in
the children's plays which were performed in the afternoons at
Christmas. They were usually very exciting with secret panels and
children getting the better of crooks, but sometimes they were about
animals like Toad of Toad Hall. What really made me feel special
was that, after the curtain came down, my mother took me 'round
behind'. There was a funny dusty smell. The actors and actresses
sat in their tiny dressing-rooms up steep stone steps. They wore
dirty dressing-gowns and took off their make-up with cold cream.
I was sometimes allowed to go on to the stage and was surprised
but somehow pleased to see how, with the curtain down and the
lights off, the set looked so unreal and sloppily painted. Sometimes
the stage hands would be hauling up the backcloths and flats into
the air and lowering others for the grown-up play in the evening: a
drawing-room with French windows or a garden with a swing and
a lake in the distance.

My mother didn't only know the actors and actresses at the
Playhouse. She was a friend of Douglas Byng and Ronald Frankau.
Douglas Byng pretended to be a lady and sang songs about being
Doris, the Goddess of Wind or someone called Flora Macdonald.
Ronald Frankau was a comedian and was often on the wireless. I
had records by them in the nursery and could imitate them. Sometimes when my parents had a party, I'd be woken up and brought
downstairs in my dressing-gown to sing their songs. I didn't mind
being woken up at all because everybody laughed and clapped,
especially when I imitated Douglas Byng.

'Flora Macdonald,' I'd sing, 'Flora Macdonald. Heavy with haggis and dripping with dew . . .'

'You'd almost think he knew what it meant,' someone would
say. I didn't, of course, but I had listened very carefully to the
intonation and, by exaggerating it, unconsciously emphasised the
double entendres.

Once, when I was brought down, Ruth Lodge was sitting on an
actor's knee and kissing him.

'Not in front of the child,' wailed William Armstrong.

My mother was also friendly with the ballet. When they were
touring, Robert Helpmann and Freddie Ashton would always come
to the house. She'd met Freddie Ashton first because he'd been
asked to do the choreography for one of the big amateur reviews in
which my mother took part, but Helpmann was her favourite. She
always referred to him as 'darling Bobbie'. My father sometimes
called him 'darling Bobbie' too, but only when my mother wasn't
there so I knew this must be a joke. My mother 'adored the ballet',
which I couldn't understand as she didn't like classical music at all.
She divided it onomatopoeically into two schools which she called
'mini-mini' and 'boom-zoom'. Mozart for example was 'mini-mini',
Beethoven 'boom-zoom'.

I was taken to the ballet when quite young and was amazed to
see 'Darling Bobbie' twisting and leaping in a way that appeared to
be against nature, but I felt no urge to become a ballet dancer
because I was told that it was necessary to start very early, that the
training was long and arduous and that even when one had become
a star, daily practice was essential. More curious was that I didn't
set my heart on the stage, an obvious escape from the worrying idea
of becoming a business man and a possible way to become famous
easily. I think the explanation was that my mother constantly
impressed on me that it was 'an insecure profession'. If anyone else
– my father, Uncle Fred, my grandparents – had taken this line I
might have resisted their advice but that my mother, who adored
actors and actresses, was against it forced me to affirm that I didn't
want to go on the stage.

The only other class of people of whom my mother spoke in her
casual throw-away voice indicating their high place in her Pantheon,
were those with titles, although these were much sparser on the

ground than members of the theatrical profession. In fact there
were only two. One was the widow of a judge, a kindly rather
boring elderly lady whose observations were, in themselves, completely banal but which my mother nevertheless aired so as to be
able to introduce the source of their origin. The other was infinitely
more dashing; a certain Lady Peggy Lacon. Maud had known Peggy
when she had been married to a plain Mr Duckworth. Then she
divorced Mr Duckworth and married Sir George Lacon, a ruddy-
faced, almost silent Norfolk squire whose principal interest was
shooting pheasants. Lady Lacon was a very glamorous platinum
blonde in the manner of Jean Harlow. She occasionally came to
stay with us and what made this both worrying and yet fascinating
was that Bill and I were always warned several times in advance
that she didn't like children! This had the effect of making me
determined that she should like me. I followed her around and
fawned on her throughout her visits in the way that a dog or cat
will often make for the one person in a room who dislikes animals.
She looked at us with indifferent dislike but confused us further by
bringing us very expensive presents. The one I can best remember
took the form of a black dude on a little plinth. There was a tiny
microphone attached to the plinth and when this was placed near
the horn of a gramophone the vibrations caused the dude to appear
to tap dance. My father thought it was a ridiculous present and must
have cost well over a pound. Although he found her 'decorative', his
favourite word to describe a pretty woman, he didn't care much for
Lady Lacon.

After the war, Maudie would frequently tell me that the thirties,
her forties, were her best time. Although there was not much money,
there was enough for her to entertain whenever she felt like it and
her social life was full and busy. This centred on the Playhouse and
the Sandon Studios Club, the Liverpudlian equivalent of the Chelsea
Arts. The Sandon occupied a wing of a very beautiful eighteenth-
century building called the Blue-coat Chambers in the centre of
Liverpool. It had been built as the Blue-coat School and was of red
brick with stone detailing, enclosing a large cobbled courtyard and
separated from the street by fine railings and elaborate iron gates.
At the back of the building was a garden surrounded by painters'
and sculptors' studios and indeed the original purpose of the club,

as its name suggested, was a meeting place for those exclusively connected with the arts. By the twenties, however, an alleged interest was considered sufficient justification. There was a long narrow unlicensed dining-room with a stained floor, oak tables and chairs and earthenware water jugs. It had a coal fire in the winter and the food, while simple, was excellent and cheap. The head waitress carried on like a grumpy old nanny and was much loved. When my mother was shopping in the centre of Liverpool or 'town' as she called it, she would usually have lunch there and would often take us with her. I was fascinated to meet painters and sculptors in their rough tweed suits, blue or rust coloured shirts and knitted ties. It was proof of another world unconnected with business.

From our perspective the point of the Sandon was the annual children's party. It was held on New Year's Eve afternoon and called the Hogmanay. It took place in the huge room on the first floor of the main block facing the street. The chief attraction was an enormous slide which you rode down on rather prickly door mats. After tea there was always a conjurer called S. Le Kessin, who wore evening dress. We didn't only get to see S. Le Kessin at the Sandon; the smarter mothers used to hire him for their children's birthday parties. To be frank his tricks, multiplying billiard balls and pulling chains of multi-coloured handkerchiefs out of his mouth, were rather tame, but he did eventually produce a ventriloquist doll called Tommy who sang 'Show me the way to go home', while S. Le Kessin drank a glass of water. At the time I didn't realise that the conjurer's name was made up of an initial, the French definite article and a surname. I thought he was called 'Esslerkessin'.

The Hogmanay party was fancy dress; the usual motley of pirates, clowns, arabs and wild men. One year, when I was about five, I had an ambitious and major failure. I was addicted to a children's strip in the *Daily Mail*. It was called 'Teddy Tail', and the hero was a rather wet mouse. His side-kick was an even less distinguished duck called 'Douggie'. That November the *Mail*, to which the Griff subscribed, offered a series of dressmakers' patterns representing these creatures, and I persuaded her to send off for Douggie Duck. It was duly made up from yellow towelling with a cardboard beak and eyes. I went to the party full of hubris, but nobody seemed to know who Douggie Duck was or even that I was meant to be a duck at all and I was much mocked and soon reduced to angry tears. My only recompense was that when my father came to pick me up it was pouring with rain, and I was able to provoke his laughter by running up and down the gutter outside the Blue-coat Chambers shouting: 'Fine weather for ducks.'

As a family we were not very lucky with fancy dress. Tom himself had once gone to a party, for which the invitation had proposed a choice between fancy and evening dress, disguised as a snowman, only to find all the other men in dinner-jackets. As a very young man he had elected to dress as an Italian organ grinder and, for the sake of verisimilitude, had gone to the trouble of hiring a live rhesus monkey from a Mr Rogers, who at that time kept a pet shop but was later to open the small and rather unsuccessful Liverpool zoo. When Tom took the monkey back to The Grange, it had broken loose, run along the mantelshelf deliberately throwing a rather good clock into the fireplace, bitten my grandfather quite badly on the hand, and run up the curtains to take up a position on the pelmet from which it refused to be dislodged. Mr Rogers had to come round, recapture it and take it away.

The year following my failure as Douggie Duck, I elected to go as Mickey Mouse and was reassuringly successful. I was so delighted at restoring my credibility among my contemporaries that I insisted on a permanent record. I was photographed one January afternoon at a local studio staring solemnly at the big camera on its tripod, its operator concealed under a black velvet hood. I stood next to a toy Mickey Mouse as a proof of my authenticity.

Later the same evening, the children's Hogmanay was followed by a New Year's Eve party for the members themselves. There was a special licence and, judging by my father's groaning recourse to Alka Seltzer every New Year's morning, it was not wasted. In preparation for this Bacchanalia, huge murals, painted by the Sandon's artists, were already in position during the afternoon. They showed, in caricature, the more notorious associates cast in the role of classical deities or historical figures, and engaged in activities just this side of decency. I was fascinated, not so much by what they were up to, as how it was possible to retain a likeness by means of such grotesque distortion. These men and women, whom I had seen lunching soberly in the club's dining-room, were here presented as skeletal or pendulous monsters, writhing or monolithic, as bald as eggs or hairy as apes, and yet remained instantly recognisable. My interest in the 'truth' of distortion was born from speculating on this mystery during S. Le Kessin's less riveting illusions.

Yet for my parents the most important annual event at the Sandon was not the Hogmanay (indeed my mother's mistrust of drink and my father's enthusiastic indulgence in it on these occasions, 'spoiled' it for her more often than not) but the annual 'cabaret'. Both of them took part, but my mother's suppressed theatricality was given full rein, and she was always the star of the night. These cabarets were no casual stringing together of acts, but specially written reviews with proper songs and sketches. The former were largely the work of a man called Alfred Francis who worked, without marked enthusiasm, for his family bakery business and managed the large central tea shop which provided an outlet for its products. He was an urbane, slightly plump man, handsome in the manners of the period, with horn-rimmed glasses and a neat moustache. His passion was popular music and he was something of a jazz aficionado. He could play the piano well, conduct and orchestrate, and his songs, with titles like 'High School Hattie' or 'Don't Play Jazz on the Bechstein Grand', while clearly influenced by Noel Coward and Cole Porter, were memorable and amusing in their own right.

Most of the sketches were written by a remarkable woman called Maud Budden. She was the wife of the Professor of Architecture at the University and one of my mother's best friends. She was of Scottish origin and had a slight and attractive Edinburgh accent. She was big and rather untidy especially about the hair. She had a frank open face with amused blue eyes. Her tongue was sharp and witty enough to make her disliked and feared by anyone pompous or pretentious enough to provoke her ridicule. Among other activities she was responsible for the words of an anthropomorphic cartoon strip in the Liverpool Echo called 'Curly Wee and Gussy Goose'. Unlike most strips this didn't rely on balloons, but unfolded its story in a series of quatrains printed below each picture. They were always neatly turned and often very funny. 'Maud Budden is a fool,' said my mother as she read them aloud to me each night before turning to the children's crossword. She meant of course the exact opposite.

The strip was drawn by another club member, an artist known only by his surname, Clibbon. He was obsessed by large busts, and the hens or ewes who were among the supporting cast of 'Curly Wee and Gussy Goose' were in consequence generously over-endowed. Clibbon carried this fetish into the Sandon cabaret where he insisted on transvestite roles as an excuse to introduce large balloons under the bathing suit that served as his foundation garment. One year he and my mother appeared as gym-slipped girls, Clibbon inevitably precocious about the figure. They had cut two skipping ropes in half and, by swinging these vigorously enough to deceive the eye, presented the illusion of surprising expertise. They sang a song which began:

> We are two little girls
> We are not fond of toys
> We'd rather be smoking cigarettes
> And mucking about with boys.

The more successful and less salacious sketches and songs from the Sandon Cabarets were recycled for three public reviews which were performed during the thirties at either the Royal Court or the Liverpool Empire to raise money for charity. They were based on the formula invented by Charlot and Cochran and were called *Murmurs*: *Northern Murmurs* (1933), *Southern Murmurs* (1934) and *Nursery Murmurs* (1935). Although too young to be taken to the Sandon Cabarets, I was allowed to watch my parents perform in the *Murmurs* despite the fact that the Griff considered some of the sketches unsuitable.

My mother was prominent in *Northern Murmurs* and stole all the notices in *Southern Murmurs*. As a result, she claimed, of jealousy among the other performers, she was given comparatively little to do in *Nursery Murmurs* and much of what material she did get was from another hand than Maud Budden's and of inferior quality. When *Nursery Murmurs* turned out to be a comparative financial and critical flop, she was far from displeased. I remember her most clearly in *Southern Murmurs* as a Liverpool flower girl in a shawl and cloth cap commenting to an imaginary assistant about her invisible customers in the style perfected by Ruth Draper.

'Here's a widder, Meg. 'and me them whites . . . Flowers, lady?

Luke lovely on yer 'usband's grave, lady. Show up beautiful against the hoak and brass 'andles, lady . . . No wonder 'e died. I'd die if I 'ad that face lukein' at me over me fish and chips of a night.'

The music for these reviews was arranged and conducted by Alfred Francis in white tie and tails. In the middle forties, when I had begun to collect jazz records, Tom rushed excitedly into the nursery where I was playing Ellington's 'Rockin' in Rhythm'. He had recognised it as the overture music that Alfred Francis had chosen for *Southern Murmurs*.

Maud tried briefly to break into radio and appeared in a few plays broadcast from the BBC's northern studios in Manchester. I can remember hearing her in the small role of a Liverpool woman deprived of her son in a play about the press gangs in the eighteenth century. It was called *Hawks Abroad*. She didn't make much progress however and soon, easily discouraged if she didn't succeed at anything instantly, relinquished her ambitions. She told us that the doorman at the Manchester studios had said to her: 'You won't get anywhere here, love, if you're not in't click.' But how, I now wonder, did she come to discuss her frustration with the commissionaire?

Her other great woman friend during the thirties was called Sylvia Maxwell Fyfe, the sister of Rex Harrison. She was married to a Scottish barrister who looked rather like Mussolini and was to become a post-war Conservative Home Secretary with a draconian belief in capital punishment and, more oddly, given Sylvia's many gay friends, a relentless prosecutor of homosexuals. Sylvia was very chic and wore pearls and scarves and little hats with veils. She radiated enjoyment and enthusiasm. She and my mother organised several parties together, usually hiring one of the rooms at the Sandon for the purpose. Sylvia had a rapid rather quacking voice which made everything she said sound amusing.

The other reference point in Maud's 'smart' Liverpool life was David Webster who lived with his parents and his friend Jimmy Bell in a handsome early Victorian terrace house overlooking Prince's Park. Maud was a little in awe of David whose plump persona and rich Dundee cake diction dominated the arts and whose circle extended far beyond the confines of the city. David, later to become General Manager of Covent Garden, was then General Manager of the Bon Marché, epitome of fashion in Maud's admittedly provincial experience. There was a restaurant on the top floor where we sometimes had tea. I loved going up in the lift and hearing the lift girls intone like a ritual the various departments in their rather affected voices. 'Going up. Next floor boys' and girls' wear, evening wear, ladies' retiring-room, restaurant.' Sometimes there was a trio playing in the restaurant led by Alfred Francis at the piano, whom I supposed to be playing hookey from his cake shop round the corner. The restaurant was in art-deco pinks and greens. The ice-creams came in metal cups on long stems.

David and Jimmy were always asked to my mother's more interesting dinner parties and usually came, but they didn't often ask her back. This rankled, but David was too much of a catch to allow her to do more than grumble. My father, on the other hand, was quite irritated by his insisting on whisky instead of gin as this meant getting in a special bottle. Yet David was such good value, so full of gossip and name-dropping tales of the world beyond the city limits, that he was always welcome, and his stately arrival eagerly awaited. He was also a member of the Sandon and in one cabaret he was concealed, with the exception of his face, inside a cast of Epstein's neo-primitive Genesis, a marble statue of a pregnant woman which had been exhibited, amidst much moral outrage, at the Blue-coat Chambers to raise money for the building's restoration. His simulation of Genesis's labour pains at the end of the sketch was considered a triumph. It took place in a green spotlight and David's final line was: 'I'm such a very young girl to save such a very old building.' My mother was fond of describing review sketches and when, as in this case, the end was signalled by plunging the stage into darkness, would cry: 'Black out!' with definitive emphasis.

These names: Maud Budden, Alfred Francis, Sylvia Maxwell Fyfe, David Webster, played as much part in Maud's conversation as her theatrical list. For me they epitomised the exciting life she led. Until I was almost grown up everything Maud did and said seemed remarkable. 'If I'm at home,' she'd say, 'all I have for lunch is Ryvita, cheese and an apple', or 'Keith Winter [a well-known playwright of the period] always says he's seen me breathing over a tomato juice at more cocktail parties than any woman he knows.'

My father fitted into her life perfectly well. He was liked by all her friends and never tried to impose any of his. Even when, later in life, she became more difficult and occasionally hysterical, he never criticised her. The only clue he ever gave of mild irritation was to refer to her as 'your mother'. The only one of her friends he actively disliked was a bossy and dwarfish woman journalist called Mary Ventris who wrote a column in the *Liverpool Echo* called 'A Woman's Note'. Tom called her 'Little Runty' and groaned audibly when he spotted her through the window waddling up the path on her bow legs – but then, my mother didn't like 'Little Runty' much either. She was just rather intimidated by her, as she was by anyone of forthright opinions. Only once, to my knowledge, did she stand up and be counted and that was when a woman criticised the actress Ena Burrell for having affairs with young men. 'She is not only a great actress,' said Maud, 'but a loyal and true friend'; and with this she left the room. She repeated this curtain line many times in my hearing, by which I deduce that she believed it to be an act of great moral courage reflecting on herself. Indeed, given her placatory and timid temperament, it was exactly that.

The other important aspect of my mother's life was her voluntary work. Part of this, the organisation of an annual charity ball at the Adelphi, her presence on appeal committees, her involvement in sales of work and bazaars, tied in with her social life, but most of it was the reverse of glamorous. For at least three days a week she sat behind a desk at The Personal Service visited by 'clients' who were in trouble with bureaucracy or felt they were entitled to grants or supplementary benefits and didn't know how to go about it. The Personal Service, which later amalgamated with the Citizens' Advice Bureau, was Maud's cause. Through it she experienced a sense of purpose and of fulfilment.

Politically she voted Conservative. Not to have done so would have exposed her to criticism, but she always said she felt 'tempted' to vote Labour in local elections, although she believed that it would be to everybody's advantage if politics played no part in municipal affairs. Nevertheless she was appalled by poverty and her instincts, while perhaps occasionally patronising, were generous and sincere. It's perfectly true that The Personal Service was run on behalf of the working classes by middle-class ladies, a concept now generally suspect. But at the time only middle-class confidence could deal with indifferent bureaucrats and red tape. Maud, so timid in controversy on a personal level, was a tiger on behalf of her clients. She knew their rights backwards and was determined they should get them.

She had become involved in social work during the First World War when she had trained under the formidable feminist Eleanor Rathbone, a cousin of the Mellys, working for the Soldiers' and Sailors' Family Association, much of whose activities were devoted to ensuring that widowed common-law wives received their pensions. Maud was not without an awareness of the ambivalence of charitable endeavours. She recalled walking down a slum street to further some enquiry and hearing one elderly 'Mary Ellen', the Liverpool name for those beshawled old women who were the matriarchs of the slums, remarking sarcastically to a contemporary: 'There goes a bit of charity for someone's back-yard.' There was, however, a tendency to use her clients as a source of mildly snobbish anecdote, to relate how a child opening the door told her that she'd 'see if the lady was in' and then shouted up the stairs, 'Eh Mam, there's a woman 'ere from der Pairsonal Sairvice.'

She also claimed to 'respect the Conservative working man'. 'Why?' I asked her in my angry teens. 'Because he votes against his interests?' As always, when criticised, she coloured and changed the conversation. It was just one of those remarks which, she'd discovered, pleased most of her acquaintances and which she'd never actually thought through. Sometimes also there was a failure of empathy. As a non-smoker she was always indignant whenever a woman, deserted, beset by debt, another child on the way, chain-smoked through an interview. On balance though, Maud did a great deal of good and was frequently asked for by name by those in recurrent difficulties. Occasionally she was genuinely surprised. 'My husband,' one woman told her, 'does it up me be'ind not to have no more kids. He empties the chamber-pot down the sink, when me mother's in the 'ouse, and he calls me a Roman Catholic bastard – now that's not nice is it?' Of course she didn't tell me about this until much later, when I was almost grown up. She saw that what made it funny was the incongruous and even restraint of the woman's reaction to this catalogue of various marital failings, but I've no doubt the advice she offered was constructive, or at any rate uncensorious.

Although her work over the years gave her more awareness of working-class life and more than most of her set, she had no working-class friends, although she once admitted rather coyly to being kissed by a one-armed liftman during the 1914–18 war. Years later, during the early days of the jazz revival, I brought home a piano player I had met at a concert. 'He must be the most Liverpool person we've ever had in the house,' she said, before adding, 'as a guest.'

On a more personal level she called on several old women, most of whom had been 'in service' and now lived in the small dark over-furnished houses off Aigburth Road with a canary for company. There was something of the Lady Bountiful about those expeditions and they always made me uncomfortable even before I was able to understand why. The old women were ever impressed by Maud's condescension. She basked a little too easily in the sycophancy. Still less did I enjoy the visits to the Home for Incurables, a charitable nursing home where 'worthy' cases were admitted to die. I hated the sweet sickly smell of the rooms, the scared old faces, the yellow hands fumbling with the bedspread. Even then I found the name intimidating, grotesquely Victorian in its determined refusal to conceal its function. It was however slightly less brutally identified than the Catholic equivalent (all the 'Incurables' were Church of England). The Catholic institution was called The Hospice for the Dying.

Maud was of course a woman of her time. It is pointless to apply today's standards to her social assumptions. Certainly she derived satisfaction from being admired for her 'selfless' dedication, but she achieved certain positive results, relieved some hardship. She didn't only visit the poor. There was also an American millionairess who lived permanently in a suite at the Adelphi. Her name was Mrs Beere and she was a tiny little woman whose amiably bemused son René, a friend of Uncle Alan's, was to die of alcoholism towards the end of the thirties. Mrs Beere was pathologically mean and expected my mother to bring her own sandwiches while she herself tucked into smoked salmon and crême caramel sent up from the French restaurant on an elaborate trolley and served by an obsequious waiter. Once, when I was about nine, Mrs Beere sent me out to buy some medical preparation from a nearby chemist. She gave me the approximate money and on returning I offered her the penny change. 'You can keep it,' she told me with an air of great magnanimity. She was very proud of her 'petite' appearance and once asked a Jewish acquaintance what nationality he would imagine her to be if he didn't know she were an American. She hoped that the answer would be French, but it wasn't. 'Jewish, Mrs Beere,' he told her with firm realism. I didn't mind visiting Mrs Beere because I was fascinated by the idea that anybody should live in an hotel, especially one so grand as the Adelphi with its 1930 Louis Quinze décor and rosy silk wall-hangings.

There was also an old plump myopic woman on Maudie's list. She had been the mistress of a famous actor, but had later become a devout Roman Catholic. She was badly off and her flat was both dusty and depressing, but the décor was pure Ballet Russe with tasselled light shades and an ottoman covered with huge cushions and grubby pierrot dolls. The cheap crucifixes and madonnas looked out of place in such louche, if dilapidated, surroundings.

From an early age I enjoyed going out with my mother even when our destination was not all I could wish. I was impressed by her knowledge of Liverpool, her sudden purposeful dives into side streets, her ascent up the linoleumed stairs of scruffy buildings full of small wholesalers to an upper floor, where there was a man who mended watches or a 'little woman' who made hats. Her dressmaker was the fattest woman I've ever seen outside a fair booth. She worked in the tiny front room of a decayed Georgian house, her mouth bristling with pins. She smelt of rancid fat. She would copy, rather approximately, photographs of clothes Maud had torn out of Vogue. My mother spent very little on herself. While some of her richer or vainer friends wore mink or sable she made do with a 'pony' coat bought in a sale or a rather beady-eyed, moth-eaten fox fur that bit its own groin with a clip. Tom, given his careful nature, did nothing to encourage her to build up her wardrobe. When I was about seven I decided to remedy this. At my request she released me at the entrance to the Bon Marché and I went to ask if it were possible to buy a fur coat for about five shillings, the amount she had 'lent' me to get her a birthday present. They told me it was not possible, but Maud pretended to be just as pleased with the ugly 'slightly shopworn' fake crocodile handbag which was within my budget.

My father's life – golf on Saturdays, snooker at The Albert on Fridays, occasional invitations to shoot or fish – naturally involved me far less during my childhood. Even my mother's interests impinged only occasionally although, as I grew older, she began to spend more time with me, to include me in many of her activities largely perhaps because I showed such a precocious and enthusiastic interest in everything she said or did. Even so the nursery remained the centre of my life, the afternoon walk the principal event of the day. Gradually things assumed a pattern. The seasons established themselves. Christmas, Easter, and the summer holidays became fixed rather than unplaced occurrences.

In 1932, when I was six and Bill was three, something extraordinary happened. My mother, then forty, had become pregnant again and my sister Andrée was born. I can't imagine that this, given my mother's age, was deliberate, but the birth was without complications and its outcome enchanting. Andrée had huge slightly slanting eyes and a snub nose. We all adored her and I felt none of the sibling rivalry which made my relationship with Bill so difficult to sustain. Nevertheless, when Andrée was at the crawling stage and we were all three playing in the nursery, she put a bead into her mouth and it became lodged in her throat. I noticed this, but was playing with some plasticine and totally absorbed. Andrée began to turn purple and it was Bill who thought to toddle on to the landing and shout down: 'There's something the matter with Andrée.' Our nanny, who had been fetching tea, ran up the stairs, up-ended her and smacked her on the back until the bead was dislodged. Everybody was rightly appalled at my indifference and so, once I had taken it in, was I. Even now the heavy smell and oily consistency of plasticine triggers off a sense of guilt.

Andrée arrived at the height of the Depression. Maud used to say that when I was born my father gave her a diamond ring, when Bill was born a platinum ring, but that when Andrée was born all he could afford to do was shave off his recently cultivated moustache. She was very touched by this gesture as she could 'never be doing with facial hair'.

6

Number 90 Chatham Street, first occupied by my great-grandfather George Melly MP in the late 1850s, was an austere Georgian corner house of some size. Many of its windows had been bricked up at the time of the window tax. Although the front door was indeed in Chatham Street, the main façade overlooked Abercromby Square with its small residents' garden.

Chatham Street and Abercromby Square had once been fashionable but the merchant princes had long since departed. Most of the houses had become seamen's lodgings, and Number 90 alone, like a Victorian whale stranded on a polluted beach, retained its original identity. The Mellys, with their passion for appropriation, referred to this one house as 'Chatham Street' or 'Chatty' for short, as though the lodging houses didn't exist.

When I was born, there were still three members of the family living there: my Great-Uncle Willy or Bill (the names were interchangeable), and his sisters Eva and Florence. Their brother George had moved out after his marriage in 1917 to a lady called Lydia Elizabeth Edwards. Four years later she went mad, or as Willie Bert Rawdon Smith put it rather more tactfully in his notes on the family: 'became a complete invalid'. Great-Uncle George died in 1927, but his wife lived on until 1932. I never met her, and am unaware what form her madness took although the Griff, rather surprisingly, let slip that she had once been invited to play bridge with her, and that 'Mrs Melly dealt all the cards to herself'. Great-Aunt Florence died in 1928 when I was two. By the time I was conscious of Chatham Street only Aunt Eva and Uncle Willy remained *in situ*.

A visit to 'Chatty', most commonly for Sunday lunch, was an intimidating experience for a child. The short walk from the 33 tram stop outside the Women's Hospital through those decaying once-handsome streets and squares, accompanied by the distant sound of a Salvation Army band, helped to build up a certain dreamlike anticipation. Standing on the porch step in front of the forbidding shiny black door, hearing the bell peel in the distant kitchen basement, Bill and I, and later Andrée, were sometimes overcome with giggles, sometimes unnaturally grave, at any rate very aware that we were on the threshold of a different world, as remote from everyday reality as Alice's Wonderland. Maud, still in awe of the older Mellys' initial disapproval, was in part responsible for our tension, but even Tom never seemed entirely at ease. Here no doubt his shortcomings as a schoolboy and business man had been made clear to him, the opposition to his marriage formulated. His defence took the form of affectionate mockery. It was the most common reaction among his generation of the family, a kind of nervous frivolity.

The door was eventually opened by Davis, curiously described as 'the head waitress', who had been at Chatham Street since 1914. Dressed in a severe black uniform with white cap and apron she nevertheless gave an impression of White-Queen-like dishevelment and calm panic. Like Gangie's Marjorie, she identified members of the family by trusting the surname as taken for granted. She addressed my parents as Mr and Mrs Tom, Gangie and Gampa were Mr and Mrs Heywood, her employers Mr Willy and Miss Eva. Davis had a rapid, very slight Liverpool accent. I never knew her Christian name or, at the time, imagined that she even had one.

Despite its Georgian exterior, 'Chatty' was completely Victorian inside. The only concessions to the twentieth century were a telephone, a wireless set and, on the piano in the library, an anachronistic little nest of art-deco ashtrays in 'jazz' colours with aluminium rims. Otherwise it was as though by stepping into the hall one simultaneously mislaid at least thirty years and, in some rooms, fifty.

Just inside the front door, crammed into quite a small vestibule, was a huge glass case of stuffed animals largely engaged in carnage: a fox looked up from dismembering a rabbit; a stoat was in the act of pouncing on a fieldmouse; a squirrel, frozen in terror, recoiled at the descent of a swooping hawk suspended from a wire. There was also a large cupboard, carved with Melly crests, and containing several boxed grey toppers, and facing it a substantial table, flanked by two of those uncomfortable little high-backed armorial chairs, and on it a silver tray for visiting cards.

All the corridors at Chatty were painted a deep shiny orange-brown. When I was very young I was terrified by a picture hanging opposite the curve of the staircase. It was probably a copy of some detail from a seventeenth-century mannerist and showed the face of a bearded old man screaming in pain or terror. The fine curve of the staircase was broken by a series of small inch-worms of metal screwed at regular intervals down the handrail to discourage young Mellys, now old or dead, from sliding down the banisters.

I knew little of the upper floors. The nursery and schoolroom were long closed up. My grandfather and his brothers and sisters were the last generation to have grown up in the house. All I knew of the nursery was derived from a late nineteenth-century water-colour at The Grange; a fire glowing behind a high fender, a dappled rocking-horse, a Noah's Ark on the floor. It's true that the drawing-room was on the first floor, a high Victorian symphony of faded gold, rose and royal blue, but by the thirties it was only used for the grandest family occasions. Its chandelier, stripped of its branches and pendant drops, was wrapped in a pendulous sheet like a great bag of cottage cheese. As those who lived at Chatty grew fewer and older, the number of rooms in general use contracted. Uncle Bill and Aunt Eva slept upstairs of course and there were guest-rooms when anyone came to stay. Davis and the servants climbed up the back stairs to the attics late at night and crept down again at dawn to black the grates, light the fires and dust and polish, but in my childhood the life of the house was effectively confined to three rooms on the ground floor: the library, the dining-room and the little morning-room, with their handsome mahogany doors.

The library was furthest away from the front door at the end of the shiny orange passage with its screaming old man. It was a room almost without colours – brown, sage-green, dusty blacks – and smelt of old leather. The only window to have escaped the window tax looked out on to Chatham Street, but there were some small French doors leading out on to a dark little garden yard with a tree in it. The light in the library was always subterranean. The nest of 'jazz' ashtrays on the piano was as incongruous as a clown at a funeral.

Although quite large, the room was cluttered. There were plants on stands and two marble statues on columns: a bust of an idealised woman with sightless eyes and a cherub with an intricately-carved swag of lace draped strategically across its presumably minuscule privates. The furniture was unmemorable and uncomfortable. Only Uncle Bill's chair with its stuffed arm-rests and curved legs had a certain distinction. It was set to the side of a steel grate next to a small table for his silver cigarette box and table lighter. It was never moved an inch. It was the library, rather than the drawing-room, which was used for family parties.

Directly opposite was a lavatory with a porcelain bowl decorated with blue irises and set into a rectangle of mahogany; let into an oval indentation on its surface was a brass plug to be pulled upwards to flush the cistern. There was also a small stand-up lavatory basin for gentlemen attached to the opposite wall, and in the bottom of this lay several small pebbles. I couldn't, I still cannot, imagine the function of those pebbles. Later, when I first heard about people 'passing' gallstones I wondered if that was what they were. The walls of this room were hung with old sepia photographs of my great-aunts in their youth, mostly seated in boats in the Lake District. As I knew that their generation never mentioned natural functions I found it odd and a little unnerving to encounter their fixed expressions gazing at me as I sat on the mahogany seat or stood at the little basin. This lavatory was used only by men and boys; the ladies were directed somewhere upstairs.

The morning-room, to the left of the front door, was small and undistinguished with wooden transom screens covering the lower half of the two windows to stop people in Chatham Street looking in and in consequence keeping half the light out. Aunt Eva did her accounts here and wrote her letters, but it was important to us in that one of the cupboards contained toys and books, the remnants of the abandoned nursery, with which we were allowed to play after lunch.

These were mostly Victorian and in many cases extremely ingenious. There was a twisted metal snake which crawled rapidly up or down a long flat rod held perpendicularly and pierced by evenly-

spaced holes. There was a monkey which performed acrobatics on
a trapeze and was set in motion by squeezing the narrow base of
the two sticks between which it hung. There were diabolos, spinning
tops with whips, bagatelle and spillikins, but our favourite toy was
a more recent addition, probably Edwardian, possibly dating from
the Great War. It consisted of two wooden ships, a dreadnought
and a submarine. The submarine was loaded with a torpedo, spring-
activated by pressing a button. The body of the dreadnought,
concealed a mousetrap-like mechanism and, after setting this, one
replaced the top deck cautiously and built up the superstructure on
top. The torpedo was fired across the carpet from some feet away
and, if it hit the target painted on the side of the dreadnought, it set
off the mousetrap, and top deck and superstructure were flung into
the air with astonishing range and velocity. It took only a second
to destroy the dreadnought and several minutes to put it back
together, but it was extremely satisfactory to operate and Bill and
I would frequently quarrel as to whose turn it was.

The books were rather dull on the whole, improving and pious
works in very small print. But there were some splendidly engraved,
hand-coloured volumes of fierce beasts and one fascinating book full
of sadistic tales about naughty children getting their comeuppance,
which even I was able to read as it deployed no word of more
than three letters, a restraint which must have meant considerable
circumlocution.

'Ned,' one story began, 'why did you get the cat and put the cat
in a bag, and put the bag in the sea?'

'For fun.'

'It is not fun for you and no fun at all for the cat.'

Needless to say this homily had no effect on Ned, but he was
eventually bitten on the leg by a mad dog and lay in terrible
agony, the jeering of the creatures he had tormented ringing in his
ears.

'Do you say it is for fun now?' asks a fly he had partially
dismembered or, to revert to the monosyllabic style of the original,
'did get the fly and did get the leg off the fly'.

While we played or read, the grown-ups dozed in the library in
the gap between lunch and tea. Everybody ate far too much at
Chatty and most of the men drank too much. The liverish, rather

disgruntled, state to which this reduced them between the enormous meals was known as Chatty fever.

It was in fact the dining-room I remember most clearly. We usually went straight in on our arrival. Uncle Bill, especially after Aunt Eva died, frequently spent the whole day there, sitting in a chair which was a pair to the one in the library, chain-smoking Turkish cigarettes through an ivory holder, a glass of brandy and soda on the little table at his side. When he had finished a cigarette he would lean forward and blow through the holder accurately projecting the dog-end into the fire. It was a completely traditional Victorian dining-room: the walls were crimson, the furniture mahogany, the pictures – a copy of a Murillo, a huge riverscape, still lifes with fruit or lobsters – all heavily framed. The dining table was enormous and would easily sit twenty people. There were huge sideboards at each end. On the other side of the fireplace there was a false door balancing the real one, with a cupboard behind it for glass and china. On the back of this door it was the custom for young Mellys to be measured at various ages; their height, name and the date pencilled in alongside the mark. I found it very strange to see my father's name next to the figures three feet six inches, and the date, 12 october 1905, or my grandfather's in 1876 when he was only three feet two inches tall.

There was seldom just us for lunch. Gangie and Gampa were often there, sometimes the Leathers, frequently several Rawdon Smiths. The volume of sound, a family characteristic, was constantly *fortissimo*.

Eva, while short and plump, was a formidable figure. Her clothes made no concession to the century. She dressed entirely in black and her voluminous dress reached the ground. She wore a locket with a coil of hair in it, a memento of someone close to her who had died. Her white hair was worn up. Her face was ruddy and plump and her slightly protruding rather luminous brown eyes and flat features gave her a distinctly pug-like look. Like her late sister Florence, she had a passion for education and, to my apprehensive terror, insisted on seeing our school reports and on setting us mathematical problems or asking us to read to her. Her comments on our shortcomings were scathing and as painful to Maud as to us. She was, however, basically kind and once our inquisition was over, adept at amusing us. Eva did a considerable amount of charitable work, but her main occupation was running Chatham Street. Her hobbies were water-colour sketching and completing enormous jigsaws. Her paintings were not up to much but everybody was expected to admire them. She usually submitted several to the annual exhibition at the Walker Art Gallery, the Liverpool equivalent of the Royal Academy Summer Show, and they were most often hung. One year, however, her contribution was rejected and, to make matters worse, a painting of a bluebell wood by Dorothy Leather, my Auntie Golly, was accepted and hung 'on the line'. Aunt Eva didn't take this at all well and Uncle Bill, never noted for tact, attempted to reassure her, in front of Dorothy, by saying that the judges obviously didn't know what they were talking about.

Eva's jigsaws came from a club and were properly made of quite thick wood. She was a complete purist. No picture or title was provided by the club, but even this was not enough for her. She would most often turn the pieces face down so that there was no help from areas of colour, and only when it was completed would she place a large board over the surface on which she had worked and turn it over to reveal 'The Changing of the Guard' or 'Deerstalking in the Highlands'. This abstract activity took up a fair amount of her time. Her jigsaw was laid out on a huge baize-covered tray on a rather rickety little table in the morning room, and one dreadful afternoon Bill and I, in our excitement over a direct hit on the dreadnought, knocked it over when the puzzle was three-quarters done.

Eva had a pocket in her throat and as, like most of the family, she ate far too fast, food would frequently lodge in it and have to be coughed up again and reswallowed. This was a noisy and prolonged operation and the convention was that nobody paid any attention, simply shouting even louder than usual to be heard. Shortly after my parents' marriage they were invited to dinner at Chatham Street and my mother, unused to Eva's retching and gasping, felt and showed her dismay. Eva drew breath for a moment to say that if Maud were upset she had permission to leave the table. Maud, who was trying hard to ingratiate herself, went crimson with embarrassment and shame.

Eva died in 1937, but her brother Bill lived on alone at Chatham Street until 1944. Willie Bert's description of Uncle Bill seems to me so succinct and plaintive that I'm going to reprint it in full, and then relate those facts which impinge on my own memory or which I learnt from my father, about the almost silent figure sitting in front of the steel grate in the dining-room on Sunday mornings.

Willie Bert wrote:

William Rathbone, George and Sarah Melly's 7th child and third son, was born at 90 Chatham Street on March 30th 1867. Known to every one as Willy, he was always rather delicate, and was educated at the Royal Institution, Liverpool. In 1883 his health broke down and he was sent for 15 months to live with Lord Dalhousie's head keeper at Panmure, which laid the foundation of his great interest and knowledge of natural history and shooting.

In 1891 he spent three months in Naples studying sponges, but had to come home as he was ill. He then spent a year in South America as Supercargo in Lamport and Holt's ships; after which he was in their London office for a year or so before joining his father's firm of George Melly and Co. in Liverpool, in January 1894, and becoming a partner in October after his father's death.

His interest in life was never business but always birds and shooting. In 1894 his uncle, George Holt, took a shooting at Llwyn Ynn near Ruthin, always referred to as The Farm, for the entertainment of his nephews (and nieces) and put William in charge. This went on till the estate was sold in 1913, William assuming more and more of the financial responsibility. It was a good general shoot producing over 1,000 head most years. All the members of the family went there year after year, his sister Florence acting as hostess.

In 1914 he took a grouse moor at Farndale in Yorkshire, but gave it up on the outbreak of war. From then until the death of his brother George, he had no shooting of his own but spent many weeks each year at Rosedale Abbey. After George's death in 1927, he became tenant of the Rosedale shoot and carried it on in the same lavish way as it had been in the past, but spending some weeks there in the spring and summer bird-watching and photographing. He was a very keen photographer and left hundreds of prints all in books duly annotated. For some years he used to prepare magic lantern slides from some of his photographs which he showed at the family Christmas party.

In March, 1932, it was decided to close the firm of George Melly and Co., and he retired from business, but at Rosedale on October 4th that year he had some sort of stroke which left him a completely different man, very silent and taking very little interest in what went on around him. Up till then he had been a very talkative man and although so handicapped by ill health, was tremendously energetic and lived life to the full. He would walk all day after grouse or partridges and then stay up half the night talking or playing cards. He was always more than generous to his nephews and nieces.

Shooting and photography were by no means his only interests. He fished, played golf and croquet whenever the opportunity offered. He said he had taken part at some time in his life in every sport except hunting.

He never married. From the time he came home from South America he suffered terribly from psoriasis. He died on 9th March, aged 76. A greater age than any of his brothers.

I was only six when Uncle Bill had 'some sort of stroke' and have therefore little recollection of the 'tremendously energetic', 'very talkative man' of earlier days. In fact I can only remember him once outside his own front door and that was when he took me, aged about five, to visit the Liverpool Zoo. This was a rather seedy and ill-stocked institution on Mossley Hill which nevertheless, in lieu of anything better, played an important role in my life, as I was and remain fascinated by zoos and had at that time some aspirations to become a keeper when I grew up.

For this expedition Willy wore pepper-and-salt tweeds and brown boots, while on his head was a large, rather shapeless tweed cap which my mother said 'looked like a sponge-bag'. We wandered together for an hour or so examining the mangy lions and tigers in their cramped quarters, the solitary elephant in its sweet-smelling shed, the few snakes, the dispirited bears. Willy, peering through his round pince-nez over his bedraggled nicotine-stained moustache, offered few observations until it was time to go. Then he said to me: 'I like this better than the London Zoo.' I turned to him in appalled amazement. Although I had not yet visited Regent's Park, it was high on my list of priorities if I should ever be taken to London. I knew there was no comparison. My uncle had said something so perverse, so unreasonable that I demanded an immediate explanation. Why? How? What did he mean?

'Not so many damned animals to look at,' he mumbled.

My father told me something of Uncle Willy before his stroke. He had been a great organiser of family outings. One summer in the early twenties there had been a circus pitched on a field off Aigburth Road. It included a lion tamer one of whose beasts, whose name was Nero, was of such ferocity that it was seldom allowed into the ring. Uncle Bill had attended the opening night and was so impressed by Nero's dangerous intransigence that he returned most evenings with as many of the family as could be persuaded to accompany him. As the circus was not doing too well and he had booked the front row for the entire run of the show, he was treated like a Roman Emperor and, like a Roman Emperor, it was the lion act which particularly interested him. Whenever he was present and if, as was most often the case, the lion tamer had decided that Nero was in too uncertain a temper to join his companions in the ring, Willy would demand his presence. 'Let Nero out!' he'd bellow, and it was done. I couldn't help wondering how Uncle Willy would have felt if a fatal accident had taken place as a result of his whim.

There was indeed an element of sadism in him. One of the few ways that we, as children, could arouse him out of his torpor was to ask him to show us the mousetrap he had brought back many years earlier from a visit to Berlin at the turn of the century. This was in the form of a Gothic church and quite large. The top could be removed to show its sinister inner workings. The mouse entered by the church door and proceeded up the nave attracted by the smell of cheese. At the foot of the altar it trod on a board which was sprung in such a way as to slam the door behind it. Having recovered from its panic, it renewed its interest in the cheese and, in pursuit of it, climbed a ladder up the inside of the tower most of which was occupied by a large water tank. At the top of the ladder, and over the tank, was a narrow passage with the cheese at the far end. The mouse excitedly scampered towards it, unaware that halfway across was a trap-door which opened, precipitating the unfortunate creature into the water tank where it swam until it drowned. What was so ingenious about the contraption, as Uncle Willy enthusiastically explained to us, was that the action of the trap, in springing back into the closed position, reopened the church door to be ready to welcome any other passing mouse and, as there was no smell of death, there was no limit to the number of rodents it could dispatch in one mission. I had proof as to its effectiveness. One afternoon Bill and I visited the dark and tortuous kitchens in the basement. In the yard, thrown there by Davis for the nourishment of the Chatham Street cats, were the drowned corpses of four or five mice, the harvest of a single night.

When he had finished explaining the mechanism of this infernal and very Teutonic machine, Uncle Bill would reset it with his constantly shaking hands, replace its religious exterior and ask us to put it back under the sideboard before relapsing into his customary silence.

This withdrawal had marked the end of a more regular family ritual than the release of Nero; the tribal visits to the D'Oyly Carte Opera Company on their biennial appearance in Liverpool, a custom much dreaded by Maudie in the early years of her marriage. This was not only on musical grounds, although no doubt for her Gilbert and Sullivan came under the general heading of 'mini-mini', but also because of Uncle Bill's noisy and extrovert behaviour on these pre-stroke outings. This was due to the fact that, unlike the majority of Savoyards, he considered the overture as a time when chocolates could be ordered and the merits of the Company discussed with members of the family however distantly seated along the row. His competence to pass judgement was founded on his golfing friendship with Sir Henry Lytton and with Miss Bertha Belmore, the two principals. Wishing to make this clear to those around him he would boom out Sir Henry's opinions at second hand. The death of Miss Belmore, far from inhibiting him, added a fresh topic. 'Harry tells me,' he'd shout, oblivious to a mounting storm of angry shushing, 'that this woman's not as good as Bertha!' Despite the end of these visits *en masse*, my father retained his affection for the operas and was delighted that in time I was to share his enthusiasm. His favourite was *Ruddigore*, which during the thirties had been dropped from the repertoire, so our first visit was to his second preference, *The Gondoliers*. I enjoyed it so much that he later took me to see *The Mikado*, *The Yeomen of the Guard* and the rest of the canon. I learnt many of the songs by heart and would enunciate them in that curiously affected mincing voice favoured by the Company. I tried, at Tom's suggestion, singing them to Uncle Willy, but he showed no more than a flicker of interest. Sir Harry had followed Bertha Belmore into the dark. Gilbert and Sullivan, like everything else except the mouse-trap, had lost their savour.

The cause of Uncle Bill's stroke was obscure but there were dark rumours. My father told me eventually that it was believed by some that, as a child, he had been injected for smallpox with a needle, insufficiently sterilised, which had previously been used on a baby infected with syphilis. It is true he never married but this is more probably because of his psoriasis, a flaking of the skin caused by the overproduction of cells, which afflicted his whole body with the exception of his face and hands. This led to terrible irritation especially at night and his only relief was to get up and take a tar bath. There was a limit to the time he was allowed to stay in the water and my father told me that once, staying at Rosedale in a room next to the bathroom, he had been awakened by Uncle Bill murmuring something rhythmically to himself and, on enquiring next morning, he discovered it to be Lewis Carroll's *The Hunting of the Snark*. Apparently the time it took Bill to recite this work coincided exactly with the period he was allowed to submerge himself in the medicated waters.

Apart from his shaking and the psoriasis, Uncle Bill also suffered from a hatred of anything sweet or sugary with the single if inexplicable exception of chocolate peppermint creams, for which indeed he nourished an inordinate passion. In consequence he was given each day his own little dish of Hasty Pudding, a kind of unsweetened soufflé, while everyone else dug into a wide choice of elaborate trifles, tarts and rich rice dishes.

As the head of the household it would normally have been his prerogative to carve the enormous joint which preceded the puddings, but his ague and general disability prevented it. With no apparent irony intended, it fell to him in recompense to ladle out the puddings which were placed in front of him after the removal of the meat course.

'Anyone want any of this muck?' he would enquire. Frequently this was one of the only three times he spoke during our entire visit. The other two sentences were 'How's yourself?' on our arrival and 'Look after yourself' on our departure. The contrast for older members of the family who remembered him as 'very talkative' must have been extraordinary.

The great occasion of the year at Chatham Street was the family party held towards the end of the week after Christmas. Almost every Melly and Smith living were present and, in the case of married women née Melly, their husbands and children also. The one notable exception was Willie Bert's mother, Great-Aunt Beatrice, who lived in southern England. After a toast to 'absent friends', Willie Bert always leapt to his feet and proposed 'My Mother' as a codicil. It was more likely her geographical rather than her 'invidious position' as a divorced woman which prevented her presence at the Chatty parties. Not that distance alone kept many members of the family away. My Great-Aunt Nell and her daughter Cousin Nell were assiduous attenders. They lived together in London in an Edwardian mansion block off the Fulham Road with eau-de-Nil walls and fine Dutch furniture, but stayed a great deal at Chatham Street and indeed lived there during the Hitler war; Aunt Nell looking after Uncle Bill, Cousin Nell driving a Civil Defence ambulance throughout the Blitz. Aunt Nell and her daughter were known as 'Old Nell' and 'Young Nell'.

Old Nell had been the second wife of Hugh Melly, one of Uncle Willy's brothers who had died in 1924, two years before I was born. He was said to have been extremely handsome. His first wife, who was killed in a carriage accident in 1890, had two daughters. She had been a Holt, a member of the shipping family. The older daughter married a Canadian and I never knew her, but the younger, Cousin Joan, married a rather noisy, ferociously right-wing but personally kindly coal-mine owner called Major Arthur Bromilow, and the Bromilows too were very much a presence at the Chatty parties.

Old Nell had three children by Hugh: Pete, who was killed in the 1914–18 war; John, who was a surgeon and took the only British Red Cross unit out to Abyssinia when it was attacked by Mussolini and who was shot on the last day of the conflict by an African rioter who, logically enough I suppose, mistook him for an Italian; and Young Nell herself.

I can remember John who seemed quite extraordinarily charming and sophisticated. He had been a friend of Vivien Leigh's and had written a drawing-room comedy which was almost put on in the

West End. He had, like many of his generation during the twenties, a passion for elaborate practical jokes. At the same time, like his mother, he was profoundly religious, and it was the application of his practical evangelical spirit which led to his death in the streets of Addis Ababa in 1936.

Old Nell was, I suppose, plain but with so glowing and saint-like a personality that she seemed to be beautiful. Like Aunt Eva she made no concessions to current fashion but her dresses, while black and floor length, were Edwardian rather than Victorian, and she always wore a tight, boned neck choker in the manner of Queen Alexandra. Unlike Eva and Florence, whose philanthropy was severely practical and objective, Nell's faith insisted on a St Francis-like involvement with those she tried to help. She was preyed on by many petty con-men who came to her with optimistic schemes for self-improvement, and when in London she would visit the embankment night after night with food and money for the down-and-outs. Aunt Eva found this approach intensely irritating, referring rather contemptuously to 'Nell's lame ducks'.

Nell was a great admirer of the Salvation Army. When the film of Shaw's *Major Barbara* came out, she and a like-minded friend staged a planned protest in the Plaza Cinema, Lime Street, and were ejected. She was also an animal rights sympathiser long before such a movement existed. She was wracked with guilt at having enjoyed hunting as a girl. It was the ride, she explained, which had been the source of her pleasure, but the ride after all was at the expense of the poor fox and even of his life. To be surrounded by relations who shot and fished with such enthusiasm, staying frequently in a house which contained the fiendish ecclesiastical mousetrap, must have caused her much pain. During the Blitz she took it upon herself to read Uncle Bill the whole of *Gone With the Wind*. Increasingly senile, I imagine he made little of it, especially as he was very frightened and confused by the bombing.

Young Nell was a cheerful person, full of fun, obsessed with the Mellys, and given to that vice of all large middle-class English families between the wars of constantly asserting that 'we are just like the Forsytes'. Young Nell never married. She lives in the same eau-de-Nil flat off Fulham Road and is still, at the age of eighty-three, known as Young Nell.

It was at the Chatty party that the remaining Riverslea Mellys surfaced: Cousins Leonard and Fanny, both old and as poor as church mice. Leonard's dinner jacket was green with age. Rotund, bustling Fanny gave us children only half-a-crown each but they were always mint half-crowns which she had drawn especially from the bank.

It was this huge and noisy party then, three generations of them, that assembled yearly for the great family feast. What happened at it was as fixed and immutable as a religious ceremony.

Before dinner the rarely used drawing-room was opened up although the chandelier remained in its shroud. Sherry was on offer. The meal was huge, even by Chatham Street standards. The youngest member of the family had to propose a toast, an obligation which made my sister Andrée almost ill with nerves when it came to her turn. Toasts completed, a long and very boring event followed. The senior member of the family recited this catch to the person on his or her right:

> Do you know the muffin man, the muffin man, the muffin man?
> Oh, do you know the muffin man who lives in Drury Lane?

To which the person so questioned replied:

> Oh, yes, I know the muffin man, the muffin man, the muffin man,
> Oh, yes, I know the muffin man who lives in Drury Lane.

Then both parties would intone together:

> Then we *two* know the muffin man, the muffin man, the muffin man,
> We *two* know the muffin man who lives in Drury Lane.

Then the person to have answered the question first turned towards whoever was on his or her right and repeated it; was answered in the affirmative and the three acquaintances of the muffin man agreed in unison that they knew him too. Unbelievably, this rigmarole continued until everybody at the table – there must have been well over thirty most years – could shout out the final chorus:

> Then we *all* know the muffin man, the muffin man, the muffin man,
> We *all* know the muffin man who lives in Drury Lane,

Some tried to enliven this incredibly tiresome chore by putting on funny accents but most, with surprising good spirits, simply played it straight. It was never suggested that it might be curtailed or dropped altogether. That would have been considered almost blasphemous.

After everybody agreed that they knew the unnaturally gregarious muffin man, the ladies went into the library and the gentlemen drank port or brandy and told mildly indecent jokes. Boys were allowed to remain in the dining-room from about the age of twelve for this initiation into masculine mores. Even Uncle Bill became quite animated and told a story about the sexual habits of the Kaiser. He also usually described a 'feller' he had seen on the stage in Paris in the early 1900s who could fart several tunes and blow out a candle at a considerable distance by the same means. Nobody really believed this, but quite recently it was revealed as fact and a book on the gentleman, 'Le Pétomane', was published proving that Uncle Bill was telling the truth.

The men, whether laughing at the Kaiser's inadequacy or pretending to believe in the exploits of 'Le Pétomane', all wore dinner jackets and the same year that I was allowed to remain behind with them in the dining-room, I wore one too. This was not new – the idea of spending money on a dinner jacket for a growing child would have appalled my father – but had been handed down for several generations. Even so I was extremely pleased with myself, despite Tom's joke at my expense earlier in the evening. I'd gone into his dressing-room, ostensibly so that he could tie my bow, in fact to solicit admiration, but all he'd said was: 'Don't annoy the little man. They're very touchy, these dwarfs!'

I must have looked rather hurt because he immediately explained the source of this mysterious but unflattering reaction. As a small child in Sefton Park he had seen a dwarf out walking with his 'owner', a showman attached to a travelling fair then *in situ*. He had scampered curiously towards it, to be met by this informative reproach. Once I'd understood it was joke I was completely mollified. I even repeated it on arrival.

When we left the dining-room to 'join the ladies', it was discovered that my brother Bill, jealous that my three years seniority allowed me to stay on, had concealed himself under the table. He told me later that he had understood nothing that had been said and grown extremely bored. In fact my own reaction had been more or less the same, but of course I wasn't letting on. 'You will when you're older,' I assured him dismissively.

The final stage of the Chatty party took place in the library. It was in two parts: 'The Great Divide' and the entertainment. 'The Great Divide' was the name given to the doling out of money in lieu of presents, a rational if somewhat impersonal solution to the problem of how to reward so large a gathering. Uncle Bill would slump in his accustomed chair. Davis would carry in a silver tray piled high with brown envelopes like wage packets. She would stand by her employer and he would pick up the envelopes at random, reading out the name written on each of them: 'Young Nell', 'Gillian Leather', 'Samuel Heywood Melly'. Each of us in turn would go forward, collect our envelope, and kiss him on his cold indifferent cheek. Each knew exactly what to expect: £50 for his generation, £25 for my father's, £10 for those in their twenties, £1 for my contemporaries. It was rather a soulless exercise, the only excitement arising from the order in which we were called and the possibility, never fulfilled, that someone might have been accidentally left out.

The entertainment followed immediately. Gangie and Gampa would offer one of 'Mrs Caudle's Curtain Lectures'; we would perform a carefully rehearsed sketch; others played the piano or recited comic monologues. One year, during Aunt Eva's lifetime, a Rawdon Smith girl – I believe it was Hope, one of Willie Bert's daughters – tap-danced to a gramophone record having first changed into shorts. Aunt Eva was visibly put out at this immodesty which must have upset Willie Bert. He was always extremely solicitous towards the old ladies of the family.

As Uncle Bill had already suffered his stroke before I was old enough to attend the Chatty parties, he had relinquished his bird-watching and photography and in consequence no longer 'prepared and showed his magic-lantern slides as part of the entertainment'. I gather that this was no great loss. Young Nell once told me that the performance lasted a long time and that the slides themselves were so blurred and indistinct that the whole enterprise had become known to the more irreverent members of the family as 'Owls in a Fog'.

During the war the Chatty parties became smaller and one year, during the height of the Blitz, there was none at all. Uncle Bill died in 1944 after several days in a coma. Davis, who had looked after him with extreme devotion, told my mother, with initial reluctance, of his end. He had regained consciousness on a cold but bright winter's evening and hauled himself up in his narrow bed to face the setting sun. 'Oh hell!' he'd muttered resignedly and fallen back dead.

I'd been to visit him shortly before this took place. On the chest of drawers was a small glass dome and inside it a stuffed thrush and a golf ball. A brass plaque on the base explained the curious confrontation: 'In 1903 W. R. Melly drove off the 3rd tee at Formby Golf Club. His ball struck a thrush in the air, killing it instantly, and holed in one.'

With Willy's death, Chatham Street was given up and its contents, with the exception of the drawing-room furniture which was left to the museum, sold or divided among the family. Uncle Bill left his body for dissection in the hope that 'whatever was wrong with me' might further medical research, but the offer was refused and he was buried in the tiny graveyard of the ancient Unitarian chapel at the Dingle, opposite the Gaumont Cinema. The house itself now belongs to the University. Passing it recently I saw, through a window, the morning-room full of filing cabinets and illuminated by strip-lighting. A girl brought in a plastic cup of tea or coffee and placed it in front of a man sorting out folders on a formica-topped table.

7

Surrounded by large late nineteenth-century houses, ringed by a sandy ride where middle-class little girls cantered self-consciously past on horses hired from a local riding school, Sefton Park forms a valley bisected by a string of lakes, the largest of which, 'The Big Lake', had boats for hire in summer and, when frozen in the winter, became black with skaters. On the other side of the lakes, dominating the landscape, is the Palm House, a large, circular, domed building of steel and glass in imitation of the Crystal Palace. When it was cold it offered a steamy refuge to expressionless men in bright blue suits and red ties, many of them missing an arm or leg. They were the institutionalised wounded of the 1914–18 war, and would sit all day smoking Woodbines on the fern-patterned Victorian benches. Behind them grew a contained circular jungle, its tropical trees and plants neatly labelled, and here and there a small marble statue of a coy nymph or simpering maiden with a quotation from a poet carved on her plinth. In summer the men sat outside on similar benches.

Statues ringed the exterior also, life-size and representing historic figures in the arts and sciences. Before I could read, my father invented false identities for those frozen worthies. A Swiss botanist, he assured me, represented the Prince of Wales, while Galileo, holding a globe of the world, he maintained to be Dixie Dean, the celebrated footballer. Beyond the Palm House the park levelled out to form a great plain big enough to accommodate the annual fair; below it a steep hill swept down to one of the little lakes.

At the bottom of this hill were two stone posts designed to discourage cyclists as there was then only a few yards across a road before the iron railings which ringed the water. I had at one time a small yellow motor car with push pedals and on one of our visits to look at Dixie Dean and the Prince of Wales my father made the following proposition. He would squat behind me on the yellow pedal car, in itself a rather precarious operation, and we would then free-wheel down the hill between the posts, whereupon I would have to turn the wheel abruptly to the right in order to avoid the railings. At five or six, for I can't have been any older, this seemed a perfectly reasonable if exciting thing to do, for I trusted Tom entirely and the danger didn't occur to me. We did it, gathering considerable speed, and shot between the posts missing the railings by a few inches. The mystery is that I cannot imagine what got into my father. It was most unlike him, and either or both of us could have been killed or badly injured. He told me not to tell my mother who wouldn't understand and I never did. Perhaps though, like Maud's driving, it is a false memory.

Most visits to the park were less traumatic. Accompanied by my mother or a nanny we usually carried with us one of those creased and crinkly brown paper bags (no longer manufactured) full of crusts cut from sandwiches, and any stale bread on the point of claiming Mrs Spilsbury's attention. This was to feed the ducks, and was indeed known as 'the ducks' bread', but very little of it reached the throng of mallards, Canadian geese and the odd swan for whom it was intended. En route, almost before we had reached the bottom of Lark Lane, my brother and I and later my sister had eaten most of it. We wouldn't have looked at it in the ordinary way, of course, but in the open air (and because it was for the ducks) it tasted delicious. The phrase 'the ducks' bread' became in time shorthand for any eating up of stale or rejected food. My mother had a loathing of waste and would finish anything left on a plate or about to be thrown away. Such odds and ends – a spoonful of steak and kidney pie, some congealed custard, a wilting salad – never reached the dustbin. 'Your mother,' Tom would say on catching her guiltily but obsessively spooning them up, 'is at the ducks' bread again.'

The Park, like much of Liverpool, paid its reluctant homage to London. The sandy perimeter ride was called 'Rotten Row'. At the end of the 'little lakes' was a cast of Kensington Gardens' Peter Pan. During my childhood, a full-sized replica of Piccadilly's Eros was installed opposite the café at the bottom of the hill which led down from the Lark Lane gates. The café was rebuilt at the same time.

The wooden 'Elizabethan' shack was replaced by a more solid art-deco structure. Peter Pan and Eros belong for me in Sefton Park. When later I saw the originals *in situ* I thought of them as 'displaced'.

There was little else of interest: a fine Victorian crescent aviary, an obelisk, two artificial 'caves' stinking of urine, a decaying Wendy House on the sward behind Peter Pan and a flat-bottomed Jolly Roger in the shallow lake below him. There was a Happy Valley and a Fairy Glen, a solemn statue of William Rathbone, after whom Uncle Willy was named, in a marble frock-coat, his hand on a marble book staring in side-whiskered indifference over the Big Lake.

The dangerous swoop down the Palm House hill apart, nothing extraordinary happened to me in Sefton Park. If I were to walk through it with a stranger to Liverpool, they would see a park and nothing else: dirty lakes, replicas of famous statues, a large conservatory, worn grass and undistinguished trees. I cannot explain, even to myself, why no corner of it leaves me unmoved.

If the park formed the 'landscape' of my childhood, the tram was its most potent presence. There are no trams in Liverpool now; they were phased out soon after the war. The point about the tram was that, because it never deviated from its tracks, the perspective of street and park was always held in exactly the same relation to the eye and gradually, through repeated journeys along the same routes, assumed the clarity of a Canaletto; the definitive view. Rattling along Park Road for example – a street of small shops, innumerable solid pubs and great soot-blackened Catholic churches – the cobbled, hilly streets of two-up two-down houses which led down to the river did so always at the same angle, and the horizon of the Mersey with its shipyard cranes on the other shore and the Welsh mountains beyond them remained fixed, imprinted on the memory with extreme precision. Trams were noisy. I could hear them whining and clanking from my bed in Ivanhoe Road, and occasionally a blue or green flash from some faulty electric contact would illuminate the night sky. The names of their destinations were printed on cloth and rolled into place behind a glass-fronted panel on both the back and front of the vehicle: Garston, the Dingle, Fazackerly, St Domingo's Pit, the Pier Head.

The tram, like the 'pushmi-pullyu' in the Dr Dolittle books, was the same at both ends. When it reached its terminus and had to go back the other way, the driver would pull on the thin rope suspended from the sprung pulley which connected it to the electric wire above, and lead it round like a giraffe to face in the opposite direction. Meanwhile the conductor, in his dark blue uniform and peaked cap, would walk from one end to the other of both decks noisily pushing the slatted wooden seatbacks, which were hinged in such a way as to reverse their position so that those who boarded the tram were always facing the way they were going. The controls too, nautical in their elegance and simplicity, were identical and there were two entrances and a set of stairs at each end.

Liverpool people never called a tram a tram. It was either a tram-car or, more commonly, the car: 'I went into town like on the car.' The tram conductors had a certain bravura. They seemed to enjoy pulling on the leather strap, strung down the centre of the lower deck, which went 'ting-ting' in the driver's cabin. They cracked their ticket punches with enthusiasm, and shouted 'I theng yow!' when offered the fare (or 'fur' as most of their customers pronounced it). The late Arthur Askey adopted that 'I theng yow' as his slogan but few outside Liverpool knew where it came from. Tram conductors' fingers were black from handling the change in their big leather satchels. The tickets were very beautiful, rectangular, printed on slightly furry paper in faded colours, pink, pale green, beige, mauve, a washed-out blue. Painter Schwitters would have loved them. Children knew how to fold them in such a way as to construct concertinas.

When I was very young there were still some trams that must have gone back to the turn of the century with outside iron spiral staircases and tin advertisements for medical products, but most of them had been built in the early twenties. They were red and cream outside and had little stained-glass panels, either red or blue and engraved like pub glass, let in to the tops of the windows. On the poorer routes there were sometimes barefoot children in torn jerseys among the customers but most of them wore big boots. There were still a fair number of 'Mary Ellens', old matriarchs of the slums in great crocheted shawls and many layers of petticoats. They wore boots too and some of them male caps. The trams smelt of stale sweat and urine but it was never a smell I disliked. It seemed to suggest to me a dangerous freedom. My mother, who could remember horse-trams, would listen intently to the uninhibited badinage in order to improve the authenticity of her performance of Maud Budden's Liverpudlian sketches. There was one mad woman who rode the number 1 or 45 very frequently. At each stop she would shout out 'The back of the baths'.

Halfway up Park Road there was a junk shop we always looked out for as its owner went in for large hand-written posters of marked originality which were frequently changed. One read: 'My dad was good enough for your dad. Let me be good enough for you.' Another: 'Get off that tram, it'll never be yours. Save your fares to buy a bike.' On the back of a tin bath hanging on a nail, he scrawled in chalk: 'Big enough to bath a bobby in'.

Trams featured quite strongly in my mother's inner life. Once, when she was a girl and the upper decks were still open, a man had spat and gob had landed in her hair. She mentioned this frequently and with shivering revulsion which was understandable enough. Spitting was still common in Liverpool in the thirties. All public transport had 'Do not spit' notices on them.

The other facet of her obsession with the tram was more mysterious. When I was in late adolescence and our conversations, frequently on the subject of sex, had become extremely open and intimate, I had explained to her, with all the smug assurance of one whose knowledge was extremely sketchy, the theories of Freud. She found them far-fetched initially, but then confessed to the following fixation. She was excited sexually by the following image: a small working-class child runs out into the road almost under the wheels of a tram. Its mother grabs it just in time, curses at it and slaps it vigorously. 'What,' my mother asked me, 'would your friend Mr Freud make of that?' She had this habit of referring to people I was enthusiastic about in this way. (Among my 'friends' at this period were 'Mr Picasso', 'Mr Joyce', and 'Mr Eliot'.) I offered what I thought might be the explanation: unidentified early sexual feelings coinciding with witnessing such a scene in reality was my general conclusion. She didn't really listen to my theory. It was too abstract to appeal to her rather literal view of life. I, on the other hand, was fascinated by so clear a 'case'. I thought about it a lot. 'Did you,' I asked her later, 'think about this scenario on the night I was conceived?' 'Yes,' she said, quite openly, 'I always thought about it when Tom . . .' I found it very odd to think that at the moment when my future existence was assured, my mother was thinking of a child pulled from under a tram, cursed at and slapped.

In the late thirties the old red and cream trams were replaced by green streamlined models with seat upholstery, springing and more silent machinery. They were called 'the Green Goddesses' and were considered an enormous improvement. They continued to run for some time after the war and were then scrapped in favour of buses. I never took to them. It's the old red bone-shakers that sway and clang through the Liverpool streets of my memory.

8

At the far end of Sefton Park, past the Big Lake with its skaters or rowers depending on the season, and across two roads, was the bottom of Mossley Hill, the grandest enclave in Liverpool. The ascent started inauspiciously with a few semi-detached houses and a tin tabernacle painted a rusty dark green, but then the great Victorian houses began, set in large grounds; many with lodges at their gates, and protected by high sandstone walls. There were three reasons for our visiting Mossley Hill: Riverslea, the Liverpool Zoo, and Cousin Emma Holt.

Riverslea was the house which the suicidally depressive, fountain-loving Charles Melly had bought for his mother and family after the death in Egypt of Andrée Melly and their return to Liverpool. Charles Melly had eight children, but with two exceptions they had either married or moved away from Riverslea by the time I came to know it. Of these emigrés the most powerful and richest was Charles's second son, Edward Ferdinand Melly.

Edward was a coal owner and lived at Nuneaton where he was twice Mayor. According to my father he had both a tyrannical will and a ferocious temper. Driving his gig through the streets of Nuneaton at the beginning of the 1914–18 war, he found his path blocked by a long column of volunteers under the command of a young lieutenant. Cousin Edward bellowed for the ranks to be broken so that he could continue on his way, and, on being refused, threatened to drive through them at a gallop. The young lieutenant drew his sword and said that if he tried he would run him through. My father considered this a brave and commendable action.

Tom was in some awe of his elderly cousin, having once suffered his serious if collective displeasure. In the early twenties Edward had taken a house on the coast of Scotland and invited several of the younger generation to stay. Among them were Tom, Young Nell, and Nell's brother John, then a medical student and very addicted to practical jokes. There was a great storm and next day, among the rocks, were huge and almost solid drifts of spume and spray. At John's instigation Nell and my father had collected some of this and persuaded the cook to serve it as a pudding that evening. It was described, quite accurately, on the individual menu cards as 'Sea Spray'.

Cousin Edward, who, unlike Uncle Bill, had a sweet tooth, helped himself to a large dollop from the cut-glass dish; the storm after his first mouthful was the equal of the night before and those responsible were threatened with a seat on the next available train south. He eventually calmed down but was not, even in retrospect, at all amused.

As a small child on a visit to Riverslea I had, it seems, a brush with Cousin Edward. I disagreed with him on some minor point in the works of Beatrix Potter and obstinately proved I was right by producing the appropriate book. My parents had trembled, but Edward unexpectedly hadn't lost his temper. I can't remember the incident myself, but it had so impressed Maud and Tom that they frequently referred to it. Cousin Edward and his third wife – he had buried her predecessors – were killed by a bomb in 1941.

Cousin Fanny and Cousin Leonard were the only two of Charles's children who still lived at Riverslea. Unlike their brother Edward, they were very badly off and the Gothic house was peeling and crumbling about them. Fanny looked like an improvident farmer's wife and had a large mole sprouting hair, something of a hazard when she embraced us. She kept hens in the overgrown garden and even, it was reported, went puffing down to Aigburth Road to buy potatoes in order to save the minimal additional expense of having them delivered. Leonard was tiny and mouse-like. He wore threadbare grey suits and a wing-collar, and had a small but straggly moustache. He exuded a rather sweet melancholy like a character in Chekhov. Indeed the whole atmosphere at Riverslea, with its decaying grandeur and faded chintz furniture, was what I later recognised to be Chekhovian, especially on a late summer's afternoon when the sun streamed through the French windows of the drawing-room and there was an air of mild regret hovering over the delicate but cracked tea service.

Beyond the windows, the garden was a jungle and very exciting to explore. Only the lawn was kept in order, and that because the Riversleas had a passion for croquet, that most ill-tempered of games, at which, Tom told me, all the envy and rivalry between the two branches of the family had found an outlet during his childhood visits. On Boxing Days too, in order to recover from the excesses of a Chatham Street Christmas Day, the George Mellys would mount an expedition to Riverslea to challenge their cousins at hockey, a perfect excuse for hacking away viciously at each other's shins. Once, during my own childhood, Leonard and Fanny had two great-nephews to stay with them and the custom was briefly, although on a reduced scale, revived. They were tough and vicious little boys and I could understand why my father had dreaded the 26th of December, a day which also happened to be his birthday. Leonard and Fanny were in themselves gentle and unaggressive. Fanny, while so comparatively poor herself, did voluntary work in the slums of Scotland Road and was, according to Willie Bert, much loved. I can believe it. She was a most cheerful and uncomplaining old lady.

Leonard and Fanny could, of course, have sold Riverslea with its large grounds and lived the rest of their lives in comfort, but I don't suppose it even occurred to them. As it was, the wallpaper was damp and peeling, the carpets threadbare. In one room was a billiard table piled high with old newspapers. I once suggested to my mother there might be several dead Riverslea Mellys buried and forgotten under them. In one of the disused and empty bedrooms in the Tower hung a trapeze. Leonard was interested only in sport. When my mother was unofficially engaged and already under siege from the disapproving Chatham Street uncles and aunts she happened to be standing behind Leonard at an amateur rugger match in which my father was playing. She was appalled to hear Leonard say to his companion: 'Young Tom's playing very badly. Too many late dances with that damn girl I shouldn't wonder.' To me he would drone on about cricket, a game which, for reasons which will become apparent, I nursed a considerable loathing. He had

been the President of the Liverpool Cricket Club for many years
and used to arrange the public school tour.

Fanny died in 1942; Leonard in 1951. The house was left to the
University who sensibly, if unimaginatively, knocked it down. I
have the catalogue of the auction of its contents, a truly surreal list
of accumulated rubbish: Lot 74: a small bronze depicting monkeys
shaving a bear. Lot 113: laundry basket containing linen and sundry
photographs. Lot 274: under-bed wardrobe containing model railway lines and preserved lizard.

The Liverpool Zoo marched on Riverslea. It had moved there
from Otterspool Park, where I can only just remember it, despite
vehement objections from the residents of Mossley Hill. The lions
would keep them awake at night. A dangerous animal might escape.
It would encourage *hoi polloi*, some of whom might trespass.

Despite Uncle Bill's seal of approval, the Zoo was what Gangie
would have called 'a poor do'. Mr Rogers, who had hired to my
father the monkey with such unfortunate results, was a big jovial
pipe-smoking man who looked rather like the late Rab Butler. As I
was among his most frequent visitors he made me a 'Junior Fellow'
(were there any other 'Fellows' I wonder, either Junior or Senior?),
and would sometimes show me around himself. In the reptile house
there was a large python called Billy. One of my privileges as a
Junior Fellow was to be allowed to drape Billy round my shoulders.
Recently, outside the Tiger Balm Gardens in Singapore, I came
upon an Indian gentleman with a snake he was prepared to hire out
for a small fee so that tourists could take each other's photographs
holding it. I was unable to resist. It was the first time I had handled
a python for over fifty years.

The Zoo was usually rather empty except on bank holidays. I
preferred it that way, resenting the noisy jostling ignorance of the
visitors almost as much as did the residents of Mossley Hill. I was
delighted one such afternoon when a lioness turned round in her
small cage and urinated vigorously over the crowd. The star turn
was Mickey, a vicious, fully-grown chimpanzee. Mickey had two
tricks. The first was to obey his keeper's command to 'blow 'em a
raz, Mick' by passing his lips against the back of his hand and

emitting a loud and prolonged fart-like note. His other trick was quite dangerous. On warm days he was to be found in a large paddock surrounded by low railings. He was tethered in the middle of this by a long chain attached to a stout post. He had two footballs and, having blown his 'raz' several times to hysterical applause, would roll one of the footballs gently towards the perimeter and then make frantic signals for someone to return it. Eventually a father, hoping to impress his children, or a young man his girl, would bend over the railings. At this point Mickey would hurl the second football with great force and accuracy at his benefactor's head.

Mickey substantiated another of the local residents' worries by escaping. He headed for Aigburth Vale and broke into an office rented by a charitable organisation with which Gampa was connected. Here he had pulled out the files and scattered the papers, and shat all over the desk and into some of the drawers before his recapture. My grandfather was not lucky with monkeys.

Aware of Mickey's trick with the footballs I knew better than to fall for it, but I did have a potentially alarming encounter with the Zoo's solitary elephant. I had persuaded the Griff to accompany me on this occasion and we were standing comparatively close to the great beast in its garage-like shed. Suddenly and without warning it wrapped its trunk round me and lifted me high into the air. The Griff gave a little cry of terror and dropped her glove. The elephant put me gently down again, picked up the glove and ate it. The Griff's panic gave way to indignation but the keeper, when we eventually found him, was most unhelpful.

'I could luke for your glove like over the next day or two,' he said, 'but you wouldn't want to wear it would you? Not after whur it's been.'

I for my part pretended that the reason the elephant had picked me up was because I had deliberately given the word of command as used by Toomai in Kipling's *Jungle Book*.

I held my seventh birthday party in the Zoo's gimcrack little half-timbered café followed by a conducted tour which included my handling of Billy, a feat which, as I'd anticipated and planned, quite impressed my school-friends.

The Zoo was never a success financially. Shortly before the war it went into liquidation and Billy, Mickey and the rest of its rather scruffy exhibits were transferred to other prisons.

Past the Zoo and Riverslea, right at the top of Mossley Hill and facing the large sandstone church with its resonant chimes loud enough, if the wind were in the right direction, to be heard in Ivanhoe Road over a mile and a half away, stood Sudley, the house and extensive grounds of Cousin Emma Holt. Cousin Emma's mother had been a Miss Bright whose sister had married my great-grandfather, George Melly. Her father, George Holt, was a partner and co-founder of the shipping firm Lamport & Holt for which Tom had briefly and reluctantly worked. George Holt was also a director of many companies and left what in those days was an enormous fortune, £600,000. A benefactor of the Liverpool University College, later Liverpool University, a collector of important pictures and an ardent Unitarian, he could well stand as the epitome of the benevolent Victorian capitalist.

Emma was his only child and heir. She never married, although the prospect of such a fortune must have offered a challenge to many an ambitious or mercenary young man. She was in fact remarkably plain with a long face, an incipient moustache, and very small eyes. At the same time she was both shrewd and self-aware. It is possible she knew that it was unlikely she would be loved for herself alone and rejected any suitors, but here I am only speculating. Her character on the other hand was original and her generosity, especially to young people, unstinting.

The gates of Sudley were actually around the corner from Mossley Hill. There was a small lodge and a long drive, with street-lamps at intervals, winding up to the house itself. This was large but low, built of sandstone in a restrained Victorian neo-classical style. The front with its Doric porch was comparatively narrow and in part obscured by rhododendrons. The main façade faced south, its tall windows overlooking a steep grass bank and narrow lawn beyond which, enclosed by iron railings, was a big field in which sheep grazed. The estate was ringed by bluebell woods.

There was an ornamental conservatory attached to the house and a walled kitchen garden with a range of greenhouses of ascending temperatures in which grapes were grown and orchids cultivated. At the back of the house was an enclosed courtyard with disused stables, one of them converted into a garage and, rather mysteriously, a row of occupied pigsties. The whole of this area, including the pigsties, was built of bright red, glazed brick, a startling effect which always induced in me a feeling of pleasurable anxiety.

Visiting Sudley, usually for Sunday lunch, was a formal experience which, like Chatham Street, intimidated my mother into using her 'church voice'. She would implore us to behave even as we yanked on the bell-pull but, being in fact less in awe of kindly Cousin Emma than any others of her generation, we usually, much to Maud's anguish, blotted our copy-books. Even Bill, in general more to be trusted than I, suddenly announced one lunch time that we had received a Christmas card of a monkey (presumably Lawson Wood's repulsive 'Grand pop'), which our nanny had said 'looked just like Cousin Emma'. Maud turned crimson.

'No, Bill,' she improvised in panic, 'I'm sure what she said was that Cousin Emma *sent* you the Christmas card of the monkey.'

This was a brave try, if unconvincing. Cousin Emma's cards were inevitably of Beatrix Potter animals, and anyway Bill wasn't going to let her off the hook.

'No,' he said emphatically, 'she said it *looked* like Cousin Emma.'

'What lovely plums!' said my mother on the edge of hysteria.

I was watching Cousin Emma closely during this exchange. I could see she was not at all angry – if anything, she was, almost imperceptibly, amused.

The interior of Sudley was far more impressive than the dark jumble of Chatham Street. Apart from the kitchen area, never visited and concealed behind a green baize door, there were very few ground-floor rooms: a little cloak-room, a library and, *en suite*, a great drawing-room, a small morning-room and the dining-room, all three facing the field with its flock of sheep.

The L-shaped hall was enormous with a parquet floor and a fine staircase curving up under a glass dome. There was a delicious smell of beeswax polish and pot-pourri. The library was dark with mahogany shelves lining every wall, and fine leather-bound books, but the three rooms facing south were brilliantly lit and furnished in restrained high Victorian taste.

There were many objects to intrigue us, notably two stuffed cranes under the well of the staircase. In life these handsome creatures had roamed the grounds, but it was the picture collection which, from an early age, excited my interest. I have been fascinated by painting since I was very small, initially I think by the puzzle of illusionism, and, unlike many children, I was always pleased to be taken to exhibitions and galleries. Nevertheless it was at Sudley, for the Chatham Street pictures were a mixed bag and heavily discoloured with varnish, that I realised the charm and possibility of a private collection.

It was, I suppose, typical of the informed taste of its period. It included a large Turner in the dining-room, several eighteenth-century portraits by Lawrence, Raeburn, Joshua Reynolds, etc., a beautiful little William Dyce and a few Pre-Raphaelites, in particular the smaller version of Holman Hunt's *Christ in the Temple*, a jewel-like picture in which the young Jesus is discovered by His parents lecturing the old rabbis. Once Cousin Emma discovered my potential liking for art she would frequently lead me round the collection and explain its history but it was the Holman Hunt that provided the climax to these little tours.

The picture wasn't hung but mounted on an ornamental easel in the hall. Attached to the easel was a large magnifying-glass suspended on a brass chain. 'You see, George,' explained Cousin Emma, 'Mr Hunt went to endless pains to be true to nature.' She then picked up the magnifying-glass and focussed it on the head of one of the Jews listening to the young Lord Jesus. 'He even,' she continued, 'painted in the cataracts on the old man's eyes.' At this she drew back the glass so that an eye increased dramatically in size. I could see the milky translucent skin over the eyeball, a demonstration I never tired of.

Holman Hunt had stayed with Cousin Emma's father and it was his host who had been responsible for the purchase by the Liverpool Corporation of the painter's grotesque masterpiece *The Triumph of the Innocents*, in which the resurrected, recently-slaughtered babes accompany the fleeing Holy Family but are visible only to the Baby Jesus as they sport around him on what looks like a rainbow-tinted water bed.

Cousin Emma went to a lot of trouble to keep us entertained.

She would read the *Tales of Beatrix Potter* and the poems of Edward Lear in her clear unpatronising voice with its Lancashire-inflected A's. Most of my elderly female relations had this slight regional intonation, but none of their brothers or male cousins displayed the least trace. I can only suppose it was because the boys were sent away to public schools in the South while their sisters were educated in the school-room by governesses. Cousin Emma pronounced glass to rhyme with 'ass' and would offer us in consequence 'a glas of mealk'.

In a cupboard in the library there was a marvellous collection of Victorian toys which she would show us but prudently refused to allow us to play with except under her supervision. There was a zoetrope, a forerunner of the cinema, with a circular metal drum which you loaded with a picture-strip of creatures in a sequence of positions. You then spun the drum round on its base and by looking through a series of little slits around the top you could watch horses apparently jumping over fences or clowns tumbling through hoops. There was a kaleidoscope and a three-dimensional stereoscope but above all – and in this case Cousin Emma wouldn't allow us even to touch it, but wound it up herself – there was an incredible musical-box. This was in the shape of a lettuce. When the music started the leaves parted and the head and shoulders of a life-size white rabbit emerged. It twitched its ears and nose, nibbled on the edge of a leaf but then, when the music finished, popped abruptly back into the heart of the lettuce whose leaves closed over it again with a click.

There must have been a large staff at Sudley both inside and out, but I can only remember Aimée, the elderly head parlour-maid, and Stanley, the grumpy old chauffeur. They both exuded tight-mouthed disapproval of everyone except Cousin Emma but especially of children. Aimée would open the front door to us as though we were the first wave of barbarians at the gates of Rome. If Cousin Emma ordered Stanley to drive us home in the sedate Daimler his back would transmit his disapproval and resentment at such a course.

On the other hand Eleanor Dodsworth, Cousin Emma's secretary and eventual paid companion, was a most cheerful person. She was the niece of one of the Brights' personal maids, and had been in the employment of both the Mellys and the Holts for many years. She liked a cigarette on the sly (Cousin Emma would allow no smoking at Sudley except by the men after dinner in the dining-room) and would respond to anything she agreed with by crying 'Eggs-actly!' Bill and I would often amuse ourselves at home by imitating Cousin Emma and Eleanor Dodsworth in conversation.

Bill: 'Eleanor, would you like a glas of mealk?'

Me: 'Eggs-actly.'

Around Easter Cousin Emma in her long dove-grey coat and straw bonnet would climb into the back of her Daimler and, with Stanley at the wheel and Eleanor Dodsworth chattering away beside her, leave Sudley behind and head north at a speed not exceeding forty miles an hour. Her destination was a house on the shores of Coniston Water where she spent the summer. It was called Tent Lodge and faced 'The Old Man', a mountain frequently invisible in mist and drizzle.

Sometimes Aimée would travel in the front of the Daimler next to Stanley. More often she would have preceded her mistress by train with the reduced staff necessary to service the smaller but by no means insubstantial house. Fires would certainly have been lit and beds aired to welcome Cousin Emma, but if it was a fine afternoon she would walk down to the lake through a pretty little wood to pay homage to Wordsworth by admiring the daffodils.

Tent Lodge was a pretty Regency box of a house so named, although I never saw the logic of it, because the corners of all the rooms were curved instead of angular. The exterior was of buttermilk stucco, the roof low, the main façade facing the lake over a gently sloping field. Next to the house, separated by a steep road, was Tent Cottage. It had a trellis porch and a monkey-puzzle tree in the garden. Here Aimée and Stanley lodged, but here were also some extra bedrooms used on those occasions when there were too many guests for Tent Lodge to accommodate.

On the hill behind the house was a home farm; at the side a kitchen garden. There were brick paths and cold houses, potting frames, piles of wicker baskets, and soft fruit ripening under nets. In fact it was exactly like the kitchen garden in *Peter Rabbit* and Cousin Emma would sometimes hint that it may well have been the source of the original. But although a great admirer of Beatrix

Potter's, and a neighbour, she hadn't got on with her personally. She had once asked her to tea, expecting a stimulating conversation about her work, much of which Cousin Emma knew by heart, but Mrs Heelis, as she had become after her marriage to a hen-pecked Hindhead solicitor, stumped in wearing dirty boots and would talk about nothing but sheep-breeding. The visit was a disappointment to Cousin Emma and the invitation never extended again.

Although it was a Regency house, Tent Lodge had been furnished by Cousin Emma's father in mid-Victorian style: a very solid dining-room, a rather fussy but charming drawing-room. The many pictures weren't a patch on Sudley – mostly pale water-colours of the Lakes or the Italian alps – but there were some of those little paintings of birds' nests and, on an easel by the dining-room window, an oil of Ruskin writing in his study at Brantwood, the next house along the lake from Tent Lodge. Gampa, staying as a small boy with his Uncle George Holt, had once met Ruskin, and the old gentleman had given him a dedicated book which Gampa had subsequently and rather irritatingly lost.

There was no electricity at Tent Lodge. Oil lamps were brought in at dusk, and on the hall table were candles to take up to the bedrooms with their walls papered with repetitive ribbons of rose buds or honeysuckle.

We stayed occasionally at Coniston either at Easter or for part of the long summer holidays. It rained a lot, but the fine days, or more rarely weeks, were extraordinarily beautiful. There wasn't all that much to do but we were never bored for long. Sometimes we rolled down the steep grass bank in front of the house until we were dizzy or 'charged the shrubberies', a game I'd invented, in which Bill and I – for Andrée was still too young – would run full pelt into the rhododendron bushes which seemed to part before us like the briars in 'The Sleeping Beauty'. We walked to the village the other side of the lake and visited the Ruskin Museum. It was not all that impressive and furthermore cost a penny to go in. There were Ruskin's collections of rather dusty minerals, his walking stick, and a few beautiful water-colours of rock formations or Venetian architectural details, but what we liked best was a xylophone he had constructed from pieces of tuned slate laid across a framework of wood and which we were allowed to play with a little felt-covered hammer.

Mostly though we fished, first collecting minnows in a celluloid trap with bread crumbs on it suspended by a piece of string at the end of Cousin Emma's jetty, and subsequently transferring them to a bucket to use for live bait. We'd row far out on to the lake in a dinghy but all we ever caught were small perch with their bright striped bodies and treacherous erectile spines. We'd carry them proudly up to the house nevertheless, although nobody was in the least interested except for the piebald farmyard cats. The excitement was to sit in the dinghy with its creaking rowlocks and faint smell of tar and to watch the red and white float bob tentatively once or twice before jerking resolutely under the water while we imagined that *this* time it was going to be a whopper. Indeed, just once, out in the boat with my father, I hooked a pike which consented to be reeled up to the surface, looked at us contemptuously with its cold eye, turned, snapped the cast, and swam unhurriedly down towards the bottom again.

I wished there had been trout in Coniston instead of perch and Tom told me that there used to be, but with the coming of the tourists it had been fished dry. When he was a small child he had gone off one misty morning to find his father who was casting from the shore. He thought he recognised him but, on drawing close, discovered it to be another gentleman. A little further on was someone else who he was sure was his father. It was not, but here, in the distance, was yet another angler. He ran towards him, but this was a stranger too. Soon he was miles from Tent Lodge and so exhausted he sat down and burst into tears. A kind man found him and took him back. Gampa had gone the other way along the shore and was within two hundred yards of the house all the time.

If we were at Tent Lodge in the summer there were other major expeditions involving grown-ups. There were picnics on Peel Island at the far end of the lake and at least an hour's row. It was a lucky little island, covered in gorse and pine trees, a marvellous place to play pirates. Sometimes we climbed The Old Man, which was steep but unchallenging, more a stiff walk than a proper climb. At the top was a cairn, a tall irregular mound of pieces of slate. You added a new one on which you'd scratched your name and the date. You could only climb The Old Man on a clear day. There were mountains all around you, cradling the flat green valleys with their

lakes and tarns, and in the distance the sea. The roofs of the village
lay directly below and across Coniston Water was Tent Lodge
itself, a neat little doll's house. Getting down was harder than
climbing up. It was difficult not to slip and slide on the rough shale.
There was a slate quarry at the bottom.

Occasionally we'd be driven to a sheep-dog trial, watching the
patient dogs circling the stupid, hysterical sheep, now creeping,
now running as they did their best to drive them all into the pens,
and time after time one sheep would turn aside almost at the gate
and belt off up the hill, allowing the rest to disperse again. There
were other entertainments at the trials, especially Cumberland
wrestling in which huge men, stripped to the waist, would move
cautiously and very slowly round each other before encircling each
other's bodies with their great arms and attempting, rather ponder-
ously, to force their rivals off-balance. Bill and I would try it when
we got back home and Bill, although three years younger, usually
won, unless I lost (but concealed that I'd lost) my temper.

Cousin Emma was not always there when we stayed at Tent
Lodge although whether she went to visit other elderly ladies or
returned temporarily to Sudley I have no idea. Like her parents she
would often lend the house to members of the family for holidays
or honeymoons. After their marriage Maud and Tom had stayed
there on their way to Scotland where Tom was to fish; an unselfish
or masochistic concession on my mother's part as she had no
interest in fishing whatsoever. On arrival at Coniston my father
developed a quinsy – a very painful boil in the throat for which
there is no relief until it bursts. My mother was so distracted she
sent for Gangie, who came hurrying north to look after 'poor dear
Thomas'. Walking with her mother-in-law in the fields, Maudie
had worried that anyone spotting them would imagine their marriage was already on the rocks. The quinsy finally burst and my
parents left for Carlisle where they were to spend a night in a hotel.
On the notice board was a letter addressed to Thomas Quinsy Esq.
Imagining it to be a joke, probably the work of John Melly, my
father crossly tore it in two only to discover, to his considerable
embarrassment, that there was a real Thomas Quinsy staying there.

Cousin Emma died in 1944. She left Sudley and the pictures to
the City of Liverpool, and the house and the collection are open to

the public. In one of the rooms the Chatty drawing-room furniture is displayed behind little ropes. She left Tent Cottage to Eleanor Dodsworth, and Tent Lodge to Willie Bert Rawdon Smith; a reward perhaps for his unselfishness in escorting her and Aunt Eva home half-way through the Sandon Cabaret. He lived there for a few years and then sold it and moved, with his wife Daisy, into a bungalow he had built in the outskirts of the village, where he stayed put until he too died.

Emma, although so kind and gentle, was not without convictions. One summer she had a running battle with the new vicar of Coniston who wanted to let girl hikers attend the services in headscarves. Cousin Emma was strong for hats. She was also at the forefront of those residents who protested about Sir Malcolm Campbell's decision to try and break the water speed record on Coniston in his boat *Bluebird*. I doubt, however, that she was among those who went so far as to booby-trap the route with submerged logs. Nor did she protest when we all got up at five on the morning of the attempt to watch Sir Malcolm roar to noisy victory in the still grey dawn, shattering the reflection of The Old Man. She just felt that Windermere would have been more suitable.

Tent Lodge and Coniston are among the green places of my childhood. There the imaginary world of Beatrix Potter and the reality on which she based it became one. I have always had this dubious need to reinforce life through art or literature, to appreciate it at second-hand, and it was at Coniston, however unconsciously, that I was first aware of this. In the little lanes between dry-stone walls I imagined meeting Mrs Tiggy-Winkle waddling along with her basket of washing, or spotting, emerging from the mound of lawn-clippings in the far right-hand corner of Cousin Emma's kitchen garden, the black-tipped ears of the Flopsy bunnies sleeping off the soporific effect of lettuces.

9

When I was four I was sent to school, a kindergarten called Camelot. It was just around the corner from 22 Ivanhoe Road and was run by a short but formidable lady called Miss Katie Yates. She was very erect, had a rather sallow skin but fine aquiline features, and carried pince-nez on a gold chain which rested on her shelf-like bosom. She had kindly but alert brown eyes, wore her hair up and spoke quietly, but with considerable authority. Her sister, although it seemed unlikely, was a great champion of the gypsies, or Romanies as she preferred to call them, had lived among them and written several books on the subject.

Miss Yates had started her school thirty years before in a room over a shop in Lark Lane where Uncle Alan had been among her first pupils. Success had enabled her to move the hundred yards to Waverley Road where she lived in a flat on the top floor. The rest of the house, which was rather bigger than ours, was devoted to the class-rooms, minimally furnished. Woodwork was taught in the cellar, and the big double room on the ground floor acted as an assembly hall and as a setting for end of term concerts and the Christmas play. There were no carpets at Camelot, but the floors of stained wooden boards were kept highly polished by a solitary, rather grumpy, elderly maid. There were few pictures, but I was early on both fascinated and frightened by a sepia reproduction of a Roman soldier guarding some prisoners at Pompeii while the molten lava fell from the air about him. It was called *Faithful unto Death* and the life-size original was in the Walker Art Gallery, although oddly enough I found it less terrifying than its smaller replica. I was extremely in awe of any destructive natural phenomena, but especially of tidal waves, earthquakes and volcanoes, none of which was likely to prove much of a hazard in suburban

Liverpool. I dreamt once of red-hot lava creeping and bubbling into the hall of Ivanhoe Road and gradually rising in level as I, with great difficulty, climbed the stairs only a step or two ahead of it. As it rose it spoke in a boily-bubbly voice. 'I'm coming,' it said, 'I'm coming, I'm coming *for you*!'

Faithful unto Death was in the assembly room, and I frequently had a chance to examine it. At nine on the dot, while we all stood in makeshift rows under the supervision of one of the mistresses, Miss Yates would make her entrance. 'Good morning, everybody,' she would say briskly, and we in our piping and ragged trebles, but with all the enthusiasm which children experience in fulfilling a ritual, would answer her in unison: 'Good morning, Miss Yates.' What then took place was some form of non-denominational prayers, for several of the pupils were Jewish or Catholic, followed by a hymn, usually 'All things Bright and Beautiful' accompanied by Miss Gibbons or Miss Edwards at the upright piano.

It was seldom however that this daily scenario went through without a hitch. Most days one of the several children who suffered from either nerves or a bilious digestive system would suddenly throw up on the polished wooden floor. At this, no matter what point we'd reached, Miss Yates would clap her hands and tell everyone else to 'turn away' – further embarrassing, I should have thought, the unfortunate child. On cue, for it was her daily chore to hover outside during assembly, the elderly maid would come into the room and mop up the mess with the dish-cloth and bucket of water which she kept in the hall at the ready. It was during these interruptions that I had the chance to study in detail the courageous centurion at his terminal post. Miss Yates would also take the opportunity during assembly to admonish, although never by name, any child who had been reported for letting down the tone of her little school. These crimes were not grave. The most heinous I can recall was someone who had been seen eating sweets on a tram.

Situated as it was in a network of streets whose names evoked the world of medieval chivalry in the works of Sir Walter Scott, Camelot paid homage to an even earlier legend. Although there were only about thirty pupils we were divided into houses – Percival, Tristram, Lancelot and Galahad – each with its coloured badge sewn on the pocket of our blazers. To begin with you were put into the kindergarten under the supervision of a very pretty girl called Kitty Coope. She was the daughter of a Church of England canon, one of those ecclesiastics sufficiently elevated for Gangie to drop his name into the conversation whenever a suitable opportunity presented itself.

I had been told that 'Kindergarten' meant 'Children's Garden'. I found it confusing that the whole school was called a 'Kindergarten', and yet we were in a class which was called 'the kindergarten', a children's garden within a children's garden. I was equally puzzled as to why Camelot was called a kindergarten at all. It was a house, its garden a scruffy little patch of grass with a few straggly laurel bushes.

Although everyone went home for lunch, when you were still in the kindergarten you didn't come back in the afternoon. The only refreshment provided by the school was a choice of hot milk or water at the mid-morning break. The milk always had a nasty skin on it and the water was served in thick mugs which somehow, although I was perfectly fond of water, made it taste brackish. You had to have one or the other and Miss Edwards made sure you drank it all up. I still can't abide water in a cup or mug.

Life in the kindergarten class was very pleasant. You crayoned in pictures in a colouring book (it was long before the days of free expression), moulded plasticine, played with a sand-pit, watched tadpoles turn into frogs in their season (what happened to the mature frogs? Were they released into one of the lakes in Sefton Park?), and did raffia work. Tom, who was very amused by anything I had to tell him about Camelot, was extremely sarcastic about the little raffia purses or place-mats that I brought proudly home. 'Miss Coope is very good at raffia,' he'd say with some accuracy, for I was very clumsy with my hands and needed a lot of 'help'. The fact that it was true made his teasing no more bearable and I would protest with increasing vehemence that I'd done it all by myself. Maud naturally and ostentatiously used the nasty little purses and set the tatty place-mats until she felt I'd forgotten about them.

Once I'd left the kindergarten, however, I began to feel less at ease. I discovered you were meant to learn, not just what interested you – I had no objection to that – but things which didn't, like adding up and dividing, French, geography and reading, The latter

I finally mastered (in memory practically overnight) and I quite enjoyed history – we used a little book entirely composed of myths: Alfred and the cakes, King Canute, the Princes in the Tower – but for the rest I refused to pay any attention at all. This both worried and puzzled Miss Yates and the staff. I was clearly quite bright, in some respects almost precocious, so why couldn't or wouldn't I learn anything? Miss Yates gave me several stiff talkings-to, but although I promised to try they had no effect at all. Severe and witty Miss Gibbons tried sarcasm; broad-beamed Miss Edwards scorn; pretty Miss Dobson persuasion, but I continued to acquire very little knowledge from these conscientious ladies.

I could, on the other hand, memorise poetry easily and recite it with dramatic if rather hammy facility. The day of the school concert at the end of each term was my apotheosis, the moment when the ugly duckling turned temporarily into a swan. Miss Yates very much dominated these occasions: 'Shall I compare thee to a summer's day', a breathless and nervous child would announce. Then it would continue, 'Shall I compare thee . . .' only to be interrupted by Miss Yates. 'Who's it by, dear?' 'William Shakespeare,' the by now thoroughly rattled child would concede before beginning again, all memory and concentration shattered.

One term, encouraged by Miss Gibbons, who had a streak of mischief behind her severe horn-rimmed glasses, I recited *Albert and the Lion*, the humorous monologue I had learnt by heart from a gramophone record and which, with my talent for mimicry, I could deliver fairly convincingly in the strong Lancashire accent of Stanley Holloway's original. All the mistresses, with the exception of Miss Yates, were delighted by this deviation from 'Fear no more the heat o' the sun' or 'I once had a sweet little doll, dears', and my contemporaries, too, enjoyed the rather bloodthirsty and callous couplets. Miss Yates, although clearly unhappy, didn't interrupt, but when I'd finished she clapped her hands for attention and told the school that although George had been clever 'in his way', she would be most displeased if she heard any child trying to imitate the accent. Having an accent at Camelot – not 'speaking properly' – was certainly on the level of being detected eating sweets on a tram.

The Christmas play was a far more ambitious project than the

end of term concert. We played it twice; a 'dress rehearsal' in front
of our nannies and an 'opening night' the following afternoon for
parents and relations. The play, which was always a fairy story,
was written by one of the staff and the costumes were ingeniously
constructed by Miss Coope from coloured crepe paper and safety
pins. One year I was a jester in blue and yellow motley and genuinely
thought that at the 'dress rehearsal' I had given a pretty impressive
performance. I was therefore all the more hurt and shocked when
Miss Yates stopped me in the corridor next morning and hoped I'd
do better in front of the parents. Did I give a bad performance or
did Miss Yates feel that I needed deflating? Perhaps both.

Miss Yates was also responsible for one of the few serious
tickings-off I ever received from my mother. I'd fallen down a flight
of stairs at Camelot and, probably because there was no carpet,
had hurt myself quite badly. Children seem to fall downstairs
frequently; I'd done it many times before but always without injury.
In a panic-stricken way I'd even quite enjoyed it: the world suddenly
fragmented, gravity set at odds, bits of stair, banister, skirting-
board, wall and ceiling jumbled up together at speed. This time
however it was not at all pleasurable and, with a bruised knee and
a bump on the head, I was so shaken that I'd been sent home early.
Maud, full of concern and sympathy, had asked me if I'd cried.
'Oh, no,' I told her airily, 'not a bit.' 'Brave little man!' she said.
'Brave little soldier!'

A couple of nights later, coming down into the lounge after tea,
looking forward to the American Colonel spitting into the fire or
another chapter from *The Jungle Book*, I was confronted by a
mother I didn't recognise, cold and grim. 'I met Miss Yates in Lark
Lane,' she said, 'and we talked about you falling down the stairs. I
said, "Wasn't George brave not to cry?" and she told me you'd
quite naturally howled and screamed. You must never tell lies,
George! There'll be no reading tonight. You must go to bed now!'
I was frightfully upset, but at the same time couldn't see what all
the fuss was about. No doubt I'd cried after my fall, but by the time
I denied it later I'd convinced myself I hadn't. I could 'see' myself
hurt certainly, but courageously dry-eyed, making light of my injur-
ies. I was not only upset by Maud's reproaches, I was also put out.
Of course she came upstairs later and 'made it all right' but I'm still

puzzled by what got into her. With her need to be liked at all times, especially by her children, her moral reproach, while perfectly justified, was completely out of character.

Jester and stairs apart, I wasn't at all unhappy at Camelot. I'd enjoyed quite a lot of it – joining the Wolf Cubs for example and prancing round the carved wolf's head in the assembly room chanting 'We'll dib dib dib. We'll dob dob dob.' During Wolf Cubs we had to call Miss Dobson 'Akela' and, although I could see little resemblance between her and the Father Wolf in the Mowgli stories, I'd liked the connection between life at school and the magic world in the dark red book with Kipling's mysterious swastika on the cover.

Bill overlapped me at Camelot by several terms, and it was irritating that he should be so much quicker than I was at learning things. Although three years younger, he was reading before I could and did well at everything else too. By the time I left I'd learnt one useful if dangerous lesson: that if you could make people laugh you could get away with almost anything. Miss Gibbons, for instance, was frequently exasperated with my lack of concentration, but I seemed able to amuse even her, and she was seldom cross for very long. Only Miss Yates was impervious to jokes. When I left at the age of seven she told me seriously and rather sadly that she was sure I could do better if I tried, that archetypal reproach of a teacher confronted by a bright but idle child.

At Camelot I developed the ability to separate areas of life one from the other, a trick for which I was to be increasingly grateful. As soon as I was home or during the holidays Camelot ceased to exist except as a source of anecdotes to amuse Tom. However, even at home things were less happy, because the nursery had become a torture-chamber. Firm but kind Bella, although she was to return later, had gone and her place was taken by a handsome fiend, a sister of the Leathers' nanny, called Hilda Cadwallader.

Hilda was a savage and chilly disciplinarian particularly at meal-times, implementing her rigid injunctions with the aid of a thin green garden cane which she flicked with great accuracy under the table to catch me, and more rarely Bill, across the calves or thighs. Her principal obsession was that if we took anything at tea we must put it on our plate before transferring it to our mouths. As forgetting to do so was to court instant and painful retribution I soon, like one of Pavlov's dogs, learnt this lesson and to this day on taking a sandwich or a biscuit automatically, however rapidly, touch my plate with it. 'Eating everything up' was another of Hilda's strict rules, a common one I know. My mother, who much to our relief would sometimes join us for lunch or tea in the nursery, would wait until Hilda had left the room to get the pudding and then rapidly gobble up whatever we didn't want off our plates. This I found, while welcome, very confusing. Was Maud on our side and if so why didn't she tell Hilda we needn't finish things we didn't like? Did she know of the existence of the thin green cane? We probably hadn't told her about it; children just don't. But if she did know, why didn't she forbid its use? I now realise that the reason was Maud's terror of a confrontation with someone of strong character and Hilda was certainly that. Andrée, still in her high-chair, was spared the rod but not a certain amount of force feeding and a slap on the leg if she persistently threw her spoon and pusher on the floor.

Our walks, too, became less interesting because on many afternoons, ignoring Sefton or even Prince's Park, Hilda would head down Aigburth Road to meet her sister, the Leathers' nanny, and spend the afternoon chatting and looking in the shops. This was very boring for Bill, my cousin Gillian and me (Andrée was still in her pram, John already at school all day) but at least it reduced Hilda's attention and left us free to scamper ahead or hide round corners. Once I stole an egg from a mound displayed on the sloping marble slab of a fishmonger's in Aigburth Vale. I don't know why I did it and was instantly so frightened that I threw it into a bush in someone's front garden. My crime preyed on me to such an extent that several months later I imagined I overheard the woman in the fishmonger's say to a customer as we passed: 'A bad little boy pinched an egg from this shop when I wasn't looking and I've told the police.'

I don't know how long Hilda was with us; certainly long enough for Andrée to be talking and sitting up at the table. But eventually she left, a day of celebration for me, and her place was taken by her other sister, May. This was, on the face of it, good news. May had been house parlour-maid before her elevation to the nursery and seemed to be a cheerful girl with a plain, friendly face and big glasses. My optimism turned out to be displaced however. Somehow the flight of stairs from kitchen to nursery transformed May into a tyrant like her sister. The gardening cane remained in use, the rules as strictly enforced. She didn't stay too long, however, and her place was taken by a sweet-natured girl called Minnie Shearer and eventually by the return of Bella, but by that time I was beyond the jurisdiction of nannies anyway.

The kitchen, both before and after May's metamorphosis, remained a refuge and a place of comfort. Following May's promotion Edna, Auntie Min's successor as cook, was joined by a very jolly girl called Ethel. In Liverpool every year there was a fancy dress dance at St George's Hall called 'The Servants' Ball'. Such a concept, such a name for such a concept, appears absolutely grotesque now but it didn't then. The Servants' Ball was a very popular function and comparatively valuable prizes were offered for the best costumes in several categories: single, couples, most comic, most artistic, etc. Edna and Ethel won the couple's prize two years running: one year as Laurel and Hardy (Edna was big and plump, Ethel small and thin) and the next year as 'The Bisto Kids'. I hadn't seen Laurel and Hardy on the screen then – I hadn't been allowed to go to the pictures – but I knew what they looked like from *Film Fun*, my favourite comic.

My comfort during the regime of the Cadwallader sisters, and indeed at all times of stress, was a small bear I'd had ever since I could remember. Its name was 'Little Ted' and over the years it had gradually lost arms, legs and eyes until hardly any of the original remained. It was repaired by my mother, no great hand with the needle, and as it also shed all its fur, it was eventually quite a repulsive object. Nevertheless Little Ted was a powerful fetish, so much so that I even took him to Stowe and later on into the navy where he was eventually lost, creating in me considerable, although suppressed, anxiety. How did I avoid teasing by school boys and seamen for having a Teddy bear? By pretending, like Sebastian Flyte, that it was a bit of camp, although in fact it was nothing of the kind but an important psychological prop. Little Ted was far more of a help in adversity than God or his son, 'GentleJesusmeekandmild'. I said my prayers because I was told to, but I gabbled through them at a fair lick especially on the cold linoleum of winter. My real solace lay on the pillow, its button eyes hanging on threads, its limbs and old woollen glove fingers lumpily stuffed with cotton wool, one ear gone, its body held together by a pair of grubby but remedial pyjamas knitted by the Griff.

God and Jesus were something of a puzzle. They lived in Christ Church, Linnet Lane, a quarter of a mile away, round the corner at the Sefton Park end of Ivanhoe Road. It was a big, rather simple Victorian church with stained-glass windows with a lot of purple and red in them. There was a stone pulpit and the Bible was on a lectern which was a fierce brass eagle. The clergyman's name was Goodeliffe. He also was rather fierce but not very old. Maud 'didn't care for him', but she went to the eleven o'clock service every Sunday and often to Holy Communion as well. Tom only went to church on Christmas Day.

When we were small we didn't go to the eleven o'clock service but to the children's service at half-past ten. Only middle-class children went to the children's service. Working-class children went to Sunday School in the afternoon. Mr Goodeliffe seems to have subscribed to the verse in 'All Things Bright and Beautiful' in which it is firmly maintained that God 'made them high and lowly and gave them their estate'.

There was a 'Children's Corner' in Christ Church, Linnet Lane. You had to say a prayer there if you went into the church when there wasn't a service on. It had Margaret Tarrant pictures in it. One of them, which we also had at home in the night nursery, was an illustration of 'All Things Bright and Beautiful' and was a bit like a coloured version of the Peter Pan statue in Sefton Park with rabbits and butterflies and a faun, but with Jesus instead of Peter Pan. Another was called 'Suffer the little children to come unto me'. Nobody told me that 'suffer' in this context meant 'allow'. I was puzzled and a little alarmed by the title, but then a lot of religion was like that. 'Our father,' I prayed, 'witch art in Heaven.' I knew witches were meant to be wicked. What were they doing practising their art in Heaven where everybody was meant to be good? In 'Suffer the little children to come unto me' Jesus was surrounded by children 'of many lands', but only one of each: a black boy, an Indian girl, a Red Indian, a Chinese boy, a Japanese girl, an Arab boy, and by far the biggest, a rather stern British boy scout. Jesus was in a white robe. He had very long hair and a beard and a light round his head. Most of the people in the stained-glass windows had lights round their heads too, but enclosed by black lines. In Margaret Tarrant's picture of Jesus it was more like a glow, as if He were an electric light bulb.

The theology at the Children's Service was naturally enough rather simple: stories mostly, which I enjoyed, especially the blood-thirsty ones from the Old Testament; a few hymns and simple prayers. Mr Goodeliffe's principal message was that if we were good we'd go to Heaven, that God loved us and saw everything we did, and that Jesus died on the cross for our sins. He told us it was the Jews who killed Jesus. This worried me a bit. I couldn't imagine the Griff or Uncle Alan and Uncle Fred doing something cruel like that, even if Fred did murder people in the Masons.

My main problem, though, was to imagine what God looked like. The best I could do was a kind of smile in the air, but if I imagined it for long the smile got fainter like Alice's Cheshire cat. Jesus of course was easier because of the pictures, but I thought he'd look very odd walking down Ivanhoe Road or shopping in Lark Lane. Perhaps he dressed differently now, at any rate when he wasn't in his house. Mr Goodeliffe dressed differently after all. In church he wore a long black dress with a white one over the top and a pretty coloured flat scarf hanging down the front, but if you met him in the street he was dressed in a suit like everyone else, and the only way you could tell he was a clergyman was by his black shirt with a stiff white collar turned back to front. Even so Jesus' hair and beard would have made him look peculiar. Tom told me that when he was younger if you saw a man with a beard you shouted 'Beaver'. Would people have shouted 'Beaver' at Jesus? Perhaps that's what they did when they mocked him before he was nailed to the cross.

Later on we had to go to the grown-up service. That was very long and boring, but it was almost worth it when you came out afterwards knowing that once Tom got back from The Albert there'd be roast beef, roast potatoes and Brussels sprouts in the dining-room or at the Griff's. We always had Sunday lunch downstairs and then Tom wound the grandfather clock.

Once, when I was about seven, I had a vision of God which was very different from the smile in the air. I had to have a tooth out and was given gas. Mr Williams, the dentist, faded away before I'd counted to six, and I found myself at the centre of the universe with all the stars round me and a kind, gentle voice saying: 'I am God. I am God.' But then the cosy universe I was enclosed in was shattered into thousands of pieces and I was faced by a limitless and terrifying void. Furthermore another, deafening, voice took over, bellowing and thundering: 'No you're not. I AM GOD! I AM GOD!' Yet despite this apocalyptic vision which even at the time, like my subsequent headache and vomiting, I put down to the effect of the gas, I wasn't so much worried by religion as simply puzzled. I just accepted it as something you had to do, like going to school.

I discovered later that my mother's theology was almost as simple as my own. When Tom died in the early sixties she believed, and it was a great comfort to her, that she'd meet him again but couldn't make up her mind if he'd be wearing his pyjamas or his old mackintosh. Tom himself was not at all religious. He still said his prayers when I was a child, but in later life got straight into bed. He always got very angry with Mr Goodeliffe on Christmas Day because he took the opportunity, given a full house, to tick off those of the congregation, of whom my father was one, who usually went to The Albert instead. In revenge, Tom would sing funny versions of the carols: 'When Shepherds washed their socks by night' and, in the year of Edward VIII's abdication: 'Hark the Herald Angels sing; Mrs Simpson's pinched our King.'

Although it was very long, I didn't mind the Christmas service much. The carols had better tunes than the usual hymns and, from our pew, I could see in the Children's Corner a lit-up crib with the Holy Family, the shepherds, the kings and an ox and ass carved from wood. I didn't mind the Harvest Festival either. It seemed so odd to see potatoes, cabbages and other vegetables and fruit of all kinds piled up all over the church like the trestle tables outside Waterworths, the greengrocer's in Aigburth Road.

Eventually Mr Goodeliffe left to tell off other fathers who only went to church on Christmas Day and his place was taken by a big man with tiny but kind eyes and a very red nose. He was called Mr Thompson. Maud liked him much better than Mr Goodeliffe and he was sometimes asked to tea. He made jokes too, something Mr Goodeliffe never did.

Tom didn't like Christmas much anyway. He hated the paper-chains and holly they put up in The Albert. He called it 'Christmas crap'. When eventually they took it down he'd come home looking very pleased. 'They've taken down the Christmas crap in The Bertie,' he'd tell us to explain his good humour. He loathed carol singers ringing the bell and would tell them, right up to Christmas Eve, that they were too early. Some of his resentment of the season may have been because his birthday was on the 26th. As a child, and indeed for the whole of his life, people tended to give him one present instead of two.

I myself had mixed feelings about Christmas Day, based I imagine on too great expectations. I quite liked helping to put up the Christmas crap in the nursery (the rest of the year it was kept in a cardboard box in the cupboard under the stairs) and especially the big green paper bells which lay flat in the box but opened up to become round and honeycombed. I also derived pleasure from the coloured glass balls we hung from the branches of the small tree we'd bought at Waterworths, although it was very annoying when they came adrift from their little silver collars and the two thin metal prongs which held them on their hooks. It was also a bonus that Hilda and later May were less strict. But nevertheless Christmas Day itself was always somehow a disappointment. It was not that we believed in Father Christmas (although I did, certainly until I left Camelot, firmly subscribe to the tooth fairy and her compensatory sixpence for a milk tooth placed under the pillow); rather it was to do with waking too early, opening stockings in the dark, going into our parents' room and being told to go away and go back to sleep. Everything turned into an act. We were expected, except by Tom, to enjoy ourselves too much, to be 'wide-eyed with wonder'. There was too much to eat at the Griff's. The Christmas cake was too rich and too soon after lunch. At the end of the day I went – willingly for once – to bed, tired, bilious and obscurely disappointed. I still mistrust Christmas and understand perfectly why Tom was so pleased when they took down the Christmas crap in The Albert. I was twice, as a child, ill on Christmas Day.

Nevertheless the Christmas holidays as a whole were full of treats. One morning, for example, my parents would take us to 'do' the grottos in the big stores. These varied a great deal depending how up-market the shop was. The Bon Marché was too grand to bother. George Henry Lee's was the most elaborate with Father Christmas reached only after a trip in a moon-rocket or a sledge-ride to the North Pole, and he wore proper baggy red trousers and boots. Lewis's was average. You walked into the grotto past animated 'Nursery Land' figures and Father Christmas allowed you to spend a bit less time on his knee before giving you your 'present', wrapped in blue paper for a boy and pink for a girl. The boys' presents at Lewis's were always rather large wind-up cars 'made in Japan'. They had nasty sharp edges and soon broke. The girls got cheap dolls resembling Shirley Temple. But my father's favourite grotto, and the one we rated least, was Blackler's, a cut-price emporium in the centre of Liverpool. Here Father Christmas, assisted by a pert fairy in a tutu, sat among no more than a few papier mâché rocks and the presents were the sorts of things you got from crackers. Father Christmas himself had a beard which clipped on over the ears instead of a proper one stuck on with spirit gum, and he wore ordinary grey trousers under his red robe. He also had a strong Liverpool accent and smelt of beer. ''Ave you been a good lad?' he'd ask. 'What yer want for chrissie den?' One year, Tom told me later, the Blackler's Father Christmas was sacked when the under-manager found him screwing the Fairy behind the papier mâché rocks. When I was very small and the grottos were the only reason I was taken to the big stores, I believed that the lifts didn't go up and down, but from shop to shop, from grotto to grotto.

The other, and indeed greater, highlights of the Christmas holidays were the pantomimes. Like the grottos, these could be graded. The Royal Court was considered the most 'artistic' with a proper transformation scene and a ballet, but we found it the dullest. Cousin Emma took a huge party of children to this, followed by a tea at George Henry Lee's. The Court Pantomime sometimes engaged Douglas Byng as its dame, a considerable bonus for me who knew his records so well and had met him personally – a fact I made quite sure all the Holt cousins appreciated. In keeping with the refinement of the entertainment – and indeed his own persona – his dames were upgraded, never the nurse, always the governess, not a cook, but a housekeeper. Given that it was a family entertainment he didn't, to my regret, recite any of his discreetly obscene monologues, but he was even so very funny, something of a relief in contrast to the gentility of the rest of the entertainment. In *The Sleeping Beauty* when the Court, covered in cobwebs, awoke after the interval, Douggie's reaction to the Fairy Queen's announcement that they'd been asleep for a hundred years reduced Bill and me to helpless, if knowing, laughter and earned us a censorious look from Cousin Emma. 'A hundred years!' said the appalled Douglas Byng, 'and I forgot to put the cat out!' Like Maud and Tom, Bill and I were very much amused by scatological humour.

We were taken to the Empire, the huge Palace of Varieties opposite St George's Hall, by Gangie and Gampa. This was a big brash show-biz panto with stars like George Formby and Arthur Askey, and lots of catchphrases from popular radio shows and advertising slogans. It was very long but always very enjoyable, and by the time the 'entire company' came on for their final bow, dressed in elaborate finery, and swanning down a high bank of glittering steps to acknowledge their applause, we had been seduced into exhausted complicity by the slapstick, community singing and exuberant vigour.

Pantomime, despite the 'I theng yows' and the references to Bovril stopping 'that sinking feeling', was still comparatively traditional. The Principal Boy was always a girl, and the demon king shot up in a puff of green smoke through a trap door, and spoke, like his opponent the Fairy Queen, in rhymed couplets. Even so my father, while always very interested in the Principal Boy's legs, complained that when he was young they didn't limit themselves to the same few traditional stories: *Cinderella*, *Babes in the Wood*, *Mother Goose*, *Humpty Dumpty*, *Robinson Crusoe*, *The Sleeping Beauty*, *Little Red Riding Hood*, *Dick Whittington* and *Aladdin*, but drew freely from a wider field. 'They did things like *The Yellow Dwarf*,' he'd tell us. He never mentioned any of the other things they did, nor indeed what had impressed him so much about *The Yellow Dwarf*, but he'd bring it out each year as a stick to beat the unimaginative limitations of the modern pantomime. Nevertheless he was always pleased when it was *Cinderella*, then as now the most hackneyed story of all, but this was entirely because of the moment when the crystal carriage emerged from the wings to take Cinders to the ball. It was drawn by Shetland ponies and what interested Tom was the possibility, surprisingly frequently fulfilled, that one or more of them might shit on the stage.

My parents themselves took us to the Christmas play at the Playhouse and the panto at the Pavilion, a seedy theatre in Lodge Lane, a rather run-down area not far from Sefton Park. Here, all memories of *The Yellow Dwarf* obliterated, Tom's relish for the tatty and the meretricious was allowed full play. There were lashings of vulgarity and in the second half the plot was more or less abandoned and everyone just performed their speciality acts. To call them pantomimes at all was really a misnomer. They were basically music-hall bills with a cursory nod towards the panto in acknowledgement of the season. We often went to see Old Mother Riley as the dame and 'her beautiful daughter Kitty' as the principal girl. Old Mother Riley's real name was Arthur Lucan. His 'daughter' was, in fact, his wife. Never beautiful and, with the passage of the years increasingly less so, she was apparently a drunken termagant who made Lucan's life a hell. On stage, though, they were in the great tradition: Old Mother Riley in her bonnet and shawl, writhing and banging her elbows together in paroxysms of anxiety as to where Kitty was and what she'd been getting up to. Then going at her hammer and tongs on her eventual return. 'You went to a museum,' she'd shriek. 'You went to a museum to see the antiques! Why did you 'ave to go to a museum to see antiques? Why couldn't you come 'ome and see your mother!'

We didn't only go to the Pavilion at Christmas. My parents loved the music hall and would take us quite often during the rest of the year. It was there we saw 'The Uncle Ronnies' and, for the first time, Frank Randle, my favourite comedian of all. Dressed as an old hiker, glasses awry, sparse hair sticking up in tufts, his absurdly skinny legs emerging from baggy shorts, belching, burping and frequently removing his teeth, he presented a hideously ludicrous spectacle. 'Eeeee,' he'd start off, holding on to his huge phallic stick for support, 'ah've supped some ale toneet!' 'A disgusting old man!' said Tom admiringly.

Some years it was *Peter Pan* at the Empire instead of a pantomime, and it was always a children's play at the Playhouse. One of these plays so impressed me that when we got back to Ivanhoe Road I reconstructed it with Bill and even Andrée, although she was only two and a half and needed a lot of direction, and we performed it for our parents. They were so amused that the following Sunday they asked the original cast to tea and we acted it out in front of them. It was a great success and the following years we repeated it. It became known as 'The Melly Version'. As I grew older 'The Melly Version' became more ambitious, with scenery and some old candle footlights from Chatham Street. School friends too were recruited and I suspect that what had once been rather charming and droll grew to be a considerable bore for the poor actors and actresses on their one day off. This never occurred to me of course, and I very much doubt if it occurred to Maud either. Mary Ventris, alias 'Little Runty', the Louella Parsons of Liverpool, was also invited and wrote it up several times in her 'Woman's Note' in the *Liverpool Echo*.

Although I'd been taken to the theatre from an early age, I wasn't
allowed to go to the cinema until I was almost seven. Maudie had
never cared much for the 'pictures' and had rationalised her dislike
into believing them to be bad for children, a potential drug. I'd been
chipping away at her resolve for some time before I succeeded. It
was my enthusiasm for wild beasts that eventually won the day.
Walking rebelliously down Aigburth Road with Hilda en route to
meet her sister, I spotted a large poster outside the Rivoli, at that
time the district's only cinema. It was to advertise a film called
Trader Horn, about a man who collected animals for zoos and
circuses. The poster was in full colour. The hero with a gun glared
with desperate courage from the edge of a swamp. Behind him an
immaculate girl in an open-necked shirt and jodhpurs recoiled in
some alarm. His desperation, her alarm were fully justified: a
crocodile glided purposefully towards them, a giant boa-constrictor
lowered itself from the branches of a tree, a lion and a leopard,
crouching in the long grass that edged the swamp, showed more
than a passing interest, while a bull elephant trumpeted its displeasure in the background. With all this at stake, I went down
from the nursery after tea determined to use whatever means I could
to break her injunction, and went up to bed triumphant. The very
next afternoon we were to go to the matinée of *Trader Horn* at the
Rivoli, Aigburth Road.

   The Rivoli had been built in the early twenties. Like the Rialto a
mile and a half away, but on a more modest scale, its inspiration
was Moorish, the low façade covered in creamy ceramic tiles. The
inside was fairly scruffy, many of the seats broken, the carpets full
of holes, a stale smell of bodies masked by strong disinfectant. The
matinée was sparsely attended; a few little gangs of noisy children

and isolated old age pensioners. Nevertheless there was nowhere on earth I would rather have been. I was 'at the pictures'.

In the event, although I was not so stupid as to let on, I found *Trader Horn* something of a disappointment. It had lots of good bits – lions caught in nets, natives digging concealed pits for elephants, a charging rhino, a lovable chimp – but what confused me was that at no point was there a scene which in any way resembled the multiple and highly coloured confrontation promised by the poster. Nevertheless I walked home with Maud as if I had successfully passed some initiation test, and boasted so much at tea that Bill became hysterical with envy and burst into angry and prolonged tears. As a result, and to my ill-repressed fury, he was taken to see *Trader Horn* the very next day! I felt I'd done all the spade-work only to allow Bill, three years younger than I was, to blub his way into reaping the benefits. Nevertheless I'd been to the pictures and there was no way now of stopping me going whenever I wanted to.

The only practical difficulty was getting people to take me, but here I discovered that most members of the family enjoyed the excuse, and also preferred this or that genre of film, so that after a certain amount of research I was soon able to cover the whole spectrum. My father, with his curiously narrow but intense tastes, liked *Mutiny on The Bounty*, which he was prepared to visit any number of times and even put up with my imitations of Charles Laughton for several hours afterwards, and gangster pictures. Maud hated gangster pictures, but quite liked Fred Astaire and Ginger Rogers and indeed all musicals. Gangie liked Douglas Fairbanks Junior pictures and costume drama in general with plenty of sword fights, but she hated the concomitant torture-chamber scenes for which I had a morbid passion. The Griff would take me to anything I wanted provided one answered in the affirmative a question dating from her youth: 'Do they speak well of it?' I didn't really enjoy going to the pictures with the Griff though, because she fell instantly asleep and I would be forced, as I thought for her own enjoyment, to keep nudging her. Sometimes Bill and I – for I had soon become reconciled to his profiting at my expense in exchange for having someone to discuss every sequence in detail – would tease her by asking if she'd enjoyed scenes which weren't in the film at all. Uncle Fred would always take me to Chaplin or the Marx Brothers. My

only sadness was being barred from films which in those days
had an 'H' (for Horror) certificate. I longed for Frankenstein and
Dracula, for the Wolf Man and The Mummy, but the only time I
could see them on the screen was when they appeared in spoofs,
most often to the discomfiture of Old Mother Riley.

The cinemas themselves for me were almost as magical as the
films they showed. The Rivoli, my first, held a special place in my
affection, but I was tremendously excited by the 'modernistic'
splendours of the big Picture Palaces in the centre of Liverpool. The
commissionaires in their paramilitary uniforms, the thick carpets,
the chrome banisters, the framed photographs of the stars lining
the stuccoed walls, the ice-cream girls in their twin spotlights during
the intermission. There were also, as a special treat, the cinema
cafés with their 'dainty teas': fish and chips with very thin bread
and butter, the scalding chrome tea pots, knickerbocker glories,
fancy cakes. In the film and the cinema I had found my faith and
my cathedral.

At some point in the thirties, and within a year of each other,
two huge cinemas were built in Aigburth Road, both within a
quarter of a mile of where we lived. This, once I had learnt of it,
was a source of great pride and anticipation. The Gaumont opened
first. It was at the Dingle, opposite the Corporation tram-shed and
the Ancient Unitarian chapel. It was built of special pale brick in
'streamlined' art deco, like a modern liner. Inside too it was luxurious but not flashy, restrained in detail, comfortably functional. The
Mayfair, despite a flat façade, and being a little farther away down
Aigburth Road – almost next door to the Rivoli which must have
suffered in consequence – was much more what I'd hoped for. In
particular it had a sensational curtain, ruched in many folds which
were lit from both above and below in a wide spectrum of slowly
changing colours: yellow with purple shadows, red with green, pink
with blue. I thought it the most glamorous effect I'd ever seen. The
cinema organ too (although as an instrument it bored me and I
longed for its grimacing practitioner to sink back into the pit so
that the programme could start) was bigger, brasher and with more
effects, both musical and visual, than its nearby rival. In the end
however, despite my aesthetic prejudice in favour of the Mayfair,
it was what they were showing which decided whether I dragged

my companion up or down Aigburth Road. The Gaumont, the
Mayfair and the Rivoli are all bingo halls now.

Although films were shorter then – ninety minutes was the average – they gave you full value for your one and ninepence: the main
film, a support feature, a comedy short or two (I was finally able to
check up on the accuracy of Edna and Ethel's appearance and
demeanor as Laurel and Hardy at the Servants' Ball), the news and
a travelogue. I liked everything but the last two. I was very bored
by a much-imitated man called James Fitzpatrick who seemed to
end every travelogue with the sentence '. . . and so, as the sun sinks
in the west, we say farewell to . . .' But my obsession was the
cartoons and especially the early Silly Symphonies of Walter (as he
was known at that time) Disney.

They still revive and show on television the formative years of
Mickey Mouse and *Donald Duck* and even, occasionally, *The Three
Little Pigs*, the most celebrated of the Silly Symphonies, but most
of them are never to be seen and yet rank, I believe, amongst the
Disney Studios' most original works. The opening of the Tatler,
Liverpool's first news theatre, was an important date for me because
it was there, despite having to sit through many tiresome features,
that the new Silly Symphonies had their premières: *The Pied Piper*,
King Midas (*The Golden Touch*), *Rock a bye Baby* (with its
bogeymen, a run-up for Dumbo's pink elephants), *Peculiar Pen-
guins*, *The Robber Kitten*, *Noah's Ark*, *The Grasshopper and the
Ant* and many more.

The fat, jostling, red letters announcing a Silly Symphony stood
out against a background like a quilted yellow eiderdown. Then
the screen went dark and an iris lens opened from the centre to
reveal a country where the flowers had flat black centres and simple
petals the colours of sweets and the trees were as plump as pillows.
Certain images still haunt me: the rats in the Pied Piper covering a
chicken carcass like a fur-coat and then retreating a second later to
reveal only the bones, like a mounted prehistoric monster in a
museum; the obscenely hairy and skinny wolf disguised as a mermaid, wearing lipstick and a gold wig, and strumming a harp in
midstream in an attempt to seduce the wise little pig in *The Lie
Detector*; the passing of the storm in *Trees and Flowers*. I loved
Mickey too; I was never as fond of the bad-tempered duck, but

have always regretted the phasing out of the supporting cast. When was the last time Minnie fluttered her long eyelashes? What became of Horace Horsecollar, Clarabelle Cow, Peg Leg Pete, and the Mae-West-shaped diva, Clara Cluck, the farmyard nightingale? I shared this passion for early Disney with Gampa who was always prepared to take me to the Tatler until I was old enough to go by myself.

All these characters appeared in strip form in *Mickey Mouse Weekly*, a comic published around 1935. In the first issue, anticipated by me since its announcement some months earlier, I discovered you could join the Mickey Mouse Weekly Club and receive a badge, the password, how to give a secret handshake, and a diploma. I had included a page of rather stilted drawings of Mickey, Minnie, Clarabelle Cow *et al.* with my application. I spent a great deal of my spare time learning to draw them by heart and was absolutely delighted to receive a personal letter back from the editor. 'Mickey and the gang sure thank you for their portraits,' it said.

I would have spent all my time at the pictures if I could but there were other activities in which I was expected to take part. Dancing lessons, for example, first at Miss Jones's studio in the centre of Liverpool. It was a proper studio with a barre and wall-length mirrors. Miss Jones was very old – she had even taught Maud as a child – and she wore a long black dress and held herself very erect. The forefinger of her left hand was in a fat bandage and according to my mother always had been. Apparently she had 'a whitlow'. I absorbed this explanation, but had no idea what a whitlow was; indeed I hadn't until a few moments ago when I looked it up in the dictionary:

Whitlow (-o), n. Inflammatory tumour on finger esp. about the nail. [Earliest form *whitflaw*, app. = WHITE + FLAW]

It makes perfectly good sense.

Miss Jones taught very formal dancing: gavottes, quadrilles, reels and the schottische. We were expected to wear black, patent-leather shoes with buckles. We danced to an equally old lady at the piano.

I didn't go to Miss Jones's for long. Perhaps she retired or Maud felt she was too old-fashioned or expensive. We moved to a School of Dancing in the suburb of Allerton beyond Mossley Hill whose proprietor was a Miss Saul, obviously a professional name as her husband, who had the kind of hairline moustache Maud 'didn't care for', also taught us. 'Ballet, Modern, Tap' it said on the board outside the semi-detached house. The studio here was the empty front room and we danced to a wind-up gramophone. It was less boring and intimidating than Miss Jones's, but I never got to be any good, and gave up as soon as I was allowed.

We learnt to swim at the noisy Cornwallis Street baths which stank of chlorine and where Maud was always worried we'd 'pick up a verruca', and we were taught tennis by a professional at the Racket Club, the smartest club in Liverpool, on a wooden court where, under an echoing glass roof, the balls made an incredible noise like guns going off. I quite enjoyed playing tennis.

We went ice skating at a rink which had been one of the centres of Maud's flirtatious social life before the Great War. I didn't like ice skating as it made my ankles ache. I much preferred roller-skating but that, somehow an inferior activity, I had to learn for myself. On Saturday mornings we were taken into town where, in the restaurant of the Bon Marché, a Miss Eyenet ran what she called her 'Fun Club'. I hated the Fun Club! Most of the time we spent doing Swedish gymnastics – one and two and three and four – but at the end of the two hours there was a bran-tub which you dug into and pulled out a present. One Saturday I won a tennis ball which had a very strong camphorated smell. I began to sniff at it on the way home on the tram, and continued to do so all day until I was violently sick on the nursery floor. It must have contained an intoxicant of some kind and what I was doing was the equivalent of glue-sniffing. I still sniff surreptitiously at tennis balls but they are always scentless.

I didn't learn riding in Sefton Park, although I could have, and in the winter I did my best to avoid tobogganing and snowball fights. I loved watching the snow fall from inside the warm nursery and the way it made the houses in Ivanhoe Road glow a specially intense shade of sooty-red, but I hated 'winter fun' and, unlike Bill who was lethal, I couldn't throw a snowball. I have never seen the pleasure of being wet, cold, uncomfortable and possibly hurt.

*

One morning, when I was about seven and a half and in my last term at Camelot, I went into my parents' bedroom and found them looking at glossy 'curricula' for Liverpool's preparatory day schools. They'd rejected St Christopher's although it was just round the corner, and the junior wing of Liverpool College, and decided on a school called Parkfield in Parkfield Road only a few hundred yards away. 'Your cousin John was there,' Tom explained, 'and Ronnie was quite satisfied. The headmaster, who's called Twyne, is a pompous ass, but most schoolmasters are. No, we think it's probably the best choice.'

That holiday I went with my mother to George Henry Lee's and bought the school uniform: grey flannel shorts and blazer, football shorts and two sweaters – one white, one black – cricket shirts and flannels, black shoes and house-slippers, a belt with a snake buckle, a cap and tie in alternate stripes of Oxford and Cambridge blue. I wasn't especially apprehensive. I'd be home every night and all day on Sundays. It was only round the corner. I could tease Bill for still being at a kindergarten . . .

I didn't know it then, but I was soon to be very, very grateful for my ability to keep the different areas of my life in separate compartments. Even the prospect of writing about Parkfield, evoking Mr Twyne, induces a mood combining gleeful rage and retrospective terror.

12

W. W. Twyne, the headmaster and proprietor of Parkfield, was a big man. Of course to children everyone looks big but he seemed so in relation to other grown-ups. He was burly but not fat, and smouldered with malevolent energy. Bald with a ruddy-brown complexion, his features were in themselves handsome, but his expression was usually one of petulant and disappointed frustration and his rages, which were frequent, distorted his face into a hideous and terrifying mask like a Japanese warrior in a print. When he was in a rare good mood, he could be surprisingly gentle and amiable. We basked in his good humour, fawned like puppies in the hope of sustaining it; but we watched him warily, knowing only too well that it wouldn't last for long.

He was a very physical man with a large store of what would now be called body language. During his rages he would pace rapidly up and down as though in a cage, turning heavily on his heel every four paces. Simultaneously and continuously he would shoot his cuff, insert the digit finger of his right hand into his collar to loosen it and then shoot his frayed cuff again. We sat frozen during this performance, wondering on whom or on how many his retribution would fall. He would accompany this ritual with a series of oaths, mild enough, even comic in themselves, but delivered with such explosive venom that we felt no urge to smile. 'My Godfathers!' he would shout, 'Ye Gods and little fishes! You people really are the limit!' and always in conclusion, 'It's the pestilential day-school system!' When we were alone together, as a form of exorcism, we frequently imitated this performance. Mr Twyne's absurd nickname, 'Twimbo', was another way we hoped to reduce him in our minds to less intimidating proportions.

The forms his physical retribution took escalated from pulling you up to your feet by grasping either the short hair over the ears or the fatty part of the cheek between thumb and forefinger and then shaking you like a rat, through knocking you rapidly and repeatedly across the side of the skull with his knuckles or the bowl of his pipe, to slippering you with your own house-slipper. Little did I think, when casually trying on a pair of those house-slippers in George Henry Lee's with Maud, that such apparently innocuous objects were to become the instruments of pain and humiliation.

'Give me your slipper!' Twyne would shout to the offender, 'Bend over!' Anything between one and six heavy blows with the heel of the slipper might be anticipated depending, not on the seriousness of the offence, but on the rage of the executant. There was nothing, and I am unable to decide if it was better or worse, premeditated in Mr Twyne's assaults. You were never sent for and beaten in cold blood for a specific crime. Nemesis was instant and completely unpredictable. Sometimes he would slipper the entire school (about forty in number), explaining to each boy, as the blow descended, the individual shortcoming which justified his inclusion in this holocaust. 'You don't do enough work.' 'You talk too much.' 'You've got a cold,' etc. This last may appear especially unfair, but it was Twyne's belief that catching a cold was a matter of choice and indicated some kind of moral failure. It was just one element in an eccentric mental system of quite extraordinary rigidity.

Twimbo was not well dressed. His wardrobe seemed to be confined to one rather shiny brown suit, although I suppose there may have been a second or even a third of identical cut and shade. He wore heavy brown shoes, a little down at heel and, in the street, a greasy trilby hat. His only tie, thin, crumpled and stained, confirmed the fact, frequently referred to in conversation, that he had been educated at Clifton College. He was rather dirty in his habits. In the winter, having blown his nose vigorously, he would bend down to dry the steaming greyish handkerchief at the gas fire, and in doing so revealed that the crotch of his trousers had worn through, allowing us the doubtful pleasure of staring in some awe at his pendulous testicles.

In one of the class-rooms, every morning at about nine fifteen, we could hear outside a loud and puzzling splash. One day, the master or mistress having left us alone 'on our honour', one of the bolder boys decided to solve this conundrum and cautiously put his head outside the window. Twyne's quarters were at the same height and on the same side of the school and, to the minute, his hand emerged from his bedroom window grasping a full chamber-pot which he emptied precipitately into the ivy below. The mystery was solved. This rather eighteenth-century gesture, while the subject of prolonged ribaldry, seemed to us out of character, but I realise now it was probably to do with his almost Swiftian disgust at bodily functions. If we needed more lavatory paper we had to approach him and, after handing it over, he would order us to carry it under our coat 'in case the Matron might see it'. One of his many aphorisms ran as follows: 'Anyone who uses a public lavatory except in a case of dire necessity is a filthy pig!'

His emptying of the chamber-pot into the ivy was presumably because it would have embarrassed him to allow the maid to do it, although at that time this was considered perfectly acceptable practice, and if he'd gone to the bathroom to do it himself there was the possibility of meeting her en route. His statement as to the only justifiable use of a public lavatory illustrates his curiously formal and indeed memorable use of language. No great lover of literature – his revealed taste was for 'rattling good yarns' (*Treasure Island*, Sabatini, Ballantyne, John Buchan, A. E. W. Mason, Rider Haggard were all he advised us to read in our leisure hours) – he nevertheless, even in his rages, relished an ornate phrase. His favourite quotation, which he ascribed to Dr Johnson, was: 'Sir, you are intoxicated by the exuberance of your own verbosity.' His own verbal reactions to a given situation were almost equally elaborate.

His voice was slightly rasping, becoming more so as his temper rose. His accent was received middle-class of the period, clipped rather than drawling but with a southern bias which sounded alien to our northern ears. All his 'a' sounds came out as 'e's'. He pronounced 'back' as 'beck', and he shortened his double 'o's' while lengthening his single 'o's'. 'Afternun,' he'd say, and, for 'often', 'orfen'. Today it is only by listening to British films of the thirties and forties that you can hear this accent in its prime, but there is a distinct echo of it in the voices of the more elderly tennis and cricket commentators on TV.

He was no highbrow. Musically, while detesting what he called 'jazz', by which he implied any form of modern dance music, he expressed enthusiasm for nothing beyond Gilbert and Sullivan and 'the old-fashioned waltz'. In his relaxed moments he admitted, with revealing candour, to a delight in the character of Dickens's Wackford Squeers and, less culpably, a liking for the work of Will Hay, a contemporary comedian who usually appeared in the role of a blustering but ineffectual schoolmaster. Indeed, although very infrequently and only at his most expansive, Mr Twyne would admit, 'despite its deplorable vulgarity', to a weakness for the music-hall.

It may seem perverse that while there were no borders at Park-field, he should have insisted that everything that enraged him was the result of 'the pestilential day-school system', but his school and its geographical situation were, in his eyes, far from ideal. He detested the North of England, making an exception only for the village of Kirkby Lonsdale on the edge of the Lake District, and ideally he would have chosen to be the headmaster of an all-boarding preparatory school in Somerset or Wiltshire, not too far from his beloved Clifton. Why and how he had landed up in Liverpool was one of the several mysteries surrounding him. We knew nothing of his family, although there were rumours of two sisters. Of his previous career all he told us was that for a time he had been an assistant master at Terra Nova, a prep school for which he admitted warm admiration despite the fact that it was situated near Southport, a rather grand resort ringed by golf clubs, but only thirty miles away.

Given that Parkfield was a day school, Mr Twyne did all he could to control his pupils even after we returned each evening to 'the softening influence of home'. We worked on Saturdays. We were forbidden to go to the theatre or cinema or even into a shop, or to associate with children from other schools, not only during the term, but for a week before the end of the holidays. For a time he even made us assemble at Parkfield on Sunday mornings to attend the eleven o'clock service at Christ Church, Linnet Lane, *en masse*, thereby adding to the boredom of the ceremony the fear of earning retribution for giggling or not paying enough attention. Some parents, however, objected to this practice, either because they wanted their children to go to their own local church or because, if they attended Christ Church anyway, they preferred to go *en famille*, and eventually Twyne reluctantly agreed to abandon the church parade.

Why did I put up with it? Why didn't I complain to Maud and Tom who would certainly have taken me away from Parkfield and sent me to a gentler establishment? In part I suppose, as in the case of May and Hilda, I had too much pride to whine, but largely it was because Twyne stressed frequently and menacingly that anyone who left had to give a term's notice and in the case of several boys who did, he offered the rest of us a practical demonstration of just what to expect. Never missing an opportunity to enlarge our knowledge of Latin, he would accompany their increased ration of hair-pulling, cheek-pinching, knuckle-bashing, pipe-welding and slippering by intoning rhythmically the while: '*Proditor, Proditoris*, masculine, a traitor'.

'We'd have paid the term and you wouldn't have had to go,' Maud said to me later when, Parkfield behind me, I told her about the extent of Twyne's physical violence, but I didn't know that at the time and wonder, even if I had, whether I'd have taken advantage of it. I have always been very obstinate and perhaps my hatred of the man had a certain ambivalence. I half-cherished his dislike of me. If I couldn't seduce him I would make quite sure I stood for everything he disapproved of.

Twyne had no degree and, so far as I know, had not attended a university, but there was no question of his knowledge and love of Latin, the only subject he taught. Any boy with a facility for the language or who worked hard at it, while not exempt from assault, tended to attract less of it. If he were also 'promising' at rugger or cricket or – even better – at both, he was in an even stronger position. Bill, arriving three years in my wake, fulfilled all these qualifications. He had in consequence a much easier ride.

'Rugger and Latin prose are all a gentleman needs,' Twyne told us – inappropriate advice I would have thought for the sons of business men and prosperous tradesmen who were his pupils. He would certainly have added cricket if it wouldn't have spoilt the rhythm of the sentence. I had immediately decided that Latin was one of those subjects in which I had no interest and was not prepared to do a hand's turn; I hated the mud and potential for injury on the rugger field and feared the speed and hardness of the cricket ball. I was a 'duffer' in the classroom and a 'rebbit' at games. These, however, were negative failings. I would quite often go out of my way to needle him.

My method was never direct. The lad I admired most in the whole school, a rather stupid and unimaginative boy called Frazer, on one occasion, during a full-scale assault from Twyne, broke loose and shouted 'Lay off!' in a loud defiant tone. I'd never have dared do that. My strategy was to prattle on in apparent innocence about what I knew was calculated to enrage him – my mother's friends in the ballet, for example. He had a profound and just conceivably suspect hatred of any activity he considered effeminate, and the ballet ranked high. I knew that Twyne would be unable to criticise my mother directly, but of course I didn't win. 'Melly Major,' he asked me, 'would you rather go to the ballet or watch a good game of rugger?' I could see the trap, but was at this point unable to recant. 'I'd rather go to the ballet, sir,' I told him. 'Give me your slipper, Melly Major!' he bellowed.

Sometimes I enraged him by accident. One teatime he heard me commiserating with a boy because his birthday always fell during termtime. Twyne beat the wooden trestle-table for silence, told the school what I'd said, and then asked every one of the forty boys whether they would sooner have their birthdays during the holidays. Each of them replied, some a little shame-facedly, in the negative. I was then hauled to my feet and beaten, my punishment confirmed by this cowed consensus.

Yet, even towards me, he would sometimes, however rarely, extend a moment of favour. '*Mel, Mellis,*' he would always decline on these occasions, 'neuter – honey'. While this lasted, and it was never for long, I would feel more than relief, almost love.

Parkfield School occupied a large Victorian stone house with a red-brick extension housing the class-rooms and dining hall. At the front there was only a short curved drive and a bed of gloomy, overgrown laurels masking the building and Twyne's piss-pot emptying from the road, but behind there was a large yard, cemented over, with an outside lavatory and a shooting gallery along one side and across the yard, through an opening in the high wall, the playing-field.

What Twyne always called 'the carriculum' was quite elaborate. Rugger and cricket of course, but also rifle-shooting in the long shed where we lay full length on our elbows on prickly mats, 'squeezing not pulling the trigger', and boxing in the basement, a hideously painful business of bleeding noses and cut lips which he always referred to as 'the noble art of self-defence'. In the summer we went swimming once a week in a hired indoor pool the other side of Sefton Park. This wasn't too bad as it involved a long Noah's Ark-like walk during which you were allowed to talk to your partner, and just to get out of the building at all was a relief, similar in impact I should have thought to that experienced by a long-term convict on changing prisons and thereby catching a glimpse of the outside world going about its normal business.

At the baths Twyne's method of teaching those who couldn't swim was, predictably, to throw them in at the deep end, hauling them out only if they were in real difficulties, and I was extremely grateful I had already mastered, at the Cornwallis Street baths, an adequate if stilted breast-stroke. If it was raining hard on the day we went swimming Twyne, rather than write off what he had paid in advance for the pool, would order a fleet of taxis 'with terrible trouble and at horrible expense' as he put it. I learnt later that the school was always on the verge of financial collapse so it was indeed an inexplicable extravagance.

Parkfield's stated object was 'to coach boys up to the standard of the Common Entrance Examination for the Public Schools' and to this end, apart from Latin, we were taught English, French, History, Geography, Mathematics and Scripture. In addition there was Music, Art and Carpentry once a week. For these 'extra' subjects teachers came in, but for the others there was a permanent and presumably hideously underpaid staff.

Two of them, Miss White (Maths) and Miss Maclean (French), are little more than names now, although I can remember that Miss White, while small and elderly, was an effortless disciplinarian and that Miss Maclean smoked a great deal and possessed a leopard-skin coat. The rest of the permanent staff remain in much sharper focus: Mr Taylor and Mr Oliver because they liked me; Miss Chesterton because I irritated her so much. Mr Taylor and Mr Oliver were both, I suppose, in their early twenties, and Mr Oliver, unlike Mr Twyne, was actually a BA, a fact heavily emphasised in 'the carriculum'. They were both keen territorial officers and amateur rugger players, and you wouldn't have expected them to take to me at all, but they did. Mr Oliver was rather good-looking in a clean-limbed kind of way. Mr Taylor on the other hand was prematurely bald with a ginger moustache and owlish spectacles, and I liked him even better than Mr Oliver. They both taught English and History at different levels of the school, and it was true that these two subjects were the only ones I was any good at. I don't think, however, that this is why they were on my side. It was more to do with the fact that they were both very bored, loathed Twyne, admired my refusal to submit to his will and, above all, that I made them laugh.

When I was still in the bottom class and, except in English and History, at the bottom of it, Mr Taylor discovered to his surprise that I could recite Shakespeare and, with Mr Twyne's reluctant permission, loaned me to Mr Oliver to take the principal role whenever the top class was stumbling its way through one of the plays. That I could read blank verse fairly convincingly didn't mean that I could understand much of it – it was more to do with my imitative facility, Tom had taken me to see *Macbeth* when I was still at Camelot, and Maud would sometimes, as a change from 'Naughty Little Briar Rose' and 'Burglar Bill', recite me some of the famous speeches in which she had triumphed at The Green Room before the Great War. I had been thrilled by *Macbeth* and moved by Maud's rendering of 'Build me a willow cabin' and 'The quality of mercy'. As a result I had caught the rhythm of Shakespeare and, provided I understood the gist of the speech, could turn in a creditable performance for a boy of eight.

Later, however, whenever I said anything which amused either of them, or recited a new monologue by Stanley Holloway, or imitated the Western Brothers – popular comedians of the time who dressed in tails, wore monocles, and drawled their way through satirical songs of aristocratic fatuity – I would be sent to repeat it in the other's class-room. If I were to meet Mr Twyne en route, they told me, I was to explain that I was needed to read a speech by Shylock or Othello. But as Twyne was always in his own class-room, stressing perhaps that while *nubio* meant 'to marry' it applied only to women, I never had to resort to this excuse. Naturally I was delighted at these expeditions, not only because I adored showing off, but also because I was in league with grown-ups in the deliberate deception of Mr Twyne himself.

Sometimes Mr Oliver became irritated at my continuous need to divert, at my untidiness or lack of concentration, but Mr Taylor never did, which was why I preferred him. The only time he spoke harshly to me was not because of anything I'd done, but because he was irritated by Gampa's admittedly rather dubious insistence on being addressed as 'Colonel'. 'He has no right to the title,' said Mr Taylor, quite red with passion. 'He was only a Colonel in the Territorial army. He would have to have been in the regular army to earn the right to be called Colonel! I would refuse, yes refuse, to address him as "Colonel". I would call him "Sir". As he is an older man I would naturally call him "Sir", but Colonel never!' I couldn't understand why Mr Taylor – although I'm quite sure he was technically correct – became so heated on the subject, but I somehow felt it was better not to question Gampa or even Tom. It would be betraying Mr Taylor.

One afternoon at tea (doorsteps of brown bread thinly smeared with margarine and jam which came out of huge tins and tasted of onions) Mr Taylor and Mr Twyne had a row. We were all, of course, riveted but were unable to work out from what they said to each other what the row was about. They were perfectly civil on the surface and both finished off every sentence with a 'sir'. But their voices were quivering with suppressed rage and Twyne's finger, always a bad sign, was constantly easing his collar. Whether as a direct result of the row, or because of a more general antipathy from which it arose, Mr Taylor left in the middle of the summer term. I cried when he said goodbye to me. I cried on the way home, and I howled and sobbed to Maud and Tom that evening.

'He was my friend,' I explained to them repeatedly as they tried, rather worriedly, to calm and comfort me, 'he was my friend!'

Bill, who was in the room, suddenly realised that he did not like all the attention I was receiving, and decided to get in on the act.

'He was my friend too!' he wailed loudly and somehow managed to burst into tears as convincing and copious as my own.

I stopped crying at once. Bill had only arrived at Parkfield that term whereas I'd been there for three years. He hardly even knew Mr Taylor! I was absolutely furious with him. It was like *Trader Horn* all over again.

Miss Chesterton, who taught Geography and Scripture, was quite young, handsome rather than pretty, and clearly very nice. Her dislike of me rankled and was based, I've come to the conclusion, on my preciousness and tendency to pronounce confident value judgements. Two examples will suffice, both of which took place at tea. Sir Henry Newbolt – Twyne's favourite poet as it happened – had just been created Poet Laureate. I pronounced magisterially that this was ridiculous. It should obviously have been Kipling. Miss Chesterton snapped that I was in no position to judge. I was very hurt.

The second confrontation was over a joke. 'Did you know,' I asked the boy sitting next to me shortly after the coronation of George VI, 'that the King has been going around with Mrs Simpson's sister-in-law?' He looked very surprised until I explained that Mrs Simpson's sister-in-law was (ha-ha) the Queen. Miss Chesterton overheard me, as she was intended to. I wasn't going to waste a joke like that on one dim boy, especially as it was the kind of joke that Mr Taylor would have sent me to tell Mr Oliver. Miss Chesterton, however, was not at all amused. She said it was disgusting and an insult to the Royal Family. I told her that I had heard it from my Uncle Fred. It was my customary ploy to retreat behind a grown-up if challenged, and this time anyway it was true. 'That doesn't make any difference,' said Miss Chesterton. 'It's unsuitable here!'

Twyne was at the head of the next table but luckily did not pick up this exchange although, unexpectedly, he wasn't a passionate monarchist. The Empire, yes. The public schools, certainly; but his enthusiasm for the Royal Family was never more than lukewarm. Of course he never admitted to this directly but several times he repeated something which struck me later as significant. 'When I was inspected by the Prince of Wales during the war,' he told us, 'I could see that he was wearing make-up. The Royal Family wear make-up!' It was clear that he found this extremely suspect. For a man, whether Royal or not, to wear make-up was almost on the level of being a ballet dancer.

The temporary staff consisted of a carpenter, a lugubrious Liverpudlian who was passionate about dove-tailing. I was as bad at carpentry as I'd been at raffia. He used to pick up whatever I was trying to make, hold it up to the bare bulb of the basement, and squint along it with one eye. 'Luke at dat,' he'd say gloomily. 'It's all cock-eyed.'

Music took place in Twimbo's sitting-room, a dusty and masculine apartment with leather furniture and an upright piano, on the ground floor of the older part of the house. We didn't learn to play instruments, just to sing, either in unison or two-part harmony, a selection of sea shanties or folksongs. We were taught by a small, cheerful and somehow pathetic lady called Miss Nangle who also accompanied us on the upright. It was all perfectly agreeable and the songs: 'What shall we do with the drunken sailor?', 'As I was going to strawberry fair', rather jolly. The only time there was a near disaster was when we were learning a new folksong allegedly written by Henry VIII. It was called 'The Carrion Crow' and one of the verses went:

> Oh wife, oh wife bring out my bow
> Heigh ho, the carrion crow.
> Oh wife, oh wife bring out my bow,
> For I mean to shoot that carrion crow.
> Twiggle Twiggle Twig Dum Twee!

The trouble was the absurd last line. Every time we sang it through, I became more and more hysterical and hysteria is catching. Miss Nangle was very patient. 'Boys! Boys! It's not that funny! Now calm down! Let's start again, shall we? One, two . . .' It was no good. Eventually we could hardly get through the first line before the thought struck us that only four lines on we would have to deal with 'Twiggle Twiggle Twig Dum Twee', and we would dissolve into giggles.

It was a hot summer's day and the sash window was wide open. We stood in a semi-circle round the piano and I was facing the window. I looked up, wiping away my tears, and saw that Mr

Twyne, who could always move remarkably quietly for so large a man, was leaning on the window-sill thoughtfully smoking his pipe. How long had he been there? Did he realise I had started the whole thing off? His expression was enigmatic, but that didn't mean anything. The fact that I had stopped laughing so suddenly had an instant effect even on those with their backs to the window. We froze like a herd of deer scenting danger. Miss Nangle, facing the piano, had no notion as to why the atmosphere had changed so rapidly. We sang through the first verse, including the refrain, as if it were a dirge. When I looked up, Mr Twyne had vanished like a ghost.

'That's better!' said Miss Nangle, 'But now it's *too* serious. It's meant to be fun! We'll try it again next week. Turn to "Bobbie Shafto".'

Miss Nangle also taught me the piano at home.

Art was my favourite subject. We were taught it on Saturday morning by a man called Captain Banks or, as Twyne pronounced it, 'Ceptin Benks'. He was short and rather dapper and quite old. He was very bald and freckled with many grave marks on his hands. He smelt strongly of scent. His method of teaching was to demonstrate on the blackboard with coloured chalks. He taught us about perspective, shading, highlights, the ideal proportions of the face and body. He would run at the blackboard, make a mark with the chalk giving it a little twist at the end, a little flourish, and then retreat backwards equally fast to examine the effect with his head on one side and a look of total self-satisfaction.

Sometimes he gave us his own small water-colours to copy. They were poor things, very wishy-washy, usually of boats pulled up on a shore. They were framed in *passe partout*. He didn't tell us much about the history of art, but spent a long time attacking the modernists whom he felt had robbed him of recognition. In particular he raged against 'the Sandon Studio artists', many of whom I knew. 'They paint purple women with green hair,' he shouted, working himself up into a paroxysm of rage.

One Saturday, instead of copying the boats, we went to Sudley with Captain Banks to look at Cousin Emma's pictures. He'd asked me to arrange this expedition and I had. I was in fact rather proud that he should have considered that a relation of mine had a collection worth visiting, especially as Captain Banks had never taken us to the Walker Art Gallery. Perhaps, though, that was because Twyne wouldn't allow it. As it was open to the public, it may have come under the same taboo as cinemas, theatres or shops.

Cousin Emma, having greeted me personally and affectionately, much to my satisfaction, asked me to introduce her to the Captain and then showed us round herself. Captain Banks bobbed and smarmed about her in the oiliest fashion; confirming her judgement, leaping back from the pictures as if he had just completed them himself, stressing constantly how privileged we were to be there. As we were putting on our coats and caps in the hall, under Aimée's suspicious eye, he took her aside and engaged her in earnest conversation. 'No thank you, Captain Banks,' I heard her say firmly, 'I'm afraid I don't feel able to take up your kind offer to paint either the house or myself.'

She told Maud later that she believed Captain Banks had arranged the whole outing in the hope of netting this commission. I was sorry for him – even at nine I could recognise pathos – but equally I was rather embarrassed.

13

The rest of the personnel at Parkfield were a cook whom we never saw, a maid-of-all-work who did everything except empty Twyne's chamber-pot, and a 'groundsman' who mowed the playing field and rolled the cricket pitch. There was also a matron called Miss McClaren. It was surely unnecessary in 'a pestilential day school' to employ a matron but I suppose she could have been responsible for the catering. She was dressed, however, as a proper matron in a kind of hospital uniform with a cap, and I think she was hired to bolster up Twimbo's dream of running a real boarding school in the West Country. She was very kind-hearted, and when Twyne knocked anyone about, a look of distress and anger crossed her open Scottish features. One term she was not there any more, nor was she replaced, but Mr Twyne, when we asked him what had become of her, dismissed her, with great bitterness and in defiance of her gender, as a '*proditor, proditoris*, masculine, a traitor'. What had she done, we wondered? Had she perhaps threatened to report him to the NSPCC?

A term or two later we acquired an even less necessary addition to the staff – a staff sergeant. His name was Rutter and he had been in the Mozambique Rifles. Thinking back on his appearance I believe he may have had some black blood: his nostrils were very wide, his mouth generous, and he had crinkly hair. His head was large, his body broad and compact, but what was perfectly obvious, to anyone with even an inkling of such things, was that he was a screaming queen. Didn't Twyne, with his phobia about effeminacy, recognise this? Is it just conceivable that he was Twyne's lover? Certainly his duties were light enough. He took PT in the concrete yard. He taught us shooting in the long wooden shed. On very wet days he would lecture, with slides, on life in the African bush. He helped out Twimbo on the playing-field or during boxing in the basement. He also cut our hair. A barber had always come in to do this during term-time, but now Sergeant Rutter took his place. His haircuts were drastic. 'Oh no!' cried my mother in only partially mock anguish when Bill and I came gooseberrying home after the Sergeant's radical application of the clippers.

He was a kind man though, and stopped Mr Twyne from throwing boys into the swimming bath by insisting on teaching them himself at the shallow end. While patently gay, he was not – and boys always know even if they don't know what they know – at all pederastic. My parents could not believe it. Sensing Maud's fascination and liking for homosexuals, he used to rush up to her on sports days or on meeting her in the street shrieking: 'Bless you, Mrs Melly,' a sentiment Twyne, who both mistrusted and disliked her, would never have endorsed. My father, on his return from the office, would sometimes imitate this greeting, And he always referred to Sergeant Rutter, although naturally never to his face, as 'Pansy' Rutter. After a couple of years he left and we were sorry to see him go. Perhaps for the reason I have tentatively and with no positive evidence suggested, 'Pansy' had acted as a restraining influence on the excesses of W. W. Twyne.

Much as I dreaded Twyne in the class-room I was at least in part protected there by others, some of them 'promising' athletes who were as unenthusiastic and idle when it came to mastering 'Letin prose' as I was myself. It was on the playing-field that some of our worst confrontations took place and it was cricket especially that brought out what he called the 'bolshie' in me.

During rugger matches, by running about a lot and making sure, as discreetly as possible, that I was in the wrong place, I could at least present the illusion of involvement. What I hated about rugger was not so much the games, which at any rate lasted a specific time, but the scrum practices on Saturday afternoons. These, when I was longing to get home, went on and on, well into the dusk, and were made all the more frustrating by Twimbo's reiterated and mendacious promise that each successive scrimmage was to be 'the last scrum of the day'. 'Show some guts, you little forwards,' he would bellow as an excuse for prolonging the muddy tedium another ten minutes. 'Guts' was the strongest language I ever heard him use, and even here he would qualify it later at tea by telling us that it was a word 'justifiable on the rugger field but not in the drawing-room' even though 'these days duchesses swear like bargees'.

His attitude to women was, I suspect, deeply hostile, and he covered this by excessively formal politeness which some mothers, but not Maud, found charming. Sometimes he would instruct us on how to greet a lady in the street. He would borrow one of our caps, which on his large bald head was already a dangerously risible spectacle, and would then pretend to walk in a somewhat military fashion for some paces before recognising an imaginary aunt or 'another boy's mother'. He would stop, smile rather savagely, and raise the cap into the air with his right hand. 'Good afternun, Mrs Clutterbuck,' he'd enunciate clearly before replacing the cap and resuming his even pacing. We were then expected, either individually or collectively, to repeat this absurd exercise, 'Mrs Clutterbuck' and all.

It was, however, in relation to sport that his misogynism became nakedly manifest. He told us that women were, by temperament, totally unsuited to playing anything, illustrating his thesis by citing the behaviour of a certain M'mselle Suzanne Lenglen, a French tennis champion of the twenties, who several times at Wimbledon had 'thrown down her reckit in pure rege'. He also told us that we must never play any game with a girl, 'not even tennis, not even with your own sister' because of the unacceptable possibility of being beaten.

Cricket, however, was a male preserve and he took it for granted that any man who had no interest in it was totally beyond the pale. Had I been more circumspect or less obstinate I could have faked it, expressed some enthusiasm if no aptitude, learnt at least the positions on the field, but I made no such concessions. If, when arranging the fielding, he directed me to silly mid-off or square-leg I made it patently obvious that I had no idea in which direction to aim. During test matches, when we were expected to sit through lunch or tea in rapt silence, listening to the commentary on the wireless, I emanated boredom and, if questioned, total ignorance as to the state of play. He could slipper me as often as he liked, but my rejection of the mystique of 'King Willow' remained absolute, the centre of my integrity.

Once, when batting, I scored a four, but was relieved, although also rather hurt, when he dismissed it contemptuously as 'a cow shot'. 'There are only two strokes in betting, Melly Major,' he remonstrated, 'Forward and beck!' He demonstrated these alternatives with an invisible bat: 'Forward and beck!'

I still know nothing about cricket, but retain and cherish a single sentence of his on the subject, not because of its content, but because of the way it was expressed – Twyne at his most baroque. 'When Jessop was betting,' he used to say, 'nursemaids would leave their charges.'

The boys who assembled under Twyne's threatening shadow came from a fairly wide social spectrum. Some were the sons of professional men: doctors, lawyers, architects. The majority of us were the children of business men. A few had fathers who had succeeded in trade – fishmongers, market gardeners, coal merchants – who had decided they could afford to turn their sons into gentlemen. Twyne was not in a position to be selective. He needed a full school to keep his shaky financial position from collapsing.

None of us was actually what he would have chosen; even the doctors and lawyers were Liverpudlians. Ideally his pupils would have been the sons of small Wessex landowners, military men and colonial administrators. He had no dreams of running a fashionable school; in fact he despised 'Society', foul-mouthed duchesses and all. He had no ambitions to boast that his boys went on to Eton or Harrow. The public schools he favoured were those modelled on Dr Arnold's Rugby: Marlborough, Repton, and of course Clifton. His ideal boy 'worked hard and played hard'. The quality he most valued was *esprit de corps*.

Naturally he became apoplectic at the idea of progressive education, reserving his especial venom and verbal exuberance for the Montessori System. This he described as 'a pimply youth in a velvet suit doing crochet in a deckchair'.

He made no secret, either, of his dislike of the industrial working classes. '*Sperno profonum vulgus*' (I hate the common people), a Latin tag ascribed to Coriolanus, was frequently on his lips.

Nevertheless he believed that they, or at any rate their children, were useful in offering us a practical opportunity to apply the lessons we had learnt in 'the noble art of self-defence' in the school basement.

It was the custom of gangs of small and ragged boys from the back streets of Lark Lane and Aigburth Road to lie in wait in the driveways of the big houses near Parkfield in order to duff us up on the way home. Twyne referred to these children collectively as 'oiks', and indoctrinated us with the idea that if we took them on one at a time and applied the Queensberry Rules, we would automatically establish our superiority. Unfortunately the 'oiks' appeared to be unaware of the Queensberry Rules. They used their elbows, heads and boots, and were not prepared to take us on man to man. Their intention was never to hurt us badly. What they hoped to do, and frequently succeeded in doing, was to humiliate what I heard one of them describe as 'dem posh kids wid dair daft caps and dair toffee noses in de ur'. It was Twyne who lusted for reports of broken noses and smashed teeth.

Despite the legendary exploits of an old boy called Barlow Major who, according to Twyne, had left three large 'oiks' unconscious and stacked neatly around a lamppost like a picture in a comic strip, most of us preferred to rely less on our pugilistic expertise than on safety in numbers. The 'oiks' were usually in gangs of three or four at most and so if we walked home in groups of five or six they usually left us alone. One evening in 1935, however, I set off by myself because I had obtained special permission to meet my father on his way home from the office and, although it was termtime, go with him into a shop in Lark Lane to buy my first bike. Twyne was standing outside the gates of Parkfield smoking his pipe, something he frequently did in the summer to make sure that we neither dawdled nor ran, at any rate until we were out of sight, and Tom, I could see, was waiting on the corner of Ivanhoe Road, some two hundred yards away. When I was approximately equidistant between them, three minute 'oiks' rushed out of a driveway and set about me. Aware of the proximity of Twyne I assumed the classic prizefighter's stance: right fist guarding the face, left arm extended, while they ran rings round me, kicking my shins and elbowing me in the ribs. There was a bellow from Twyne as he became aware of the fracas. He ran down Parkfield Road, an intimidating if absurd spectacle, yelling: 'Keep a straight left, Melly Major!' Seeing and indeed hearing him coming, the 'oiks' scampered off, passing within a few feet of my father, towards the safety of Lark Lane. One of them was triumphantly waving my cap. Tom was convulsed with laughter, Twyne out of his mind with rage. 'Why didn't you stop them, Mr Melly!' demanded the furious Twimbo.

'Because I was laughing too much,' said my father. Twyne turned silently on his heel and strode off back to Parkfield. Despite the fact that Tom had been educated at Marlborough, Mr Twyne obviously believed that he was wanting in *esprit de corps*.

Although I didn't like being duffed up, I envied the 'oiks' their freedom, their torn jerseys, the fact that they could stay up as late as they liked and roam the streets. I know this incident took place in 1935 because that night, lying in bed, my beautiful new bike in the little shed in the back-yard, I could hear some of them, possibly even the same gang, singing profane words to a Salvation Army hymn as they swaggered back down Parkfield Road.

> Will you come to Abyssinia will you come,
> Bring your own ammunition and your gun,
> Mussolini will be there
> Popping bullets in the air.
> Will you come to Abyssinia, will you come.

14

I forget which boy it was that, when I was about nine, suggested that he put his hand up my trouser leg and 'rubbed up my dick'. I resisted his invitation initially, it seemed both meaningless and 'rude'; but when he promised me I'd like it, and furthermore I somehow began to feel curiously excited at the idea, I let him do it. As soon as he started to tickle and rub my privates I could feel my 'dick', small as it was, grow hard, and a minute or two later a delicious sensation, starting at the base of my spine, flooded through my whole body. I had experienced, although I'd no idea what it was, my first induced orgasm, but naturally, as I was still several years from puberty, there was no sperm. I felt no hesitation therefore in gratefully doing him the same service. I watched with interest how his eyelids fluttered and he gave a little moan when he achieved what he called 'the funny feeling'. Although temporarily incapable, I couldn't wait to do it again.

I soon discovered that this habit was widespread throughout Parkfield, especially among the older boys. It had, I learnt subsequently, been imported by a boy called Warren, the school's best cricketer, as it happens, and big for his years. He had learnt about it from an older brother who was at public school. There were a few boys in the school who would have no part of it, but most of us were at it all the time – in the outside lavatory, in the changing-rooms, even during class behind the high tip-up desks. It didn't take very long, and we'd no idea of its significance beyond the pleasure involved, but we never stopped. It was like a comforting secret to set against the harsh and spartan world of Twyne.

That it should remain a secret we knew instinctively. A certain guilt about our privates had been inculcated since we were toddlers, although without any explanation as to what we were meant to feel guilty about. Even my mother, with her advanced views on nudity within the family, would tell me and Bill not to touch 'our obies' if she saw us doing so. I've no idea why she called the penis an 'obie' but she did. Alternatively it was known as a 'dumbelow' although this, she told me, derived from a misunderstanding of Uncle Fred's when he was a little boy. The Griff, while giving him his bath, would tell him, having herself washed everything else, to soap himself 'down below', and he misheard it as 'dumbelow' which he concluded to be a name for his 'arrangements'. Of course this demystification of the privates by the use of whimsical names was not confined to the thirties and persists even today. You hear even the most progressive mothers refer to their child's 'willy'.

I soon discovered, although I found it less exciting, that I could 'rub up' myself, and this explained to me why my mother sometimes rushed into my bedroom and whisked back the sheets and blankets with a cry of, 'Where are those handymits?' The myth of the evils and dangers of masturbation was universal then.

An orgasm, while the means to achieve it was new, was an experience I remembered from a dream I had when I was only five or six. I found myself as a pig in a dirty sty at Uncle Percy's farm and derived enormous satisfaction from rolling and wallowing in my own dung. I awoke to what I now recognised as the same feeling I got from 'rubbing up'. I'd also been very interested in my privates. I once dreamed, but believed it for many years to be factual, that I was sitting in the nursery and had discovered a way to remove from my testicles the two hard little balls I could feel under the skin. These turned out to be brightly coloured beads of a curiously electric puce, and I spent a happy time rolling them about the green cork floor before realising, in a panic, that I'd no idea how to put them back. The beads at least were real, part of a game in the nursery cupboard, and it was one of them that Andrée had swallowed and on which she had nearly choked to death.   .

At Parkfield we were entirely unromantic about our sexual partners; that was to come later at our public schools, but we did develop purely physical crushes. These led to curious liaisons across the usual lines of interest. Warren himself, for instance, captain of cricket and a brilliant 'all-rounder', became a close friend through this shared interest whereas before it would never have occurred to him to spend his time with 'a rabbit' who couldn't throw overarm. There was a certain amount of selective rejection too. There was one boy I liked very much but refused to engage in sexual activities with because he had plump, wet hands, was overweight, and wore pebble glasses. Equally it took me a long time to persuade a very randy and in truth rather neolithic-looking boy, the son of a timber merchant, to have anything to do with me. Another mystery: why did I find him attractive? He had a low forehead, small eyes and a heavy jaw. All I knew was that I did.

Taking a leaf from the 'oiks' book, I invented a parody of the title song of a film in which George Formby played the gormless lead. Both the song and the film were called *It's in the Air*. Holding an imaginary ukelele and assuming Formby's innocent grin and Lancashire accent I sang:

> It's in the dick
> That funny feeling that's so quick
> To tickle like the heck
> At the back of the neck,
> It's in the dick.

This became something of an anthem to the rubbing-up brigade and we would hum or whistle the tune publicly about the school with looks of knowing complicity.

With all this going on, it was only a question of time before Twyne found out, and when this eventually happened I was a witness. At the back of the school was a small quad, a patch of grass with a conservatory along one side. Overlooking this area was a basement which formed the lower changing-room, whereas the conservatory was used as the upper changing-room.

I was in the lower changing-room, usually a hive of sexual activity, and while changing into my hated flannels I happened to glance out of the window only to spot Twyne tiptoeing across the grass. He stopped outside the conservatory and peered in. There was a moment's delay before he jumped in the air, banged on the window, and rushed into the body of the school yelling, 'Ring up the school doctor!'

I guessed, of course, what had happened, and it was confirmed during the game. Warren, who was in the upper changing-room and, as I'd expected, involved, was fielding opposite me. At each over, as we crossed on the pitch, he managed to tell me the story in single sentences. Apart from his request for the school doctor, an instantaneous reaction which he had not followed up, Twyne had done nothing: no hairpulling, no slippering, simply the order to get changed at once delivered in a neutral if icy tone.

After tea the staff left the dining-hall in a rather self-consciously casual way, and the whole of the lower changing-room were ordered to take the few very small boys who went home half-an-hour earlier, to wash. Later I asked Warren what Twimbo had said. 'Oh, that we'd go blind, and lose a vital fluid out of our backbones and stop being able to play games well,' he told me. Nobody believed this, and quite soon we started 'rubbing up' again only with rather more circumspection. The only thing which puzzled me was why Mr Twyne imagined that vice was the sole prerogative of the upper changing-room.

For a surprisingly long time, until I suppose I was about ten, I made no connection between 'rubbing up' and procreation. My knowledge of sex was non-existent. Maud, when I'd asked her about how babies were born – for Tom played no part in answering any of our more serious questions – didn't try to fob me off with storks or gooseberry bushes, but her answers were 'The Daddy,' she said, 'loves the Mummy so much that a baby starts to grow in her tummy. It's there for nine months and then it's born.' Perfectly correct as far as it went, but I believed in consequence that all that was involved was an act of will. My ignorance was eventually dispelled, not at home but at school, by a very serious boy called Rice. He was as hopeless as I was at cricket and Twyne, in exasperation, had told us to go to the nets at the far end of the playing-field and practise batting and bowling. Ever the proselytiser, I was questioning him as to why he took no part in our sexual activities. 'Because,' he said, bowling a wide which would have brained the umpire, 'I believe sex should be used for its true ends – the making of children.' He could see from my face that I hadn't the faintest idea what he was talking about, and he proceeded, with admirable scientific detachment, to enlighten me. Frankly I couldn't believe him. Had Tom done *that* to Maud? Had all the Parkfield mothers

and fathers done it? Had the Griff done it, and Gangie and Gampa?
No, it was impossible. It was my turn to be censorious.

When I got home I asked Maud outright and she, who had read
or been told that you must answer such questions honestly as they
came up, confirmed everything he'd said, only stressing that what
was important was the presence of love.

'Is it nice though?' I asked.

'Yes,' she said, rather wistfully. 'It's also very nice.'

I went to bed in such a mental turmoil that I didn't even bother
to rub up.

It didn't take me long to make the various connections. Men and
women did it because it gave them 'the funny feeling', but you
didn't have to do it with a girl to get that although it must be best
if you could. I also discovered that most of the boys whom I
hastened to enlighten already knew about it, and the various jokes
they told, which I'd laughed at but hadn't understood, suddenly
made sense. Having broached the subject, I questioned Maud endlessly, and gradually extended my sexual knowledge into quite
esoteric byways. She told me about gays and lesbians, why some of
her men friends lived together, and so on. She preached tolerance
and understanding and revealed, although involuntarily, her own
largely unfulfilled sexuality. A lot of things began to fall into
place: what Douglas Byng was actually singing about, many of the
references at the music-hall. Of these areas the boys at Parkfield
knew nothing. I was in a position to enlighten them and, always
delighted to be the centre of attention, didn't hesitate to do so. It
was even more satisfactory than going on about Maud and Tom
letting us see them with nothing on.

15

As a result of all this rapidly acquired and mostly ill-digested knowledge, I began to have crushes on girls. Most of them I recognised to be fantasy figures: film stars, actresses, lady acrobats, whom I would never meet but who could be thought about when 'rubbing up' – for by now this was no longer sufficient unto itself. I had to have a scenario. Much more frustrating were the girls I knew who were in their late teens or early twenties, for I had no interest in my giggling or snooty contemporaries. I became obsessed with several of them, but realised at the same time that they were unlikely to be remotely interested in a boy of nine or ten.

Of these perhaps the one who gave me the most anguish was a tall twenty-year-old Irish beauty with very white skin, jet black hair and huge blue eyes. Her name was Miss Simpson and she had come to teach at Parkfield as a replacement for Mr Taylor. She didn't stay very long, perhaps only a year, but during that time, whatever perils the day might hold, I actually hurried to school with an eager heart. Nor was it only at Parkfield that I saw her. She would sometimes come to the house. My mother collected pretty girls, whom she called collectively 'the young lovelies', to 'fill up' her straight dinner parties. She had met Miss Simpson at a school sports day and my father, whom Maud always liked to please, admitted to finding her 'decorative'. She was asked once and, having 'scored a hit', joined 'the young lovelies' on a permanent basis. Tom called her 'the Duchess', pinning down her employment at Parkfield to 1936, the year of the Abdication, which would mean that I was ten years old.

For me a side benefit of the Duchess's success as a 'young lovely' was the rage and anguish it caused Twyne. He mistrusted and disliked my parents and for one of his staff to be invited to their dinner parties seemed to him an outrage. I made sure he knew of it, too. Maud would ask me to see if Miss Simpson was free the following Wednesday, and I deliberately invited her in Twimbo's hearing. 'Sure,' said the Duchess in her soft brogue, 'wouldn't I be delighted.' Twyne could do nothing. His staff were free to spend their evenings as they wished, but he could later be heard muttering that 'nobody could be expected to do their jobs properly if they spent their nights in dissipation.'

Miss Simpson accepted my worship with tact and charm. Once I tried to declare myself. We were sitting in adjoining deckchairs watching a school match with Bishops Court, a Catholic establishment from Blundellsands. (I never minded school matches because I was not in the team and there were special buns for tea coated with sticky white or pink icing.)

'Miss Simpson,' I said in a fake blasé voice, 'perhaps you don't realise this but boys my age, not all boys perhaps but some, have strong sexual feelings.'

'Is that so now?' said Miss Simpson without displaying either excessive interest or dismissive indifference. 'Well, it's unfortunate for them, but then haven't they got their lives ahead of them?' She gave me a sweet and understanding smile which didn't help much. 'Hadn't we better pretend to take an interest in the game, boring as it is. Twimbo's got his eye on us, and we'll both be in his bad books.'

I ate a lot of sticky buns for tea and was fascinated, as always, by the way boys from Bishops Court crossed themselves before sitting down.

It wasn't all Wackford Squeers or Wedekind at Parkfield. There was also friendship and enmity, the discussion of films seen in the holidays, hobbies, games in their season, smuggled comics, the usual traffic of small boys everywhere. Comics, or 'penny dreadfuls' as Twyne, with typical archaism, chose to call them, were banned and I usually read mine at home. Defiant in spirit, I was very cautious when it came to breaking rules. Unlike some boys, I never went to the pictures during the term, but then I did live very close to the school. I doubt if I would have done so no matter where I lived, because I believed that, like God, Twimbo would find me out.

Leaving aside my own personal obsession with *Mickey Mouse Weekly*, the most generally popular comics were the *Beano*, the *Dandy* and *Film Fun*. Fond as I was of Big Eggo (a greedy ostrich), Keyhole Kate, Desperate Dan (who ate whole cow-pies with the hooves and horns sticking out), Lord Snooty and his Pals, and Pansy Potter, the strong man's daughter, all of whom appeared in either the *Beano* or the *Dandy*, my favourite was definitely *Film Fun*. Apart from its link with the pictures, it gave double value in that it was possible to follow the stories by racing through the balloons issuing from the characters' mouths over breakfast, reserving the more expansive text printed under each frame until I returned home. Then I could read at leisure and with a clear conscience for there was one great advantage about Parkfield: although we came out later than most schools, Twyne did not believe in homework.

Laurel and Hardy took up the front and back page of *Film Fun*. Inside were other single-page adventures featuring, among others, Schnozzle Durante and, more esoterically I would have thought, as their films were generally only released in the North of England, George Formby, Old Mother Riley (and her beautiful daughter Kitty), and even Frank Randle.

The stories were more often than not concerned with what the text described, with almost Twyne-like elaboration, as 'temporary pecuniary embarrassment', solved, after several vicissitudes, by a rich uncle handing over a five-pound note with '£5' printed boldly on it. This was inevitably spent at either 'The Hotel de Posh' or 'The Hotel Stuffem', two establishments where the cuisine appeared to be limited to a turkey (or was it a very large chicken?), a huge dish of mash with sausages sticking out of it, and a bowl of fruit with a prominent pineapple. Laurel and Hardy usually shared their good fortune with two identical girls dressed, unfashionably, in the 'flapper' style of the twenties. Nobody ever 'said' anything in *Film Fun*. They 'chortled' or 'guffawed', 'growled' or 'yelled'. The background detail was also worth studying. When the characters were still 'broke', there was usually a thin cat somewhere in the picture gnawing ravenously at a fish reduced to its head and skeleton.

Apart from comics there were conkers in the winter term which were allowed at Parkfield and, for a time, the renaissance of that craze of the twenties, the yoyo, which was banned. Tom surprised me by his expertise with the yoyo, a skill he had acquired in his youth. He could even do 'round the world' whereas all I could manage was to make it go up and down on its string and even then with ever-decreasing momentum.

My two best friends at Parkfield were both the sons of doctors. One was called David Hurter who was rather small and very serious. Tom called him 'Mr Penny' after a character in the popular radio programme 'Monday Night at Seven'. Hurter – for although we were close Twimbo's embargo on first names tended to apply even during the holidays – had a jolly mother who adored him. Their mutual passion was catching moths and I accompanied them on several expeditions to the heaths around Southport or the woods and fields of the Wirral. I enjoyed catching the moths in a net and dreamed of discovering a new species, but found it difficult to remember the names and distinguishing characteristics of those we came across and, although a dab hand with the killing bottle, I was useless when it came to mounting the specimens once I'd got them home. Still for Hurter's sake I persisted for several years.

Desmond Julian's father was a homeopath, at that time considered an eccentric if not positively harmful form of medicine. Desmond had an older brother called Adrian who seemed to me the epitome of knowledgeable sophistication, and a charming sister called Pauline. His mother was warm and loving and they were indeed a most attractive family. I went on summer holiday with them once in Anglesey and Adrian explained to me, quite without prurience, why Pauline couldn't swim that day; another fact to add to my growing store of sexual knowledge.

Twyne didn't like the Julians any more than he did us, not in their case because of any theatrical connection, but because he thought the Doctor to be dangerously left-wing. In fact Dr Julian subscribed to Sir Richard Acland's Commonwealth Party, but anything less than a total commitment to the extreme right of the Conservatives was, for Twyne, tantamount to carrying a Communist party card.

Hurter, Julian and I formed a dissecting club. Both of them wanted to become doctors like their fathers, and it was the period when I, who couldn't even mount a moth without the wings coming off, saw myself as a famous surgeon. Part of the reason for founding

the dissecting club was in opposition to a boy called Nicholas who
had started a model aeroplane club. Hurter, Julian and I all detested
model aeroplanes, and we also thought Nicholas far too bumptious
in general. I approached my father's first cousin, Dr George Rawdon
Smith, to ask for his help and he gave us the small dissecting table
he had used as a student and a set of rather rusty surgical knives.

We met at our house on Sunday afternoons and went upstairs in
procession accompanied by Hurter playing his recorder. There we
cut up (or in my case hacked up) a rabbit or pigeon purchased from
Glendennings, high-class fishmongers and poulterers, of Lark Lane,
preserving the organs in jars of formaldehyde, before marching
down the stairs again for a large tea. Among the rabbits' brains and
pigeons' hearts was our prize specimen, Bill's appendix which, after
prolonged haggling, I had bought from him after his emergency
operation for one shilling and sixpence.

Maud didn't mind us cutting up pigeons and rabbits, but she
drew the line when she discovered that I had been to see a vet and
reserved a dog he was about to put down. She made me ring up the
vet, much against my will, and cancel it. The dissecting club, like
the model aeroplane club, gradually petered out, but both Julian
and Hurter eventually became doctors.

Julian, who was a little older than I, left Parkfield just before the
war. Shortly afterwards Twyne, reading in the *Daily Telegraph* of
the Russian non-aggression pact with the Germans, jumped to his
feet, threw the paper on the floor and shouted: 'The Julians ought
to be shot!'

16

At some point in the mid-1930s Maud and Tom decided that, with Andrée beginning to grow up, 33 Ivanhoe Road was becoming too cramped and that they should move. They first considered buying a very beautiful old house at the entrance to Fullwood Park, a private residential drive curving down from the bottom of Aigburth Road to the river. The house had been built in 1666 and was in bad repair, and Tom, ever cautious financially, decided against it. I was very disappointed as I was sure it must have had at least a couple of secret panels, one of my fixed obsessions. It was eventually bought by a prosperous doctor who immediately knocked it down and built a hideous villa faced in yellowish-brown pebble-dash. He even put a plaque up on the side reading: 'Built 1666. Rebuilt 1936', to advertise his crime.

It was surprising that Tom agreed to buy a house at all. He had always maintained that he preferred to rent so that the landlords and not he were responsible for any repairs. I've no idea why he was so nervous about money – he knew that he would eventually inherit a substantial amount – but nervous he was. He even got quite cross if he felt we were using too much lavatory paper. 'Quite unnecessary,' he'd remonstrate; 'all you ever need is two up, two down and a polisher.'

Eventually they settled on a very ugly but large late-Victorian house in Sandringham Drive, next door to York Mansions where the Griff had her flat. About forty years old and very solidly built, it was structurally sound and cost only a thousand pounds freehold, reasonable even in those days as there was almost half an acre of ground at the back. Faced with sandstone, it had bay windows and awkwardly pointed eaves. There was a large porch at the side leading through to a decrepit conservatory mounted on tall brick foundations with wooden steps down to the garden. The front, while badly proportioned, was at least symmetrical, but the back was a mess with haphazardly placed windows and naked drain-pipes. It was, however, an undeniably solid property and inside, the rooms, as in so many Victorian houses, were large and well-lit.

Maud decided the way to deal with it was to 'modernise' it. She had most of the walls papered in cream and the woodwork painted shiny black. She replaced the elephantine newel post by a straight elongated cube and boxed in the ornate heavily carved banisters with plywood. She did the same for the doors, changing their large round china handles for angled chrome or bakelite. She also boxed in the elaborate plaster friezes and ripped out most of the fireplaces, replacing them with gas fires. In the lounge she installed a modern grate with geometrical cream and brown tiles. She carpeted the hall and staircase in 'apple' green and had the outsides of the doors and the boxed-in staircase painted to match. For the main rooms she had curtains made which went down to the ground and had square pelmets covered in matching material. She made two bathrooms: hers and Tom's was called 'the green bathroom' because not only were the walls green but so were the bath, washbasin and lavatory – the *dernier cri* in 1935 – and the cistern of the lavatory was not high up the wall but behind the basin itself, another novelty at that time. The adjacent 'blue bathroom' for the maids and children was far less grand. It had ordinary white fittings, and only justified its name because the walls were painted a rather raw blue. The top floor, which we didn't use, she blocked off with a cheap door and more hardboard, in case one of us ever needed a flat. It was in one of those empty, undecorated rooms that the dissecting club held its weekly sessions.

With the exception of a large divan for the lounge and some furniture for Andrée's pink, sprig-muslined room, she had to buy very little. What had seemed cluttered in Ivanhoe Road proved quite adequate here. When I used to stay at home during the fifties it seemed shabby and dated but, freshly decorated inside and out, the effect for suburban Liverpool was quite 'daring'. This was confirmed by Aunt Eva's state visit. Looking very out of context in her floor-length black bombazine dress and jet jewellery, she went 'over the house' without comment, only to pronounce magisterially on leaving that it was 'far too modern'. Maud had aimed at modernity and should have taken it as a backhanded compliment, but given her insecurity in relation to the older Mellys she was quite upset. Most people, however, found it 'very exciting', if, in some cases, 'a little extreme'.

In the basement, running along the whole of the back of the house, was 'the big room'. It had a fairly low ceiling, two central columns taking the weight of the building, eight windows and a door into the garden. Maud did no more than paint it cream, build a wooden wall-seat right round it, and put in a gas fire at each end. She knew very well what she would use it for. She would hold a series of huge parties.

Meanwhile it was a marvellous room for us. We had a full-length ping-pong table which, when stood on its side and drawn on with coloured chalk, doubled as the scenery for the later 'Melly Versions', while the space between the two columns formed an ideal proscenium arch. There was of course no secret panel, but in compensation there was a trap-door in a corner of 'the big room' with a steep little ladder leading down into the foundations and, at the front of the house, extensive cellars. In one of these was a large boiler and a pile of coke, for there was an antiquated but perfectly efficient central heating system, in itself a rarity in pre-war Britain where frost patterns on the windows and chilblains on toes and fingers were accepted as the norm in winter. It had to be very cold, however, before Tom felt there was sufficient justification for lighting it.

The garden consisted of a long narrow 'top lawn' which ran parallel to the garden of York Mansions. At the end, flanked by two ugly Victorian urns, were some steps leading down to 'the big lawn' with a herbaceous border along one side and a kitchen garden beyond. Across 'the big lawn' some more steps led up to a garage on a cement plateau and, for access, there was a sandy lane running up the other side of the Griff's, with a double gate at the top leading out again into Sandringham Drive. Tom took over the garden and became quite keen on it. It was a bit too big for him and he wasn't very interested in vegetables, which anyway grew badly in the sour Liverpool soil. In consequence the kitchen garden behind its 'rustic' trellis of rambler roses looked, with its little wooden hut, like an ill-tended allotment, but he mowed the lawns and took a lot of trouble with the herbaceous border. Maud raided this a great deal for the house, but it caused little friction as what she was after in the main was a tall plant called Golden Rod which he considered to be a weed and would like to have uprooted, but which she thought looked 'very dramatic' in a big beige jug on the square piano in front of the burnt-orange curtains. There was a little wooden gate leading into the Griff's so we could play there too and, when we got a bit older, some neighbours, the Brocklehursts, had a door made in their fence on the conservatory side of 'the top lawn' so that we could use their hard tennis court. From a small terrace house with a back-yard and an 'entry' we suddenly had all this. How we could afford it remains a mystery. Had Tom come into some money from an uncle? Had Gampa advanced him some? Or was it that, with the Depression over, he was doing much better in the buying and selling of wool futures?

Yet despite enjoying our new-found grandeur, and because I was already nine or ten when we moved, it was Ivanhoe Road which remained for me 'the house'. Many of the incidents and conversations with my mother which must have taken place at Sandringham Drive I remember as happening in Ivanhoe Road. I was convinced, for example, that Gampa died when we were still there, but reading in Willie Bert's pamphlet that this took place in 1937 I realised that it must have been after we'd moved. Andrée confirmed this. Although not told about Gampa's death at the time, she remembers going into the spare room at Sandringham Drive and finding Gangie praying at the foot of one of the twin beds with their shot-silk covers. It remained fixed in her mind, although she was barely five, because she found it so strange that Gangie should be saying her prayers in the afternoon. But then Andrée can hardly remember Ivanhoe Road at all. Just the pram room, she says, and mostly only its rubbery smell. A further factor in my confusion perhaps was that both houses had the same furniture arranged in much the same way.

Where was it, for instance, that I gave up listening to *Northern Children's Hour* in favour of Henry Hall and his orchestra? I'd loved Children's Hour especially *Toy Town* and a programme called *Out With Romany* in which 'Auntie' Doris and 'Auntie'

Muriel pretended, in a Manchester Studio, to be out on a nature ramble with a rather posh gypsy and his extremely well-trained dog, Rack. Fooled by a convincing recorded background of bird song, Bill and I firmly believed that they were really in the country, although we were surprised and impressed by the number of creatures – hedgehog, fox, badger, otter, woodpecker, stoat, etc. – that Romany, in his stage whisper, managed to bring to the attention of the two 'Aunties' in only half an hour. Quite suddenly, though, I abandoned Rack and his master, Larry the Lamb and Mr Growser, for the suave bespectacled Hall. At first I only liked the comedy or novelty numbers like 'The Teddy Bears' Picnic' and 'Hush, Hush, Hush, Here Comes the Bogey-Man!', but soon developed a taste for ballads: 'The Isle of Capri', 'Red Sails in the Sunset', 'The Story of Love', and particularly 'Pennies from Heaven'.

Miss Nangle, whom Tom had nick-named 'Niddy Noddy', had taught me the piano at Ivanhoe Road and continued to do so for a time at Sandringham Drive. I showed no aptitude for it and hated the simple classics I was expected to learn. Finally I delivered an ultimatum. I would only carry on if I could learn to play dance music. Niddy Noddy reluctantly conceded and I bought, from the music shop in Lark Lane, a song copy of 'Pennies' with a pale blue art-deco cover and a round inset photograph of the young Bing Crosby in the bottom right-hand corner. I thought I'd be able to play dance music at once but found out it was just as difficult as 'The Merry Peasant' or Brahms' 'Cradle Song'. Eventually I was allowed to give up music altogether, although I prevaricated about this for several weeks because Maud had often said that 'poor Miss Nangle is very badly off'. Finally, in defensive tears, I told her, and it was perfectly all right. She said she'd hated having to teach me dance music anyway, and that as I'd no talent even for that, it was really a waste of time for both of us. From then on I saw Niddy Noddy only at Parkfield and, as a bonus, the duets with the Griff came to an end too. Mrs Oochamacootch was no longer in a position to reprimand her partner Mr Umpty Plum, now that he had retired from the concert platform.

I kept the song copy though and bought others when I wanted to learn the words. For some reason I can 'see' the cover of 'Pennies from Heaven' superimposed, like a pop collage, on the sky above a road that led up from Aigburth Vale to the bottom of Mossley Hill. Perhaps one day I noticed that the sky was exactly the same shade of blue.

The wireless played an increasingly important role in Bill's and my life after we'd moved to Sandringham Drive. We wouldn't have missed *In Town Tonight* ('Once again we stop the roar of London's traffic to bring you some of the interesting people who are IN TOWN TONIGHT'); *The Palace of Varieties* with its signature tune 'The Spice of Life', and especially *Bandwaggon* with 'Stinker' Murdoch and Arthur Askey. Big-hearted Arthur and Stinker lived in a flat on the top of Broadcasting House. They kept a goat and two pigeons up there, and their char's daughter was called 'Nausea Bagwash'. On each programme Arthur would sing one of his 'silly songs', the most famous of which began like this:

> Oh what a wonderful thing to be
> A healthy grown-up busy, busy bee . . .

In the last programme of the series Arthur and Stinker had to move out of their flat and, despite the fact that I must have been at least eleven, I burst into tears.

Maud and Tom held a huge house-warming party in the Big Room; Tom never seemed to mind lashing out on entertaining. *Tout* Liverpool was there as well as many visiting theatricals. Ronald Frankau came and did a free cabaret with 'Monte Crick at the piano', although Maud, while grateful, really felt he went too far. 'I like a bit of spice,' she said, 'but he sang a song about balls in front of all those young girls!' Nevertheless the party was favourably reported at length, not only by Mary Ventris in *The Echo*, but by her friendly rival Kitty Russell, who wrote a column called 'Rumour' in the *Liverpool Evening Post*. Cousin Emma sent over a van-load of potted plants from her greenhouses so, for the only time in all the years we were there, the conservatory looked like a conservatory rather than a dumping ground for the detritus of the house and garden. There were so many cars parked in Sandringham Drive that the police came to find out what was going on. They told Maud they thought it must be a Fascist meeting.

One of the uses to which the conservatory was put, after the van

had collected Cousin Emma's potted plants, was as a place for me
to keep my lizards. I'd always wanted to own reptiles but there just
hadn't been room at Ivanhoe Road. Now I bought a vivarium, built
a little rockery in it and turned one of the dissecting club's kidney
bowls into a pool, and it was done. The lizards, bright green and
about ten inches long, came from a pet shop in Park Road, and
were fed on meal worms from the same source. They became very
affectionate. I used to walk around the house with them sitting on
my shoulders, a habit which once gave a nasty shock to René Beere,
friend of Uncle Alan and son of Mrs Beere, the stingy millionairess
who lived at the Adelphi. René Beere, while extremely amiable and
no trouble, was a bad alcoholic. He had come to dinner and was
just knocking back his third gin and tonic with my father when I
came into the room with the lizards about my person. Poor René
did a double-take and the ice began to rattle and crash against the
sides of his glass. 'It's all right, René,' said Tom, recognising the
cause of his panic; 'they're real.'

Unfortunately, possibly because the conservatory was too cold
for them, the lizards died and, although I replaced them once or
twice, they continued to die and in the end the vivarium was
left untenanted. We weren't lucky with cold-blooded pets. Our
succession of tortoises, always called Ptolemy after Jeremy Fisher's
guest, never survived a winter. With the death of the last lizard the
cast of my bed-time prayer, both quick and dead, was complete and
remained unaltered until I lost any semblance of faith. It went:

> God bless Mummy and Daddy,
> Dear little Bill, dear little Andrée,
> Gangie, Gampa and Gaga,
> Uncle Fred and Uncle Alan,
> Jock, Zip, Ptolemy and the lizards,
> All kind friends and relations,
> And make me a good little boy.
> Amen.

The fact that I continued, until the age of about sixteen, to refer to
myself as 'a good little boy' would seem to suggest either that I was
a moron, or that I wasn't really thinking much about what I was
saying before joining Little Ted between the sheets.

More successful was my career as a breeder of budgerigars. I started with two in a small cage in the nursery and graduated to a proper aviary in the garden with nesting boxes and lots of perches. We bought the aviary by mail order from an advertisement in the *Radio Times*. Tom and I tried to put it up ourselves with the help of the enclosed plan but we had to give up and send for the carpenter, Mr Hughes, whom we called 'Good 'eavens' because that's what he always said, in his light Lancashire accent, whenever we asked him to do anything. He said it now when he saw what a muddle we'd got into trying to erect the aviary, but he had it up in no time, and the budgies bred like mad – various blues, green, yellow and even white. I sold them through the pet shop where I'd bought the lizards and made quite a lot of pocket money.

Later, during the war, my father got rid of the budgies, added a rather untidy wire-netting extension to the aviary, and bought some hens which he called 'The White Sisters', not only on account of their colour but also because they reminded him of some nuns of that order who had bought the house next door from the Brockle-hursts and turned it into a Convent. The feathered White Sisters weren't anything like as successful as the budgies. They laid very few eggs and what they did lay were extremely small and the shells, despite enormous quantities of grit, were disastrously thin.

Shortly after we'd moved into Sandringham Drive we had to put down Joey, our enormous, much-loved, neuter tabby cat, who had become almost blind and more or less incontinent. He was replaced by a ginger kitten not especially prepossessing, even at an age when most kittens are fairly irresistible. He was called 'Ginger', the lack of imagination indicating the low regard in which he was held. Ginger grew up to be a truly unattractive cat. He was ravenous but scrawny, slightly cross-eyed and, as his teeth didn't fit properly, he dribbled continuously. Needless to say he was exceptionally and obtrusively affectionate, being especially fond of Maud who would occasionally feel obliged to stroke him once or twice with the same expression on her face as if he were a very large black widow spider.

Ginger had the habit of pacing from room to room with his tail stuck perpendicularly up into the air as though determined to display his sphincter muscle, admittedly clean and neat, but of an unpleasing pink which clashed badly with the surrounding ginger fur. Maud was particularly dismayed by this spectacle, but one day, when there was something she desperately wanted to happen, or alternatively not to happen, said that, if she knew for certain her wish would be granted, she would be willing 'to kiss Ginger's arsehole'.

She could never, so far as I know, bring herself to put this to the test. If she had, and her sacrifice had proved worthwhile, it would have meant, among other benefits, that the Second World War wouldn't have taken place. Later on Ginger was partially run over by a tram when he was crossing Aigburth Road. He recovered more or less, apart from a slight Byronic limp, but his tail was completely paralysed and now trailed behind him as he dribbled from room to room in search of affection. This would have made Maud's task even less enviable. She would have had to lift this limp and useless appendage first before attempting to influence the course of history.

For each of us, except for Andrée, Sandringham Drive had both advantages and disadvantages in relation to Ivanhoe Road. For Maud it was too close to her mother, although she must have known this when they bought it, and the Griff was therefore in an easier position to exert her imperious will. On the other hand the size of the house at last allowed her to become a hostess on a scale denied her in Ivanhoe Road.

For Tom it was a bit further from The Albert but closer to Jack and Maisy Forster's so he was more able to slip in there for a gin or two on his way back from the pub. This incidentally was certainly on Maud's list of disadvantages. They didn't row much as far as I know, but when they did it was usually about Tom's boozing. 'That bloody drink!' I heard her shout in pain and rage one evening as I was passing the lounge, and then Tom, equally angry, stormed out of the room and subsequently the house, slamming the front door. I was very upset at this rare explosion and much relieved when, five minutes later, Tom returned and apologised.

Another advantage for my father was that it knocked a good ten minutes off the time he took to get to and from the office. He used to have to walk down to the bottom of Lark Lane or Parkfield Road and catch a tram. Now he could take the overhead railway from the Dingle, a beautiful bit of early twentieth-century engineering, later pulled down, which rattled along above the still prosperous docks and past the great berthed liners.

For Bill and me, it was a slightly longer walk to Parkfield, but in recompense we were less likely to encounter Twyne during the holidays. Frustratingly the bottom of the playing-field with its tall wooden fence faced on to Alexandra Drive and was only a few yards from the entrance to Sandringham Drive. In the winter, when it was dark, we sometimes risked running down the field and vaulting over a low side-wall into the shrubbery of that house which I associated with Monte Carlo. It was an exciting and exhilarating dash, and we were never caught.

For Andrée there were no points of comparison, but she some-times behaved oddly in relation to the new house. When the builders were still in, we'd gone there for a picnic in the garden, and when it came to be time to go home Andrée, who was about four, refused to move. She just lay curled up on the grass apparently deaf to pleas and threats and in the end Tom, who had become quite worried at her silent embryonic obstinacy, had to pick her up and carry her all the way back. A few years later, when Tom was getting out his key to open the front drive, Andrée suddenly dropped her knickers and deposited a neat turd in the drive. Tom was quite put out and made her pick it up in a laurel leaf and throw it in the shrubbery.

He called it 'untypical' and indeed it was. With her snub nose and enormous slanting eyes she was growing up, like the little girls in the advertisement for Pears' soap, 'to be a beautiful lady'. Very funny and observant, full of affection, at times painfully conscien-tious, adored but unspoilt, she might have been considered almost too perfect, and perhaps the occasional gratuitous gesture like the turd in the drive was her unconscious revolt against that possibility. Maud who, as the Griff never failed to point out, didn't bother much about her own appearance, was rather clever about dressing Andrée. She didn't try to make her look winsome and frilly, but bought her rather severe clothes and had her dark hair cut straight, although sometimes she added a huge brown Minnie Mouse bow on one side.

Like everyone else, I loved Andrée, but I wasn't always very nice to her. I sometimes couldn't resist snapping her hat elastic, but my cruellest tease was based on my discovery that, although extremely quick in every other direction, she couldn't understand the mechanism of the joke. She probably would have done so in time, but having realised that the nervous laughter with which she hoped to conceal this fact was entirely spurious, I not only asked her to explain what she was laughing at, but worse, made up 'jokes' with no point at all to trick her into pretending she had got the point. As a result even today if anyone says to her: 'Have you heard the one about . . .' she is overcome by panic. Otherwise we became extremely close as she grew older, but although my influence, my Byronic adolescent attempts to mould her as an *alter ego* were dangerously manipulative, Andrée has always been too intelligent, too certain of her own moral position, not to remain her own woman. If anyone it was Maud, with her burning unfulfilled theatrical ambitions, who was a more serious threat to Andrée's identity but here too, at times under considerable pressure, she has always managed to preserve her centre.

Bill had his emergency appendix operation a couple of years after we'd moved to Sandringham Drive. He was rushed off to hospital and for some hours his life was in the balance. I sat up in bed in our twin room talking to Ginny Duckworth who was our 'paying guest' at the time and her fiancé, Larry Rathbone. We told dirty jokes to keep our minds off it, but I was increasingly conscious of Bill's neat and empty bed, and in the end we just sat there more or less silently listening to the hissing gas fire and wondering if no news really did mean good news.

At about four the phone rang. Is there a more sinister sound than a phone ringing when you know why, and that there are only two alternatives? It was Tom to say they thought it was going to be all right. I have questioned Maud's assertion that the long night of tension instantly changed my relationship with Bill but, while we still had rows, and I at least remained very competitive, we certainly began to get on better from about that time. We'd come home from Parkfield together, play ping-pong (the only game at which I have ever developed any skill), listen to the wireless or, on summer evenings, get through a couple of sets of tennis on the Brocklehursts' court with no more than a little mild bickering as to whether a ball was in or out. Every night before we went to sleep, we'd hold what we called the 'daily chat', much of it devoted to the immediate eccentricities of Mr Twyne or, in the holidays, an analysis, frame by frame, of any film we'd seen. We gradually became friends – even at times conspirators.

Ginny Duckworth, the 'paying guest' who sat up with me the night 'dear little Bill' had his brush with death, was the daughter of Lady Lacon, Maud's friend who 'didn't care for children'. She was a tall girl of about twenty with enormous brown eyes, very long legs, and an interestingly sulky expression and, after the Duchess had left Parkfield, she was the next person I fell in love with.

Despite the fact that he was always perfectly friendly, I hated her boyfriend, Larry Rathbone. He was actually a distant cousin of my father's, but for me, with his loud laugh and swept-back blond hair, he was simply a rival with every advantage on his side. When they had a row – and they had quite noisy rows – I was ecstatic. Despite my calf-eyed devotion and gifts of Black Magic chocolates, Ginny seemed quite fond of me. She would let me sit and talk to her while she wandered round her bedroom in her underwear and pulled on her stockings.

By the time I was twelve I was allowed to stay up for grown-up dinner and, as my parents were out at least three nights a week, Ginny and I often ate alone. She didn't get on all that well with Maud, who thought her 'moody', and Ginny was sometimes quite critical of her. I found this wickedly exciting. No one, except the Griff, had ever found any fault with Maud in my hearing except, by inference, Mr Twyne, and that I took to be in her favour. Ginny, for instance, pointed out that, when my parents weren't there, Maud took a lot less trouble about what we had to eat. In particular the puddings were almost always based on the banana. Sometimes these were mashed with cream, sometimes cut in two with ice-cream down the middle, sometimes chopped up with nuts. I called these puddings 'Sherlock Holmes and Dr Watson' because they were always bananas in different disguises. We had quite a few little shared jokes of this sort at poor Maud's expense, but I would have gone to any lengths, any treachery to please Ginny. Before I went up to bed and the 'daily chat' she let me kiss her a tense goodnight. In the end she married Larry Rathbone and I didn't see her any more.

I was already at Parkfield when we moved to Sandringham Drive.

One night I slept surrounded by rolled up carpets and packing cases at Ivanhoe Road, and the next in the new house. I was quite excited but, several times during the first few weeks, if I wasn't concentrating, I'd find myself crossing Parkfield Road and be half-way down Ivanhoe Road before I realised I was going the wrong way.

Once Bill was born we no longer spent the summer holidays in boarding-houses at seaside resorts. From 1933 on, unless invited for a week or two at Tent Lodge, we went for a month to North Wales followed by a month in Trearddur Bay, Anglesey.

The reason we went to North Wales was that, following his stroke, Uncle Willy had no further reason for taking a shoot in Yorkshire, but instead rented a series of large houses in the Clwyd Valley with nearby trout and salmon fishing for the benefit of the family. This was very unselfish of him as he no longer fished either, nor indeed ventured out. As far as he was concerned he might as well have stayed at Chatham Street and saved his money. As it was, he just sat in a chair chain-smoking his Turkish cigarettes, drinking his whisky and soda, saying little beyond. 'How's yourself' when you got there and 'Look after yourself' when you left, and eating his hasty pudding. It was his sister Eva who ran the place, ordering the enormous meals, supervising the linen, arranging the flowers and, for her own pleasure, painting watercolours and spending hours on end over her great jigsaws.

The older members of the family – Gangie and Gampa and Old Nell – were in residence the whole summer, but the next generation – the Leathers, the Rawdon Smiths and us – were invited to the house for a week or so and then, if we wished to take advantage of the fishing, were expected to rent a farm or cottage in the neighbourhood, although this didn't preclude going over for as many meals as we chose. It was a reasonable and amiable arrangement. The first year Willy took a huge house called Bodrhyddan belonging to an Admiral Rowley-Conway. It was so big that the Admiral didn't have to move out, but simply confine himself to one wing. He in no way imposed himself, but now and then you would catch a distant glimpse of an erect red-faced figure with two King Charles spaniels at his heel crossing one of the clipped yew walks in the large formal garden.

I was too young to ask about the date of the house but from my memory of mellow red brick and slightly cumbersome renaissance detailing I'd guess it to have been built during the Restoration. Inside there were suits of armour and weapons arranged in patterns on the wall, and great bulbous-legged chairs with either embroidered or worked leather seats and backs. I had high hopes of finding a secret panel, but did not.

What amazed me about staying at Bodrhyddan was the breakfasts. I was used to vast lunches at Chatham Street but had never breakfasted there. Coming down that first morning I found porridge and every known form of cereal, boiled eggs on little stands, toast and four sorts of bread, but what really threw me was the long line of silver chafing dishes on the massive sideboard: bacon, fried eggs, poached eggs, scrambled eggs, kippers, breakfast trout, haddock, kidneys, sausages and kedgeree and, on the table, several kinds of marmalade, honey and quince jelly. I've always been greedy and loved breakfast. The amount I put away even aroused the interest of Uncle Bill. 'You enjoy your food then, young feller,' he said despondently as he shakily buttered a slice of toast.

The presence of Old Nell was a great help to the other grown-ups in keeping the children off their backs. It was her custom to purchase a huge quantity of plain white postcards and, with the help of scissors, stamp hinges and a box of water-colours, build a whole model village with a church, a pub, a wishing well, a manor house and several cottages. We would sit watching her for hours, occasionally encouraged to take over the simpler tasks although most often she had to do them all over again. Another thing that surprised me about Old Nell was that she could make a boiled sweet last for hours.

That year, 1933, I was considered too young to be taken fishing, but Tom used to let me go out shooting with him in the evenings and I was allowed to 'beat' for him, knocking the tree trunks on the far side of a wood to drive the clattering wood pigeons towards him. One day I found a cow's horn in a field on one of these expeditions and fitted it on the end of a stout stick. I called this my 'wandering stick' and would set off by myself into the great park with its red and white chestnut trees to explore the surrounding countryside. I wore white that year and, on my head, a small kepi which I had purchased on a visit to Rhyl. White is not the best colour in which to remain unobserved by shy birds and mammals, but on my return, taking a leaf out of Romany's book, I would pretend to have watched a vixen playing with her cubs at the den's mouth or a badger, untypically abroad in the middle of the afternoon, rooting for grubs. I don't suppose anyone, except Maud, believed me, but no one was so impolite as to call me a liar.

I spent a lot of time, too, exploring the outhouses of Bodrhyddan. If you opened the stable door quietly when the horses were all out in the fields, there were almost as many rats as in Disney's *Pied Piper*, swarming all over the mangers. I told Tom this and he used to go with me into the stable yard with his shotgun. I'd then fling open the top half of the stable door and he'd fire both barrels, sometimes killing four or five rats at a time. Once I found a beautiful plant growing behind an abandoned pigsty. It had lustrous black berries but I'd been told never to eat anything I wasn't sure of. I took Gampa to look at it, who told me it was deadly nightshade.

Some mornings, very early, Gangie and I would go mushroom picking in the misty fields. They were added to the gargantuan choice at breakfast. When we didn't go picking mushrooms, Bill and I loved to get into bed with Gangie and Gampa when they were drinking their morning tea. Gampa wore a night shirt and they both smelt of warm biscuits.

One Saturday afternoon at Bodrhyddan there was a fête. In the yew garden there was a big bush clipped to look like a blackamoor's head. For the fête the gardeners had hung gold hoop ear-rings from its dark green ears and inserted big rolling eyes and white teeth. I'd discovered these objects in a loft and wondered what on earth they could be. I was told they were very old.

Gampa gave me five shillings in pennies. I rolled them down a shute on to a board with different numbers on it. If a penny came to rest on a number and not on one of the squared lines which divided them, you won. I was very lucky and won a pound. I rushed off to tell Gampa and found him chatting to Admiral Rowley-Conway who, for once, wasn't hiding in his wing. Gampa said he was very pleased. Then I went back and lost the lot. When I told Gampa this he gave me a lecture on gambling. 'Always stop when you're on top,' he said quite crossly. I've never been able to do that. That's why I still gamble very little and always for an amount I've decided to lose in advance.

I loved being at Bodrhyddan. I think that year we stayed the whole month. The house was so big we didn't have to move out. There was room for any number of Mellys, Rawdon Smiths and Leathers. I told everyone at breakfast on our last morning that I'd decided I 'preferred the country to the seaside'. They all laughed, but I did, and still do.

Uncle Willy didn't take Bodrhyddan again. For the next four years he rented a house called Hafod. It was a yellow-washed manor with a stable yard and a tennis court, but it was nowhere near as big. Most years we stayed at a farm nearby, but in 1937 Tom rented a rather 'modernistic' villa called Lount Cottage on the outskirts of Denbigh. Almost every morning Gampa sent the car over to take us into Rhyl or Prestatyn to swim in the big open-air baths. Sometimes Gangie and Gampa came too. Afterwards we usually went back to Hafod for lunch and spent the afternoon there.

Once I went out sketching with Gangie and Aunt Eva and they had a splendid row. Gangie chose to paint part of a barn and a bit of field beyond. It turned out very well. Aunt Eva took on a wide panoramic view with woods and distant hills and it went wrong. She was already gobbling like a turkey-cock with irritation when Gangie, never exactly noted for her tact, said rather smugly that perhaps she'd been 'over-ambitious'. Aunt Eva, mottled with rage, knocked over her spindly little easel and threw her paint-box in a ditch. They didn't speak for two days.

John Leather was at Hafod one year. He had an airgun. We discovered that if you suddenly raised the lid on the corn bin in the harness room there was always a mouse scurrying about on the top of the hard shiny corn. It immediately began to burrow down into it, but if you were quick to aim the muzzle at its fast-vanishing backside and pulled the trigger it more or less disintegrated. We always felt guilty about this afterwards, but it didn't stop us doing it again. We spoke hypocritically of 'keeping down vermin', and I tried to think it was just the same as Tom blasting off at the rats at Bodrhyddan, but somehow it wasn't.

In 1935, for the first time Tom and Gampa took me fishing, something I'd begged them to do every year. We drove down a little lane one fine afternoon and Kane had to stop the car when a mother duck and about six babies in her wake emerged from the grass and waddled processionally across. We got to the fishing hut by the River Clwyd and Tom and Gampa put up three rods. They tied on flies for themselves and a big worm for me. I sat on the bank watching my float and listening to them bickering as they fished. Tom was the more impatient. He cast all the time. Gampa reproached him. 'What's the point of flogging the water, Tom? Wait for a rise.' I found it quite funny but a bit disorientating to hear my father told off like a small boy. Then my float bobbed. I did nothing. I knew from catching perch at Coniston that you didn't strike until it went under. It was most likely to be an eel. Gampa said I'd probably only catch eels. The float bobbed again a few times and then moved steadily down towards the bottom. I struck and gave an excited yelp as the rod bent double and the line came screaming off the reel. Tom and Gampa, shouting advice, ran towards me along the bank.

Twenty minutes later my first trout, three pounds in weight, lay on the grass in all its speckled glory. How responsible was I for landing it? Very little I should think, but they never took the rod off me. I believe my father stood behind me, his hands over mine, guiding them as to when to reel in, when to hold, when to let the fish run. Gampa netted it. When we got back to Hafod, Gampa wrote down in his fishing book:

DATE	RIVER	FISH	FLY	WEIGHT	REMARKS
Aug 15 1935	Clwyd	Brown trout	worm	3lb	GM's first trout

After that Tom taught me to fly-fish, but I didn't have much success to begin with. The year we took Lount, there was a little stream at the bottom of the concrete gnome-ridden garden. I was convinced there were trout in it, and cast away there hour after hour. One day Tom told me he thought the trouble was there were too many leaves and too much rubbish floating down the stream. He bought wire netting and some posts and we spent a morning erecting a barrier across it, both at the top end and, more mysteriously, at the bottom. Two days later I hooked and landed a trout unaided. It was only six inches long but I had done it all by myself and insisted on having a photograph taken. It came out rather blurred, but you can just see the trout. I am holding it up by the tail, the rod in my other hand, and looking very proud and solemn. What Tom didn't tell me for ages was that there were no trout in that stream. He'd gone out one evening to a trout farm and bought half a dozen. The wire-netting barriers had nothing to do with either leaves or rubbish. They were to prevent the trout he'd bought from swimming away.

There was a terrible plague of wasps in the Clwyd Valley that year. At dinner at Hafod everybody was complaining and Maud said she'd found a way to deal with them. She'd put jam jars everywhere, half-full of water with some jam smeared round the inside rim, and the wasps went into the jars for the jam, fell into the water and slowly drowned. Later that night Old Nell drew Maud aside. Had we got a maid with us at Lount? Yes. Were we on the phone? Yes. Well, would Maud mind ringing up the maid before she went to bed to ask her to make *quite* sure that all the wasps were properly drowned? Maud actually refused. She said she'd have felt too much of a fool.

Towards the end of our stay that last year Aunt Eva was taken ill. Before we left for Trearddur the three of us went in to see her in bed. There was some purple clematis that grew round her window at Hafod. I remember thinking how pretty it looked framing the 'ambitious' hills beyond. She looked very flushed and was wearing one of those buttoned-up Victorian night dresses which were to become so fashionable thirty years later. Then Tom honked the horn outside and we went downstairs. She died at Chatham Street that November aged eighty-three. Within a fortnight Gampa, seventeen years her junior, was also dead. Aunt Eva left Andrée, then five, a hundred pounds, 'because she looks like me'. She didn't look like her at all, but it was kind of her. Having lost a brother and a sister in under a month, Uncle Willy sank even deeper into lethargy.

With no one left to run it, he never again took a house for the summer. In 1938 we went to Coniston for a few weeks and spent the rest of the holidays in Trearddur Bay.

Anglesey is an island off the north-west coast of Wales. A sensational bridge, flung across the beetling Menai Straits, links it to the mainland. It has few trees and what there are have been bent almost double by the strong prevailing winds. There are fine beaches, mile after mile of golden sand fringed by dunes, and steep cliffs honeycombed by caves. The farms are white-washed and crouch low against the ground as though afraid of being blown away in the winter storms. There was little attempt to encourage the trippers and there were then no caravan sites. The only port of any size is Holyhead where the ferries set off for Ireland full of drunk men with red faces and bright blue suits and potentially seasick nuns. There are many golf courses.

For all these reasons, except for the presence of the Irish who anyway got straight off the train and into the boats, it was fashionable among the *haute bourgeoisie* of the North of England. 'It's like Brittany,' they told each other, 'or Normandy.' Certainly there was fine sea-food: lobsters, crabs, even local whitebait. We went to Anglesey year after year after leaving Uncle Willy's, and Tom, who tended in part to commute from Hafod or Bodrhyddan, took his main holiday there. The Griff too would spend a fortnight with us, and Uncle Fred and Alan would come down for a weekend or two. We usually rented a house, one of those basic white seaside villas with the hall full of sand and metal windows corroded by salt. When I said I preferred the country to the seaside I was thinking particularly of Anglesey. It was healthy, 'unspoilt' and bracing and it bored me stiff.

Trearddur Bay itself is only a few miles from Holyhead. Many friends of my parents were nearby and there was a great deal of golf and bridge, neither of which interested Maud, and a lot of drinking which she feared and detested. I think she disliked holidays in Anglesey as much as I did.

Every day, unless it was raining hard, we went swimming. We were meant to like that, but the sea was always freezing. We came out with our teeth chattering and Maud was waiting with one of those rough towels with yachts printed on it and a ginger biscuit which was meant to warm you up. We had a raft one year and Bill, who was about four, climbed on it just before the tide turned and began to drift out to sea. He sat there perfectly calmly, seemingly unaware of being in danger. I drew Maud's attention to his diminishing figure. She was fully dressed and wearing a heavy mackintosh but she plunged in, swam after him and pushed the raft back to shore. A man congratulated her, as she stumbled, wet and exhausted, up the beach: 'Very brave of you, Madam, to rescue that little boy.' Maud, although out of breath and on the point of collapse, could never resist a good curtain line: 'Little boy?' she said. 'It's my son!'

It would be unfair to say I experienced no moments of pleasure at Trearddur. In fine weather it could be dazzlingly beautiful. Once, walking inland, I passed a windmill and found myself in a long gentle treeless valley, its slopes bright with clover and stained with poppies, fading into a blue haze in the distance. Whenever I think of the line 'Over the hills and far away', I think of that valley.

I was interested in rock pools too. I would lie full length on the damp seaweed, popping the little bladders in the long fronds and staring down into the water at the transparent shrimps, the tiny dark green crab and the rose-pink sea-anemones which closed up into little balls of jelly if you threatened them with a stick.

We did a lot of fishing, although after my three-pound trout and in comparison to casting a fly, it seemed far too easy with its big hooks, strong traces, and a wooden frame with the line wound round it instead of a delicate split cane rod. Tom and I, when he wasn't knocking them back at the golf-club, used to go and sit on a ledge just below a cliff top and pull up inedible multi-coloured fish, apparently some species of rock-bass. I didn't much like putting on the worms we used either. They were segmented with many horrid little legs and they bit. We bought them from a man with a wooden leg in Holyhead.

Sometimes we went out after mackerel in a motor-boat. I liked the getting there: bounding over the water with the cliffs and houses bobbing and lurching away behind us and the people on the beach getting smaller and smaller. But once we'd stopped and hit a shoal it soon became monotonous. The fish were beautiful – striped, streamlined, blue, green and silver – but they were so eager to get caught that they grabbed the feathered lures almost before you could get them back into the water. It was too easy to be satisfactory. I preferred prawning: scraping the straight wooden edge of the net up the underside of rocks and lifting it out of the water to find out how many hopping crustacea I'd dislodged.

We were also taught riding by a Mr Jones, a handsome black-eyed Welshman with a great deal of patience. He needed it with me. The horse I tried to ride was in no way temperamental, just obstinate. Despite my trying to follow Mr Jones's advice about using my knees and letting him know who was boss, it did exactly as it wanted, turning right when I wanted to go left, and grazing whenever it chose, no matter how hard I tugged on the reins. In the rough fields around Mr Jones's riding school one year there was a plague of striped black and yellow caterpillars. I put one in a match-box to take back to Parkfield to show Hurter, but somehow it escaped.

We weren't alone in Trearddur. There were several of our contemporaries, the children of our parents' friends, some of whom I liked in Liverpool. Here all they ever wanted to do was play ball games on the beach which was exactly what I hated. Sometimes they chanted 'Sissy Parkfield' at us. It seemed hard when I loathed Parkfield so much to have to defend it during the holidays.

One morning in a hen-run on the edge of the garden of the house we rented, I came across a disturbing spectacle. On the grass in the middle of the run squatted a large toad, although how it got there I couldn't imagine. The hens, about half a dozen in number, were pecking it to death, but not in any concentrated way. They would strut around for a bit, making their stupid noises, preening their feathers, scratching here or there and then one of them, quite casually, would stab at it a few times with its beak. The toad just sat, seeming to grin, gradually coming to bits but still breathing. I could do nothing. If I rescued the toad, I thought, it was too far gone to live. I couldn't kill it either – that would mean associating myself with its beady-eyed assassins. I remained, watching in rapt horror, until it was obviously dead. Whenever I read of gratuitous cruelty I see that toad.

As the thirties drew to a close, Ginger's arsehole was under increasing threat. Sitting in the Tatler, waiting for the latest Disney, I saw Spain bombed, Hitler and Mussolini, Auden's 'fashionable madman', strutting and ranting. Because of my mother's blood we were more aware of the increasing persecution of the Jews than most middle-class Liverpudlians. I don't know how it came about but for a few months we even took in a Jewish refugee. Vicki was a young man from Berlin, neatly dressed and speaking perfect if pedantic English. He told us what made him decide to leave Germany: the burning of synagogues, the looting of shops, university professors forced to clean out lavatories in front of jeering crowds, the casual use of rubber truncheons. Hearing this did Tom no harm. He'd been inclined, like a lot of people, to dismiss much of what he'd heard or read as exaggerated. Nevertheless, on a personal level, Vicki drove my parents mad. Humourless and pompous, he constantly 'held the floor', the gravest crime in Maud's almanac. Much to their relief he didn't stay very long. Highly qualified in chemistry, he landed an excellent job in Leicester.

Somehow, although it was increasingly likely there would be a war, people managed to put it out of their minds most of the time. My parents continued to entertain. I went five times to see *Snow White and the Seven Dwarfs*. My mother organised a successful appeals year for the Personal Service, including a sale of work in a house belonging to Toc H in Rodney Street. Gangie and Gaga, still Mrs Melly and Mrs Isaac to each other, each ran a stall. Gangie was in charge of knitware, Gaga sold home-made chutneys and jams. There was something about sales of work which very much irritated Tom. He was obliged to go, of course, but explained to me sarcastically, when I asked him what a sale of work was: 'It's your grandmothers playing shop.'

From being unable to read, I had now become an obsessive reader, but my parents' library was no treasure trove. There were Maud's prizes from Belvidere High School for Girls: *Hiawatha* in blue leather, *The Works of Tennyson* in limp calf, and a number of theatrical memoirs by people she'd known, many of them dedicated to 'Darling Maud' in extrovert calligraphy.

Tom's contribution to the shelves was mainly Leslie Charteris's 'Saint' books, and a number of 'dossiers' of imaginary crimes with little cellophane envelopes in them containing 'real' clues: a lipstick-smeared cigarette butt, a torn-off button. There were, however, as always with Tom, a few surprises: the short stories of Damon Runyon for instance, which he bought as they came out, and a first edition of Waugh's *Vile Bodies*, his favourite book. It was typical of him that he never read, or was curious to read, any other book by Waugh, or at any rate not until *The Loved One* was published in the late forties. Maud even had difficulty in persuading him to read *Rebecca*. 'I knew he'd love it,' she'd tell people, so I kept leaving it about, even in the lavatory at Trearddur, but he wouldn't open it. When he did, of course, he read it cover to cover at one sitting.' She told this story a lot. She seemed to believe it reflected some credit on her.

Although my parents didn't buy books, they both subscribed to Boots. Maud liked Warwick Deeping, Gilbert Frankau (brother of Ronnie), and J. B. Priestley. Tom read mostly thrillers and detective stories: Edgar Wallace, Dorothy Sayers, and Agatha Christie but only if Poirot wasn't in them. Maud, too, could sometimes break out of her middle-brow corral; she adored *The Diary of a Nobody* and instantly saw the point of *Cold Comfort Farm*. I read all these; sometimes Maud and Tom had to fight to get their own library books back; I read the William books, E. Nesbit and Arthur Ransome, any collections of ghost stories I could get my hands on, and *The Story of San Michele* which I thought a masterpiece.

From being relieved that I had learned to read, Maud became worried at what had become an addiction. 'No books!' she'd shout through the bathroom door, and she'd come into the 'boys' room' several times each night to make sure I hadn't turned the light on again.

The other thing that worried her was my stomach. Given that I was eating a cooked breakfast, a substantial if disgusting lunch at school, a huge tea and a grown-up dinner at night, it was hardly surprising that, while remaining rather skinny in general, my stomach had swollen up like a tight balloon. Fearing a tumour, she took me to the doctor. While he was examining me he asked me what I ate on an average day. I told him. He didn't bother to go on with the examination. I was advised to eat rather less and my stomach disappeared for twenty years.

Maud was also much preoccupied during the later thirties with the difficulty of finding suitable 'staff'. 'Going into service' was becoming less popular and she was forced to employ girls she would have rejected instantly a few years earlier. There were two Irish sisters, for example, who gave her a great deal of trouble. They were called Nelly and Norah and had very thick Dublin brogues. Nelly, the parlour-maid, was handsome in a bold raw-boned way. Norah, the cook, was fat, dumpy and hysterical. They fought all the time. There'd be a crash in the night followed by screaming and shouting. Maud would get up and rush into their bedroom to find out what on earth had happened. Usually Nelly had thrown a water carafe at Norah or vice versa.

Nelly liked mischief. She read the Bible as if it were a dirty book because, back in Ireland, her parish priest had told her it was a sin for lay Catholics to do so. Swearing me to secrecy, she would wait until my parents were out and then use 'the green bathroom' instead of 'the blue'. Eventually Nelly scored a bull's-eye with the water carafe, cutting Norah so badly that she had to have stitches, and Maudie decided that enough was enough.

Molly, the house parlour-maid who followed was, as Maud admitted, a very hard worker, but she was extremely noisy and had a very strong Liverpool accent. She was also enormous. She sneezed a great deal about the house too, making no effort to control it, despite Maud asking her continuously if she could possibly use a handkerchief. 'A-a-a-a-CHEW-ER!' was what it sounded like.

I was especially fond of Molly as on her day off she would take me to the pictures. We often went twice; to the matinée at the Gaumont and the evening performance at the Mayfair, and had fish and chips in between. It never occurred to me that it was odd for a twenty-year-old girl to choose to spend her day off with a twelve-year-old boy, but in retrospect I suppose it was because she was so fat that no one of her own age ever invited her out. She was very cheerful, though, and good fun too. If we both liked a film very much we'd sit through it again. Molly left to work in a factory where they paid a great deal more money.

Then Auntie Min came back as 'cook–housekeeper', and was given the flat upstairs. Her husband Tom moved in too, still working on the railways and silent as ever. Once Maud and Tom, after a party, brought back several members of the ballet for bacon and eggs (I don't know who cooked them – it certainly wasn't Maud) and found Tom Roberts, just off shift, drinking tea in the kitchen. 'I thought,' 'darling Bobbie' told Maud later, 'that it must be your handy man, but then I thought, "What was he doing being handy at four in the morning?"'

Bella, too, returned after Jack's death, bringing Beryl with her. This was lovely for Andrée as it meant she had someone more or less her own age to play with. Beryl was very good at playground games, especially one that involved bouncing a ball against a wall, and gradually increasing the number of actions performed between each bounce. 'One, two, three, a footsie. Four, five, six, a footsie. Seven, eight, nine, a footsie. Ten, a footsie, post the ball,' she chanted. 'Darling Bobbie' happened to catch this too. 'The child's a genius!' he cried.

In 1937 Tom gave Bill and me a choice. Cousin Emma had offered to pay for us to go to London for three days to watch, from a balcony in the Mall, the Coronation procession of King George VI or, if we preferred it, to spend a whole week in London at a later date. It was typically generous of Cousin Emma to offer such a treat and typically imaginative of her to give us an alternative. It didn't take us long to decide we'd prefer a whole week and no Coronation to only three days and a view from the Mall. Tom was to go with us and we were all going to stay with Aunt Maud Bradley who lived at Hammersmith. Bill and I both got very, very over-excited as the day drew closer.

I've never discovered exactly who Aunt Maud Bradley was. She came at least once a year to stay with Gangie so I suppose she may have been a sister. She didn't look at all like her though, because Gangie was very pretty, and Aunt Maud Bradley wasn't at all. 'An old boiler' was the rather unkind phrase people used to describe elderly ladies who looked like Aunt Maud Bradley in those days. She didn't actually live in Hammersmith either. She had a flat in a mansion block in Barnes but overlooking the river and Hammersmith Bridge. I thought the bridge was lovely, like a bridge in a pantomime, but the Thames itself was one of the few things in London I found really disappointing. I thought everything there must be bigger as well as better, but the Thames turned out to be far narrower than the Mersey.

I suppose Tom paid some of Cousin Emma's money to Aunt Maud Bradley to have us to stay, but she didn't spend much of it on food. For pudding, every time we ate in, which was as often as Tom could get away with it, there was always the same bowl of fruit salad and all Aunt Maud did was to empty another tin on top of what was left. Tom said he was surprised and indeed disappointed that it hadn't fermented. We didn't actually see all that much of her except when we got home. Her own 'treat' was to take us to *Gunga Din* at a cinema in Hammersmith Broadway. I was pleased to see it, because I'd read about it in Fat Molly's *Picturegoer* and knew it wouldn't be on in Liverpool for ages, but the picture house impressed me even less than the Thames. It wasn't anything like as grand as the Mayfair or the Gaumont. It was more like the Rivoli.

Aunt Maud Bradley also came with us to the Zoo, the highspot of the visit as far as I was concerned. It was a boiling day (the whole week coincided with a heat wave) and we wanted to see everything. That is to say that Bill and I wanted to see everything. We rushed from Mappin Terrace to the sealions. We banged on the glass in the reptile house although it said we shouldn't, and made the cobra rear up and open its hood as in *The Jungle Book*. We fed buns to the bears and had a ride on an elephant. We not only exhausted Aunt Maud Bradley but Tom too. When it was almost time to go we discovered we'd missed out the hippopotami which were in the North Gardens and this meant running through a tunnel under the

road. Tom and Aunt Maud Bradley were sitting on a bench near
the Aquarium. We were amazed that he'd rather sit on a bench than
see a hippo, but he said he would.

It was a London I was never to experience again – tourists' London.
We went to the Tower, and Madame Tussaud's where I was critical
of the Chamber of Horrors. There was only one proper torture – you
pulled back a curtain and there was a Turk hanging from a hook
through his stomach – and the murderers looked quite like ordinary
people. We enjoyed being taken to the Regent Palace Hotel for lunch
afterwards, though. One of Maud's 'boyfriends' who had moved to
London took us. For five shillings each you could eat as much as you
liked and there were fifteen courses. Bill and I managed twelve
apiece. Tom said it made him feel quite liverish just to watch us.
Maud's ex-boyfriend said, 'What appetites, dear.'

Tom took us to see a revue at a big theatre. The star was an
actress called Frances Day. She was very pretty and imitated several
film stars. Tom had chosen this revue because he'd met Frances
Day on a boat going to Portugal where he had a client in the wool
business. He said they became quite friendly and she'd called him
'Mr Woolly Man'. I asked if we were going to go round and see her
later as we did with friends of Maud's. He said no. She mightn't
remember him and besides Aunt Maud Bradley was tired and
wanted to get back to Hammersmith.

One afternoon we had tea at the House of Commons with David
Maxwell Fyfe, our local MP. Afterwards we went and watched a
debate from the visitors' gallery. It was an important debate to start
with and I recognised several of the members from the cartoons in
the newspapers and the newsreels at the Tatler. Churchill was there,
and Neville Chamberlain, and Lloyd George with his long white
hair and moustache. After a while, though, a man got up and spoke
with a Welsh accent about snobbery in the British Navy, and most
people, rather rudely I thought, walked out.

At the end of the week we thanked Aunt Maud Bradley and
caught the tube train back to Euston, changing in the middle on to
another line. Tom got into a panic on tube trains because he always
worried that we'd get lost and go to the wrong station, but we
didn't. Bill and I recognised several of the names on the map above
the window of the carriage from having played Monopoly. On the

train back to Liverpool I suddenly wanted to eat an orange more than anything in the world. I didn't usually like oranges very much, but I could hardly wait to get to Lime Street so that I could peel one and pop the segments in my mouth.

I didn't get back to London until almost ten years later. It was a different place, scarred with bomb damage, grey, its paint peeling, everything rationed.

In a way we got to see the Coronation after all. When we went back to Parkfield Twyne told us that he was going to break his own rule and take the whole school to the Mayfair to watch it in colour. I was absolutely amazed, but immediately asked him if we were going to stay and see the whole programme. He said he'd have to find out if the main film was suitable, and told us a few days later that it was not. It was a comedy with Tom Walls and Ralph Lynn, and I was furious at missing it, but there was nothing to be done. On the appointed afternoon we filed in to the Mayfair, me displaying my savoir-faire by making it obvious I knew my way around, and listing the films I'd seen there since it opened. We sat through the Coronation which was very long and quite boring, and then filed out again as the titles came up for the main feature. Hoping to catch at least a glimpse of the suave Walls with his little moustache and Ralph Lynn with his monocle and 'silly ass' laugh, I looked over my shoulder until we were right out in the foyer.

Munich happened: Chamberlain in the Tatler waved his piece of paper, and most people thought it marvellous. Bill and I discovered a new milk-bar where you could ask for a free sample. Tom dug a shelter into a high bank in the garden well away from the house. It had sandbags round the entrance and a tin roof on which he piled the earth back. It was useful to play in. Fred, Alan and Tom volunteered to become air-raid wardens if there was a war. The authorities tried out the sirens a few times.

The weekend that war was declared, the ballet was back in Liverpool. 'Darling Bobbie' and Freddie Ashton were spending the day with us. We listened to Chamberlain on the radiogram. The grown-ups seemed very sad, not a bit excited. Ginger, beyond helping us now, rubbed against Maud's legs. She smiled a lot at us, but they weren't proper smiles.

Tom told us that next day he and Maud were going to drive us down to Cousin Arthur Bromilow's in Shropshire and then that Mr Twyne had arranged for Bill and me and the rest of the boys from Parkfield to go to a public school nearby, at any rate for the following term, and that Andrée would stay with the Bromilows and go to the same school as their granddaughter Bridget. He'd obviously known all this in advance.

An hour after the war was announced the siren wailed, and we all went and sat in Tom's air-raid shelter, the only time it was ever used, waiting for the sound of the bombers. After a while the all-clear sounded, and we went back into the house and had lunch. Tom said perhaps it was just a trial to make sure that people didn't panic.

Next day we got up early. All the staff had gone and Maud, for the first time in her life, tried to cook sausages for breakfast. She didn't know about pricking them, and turned the grill on full to make it quicker, so that they all exploded. We thought this was very funny, but then Maud burst into tears so we stopped laughing.

We drove down to Cousin Arthur's in the old 1920s car Tom had bought for the summer. He never bought a new car; he'd spend about £10 on what he called 'a heap' and then sell it again after we got back from Trearddur, although this year we hadn't been there. It was a beautiful day. We got to Cousin Arthur's in time for tea in the garden. We sat under a cedar of Lebanon eating toast and honey in front of the pretty Georgian house in the bright sunlight. The grown-ups listened to the news all the time. I drew a caricature of Hitler which I thought was quite good. I showed it to Maud who said she didn't know why I wanted to draw such a horrible man. Somehow the Bromilows managed to find us all somewhere to sleep that night. Next morning Maud and Tom said goodbye to us and drove back to Liverpool in 'the heap'.

Tom said later that neither of them expected to see any of us again.

That same afternoon Cousin Arthur drove Bill and me to Oakridge, a minor public school on the Welsh borders, and over the next day or two the boys from Parkfield reassembled in this unfamiliar place. Twyne was already there to greet us, although that is certainly an inappropriate word for his gloomy if uncharacteristically restrained presence. He told us that once the term had started, which was still ten days off, we would be subject to the rules and regulations of Oakridge, although of course initially under his supervision. He also explained that in a few weeks he would be leaving us to find premises in order to reopen Parkfield as soon as possible. He hoped we would work hard and play hard. We slept that evening in a dormitory which had been set aside for us, and wondered if the bombers were over Liverpool, some sixty miles away.

Oakridge was a comparatively new seat of learning but was determined to overcome this by embracing the public school ethos at its most unyielding. Beating and fagging were held to be sacred principles; there was a school song made up from those lush Victorian harmonies guaranteed to bring a tear to the eye of the managers of rubber plantations at sundown; and a great number of rules about which piece of grass you could walk on and what buttons you could do up. The headmaster was a towering Olympian figure with a raw red face, and the buildings were unfashionably Gothic and already convincingly choked with ivy.

On the first morning of term we went down to breakfast in the usual place only to find we were expected in a different hall on the other side of the school. Those of us who had cut it fine were in consequence five minutes late. Immediately after breakfast we were sent for by our new housemaster and given three strokes of the cane. He was a jovial and savage little man called Shorte and appeared to think we should enjoy the beating almost as much as he did. It was like that all term. I'd never been beaten with a cane before, or heard the dreadful preliminary swish as it parted the fusty tobacco-laden air of Mr Shorte's study. I was to learn to know that sound well before I'd mastered the complicated structure of rules in a large school, and even after that for comparatively trivial offences.

In time we settled in. There was a school chaplain who fascinated me. He was very High Church – even Gangie might have had reservations about the amount of incense and lace he favoured – and he wore a soutane at all times. He was also very unprepossessing with a leathery yellow face and a soft insinuating voice, but what distinguished him most was his Rabelaisian relish in lavatorial and excretory jokes. I'd no objection to this – on the contrary, but I didn't hesitate to use it as a Twyne-tease. 'The chaplain,' I told him with a mixture of mock horror and surprise, 'tells us lots of jokes about lavatories, sir. Why is that, sir?' Twyne was as shocked as I'd hoped, but he couldn't of course say much. 'Disgusting,' he mumbled, and turned away.

With all of us sleeping in the same dormitory, our sexual activities were resumed and indeed extended. One night I was in somebody's bed when the door was flung open and there stood Twyne silhouetted against the dim light from the stone passage. I slid out of the bed and began to crawl towards my own, wondering if I could possibly make it before Twimbo, who was walking down the dormitory on a tour of inspection, discovered it empty except for Little Ted. Under one of the intervening beds I fortunately encountered a pair of rollerskates, which went crashing out across the wooden floor like a runaway train. Twyne, with a cry of 'My Godfathers!' ran back to the entrance of the dormitory to find the light switch and, by the time he did, I was safely back in my own bed, apparently asleep.

A week or two later he left and we heard that he had rented a house on the outskirts of Southport in the suburb of Birkdale which, being fifteen miles from Liverpool and a completely residential town, was considered fairly safe should the bombing eventually start. He would reopen Parkfield in its new premises the following term. Towards the end of the current term at Oakridge, the

Olympian headmaster descended from the clouds and began to address himself benignly to us Parkfield boys. He indicated that he would be far from displeased if we chose to suggest to our parents that he might be willing to accept us into the school, even those of us rather younger than was usual. 'In the heart of the country . . .' he stressed, 'not a major city within sixty miles and, in the case of brothers, special arrangements . . .' Bill and I talked this over and decided we'd rather go back to Twyne. In the end I think only two or three boys, *proditores* it goes without saying, took advantage of the headmaster's offer.

It may seem perverse that I should prefer to return to Parkfield, but I had several sound reasons. Apart from the fact that the slipper was minimally less painful than the cane, I'd only two terms left to go. If I were transferred to a public school, and one which I actively disliked, I would find it that much more difficult to leave and go elsewhere. Also I hadn't liked the way the headmaster beamed at us and patted our heads and recruited us to solicit our parents. All I hoped was that, wherever Maud and Tom did decide to send me, it would be nothing like Oakridge.

As there was still no sign of any bombing we went back to Liverpool for the holidays; something no one would have thought remotely possible only three months before. Singing the syrupy Oakridge school song in the chapel, while the scatological Chaplain ponced about genuflecting like a weasel, the only tears I felt were those of relief.

Parkfield's new premises were a large detached Edwardian house of red brick, white plaster, intricate half timbering and ill-proportioned little towers. The staff, apart from Twyne himself, was reduced to two: an eccentric Maths master called Mr Corelli who looked like Einstein, and loved his subject so much that he managed to make it interesting, even to me; and a depressive Lancastrian who taught everything else except Latin. There was no games field, but we shared one with several other schools a quarter of a mile away. There were no extras: no art, no music, and the food was almost inedible.

Twyne seemed for him comparatively restrained, but he had his moments. We petitioned for a wind-up gramophone, and most of us brought some records. Among my contribution from the nursery pile was a very old and scratchy recording which had probably once belonged to Gampa. It was called 'Yes, we have no bananas'. We were playing this one evening when Twimbo burst into the room.

'Take that record off, Melly Major,' he shouted, 'it's distinctly vulgar.'

'But, sir,' I said resorting to my usual tactic, 'my mother chose it.'

Twyne's reply very much amused Maud and Tom when I repeated it to them. 'Mrs Melly,' he said, 'is a very Bohemian woman.'

We were allowed, at our parents' request, to go home sometimes for the weekend, but Twyne hated it. Although not one bomb had yet fallen on Liverpool, he would tell us, as we set off for Birkdale Station, that we were 'entering the lion's jaws'.

The summer term of 1940 was my last at Parkfield. I had passed, on the strength of my English and History papers, my common entrance and that September left Lime Street Station on my way to Stowe.

Twyne had very much disapproved of my parents' choice of school. In his view, as far as the public schools went, it was practically on a par with the Montessori System. There were, he understood, no traditions and the headmaster, J. F. Roxburgh, was not only a dandy but addressed the boys by their first names. While games were played, they were in no way a fetish. The arts were encouraged, and so on.

He was more or less right, and the reasons for his censure were exactly why my parents had chosen it. There was still some beating, but I was beaten less in the whole of my time at Stowe than I was in one term at Oakridge. As for fagging it didn't involve the master–slave relationship of the more traditional schools, but just meant that you dusted a senior boy's study twice a week for your first few terms.

On my arrival J. F. sought me out, called me 'George', and said he hoped they'd make me happy. Most of the boys and masters were friendly, and in the Art School I found a heady and experimental atmosphere which suited me down to the ground. For some reason, to have come from Liverpool and to sing its praises excited some teasing, but otherwise there was nothing that didn't delight me. I came home for my first holiday right over the top, spouting Eliot and Auden and raving about Picasso and Matisse. I calmed down in time but I was, for the moment, what Maud called 'an affected bit of goods'.

During the preceding term the bombing of London had started in earnest and that August it was the turn of the provincial cities. Up until then Tom, Fred and Alan, as chief air-raid wardens, had little to do except make sure that people observed the black-out. They'd spent a great deal of time in a rather rough pub down by the docks where Tom had become almost as much a fixture as at The Albert, while Fred and Alan scored a great hit at a Wardens' hot-pot supper by singing a parody, written by Fred, of 'Side by Side'. The middle eight bars went:

> We'd rather have our wardens
> Than any other wardens in town.
> We're touched by their loyalty and devotion,
> And very often touched for half-a-crown.

The conclusion was especially well liked:

> When you knock and ask a man to put his light out,
> He feints with his left and puts his right out.
> So wardens in blue, always march two by two,
> Side by side.

Now, however, with heavy raids every night and the docks on fire there was no time for hot-pot suppers. My father and uncles were up all night and returned grey with fatigue and covered in dust for a few hours' sleep before setting out again at dusk.

We didn't use the shelter Tom had dug in the garden, but took refuge in the Griff's cellar together with those other residents of York Mansions who had remained in their flats. The Griff took it all very calmly, largely I think because she couldn't believe that Hitler would have the nerve to harm her. One night Mary, the Griff's parlour-maid, was coming down with a tray of tea, having left the door at the top of the cellar steps open, when a bomb fell somewhere in Park Road. The blast blew her down the last few steps and the tray flew up into the air. Mary wasn't hurt at all and the Griff, having first briefly commiserated with her, then expressed her satisfaction that it wasn't the best china.

After a week or two of this Tom decided that we ought to be evacuated again, preferably somewhere not too far away so that he could join us when not on duty. His solution, while practical, appalled me. He rented Parkfield for the rest of the school holidays with Twyne in situ. Having just escaped, I was going to find myself again under that hated roof. I would much sooner have sat out the blitz in the Griff's cellar.

In fact it wasn't too bad because I realised, almost at once, that Twimbo had no jurisdiction over me whatsoever. He was like a sorcerer who had lost his power, whereas I could make quite certain that everything he had suspected about Stowe was absolutely true. He twice offered to 'coach' me in Latin and I refused outright. After that he left me alone. Tom, during one of his weekends off, made a discovery about Twimbo.

'Do you know what he does every evening?' he said. 'He goes down to the Scarsdale Hotel, sits in the bar and soaks up whisky.' Drink would, of course, explain a great deal of his behaviour. Twyne, though none of us had ever suspected it, was a serious boozer.

I had lunch some years ago with a publisher a few years younger than myself and discovered that he had been a boy at Parkfield in the early 1950s, during its final years at Birkdale (for Twyne never moved back to Liverpool). Once we'd established this, our publishing venture was forgotten. People at nearby tables were rather startled to hear two apparently sane men shouting: 'My Godfathers!' and 'Ye Gods and little fishes!' at each other. What the publisher told me – of which I'd no idea – was of Twyne's end. He had written to all the parents saying that, for various reasons, he was in financial difficulties, but if they could see their way to advance a term's fees all would be well. Most of them had, and during the holidays Twyne had drunk himself to death.

That evacuated holiday in Birkdale, I decided one afternoon to dress up in some of Maud's clothes, make my face up, and walk with Andrée, then eight, into Southport. I've no idea why I wanted to do this. I have never been attracted by transvestism and, with this solitary exception, have only worn drag at fancy dress parties where it was requested and once, as a joke, during the last evening of a season at Ronnie Scott's. This day, however, I went to pick up Andrée and we set off down Waterloo Road, me tottering along on Maud's court shoes, Andrée with strict instructions to remember to call me 'Auntie'. On the outskirts of Southport proper were two back-to-back public toilets sited on an island in the middle of the road. Holding Andrée firmly by the hand, I entered and used the Ladies. We then walked on into Southport, where we had an ice in a fashionable café in Lord Street and returned home.

During the writing of this book several events have taken place, on both a public and personal level, which have made parts of it no longer currently accurate.

In Liverpool, during the Toxteth riots, the Rialto cinema, which I passed with Carol Ann, and the Racket Club, where I learnt to play tennis on the wooden court, were both burnt down.

Just before Christmas 1982, Alan Isaac, eighty-five years old, had a heart attack and died in hospital four days later. He had been active right up to the end. His final message to me, transmitted by a friend of his during the interval at Ronnie Scott's, was, 'Tell George I'm still battling.'

A few months later, in a nursing home in Surrey, Maud died at ninety-one. Her memory had been going for some time; whole areas of it drifting away like icebergs from a thawing ice-cap. Brighton, where she'd lived for fifteen years after Tom's death, gone. Cranleigh, where she'd spent the last five, gone. Most of her sixty-eight years in Liverpool, cracking up, melting.

At her ninetieth birthday party, Andrée, Bill and I, and most of our families, were there. She seemed a little unsure about what exactly was going on but after we'd had tea, I said to her, 'Now Maudie, if you've had enough birthday cake, I'll tell S. Le Kessin he can come in and do his conjuring tricks.' Maud paused for a moment, and then began to laugh quite heartily. 'S. Le Kessin,' she said, 'I haven't thought of him for years.'

RUM, BUM AND CONCERTINA

I

I was sitting, less than a month off my eighteenth birthday, on the lavatory of the 'green bathroom' in my parents' large comfortable ugly house in the Victorian suburbs of Liverpool, and I was crying bitterly.

The reason I was crying was because I'd just read a letter from a man called A B Clifford who was a housemaster at Stowe, the school I'd just left and, more relevantly in this context, Officer in Charge of the JTC there.

JTC stood for Junior Training Corps. When I'd arrived at Stowe, about a year after the beginning of the war, it was still called the OTC, but this had been changed to meet the democratic temper of the times. Officers' Training Corps had suggested rather too blatantly that all public schoolboys were automatically officer material.

Changing an initial didn't mean changing anything else though. The ancient Drill Sergeant still called us 'sir', and we dressed up every Tuesday afternoon in 1914 uniforms, with puttees and brass buttons. In the summer there were occasional 'field days' when we charged about the drowsy Buckinghamshire countryside pretending to shoot each other, while perspiring umpires decided whether or not we were 'dead'.

Playing these Henty-like games made it difficult at times to remember there was a real war on and that boys we'd known well had been killed in it. Like their more fortunate contemporaries most of them had done their initial training at either Oxford or Cambridge, an arrangement that assured them of a place after the duration if and when they returned. They'd usually come down during this academic interim looking carefully languid in their new Brigade of Guards' uniforms and, more often than not, enviably drunk. Then they'd be posted and a few months later we'd be told, in Chapel, that they'd been killed on active duty. A talented boy of Norwegian origin who liked to paint still-lifes in the school art-school in what he called 'masturbational Pre-Raphaelite detail' was blown up in Africa. A debating society wit, as humane as he was clever, was mown down in Italy. Then, for a moment, we'd realise, with morbid but not unpleasurable intimations of mortality that, if the war went on long enough it might be our name that J F Roxburgh was reading out with a distinct and untypical tremor in the famous, much-imitated drawl.

Yet in my case, however much I might fantasise along these lines, I was enough of a realist to know that if I fell it wouldn't be in a commissioned uniform. I was patently not officer material. My puttees fell down, my buttons were either dull and smeary or, if halfway bright, the Duraglit had spread greasily over the surrounding khaki. Worse, I was always losing things and indeed, during the last week of my final term when the time had come to hand in my uniform, I'd discovered that I was short of a brass-buckled belt and one boot.

Thinking myself safe because I wasn't coming back, I'd concealed the loss from the retired Sergeant in the 1820 Gothic armoury and left school in high spirits with several of my contemporaries; all of us defiantly puffing away at Black Balkan Sobranies through the taxi window. My confidence was misplaced. The missing items were noted and reported to Major Clifford. He bothered to write to me during his holidays, not only demanding I paid for their replacement but warning me, in an icy rage, that he intended writing to my future Commanding Officer at the Navy Shore Establishment, Skegness, informing him of my perfidious carelessness and suggesting some suitable punitive action on my arrival there.

Unaware of what this might lead to, despite a brother and a father currently in naval uniform, my notions of the Senior Service were still coloured by the Charles Laughton version of *Mutiny on the Bounty*; I wept and continued to weep until, as I'd probably intended, my mother heard me and rattled the Bakelite handle of the bathroom door to ask me what was wrong.

Given that I was almost eighteen it may suggest a certain emotional immaturity to cry quite so desperately for so slight a cause, and the truth is that, while rather tiresomely sophisticated in some directions, I was extremely undeveloped in others and had, I would say now, an emotional age of about thirteen. Even if Major Clifford had carried out his threat it was extremely unlikely that a senior officer in command of the entire Royal Navy intake during a major conflict at a particularly crucial moment could have spared much time to work himself up over the loss of two items of archaic military equipment at a distant public school. Predictably, when I got to Skegness not a word was said about either belt or boot.

My choice of the Navy is also indicative of my thinking during that period. It had nothing to do with my younger brother's success as a Dartmouth cadet nor my father's shore-based commission in the RNVR. It was for no other reason than that I found the uniform 'more amusing'.

Wearing plum-coloured corduroys and a pale pink shirt (school uniform had been suspended at Stowe during the war), I had explained this a month or two earlier to an outraged Admiral in Cambridge. I'd been sent to see him by the school in the hope that he might recommend me, like most of my contemporaries, for the year's training while attached to a college. Enunciating with dangerous care, he told me he felt unable to do so. Otherwise I had a pleasant day. I took an actress from the local rep out to lunch – I'd met her through my mother when she'd been at the Liverpool Playhouse. I went to visit some pretty twins who painted identical whimsical pictures of cats in a studio flat in Petty Cury – I'd a letter of introduction from the couple who ran the Stowe art-school. Then I'd gone back and explained to J F Roxburgh, as sympathetic and ironic as ever, that the Admiral and I hadn't really hit it off.

All in all then I was fairly confident that I would be wearing my 'amusing' uniform for as long as the Navy chose to keep me.

The journey to Skegness, a meander across wartime Britain involving a change of stations at Manchester, dragged on interminably. On the second leg I shared a carriage with a robust middle-aged Lancashire woman in a pixie-hood. She had two children with her, a baby and a toddler whom she used as props in a monologue aimed at demonstrating how rough yet warm-hearted were her maternal feelings. The baby was changed twice, with suitable comments on its copious stools. The little girl in her pink cardy understandably whined a great deal and was threatened or placated according to whim. At every stop – and there were many and all of uncertain duration – her mother, with the single-minded insistence of a radio comic launching a new catchphrase, yelled at her to 'gerraway fra' that door'.

I smiled at her occasionally in hypocritical if solicited endorsement. At the same time I neutralised much of my irritation by reminding myself that she was working class. My priggish if emotional left-wing sympathies, springing in the main in reaction to the Fascist sentiments of a hated prep-school headmaster, automatically awarded good marks for humble social origin. The fact was that I'd never met a member of the proletariat who wasn't a nanny, tram conductor, plumber or school servant.

Neither was I in any position to criticise anyone for role-playing. The book I was reading, Corvo's *Hadrian VII*, and the other books I'd brought with me were as much to advertise my tastes to anyone who might share them as for their literary content. And so we sat there as the Lincolnshire landscape grew flatter in the heat, she playing mum, me sensitive aesthete, until at last, at about five-thirty in the afternoon, the train pulled into Skegness Station. I found the pass the Navy had sent me, and drifted towards the exit.

Although turned down for Cambridge I was still what was known as a 'Y scheme' rating; that was someone who was at least to be considered for a commission; a categorisation based entirely on the fact that I'd been to a public school for, aside from my unfortunate brush with the Admiral, I'd no other contact with the Navy, taken no exam, attended no further interviews. Nor was there anything in my scholastic record to suggest a future officer. On the contrary I had managed to fail the elementary maths paper in my School Certificate and had made no attempt to take it again.

Even my having been accepted for the Navy at all was something of a privileged fiddle. Although entitled to state a preference, if you waited until you were called up you had no control over which of the services claimed you and at that time, just before D-Day, it was more than likely to have been the Army. If however you were still at school you could volunteer for whatever branch you wanted at seventeen, thereby ensuring acceptance. Simultaneously you entered a plea to be allowed to finish your education; a ploy which almost automatically deferred your service until the time you'd have been called up anyway.

That was how I found myself rattling toward HMS *Royal Arthur* in a small naval bus which had been waiting outside the station for the new intake. I looked out at the almost deserted resort, the pier peeling, the rock and souvenir shops shut for the duration. Despite my tears of a month before, I wasn't in any way worried, simply curious.

What initially confused me about HMS *Royal Arthur* was the immediate sensation, later confirmed, of a certain architectural frivolity completely inappropriate to a Royal Navy Shore Establishment. The rows of huts, the great concrete messes, the straight paths – even the formal flower beds – were explicable enough, but it was possible to see that, under the khaki or grey paint of the exterior of the buildings, were traces of shocking pink or baby blue, while the interior of the communal structures proved even stranger. On arrival, still in our civvies, we were marched to 'Collingwood Mess Block' for a meal. We queued up in a large lobby to draw our knives, forks and spoons through a hatch. The ceiling of the lobby was painted to represent a summer sky with fluffy white clouds passing across it. In the centre of the room, rooted in the bare floorboards, was a large and comparatively realistic tree. Part of the plaster from which it was constructed had fallen off to show a skeleton of wire-netting and metal scaffolding. The upper branches in no way tapered off, but terminated abruptly on contact with the painted sky. The serving hatch, through which a rather gloomy WREN Galley Rating passed us our eating irons, was framed by mullioned windows let into the elaborate façade of an Elizabethan inn with a sign reading 'Ye Olde Pigge & Whistle' projecting out over our heads. The dining hall itself made no effort to carry through this Merrie England ambience; it was an exercise in wholehearted if cut-price Odeon Art Deco. Our initial medical examination, on the other hand – 'Have you ever had a venereal disease? Bend over. Cough' – took place in a plaster-of-Paris cave embedded with papier maché skeletons and treasure-chests.

As I soon discovered, HMS *Royal Arthur* had been built for

another function. It was one of the first of Billy Butlin's holiday
camps, all of which had been taken over by the Navy. Planned for
the regimented pleasure of the Fairisle-jersied civilians of the late
Thirties, they needed no more than a few coats of drab paint and a
whaler on the swimming-bath to become wartime shore establishments. The redcoats were transformed into Petty Officers. The
intercom system, through which the campers had been hi-de-hied
to meals or jollied along to enter the knobbly knees competitions,
now barked out our orders. The first morning, just to make quite
sure we knew we were no longer subject to individual logic, we
were made to get up at 0530 hrs. As a public schoolboy I was
initially less thrown and unhappy than most of my working-class
contemporaries. Being used to being away from home I was less
homesick and, despite Stowe's comparatively liberal approach to
discipline, I found it that much easier to accept illogical orders. On
the debit side, I was less able to cope for myself. I lost more, looked
grubbier and more untidy, and found it impossible to lay out my
bedding and equipment with the required Mondrian-like precision.
Luckily, however, I was an instinctive and practised tart and most
of the Petty Officers were, platonically at any rate, easily seducible.

Our Chief Petty Officer was a case in point. He looked rather
like W C Fields and was quite old. Given his experience I suppose
that he must have been near retiring age even by wartime standards
or he would surely have been given a more taxing job than marching
ninety young men around an intake camp. I fell for him because he
combined a truly inventive obscenity with human sympathy:
'You're a fine specimen of hu-fucking-manity!' were the first words
he spoke to me directly; and because, despite my patent inadequacies
and determination to become a licensed jester, he quite clearly liked
me.

Throughout the three-and-a-half years I was to spend in the Navy
I found that, in general, Petty Officers and Chief Petty Officers, if
not religious maniacs or just nasty by nature, tended to be reasonable men. Long association with the sea and its ports had given
them a certain tolerant sophistication, part cynical certainly but
affectionately so. They had learnt to mistrust the moral imperatives
of any one place because they had seen them replaced by others,
often equally rigid and ridiculous, elsewhere. They made allowances

too for us temporary sailors. We were there because we had to be. One day the war would be over and the Navy its old self – a machine for sailing in. The same attitude was common among regular ratings, especially those with long-service stripes. Many of them had been Petty Officers in fact but had been reduced to the ranks for some detected misdemeanour: habitual drunkenness, too open a penchant for young lads, jumping ship or failure of duty. They did, if very old, look a little absurd in bellbottoms but they were jolly fellows although in some cases a little pressing in their affections.

Warrant Officers on the other hand I could seldom abide. Martinets, sticklers for the letter of the law, hard resentful men who realised that they had risen from the ranks on merit but had been blocked for a commission on class grounds. Caught uneasily between the relaxed bonhomie of the POs' mess and the easy formality of the wardroom they were punctilious in their insistence on outer form, correctitude, the marks of respect as laid down by King's Regulations. In particular the presence of public schoolboys on the Lower Deck had a quite unsettling effect on them. Their perfectly understandable resentment at having to salute men much younger and less competent than themselves over the years tempted them to take it out on conscripts from the same social background as their 'superiors' yet, in fairness, their respect for the rules prevented them from yielding openly to the temptation to harass. It was just that if, as a middle-class rating, one erred, their reproaches or application of the primitive remedies available were delivered with a certain thin-lipped satisfaction not unlike that of a colour-prejudiced yet rigorously self-disciplined policeman happening upon an immigrant engaged in some provenly criminal act, or a moderate anti-Semite reading in a newspaper that a Jewish financier has been arrested for fraud. Retrospectively I can sympathise with those Warrant Officers but at the time, trapped myself in a web of confused class feelings, I teased them and yet resented it when they reacted as I'd intended.

With the Upper Deck it was easier. They behaved in general as if they were prefects and the middle-class conscript ratings were new boys. Occasionally, usually when slightly drunk on unaccustomed amounts of pink gin, some young sub-lieutenant would tell me, with an air of considerable condescension, that he'd known my brother at Dartmouth. There was also the odd officer, usually rather senior, who allowed himself to talk on a personal level to individual ratings. On the whole though contact with the Upper Deck remained minimal. Collectively we referred to them as 'the pigs' but, except in the case of a particularly officious or unpopular officer, the epithet was dismissive rather than venomous.

The only officer obliged to remain in contact with the Lower Deck on an approachable basis was in fact the Chaplain. It was he who organised any extra-maritime activities such as art shows or drama groups, and of course he was also responsible for our spiritual well-being. When I first joined the Navy I was still a vague believer in the existence of a personal God. After a great deal of hesitation, and considerably later than most boys at Stowe, I'd been confirmed, though I have a suspicion that my doubts and eventual decision to accept communion were largely based on attracting additional attention. I was aesthetically moved by the King James Bible and the *Book of Common Prayer*. I adored wallowing in the juicy harmonies of Victorian hymns, but the discovery that the Surrealists violently opposed Christianity had begun to shake my already pretty ramshackle faith, and the address to the new intake of ratings at *Royal Arthur* by the camp Chaplain did little to prop it up. 'God,' he told us in an insane parsonical bray, 'is the Highest Officer in the British Navy.'

Our Chief Petty Officer was a sceptic. On Sunday mornings he told us: 'You can crash your swedes until 0830 hrs, that is unless you wish to attend 'oly Commotion.'

Before our first Church Parade he told Roman Catholics to fall in at the front, and then asked if there were any Jews. There were two.

'Well, we 'aven't got no Rabbi,' he said, 'you'll 'ave to listen to the wireless,' and they were dismissed and told to stay in their chalets until the Highest Officer in the British Navy had been suitably piped aboard.

We were meant to be at 'Skeggy' for a fortnight before going on to another camp near Ipswich for further training. During this period we were marched about endlessly. 'Come on! Come on!' yelled our Chief when we were tardy at falling in. 'If you'd let go of yer cocks you'd get around a bloody sight quicker!' We had our

urine analysed several times and were shown a film about the effects
of VD – 'You're off to the pictures now to learn how to whip it in,
whip it out and wipe it!' Due to the size of a screen designed for a
full holiday-camp at the height of the season this proved a rather
unnerving experience and several ratings fainted. I wasn't among
them, but I did become hysterical with suppressed laughter while
watching a silent documentary on the correct way to brush your
teeth. The enormous lips opened to reveal teeth the size of important
Victorian tombstones while a huge brush moved slowly up and
down them, and a little later a King-Kong-sized finger with a
surprisingly dirty nail massaged the gigantic gums. We were looked
at by psychiatrists to whom I swanked about my fondness for Eliot
and Baroque architecture, but who all agreed with me instantly that
I was sensible to favour the Lower Deck.

At 0830 each morning we fell in on the parade ground to salute
the flag, another occasion that could prove dangerously risible. This
had nothing to do with the Union Jack itself. It was still over twenty
years before it was to become a fun object and, although I would
never have admitted it at the time, with the war on the turn there
was something rather moving about its brisk and fluttering progress
up the flagpole. The danger came immediately after the Marine
band's version of the National Anthem. This, while rather elephantine, was efficient enough but it was followed, whether because of
a general order or a local whim I never discovered, by the National
Anthem of one of the Allies. When it was the turn of an occidental
nation this sounded well enough, but the anthems of the East,
involving as they did a different scale and rhythmic tradition, could
lead to some uncertain and gong-punctuated noises.

Giggling is rarely a solitary occupation. It depends on mutual
feedback; a painful attempt to suppress one's own snorts, tears and
whinnies conflicting with an unpleasant desire to see one's co-giggler
reinfected. I had in fact found a friend, someone to laugh with and,
for all my determination to crash the class-barriers, he was, typically
enough, another public-school rating.

His real name was Graham but the class rechristened him Percy
or The Professor. He had a high-pitched definitive voice, a very
slightly androgynous walk and rather wide hips. We'd met in the
Camp dentist's waiting-room where I'd been sitting prominently

reading a collection of Osbert Sitwell's verse. Percy, from the other side of the room, told me that he thought less than nothing of Osbert and not much of Edith either. Auden was another matter. I hurriedly agreed with him – a selection of Auden was among my collection of lures and baits – and he strolled across the room to sit next to me, ignoring the friendly if derisive whistling and kissing noises of our fellow conscripts. These were not only because he was distinctly effeminate in both voice and gesture but also because he 'spoke posh'. This was a perpetual hazard in the Navy. The first day or two in a new mess one was constantly lampooned, especially at meals. 'I say, old man, be a sport and pass the jolly old salt, what?' – that kind of thing. It didn't last long, partly because it became boring if ignored but also because it was based on similar foundations to my own idealisation of the working class en masse – unfamiliarity. For most of the Lower Deck a posh accent was equated with authority: the officers themselves, schoolmasters, bosses, BBC announcers, politicians and, in some cases, magistrates. Now for the first time the owner of a posh voice was vulnerable, equal. Yet because of this, provided we were neither openly arrogant nor patronising, there grew up a collective pride in having us as part of a mess. This pride was sardonic rather than subservient. Long words, for example, were a never-failing reason for incredulous laughter or derision and, in our turn, many of us were tempted to play up, to ingratiate through exaggeration. Very often, running parallel to the mockery, a protective attitude developed. They felt sorry for us in our helplessness, the result of our sheltered upbringing. This too, at any rate for people like Percy and myself with our rather passive homosexual natures, appeared both flattering and pleasurable. The Chief himself projected both the mockery and the protective element.

'All right, Georgina,' he'd tell us while handing out jobs, 'you and Percy can go and clean out the 'eads together, but don't play with each other's squeegees.' Where the Chief was completely inaccurate, however, was in suggesting that Percy and I had any interest in each other sexually. What we shared were the same tastes – a liking for butch and pretty heterosexual lads, or at any rate those who gave the appearance of heterosexuality.

This is not a case history, nor am I competent to analyse why, at the age of eighteen, I was still more or less completely gay, but perhaps a few pointers might help. To begin with my mother preferred in general the company of homosexuals. In provincial Liverpool they seemed to her to be more amusing, better company, more creative than most heterosexual Liverpudlians, and her fondness for the theatre and, more particularly, the theatrical atmosphere added to her circle a number of visiting firewomen all as camp as Chloë. From my earliest years therefore I had learnt to equate wit and creativity with homosexuality even before I knew what it was. My father, it's true, was heterosexual but extremely tolerant. He once told me he'd been on a jury in a case of sodomy but that the accused had been acquitted. I asked him if they were guilty. 'Oh yes,' he said. 'but half the jury didn't think it was possible and the rest of us didn't think it mattered.' He had his own hearty heterosexual friends certainly, draught Bass drinkers in the main, but he saw them mostly in pubs. As host he presided over a largely gay ambience or one where at any rate there was no stigma attached to deviance.

My loathed prep-school headmaster, already remarked as initially responsible for my left-wing bias, confirmed me in my admiration for effeminacy through his hysterical and possibly ambivalent hatred of it. I was on one occasion slippered in front of the whole school for insisting, despite warnings, that I would prefer to go to the ballet than watch a game of rugger. In the face of such a brute I felt impelled, as far as a twelve-year-old boy could, to defend all those beautifully dressed, graceful, funny friends of my mother's.

At the same time that very prep school, particularly after its evacuation to Shropshire at the beginning of the war, was athrob with sexual experimentation of all kinds. By the time I went to Stowe at the age of fourteen I was aware of (if in some instances uninitiated in) every variation of homosexual lovemaking. Yet at this date I hardly equated our pre-adolescent fumbling with those gay and witty young men I knew to be, in the fashionable slang of the time, pansies. Stowe bridged this gap, or at least an aesthetic set at Stowe did so. Wilde, Beardsley, Firbank, Proust became, by association, our mentors. We called our physical relationships 'affairs' and wrote each other poor if purple verses.

I left Stowe a convinced homosexual, believing and accepting that I would always remain one. I felt no shame; on the contrary I considered myself part of an élite, a freemasonry whose members held most of the keys to what was truly creative and exciting in the grown-up world. But, while genuinely attracted by boys, I was not inwardly entirely committed to my own sex. Even from quite a small boy I'd fantasised about girls, usually circus or pantomime performers and, at the cinema, the more obvious platinum blondes, bar-room whores and Busby Berkeley chorines. Yet somehow I managed to convince myself that these fantasies in no way impinged on the purity of my homosexuality. The reason, I suspect now – for at the time I merely avoided correlating the two elements – was a pretty firm conviction that I would never be able to persuade a girl to say yes. My nature has always been to avoid any situation in which I thought I might fail.

I'd also developed several painful heterosexual crushes during my later childhood: a golden-skinned, violet-eyed Burne-Jones girl who'd spent a holiday with us in the Lake District the first summer of the war and, a year or two earlier, a sultry, long-legged paying guest, the daughter of a friend of my mother's who, whether provocatively or because she failed to recognise the explicit sexual feelings of a precocious ten-year-old, allowed me to sit and watch her put on her make-up wearing only her bra and cami-knicks, and for whom I bought Black Magic chocolates whenever I could afford it.

Yet these girls, and others less obsessively desired, were all eighteen or nineteen, in practical terms as inaccessible as the proud girl on the trapeze or the platinum-blonde Hollywood vamp. Boys on the other hand presented no such problem and, as I grew older, men too became viable. After all, it was they who might want me. I could refuse or accept and, even if I found them not especially attractive with their stubble, thinning hair and sagging flesh, I derived satisfaction from feeling myself wanted, from flattery, from having something to give. Ideally, however, I preferred those of my own age or a little younger, thought of myself as Oscar Wilde, making up what I might lack in beauty – for I was never physically vain – by charm and wit. I was also, for all my emotional passivity, in this area the active partner. A too-early and impetuously executed experience of sodomy had made it impossible for me to be buggered without fainting.

In the realm of friendship I was never committed solely to fellow pederasts. In fact my closest friends were usually, while of necessity uncensorious of my proclivities, heterosexual. In them, however, I sought an iconoclastic spirit. They all despised pomposity, taboos, fake emotions. They were expected to lead or goad me on to acts of outrage, to defy authority, to unmask humbug. I remained, during my naval days, in correspondence with several of them and we met, when on leave or stationed near each other, whenever possible. My mother, in general, tended to prefer my homosexual friends. They were better mannered, fell more readily under her spell and didn't, except in the sexual sense, attack or offend society so aggressively. She felt the others were apt to 'encourage me'.

Percy and I shared a common enthusiasm for the cinema and literature. He however was a classical music buff while I, despite a short-lived period in my teens when I sat, outwardly intense, inwardly bored silly, through a season of concerts at the Liverpool Philharmonic, was not. He was completely unmoved by jazz or blues, already my ruling passion, and like many extremely musical people was comparatively uninterested in the visual arts.

He was a severe literary critic, applying to individual poems, for example, a close analysis far removed from my own vague emotional response. I showed him with some pride a long poem on Prometheus I had written in Spenserian stanzas which I had entered successfully for a prize at school. 'It's no good,' he snapped, and showed me a poem by a schoolfriend of his about waiting at night on a lonely station platform. I had to admit it was a real poem, not a limp romantic pastiche, but I didn't love him for it.

Films were a less contentious area. We were united in our admiration for Bogart in particular and the American crime thriller in general. We both admired Welles without reservation; at Stowe I had once reduced a small boy to tears because he had admitted to finding Citizen Kane boring after a Saturday night showing in the gym. We both loathed war-propaganda films – even the Bogart pictures of that period were often flawed by a five minute 'message' tacked on at the end – and we particularly abhorred the cycle of

Hollywood 'occupation' movies with their unpleasant mixture of schmaltz, sadism and complete unreality.

We both enjoyed, although perhaps with a certain condescension, low pubs and music halls. Although we quite liked the ENSA shows in the camp theatre, we preferred a small, extremely tatty hall in the town itself where the comics were both blue and hopeless, the jugglers dropped their props, the performing dogs ran off stage, and the chorines, some openly chewing gum supplied no doubt by American airmen from one of the nearby USAF bases, were just as openly contemptuous of their simple routines.

If asked at that time my aspirations I would have said – despite Percy's rejections of 'Prometheus' – 'to be a writer'. After a few pints, and I became inebriated in those days on an enviably small quantity of cheap flat mild, I was convinced that I understood the poetic significance of everything: the mahogany and engraved glass, the pool of beer on the bar, the faded fly-blown pre-war advert for gin, cigarette smoke, overheard fragments of conversation. Sitting in that music hall, enchanted by a tatty backcloth of a 'modernistic' cityscape or noting how the footlights by reversing the pattern of light and shade on a comedian's face emphasised the dead, puppet-like quality of his act, I would say to myself very solemnly: 'one day I must get this all down'.

I didn't actually write anything however. Admiration for others inhibited me. I believed that until I felt myself able to equal the interplay between inner and outer reality in the opening paragraphs of Joyce's *Ulysses* there was no point in starting, and I wasn't quite ready for that yet. One day, I was convinced, I would sit down with a notebook and several sharp pencils and write, without hesitancy, the opening sentences of the greatest novel of the century. Until then I was 'living', 'absorbing impressions', and limbering up for the obligatory spell of 'silence, exile and cunning' at some later date. The point was that, like most protected youths with literary interests, both Percy and I saw everything through established writers' eyes. In Skegness, admittedly livelier than most resorts due to the presence of military and naval establishments nearby, and no longer heavily fortified against invasion, we would chant 'August for the people' as we reeled its near-empty streets.

At a 'talent night' in camp Percy, despite his indifference to jazz,

condescended to accompany me on 'Frankie and Johnny', a ballad
he would allow some virtues as Auden had included it in his
anthology of folk poetry. Percy's classical training meant that his
version was rather stiff and academic. My singing was more enthusiastic than tuneful, but we won for all that and were asked to stage
a repeat performance in the Petty Officers' mess by our Chief, where
we were made much of and treated to a great deal of beer. Yet
despite our success I was unable to convince Percy that there was
anything in jazz. I was not however alone in my enthusiasm. I soon
found out that the rediscovery of Morton, Oliver, early Louis and
Bessie Smith was not, as I had imagined, a local phenomenon
confined to a small group at Stowe. When I whistled, recognisably
if only approximately, a chorus from Louis' 'Kneedrops' in the
NAAFI, it was identified by a young Glaswegian and later, after
I'd sung 'Frankie and Johnny', other ratings came up and admitted
to a keen interest in the music. Jazz, it seemed, was a widespread
minority passion that cut across all traditional class and cultural
barriers and through it, without thinking about it, I discovered the
key to the door I had been trying to force: communication with
some of those whom my mother, reacting to my insistent and
provocative hymning of their praises in every letter I sent home,
had taken to describing as 'your friends, the working classes'. At
the end of our second week, the time we were due to be transferred
to Ipswich, we were told that there was a bottleneck and that we
would be staying at Skegness for up to five weeks more to do
intensive square-bashing, PT and some elementary seamanship. I
went home for a few days' leave. Shortly after I got back to camp
we had a nasty shock. The reason for our hold-up became clear.
The Navy had drawn too many Ordinary Seamen. We were to be
made either cooks, writers or stewards or, if unsuitable for any of
these roles, redirected into the Army.

The explanation was, in human terms, something to be grateful
for. The number of casualties among naval personnel during the
D-Day invasion hadn't been anything like as heavy as expected, in
fact almost negligible. In consequence the Navy had quite enough
fully-trained ratings and didn't need us. At the time though, while
perfectly aware that this was why we were to be transferred, I can
remember feeling nothing but frustration. Cooks, stewards and

writers didn't wear bellbottoms. They wore a uniform rather like a shabby chauffeur, dark blue with a white shirt, black tie and a peaked cap. Furthermore the writers, the branch into which despite no ability whatsoever in maths or methodical clerical work I was enrolled, contained a majority of the one class I believed it somehow perfectly defensible to despise: the *petit bourgeoisie*.

In my indifference to the progress of the war, first at school and then in the Navy, I was by no means alone among my generation. Beyond the normal self-absorption of adolescents, I think our failure to consider the implications of losing was based on an inability to conceive this as a possibility. This was not surprising, even for those of us who thought of ourselves as rebels. Since our childhood we had been indoctrinated, both openly and implicitly, to believe in Britain's superiority.

Being half Jewish, I'd every reason to fear and hate Hitler and was, theoretically at any rate, an anti-Fascist, but the tone of British propaganda during the Second World War, at any rate until the discovery of the extermination camps, was either practical – 'Dig for Victory', 'Lend to Defend the Right to be Free', 'Britain Can Take It' – or mocking. Hitler, Goering and the rest were ridiculed in cartoons, songs and comedy shows on the wireless. 'Adolf, you've bitten off much more than you can chew,' sang Arthur Askey. Fougasse's warnings against careless talk showed the Nazi leaders sitting rather cosily on a bus listening to a pair of garrulous housewives giving away secrets on the seat in front. There was none of the anti-German hysteria of the 1914–18 war. No dachshunds were kicked in the streets. Beethoven, far from being banned, was responsible for the V-for-Victory musical symbol. Rommel was even promoted as 'a good German', a worthy opponent, and the German troops respected whereas the Italians, with their lack of enthusiasm for the conflict, were despised.

I was too young to take in Dunkirk, but found Churchill's rhetoric and *persona* curiously unreal. Even the bombing – and I sat through several weeks of that in my grandmother's cellar under the block of flats next to our house in Liverpool (the smell of damp still evokes the crump of falling bombs) – felt more like a natural phenomenon than the destructive and deliberate work of man. 'Jerry's late tonight,' people would say almost affectionately. Nor did the hearty joviality or the purposeful grim tones of the newsreel commentators make the war less distant or more real. I was still a child when it started and it seemed to have been going on for ever. The disappearance of bananas meant as much to us as the Battle of Britain.

On the other hand my contempt for the lower-middle classes had nothing to do with the war, nor was it confined to me. It's an old heresy, and one that still exists, to believe that the upper classes and the working classes are alike in their freedom from convention, are somehow 'real', whereas the lower-middle classes are the prisoners of their own aspirations, castrated by their pretensions, fair game for teasing and shocking. Through holding this belief it is possible to suck up to the aristocracy and patronise the working classes and feel unsnobbish while in fact indulging one's snobbery shamelessly at the expense of suburban commuters and their families.

Worse, most of this snobbery is based on taste, on the crooking of little fingers and non-U vocabulary. It's not really the sense of propriety, the admittedly narrow outlook, the opportunist morality that goads the intellectual, and all these defects are perhaps more strongly in evidence in the suburbs than in any other sector of the community. It's the garden gnomes, the love of light classical music, the chiming doorbells, the ritualistic washing of the car; these are the butts, the excuse for mockery. Of course the assertive belief that their standards are right, that their measure of taste is unassailable, can be irritating. In the Navy I was constantly under attack from the *petit bourgeoisie* for preferring jazz to, say, the *Warsaw Concerto* and I retaliated cruelly and contemptuously, wrote home sneering at those I called 'the tomato-growers', while at the same time deceiving myself that I was socially without prejudice. To find myself a writer, a clerk, in a badly-cut suit with a collar and tie depressed me immeasurably and, to be truthful, I was aware too that dressed like that I would be an object of less interest to homosexuals. For them, traditionally, bellbottoms were in themselves something of an aphrodisiac. There was nothing to be done, however, and having handed in our ordinary seamen's uniforms and drawn our hated fore-and-aft rig, Percy and I were sent to do the first part of our writers' training course at a camp on the outskirts of Malvern.

2

HMS *Duke*, a shore establishment, had been built as such and lacked in consequence those bizarre touches which helped relieve the austerity of the requisitioned Butlin Camps. It stood a little outside the town and depressed me instantly. For the first few weeks Percy and I were in different classes and couldn't even go on shore leave together. Later we were able to appear at 'Commander's Requests and Defaulters' for permission to rejoin each other and, at the price of a raised eyebrow from the officer on duty and a confirmatory smile from our Petty Officer, our request was granted.

On board, as we soon learnt to refer to the rigid geometry of the camp, we were taught nothing as yet in connection with our future role as the Navy's clerks but, in the company of cooks and stewards, sweated and cursed yet again through our basic training. This was reasonable enough. HMS *Duke* was after all the intake establishment for all fore-and-aft men and, by relinquishing our bellbottoms, we were officially new entries. It was dispiriting though and lacked that salty obscenity that had made the rigours of Skegness acceptable.

A season in hell among the tomato-growers was how I saw it, and my sense of snobbish outrage was fed by discovering that, whereas seamen turned in wearing their underwear, a practice which struck me as cheerfully squalid and which I soon adopted in preference to my pyjamas, my fellow clerks wore pyjamas *over* their underwear.

The traditional cry 'Show a leg' derives from the sexually permissive eighteenth century when sailors were allowed to cohabit with women between decks. On this command, the hairless leg of a doxy extending sleepily over the edge of a hammock entitled its owner to snooze on. They shouted 'Show a leg' at 0630 every morning on

HMS *Duke*, but mechanically and with no indication of awareness as to its original meaning. In fact the whole rhetoric of this bout of training lacked edge or colour. Our very Petty Officer, dispirited by the slightly priggish reaction of the more strait-laced writer trainees, abandoned any pretence to originality and fell back on those well-worn military clichés already familiar to me from a number of wartime films in the Crown Film Unit tradition.

'If yer don't pull your fuckin' socks up,' he'd shout with the minimum of conviction, 'I'll 'ave yew runnin' up and down that fuckin' 'ill ! It needs flattenin'!!'

The hill in question was truly enormous. It towered over the town nestling on its lower slopes, and this should at least have given the Petty Officer's uninventive threat the virtue of maximum exaggeration. It didn't, because the Malvern Hills, while certainly steep and at that time of the year generously splashed with extravagant browns and oranges, managed to avoid the grandeur to which their scale entitled them. They had the look of those reproductions of watercolours you could buy from the larger branches of Boots; an easily digested aesthetic calculated to appeal to those retired military men and elderly ladies with small private incomes who had elected to spend their later years in Malvern's innumerable private hotels and boarding houses and were largely responsible for the spa's air of moribund gentility.

The presence of a naval camp, while no doubt accepted as a patriotic necessity, may have initially distressed the residents, but the Navy's choice of personnel was as tactful as possible. The largely abstemious writers, in their very appearance reassuringly suggestive of more prosperous times when a chauffeur waited to receive his orders for the day, sipped their halfs of bitter quietly in the orderly public bars. They posed no threat. If HMS *Duke* had been a training camp for Glaswegian stokers the recognised need for sacrifice in our hour of need would have been stretched to breaking point.

The only evidence in Malvern that the average age of the entire civilian population wasn't around seventy was provided by a number of schools in the area. In particular there was a girls' school, which allowed its sixth form out on Saturday afternoons. They'd walk, whispering excitedly arm in arm, up and down the mountainous High Street, sit in cafés lost in moony reveries or, after mysterious glances and long pauses, burst into irrepressible shared giggles. Percy and I would walk past them as we strolled the streets, waiting impatiently for the pubs or cinema to open. We'd sit, sipping coffee and watching them tucking into powdered scrambled eggs on toast or 'fancy cakes' made from soya bean flour and filled with synthetic cream. Percy found them irritating, but I, with my more ambivalent sexual identity, was mildly excited by their purple blazers, shirts and ties, grey flannel skirts and black woollen stockings and would sometimes murmur with wistful lasciviousness a phrase I'd heard used by great aunts when I was a small boy – 'She married straight out of the schoolroom'.

We endured our training and, although my sluttish appearance led at times to a mild reproach, we could by now perform our drill and tie our repertoire of knots without even thinking about it. I had expected to be morally shocked by bayonet practice, the only addition to the Skegness curriculum, and no doubt had I been conscripted into a fighting regiment I would have been appalled. Here, however, among my fellow pen-pushers, the pale cooks and weedy stewards, the exercise lacked all realism. Even the Petty Officer in charge found it difficult to keep up the pretence of ferocity. 'H'imagine you've got a German h'on the h'end of that,' he'd yell as we jabbed feebly away at the suspended straw-filled sacks, but it was perfectly obvious that neither he nor we could imagine any such thing. Neither, given our naval futures in pay depot, galley or Officers' Mess, was the situation likely to arise.

Life in camp was a kind of limbo, not unbearable exactly but more or less unpleasant depending on how early or how cold it was, or whether what we were doing involved painful physical effort. Yet I can remember one moment when I was suddenly aware of being intensely, almost impossibly, happy. I was one of a number of ratings marched down to a railway siding to transfer some stores, potatoes I believe, from a goods van to one of the camp lorries. It was a warm and sunny October afternoon. I was eighteen, and somehow the stationary, rusty goods train, the overgrown banks of the railway cutting, the noise of the cinders crunching under our feet, the blue cloudless sky, the rhythm of the work, a sense of physical well-being – all fused to become one of those rare, almost painfully ecstatic experiences which stay in the mind for ever, and are all the more mysterious for having no logical or overtly emotional explanation.

'Liberty Men' is the name for sailors on shore leave and once at liberty Percy and I headed for the cinema. This formed part of what would now be called a complex: a handsome Victorian building with a heavily-marbled hall under a fine iron and glass roof and with a fountain of nymphs and cherubs extinguished for the duration, for at a time when patriots were advised to paint a line only a few inches above the bottom of their baths no fountains played or trickled. The cinema was small but, whether by chance or because whoever booked the films was an enthusiast, the programmes were uniformly excellent. Bette Davis in *Look Stranger* sent us beside ourselves with camp enthusiasm, and it was here too that I first watched that great mutilated masterpiece, *The Magnificent Ambersons*. We sat in the warm dark, almost alone, for even at that time when cinemas were always full, Welles was box office poison. So it was for us that the Ambersons lost their fortune and to us that the master, having introduced his actors and technical credits, thundered out that last great megalomaniac cry – 'I wrote and directed this picture. My name is Orson Welles.'

One afternoon on shore leave, alone for once (perhaps Percy was on leave in Aldershot), I went to look at a British Council travelling exhibition of Blake and Fuseli. Both were artists I admired; both after all had been praised by the Surrealists, or by Herbert Read at any rate, and the latter provided a chapter in Sacheverel Sitwell's *Splendours and Miseries*, a book I'd chosen as my prize for writing the poem about Prometheus which Percy had so despised.

Among others peering at the pictures was a family, the father ruddy and bearded, dressed in the tweedy homespun style of an Osbert Lancaster Hampstead intellectual, his short pleasant-looking red-haired wife and a small son. 'That,' I heard the man announce firmly and resonantly, 'is a bloody fine piece of work by Billy Blake,' and he jabbed with the end of his pipe towards one of Fuseli's nightmare ladies smiling in a most ambivalently malicious way under her elaborate coiffure.

Absurdly, and on occasion dangerously, I've never been able to stop myself pedantically correcting people's incorrect information. Once, aged about ten, I'd narrowly avoided having my ears boxed by an irate father at the Liverpool Zoo when I'd told him that 'dat leopard' he was pointing out to his small son was in fact a jaguar. This time too I sailed in. 'Actually Fuseli,' I murmured. The man took it well. He looked for a moment at the single sheet of the catalogue to check up, found out I was right and shouted: 'Bugger me! So it is, and who are you?' I told him my name and was asked to tea. His name, he told me, was Donald Cowie and he was an author. He was a publisher too. Fed up with what he called 'the bloody freemasonry of publishers' he'd founded the Tantivy Press and, with remarkable persistence and serendipity, had unearthed pre-war stores of very beautiful paper lying in small and mostly rural paper mills. On this he had printed and published a large body of his own work, most of it light satirical verse in a traditional mode and, as bookshops were starved for anything to put on sale in those paper-rationed days, he did extremely well.

Theoretically, as an enthusiastic if ill-informed admirer of the Surrealists and a rather precious young man in general, I should have detested both his work and him. I was, however, in part impressed by his scatological and sexual Rabelaisian turn of phrase, and equally won over by his kindness and the way in which he treated my aspirations to become a writer with apparent gravity. Always a chameleon, I found myself, in his company, assuming a bluff and noisy neo-Georgianism redolent of beer and wenches and long tramps through damp bracken. I was impressed too at his output (albeit self-published), and by his friendship with the then celebrated Professor Joad, a popularising philosopher, the mainstay of the BBC's Brains Trust and, according to Donald, as randy as a goat, as drunk as a judge, and much given to climbing up lampposts and similar japes.

Later, Joad was savagely discredited, quite absurdly in my view, for riding on a train without paying for a ticket, but at the time he was a national figure almost as famous as Tommy Handley, and much imitated for his philosophical catch phrase 'It all depends what you mean by . . .' and his rapid, precise – if rather high-pitched – delivery. For the friendship of a writer who knew Joad, I was prepared to put aside any reservations. Not so Percy. I only took him there once, but it was a sour disaster. Percy's literary seriousness was appalled by Donald's facility, while his equally puritanical homosexuality was offended by Donald's uxorious celebration of heterosexual monogamy. There was one sentence in particular, a sentence which began 'Last night my fingers were exploring the nocturnal interstices of my wife . . .' which turned him crimson with embarrassed distaste. His comments afterwards were withering on both an aesthetic and personal level. We had begun to drift apart.

Not that Donald Cowie was the sole reason for that. More important was a new friendship with a tall boy from Wolverhampton, a warm-hearted, slightly cynical person with a lopsided grin and the look of a younger Joseph Cotten. His name was Harry Wakefield and like me, but with more natural aptitude, he was training to be a writer. I fell head-over-heels for Harry and he, while interested only in girls, was prepared to accept my adoration in return for the amusement I provided him and, I believe, genuine affection.

All through my life I have been attracted by people like Harry Wakefield, at first, although fruitlessly, in the sexual field but soon (sex more or less sublimated if not all that far below the surface) as platonic friends.

Harry knew a great deal more about jazz than I. It was he who pointed out that if I really liked improvisation above all else, both Muggsy Spanier and, come to that, Duke Ellington and Jelly Roll Morton, relied in the main on arrangements, so in praising them I was talking nonsense and must either revise my opinions or discard them. This really threw me, but he added that as, within the scored passages, there were plenty of holes for improvising, why not admire both their skill as composers *and* the brilliance of their soloists? This view seemed and seems to me extremely sensible and although for many years I remained suspicious of the saxophone, I soon became less rigid and more open.

At all events it was with Harry's star in the ascendancy, and Percy's in decline, that we finished our basic training as writers and were sent home on leave. As for the Cowies, we kept up a correspondence for some time and indeed, when a sortie North on a bookselling expedition took them near Liverpool, I was able to repay some of their hospitality by asking my parents to put them up. My mother didn't 'care for his beard'. My father was very amused and indeed impressed by the fact that, under various pseudonyms, Donald wrote all the critical puffs on the dustcovers of his own work and, more conventionally, the publishers' blurb as well. But distance and diverging views soon put an end to our letters, and I never met nor indeed heard of him again.

3

My leaves in Liverpool have by now fused into one long leave. The Blitz was long over and the northern port had never suffered under the doodle-bug attacks which had, until the success of D-Day, made life in London and the South so nerve-wracking a phenomenon. Still the sense of being at war persisted: the gaping bomb-sites as yet nude of weeds, the partial black-out, the notices in the butchers' windows announcing what numbers in which streets were entitled to offal. On arriving at Lime Street Station I'd board a 1 or 33 tram-car, and walk with my kitbag over my shoulder and my ditty-box (a small cardboard suitcase) in my hand towards the comforts of home. For ten days or so I'd see my relations, chat to my small sister, stroll the public parks of my childhood, and go to the theatre with my mother or a friend of hers, a fat, highly literate and intelligent queen who had decided to take in hand my education and plied me with books, magazines and advice.

At the end of each leave, my woollen underwear restored to approximate whiteness (for my own efforts at dhobying never achieved more than what I called 'hammock grey'), I'd stagger back down to Lime Street to face the long journey back to wherever I was stationed. 'Leave,' they told us frequently in the Navy, 'is a privilege, not a right.'

This time my destination was the writers' training camp at Wetherby, a small town near Leeds in frozen Yorkshire. It was the week after Christmas.

It wasn't exactly that I'd no intention of passing my exams at HMS *Demetrius*, an establishment appropriately far from the sea. My moments of revolt, rare but extreme, have always been public, either the end result of accumulated angry frustration or the unpremeditated effect of a rush of adrenalin through the system. The notion of deliberately faking stupidity was foreign to me. Nor, in this case, was it necessary. My mathematical sense has always been shaky. I can't add up a row of figures twice and reach the same answer. I'm not however one of those who try to present this failing as a virtue: the proof of unworldly, seer-like preoccupations. It's very irritating and has cost me dear. I comforted myself on this occasion that at least I'd pointed it out in advance to those who had insisted on allocating me to such an unsuitable role and did my best, given a persistent inability to concentrate on something which doesn't interest me, to work out how much pay less tax would be earned by a first lieutenant, acting-captain of a motor-torpedo boat, with a wife, two children and a dependent mother. The lieutenant, had he existed, would have become somewhat nervous as each pay-day drew near, never knowing whether to expect a salary rather higher than an Admiral of the Fleet, or considerably less than the expectations of a Victorian crossing sweeper during a heatwave.

As each exam approached I reacted, as I'd often done at school, by a series of genuine but undoubtedly psychosomatic diseases. Glands swelled, teeth abscessed, flu struck. Harry and Percy were almost ready to pass out before I'd taken and failed my first test.

Happily, the camp's Training Commander, a squat, ruddy-faced, blue-jowled Jewish officer given to twinkling, found me absurdly amusing or, more accurately, amusingly absurd. I'd first come to his attention when a prudish lady sorter in the Wetherby post office had sent back with a complaint an envelope addressed to my mother which I'd decorated with some sub-Rex-Whistlerian cherubs modestly, indeed almost vestigially, hung. He'd returned this to me, forced, because the complaint had been official, to issue at least a formal reprimand, but making it perfectly clear that he thought the woman was a prurient fool. He suggested that in future I confined my *putti* to inside the envelope. From then on he kept a sardonic eye on my antiprogress. He gave the impression of boredom and impatience with his job, and at least my passionate defence of my right to give male cherubs appropriate if minute sexual organs made a change from deciding what to do about ratings late off shore, or cooks apprehended smuggling out a pound of butter on weekend leave.

Our next encounter seemed more serious. At Christmas, after a beery dinner served to us, as was the naval custom during that period of traditional misrule, by the officers, Harry Wakefield and I fell asleep on the same bunk and were roughly awoken by a fiercely heterosexual Warrant Officer who had long suspected and resented my propensities. He put us on a charge but the Commander would have none of it.

'Far too drunk to have done anything about it even if they'd wanted to,' he commented dismissively. Our accuser reddened, and Harry and I, he with justifiable innocence, me at any rate technically not guilty, saluted, turned about and marched out of the room.

In between working up to being ill during exams or recovering after them, I quite enjoyed Wetherby. Physical exercise was minimal. Football was voluntary, and even the obligatory twenty minutes of PT before breakfast required no more effort than was necessary in order not to freeze. The classes were boring enough but there was a reasonably warm canteen, a piano player stumbling through boogie-woogie, the tick-tock of ping-pong balls, Harry or Percy to chatter to over the watery pints of NAAFI mild. The war too had begun to swing in our favour. We didn't talk about it much, but it meant a diminution of possible risk and that was cheering.

So we sat, played dominoes, talked about jazz or painting, speculated as to why the smoke was blue when it curled up from the end of a cigarette but grey when expelled from the lungs, indulged in horse-play, listened to Bechet or Jelly Roll on a gramophone borrowed from the Chaplain; inadequately, in my case, washed our underpants, gave blood to a travelling unit known as 'the mobile Dracula wagon', slept heavily on 'make and mends', masturbated often, and got drunk in Leeds or Harrogate.

Harry and I didn't often go to Harrogate. A refuge for the elderly, it seemed too like another Malvern although we were temporarily impressed and amused by its enormous Edwardian hotels where a few old ladies ate their meagre lunches in the Baroque wastes of the under-heated dining rooms, and a palm court trio, wearing cardigans against the cold, scraped out selections from *Floradora* or *The Yeomen of the Guard*.

We much preferred Leeds, a wide-open city with enough tarts and drunkenness to earn itself one of those 'revealing' articles in

the *News of the World*. Although the war continued, there was
now no question of an air-raid and modified street lighting had
been re-introduced. This made our reeling sorties from pub to
dance-hall to pub to café to YMCA or Salvation Army hostel less
hazardous, and revealed also the Victorian Gothic fantasy of the
town. In the city square, a platoon of solid nymphs held lamps
aloft. There were elegant glass-roofed arcades to explore and a
huge town hall, a sooty metaphor for the civic pride of the High
Victorian dead.

I discovered eventually that you could take a tram out to a large
Elizabethan manor house on the outskirts of the city where the
Corporation housed many of its treasures including what was, for
those days, a rather adventurous modern collection.

The tram-ride itself was a dreamlike pleasure. The last few stops
were among woods, the rattling tram was old and Emmet-like, with
an ornate spiral staircase and little panels of engraved blue and red
glass above the windows. The house, Temple Newsam, had Latin
mottoes picked out in stone around the parapets of the great courtyard. It was usually empty, and Harry and I wandered its crimson
rooms full of Rubenses and Canalettos and roped-off eighteenth-
century furniture, and spent a long time admiring the Graham
Sutherlands, Henry Moores and Paul Nashes in the modern collection. Later, after I had met the Surrealist Group in London, I
rapidly recanted my admiration for these artists, apostates all, and
shamefacedly tucked away those oblong Penguin Modern Masters
which extolled their work, but at Wetherby I still found anything
'modern' admirable.

Culture in the afternoon then, a habit I was to keep intermittently
throughout my naval career because, for one thing, it was very
economical, and vice, or at any rate aspirations to vice, in the
evening.

Vice in Leeds, that last winter of the European war, centred for
us on The Dick Turpin, a garish public house in the Thirties' cream
and green, not far from the city centre. Percy came once and didn't
like it, but Harry and I did, and in no time were on friendly terms
with the rather drab and pathetic little whores and their lord and
master, a Spanish pimp called Tony Angelo.

As to why I was so impressed, the answer, I suppose, lay in my association of whores with the Storyville era in the history of New Orleans jazz. To talk to real whores and pimps seemed to me to create some kind of spiritual link with Buddy Bolden, Tom Anderson, Lulu White and Jelly Roll Morton.

There was one girl with whom I became quite friendly. She charged, she told me, three guineas, a curiously pedantic sum, but threw in breakfast and kept the place spotless (or so she said, for at three guineas a throw I hadn't the means to find out even if I'd had the inclination). She was worried because she had no identity card. She despised good-time girls 'who "go" for nothing'. I listened to her for hours, hearing the tinkle of the whorehouse piano in my mind's ear and, about once a night, in exchange for buying him a gin and orange, I was allowed a few moments' audience with Tony Angelo himself. Dressed in a wide-lapelled black-market suit, wearing a mauve silk shirt, kipper tie and pointed leather shoes, sporting an amazing amount of jewellery, heavily-scented, his Brylcreemed hair worn long for those days, his hairline moustache almost invisible in its precision, he seemed to me the most glamorous person I'd ever met. His arrogance too was God-like. When I asked him, rather nervously, about his reaction to that article in the *News of the World*, he'd shrugged dismissively. 'I not frightened of those beeg fat City Halderman,' he said examining a beautifully manicured nail, 'I know too much haybout them.' City corruption too, I thought to myself. Here I am talking to a man described in the newspaper as 'a slimy foreign beast earning a fat living from battening on to women of a certain sort', and he feels perfectly safe because he knows too much about the City Fathers. Orgies in the Mayor's parlour perhaps? Gross old men in their sock suspenders chasing Tony Angelo's tarts round a solid mahogany table with the mace on it? I wished he'd tell me more but, the gin and orange once dispatched, the audience was at an end.

One night too, five vicars marched in. Hearty and unshockable, they had come to fight the good fight.

'Come to save me fookin' soul!' yelled a very drunken girl from Bradford.

'If I can, sister,' said the leader of the troop bravely.

A year later, my atheism confirmed by Surrealist doctrine, and my anti-clericalism fed at the same source, I would perhaps have felt it necessary to insult the Men of God in imitation of Benjamin Peret in that famous photograph, but that night I was prepared to dismiss their prayers and hymns among the indifferent clientèle of The Dick Turpin as 'noble but misled'. I wrote as much to my mother, adding pompously that I found 'negative stupidity and the belief that civilisation was a refrigerator in every home, worse sins than drunkenness and copulation'.

I was in love with squalor then, and scoured the city for it, usually finishing the night drinking Camp coffee in a filthy little café. We'd struck up an acquaintance with an old woman there called 'Cigarette Liz'. She wore a cap and stank of mildewed pennies, a complaint she put down to a canker.

'Me 'usbands used ter beat me,' she croaked. 'All me 'usbands did, but they all knew about me money and drew out insurance policies. There'll be four or five of 'em wrangling over me when I'm gone.'

I listened attentively. She went on: 'There was a rat wot lived in me tent when I camped out on the waste-land.' The Waste Land! The rat's foot stirring the bones in the cellar in 'The Straw Men'! The literary echoes produced an immediate know-all *frisson*. I must remember to point them out to Percy next day, I told myself.

'Did you feed 'im, Liz?' asked the enormous, pregnant proprietress; her ninth she'd told me.

'Yes. On fish. You should have seen 'im swim. Fookin' water-rat he wus.'

Dickensian cackling.

'There was a rat wot used to come in 'ere,' said the café owner, not to be outdone. 'Used to come in this very shop and go "wee wee" at me. " 'Ere's me rat," I'd say, but the young chap wot 'elped with the chips said: "Bugger you and your rat!" That's what 'e said, "Bugger you and your rat!"'

Harry, like most of the heterosexuals I became fond of during that period of my life, did his best to convince me that girls were better value. In fact, while at Wetherby, I was not particularly active anyway. Most of the writers were extremely prudish, and although Percy and I had once spent an evening out with two stokers from the camp's ship's company, it had led to little more than some heavy petting behind the boiler house, for by the time we came back on board we were far too drunk to get anywhere at all. Yet Harry's proselytism continued. It wasn't that he was in any way censorious. It was just that he believed it to be the lack of heterosexual experience rather than choice or inclination which dictated my propensities.

With what he believed my interests at heart, he would occasionally drag me away from The Dick Turpin and we'd spend the evening cruising a flyblown dance-hall where under a revolving globe of faceted mirror-glass, we'd try to chat up those girls too homely not to have been commandeered by the infinitely more glamorous and far better paid American service men. One night, just before Christmas, we scored; Harry's girl being, of the two, by far the prettier. This I accepted as inevitable, Harry being not only better-looking but more at ease when it came to exchanging that mocking *badinage* which conversation demanded. We left the dance-hall after 'The King' and bought them fish and chips. Then, following a rather inconclusive snog under some railway arches, put them on the last train to the nearby woollen mill town where they lived and worked.

Before their train left, Harry's girl had proposed a date, mine looking considerably less eager, and we'd agreed to make a foursome of it some ten days later. On our train back to Wetherby I'd expressed considerable dismay at the prospect. I'd found my experiences the reverse of satisfactory, let alone aphrodisiac. It's true we'd kissed but, as I told Harry, her mouth tasted of batter from the fish and chips we'd bought combined most unpleasantly with the Fulnana cachous she'd been sucking. Furthermore, I didn't like having her virulent red lipstick smeared all over my face and collar. There was no question either of 'going further' – a tentative attempt to feel her breast had been repulsed with a sharp slap across the wrist. Not that this had worried me particularly. She'd seemed to me both lumpy and pasty, her conversation limited to Palais catchphrases, and she'd cost me a lot of money as well. I added that personally I'd sooner have spent it getting pissed in The Dick Turpin.

I sat back on the dusty cushions of the unheated local train and sulked. In the mirror above Harry's head I could see the lipstick smeared across my collar. Harry laughed. Had I forgotten we were going on leave, next week? They'd no intention of keeping the date, no more than we had. That was just a polite convention. His didn't come across either. A prick-teaser and a waste of time. The next evening ashore we'd go to The Dick Turpin.

Christmas came. Paperchains in the NAAFI. Carols in the tin church. Harry was particularly affectionate as he knew I'd felt silly and inadequate, and he thought it was perhaps his fault. It may have been this that persuaded him to let me share his bunk after our turkey and plum pudding; an act of kindly expiation which led us close to the edge of disaster. Then, when that half of the trainees who'd been on leave returned, the rest of us set off for our four days at home; Harry to Wolverhampton, and me to Liverpool.

I was due back on 31 December and, no doubt because another exam was looming up, developed *en route* an agonising toothache. It was a Sunday and, after I'd changed stations, running between City and Central, each step jogging my tooth most painfully and sweat pouring down my face, I discovered that my efforts had been in vain. I had three minutes to spare to catch the nine o'clock train to Wetherby. It being a holiday, the ticket collector told me, with that smug satisfaction which all petty officials derive from transmitting unwelcome information, it wasn't running. The next one was at 6 am. 'A lot of your lads made the same mistake,' he added. 'They weren't best pleased. None of 'em!'

I turned, resigned to a night at the YMCA, to find myself facing two viragos.

'Why didn't yer turn up to keep yer date today?' snapped mine.

'Aye, and where's 'Arry?' demanded the other

Harry's 'polite convention' had crumbled. Clearly his charm had persuaded his girl that he had meant it and she'd dragged mine along to prove it. Typically enough it was mine who was the more furious. I calmed them down – unexpected leave (lie); here was my pass to prove it; no way to get in touch (true); Harry desperate but his mother was none too well (two more lies). Gradual resignation on the part of the girls.

Would they like a cup of tea? Yes. Their train wasn't until 10.20pm and so off we went and, with no need to prove myself sexually, we had quite a pleasant three-quarters of an hour, chatting away in a café near the station. They told me about their work, 'the toil' they called it, in a woollen mill, and what film stars they liked and how one of them, Harry's, had been going steady with a soldier but had broken it off because he was 'so thick', and then, at 10.15, we strolled back companionably to the station, arm in arm, and I felt quite a dog. Two girls, one on each arm. Even my tooth hardly bothered me.

They got the tickets out of their Dorothy bags and we approached the barrier. Another official, dead ringer of mine, smiled with grim delight. 'Aye, 10.20 *most* Sundays,' he agreed, 'but Good Fridays, Christmas Day and New Year's Eve she pulls out at 10.10. There won't be another now until morning.'

Both girls burst into instant hysterics.

'What will me dad say!'

'Oh bloody 'eck!'

'You've never seen me dad wild!'

I tried to reassure them. Led them to a telephone box and sent off identical telegrams to their fathers: 'Don't worry. Missed train. Spending the night in Girls Friendly Society Hostel.' 'Love Barbara' in one case; 'Love Margaret' in the other.

The woman taking it down, recognising a masculine voice, read them back to me with disapproving scepticism. She also told me neither telegram would get there before morning anyway, but I thought it judicious to keep this from Barbara and Margaret, who were beginning to look, if not cheerful, at any rate glumly resigned.

I looked up the hostel and found it to be in a distant suburb. Taxis were predictably hard to find but at last we got one going more or less in the right direction, although we had to share it with two randy soldiers and an old drunk, who kept asking what was wrong with a drink on New Year's Eve at defensively frequent intervals. We eventually found the hostel, all lights off and in no way suggesting anything even minimally friendly. I rang and knocked for ten minutes. Eventually a sour elderly woman answered the door. She was in a dressing gown and a filthy temper. At first she refused to take them in. 'Very well,' I said, 'my mother is a prominent social worker in Liverpool. She'd be most interested to hear that two girls had been refused admittance on a dark winter's night. Could I have your name, madam?'

Yet again that unfair confidence which is the birthright of the middle classes won out. She took them in, both expressing their gratitude, she admonishing them for their noisiness, rattling out the rules of the establishment.

So there I was alone in the laurel-haunted drive of a large Victorian private house on the edge of a city. My bad tooth, forgotten during the necessity for action, reminded me of its existence.

It took me forty minutes to walk back into Leeds. The streets were full of maniacs, people being sick, others roaring out the songs of the day. I caught myself reflected, looking desperate, in the window of a big store with a street lamp behind me. I'd never felt more miserable in my life.

The YMCA was full but they let me sit on a wooden chair with my tooth giving me hell. I caught the 6am train back to camp, but was in no trouble for being late as so many others were in the same boat. The tooth came out the next day. It had been abscessed badly, and they used procaine, a new local anaesthetic. I was well enough to take the exam, but predictably failed it. Harry and Percy had meanwhile both passed their finals.

A month later, the Commander sent for me. I'd flunked it again. Harry and Percy had both been drafted. There seemed no way I would ever escape from HMS *Demetrius*. I was beginning to feel a certain despair.

'Quite clearly,' said the Commander, looking through my file, 'there's no point in you going on like this. I suggest you get back into bellbottoms; in fact I've applied for you to do so. I don't think they'll say no and I can see you're not exactly against the idea' – this was obvious as I was grinning broadly and trying hard not to jump up and down – 'Meanwhile, you can join the ship's company on a temporary basis and make yourself useful in the galley.' I saluted and once outside his office began to leap and gambol along the neat paths like a clumsy foal in the pale February sunlight.

For the next five weeks I worked in the galley, my hated fore-and-aft uniform becoming greasier and greasier. My colleagues were four WRENS, René, Joyce, Black Bess and Bambi, all of whom immediately accepted me as one of the girls. Together we mopped and squeegeed the concrete floor – we were meant to call it the deck but never did so – peeled mountains of potatoes, sliced the huge grey loaves of bread, and loaded and unloaded the washing-up machine, which smelt of babies' nappies. I soon learnt to ignore the sudden clockwork-like emergence of one or more of the enormous cockroaches who lived behind it. We also did a lot of skiving and sat for hours at a time drinking ki (naval cocoa) and smoking like chimneys. I was riveted by the erotic adventures of René, Joyce and Black Bess, which they described with a remarkable lack of inhibition. Bambi, although by far the prettiest, contributed nothing to these revelations beyond an occasional 'That'd be telling' or 'Wouldn't you like to know,' and then only when pressed by the others. I suspected that, while without censoriousness, she was saving herself for Lieutenant Right.

From the rest of the ship's company, the stoker, electricians and sick-berth attendants, I learnt several dodges unknown to the transient trainees. By applying to attend the Methodist Chapel in Wetherby, for example, it was possible to dive smartly down a side alley while the rest of the column marched up a certain narrow street and to spend the Godbothering hour in the back room of a friendly pub, rejoining the genuine Nonconformists at the same point during their march back to camp.

I finally made it with one of the stokers, and wrote to tell Percy at his new posting in Colombo. I often wondered if he knew what I was on about. On account of the censors I felt obliged to be what was perhaps impenetrably oblique.

When my transfer came through, a very nice Leading Seaman, who had been responsible for the discipline in my class during my abortive attempts to become a writer, invited me to join the local batch of successful trainees for a final piss-up in a country pub. We got very drunk and all I can remember of the evening was a chill but brilliant sunset lighting up a stained-glass window let into the pub door. It represented a fox holding a fat goose in its mouth. How I got back to camp I can't imagine, but the next day, with a formidable hangover but otherwise extremely happy, I set off again for Skegness.

4

To return seven months later to Skegness was like one of those recurring dreams in which the details are a little different each time. I knew my way around this time but I still had to move, like a somnambulist, through the same routine: same films on VD and the correct way to brush the teeth, same elementary drill and seamanship. God remained, according to the same chaplain, the Highest Officer in the British Navy. Yet there were changes too. Although the war was still on, its successful conclusion, in Europe at any rate, was only a matter of time. They'd cleared the barbed wire from along the sea front and were digging out the anti-tank traps on the beach. They'd even re-opened the small funfair; the proud shabby horses revolved on the merry-go-round for the first time since 1939. The ghost trains banged through the double doors into an innocent world of shrieks and spectres. Back in my bellbottoms I felt reborn.

It was spring by now. I lay on the grass smoking, reading or staring up at the blue sky. The goldfish gleamed among the reeds of Billy Butlin's neglected boating-lake. The sea's horizon no longer held its threat.

In the newspapers and on the newsreel in the cinema where I went to see James Cagney in *The Roaring Twenties*, they showed us for the first time the appalling images of Belsen: the stumbling living skeletons with their bald heads and huge empty eyes, the bulldozers scooping up the mounds of dead. As far as I can remember, they hardly affected me, seeming no more real than the briefly illuminated bug-a-boos in the Skegness ghost train. How could I weep over a poem and remain indifferent to this proof of what humanity is capable of? I am unable to answer. In this respect the nineteen-year-old self that I am trying to recreate or understand is a total and repellent stranger. What did he feel as the camera explored the gas-chambers and the ovens? I can't remember. I'd like to think it was too horrible to grasp, but fear that it may be simply because I can't face up to my own self-centred lack of imagination. I wrote home praising *The Roaring Twenties*. As usual, I also asked for a small sum of money on some rather flimsy pretext. Waiting for my draft, this time to another Butlin's camp in Pwllheli, North Wales, I was given a stick with a nail in the end of it for collecting waste paper.

I'd made a new friend, this time of undeniably working-class origin. His name was Tom Dash and, although he was a grammar school scholarship boy, his father was a dustman who lived in a pre-fab in Dalston. 'My old man's a dustman,' Tom sang in an exaggerated Cockney accent. ' 'E wears a dustman's 'at!' Writing to my mother I suppressed the scholarship but emphasised his father's profession. 'He's very clever though,' I added, 'and is teaching me about a political theory called Anarchism which I find very convincing.' I knew how to tease my mother.

Actually I did find Anarchism convincing, or at any rate in so far as I was able to concentrate on the pamphlets published by Freedom Press which Tom had lent me. One of them, I was delighted to discover, was by Herbert Read, who had also edited the Faber Surrealist anthology I had found by chance in a Liverpool bookshop during the school holidays some three years earlier and carried with me everywhere since. Already believing myself a Surrealist I could now, without fear of being labelled inconsistent, declare myself an Anarchist as well. Tom saw no reason to return the compliment. His Anarchism was less romantic, based on his hatred of class oppression, on his memories as a child of Mosley's march through the East End (he had no trouble in reacting to Belsen). He found Surrealism irrelevant to the struggle, even suspect.

After the relaxed atmosphere of Skegness, HMS *Glendower* came as a nasty shock. For the first three weeks, it rained and drizzled non-stop and this coincided with more bullshit, discipline and physical unpleasantness than I had yet encountered. We had to get up at 6.30am, go everywhere at the double, and perform such dangerous feats as clambering up the sixty-foot main-mast erected by the swimming-pool, and climbing hand over hand upside down along a rope suspended unpleasantly high from the ground. Bell-bottoms or no, there were times when I almost regretted my inability to add up and envied Percy and Harry sitting in their nice offices filling in ledgers. Falling into my bunk each night, aching all over and completely exhausted, it seemed only about ten minutes before they woke us up again. There was no shore-leave either. No time to read or think.

What they were doing, of course, was breaking us down as individuals in preparation for turning us into sailors. What I tended to forget was that my fellow sufferers had only been in the Navy for a week or two. I'd been spoilt, softened by months of cushiness and tolerated skiving.

Then, quite suddenly, things improved. We got up an hour later; the dawn was getting earlier too. The sun shone and across the parade ground Snowdon, until then invisible, rose snowcapped into the sweet spring air. I felt fitter than I ever have before or since, and mentally buzzing with new ideas as yet only partially formulated. Anarchism for instance. What a beautiful concept! A rational world in which what you made was for use, not profit, and all you took was what you needed. Love was the only law. Money unnecessary. Crime – once envy, greed, and private possessions no longer existed – would be unnecessary. Why steal when you could take freely? Free sexuality would extinguish jealousy. Nobody would mind who his father was because children would be the beloved responsibility of all. War would be unthinkable; police, spies, informers, politicians redundant. It was simply a question of convincing enough people that they held the power to free themselves from their chains. They must be taught – no, persuaded – that it was useless overturning one political system simply to embrace another. Communism, Tom had pointed out, was simply one more form of tyranny. Until then I hadn't realised this. As Communism was one of the several subjects which brought my hated prep-school headmaster to the edge of apoplexy, I thought it must be defensible. Not so, said Tom. Marx might have claimed that the end-product of Communism was the withering away of the State but the reverse was true. He gave me Koestler's *Darkness at Noon* to read, and Orwell's *Homage to Catalonia*. I found them much easier to grasp than the political pamphlets, and took his point. Long live Anarchism! Down with the State!

Surrealism also. Perhaps Tom was right to reject it personally. After all there would be a lot of spade work necessary to dismantle the apparatus of power, to help the Workers' Syndicates supplant the bosses, to distribute food and raw materials, but at the same time purely practical activities were not enough. 'Change life,' the Surrealists had ordained. 'Tell your children your dreams!' From the few texts I'd read; from the reproductions of Ernst, Dali and Magritte I'd studied; I had derived amazing certainty that the marvellous was all about us, that if only we could escape from that mental labyrinth built in the name of morality, religion, patriotism and the family, we could all become poets; move through a universe where dream and reality were indistinguishable. If Anarchism was to provide the sustaining bread of life, Surrealism would pour out the intoxicating wine.

All this filled my head as we learnt how to clean a rifle, knelt at Church parade, or saluted the Quarter Deck, and it never occurred to me to translate my revolutionary fervour into practice through some act of refusal or defiance. I had only to shout a blasphemy in Church, refuse to salute the Quarter Deck, or throw down my rifle to prove that the status quo was as determined to protect itself as Tom maintained. I did no such thing, and nor did he, but as we argued and theorised, a true Anarcho–Surrealist was about to leave Skegness to join us. I knew him too. He had been at Stowe with me. His name was Tony Harris Reed.

Tony had already played a formative role in my life. Thin and almost colourless in physical appearance, he had the questing expression of a hungry ferret and, ferret-like, was prepared to track down an idea through the most complicated system of burrows. Nor was he against sinking his teeth through to the bone of the hand of anyone in authority foolish enough to try and handle him after his re-emergence. A true black humorist, he would carry a dislike to extreme ends, in no way disdaining so childish a ploy as letting down a hated master's bicycle tyres, and yet at the same time using his considerable inventive powers to build up such an exaggerated picture of the man's minor eccentricities as to reduce us all to mocking laughter at the very mention of his name.

One of his butts – an admittedly pompous history tutor, but in every other respect comparatively harmless – reduced Tony to a state of near hysterical rage, and was metamorphosed into a figure of Ubu-like proportions. The unfortunate man had a dark, ruddy complexion which contrasted startlingly with his cropped snow-white hair and neat moustache. Tony decided he looked like the negative of a photograph. He also put it about on no evidence at all that his wife, a plain lady of no doubt entirely conventional morals, was not only an insatiable nymphomaniac but a thief to boot. In support of the latter theory he claimed that, following her by chance along an obscure path from the school's wartime fuel supply to the married masters' houses, he had at first thought her to be pregnant – no doubt the work of some precocious sixth-former or a randy if indiscriminate junior master – but then noticed how, every now and then, a piece of coal would fall from under her bulging mackintosh. During our readings from a translation of Plato, Tony, while remaining completely po-faced himself, would imitate quite blatantly the man's affectedly clipped drawl, reducing the rest of us to ill-suppressed handkerchief-in-mouth splutterings.

He'd also cultivated a vendetta against the President of the Debating Society, a maths master of superficially liberal principles as long as everything that was said remained within certain limits. Noticing that the American popular singer Frank Crumit had died, I proposed, and Tony seconded, that in future the President should wear *in perpetuum* a black tie in his memory. The master claiming, quite correctly, to fail to see any relevance in our motion refused, but was voted down by a carefully canvassed majority. From then on, whenever he failed to observe the rule, Tony or I would jump up to protest vigorously during 'any other business'.

The main target for his anarchic disrespect was less expected. It was Robin and Dodie Watt, the Canadian couple who ran the art-school, a modern concrete building behind the chapel, a refuge where anybody during his spare time could go and paint or argue, a haven for generations of Stoic aesthetes and for unconventional masters as well.

Robin Watt was a quiet man who painted portraits in the style of a less exuberant Augustus John. His wife Dodie was a far more positive character. She drew well, was both kind and protective to her protégés, and managed to stimulate a great deal of interest and excitement in art in general and certain aspects of modernism in particular. She had however certain very defined ideas about what was and what wasn't acceptable in painting and, to make sure we all toed the line, would pin up paired reproductions which we were expected to divide into good, bad, or in some cases of equal merit. For example, a Matisse was 'good', a Holman Hunt was 'bad', but apples by Cézanne and Courbet were both 'good'. If we went wrong she'd explain why and, as she talked well, it proved an extremely effective form of visual brainwashing.

Arriving at Stowe, rather apprehensive, and feeling both provincial and lost, I found the Watts and their art-school an unexpected haven, and was soon preaching their gospel during the holidays not only to my mother and small sister but also to my various Liverpudlian relations, including a rich cousin of my grandfather, who took it pretty well considering that my lecture took place in a large drawing-room hung with original Pre-Raphaelites collected by her father, a nineteenth-century ship-owner.

At first Harris Reed was equally under the spell of Robin and Dodie Watt. Indeed he produced with remarkable facility a huge number of precocious pictures in the style of those painters we were taught to admire. Yellow crucifixions against pink landscapes in the manner of early Gauguin yielded to cubist still-lifes on up-tilted table-tops after Braque. Matisse nudes jostled Chagall lovers. Picasso harlequins sat amidst Derainesque landscapes. The rest of us were dazzled by his eclectic brilliance although the Watts, while by no means wishing to discourage so receptive a disciple, felt he ought to spend a little more time improving his rather shaky draughtsmanship.

Given that Ma and Pa Watt, as we had come to call them, were our mother and father figures, there came that inevitable moment during our later adolescence when we began to question their authority, and here Tony turned what might otherwise have been little more than a series of mild disagreements on the relative importance of this or that painter into a full-scale revolt.

It was my discovery of Herbert Read's book on Surrealism that acted as the catalyst. I'd brought it back to school in a state of high excitement and carried it, like a trusting puppy, to the Watts for their approval. They were of course both aware of Surrealism, having visited that pre-war exhibition in London which had led to the publication of Read's anthology in the first Place. Furthermore, in the art school library was a copy of ELT Mesens' *London Bulletin* – No 1 which contained a reproduction of Magritte's *Le Viol* which Ma and Pa Watt dismissed as sensationalism – and, more damagingly, 'literary' – although personally and secretly I'd found it both disturbing and impressive.

It was a weekly custom of the Watts to hold, in their own room, a discussion-meeting-cum-sketch-club and it was here that I produced my book. There were about eight of us there, including Tony and Guy Neale, the third member of our little clique. It was Guy who'd first introduced me to jazz. I'd shown both Tony and Guy the book earlier, and they had shared my enthusiasm. Ma Watt looked rapidly through the reproductions, screwing up her eyes behind her glasses as was her habit. She was almost entirely dismissive. 'Old hat' was her first condemnation of the movement as a whole. She was willing to allow that Klee, Miró and of course Picasso were OK, but she dismissed Dali, Magritte and Ernst as 'no damn good'. Robin mumbled his agreement. I felt very depressed but then, in an unprecedented way, Tony and Guy began to argue quite forcefully. Ma Watt stood her ground. 'Silly Freudian images painted as photographically and as badly as the Pre-Raphaelites.' Taking courage from my bolder friends, I too began to question the whole aesthetic grid through which Ma Watt judged pictures and the meeting, usually so civilised, finished on quite a sour note. The following week, despite considerable grumpiness from both Ma and Pa Watt as to the value of what we were doing, Tony, Guy and I began to turn out pictures in the orthodox Surrealist manner.

Tony didn't let things rest there, however. Taking advantage of Ma Watt's absence (I believe she suffered from migraines), he asked the more easily persuaded Robin if we could use the small sculpture room for a Surrealist exhibition. He tentatively agreed, thinking that we intended to do no more than hang up our pictures. Not so. The following Thursday, the Watts' day off, we set to work with full iconoclastic enthusiasm. We jammed a large doll's head over the taps of the sink so that the water poured out of its neck on to a piece of coral. We smashed in the breasts of a classical plaster-cast bust and put tins of condensed milk in the cavities. We dragged in a dustbin and filled it with the dismembered limbs of the school's skeleton, painted shocking pink. We scattered dead leaves all over the floor. We hung our pictures too of course, but copied out various Surrealist texts below and above them in poster paint. We also imported two or three gramophones and attached various incongruous objects from the still-life cupboard to their slowly revolving turntables. We were rather pleased with the general effect.

Next day we hid behind a low cupboard on all fours waiting for the Watts to arrive. Unfortunately, believing the art-school to be empty, Ma Watt allowed herself the luxury of a discreet fart and Pa Watt, following in her wake, asked if she'd 'pooped'. This set us off into audible giggles. Ma Watt ordered us out from behind the cupboard, told us off for being childish; and asked us suspiciously why we were hiding there anyway. We told her we wanted to hear her reaction to our Surrealist exhibition without her feeling inhibited. 'What Surrealist exhibition?' she snapped. Her husband explained that he'd said we could hang our pictures in the sculpture room.

Snorting with irritation at his compliance, she threw open the door. We needn't have shown any fear as to the inhibition of her reactions. She went puce with rage, told us to clear up 'that damn insulting mess!' and barred us from the art-school for a week. Tony was delighted. We'd proved her bourgeois conformism masquerading as tolerant modernity. It was up to us now not to go crawling back. We didn't show up for the rest of the term. I decorated my study with the bust with the condensed milk-tin breasts and we met there to play our jazz records – Ma Watt had objected to the seriousness we'd showed in that area too. 'It's just fun music,' she'd complained.

Eventually Guy and I made it up with the Watts, but Tony Harris Reed never did. I looked forward to his arrival at Pwllheli with rather anxious anticipation.

At first sight, but this was not unexpected, Tony looked unexceptional. His uniform fitted him, his hat was on at the prescribed angle. He hadn't even bothered to bleach his collar. I introduced him to Tom and the rest of my circle of friends. He and Tom didn't really take to each other. Tom's idealism, which had, during the past few weeks, coloured my own thought-patterns, seemed rather wet to Tony's way of thinking. *His* Anarchism was more mocking and subversive. He had little belief in the effectiveness of political or anti-political action. On the other hand, since I had last seen him, he had rooted out a great deal more information about Surrealism, discovering for example that there was an active group in London led by the Belgian poet and collagist ELT Mesens, then 42, the friend and entrepreneur of Magritte, and the publisher of the pre-war *London Bulletin*. In the back of the *New Statesman* he found an advertisement for several recently published pamphlets and broadsheets, as well as a book of Mesens' own poetry and another by Paul Eluard, translated by someone called Roland Penrose. Tony had some money and I, as usual, wrote home for some, and we sent off for these in high anticipation.

Meanwhile, under Tony's sharp eye, life at HMS *Glendower* began to assume a more hallucinatory aspect. He was quick to recognise the potential, as 'a Surreal personage', of a boy I introduced him to with the curious name of Arding Jones, and it was he, rather than Tom, who became an intimate.

Arding Jones was as odd as his name. He was tall, hawk-like and with a really depressing acne-scarred skin. He'd been to public school and was superficially a traditional rugger-bugger, but he fancied only pretty working-class lads. To make his life more difficult, however, he was reduced to a ferocious rage by working-class accents irrespective of their region of origin, a dilemma he solved by taking out his fancy and spending a great deal of money on the pictures, beer, cinema, etc, *on condition the boy didn't open his mouth once*. Stranger still, he was never without a companion usually, to me, most enviably desirable. I had found this rather shocking, although I liked Arding well enough, but Tony relished the absurdity of it. The long silent evenings, full of loving glances, but with no verbal communication, he said, must be intensely erotic.

Among Arding's other peculiarities was his insistence on masturbating twice a day at exactly 11am and 3pm (or 1500hrs as the Navy insisted we call it). As a rule this presented little difficulty. If we were in class studying gunnery or semaphore signals, he would simply ask to go to 'the heads'. Occasionally however there would arise a situation which presented what one might imagine to be a more tricky problem. One morning we were all detailed off to help a local farmer thin out some root crop, and 10.45am found us isolated in the centre of an enormous field with another hour and a half to go before the lunch break. Amused expectations arose, for everybody knew of Arding's clocking-in time. At 11am precisely, he left the furrow, marched smartly a distance of some ten yards, lay down, undid the flap on the front of his working bellbottoms, and set to entirely uninhibited by our noisy encouragement, and appearing in no way disconcerted by our ironic applause at his success.

The final, and in some ways most unlikely, facet of Arding's character was a fierce republicanism. This was in no way unsympathetic to me, as a Surrealist and an Anarchist: the centrist argument that a monarch, above parliamentary or political affiliations, was the best defence against totalitarianism naturally held no weight. Even so Arding's ferocity, bordering on mania, astonished me. He wouldn't even refer to the King by name; he called him 'Korky the King', a form of alliteration he'd based on 'Korky the Cat', a character in the *Dandy* comic. In particular his subterfuges to avoid standing for the National Anthem, except when completely unavoidable as on the parade ground, went to any lengths and he would sooner miss the last five minutes of a film than remain at attention during what he always called 'Korky's tune'. Sometimes we were caught out; a film came to an end without the usual slow fade-out or give-away swelling chords, but even then he would rush agitatedly up the aisle muttering angry runes and imprecations like a vampire confronted with a crucifix. I felt obliged in his company to follow and, indeed, one night we ran into the erect form of a Warrant Officer who took our names and numbers, and we were reported and given three days' 'number elevens', that is to say, confined to camp and put through an hour of punitive drill to boot. Arding was in no way contrite. He blamed it all on Korky.

Arding liked neither jazz nor Surrealism but he, Tony and I spent a lot of time ashore together. Not that I deserted Tom. I went ashore with him too, but had to admit to myself that our evenings together lacked something of the hysterical and mythical quality of my nights with Arding and Tony.

Tony in his own right had begun to operate effectually. Strengthened by the Surrealist canon – for the books had arrived and we spent many hours absorbing their message – we both declared ourselves convinced atheists, and Tony's first practical demonstration of our new-found freedom from 'Judaeo-Christian mysticism' was to steal some bottles of admittedly unconsecrated Communion wine from the chapel, and we all got extremely and indeed disastrously drunk in his chalet.

We had also decided that we should write to Mesens in London pledging our fealty to Surrealism and, to this end, Tony began to make some beautiful if excessively Ernst-influenced collages – I remember one in which some Victorian sportsmen were engaged in shooting at a flying turtle – while I had begun to write poetry of what I hoped was a genuinely Surrealist flavour. 'The egg is always surrounded by birds,' one of my poems concluded. 'The gun by corpses, the bicycle by lovers / We are going to ascend in this ornate balloon / Much to the astonishment of the ladies and gents.'

When we had created enough collages and poems, we sent them off to the address printed on the Surrealist pamphlets and waited anxiously for a reply.

Meanwhile we strove, within the limits imposed by the Navy, to live the Surrealist life. There was, for example, the visit to the Abyssinian princesses. Rumours reached us from one of Arding's lads (for there was no embargo on their speaking to us when he himself wasn't within earshot) that in the nearby village of Criccieth, three young 'darkies' had been sighted riding their bicycles through the chapel-haunted streets. This in itself excited me. Through jazz, anyone black had become sacred and I was always writing home to tell my mother that I would marry only a negress, and that there was no question that if Bessie Smith had still been alive it would have been her. (How the Empress of the Blues would have reacted to my proposal never occurred to me then.)

A little later I found out something more concrete about the three girls. They were grand-daughters of the 'Lion of Judah', and this, as I explained to Tony Harris Reed, gave me an entrée. My father's cousin, John Melly, a witty life-loving man of strong Christian principles, had taken out, in his capacity as a doctor, the only British ambulance team during the Abyssinian war. He had unfortunately been killed on the very last day, shot by a drunken Ethiopian who'd mistaken him for an Italian, but he was considered to be a great hero by both the Emperor and his people. (There is a John Melly Street in Addis Ababa and a wing of the hospital is named after him.) We had, therefore, every excuse to call on the Lion's grand-cubs. I proposed that it would be truly 'Surreal' to visit them in a Welsh village wearing our best bellbottoms. Tony agreed and, on the next make-and-mend, we walked between the lush Welsh summer hedges to the little town and, after a couple of enquiries of extremely voluble locals, found our way to their modest lodgings.

A suspicious Welsh landlady with a small but definitive beard answered the door and, after listening to our explanation, showed us reluctantly into a small parlour while she went off to fetch the princesses' governess. It was a very Welsh parlour, hung with admonishing texts promising a far-from-reassuring future life. There was a table in the window with a potted fern on its dark-green bobble-edged cloth and many faded sepia photographs of the dead. What undid us though was a large Victorian steel engraving above the mantelshelf. It showed a small child wearing a nightgown and in the act of embracing a presumably symbolic sheep. The sheep in its turn regarded the child with what I presume the artist intended to be an expression of loving anthropomorphic piety but, to our eyes, it seemed almost grotesquely lascivious while at the same time extremely shifty. We began to giggle, and the sudden entrance of landlady and governess discovered us almost helpless with hysterical laughter. This made our task the harder. The governess was Scottish, with pale ginger hair and a forbidding expression, but we managed eventually to persuade her that I had a genuine reason for meeting her charges, and we were asked reluctantly to stay to tea.

This in fact proved quite a success. The princesses were very beautiful, their glowing black skins and fine features appearing doubly exotic in the dusty little dining room, with its ticking marble clock. They were also full of high spirits and Tony and I made them laugh a great deal so that even the governess allowed herself an occasional frosty smile. Indeed one joke led to a minor disaster. Princess Ruth, the youngest, had just swallowed a mouthful of orangeade when something Tony said caught her unawares and she performed the nose-trick.

'Dearie me!' said the governess, busy with a handkerchief. 'Poor Princess Ruth has been quite overcome.'

Our training continued, but became a little easier. On the cliffs at the edge of the camp we learnt to fire a mounted anti-aircraft machine-gun. Our instructor was a short and tubby Geordie Petty Officer who demonstrated the effectiveness of the weapon with a certain practical ferocity.

'Yer see that shite-hawk,' he said, pointing to a lone seagull flying from left to right across the middle distance. We agreed we did. He fired a short burst.

'Well now yer doant!' he told us with savage satisfaction. Tony and I wondered how many innocent shite-hawks had involuntarily sacrificed their lives in this way in the service of democracy.

One day, the war in Europe was over. It wasn't a night we were due to go ashore, nor was it an occasion I can especially remember. Everybody got rather drunk. Some chalet windows were broken and a few wire litter baskets set on fire. Next day training continued as usual. There were still the Japanese. The arrest of the chief Nazis, the discovery of the charred bodies of Hitler and Eva Braun in the Berlin bunker, seemed almost a logical and commonplace conclusion to the whole phantasmagoria. Tony and I felt more concerned about waiting to hear from the Surrealists in London.

We had meanwhile acquired an enemy, a Warrant Officer, the same man who had apprehended Arding and myself leaving the cinema during the National Anthem. He, disliking our levity, our background, and our rather flirtatious relationship with the Petty Officers, did what he could to harass us. One day Tony devised a very typical revenge.

We had found on the shore, during our long and excitable walks in pursuit of the 'marvellous', a large dead starfish and brought it back to camp. Then one of us put forward an idea for a Surrealist object. We would buy a common mousetrap and put the starfish in it as though it had been caught. This we did and so pleased were we with the effect that we decided to take it into Pwllheli and have it photographed – intending, if the result was satisfactory, to send a print to London in pursuit of the poems and collages and in the hope of expediting our yearned-for acknowledgement. Tony decided, however, that we could draw a subtle advantage from this activity. After making sure our enemy, the Warrant Officer, was to inspect the Liberty Men, he placed the object in an empty tickler tin and persuaded me to conceal it in my mackintosh pocket in so furtive and yet obvious a way as to lead to certain detection.

'Tickler' is naval slang for duty-free tobacco and in those days every rating was entitled at regular intervals to a large tin, at an extremely modest price. This was a great help financially but naturally enough, given the rarity of cigarettes in 'Civvy Street', there was a considerable temptation to smuggle one's ration ashore in order to sell it at an enormous profit, and to help dissuade us from this course the penalties, if we were caught, were correspondingly severe.

Tony knew that our enemy, the Warrant Officer, who always inspected us with particular thoroughness, would be sure to find the tin, and so he did.

'What have you got in that pocket, Seaman?'

'A tickler tin, sir.'

A grim smile of satisfaction spread across his face as he told me to pull it out. The rest of the Liberty Men were torn between resentment at being held up and pleasure in the discomfort of a fellow rating. Making much of it, I finally and apparently reluctantly pulled the tin out of my pocket. He asked me, very sarcastically, what was in it. I told him the exact truth – a star-fish caught in a mousetrap. A wild incredulous whoop of laughter rose from those near enough to hear my answer. It was relayed in whispers to those further down the ranks. Our enemy turned extremely red. He took the tin and opened it. He extracted our object. He looked at it, replaced it, and handed me back the tin. He next asked me why I was taking it out of the camp. 'To have it photographed, Sir,' I explained. More laughter. He ordered silence, completed his inspection and let us march ashore. Tony and I were cock-a-hoop. Our cruelty caused us not a moment's pause. Like schoolmasters, Warrant Officers were fair game. The photographs were unsuccessful; the local photographer, usually confined to the recording of weddings, funerals and Eisteddfods, was unwilling to accept the commission in the first place and the result, after we talked him into it, reflected his suspicious bewilderment.

At long last a short letter arrived for us from the Surrealist Group in London. It expressed interest in, if no great enthusiasm for, our work, and suggested that if either of us was in London in the future, we should contact the secretary, Simon Watson Taylor, at a Chelsea address. We were a little disappointed. We'd both hoped to receive something more positive, and we were depressed too that the letter was signed only by the secretary to the group, and not by ELT Mesens himself. Still at least we'd heard; at least we had an entrée.

Shortly afterwards we passed out as Ordinary Seamen, and after a few weeks hanging about as officers' messengers, or Quarter-masters' mates, we went sent home on a fortnight's leave. Tony, a Portsmouth rating alas, would then report to his home barracks, I to Chatham, a town I knew to be intoxicatingly close to London. I only hoped I would be stationed there long enough to make at least some initial contact with the Surrealist Group.

5

I arrived at Chatham barracks on a dank July evening. My hammock and kitbag weighed me down and I had bad dhobi itch as well. Dhobi itch is a weeping rash in the crutch caused by failing to rinse the suds out from one's underpants. It is a most dispiriting complaint.

I reported to the Petty Officer on duty. He told me the barracks were full and that I was to sleep on HMS *Argus*, a superannuated aircraft carrier rusting away in the dockyards adjoining the barracks, and which was in use as an overflow base. 'Don't bother to make yourself cushy though,' he advised me with a wolfish smile. 'We'll 'ave you out East before the fuckin' week's out.'

I tried to appear enthusiastic at this prospect, picked up my hammock and kitbag again, and walked bow-legged and in some discomfort through the dockyard gates in the direction indicated. Twenty breathless and sweaty minutes later I found the *Argus* looming up into the darkening drizzle, and staggered up the gangway on to the Quarter Deck. Formalities completed, I was shown my Mess Deck and later, after a revolting supper of what appeared to be camel's entrails, slung my hammock for the first time. Bearing in mind what the Petty Officer had promised, I left my kitbag packed. After a few days of digging about in it to find things I needed, I slowly transferred its contents to my locker. I was to remain on HMS *Argus* for over a year.

The *Argus*, as I soon discovered, was a den of skivers, misfits and lunatics, a floating, tethered thieves' kitchen. Our Captain, an elderly and scrawny religious maniac risen from the ranks, seldom left his cabin and could be heard, during the night watches, loudly declaiming the more bloodthirsty passages from the Old Testament. Despite his age and length of service, he was still – and understandably – a Lieutenant. The rest of the ship's company were all involved in a conspiracy to remain exactly where they were, tucked snugly away, a cosy and corrupt community dedicated to mutual aid. Among them I soon became friendly with an open-faced and charming rogue nicknamed Wings and after a short time I became his official winger. The expression 'winger' means, at its most innocent, a young seaman who is taken under the wing of a rating or Petty Officer older and more experienced than himself to be shown the ropes. It can also, although far from inevitably, imply a homosexual relationship, and in our case this was so, but on a comparatively playful and lighthearted level, mostly confined to rum-flavoured kisses when he returned on board.

Wings filled me in on many useful dodges. For example he advised me never to attend the regular pay parades in the barracks. At these parades suspicious marines stalked about seeking out ratings who might be posted to ships about to sail East. Far better to attend the miss-musters parade when those who had been on watch duty drew their money, and only a bored officer and an equally indifferent Petty Officer were present.

To ensure this end he advised me to land a watch-keeping job and I soon managed it. A friendly Chief Petty Officer made me a boatswain's mate. This proved to be chilly and monotonous; twenty-four hours on duty; four hours watch and watch about on the open Quarter Deck, checking the leave passes of ratings going on or coming off leave and saluting, and occasionally physically assisting aboard, the officers. The advantage was that after coming off duty I was entitled to forty-eight hours' shore leave – quite long enough to get up to London – and that every other weekend there was seventy-eight hours off, time enough for me to get up to Liverpool.

Wings had advice here too. As to London he suggested that, if I decided I had a future as 'rough trade', I should haunt either a pub in Victoria or another in Piccadilly. He himself had been successful in both of them. He told me that if picked up by an old queen who, in the morning, turned out to be less than generous, he usually knocked him about a bit and then walked off with whatever he fancied. He insisted that it was common practice and furthermore it was his view that 'most of the old buggers' expected it or even enjoyed it. I was really shocked at Wings and did not believe him, or at any rate chose not to. In another branch of petty criminal activity, however, he was to prove extremely helpful.

Getting to London presented no difficulty; it was quite cheap by train or you could hitch-hike. On the other hand, a return ticket to Liverpool was comparatively expensive and, with only four free travel warrants a year, it looked as though I should, yet again, have to cadge off my parents. 'No need,' said Wings when I had explained my dilemma, and he demonstrated an ingenious method whereby, with the aid of a local return ticket, ink remover, diluted Stephen's green ink, and some reliance on the dim lighting at station barriers and the senility of the wartime inspectors, you could get to any major provincial station and back for approximately five shillings. I practised this deception many times during my *Argus* period. So did many of my fellow ratings, but as far as I can remember no one was ever caught out.

You might wonder why, with London so close and ready to be explored and conquered, I should wish to return to Liverpool at all except for long leaves. The answer was that, while certain that in the end I would become the toast of the town, I realised it might take a little time and meanwhile it was a solace to be able to return home where my mother's unfailing belief in my eventual triumph, the comfort of friends, the admiration of my fourteen-year-old sister and, above all, the familiar port heavy with childhood associations, would help to restore my confidence. To be frank I was a little in awe of London; a state fostered equally by my father's reluctance to visit it except when his business as a woolbroker had positively demanded it, and my mother's pre-war expeditions which, on her return, loaded with toys from Hamley's, she painted in the most brilliant of colours. 'I did eight shows in six days,' she'd tell us excitedly, 'and went three times to the Savoy Grill with Rex Evans [a night-club owner and performer of the period] and had lunch at the Ivy twice with dear Bobby.' It sounded rather formidably sophisticated. Also, every time we went to our dentist, a Mr Williams who had his surgery, like many of the medical profession in Liverpool, in Rodney Street, a rather beautiful Georgian terrace, she would say that they were 'just like London houses'. Sitting tipped back in Mr Williams's dentist chair, while he chattered to my mother about the latest production at the Playhouse and did painful things inside my mouth, I would imagine that the sky over London must look much as it did above the opposite side of the street and, as I was to recognise much later, the word 'London' had become subconsciously associated, and a little anxiously, with dentistry.

It was therefore with a certain tentative apprehension that I began to explore the metropolis. It was true that I had visited it once before. When I was ten, Emma Holt, a rich and kindly cousin of my grandfather, had offered us a choice: she would either pay for my father to take my brother and me up to watch King George VI's coronation procession from a balcony in the Mall or, if we would prefer it, we could spend a whole week in the capital later in that same year. After some debate we chose the latter, stayed with an aunt in a flat overlooking the river at Barnes, and exhausted my poor father by racing round the zoo, Madame Tussaud's, the Tower and other traditional 'sights'. There was however little to compare between this protected and sponsored expedition as a child and my return, almost nine years later, as a solitary seaman. It's true that there were relations of my mother's living in flats, mainly in genteelly unfashionable areas, and friends of hers too with more central addresses and connected with the arts, but obstinately, before contacting anybody – even the Surrealists – I wanted to get at least the feel of the place, to establish at any rate the broadest outline of its central geography, and so for the first month I did little more than walk the streets, visit the museums or, getting on a tube train, travel at random, emerging from any station familiar by name, usually because it figured in 'Monopoly'.

I also tried to follow Wings' example (we never went 'up the Smoke' together, as for one thing he was on the opposite watch from me and, for another, he considered, quite rightly, that my middle-class effeminacy would reduce his impact as rough trade). Perhaps for this very reason I was not a success with the corseted and discreetly rouged old gentlemen who combed the gay pubs. Occasionally one of them would offer me a half of Guinness, but he would soon lose interest and move towards a more masculine fellow seaman or haughty guardsman, leaving me to my *New Statesman* at the marble-topped bar. While rather hurt, I was not entirely unrelieved either. The point was that, while coming on as what Bessie Smith called 'a skippin' twistin' woman-actin' man', my real taste was also for butch young men, but with myself in the masculine role. Much later a perceptive if rather coarse-minded rating expressed this with obscenely poetic exactitude: 'You're not a brown 'atter at all,' he said. 'You're an arse-bandit what acts like 'e was a brown 'atter!'

One night, it's true, I did make a conquest. Having forgotten to book in at the Union Jack Club (1/6d a night), I was sitting shivering on a seat in Leicester Square when a small, middle-aged respectable-looking man wearing glasses and a Crombie overcoat approached me. After offering me a cigarette, he followed it up with a sofa, which I accepted, in his flat in Dolphin Square. I wasn't deceived by the sofa and was glad to be warm and comfortable, but wished he had not brushed his teeth so thoroughly as the taste of Gibbs' Dentifrice was overwhelming. At breakfast in the dining room next morning, for I was on a forty-eight hour pass, I had the mild jitters as I knew that somewhere in that huge 1930 rabbit warren of flats there lived a great friend of my mother, an elderly and obsessively respectable actress who would certainly feel it her duty to report back. That morning, however, she must have taken her breakfast in her flat (Meissen figurines and old playbills), and I left fed and rested for the Victoria and Albert Museum. My closet queen made no effort to arrange another meeting, nor did he offer me 'a present'. I was clearly a final resort; a sheep in wolf's clothing. He would have much preferred Wings and his ilk. For my part I looked speculatively round his flat. What would Wings have taken? The ivory-handled hairbrush? The heavy 'portable' wireless? It was purely academic. The idea of threatening someone of approximately my own class who, that toothpaste flavoured half-hour apart, had behaved like a kindly if boring uncle or friendly housemaster was out of the question.

Once I'd established what I thought of as 'the magic square' – that is to say the relative positions of Regent Street, Oxford Street, Park Lane and Piccadilly – I felt secure enough to begin to ring people up. At first it was cousins of my mother; gentle middle-class, middle-aged Jewish ladies who had a spare bed or at least a sofa, but later, as the parks, Soho and Chelsea assumed their approximate location on my mental map, I took to visiting her more artistic friends: a theatrical producer with a flat in the King's Road, a butch actor and, above all, David Webster who had just come down from Liverpool, to a chorus of vicious screeching from most of the musical establishment, to take up his position as Managing Director of Covent Garden.

I had known David since I was a little boy and like most of my mother's circle had been encouraged to call him Uncle David, a form of address which, now that I was about the same age as many of his younger friends, I was firmly forbidden to employ.

David was and always had been plump, he had gone bald early; my parents had known him from a very young man and told me that he had always looked exactly the same. He was not especially scrupulous about his person: his nails were, as my mother said, 'in mourning', his suits, while well cut, had their collars powdered with dandruff. This was of no importance, however, because he had been born almost unfairly endowed with charm and wit. In the Liverpool of the Twenties and Thirties he ruled the artistic roost. The son of small Scottish shopkeepers (and although in many ways extremely snobbish, he'd never tried to hide them away or upgrade his social origins), he soon proved himself to be brilliant in many directions and with particular flair and feeling for the arts. After graduating from Liverpool University, he'd become extremely active, directing and acting in plays. 'His feet,' said my mother describing his appearance as Becket in Eliot's *Murder in the Cathedral*, 'were none too clean.' He'd also taken part in cabarets organised by the members of The Sandon, a club connected with the arts, and here his appearance as Epstein's *Genesis* in labour under a green spotlight was long remembered. But it was more probably his chairmanship of the Liverpool Philharmonic which had led to his present, much questioned, position.

Unlike his parents he hadn't a trace of Scottish accent, but there was a certain precision combined with richness in his delivery which hinted at his Caledonian roots, and eliminated any possibility of a Liverpudlian background. He had, from early in his life, cultivated the friendship of artists and writers. Edith Sitwell sent him her books with warm dedications on the fly-leaves and he had a great many amusing stories to tell about his various encounters with Mrs

Patrick Campbell in her later years. His house, in a Victorian suburb of Liverpool, seemed to me, as a child, the essence of sophistication. The drawing-room had a white carpet, there was a Matthew Smith still-life over the grand piano and, lounging elegantly about, beautiful young men, all of whom were creative in some way. This one played the piano, that one designed ballet sets. Outside, the sunlight itself seemed less raw, more urbane, than anywhere else in Liverpool.

David, however, believed in work. He needed money to defend his life-style and was not ashamed to earn it in commerce. To this end he had risen to become Managing Director of Bon Marché, Liverpool's most fashionable big store. I adored Bon Marché. The ground floor smelt of scent and rich furs and here too, shopping with my mother, one was most likely to come upon Uncle David sampling the home-made chocolates, for he was, it must be admitted, extremely greedy.

Both chocolates and David Webster figured in my first grown-up homosexual experience. Early in the war, while still at Stowe, I had been asked to act the role of Lady Macbeth; it was to be directed by Professor G Wilson Knight, the distinguished, if eccentric, Shakespearean scholar who was at that time one of the strangely assorted staff. I learnt the part in the holidays and, wishing to appear one-up on my return to school, asked David if he would give me some advice. He had himself directed and played Macbeth some years before, casting my mother, who was in fact rather irritated not to have played Lady Macbeth, as the third witch. Sixteen years old and alone with David in his drawing-room . . .

'I have given suck and know how sweet it is . . .'

'More passion, dear. You sound as if you are opening a garden féte. Have another chocolate.' For, despite rationing, there was a big box on the low glass table and they were proper chocolates too, each in its little crinkly nest and some of them wrapped in gold paper.

Then, when we'd finished, he kissed me on the mouth. I hadn't really enjoyed it, but revelled in the idea of it. Since I was thirteen, I'd been making eyes at all my mother's friends I knew to be gay and finally one of them had responded, so I ran home to tell my ten-year-old sister. I'd already sold her the glamour of homosexuality and we'd go for long walks in the parks appraising the raga-muffins in their torn jerseys. 'How much more beautiful,' I'd say to her, 'is the word "boy" than the word "girl",' and she, flattered to receive my attention and confidences, would solemnly agree.

Now, via a wartime stint at the Ministry of Production under Sir Stafford Cripps, David had left Bon Marché for the Garden to prepare for its re-opening after its wartime metamorphosis into a dance-hall. He had moved into an impressive modern house near the BBC. The attacks on him were both underhand – 'the homosexual haberdasher' was a particularly snobbish epithet – and unrealistic. He knew, after all, a great deal about opera and ballet and he had many friends in both worlds. Furthermore, through his experience in running a big store, he had a grasp of business, of costing, of handling people in organisations, which was denied to the more obvious candidates for the job.

When I rang him the first time, he was kindness itself and immedi-ately asked me round for a drink. I felt able from then on to call him whenever I wanted to, while at the same time aware that it would be a mistake to presume too often. Despite Lady Macbeth and the chocolates, I was not really his type. Partially to my relief, partially bruising to my vanity, he never made a pass at me again.

6

My real reason for not contacting the Surrealist Group immediately
was that I feared – as I still fear – rejection, and reading the
formal, icy attacks of André Breton on those he found inadequate
or hypocritical (a style of vituperation echoed in those English
pamphlets which Tony and I had pored over in Pwllheli) in no way
reassured me. The thing was that I believed – and to this day still
tend to believe – that everybody shares my obsessions. For example,
on one of my first visits to London, I had approached a policeman
in Regent Street and asked him, to his justifiable astonishment,
where Freddie Mirfield and his Garbage Men were playing that
night. Mr Mirfield had only made one record, a rather weak
approximation to Chicago jazz, although in retrospect of some
historical interest in that among the other Garbage Men was a very
young clarinettist called Johnny Dankworth. It is very likely that
the band was a pick-up group, certainly they never made another
record, and yet I took it for granted that, because I knew about them,
they would be playing every night in London at some well-known
dance-hall. In the same way I visualised the Surrealists, those
wizards who at any moment were about to change the world, as
occupying a large headquarters hung with masterpieces, full of
studios where some people painted or constructed objects and
others wrote poetry of crystalline purity or issued manifestos of
impeccable revolutionary fervour, and where rooms were set aside
for acts of erotic delirium.

I hesitated, therefore, to ring up Simon Watson Taylor at his
Flaxman number, believing that I might be found wanting immediately, denounced for wearing a uniform, or unmasked as a homosexual, a deviation I gathered Breton disapproved of because of the
frivolity and aesthetic freemasonry of people like Cocteau and their

tendency to exploit the more superficial aspects of Surrealism for purely fashionable ends. I didn't admit to this reasoning, pretending to myself that it was important to wait until Tony Harris Reed could join me, and to this end wrote to him frequently to establish a date when he had both sufficient leave and sufficient money to make the journey up from Portsmouth. He answered noncommittally but the truth was that, although later on he did meet Mesens on one occasion, his enthusiasm was already waning and he had begun to apply his sardonic concentration to another of his interests – racing. Comparatively soon, we lost touch, but I met him some years later in a pub, dressed in the loudest of checks, and earning his living as a newspaper tipster, calling himself Major in line with his profession.

In the end, therefore, I plucked up my courage and rang Simon Watson Taylor from a phone box in Chatham dockyard. He sounded polite if rather abrupt and I arranged to go to his Chelsea flat the following Saturday at midday. It was my usual custom then, if the weather was fine, to hitch-hike into London from the outskirts of Rochester. It was too unreliable a method to risk on the way back because one had to report on board at a specified time, but drivers, both commercial and civilian, were still generously disposed to picking up servicemen and it saved quite a lot of money. That day, nervous but excited, clasping my ditty box, I left the dockyard and was soon sitting high up next to an old lorry driver whose false teeth were so poor a fit you could hear them forming fours above the roar of the engine. As he had to turn off towards the docks at Blackheath he dropped me at the top of the hill that falls away towards New Cross, and I stood there looking down at the bomb-scarred city below me glittering in the winter sun. In my ditty box were a bottle of ink, a pen, a grubby towel, a sponge bag and a new poem typed on a naval typewriter on pink paper. It was called 'The Heir':

> Naked, he makes small red tears.
> A monster (with beautiful eyes and hands),
> Who blames his father.

I felt like a Surrealist Dick Whittington, and a little later thumbed a lift in a car that dropped me off at Charing Cross where, after a few minutes at the stop outside the anti-vivisectionists' headquarters, I caught a number 11 bus to Chelsea and rang the bell of Simon's flat in Markham Square.

Simon was a few years older than I. He was small but neatly made, full of aggressive energy fuelled by alcohol, controlled by discipline. He was dressed in a well-cut conservative tweed suit with an expensive shirt and tie. His eyes blazed with intelligence. His hair was short, cut *en brosse* by an excellent barber. His humour was icy. I found him impressive and rather intimidating. His flat, however, was something of a disappointment. There were a few etchings by Miró and Dali but little sense of fantasy and the furniture, while comfortable, was banal in the extreme. We talked for some time and I, in my usual, parrot-like wish to make appropriate noises, declared my adherence to Surrealism in a solemn style deriving from the translations of Breton's ornate classic French into a rather stilted English. Simon listened to me with sardonic kindness and only when, to curry favour further, I attacked homosexuality did he correct me by saying that several of the greatest Surrealists, Crevel for a start, had been queer or at any rate bi-sexual and that it was only Breton who had found it necessary to rationalise his own feelings of repulsion towards that particular deviation. The only trouble with the human body, Simon said, was that there were not enough holes in it for the exploration of human pleasure.

I must have been maddening, but it was clear after an hour that he had taken a liking to me and a friendship was established that has lasted to this day.

It seemed to me perfectly natural that after a time he should open a cupboard on whose shelves were neatly arranged, each in its cardboard cover, the most enormous and amazing collection of rare 78rpm jazz and blues records including many original Bessie Smiths. As he was a Surrealist, I thought, *of course* he'd like jazz. He declared his belief in Anarchism too, and promised to introduce me to the London Anarchist Group some of whom had only recently been released from prison for causing disaffection among the troops through their publication *Freedom*. I expressed my eagerness, but was even more excited when he suggested that I might attend the next Surrealist 'séance' the following Monday in a private dining room of the Barcelona Restaurant, Beak Street.

He had an appointment in the afternoon; somehow Simon's appointments always impressed me as very portentous and serious; but first he offered me lunch and we walked along King's Road to a rather disgusting little restaurant (even by the standards of the time) called the Bar-B-Cue where we ate Spanish omelettes under a poor mural of cowboys roping steers. I was, I must admit, in a state of delirious excitement at lunching with the secretary of the Surrealist Group in England.

In the Bar-B-Cue was an extraordinary figure, surrounded by an admiring circle of bohemians, whom we joined for coffee. 'Mr Watson Taylor,' said this person, 'sit down and tell me the story of your life, and introduce me to your friend in bellbottoms.' It was obvious to me that Simon, while heterosexual himself, knew this man. I had made a considerable tactical error in assuming that all the Surrealists shared Breton's mistrust of deviation. His name was Quentin Crisp and he was then I should guess in his middle thirties. Being in Chelsea he was unshaven and rather grubby, the nail varnish on both finger and toe nails, the latter peeping through gilt sandals, cracked and flaked, his mascara in need of attention, his lipstick of renewal. He had, however, a wistful, frail beauty and a wicked wit. His hair was henna red, a common enough sight now but unseen then on ostensibly male heads. I thought him extraordinary and suspected – rightly so as it turned out – that he must have the courage of a lioness to walk the streets of London. Indeed, he was frequently insulted, sometimes assaulted and now and then was in trouble with the law who objected, not to any overt act, for there he was very discreet, but to his appearance in general.

My equation of Chelsea with grubbiness may seem too broad a generalisation, but it was exact in relation to Quentin. He lived in an amazingly squalid room somewhere off King's Road and in the quarter saw no reason to do more than slap cosmetics over the grime. When visiting North Soho, however, his other habitat, he was always clean and chic, first bathing in a friend's flat – for he had no running water of his own – and then applying his make-up with impeccable art. We became friends instantly (I'm not denying that the sailor suit may have been something of a turn-on), and when Simon left for his appointment, Quentin suggested we went to the cinema to see 'one of Miss Hayworth's films'. And so we did, arousing many a curious glance. Later, like Quentin, I too added the Bohemian cafés and pubs of Charlotte Street to the diverse worlds available to me on leave, but for the moment I thanked him for taking me to the pictures and took a bus to South Kensington to visit an old school friend of mine called Robin Westgate, a Lieutenant in the Guards. We had a nice dinner and I stayed the night in his parents' sparsely furnished London flat, but there was hardly a moment when I wasn't thinking about my meeting with the Surrealists the following Monday.

I was actually meant to be on watch that day, but so adaptable was life aboard the *Argus* that I was able to come to an arrangement with my 'oppo'; he was carrying on with a married lady in Gillingham whose husband worked nights on Tuesday so it suited him very well.

I went up to London around noon and spent some hours in the Victoria and Albert Museum looking at original Lautrec posters in the Print Room. I forget who'd told me about the Print Room but it was open to the public and they brought you whatever you wanted to examine. This fulfilled several functions in my London life at that moment. Firstly it was free so it was a way of staying warm and interested during the day and saving the evenings, as I had done in Wetherby, for drinking and, with luck, debauchery. Secondly, I could examine, in the original, the work of artists who interested me, and linked to that, but rather shamingly, I was aware of the effect of a sailor in bellbottoms asking for comparatively esoteric artefacts, thereby astonishing and pleasing the librarians and the elderly scholars. 'So you're a Tiepolo fan too,' one of them had said on a previous visit. The Lautrecs, however, were not such a good idea. What I hadn't realised was that some of the posters, which I'd known only in postcard reproductions or in the meagre little books of the period, were very large and I had to have the librarian's help in spreading them out, thereby incommoding the gentlemen examining Persian miniatures or Fuseli drawings, forcing them to move, grumbling, into the corners of the room.

When they closed the Print Room I caught a tube from South Kensington reading, with mounting excitement, one of the Surrealist publications I carried everywhere, and filled in the time in a news theatre and various pubs, in many of which I was stood drinks. Then at eight o'clock precisely, for I had earlier made an expedition to be sure exactly where it was, I entered the restaurant and asked the plump Spanish proprietor where the Surrealists met. 'Mr Mesens,' said the man, 'he go upstairs but no one arrive yet.' To retreat? No, I thought, better go up and drink a glass of wine. I was sure it would be taken as a sign of enthusiasm and commitment. I walked up into a rather dingy room with a large table and sat down at one of the laid places. I was a little drunk from excitement and the beers I'd swallowed. I thought of the pre-war Surrealist 'séances' at the Café de la Place Blanche in Montmartre. The magisterial Breton, Paul Eluard, Aragon before his traitorous defection to Soviet Communism, Max Ernst, 'the most marvellously haunted mind in Europe', Peret, Miró, Souppault; all those names I had read of, learnt, and in the main mispronounced, from the Herbert Read anthology I had discovered in that Liverpool bookshop.

Mesens, too, with his insistence on the use of his three initials, ELT, friend of Magritte, editor of the *London Bulletin*, the magazine in which I had first clapped eyes on a reproduction of *Le Viol*, he would actually be here! I drank three glasses of very sour red wine in quick succession.

There were voices, foreign voices, on the stairs. I forget who came first but I remember everybody who attended that delirious evening: Simon of course, and his sister Sonia, who wore her hair in what would now be called an 'Afro' and had a black boyfriend, Antonio Pedro, a Portuguese painter; two young Turkish poets, Sadi Cherkeshi and Feyyuz Fergar; the writer-cinéaste Jacques Brunius, pipe-smoking, with a long, intelligent, melancholy face and a seductive French accent; and Edith Rimmington, a rather cosy-looking lady whose pictures were nevertheless disturbingly sexual in impact. There were also various girlfriends, all of whom seemed to me extraordinarily glamorous and, I speculated, probably expert in the more erotic games of love and then, finally, ELT Mesens and his wife Sybil, he apologising in a strong Belgian accent for being late due to the difficulty of finding a taxi in Hampstead. My eyes shone, my spirits soared. I muttered to myself the famous image from Lautréamont: 'As beautiful as the chance meeting of an umbrella and a sewing machine on the dissecting table.'

ELT Mesens, a name which, since Tony and I had first come across it in our pamphlets, seemed to carry an increasingly mysterious weight, was at first sight not especially impressive. Aged then about forty – 'I was born in 1903 without God, without King, AND WITHOUT RIGHTS!' – shortish, plump, neatly if conservatively dressed, meticulously shaved and manicured, his shoes well polished, his hair oiled and brushed back, he had the look of a somewhat petulant baby or of a successful continental music-hall star. His wife Sybil was about five years younger, a handsome, slightly gypsyish woman with an olive skin and fine aquiline features dressed, for that austerely shabby time, with fashionable reticence. Together they presented a certain urbanity far removed (with the exception of Simon, whose style was more suggestive of a country squire visiting London for the day), from the comfortable shabbiness of the other Surrealists. It's true that Edith Rimmington had an expensive fur coat, but she seemed so cosy and provincial, not unlike some of my mother's less dashing Liverpudlian friends, that its effect was negated. Sybil didn't seem cosy at all. She had something of the tension of a beautiful bird of prey, and ELT, despite Simon's carefully thrown away introduction, soon established himself as the most formidable figure there. He shook hands with me (this hand I'm shaking has touched that of Breton) and sat down, as if by right, at the head of the table. The boss of the restaurant came up and took our orders for which we all contributed a pound; there was a law in force which forbade a restaurateur to charge more than five shillings per head, but by adding whatever the patron thought the client would accept to pay for wine or cover charge, this was easily sabotaged. Feeling like a very minor and impoverished disciple at the Last Supper, I ate my way through a rather under-populated paella, straining my ears the while to try and catch what Mesens was saying at the other end of the table, and chatting to those on either side of me. The girl on my left was Sadi Cherkeshi's mistress. She had short hair and a friendly gamine appeal, but it became clear to me that her principal interest in Surrealism lay behind the Turkish poet's flies. Antonio Pedro proved more willing to listen to my questions and explain who everybody was and what they did, and I was also extremely amused by his vivid Portuguese English. I remember him, that first evening, declining trifle for pudding – 'It is the 'orrible custard and the bread of yesterday' – and also answering my query as to whether the scream of cats in sexual congress on an adjacent Beak Street roof-top was caused by pleasure or pain with: 'Pleasure for the cat, and pain for the cattess' .

Yet cats and custard apart, I cannot truthfully say I can describe exactly what was said and done that first evening, partly because I was rather drunk and a bit mad with excitement at being there at all, but chiefly because as, over the next few months, I managed to wangle almost every Monday off, I attended most of those evenings at the Barcelona Restaurant, and while certain monumental rows, solemn games, mass ejection by the proprietor, messages from abroad, discussions over future activities or publications, even expulsions took place, it now seems, almost thirty years later, as though it were one long evening instead of a series taking place in the few months between the end of the German war, and the dropping of the first atomic bomb.

When I first heard it, the expression a 'Surrealist séance' seemed totally confusing. It suggested table-tapping, trumpets in bird-cages, yards of regurgitated cheese-cloth, and the shrill voices of child guides. I wondered if the intention was to evoke such phantoms as Lop-Lop, Max Ernst's bird–king, or the disturbing spheroid-headed 'personages' of de Chirico. I subsequently discovered that the French meaning of the word was simply 'a meeting', and yet there remained something mysterious about those Mondays. They did indeed reflect a certain spiritual state of mind.

After eating, drinking and general conversation, Mesens would propose a subject. Although he had come to England in 1936 and lived here ever since, he had retained his strong Belgian accent and, despite a wide and vividly-used vocabulary, constructed his sentences as if they were in French. He particularly enjoyed provoking noisy disagreements. One of the more memorable arose out of his suggestion, couched more in the nature of a command, that no member of the group should write or draw for anything except official Surrealist publications. This was all very well for him; his war-work for the Belgian section of the BBC over, he was preparing, with financial backing, to reopen in new premises the gallery he had run before the war; but many of the rest relied on journalism to a greater or lesser extent: Brunius, for example, wrote on the history of the cinema, and even I had begun to review art exhibitions for the *Liverpool Daily Post* at a guinea a time. The opposition to ELT's near-edict was vociferous and prolonged, and included many threats of resignation and counter-threats of expulsion. In the end, however, the breach was healed.

Most meetings were calmer. I enjoyed especially playing 'Exquisite Corpses', the Surrealist version of 'Heads, Bodies and Tails' combined with Consequences. Opening one of these I discovered someone had written 'Love is fucking' as their contribution. I was astounded. Who could it have been? I looked around at these grown-ups, serious people, some of them the same age as my parents. In the Navy of course the use of the word as an adjective was monotonously obligatory, but here it was used precisely, with deliberation. 'Love is fucking.' I couldn't get over it although I was careful not to betray my astonishment.

After I had served my apprenticeship, Mesens encouraged me to read my poems aloud. These, written aboard the *Argus* during the night watches, offered me an opportunity to dramatise which I was not slow to take up. In one poem there was a line: 'You are advised to take with you an umbrella in case it should rain knives and forks'. One evening I collected a great deal of cutlery from a sideboard and, on reaching the image, hurled them into the air. The effect was very satisfactory, the noise formidable, but while the Surrealists' applause was still resounding in my gratified ears, the proprietor of the Barcelona rushed up the stairs and ejected us all. Mesens was delighted as this gave him, and others, the opportunity to indulge in that other Surreal tradition, 'the gratuitous act', in this case insult. Later in the week the proprietor, not wishing to lose the custom of so large a party on a regular basis, made it up and we were allowed back.

Another near-disaster for which I was responsible took place in the street when we had left the restaurant. I proposed that we should go to a telephone box, choose a number at random and, if and when the subscriber picked up the phone, recite a line from a Surrealist text and then replace the receiver. This was enthusiastically received but when, as the originator of the prank, I was assuring a puzzled gentleman in Ealing that 'The stones are full of guts. Hurrah! Hurrah!' (Jean Arp), a policeman approached and asked to see the identity cards or passports of all present. His confusion was absolute, his desire to translate it into some punitive action apparent. What was a British sailor doing with a group of people of Turkish, Belgian, French and Portuguese origin? However, all our papers were in order and, as I'd hurriedly severed my connection with the crossly perplexed ratepayer in W5, there was nothing he could do except tell us to move on.

After some months the meetings began to be less well attended. Simon who, despite the fact that he was the most aggressive in combating ELT, was also the most active member when it came to organisation, went away to the Middle East as part of a touring company, entertaining the troops in a production of *Pink String and Sealing Wax*, for he was at that time an actor. Mesens himself was becoming more and more involved in the renaissance of the London Gallery. A lease had been taken on a five-storeyed Georgian building in Brook Street. It was narrow, very pretty if rickety, and in considerable disrepair. The long fight for permits and the frustrating search for building materials were beginning, but the Mesens were soon able to move into the top-floor flat and as by this time I had become very much their protégé, I had another place where I was welcome, another settee where I could sleep.

The meetings became fortnightly, then monthly and eventually ceased altogether, but I didn't really care. I was now 'le petit marin' and, ELT assured me, certain to make my mark on the Surrealist movement. He added that not everybody in the group held this view however. One, whom he refused to name, said that he thought I 'would never be more than the English Cocteau'. I assumed indignation, but was actually rather pleased.

I now had several earths and, fox-like, chose to keep moving. The Mesens' was certainly the most comfortable and not only was Sybil an excellent and imaginative cook but I was also taken quite often to dine at a restaurant of which I had heard my mother speak in awed tones, The Ivy. Here I was amazed to find that the bill could be as high as thirty shillings a head without wine, and was equally surprised at the amount of time ELT and Sybil were prepared to invest in deciding what to eat.

Back in their flat I helped hang some of ELT's remarkable collection (the bulk of it had been stored in the cellars of the Palais des Beaux Arts in Brussels where it had luckily escaped the attention of the occupying and modern-art-hating Nazis), and at last was able to examine at close quarters those painters I had admired so passionately. While we worked, washing glass smeared with the dust of six years, spraying and revarnishing canvases from which the images emerged with renewed clarity, he talked to me about the old and heady days in Paris and Brussels: about Ernst's near-murderous jealousy of Miró, of Tanguy's drinking habits, of Magritte's meticulously bourgeois life-style. I was enthralled, yet I didn't choose to spend all my time there. For one thing I was worried that I might overstay my welcome. Edouard, even in those days, was a heavy drinker and, in drink, of uncertain temper. For another I was eager for experience both sexual and social, and the Mesens lived, I then thought, rather too ordered and domestic a life to satisfy me. For example I was extremely impressed to discover in his collection Magritte's *Le Viol*, that representation of a woman's body replacing her face, which had struck me as so marvellous when I had come across it reproduced in the *London Bulletin* in the art-school library at Stowe but, when I offered to hang it, Sybil refused. At the time I thought this mere prudery. The idea that she might dislike it on the grounds that it reduced her sex to a purely physical cipher never occurred to me.

London was beginning to acquire a meaning, a pattern. I found myself fleeing to my Liverpudlian womb less often. The kindly elderly Jewish cousins, no doubt to their relief, saw me infrequently. Not so however a connection of my father's family, a girl, some seven years older than myself, whom I imagined to be the black sheep of the family. Her name was Paulie Rawdon Smith, the daughter of a rather stuffy Liverpool doctor. Meeting her by chance on my way to the Victoria and Albert Print Room, I discovered she had a mews flat close by where I was welcome any time. It was with Paulie that I came to know the pubs and cafés of Soho, re-meeting in this context the immaculately clean Quentin Crisp: 'Mr Melly, I've been led to understand that Miss Rawdon Smith is your cousin.' Here too I came to know many a famous old Bohemian bore such as Iron Foot Jack, with his pocketful of yellowing press-cuttings.

Jack, dressed in a wide hat, cloak and knotted scarf and smelling like a goat in rut, claimed that his six-inch iron foot was the result of losing part of his leg to a passing shark, an unlikely explanation as he had retained the foot itself. He had a juicy Cockney accent, boasted of occult powers, and lived with a series of old crones whom he used as an excuse for hinting at a Crowleyan sexual virility. 'There are occult practices,' he told me every time we met, 'that it is best the general public know nuffink abaht. When I had my stewdyo in Museum Street . . .' More interesting was a woman called the Countess Duveen, old and bent, with some indication of a former beauty. She spoke in a grand but rasping voice, kept herself going on the insides of benzedrine inhalers and cadged cups of tea, earning her living from scavenging in dustbins or on bomb sites. She sold me a carved wooden bird of East European peasant origin for sixpence. It had once had a string which, when pulled, made its head jerk up and down to suggest that it was pecking grain, but the string had long since perished and the head sagged permanently forward. 'Isn't it a saucy pussy!' the Countess had cried by way of sales talk. I resisted buying what she described as 'a hand-sewn gentleman's kid glove' on the grounds that I had two hands. 'I think,' she announced despairingly, 'that I know where I can find the other one.'

Quentin, Iron Foot Jack and the Countess Duveen confined themselves to seedy cafés chosen for how long you could stay there without buying more than the odd cup of tea. In the pubs, especially The Fitzroy and The Wheatsheaf, I met a less derelict collection. The occasional *bona fide* lion I recognised but never dared approach: old Augustus John with his baleful swivelling eye, Dylan Thomas oozing drink and talking frenetically in his parsonical, obscenity-larded posh Welsh bray. Others seemed more accessible: Maclaren Ross with his cloak and silver-topped cane, Nina Hamnet, rushing impulsively from one watering-hole to another for fear of missing out on something. My old schoolmaster, John Davenport who, depending on how drunk he was, would either hug me warmly or cut me dead, and a variety of queens, anonymous earbenders, young painters, writers and poets, and the more commercially-minded sectors of the armed forces, mostly sailors or guardsmen.

It was a scruffy, warm, belching, argumentative, groping,

spewing-up, cadging, toothbrush-in-pocket, warm-beer-gulping world which I found less taxing if also less stimulating than the Surrealist ambience. I slept occasionally with a man who made masks. He had amazingly tragic blue eyes, stubble under his make-up and smelt of pungent but not unpleasant sweat. He lived in Frith Street in a tatty but inventive flat with bare boards, shawls, incense, and his own artefacts grimacing in gilded candle-lit rictus anguish: a setting which twenty years later would have seemed a commonplace hippy pad, but at the time was, for me at any rate, unique. Here, after the pubs and coffee shops closed, a tough homosexual world gathered to bitch in the accents of Birmingham or Newcastle. As dawn broke we would all collapse in each other's arms on stained mattresses under grimy blankets which had been 'liberated' from hospitals by a skeletal consumptive boy who worked as a porter at the Middlesex. I should say my cousin Paulie was not part of this scene.

However, it was with Paulie that I first discovered the Caribbean Club in Denman Street. This place, a lobby bar and a low but large room with a bandstand at one end, was primarily West Indian, with a few black GIs and some white members, mostly girls of rather painful refinement whom in retrospect I imagine to have been tarts. The owner, Rudi, was one of those between-the-war blacks whose English was exaggeratedly Oxbridge, whose clothes were excessively formal, and who once a night would sing, in the rich baritone of Paul Robeson, such sophisticated night club ballads as 'East of the Sun and West of the Moon'. The rest of the music was more jazz-oriented. A trio led by Dick Katz, smiling like Carroll's Cheshire Cat, played a selection of tunes ranging from Fats Waller to the newly emergent Bebop. Sometimes I would sing a blues, tolerated by the clientèle for my gauche sincerity. The man at the door called me 'Admiral'; the barmaid, as long as I had money to drink with, allowed me to flirt with her. I was eventually given an honorary membership. 'Now,' I thought to myself, 'I've really made it. I am a member of a London Club!'

Another bed, or in this case two chairs, I found in Margaretta Street, Chelsea, in the room of the Turkish Surrealist poet, Sadi Cherkeshi. Unlike Simon, who tended to put me off by explaining that 'his mistress' was staying the night and it would therefore be 'inconvenient', Sadi didn't mind me lying in the dark, ears agog, listening to him screwing his girl. I felt no end of a liberated, tolerant and, to be frank, stimulated creature in this role. In the end, however, it was the household which was to prove more central to my life. At its head was an elderly man called Bill Meadmore who wrote biographies, ghosted memoirs and worked for Customs and Excise. Long-haired and irascible, married to a kindly, quietly realistic, humorous woman called Dumps, he was the progenitor of three daughters and the owner of two unreliable cats. Bill and I found ourselves on immediate terms. Not that we agreed about anything. Bill, despite Sadi and, before him, Simon as lodgers, hated Surrealism and indeed modern art in general. He liked Sickert and, in lieu of the means to buy his paintings, had acquired the work of his followers, in particular those of Clifford Hall, a gruff, bearded man with whom I had many a furious argument stimulated, when there was any danger of it flagging, by Bill's mischievous intervention. It seemed inevitable that one morning, on going to the bathroom, I should come upon Quentin Crisp relaxing in an unpatriotically full tub, Bill Meadmore's being one of those houses where he prepared himself for a sortie up West. Surrealism, Soho, the Caribbean Club, the Meadmores, Quentin, my second cousin – I felt that I had begun to discover, in the seeming chaos of the 'Smoke', a secret village. As spring came however, I was to happen upon a very different world.

7

Robin Westgate, the school friend I had been to see on the evening of the day I had first met Simon Watson Taylor, was responsible for introducing me into a milieu far removed from the austere if original morality of the Surrealists or the boozy promiscuity of Soho.

Robin was of a fragile beauty which I had long associated with Wilde's Dorian Gray and was soon to identify with Waugh's Sebastian Flyte. His manner was correct, diffident and charming, but his opinions, even on so simple a matter as the weather, while seemingly delivered with clipped precision, were so qualified as to leave the listener unable to decide whether it was fine or not. His parents lived mainly in a manor house in Essex. His mother was what is called well-connected. His father, a retired Major with a moustache, while almost completely silent, somehow managed to project a deeply-grained and melancholic pessimism. I can only remember him addressing one remark to me directly. I had come to see Robin in the Westgate's *pied-à-terre* in South Kensington and found his father sitting alone in a deck chair in the under-furnished drawing room. I was wearing a cardboard bird's mask which I had bought in King's Road and which I believed, in conjunction with my bellbottoms, transformed me fairly convincingly into one of those 'personages' from an Ernst collage. Major Westgate looked at me without showing much reaction but eventually asked me, without any real conviction, if I didn't think that my metamorphosis might be construed as 'an insult to His Majesty's uniform'. Before I could answer Robin came in and Major Westgate relapsed into his customary shell.

Mrs Westgate, on the other hand, was the opposite of inhibited. A great beauty with an unfair amount of charm, she would ask my advice about everything, no matter how intimate; a trait which, directed at someone as young and inexperienced as I was, could not but fail to seduce me utterly. Most of the time, however, Major and Mrs Westgate were in Essex but, as Robin was stationed at Chelsea barracks, he stayed in South Kensington when not on duty and I, from time to time, stayed with him.

At school we had never in fact had an affair, but as everybody thought we had, I had gone to no trouble to put the record straight. To be exact I had cast Robin as Bosie to my Oscar, taking it for granted that this role-playing would be to his liking. Now I would be less sanguine. Robin's ability to fall in with everything or, to phrase it more negatively, his inability to assert himself, makes it difficult to be sure. Yet he had no hesitation in behaving unconventionally providing someone else made the running, even though the consequences might have proved awkward or even disastrous. For example, commissioned officers were not allowed to associate with enlisted men, yet Robin never put up any objection to appearing in public wearing his Guards' uniform with me in bellbottoms. We took considerable liberties, walking up Piccadilly for example arm in arm whilst eating ice-cream cornets and, on another occasion when Robin and a platoon of his men were, according to some ancient tradition, guarding the Bank of England overnight, he even went so far as to ask me to dinner there. It was apparently his privilege to invite a guest to help relieve the tedium of this chore, but the Sergeant who escorted me up to the small but formal dining room, with its regimental silver and excellent wine, made it quite clear that he found an Ordinary Seaman an unacceptably bizarre interpretation of this right.

Much more dangerously, he came with me to an Anarchist meeting in the upper room of a public house where I had accepted an invitation to speak. The Anarchists, now released from prison, were as idealistic as I had hoped and I was completely bewitched by a woman called Marie Louise Berneri, the beautiful daughter of a revolutionary murdered by the Communists, and the wife (or companion as they preferred to call it) of one of the English comrades. She – and indeed all of them – had an unsentimental goodness and a true vision betrayed alas only by the age-old political and/or religious machinery they hoped to dismantle, and by the willing servitude of the slaves they longed to free. Nevertheless, their philosophy was regarded with great suspicion by the authorities in general, and MI5 in particular, and it was completely unacceptable that a member of HM Forces should subscribe to it. This, much later, I was to discover, but at that time, with blind naïvety, it never occurred to me that I was doing anything untoward. Yet dangerous as it was for me to declare my allegiance to Anarchism, Robin's presence, in his smart uniform, was surely far more of a hazard. He sat there, however, as calm as in his mess, listening to my near-tearful histrionics in the name of freedom, and not even flinching when, in what I considered a daring *coup-de-théâtre*, I first played and then smashed a record of the National Anthem I had bought for the purpose in the HMV shop in Oxford Street. Perhaps in Robin's case it was a profound ennui, possibly inherited from his father, that made him ready to accept whatever anybody proposed. Perhaps it was simply good manners carried to an unprecedented extreme.

Given his parents' empty flat, we finally went to bed together without, I suspect, much enthusiasm on his part although, for a full decade to come, we would occasionally repeat the experience when the circumstances were right. Later he was to take to girls but, like myself, like many public schoolboys of the period, he was then entirely gay, and his physical beauty was such as to ensure him an immense success, while his good manners prevented him from ever saying no. Meeting him once in the company of the young Lord Montagu, also in the Guards, I took them to tea with David Webster. David looked at them with unconcealed admiration. 'I don't know how you do it, dear,' he murmured to me. 'Two of the prettiest things in London.' I glowed with pride.

Robin's main liaison at the time was with an old Italian baron who didn't approve of me at all. I was invited for dinner, but as I preached Anarchism and Surrealism non-stop the invitation was not repeated. I was fascinated, however, to see scattered about the rather gloomy, if luxurious, flat a great many signed photographs from the Pope. This fed my fantasies of the sort of Buñuel-like corruption I longed to discover. I breathed in deeply the pot-pourri-scented air and imagined the day of reckoning on the barricades.

Most of Robin's friends, especially as they seemed to like me, produced no such visions of liberating revolt. In truth, chameleon-like, I fell in instantly with their easy-going manner, revealing just enough of my Anarcho–Surrealist leanings to amuse them. It was in such a mood that one fine spring morning, while I was spending part of a weekend with Robin, we strolled across Hyde Park, along Oxford Street and up Portland Place to meet a friend of his whom he felt sure I would appreciate. It was a sunny morning and the trees in Regent's Park were just beginning to hint at greenness. We turned into a Nash Terrace and rang the bell of a large cream stuccoed house. A butler answered it, seeming in no way surprised to find a Guards' officer and an Ordinary Seaman standing on the doorstep. We walked through a hall and got into a lift. The house, Robin explained, belonged to his friend's parents but he had a top flat in it. We rose five floors and emerged into a rose-pink world where, standing with a Pimm's in his hand, beautifully dressed, discreetly made-up and smelling divine, was a man whose face, before he had said a word, suggested something witty and outrageous. Robin introduced us and told me his name was Reggie Kestrel.

Reggie was then in his early thirties, which seemed to me quite old, but as he took a great deal of trouble with his appearance he looked much younger. He was so obviously gay that the Services were out of the question but, as he also suffered from flat feet, the authorities had gratefully rejected him on this ground. Now, relieved from the necessity of doing anything, he was devoting his life to pleasure as far as he could manage on what he claimed was an extremely inadequate allowance from his father. He belonged therefore to that class of person whom the post-war press had already begun to refer to as 'drones'; a category at one time admired or at any rate tolerated, but only minimally less despised than spivs or black-marketeers in the grey dawn of the age of austerity.

His lifestyle, deviation apart, was that of an Edwardian man-about-town. Rising late and bathing long, he eventually sauntered up to the West End to drink hot chocolate in Fortnum's with his circle. He lunched in Soho, usually at Le Jardin des Gourmets where he would flirt heavily with the waitresses (waiters, due to either their nationality or conscription, were a comparatively rare species), in the hope, usually successful, of cajoling out of them an extra, and illegal, slice of gâteau generously ladled with cream. Reggie

was childishly greedy and was beginning to develop a small but
definitive pot, a phenomenon which, as he was also quite vain,
caused him a certain amount of impotent anguish. In the afternoons
he would go to the cinema, preferably the Curzon, while his evenings
were devoted to drink and sex. Superficially this might appear a
rather monotonous way of life but he illuminated and transfigured
it through his dazzling wit and sense of fantasy, so that even the
most trivial encounter became an excuse for high camp anecdotes
in the style of Firbank, his favourite author.

Reggie and I started an affair at once. Physically he was in no
way my ideal, but his sense of fun and the sybaritic luxury of his
surroundings were more than adequate compensation. Brought up
to standards of adequate middle-class comfort, I was overwhelmed
by his silk sheets, handmade shirts, rich ties, innumerable suits, and
especially by his bathroom with its huge bottles of Prince Guerlain,
French soap (a present from a thoughtful friend who had helped to
liberate Paris), and its vast warm towels. Nor was I unimpressed to
discover he was an Honourable. His father, patrolling the house
under Reggie's little nest, was a peer of the realm and, despite my
knowledge that to a Surrealist and an Anarchist this was not so
much irrelevant as deplorable, I found it absurdly glamorous.

I was eventually introduced to his parents, a course Reggie found
preferable to bumping into them fairly regularly in the hall or lift.
His father looked like a rather dated caricature of an elderly English
aristocrat, having a red face and bristling white moustache, and
wearing rather old tweeds much patched and mended. His mother
was American, a small, animated, prettily bird-like woman who
conducted the tea from behind a battery of silver teapots, hot-
waterpots, milk jugs, cream jugs, sugar basins, slop basins, tea
strainers and sugar bowls. I was careful to call him 'sir', and they
seemed to accept me as Reggie's friend, but I was however puzzled
as to how much they knew about his propensities. In this, as in
much else, I was naïf.

Often in later life, people have asked me if I have ever been to an
orgy or, as the Sixties preferred to call it, become involved in 'group
sex' and, thinking in terms of heterosexuality, I've always said no,
or at any rate only to the extent of a threesome or as a quarter of
an interchangeable quartet. In fact at this period of my life I was

fairly frequently a participant in mass homosexuality but, thinking of it as simply an extension of schoolboy activities, I never associated it with an orgy, a term I felt to imply a Roman profusion of grapes, wine, buttocks, breasts, marble *chaises-longues*, and squiffy laurel crowns. At Reggie's, however, there were fairly regular orgies involving Guards' officers and other ranks, plus interested civilians, and I found them perfectly acceptable and guilt-free. My speculations about Reggie's parents in no way extended to their butler Grope who not only appeared to think nothing of serving breakfast in bed on mornings when we were alone, but was equally detached in proffering cups of coffee to a writhing mass of bodies or actively horizontal couples strewn around the flat. Despite his rather bland if precious manner, the moonfaced Grope knew his place. He showed no more excitement than if he had been present at a more conventional 'at home' and never attempted to participate. He was, in the true sense, a gentleman's gentleman. As to my doubts as to how much Lord Kestrel was aware of what was going on, these were soon resolved, but the cause of his angry confrontation with his son was not so much to do with what was going on, as with the accompanying noise.

I had, of course, tried to interest Reggie in jazz but he didn't really like it, and particularly not as a background to sensual activity. Here he favoured Edmundo Ros played at full volume on a radiogram. There were no LPs then of course but, by stacking up twelve 78s, he was ensured of about forty minutes' worth of rumbas, sambas and cha-cha-chas and eventually somebody would turn the lot over. The insistent rhythm plus people falling off beds or over each other, shrieking or giggling, knocking over glasses, and banging away all over the flat was quite enough to wake His Lordship a floor or two below and, though Reggie theoretically asked his guests not to make too much noise, the amount of Pimm's No 1, the drink he usually provided to make things go, ensured that in practice no one took much notice of this request.

On the night in question I had fallen asleep up a very pleasant boy in the RAF. In the ensuing débâcle I found the time to apologise for this breach of sexual manners and he accepted my apologies with good grace – not that there was much time for recrimination even if he had wanted to. His Lordship was standing at the entrance to the flat wearing an ancient fawn dressing-gown with a frayed plaited cord, striped pyjamas and very old leather slippers and shouting at his naked son that everybody must get out at once or he would call the police. Meanwhile, panic-stricken, Reggie's guests were struggling into their uniforms or civvies and hurrying down the stairs. By the time I was dressed – bellbottoms are quite complicated when it comes to getting them on in a hurry – Lord Kestrel, still in his pyjamas, was standing on the right of his front steps shouting abuse at the departing orgiasts while on his left Reggie, who had by this time put on an expensive silk dressing-gown I had watched him choose in Burlington Arcade, was apologising profusely for his father's boorishness and asking us all to be sure to telephone him next day. As it was far too late to bother anyone else, I staggered as far as the Union Jack Club, where there was luckily a bed available. I woke next morning at 7am in time to catch the sailors' all-night-in train back to Chatham, to discover that everyone else in the large dormitory was Chinese, a rather unnerving experience while suffering from a ferocious hangover. I rang Reggie later; he said his father had calmed down, and I was perfectly at liberty to come and stay with him the following weekend. I did so, taking with me, as a precaution, some flowers for Lady Kestrel. Although as monosyllabic as usual, Lord Kestrel made no reference to the event.

So warm was my reception that I felt emboldened to open my ditty box and get out a copy of *The Liverpolitan*, a small monthly magazine which had accepted two of my articles: one on why I loved Liverpool, the other on a British Council exhibition of Paul Klee which I'd seen on leave a month before. I was very proud of these pieces and suggested I read them both aloud to Lady Kestrel, who was polite enough to listen without yawning and to compliment me at the end. I was even more delighted, however, when on a visit to David Webster a day or two later, I found I'd no need to open my little case. With what in retrospect strikes me as kindly tact, he had placed *The Liverpolitan* on the top of a pile of other publications on a low glass table. 'I've read your little pieces, dear,' he said as he poured me out a drink. 'The Klee piece is a tiny bit naïve but the Why-I-love-Liverpool bit has something.' He picked it up and opened it. 'You do go on about the poetry of the local *patois* rather too much,' he complained, 'but I quite like the rest.' He began to chuckle. '"When on leave in London",' he read out, '"I have a very gay time". Now that, dear, I'm inclined to believe, but you really shouldn't let everybody know . . .' I nodded but I didn't really know what he was talking about. I'd never heard the word 'gay' at that time. 'Queer' was in more general use even among homosexuals – and indeed above his desk David had hung, firmly between inverted commas, one of those pokerwork mottoes of the kind displayed behind the bar by facetious publicans. It read: 'All the world is queer except for me and thee and even thee's a little queer!' I actually found David over-critical, as indeed I had while rehearsing Lady Macbeth with him three years before. ('He is willing to listen to any amount of praise,' wrote Pa Watt, the art master, in one of my reports, 'but seems unable to believe that anything less than complimentary could possibly refer to him.') Nevertheless, he placated me by adding that, no doubt, after my demob I would 'take his place in Liverpool'. I was by this time already beginning to think that I must live in London anyway and yet, remembering what a glamorous figure David had seemed to me as a child and adolescent, I could not help but be pleased.

The reason I'd gone to see David on this occasion was actually practical. Covent Garden was to reopen. He had offered my mother two tickets and she had decided to come down and take me. I was thrilled about my mother coming and excited about introducing her to all the friends I'd made and all the places I'd been. I thanked David warmly, and returned to Reggie, who was lying, looking rather put out, in a hot scented bath.

The reason Reggie was put out was that he had discovered he had caught a dose of crabs and, probably correctly, blamed me. I feigned frivolity.

'That'll teach you,' I said, 'to sleep with the Lower Deck.'

I was, even so, rather humiliated. There was something distinctly unpleasant about finding oneself not only a host to parasites but a transmitter to boot. Immediately he'd told me, I began to itch, and a short search was rewarded. I looked with fascinated repulsion at the almost transparent creature, no bigger than a pinhead, wriggling its legs on the black marble wash basin. I knew about crabs, of course: they were very much part of naval mythology and were

referred to by such synonyms as 'fanny rats', 'minge mice', 'mobil-
ised blackheads' and 'mechanised dandruff', but to have heard
about them was quite different from catching them. I asked Reggie
what you did to get rid of them. He told me rather snappily that he
would go to his doctor, but that the best thing I could do was to
report to sick bay.

Luckily before taking his advice I confided in Wings. 'If you do
that,' he told me, 'they'll shave your bush off, paint you bright
fucking blue and confine you on board for a fucking week. There's
a chemist in Chatham High Street that'll settle for the buggers.'

I was more than grateful to Wings, as with Covent Garden
opening only two days ahead the last thing I wanted was to sit on
the *Argus* with no pubic hair and azure balls!

I found the chemist on the way to meet my mother forty-eight
hours later. I told him what was the matter and he invited me into
his back room which was full of stacked boxes of wartime lavatory
paper, Cow & Gate rusks and cartons of Brylcreem. He had a jar
of white ointment with him and a little brush. It was clear that he
enjoyed this profitable side-line. I dropped my trousers and he made
a quick and expert inspection.

'Oh yes, sir,' he said, 'you *have* got 'em!' As he applied the
ointment he told me that I was lucky to catch them early. 'I had a
Petty Officer in last week,' he said. 'Now 'e'd neglected them for
weeks. They'd got up into 'is chest 'air, 'is armpits *and* 'is beard.'
The ointment stung quite badly but then died away to become a
rather pleasant glow not unlike that experienced a few minutes
after a school beating. It had a chemical smell just verging on the
pungent.

'Don't pull your trousers up yet, sir,' he advised. 'Let it work its
way into t'roots. That's where they lay their eggs.' He went into
the shop to sell a lady some toothpaste and a hairnet. He came
back, dived into my bush and pulled out a dead crab, which he
showed me, with all the pride of a successful fisherman, on the top
of one of the cardboard boxes.

'There you are, sir,' he said. 'Dead as a bloody doornail. You
can get dressed again now.'

I did so with some relief. It struck me that he was almost certainly
a closet queen, and that part of his interest in the slaughter of

crab-lice was that it enabled him to handle the genitalia of the Fleet. As I did up the front flap of my bellbottoms he said something to confirm this and to make me very glad that I had given him no encouragement to pounce.

'If you don't mind me saying so,' he observed, 'you're very well hung, sir!' Admittedly rather flattered, I ignored this ploy, paid him five shillings and left to catch the train and pick up my mother, who was staying for several days with one of those Jewish cousins of hers whom I had lately chosen to ignore.

The reopening of the Royal Opera House, Covent Garden, was an extraordinarily glamorous affair. Admittedly there was a strong smell of mothballs and the choice of *The Sleeping Beauty* seemed particularly apt as, with clothes rationing still very much in force, most of the women seemed to have recently awoken from a spell of at least six years' duration. Even so jewels, redeemed from bank vaults, sparkled like miniature versions of the great chandeliers above, and famous faces acknowledged each other at every turn. Standing aside at one moment to let a gentleman pass through a doorway I, or more likely my uniform, was rewarded by a dazzling smile from Noël Coward.

After a satisfactory gawp in the bar, along the passages and on the staircases, we took our seats. Programmes rustled. We rose for latecomers who apologised their way along the rows. The musicians infiltrated the orchestra pit and tuned up. The conductor entered and acknowledged his applause, and we stood again for a roll of drums heralding simultaneously the National Anthem and the arrival of the Royal party. Standing ovation for same: the King looking tired and drawn, the Queen smiling as if at intimate friends; acknowledgement of my mother's confession that she felt 'quite chokey'; self-censorship of the fact that I, the Surrealist–Anarchist, felt the same; the dimming of the lights; the clearing of throats and discreet release of waistcoat buttons grown tighter during the duration; heightened excitement at the dramatic effect of the footlights on the great red curtains with their gold ciphers at the corners; the buzz of conversation dying in an instant at the triple click of the conductor's baton and then, at last, with that unique urgency of music heard in a theatre, an experience quite different from that in any concert hall, the opening chords of Tchaikovsky's overture throbbed out into the rosy darkness of the auditorium.

I quite enjoyed the ballet; it was an enthusiasm of my mother's which, during my adolescence and my total identification with her interests, I had persuaded myself I had shared, although even then I had preferred modern works like *Façade* to the great classical three-acters with their swans and Willis. Now that I was trying to sever, or at any rate stretch, that psychological umbilical cord, I had come to admit to reservations. Besides I had learned from Mesens of Breton's disaproval of the art as a 'bourgeois spectacle' and of how, when Diaghilev had commissioned Ernst and Miró to design the set and costumes for Constant Lambert's *Romeo and Juliet*, the two artists had been temporarily excluded from the movement and the Surrealists had made a noisy protest from the floor. I'd no intention of doing that, but reminded myself to warn my mother not to mention where we'd been to Mesens when I introduced them next day. Meanwhile I tolerated the 'bourgeois spectacle', slightly alarmed by the thought that there might be some parasitic life still active in my pubic hair.

My mother stayed several days in London, her first visit since the war finished, and I was determined to demonstrate my worldliness and *savoir faire*. The meeting with Reggie was a great success. He was exactly the sort of queen she liked, witty and friendly and with a potential title as well, but the meeting with Mesens was far less successful. Edouard took us to The Ivy, by which she was quite impressed because of its theatrical reputation but, whereas she found Sybil very sympathetic, ELT's tendency to 'hold the floor non-stop', as she put it, bored her to distraction. She thought him 'heavy going' and 'opinionated' and, knowing little and caring less about Surrealism, she found the evening to be something of a strain.

I took her to the Caribbean as well but she didn't care for that either, finding it too dark. It was Reggie she approved of. 'So amusing,' she said, and so he was, but my relationship with him was about to end, sexually for ever, socially for a short but bitter time.

In Reggie's sitting-room was a large photograph, taken in the misty Bond Street style of the period, of a very beautiful young man. It was, he told me, his best friend, Perry Edgebaston, who was away in the country. I gathered he was rich as well as beautiful, and I had a feeling that I'd seen him before. Reggie said he'd be back in London soon and of course I'd meet him.

The day of Perry Edgebaston's return Reggie gave a party for him and I asked if I could bring a school friend of mine called Guy Neale who, although entirely heterosexual, even at Stowe, was sophisticated enough to do no more than raise an amused eyebrow if the party developed along the lines that Reggie's parties usually did.

I have mentioned Guy before as it was he who had first played me a jazz record in his study some four years earlier, and who was furthermore the cleverest of the Anarchic trio of whom the other members were Tony Harris Reed and myself. I had remet him by chance several weeks before in Sloane Street. Guy, who was wearing the uniform of a Corporal in the RAF, told me that he was working in Harvey Nichols, the upper floors of which had been commandeered for the duration, and not yet relinquished. He had given me his office telephone number and we had spent several evenings together. There was something Sphinx-like about Guy. He was tall, rather reserved, and his eyes were of a penetrating pale blue with curiously-shaped pupils, more like a cat than a human being. He said little, but what he did say was original or witty, the words chosen with great care as if they were precious objects and too rare to squander. He painted small, strange, very personal pictures of figures wearing pastel clothes moving purposefully but mysteriously about rather sombre landscapes, and had sold one to Mesens after I'd introduced them. I liked to introduce Guy to everybody, because he was one of those people whose approval I actively solicited, and I would bring him parts of my life as a puppy brings in bones to lay at the feet of its master and looks hopefully up at him wagging its tail.

At school his interest in jazz had led him to learn to play the blues and he had formed a small band with which I was sometimes allowed to sing. It was in this role that he gained the sobriquet of 'Jesus', partially because we felt that jazzmen must always be called something strange like Muggsy or Pee Wee, but mostly because his manner of greeting or leaving his acquaintances involved a smile of beatific benevolence accompanied by the raising of the right hand in benediction. Now in London, we had begun to see quite a lot of each other.

He enjoyed drinking, although only gin, but whereas alcohol worked on me to produce a manic excess, a state he did nothing to discourage, in him it led to no more than a heightening of his verbal fantasies. One night, in a Fitzrovian restaurant, he had pointed out Cyril Connolly, or 'Saint Cyril' as we called him out of respect for his editorship of *Horizon*. Very drunk, I crossed the room and knelt at his feet. 'Thy blessing, St Cyril,' I invoked, 'grant us thy blessing.' Connolly looked rather perplexed to find an Ordinary Seaman carrying on in this bizarre way, but suggested amiably enough that I write something about naval life and send it to the magazine. I thanked him, rose unsteadily and staggered back to Guy, who had initially suggested the whole absurd enterprise knowing that, in my condition, I would carry it out immediately. It was he, too, who discovered a talent competition to be held in the Paramount dance-hall in Tottenham Court Road and proposed that, as his piano playing had considerably improved, and I had boasted to him of my success as a singer in naval concerts, we should enter in the hope of winning the ten pounds prize money. We did so under the name of The Melly Brothers but were not even placed. Years later Guy, who enters and leaves my life at irregular intervals, told me how amused he'd been at my insistence on this billing. 'It never occurred to you to call us The Neale Brothers,' he said, 'not for an instant, but then it wouldn't, would it?'

So Guy and I went to Reggie's party for Perry, who arrived rather late looking more beautiful than any boy I'd ever seen. I *had* met him before. He'd come down to Stowe during my final year with one of those parties of trainee Guards' officers who were allowed to spend six months at Oxford or Cambridge to establish their right to return there if and when they came back from the war. I'd come upon Perry sitting on the steps of the Egyptian Entry on the North Front. He was green with drink but even so memorably glamorous. I'd asked him if I could help him and he'd managed a wan smile before turning aside to be sick. Not the most auspicious first meeting but I'd never forgotten him and here he was.

We began to chat and he explained that the reason he'd been out of London was because he'd been to a first night disguised as a Portuguese princess and somehow the *News of The World* had heard about it and was trying to track him down. After a short time we found we were holding hands, a little later kissing, and suddenly I found myself telling him I'd fallen in love with him and he admitted the same to be the case with him. I said we must tell Reggie, so we waited until everybody had gone and there were only Guy, Reggie, Perry and me left and then I told him, and he was very angry indeed.

You might wonder why I found it necessary to tell Reggie at all. He didn't object to casual promiscuity and anyway I could have come up from Chatham without telling him to stay with Perry. I suspect my real reason was largely selfish. I wanted to sleep with Perry right away, but of course I had to rationalise it as the straight thing to do. After all this was love. I needed to commit myself, to avoid anything dishonest or underhand.

Reggie was sitting at his dressing-table when I broke the news. Guy, who'd liked him instantly, was sitting on the bed. Reggie began screeching about treachery, breaking off only to ask Guy, who politely declined, restating his total heterosexuality, to stay the night. Meanwhile, as a physical expression of his anger, he was slapping on rouge and eye shadow and spraying himself with expensive scent. He turned suddenly and drenched Guy with it too, a phenomenon which, as it was very strong, must have taken some explaining away in the RAF office in Harvey Nichols next morning. Perry was a traitor, Reggie told him, and I was an ungrateful little slut. He never wanted to see either of us again. I regretted this but not enough to recant and soon found myself in Perry's service flat in Tite Street and a minute or two later in Perry's huge Jacobean four-poster with its carved cherubs and swathes of fruit.

Next morning I woke to find the curtains being drawn by a white-coated, wizened youth with a very bad complexion and a compliant air. He vanished and returned with breakfast for two on a tray with legs, and most of the newspapers. When he finally disappeared for good, I asked Perry what his attitude was to finding him in bed with a sailor. Perry told me he was quite used to it and not just sailors. Servicemen of all nationalities had left their hats or caps on the hall table, and on one rare occasion when Perry didn't pick up anyone, the waiter had come in with the double breakfast and, with considerable incredulity, had said, 'Alone sir?' before going off to rearrange his tray. Later on we decided to christen this dwarfish figure Fairy Grogblossom after the character in Beach-comber.

I had the day off and so began to get to know Perry a little and to find him more and more enchanting. I was surprised by his flat. The furniture at Reggie's was Harrods 1930s Regency, but Perry's, brought down from his country house in Hampshire, was all real and splendid stuff. To me though it looked rather shabby; the gilt chipped here and there, the original chair covers in need of replacement – the oldest furniture I had till then seen in use, rather than in museums, was Victorian. I was impressed by the flowers however; masses of lilies or orchids in every corner of the room.

Perry and I left it a day or two before making it up with Reggie, but from then on saw him most days we were together. The morning chocolate in Fortnum's, the lunches or dinners at the Jardin des Gourmets were resumed. We all went to the Palladium to see a bill headed by the great Tessie O'Shea wearing a dress of splendidly opulent purple and orange, and along to Eton for a day of wine and sun which I was quick to equate with the visit to Brideshead paid by Charles Ryder (me) and Sebastian Flyte (Perry), in Waugh's recently published book. I have always had this bad habit of com-paring every situation in my life, every landscape or building, with something in literature or painting. It's as if I can only see or experience anything through these grids.

I was really proud to be with someone as beautiful as Perry. I even invited him to tea on the *Argus* and he came, driving down from London in his great Bentley for which, somehow, he always seemed to find petrol. We'd made the mess very pretty with a tablecloth 'borrowed' from the officers and, while my messmates treated this visit with a certain sardonic amusement, they were very nice to Perry and afterwards showed him everything including the engine room, now only used for heating as the *Argus* would never sail again. The old stoker in charge became very skittish as he explained the machinery, obviously revelling in being able to exploit the sexual symbolism so easily to hand. Later this man, a Geordie as it happened, became a perfect pest, showing up when I was alone

on night watch and making insistent propositions which I had no
intention of accepting. He wrongly believed that this was because I
thought his age might have affected his virility. 'When ah git gahin,'
he told me, 'Ah'v got a barkboon lak a fookin elephant.'

Perry was very touched by the sailors' ease and friendliness and
I was pleased too.

One thing that amazed and rather worried me about Perry was his
extravagance. Being an exhibitionist, I thoroughly enjoyed strolling
down Piccadilly with him, both of us carrying huge bunches of
flowers bought at Harrods, but I was appalled by what they'd cost
and I tried to help him mend his ways. 'Perry,' I wrote to my mother,
'was about to spend twenty pounds on a vase, but I stopped him
and found him a perfectly adequate one in Chelsea for a pound!'
What I didn't realise was that Perry probably didn't find it adequate
at all but was too nice to say so. I assumed that everybody shared
my middle-class tastes and my belief, if frequently betrayed in the
event, in such middle-class virtues as thrift and making do.

How in love was I? I believed totally. I carried Perry's photograph
in my wallet, showing it to sailors in exchange for their thumbed
and creased snaps of 'the tart' or 'the wife'; I rang him frequently
from the urine-scented public phone-box in the dockyard, and felt
a rising sense of excitement as the train from Chatham rattled
across the Thames towards Victoria Station, and yet when the
break came I felt little more than mild remorse and was able to
weep only a few self-pitying tears. Admittedly there was by then
something else happening in my life, but I'd expected to feel at least
some despair. Not for the first time nor the last did I feel that there
was a dimension missing in me. I suspected an emotional frivolity,
an inability to scale heights or plunge into chasms. I can cry easily
enough but, whatever people say or do, I feel cheerful again in an
almost obscenely short time. I have never experienced the gnawing
rodents' teeth of jealousy, but have equally missed out on a passion
that transforms the landscape. My emotional life, like Coward's
Norfolk, has been flat. As to why Perry and I broke up, although it
would no doubt have happened anyway, the fault was mine; an
example, on a more involved scale, of the 'Melly Brothers' syndrome.

I'd asked him to stay with me in Liverpool and he'd come. It had been perfectly all right, although my mother had found him less 'her cup of tea' than Reggie, but it hadn't occurred to me that Perry wouldn't share my view of this port as the centre of the universe. I took him around to meet my remaining great-aunts, uncles and cousins sitting waiting for death in front of flickering steel grates in Victorian squares or decaying Gothic mansions. I took him on walks through public parks which for me pressed every Proustian button. We drank with my father and his friends in a public house called The Albert, which was for me the exciting proof that I had grown up. I encouraged my mother to tell him stories of her theatrical friends and the parties she gave for them in the Twenties and Thirties. I introduced him to my circle of homosexuals, proud to impress them with so beautiful a friend, and Perry, having very good manners, never let me know that he found any of it less memorable, less extraordinary than I.

Later, after a lot of unsubtle hinting, he asked me to stay the weekend with him in Hampshire. A large Georgian house at the end of a long drive; his mother kind and talkative, his sisters reserved but friendly enough. A butler unpacked for me. An elderly American, a fellow guest, observed how he liked to put out half a cigarette before going to sleep because, relighting it in the morning, it had acquired 'a nice spicy taste'. I was impressed by portraits of earlier Edgebastons, Victorians glowering hairily through discoloured varnish, a Regency romantic with open collar and flowing dishevelled locks, sensible Georgians in front of wooded prospects, melancholy Jacobeans, sly Elizabethans, and furniture that seemed to demand silk ropes across it.

I sucked up to Perry's mother like anything. She responded. Had I a great-uncle who had been an MP? A Sir George Melly? No, he was my great-great-uncle (I suppressed the fact he had no knighthood), a Liberal representing Stoke-on-Trent. That would be he, and she remembered how, when she was very small, Sir George and her grandfather, both very old gentlemen, had walked arm in arm on the terrace after dinner. I glowed with snobbish pride. The Anarchist and the Surrealist never even stirred in their sleep.

On returning to Chatham I wrote a fulsome bread-and-butter letter to her, and a passionate affirmation of love to Perry, who had decided to stay on for a week or so. In the letter I proposed a programme: on my weekends off he and I should spend one in Liverpool, one in London and one in Hampshire with his mother. I took it for granted he would fall in with this scheme. Undoubtedly it helped him make up his mind that it was time for Fairy Grogblossom to serve breakfast to a more varied cast. Next time I saw him he told me an alarming tale, which I believed then but which, in retrospect, I think may have been a kindly if inventive fiction. I had, it transpired, put the thank-you letter and the love letter in the wrong envelopes. His mother had passed my letter to him along the row of sisters at the breakfast table, announcing rather icily that there seemed to have been some mistake. He had sent my letter to her in the opposite direction. She had not read it and had said no more on the subject, but there was no question of my revisiting the house. I asked him twice more to Liverpool, but he made excuses. In London he became more evasive, and finally, with a certain incredulity, I realised it was over. I asked him point-blank. He didn't deny it. I cried a bit. He was kind but firm. A week or two later I rang up and suggested a drink. He accepted and afterwards, for a time, we met occasionally. I saw less and less of Reggie too. The Surrealist and the Anarchist woke each other up. I began again to visit the Mesens more consistently. I didn't know it but a new chapter in my sentimental education was about to open.

8

I had not exactly lost touch with the Surrealists during the Kestrel/ Edgebaston episode. It was just that I had seen them less often. Nor had I allowed the world of Harrods and Gunters to destroy my belief in the Surrealist dream or my increasing pleasure in the Surrealist sensibility. Even while eagerly en route to Perry, I had never forgotten, crossing the Thames, to look out of the train window at a building that never failed, or fails, to give me a distinct *frisson*. It is a pumping station, built by some romantic nineteenth-century engineer-cum-architect. It consists of a tall chimney resembling an Italian campanile, but the most extraordinary feature is the pump-house itself. It looks like an imposing French town house with a steep Mansard roof of tiles imitating fish-scales. The house is, at first sight, on two floors with high, regularly disposed windows but, on looking in, you recognise that the façade is only a shell. There are no floors. The entire structure houses elaborate nineteenth-century machinery of great, rather sinister beauty.

In Chatham, too, walking through the dockyard on summer evenings where conspiracies of rusty, geometrical, nautical objects cast their lengthening shadows across the open spaces between railway-like sheds and dry docks, I was possessed by that nostalgic sense of the enigma which permeates the early pictures of de Chirico. I'd acquired my first picture, a little *frottage* of a bird by Ernst. I'd bought it on hire purchase from Roland, Browse and Del Blanco with money I'd earned from writing art reviews for the *Liverpool Daily Post*. Typically Mesens told me I'd been overcharged, but later on was delighted when I persuaded my father to give me forty pounds to buy a *Personnage avec des insects* by the same painter. I took these back to Liverpool on one of the slow night trains, placing them opposite me on the empty seat, staring at them as the train crawled through Rugby and Crewe. Ernst, I thought, Max Ernst, 'the most magnificently haunted brain in Europe', made these things. They are now mine. They have travelled deviously from his studio in Paris during the Thirties to this dimly-lit railway carriage and will soon hang at home. I scrutinised them with hallucinatory intensity. How real was my emotion? I was alone, it's true, but how theatrical were my feelings? I can no longer say. Registering those images, I felt them to be my own passport to the domain of the marvellous. The train rattled over the worn points. The dawn was breaking as I carried them up the platform at Lime Street towards the waiting taxi.

The fact that my father had been persuaded to give money to buy a picture interested ELT considerably. I must eventually learn a trade. Had I thought of becoming an art dealer? Actually I hadn't, but he began to convince me that it was an excellent idea. Admittedly, he pointed out, if I came to him as a trainee I would at first be paid very little, but I would soon advance, and furthermore our continuing intimacy would enable me, after gallery hours, to assist him with Surrealist 'interventions' both literary and active. I told him I had thoughts of becoming a journalist but he and Sybil soon shamed me into relinquishing the idea. The press were hyenas, scandalmongers and, to quote Edouard, 'idiots first-class'. I put aside the image I had of myself on the *Liverpool Daily Post*, living at home for next to nothing, proud of my beer-stained mac, nicotined fingers, and a sweat-stained trilby worn at a rakish angle. I saw myself now in a gallery, persuading the perceptive rich to collect Ernst and Magritte; my reputation as a poet supported by my guile as a dealer. So persuasive was ELT's argument that for ten years I 'forgot' that I could write and had been published. Next time I was on leave I spoke to my father about joining the art world and he suggested I ask Edouard and Sybil up to Liverpool to talk it over.

They came, Mesens infuriating my mother by his inability to spend less than three ritualistic hours shaving, bathing and dressing, but my father got on well with him, and by the end of the weekend had agreed to buy me into the gallery at the price of nine hundred pounds to invest in pictures after my demob. I was quite surprised by this as, outside the pub, where he was very open-handed, he was rather cautious with money. Nor was he so convinced by modern art as to think of it as an investment. I asked him later what made him decide to do it and he explained that his father had bought him into a business he didn't even like and at least I was enthusiastic. Later he began to appreciate certain painters, Magritte in particular, and after I had acquired *Le Viol* he was always taking me into a pub near his office to see a barmaid who he thought looked 'just like it'. He even began, in imitation of Mesens, to make collages, some of which were both inventive and poetic. 'Tom,' said Edouard, 'is a good old boy.'

I now had a job to look forward to, but as yet there was no prospect of my demob. At some point during the previous year the atom bomb had finished the Japanese war, but I have no clear recollection of when or how I spent VJ night. This is odd because it meant that there was no longer any danger of my being drafted to the Far East to face active service, but I suppose I had become so convinced that I would remain on the *Argus* for ever that I had stopped worrying. When, in a year or so, it was time for my demob, I would drift up to the barracks and remind them that I existed, but first there were all those who had been conscripted before me to release into Civvy Street. My life was pleasant enough for me to feel in no hurry – and besides, something extraordinary had happened to me, something which entirely dispelled my fast-fading regrets at my rejection by Perry Edgebaston. I had had a woman, and that woman was Sybil Mesens.

One afternoon in their flat, hung now with pictures and furnished with Regency furniture, Edouard and I were discussing sex. As a Surrealist he was naturally in favour of the poetic eroticism inherent in all sexual activity and in its non-rational aspects. The Surrealists had always insisted on the right to act out their desires without reference to traditional moral structures, and with complete contempt for the notion that the only reason for yielding to our instincts was for the procreation of children. I remember asking him, that misty autumn afternoon, why Breton had therefore condemned homosexuality; I had long confessed, rather to Sybil's disapproval, my own propensities. After all, I argued, homosexuality actually precluded the creation of children. Edouard reiterated the undesirable freemasonry of homosexuality in the arts, but told me that in fact, among Surrealists, bisexuality was quite common. Eluard, in particular, had enjoyed frequent *partousses* with his wife and other friends. Group visits to the brothel were not unknown, but no one ever confessed to Breton. He, arch advocate of total freedom, the eloquent defender of *l'amour fou*, was, in practice, something of a puritan. It was one thing to write a pamphlet in defence of Charlie Chaplin's fondness for cunnilingus – one of his divorces had raised this issue and the Surrealists had come out strongly on the comedian's side, with a manifesto called 'Hands off Love'; but somehow, when it came down to it, André was over-fastidious, albeit defending his position behind the most elaborate and obscurantist smoke-screen. The rest of the Surrealists felt it easier to put his theoretical precepts into practice behind his back.

Sybil was reading a green Penguin detective novel while this conversation was in progress. Edouard resented in her only three things: her singing of Anglican hymns while doing the housework, her fondness for purist abstract art, and her refusal to read anything except what he called 'teckies'; she seemed restless and vaguely irritated with what we were talking about. She shut the book and said quite casually: 'For Christ's sake stop going on about sex. If you want a fuck, George, come in the bedroom.'

I couldn't have been more surprised and looked nervously at Edouard to see how he reacted. He shrugged and said: 'Why not?'

I was to realise, long after, that they must have discussed it before and perhaps that part of Sybil's reason was to wean me away from my total commitment to arse. At the time, however, I believed it to be entirely spontaneous. I followed her into the bedroom and we undressed. She was in her later thirties and had a fine body. To my twenty-two-year-old eyes, time had just begun to stake a claim on her; there was a crease under her buttocks and a few lines under her eyes, but she was very handsome, very uninhibited and, rather to my relief, I found I had an immediate erection. I knew, from conversations with my shipmates, what to do: I went down on her and vice versa, kissed and probed and entered. She moaned and moved under me. Looking up at one point I saw ELT had come into the room. He had taken off all his clothes except for his socks and was displaying signs of obvious excitement. It was evident that he too had enjoyed those sessions with the Eluards in pre-war Paris. 'You are fucking my wife!' he shouted with fervent satisfaction.

Even then I registered some hidden amusement: that detached sense of the absurd which had always accompanied my pleasure in sex and has made it impossible for me to understand, let alone identify with, the Longfords and Whitehouses of the world. This, however, in no way marred my pleasure and, when Sybil's movements and breathing began to accelerate and her features to change into a mask of rigid lust, I came into her at what proved (but then after all there is not really much difference between hetero- and homosexual climaxes) the right moment. As I rolled off, Edouard took my place. I watched him with interest and soon felt some restirring of desire. I was particularly impressed by his orgasm, during which he shouted some French blasphemies and rolled his eyes like a frightened bullock cornered in a market place. Indeed for some years I consciously affected this performance until Mick Mulligan persuaded me that it looked absurd rather than convincing.

And so, high above Brook Street, we made love in various combinations and positions while the light faded, and on many other occasions too, but crossing the transsexual barrier didn't convert me overnight. I continued for some years to prefer boys and even now, while for a long time inactive in this direction, I find myself staring wistfully at young men from time to time. I had somehow imagined it would be a very different and superior experience – more intense – but it was not. What it did though was to give me the confidence to try again when the next opportunity came; to realise that girls liked it too. To make it with a couple proved an ideal introduction. A mixture of the familiar and the unfamiliar proved less traumatic, less of a jump, and I remain ever grateful to Sybil and ELT for their sexual generosity that afternoon thirty years ago.

During the months that followed, now that I'd made it clear I knew it was over, I saw something of Perry, Reggie and Robin. I went to Anarchist meetings from time to time. I went to see *Sweet and Low* and marvelled at Hermione Gingold's ability to make everything sound so rude. I drank, whenever I was up West, in the Caribbean. I trekked to Hampstead to see French films at the Everyman. I met up again with Percy and spent a weekend at his house with his nightmare mother in Aldershot on leave. My fat homosexual friend from Liverpool took me to the opening post-war season at Stratford-upon-Avon. We stayed at The Gloriana boarding house. In order to explain why we were sharing a room, he told everyone I was his nephew. I adored the plays, and paid willingly for my pleasure. 'Lovely boy,' he whispered in the Warwickshire night. It was a considerable compensation to be thought this, even in the dark.

Mostly, however, I saw the Mesens and in training for my future career followed ELT around as he began to wheel and deal in an art world just beginning to wake up from its wartime hibernation. He had organised an exhibition, 'The Surrealist Eye', at a gallery of a sympathetic dealer who specialised largely in primitive objects. None of the pictures sold; most of them were beautiful. Surrealism was right 'out' in 1946.

'Edouard,' I wrote to my mother, 'took me with him to buy two paintings by Paul Klee (pronounced to rhyme with "hay" not "tea"). They cost him £50 the pair. He took three-quarters of an hour beating down the price from £54 and was very pleased.' I found it rather odd that 'the poet' Mesens should derive such pleasure from haggling over so small a sum and boast about it to me at such length over several gins in a pub off Bond Street.

Later we met Lucien Freud, whom Edouard told me he found to be the only interesting young painter in London, but 'very perverse'. He said that he felt Lucien's main object in life was acting against the theories of his grandfather, the great Sigmund. Lucien, while unshaven and shabby, nevertheless projected considerable *panache*. His guttural Rs advertised his Austrian origin, but his English was otherwise faultless if idiosyncratic. His pale eyes, moving restlessly around the Chinese restaurant where we were dining, seemed more like those of a hawk than of a man. They appeared to see through you rather than look at you. Several of his views I found suspect or dotty, but there was no doubting his sincerity as an artist. His passion was to realise, at whatever cost and with ruthless determination, his intense visionary obsessions. Edouard tried hard to solicit his support for the Surrealist canon. Lucien would not be drawn. His amorality, except when it came to his work, rejected totally the idea of any moral imperative.

Eventually ELT went home but Lucien and I sat on. I was much flattered by his interest and unaware that it might have been the product of insomnia. I told him about my perplexity at Edouard's pleasure in bringing down the price of the Klees. He didn't find it out of character at all. He told me he thought Edouard was very unhappy and that his businesslike behaviour was intended to deceive himself and the world. I have sometimes found Lucien's verbal judgements (as opposed to his visual probity), wide of the mark or even totally at fault, but he was right about ELT. Inside that extraordinary man a poet fought with a shopkeeper, a drunken Anarchist struggled with a man who would check a restaurant bill four times. Mesens influenced me and has obsessed me more than anyone else in my life. The surface of my table in the hotel in Berlin where I am writing this at 2.30am is a homage to his insane sense of order and fantasy, but indeed he was not happy. He needed success like a drug, he rejected success like a monk. His tension drove him to the bottle. He was part saint, part demon, a monster I loved until the day he died of alcoholic poisoning in a Brussels hospital in 1971. In dreams he is my most frequent resurrectionary visitor.

I said goodnight to Lucien and walked towards Victoria Station, where I'd booked in at the Union Jack Club as I was due back on board at 0800hrs. In Regent Street two grotesque old whores were pissing in the gutter. 'Don't look sailor,' they shouted, rather unnecessarily, 'we're 'avin a piss.'

When I got back to *Argus* I found the ship's cat had done a shit on my hammock. I was not pleased but, before the end of the day, I was to receive an infinitely more traumatic shock: the Navy had discovered I existed. I was posted to a sea-going ship.

I was on watch on the Quarter Deck when I spotted, scurrying along the dockside, a small and agitated Lieutenant with a file in his hand, projecting much of the fussy panic of Alice's White Rabbit. He eventually found his way aboard and after I'd saluted him he asked my name and number.

'Ordinary Seaman AGH Melly, CJX/732558,' I told him.

'Well, where have you been for the last year?' he asked me accusingly.

'Here, Sir,' I said.

He rifled through his papers, muttering that they'd had me down as a writer. I explained that I had indeed been a writer but, after failing every exam, had been transferred back into bellbottoms. He looked as if he'd have very much liked to have put me on a charge if only there'd been one relevant in King's Regulations. The best he could do was to accuse me, accurately enough, of not bringing myself to the attention of the naval authorities. I remained silent, excusing myself with fake efficiency to examine the credentials of a Petty Officer returning from compassionate leave.

The White Rabbit stood by, impatiently cracking his knuckles. 'Well, now you *have* turned up,' he squeaked crossly, 'you are to report at noon to the main barracks with your kit' (I thought with some dismay of my hammock with its all-pervasive smell of cat shit) 'with a view to joining, as soon as possible, the ship's company of the cruiser *Dido*, part of the Home Fleet, and currently at anchor at either Portsmouth or Southampton.' (The Lieutenant seemed to specialise in haziness as to detail.)

My 'cushy number' was at an end, but I felt no justification in complaining. It was well over a year since the Petty Officer on duty at the entrance to Chatham Barracks had told me that he'd ' 'ave me out East before the fuckin' week's out'.

9

After a day of medical and dental check-ups, of long waits in offices to have papers stamped and travel warrants issued, after a night in barracks among uniformed strangers, I reported at 0815hrs to be driven down to Chatham Station in a naval bus. There was one rating on draft with me bound for the same ship. I was delighted to find out it was Tom Dash, as plump and grubby as ever, with the same mole halfway up his nose. I was delighted because I knew him. We hadn't really got on all that well at Pwllheli towards the end. His refusal to compromise, his working-class chauvinism, his reproachful attempts to dictate who I saw and what I said and did, made me frequently both angry and guilty. He could be charming, though, and funny, but only when alone. The sound of a middle-class voice, the expression of a middle-class attitude, turned him sullen and boring. He mistrusted my gregariousness, was ever alert for any bourgeois weaknesses.

We held at least the love of both jazz and Anarchism in common, and there we were struggling into the van carrying, not only our hammocks, kit-bags and ditty boxes, but our wind-up gramophones and cases of records as well. I'd almost lost touch with Tom since our training camp days. We'd met once in London and he'd taken me home to his parents' prefab in Dalston but it had not been a success. His father, the dustman, looked at me with silent and gloomy suspicion. One of Tom's posh friends, he'd decided. Tom's cleverness, I suspected, had made him something of an outcast there too. Nor did he want to meet ELT — nor even the Anarchists. Now we found plenty to talk about. On the train to Portsmouth we played each other new records we'd bought over the last year. Outside the carriage windows the sky darkened and the trees began to claw the air. We arrived in a storm. There was no bus to meet

us so we took a taxi. They weren't expecting us at the dockyard but told us, with that grim satisfaction of those who are the
bearers of bad news, that the *Dido* had sailed that morning for
Portland.

We tried the barracks, who didn't want us at all, but finally said
we could sling our hammocks in one of the offices. As we weren't
there officially, they told us, would we kindly fuck off ashore for
the evening. We left our things, fought our way in a head wind
across the dock road to a dirty little café for greasy pie and chips
and then into a squalid and unfriendly little pub next door, where
we got very drunk on mild. Staggering back through the howling
darkness we missed the entrance to the barracks and found ourselves
soaked to the skin and hysterical with laughter, tripping over some
railway goods tracks leading down to a jetty and assaulted by angry
waves. Somehow we found our way back and, as there was a smelly
coke fire still smouldering in the office, were able to dry out our
uniforms while we slept.

Next day we awoke with splitting headaches and mouths like
Turkish wrestlers' jockstraps to face a freezing blue sky washed
clean by the storm and, returning to the station, spent the day
meandering westward along the south coast in a series of ancient
and unheated trains. At dusk we arrived at Portland, and there lay
the *Dido* at anchor in the Sound. A liberty boat, full of cheerful
ratings, tied up at the dockside and we, rather gloomily, took their
place and were rowed out to the ship. Stumbling up the gangway
to report, I became very much aware that, for the first time since I'd
joined the Navy over two years earlier, I was aboard a commissioned
vessel.

To begin with it was total confusion, but after a day or two it
began to make a little sense. I came to realise that everybody in the
ship's company held a different if partial view. For the stokers and
engineers, it was the engine-rooms and propellers that signified; for
the gunnery officers and ratings, the neatly stacked shells and
turrets; for the electricians, the ship was a nervous system of cables
and power points; for the writers, a list of names, each entitled to
different rates of pay; for the cooks, the galleys and store rooms;
for the Master at Arms, rebellious stirrings and acts prejudicial to
naval discipline; for the Captain and senior officers a view of the

whole, detailed or vague, according to their competence; for the ship's cat, areas of warmth and comfort, and a jungle where the prey squeaked and scurried behind the bulkheads and sacks of provisions.

Yet there were also intricate private relationships, both official and unofficial. Every mess had its friends, enemies, and neutrals. Shared duty led to liaisons or enmities. Between ranks, commissioned or otherwise, there were tensions, tolerance, fierce vendettas fought out with the aid of King's Regulations or the sympathetic bending of the rules. There were rogues, poets, morons, conformists, wits, psychopaths, religious maniacs, revolutionaries, buffoons, arse-lickers and good men, all within the outer bulkheads and between the decks. The *Argus* had been no more than a hulk in which we associated out of self-interest and to avoid notice. The *Dido* was a real community, a steel village. At first enormous and confusing, it soon became cosy, not as intimidating as a battleship, not as cramped as a destroyer.

That first night, however, was a mere jumble of impressions and none of them pleasurable. We were shown our lockers, and our mess, ate some disgusting supper where my attempts to make conversation were blocked by the 'I say old boy, what, what,' treatment, told we'd have to rise and shine at 0530hrs to scrub the decks, and slung our hammocks, too tired even to unpack. As soon as the tables were cleared I fell asleep, rather apprehensive about what tomorrow might bring. My basic training was so long ago I'd forgotten almost everything. I felt very much the new boy.

I was woken by the Tannoy telling me to rise and shine and suggesting we all took our hands off our cocks and transferred them to our socks; a hoary nautical joke which seemed rather less than hilarious at such an hour. On deck it was still pitch dark and there was a medium squall blowing. I was detailed off to sand and canvas the gangway, and then wash it down with cold salt water. While at work on the bottom platform, a large wave soaked me to the skin. I thought regretfully of the *Argus* rusting fuggily in distant Chatham. By the time we'd finished, a few streaks of baleful light offered the minimum in cold comfort along the eastern horizon.

Breakfast made me feel more cheerful, and afterwards I unpacked my kit-bag and stuck up a reproduction of Magritte's *Le Viol* on the back of my locker door. I'd changed my soaking overalls for rather creased number twos, and had a shit and a smoke in the heads, which were doorless and much favoured as a conversation centre, most of the emphasis resting on the erotic adventures of those who had been ashore the night before. Sitting directly opposite me, and regaling the company with such a tale, was a rating I recognised as belonging to my mess. He was large and had the look of an outsize, extremely decadent cherub, but his use of erotic metaphor was far superior to the usual rather tedious norm.

'She was as tight as a mouse's earhole,' he was saying in a flat Midlands accent, 'but so wet that when the cinema organ come up,' and here he splayed out his fingers and looked through them, '. . . I could play stained glass windows.'

After I'd washed and shaved and done my teeth, Tom and I went off to see the Master at Arms to be detailed off for jobs. I had met this man briefly the night before, and thought him as frightening as an ogre. He had a ferocious eye, a snarl and a very black beard. Much to my surprise his office was full of large felt animals – rabbits, teddy bears, and monkeys – which I found inexplicable, but discovered later that he made them for sale and that it was considered judicious insurance to buy one for a child, whether real or fictitious, before going on long leave.

He was very sarcastic, particularly as neither of us had taken any specialised courses, and possessed in consequence no skills beyond basic seamanship. As I was what he called 'posh ignorant', he made me Officer of the Watch's messenger, a cushy enough job with many a chance for skiving while pretending to look for somebody. Tom was put in charge of a cupboard full of mops and squeegees and had to polish a certain amount of brass-work. We left the Master at Arms, 'the buffer' as he is known in naval terminology, with some relief. 'If I had the wings of an angel,' runs a nautical parody of a lachrymose Victorian ballad, 'And the arse of a fucking great crow, I'd fly to the top of the mainmast, And shit on the buffer below.' I felt further acquaintance with the *Dido*'s Master at Arms might well give these words a certain sincerity and I was pleased to escape from both him and his beady-eyed toy animals.

*

Being Officer of the Watch's messenger didn't excuse me from general duties like swabbing decks, painting ship nor, during gunnery practice, a position in the magazine chamber heaving shells and charges from their racks to the hoists. We put out to sea to do this a day or two after I arrived and very unpleasant it was. Choking from cordite fumes, stomach and arm muscles on fire, the machinery making regular snoring noises like the Red King asleep as it shot the ammunition up to the gun turrets far above, and then the thundering and monotonous vibrations, while enough money to buy a Rembrandt was blown through six barrels.

At 2015hrs a shell jammed, and we were ordered to climb to the top of the turret to remove it. To do this we used an instrument like a giant's flue brush. It was pitch dark and the wind howled like forty devils. Nor was the worst over. Crawling down to the mess in expectations of a warm supper and a fuggy unwashed sleep in the grey blankets of my hammock, I discovered that some newly arrived rating with no seatime (it could have been me but, as it wasn't, my indignation was the equal of anyone else) had been feeling queasy and opened the porthole for a breath of air. With the high sea running, a wave had swept him backwards across the entire mess and by the time those present had got the porthole shut again there was a foot of water to be mopped up. Supper was a cold pie. On the wireless a crooner sang of moonlight and roses. Before crashing I went up on deck to smoke a final cigarette. It was bitterly cold but much calmer. One of the fleet had turned its searchlights on. In its blue beam the seagulls mewed sadly as they wheeled and turned.

Once the gunnery practice was over things became much pleasanter. In a few weeks we were going to sail to Chatham for Christmas, and I was due for a fortnight's leave so that was something to look forward to. Then we were off to the Mediterranean for a goodwill cruise and I was really pleased about that, as I had never been abroad at all. My father had travelled as a young man (he had started his business life in the family shipping firm) but, during my childhood in the 1930s, he was far too broke to consider foreign holidays, even if my mother had been in favour of them, which she was not. She had a terror of the sea, and had only once been out of

England and that as a child to the Isle of Man. So it was Wales or
the Lake District for us each summer and that was why I was so
excited about the cruise.

Meanwhile we sailed rather aimlessly along the south coast,
putting into Portsmouth for a couple of days, stopping at Weymouth
for no obvious reason. It was a cold stormy winter in 1946. The
ship rolled and staggered very badly at times, and I was quite often
sick. I particularly loathed that curious feeling of weightlessness
followed by the nauseating reassertion of gravity. My Mess Deck,
badly ventilated, was hard to take in the mornings; a *mêlée* of
armpits, hairy calves, meaningless obscenities, farts and coughing
fits. My fellow ratings, who the night before had seemed in most
cases so charming and in some so attractive, were transformed into
red-eyed, green-toothed, pustular horrors. Me too; my feet dirty
from the midnight rush to be sick in the heads, I stood in my grey,
slept-in underwear and scratched my arse. None of us bothered to
wash before our greasy breakfast.

By mid-morning stand easy things had become more bearable. I
had already scurried about the ship bearing messages on behalf of
the Officers of the Watch, making frequent detours to chat with an
increasing circle of friends or acquaintances. On my own Mess
Deck I had come to know the rating whom I'd heard describing his
erotic games in the cinema, and a genuine if occasionally frightening
original he'd turned out to be. He was called 'the Baron' and came
originally from Leicester. His title sprang from his sparing use of
the word 'baronial' as an adjective of high praise. Returning on
board, he would quite often produce some 'liberated' object from
under his mac or greatcoat and offer it for sale.

'Who,' he'd enquire, 'wants to buy this baronial coffee pot?'

On the other hand, anything he disliked, and that included almost
everything connected with the Navy, he described as 'Mongolian'.
The Officers, the Petty Officers, the food, the Mess Deck, the ship
itself, were all decidedly Mongolian. This was predictable, but less
so was the catalogue of what the Baron considered to be baronial.
'Big eats,' the naval expression for a large meal ashore, usually a
steak with an egg on it and a mountain of chips, was to be expected.
Grog likewise, and sex, especially in its more bizarre manifestations
(it was the Baron who introduced me to the expression 'a yodel in

the canyon' to describe the practice of going down on a woman).
But in other directions his tastes were more individual. He read a
great deal, mostly the English classics, and had a good eye; the
baronial coffee pots and other objects he offered for sale were never
ugly, and abroad he refused to buy any of the trashy souvenirs
which most sailors staggered home with as presents for 'my party'
or 'the old lady'. It was however music that especially possessed
him, more specifically grand opera and (most baronial of all) Johann
Sebastian Bach, a composer he admired so much as to insist on
calling him by his full name at all times.

When years later I read *A Clockwork Orange*, the anti-hero, with
his passion for 'Ludwig Van', immediately reminded me of the
Baron, and when the film came out and people said they couldn't
believe that someone so in love with violence, so coldly psychopathic, could also adore classical music, I was able to contradict
them, because the Baron was at times very dangerous indeed.
Personally I only experienced this once, when some remark I made
in the showers offended him, and he threw a bucket of near-boiling
water over my feet, but ashore he was constantly and consciously
involved in fights. I knew him to carry a knife, and there were times
when his face, for all its cherubic innocence, turned very ugly indeed
and I was aware that, behind the china blue eyes, a wild beast was
insecurely caged.

The Baron was feared on the Mess Deck. Coming aboard, dangerously drunk, he would pull out his gramophone and play an aria or
a prelude and fugue and, even at three in the morning, no one dared
to object. Once someone was injudicious enough to suggest, very
unaggressively, that he turn it in. The Baron produced his knife and
very slowly and carefully sawed through the seaman's hammock
rope. There was a crash and a surprised oath as the unfortunate
man bounced off the mess table on to the deck, but he knew better
than to protest. Putting away his knife, the Baron continued to
listen with rapt attention to the divine mathematics of Johann
Sebastian.

The boiling water apart, the Baron was in general my champion,
although at times this was something of an embarrassment. Almost
my first day on the Mess Deck, I was studying, with a certain defiant
ostentation, a new book on Picasso and arousing in consequence

considerable scorn among my mess-mates. I quite welcomed this as it gave me a chance to lecture them, to try and make them see why there was nothing absurd in the artist's distortions, but before I could launch into it, the Baron grabbed my principal mocker by the collar.

'Anyone who says a word against fucking Picasso,' he murmured gently, 'gets fucking done over. Have you got that, shirt?' The shirt in question admitted he had (the Baron called everybody 'shirt' or 'horse' regardless of sex or status). From then on nobody on C Deck ever murmured a criticism of the Spanish painter.

Nor was the Baron's protection confined to aboard ship. In a pub in Portsmouth one night I was declaiming and no doubt misquoting Shakespeare when the fat old landlady decided she'd had enough. Looming suddenly over me she told me to get out. The Baron rose from another table and tapped her on the shoulder. She spun round to face his calm yet dangerous regard. 'He can stay, horse,' he told her with mild menace, 'and he can recite baronial Shakespeare,' he continued, 'and if you say another fucking word against it, I'll thump you right between your Mongolian fucking tits.' He sat down again and the old woman retired hurriedly back behind the protection of the bar.

Yet despite or indeed because of the Baron's determination to protect me against slight or insult, I usually avoided going ashore with him. This didn't actually offend him. A night without a brawl seemed to him incomplete, but he knew I in no way shared this view and, if I had been dragged in by accident, I might well have got seriously hurt. Nor was I any help in his sexual forays as, with my rather obvious effeminacy, I could easily give the rather tough women he favoured the wrong impression as to his own inclinations; for, despite complete sexual tolerance, the Baron was entirely heterosexual. If we met ashore by chance, and he was not yet too drunk, we'd greet each other affectionately. If I realised he was far gone I would do my best to avoid him. Any contact with the Baron was potentially dangerous, but his originality, his wit, his edge, made it a price – within limits – I was prepared to accept.

'You realise, of course, that if what you claim to have done was true, and what you assert you would like to do was meant, it would be impossible for us to remain friends or even acquaintances.'

The speaker was an enormous young man over six feet tall. He had a nose like the Duke of Wellington, a deep voice betrayed when amused by a surprisingly high-pitched giggle, and that serious and civilised approach to life, marred only by a certain pomposity, which is characteristic of those educated at Winchester. His name was Gerald Aylmer, his nickname 'Felix', after the celebrated actor of the time Felix Aylmer, and this prefect-like explosion was provoked by overhearing in the showers a discussion between an elderly Leading Seaman and myself as to the physical beauty of a boy-rating who had just joined the ship and whose skin, as the killick put it, was 'as smooth as a tombola ticket or a wardroom plate'.

I told Felix that what I said I'd done was true, and what I said I'd like to do was equally accurate if, alas, not necessarily feasible, and that he was not a ship's prefect or responsible for house spirit on board the *Dido*. Suddenly he laughed and agreed that my sexual tastes were indeed no concern of his, and would I like to go ashore with him that night? So we did, and got roaring drunk and became the best of friends.

Felix was a remarkable man. His father was a retired Admiral living, as I was to discover, in a village near Weymouth and, as Felix was extremely clever, he could certainly have obtained a commission. I was sometimes puzzled as to why he should have chosen to remain a rating (he was in charge of the ship's charts) but eventually came to the conclusion it was because he was a convinced Socialist. There was a kind of dogged nobility about him, an admirable probity which made me feel flimsy and frivolous, but in fact, once he had recognised and rejected the sixth-form prudery which had sparked off his outburst in the washroom, he revealed a love of gossip, a delight in alcoholic excess, and a shared enthusiasm for many modern authors, in particular W H Auden, which quickly reassured me.

The chart-room was high up in the ship, conveniently near the bridge, and Felix, when we were in harbour, was allowed to sleep in it and use it as a kind of study. As our friendship ripened I was invited frequently to visit him there, sometimes with Tom or other friends, sometimes alone. It proved a blessed retreat from the hurly-burly of the Mess Deck.

Felix was committed to the recently elected Labour Government, and would argue with me frequently as to the need for reformist and gradual political re-education, for the virtues of austerity and control, of the undoubtedly boring but entirely necessary work of committees and sub-committees engaged in such work as the implementation of Lord Beveridge's recommendations for a National Health Service. He viewed my Anarcho–Surrealism as an amusing aberration. He had read History and drawn his conclusions. Nevertheless, he was not uncritical of the Government when he felt them to be at fault and one morning, delivering a message to the chart-room, I found him, the colour of a turkey cock, growling over a copy of the *Daily Mirror*, a paper he had hitherto championed for helping persuade the electorate to reject Churchill. The reason for his anger was an article supporting Ernie Bevin's blockading of Palestine and the harassment of the Jewish refugees. This appalled Felix on grounds of both reason and sentiment. I told him that actually I knew little of the rights or wrongs of the question, feeling only that, after the horrors of the death camps, my mother's race was surely entitled to every consideration.

That evening Felix, the prototype WASP, lectured Tom and myself on the history of Zionism, and in particular on our moral need to honour the Balfour Agreement whatever the political inconvenience in doing so. He spoke well and eloquently (he was later to become a history don), and the upshot was that we all three solemnly undertook to refuse orders, if sent to the Mediterranean, to prevent refugees from reaching their promised land and, more immediately, to write a letter of protest to the *Daily Mirror*. Our first undertaking was luckily never to be put to the test although I hope and believe we would all three have honoured it. The letter, however, was both written and dispatched. Servicemen were not of course allowed to communicate with the press, but we asked the editor to inform his readers that we had supplied him with our names and ship. This was an unnecessary precaution as the letter itself, written mostly by Felix, closely argued and of great length, remained inevitably unpublished. It might have appeared in print in *The Times*, *Guardian* or *Telegraph*, but there was no possibility that the popularist *Daily Mirror* could have seen its way to use up its still-rationed space on so weighty a reproach. Felix, however, felt the better for writing it.

Tom and Felix got on moderately well. Both were keen on chess and would play together up in the chart-room while I – whose mind has always found it difficult to remember the moves, let alone plan strategy – read or wrote. They were never close however. Something abrasive in Tom, probably his resistance to the middle classes, forced him to try Felix's patience whenever things seemed smooth or pleasant. My patience too. There were times I hated Tom. Nevertheless it was with him I went down into the cable-locker flat to play our records. For one thing, Felix was not very interested in jazz, and here at least Tom and I could forget our differences, and sit listening to Jelly Roll, Louis, King Oliver, Bessie, Muggsy, Sidney Bechet on the wind-up gramophone among the great coils of the anchor chains.

'I ain't here to try and save your soul,' moaned Bessie in ecstatic glee, 'I'm only here to try and save your good jelly roll.'

The difference between proletarian Dalston and middle-class Liverpool was temporarily erased. The joyful hedonism of the stomps and marches, the catharsis of the blues were all that mattered.

Yet whereas my theoretical admiration for the working class was frequently and provokingly stretched to breaking point by Tom, my third great friend on the *Dido* sprang from exactly that area which I somehow felt it was all right to despise – the *petit bourgeoisie*.

Edward Wood came from Arnos Grove. His parents lived in a semi and his father worked in a bank. He too had done so before being called up and was to return after his demob, but he blew every theory I held about the sterility of the lower-middle classes sky high, or at least he would have done had I found it possible at that age to compare my theoretical stances with my feelings and experience. Edward was funny, mildly subversive, freshly good-looking, completely heterosexual and almost unfairly charming. It's difficult to describe Edward's golden charm. It was just that he emanated what the hippies, still at the time in their wombs or prams, were to call 'good vibes'.

These then were my friends, with the Baron as a kind of unreliable third option and the ship's writer, a Bambi-eyed South London gay, as a confidant and sometimes lover when I really needed to let my

hair down. There were others I was fond of, particularly a Welshman called – without, I'll agree, any startling originality – Taff, but
as Taff was a constant deserter and in consequence either in the
ship's cell waiting to be court-martialled or else doing time in the
glasshouse, our friendship had little time to mature.

My relationship with the Petty Officers and Chief Petty Officers
was, as usual, cordial, if flirtatious. When in harbour, for they
would in no way trust me to steer the ship, I became temporary
Quartermaster, a watch-keeper's job involving little more than
making announcements through the Tannoy ('I wish you wouldn't
say "wakey, wakey" so fuckin' womanish,' complained one grizzled
Petty Officer. 'It's fuckin' embarrassin' getting up wiv an 'ard on').
As for the officers I found them quite difficult to deal with because
they were structured to think of ratings as working class, and swung
between a somewhat awkward and patronising acknowledgement
that I was not when they were drunk, and a prefect-like severity
when faced by my failings as a seaman.

The Captain was a harmless, rather short man with whom I had
little contact, but the Commander – a tall, introspective figure –
took, for reasons I have never been able to fathom, a paternal
interest in me, and did all he could to make my life agreeable. He
was also responsible, on several occasions, for rescuing me when I
could have found myself in some trouble. Both times my peril was
due to the machinations of my one serious and implacable enemy
on the *Dido* – inevitably, it would seem in my case, a Warrant
Officer.

My first contact with this man was when I had been detailed off
to mop up a quantity of water that had been spilt on the Quarter
Deck. On my knees, dreaming of something else, I became aware
of a pair of highly polished shoes standing nearby. Looking up I
saw a thin, bitter-faced man regarding my activities with sardonic
interest. 'You have never watched your mother mopping up your
kitchen floor, have you?' he said mildly. I admitted I hadn't. 'She
had a maid to do that I dare say,' he suggested. I agreed she had.
He asked me if I'd been to a public school. I admitted it. 'I thought
so,' he said and then explained that he had reached these conclusions
by watching the way I was mopping up the water into the cloth
only to squeeze it out again, well clear of the bucket. I looked

down again to make sure he was right and had to agree it was so. I smiled up in what I hoped was an ingratiating manner but this seemed to trigger off a great deal of controlled anger. A nerve pulsed in his left temple as he ordered me icily to my feet. I got up. 'At attention,' he snapped, 'and give me your name and number.' I did so. 'I'll be watching you, Ordinary Seaman Melly,' he snarled, 'I'll be watching you from now on. Now mop up that water.' And he strode away.

From then on he kept his promise, and for my part I accepted the war and enjoyed it. For example I developed a slight eye infection and the Medical Officer said I should wear dark glasses on deck. I went ashore and bought a pair with extravagant up-swept pale pink rims. Most of the officers and the crew found these an excuse for humour at my expense (something I've never minded), or simply comic in themselves. Not so Warrant Officer Perkins. He stopped me and told me to take them off. I refused and produced the Medical Officer's chit. He ordered me to replace them. I questioned his right to specify the kind of dark glasses I should wear especially, I added, as the Commander had told me he found them 'endearingly absurd'. Perkins turned on his heel. He could afford to wait his chance.

The rest of the ship's company has faded from my mind. I remember the leading seaman in charge of our mess, one or two faces remarkable for their beauty or ugliness, the Chaplain, a Welsh-man given to freewheeling *hwyl* in his short sermons in the rec-reation space but enthusiastic about the arts and, as was to be proven, distinctly liberal in his attitudes. There was one rating, however, whom I remember clearly. He was the Earl of Dudley's son and referred to, by most of the Petty Officers, as the ''orrible Peter Ward'.

Peter Ward had been evacuated at the beginning of the war to Canada and had acquired a slight Canadian intonation. He had not acquired any democratic principles though and, as a conscripted rating on a cruiser, found himself surrounded by those who exor-cised their unease at his title and arrogance by continuous mockery. This seemed to roll off Peter's back. What he found far more distressing was having to behave as an inferior to the officers while they, in their turn, sensing his ill-suppressed contempt, went out of their way to see he jumped to it. Looking around for a friend he chose Felix, who had gone to Winchester and, in that his father had been a Admiral, was by definition upper-middle class. Being friendly with Felix he was forced, at times, to be at least fairly friendly towards me, but my lack of form distressed him, my political views and belief in sexual freedom appalled him, and my friendship with Tom or the Baron made me unacceptable when in any company except Felix's. Even here though the stronger links between Felix and myself, our literary interests, drove him into a sullen rage as above all else Peter was a most committed philistine.

It was with this cast of characters that we cruised up and down the south coast during the winter months.

Edward, Felix and I had begun to draw our rum ration and, before going ashore, we would all give three tots to one of us in rotation, believing that the resultant intoxication would produce a feeling of uninhibited fantasy that would take us all into absurd adventures. This it frequently did. One night in Weymouth we staggered from The Boot, a public house preferred by the Baron to the even more baronial Belvedere, aware, with some relief, that he himself would be in neither as he had been sent to his native Leicester to give evidence at the trial of a mate accused, no doubt with every justification, of stealing a car ('the judge was a right Mongolian cunt,' explained the Baron on his return). In the Belvedere was a collection of very mangy old whores and we sat drinking brandy, and listening with delight to their Rabelaisian banter. One toothless Irish lady, with stringy hair cut like a man and pyjamas worn under her trousers, was asked by a drunken Yorkshire Petty Officer how much she'd charge for 'all night in'.

'All night in what?' she asked him. 'We got rabbits in the bloody air-raid shelter!'

'But lass,' he persisted, 'I've got eighteen inches.'

'Uncontrollable passion eh? Well wrap it round your neck and throw snow balls.'

A few weeks before Christmas we met up with the entire Home Fleet for a rehearsal of an event which was to take place in February. The King and Queen were to visit Canada and we were to cheer them off. We were lined up and told that after the salute (to be represented on this occasion by five instead of twenty-one guns), the bugler would sound off a 'G'. We would then raise our caps at an angle of forty-five degrees, holding them by the brims, the arms fully extended and, when the officer on the bridge shouted 'Hip, Hip,' we would yell 'Hurrah' three times, replace our caps and stand to attention. A small sloop representing the *Vanguard* passed between the two lines of ships, and we raised three feeble cheers. 'Not bad,' said the Commander through the loudspeakers, but then he was always agreeable to everyone.

My Anarchic sentiments thoroughly stirred by this chilly exercise, I went down to the Mess Deck and scribbled the beginning of a letter to my mother: '. . . for whose benefit? The King's? Ours? The sentimental heart of the great British public stuffed with *Daily Mirrors*? No wonder constitutional monarchy, particularly the English brand, so appeals to Salvador Dali!'

Then I went up to the recreation space to play tombola, the bingo of the Navy, with the Baron, who always insisted on calling it 'Thomas Bowler'. I won ten shillings. After supper I picked up an American comic. Adding to my mother's letter I commented: 'Featuring supermen and desperate criminals who discover how to destroy the world, these bright gaudy pages crammed with sadism, near-rape and death are a wonderful psychological mirror. There is even a Surrealist interest, *eg* "Like evil things spawned by the brooding marsh".' Now if only I'd pursued that line, taken it as the subject for the article nervously solicited by St Cyril in the restaurant, I might have earned my place as the first prophet of English pop art, but I didn't. I slung my hammock and the next day we upped anchor and sailed for Chatham and the Christmas leave.

Christmas was as it had always been. Lunch at my maternal grandmother's, where my father complained, as usual, that Uncle Alan's cocktails had too much orange in them and not enough gin. Even so there seemed to have been quite enough gin for my grandmother, who made a speech, after the pudding and mince pies, in somewhat incoherent praise of the police, sentiments hardly likely to appeal to my Anarchist sympathies.

A more expected assault on my convictions came when Uncle Alan himself, always a convinced patriot, insisted on everybody listening to the King's speech to the soon-to-be-dissolved Empire, and then on us all standing, he inadvertently wearing his pink paper hat from a cracker, for the National Anthem. I had threatened my mother to remain seated that year but, in the event, compromised by pretending that the unaccustomed richness of the lunch necessitated a diplomatic visit to the lavatory.

Leave over, I returned to the *Dido*, looking forward to the spring cruise in the Mediterranean, and with a watchkeeper's job which would allow me over the next few weeks to renew the pleasures of the capital.

The London Gallery was beginning to take shape. Edouard had been to Belgium and returned depressed by Surrealism there: 'Very provincial,' he grumbled, and he was furious too that Magritte, in the after-glow of wartime resistance, had joined, for what proved to be a very brief period of time, 'the Stalinists'.

Reggie and Perry were much as before, although Perry told me he was thinking of taking a job, an idea I actually found quite shocking. I revisited Soho, and the Caribbean Club, but now that I was to come and work in London, I found myself beginning to view the city in a new light. I had begun to think of myself as a native.

Halfway through January disaster struck. The ferocious black-bearded Master at Arms sent for Tom and me and told us in his office, largely denuded of toy animals by the Christmas rush, that two ratings of the battleship the *Duke of York* were being loaned to the *Dido* for two months to do a gunnery course, and that two ratings from the *Dido* must be handed over in exchange.

'I know you're mates,' he said, 'and I also know that, with the exception of the 'orrible Peter Ward, you are the most useless pair of fuckin' articles on the ship, so you it is. In repayment of my kindness in sending you off together I shall expect from you, Ordinary Seaman Melly, two free tickets for the Chelsea Arts Ball where I am led to believe a great deal of shagging is the order of the day. You will join the *Duke of York* next Thursday when we reach Weymouth. Any questions? No? Then piss off!'

We thanked him and did as he advised, but I had mixed feelings about two months alone with Tom. I was also upset not to have Felix and Edward to go ashore with as, despite the fact the whole of the Home Fleet was cruising in the Mediterranean, the ships were not necessarily going to the same ports. However, there was nothing to be done, and the following Thursday morning found us sitting in a cutter, one of whose crew was indeed 'the 'orrible Peter Ward' himself, covering the three hundred yards that separated the two ships. There was a gale-force wind, and it took over twenty minutes to reach the *Duke of York*. We climbed the enormous gangway to discover a fo'c'sle like a limitless plain. I was immediately frightfully homesick for the dear little *Dido*, which I had once found so alarmingly large, and I especially hated that instant loss of identity which is the effect of joining any new institution whether a ship or a school. The next day we got up at o6oohrs to sweep the deck prior to saluting the King. It was very cold and I got my feet wet. Tom and I, sitting down to breakfast without washing, a normal practice on the *Dido*, were shamingly ordered to go and do so by the mess killick, a Leading Seaman.

At 1100hrs we fell in. The two lines of the Home Fleet stretched as far as I could see, battleships, cruisers and destroyers fading into the distance. They fired the full twenty-one guns this time, and between the heads of two stokers who were pretending to commit sodomy I caught a glimpse of the King as he passed by a hundred yards off, standing on the deck of the *Vanguard* and saluting his acknowledgement of our rehearsed cheers. One of the stokers had a huge and angry boil on the back of his neck.

The next day we sailed for the first post-war Home Fleet goodwill cruise of the Mediterranean. I had the first watch on the bridge that night: black sea, white spray, brilliant stars. The following morning, in the Bay of Biscay, we ran into what a Chief Petty Officer assured me was 'the worst bastard storm' he'd ever encountered in thirty years of service. Apart from our watchers we were forced to stay down below for four days and nights. In consequence there was nothing but the slow sickening roll from side to side, the vile taste in the mouth, the repetitive Mess Deck obscenities, uneaten meals congealing in fat, spew in the heads and flats, pale-faced creatures barging into each other like zombies, and the throbbing of the machinery. Nobody washed or shaved. Only during my watches on the bridge, stirred by the raging seas, could I feel any exhilaration or purpose in living. I was sad when my four hours were up and I had to go back into the foetid hell below decks.

Then one morning we woke to find the sky a warm bright blue, the waters calmed and sparkling, to port the mountainous coast of Spain. Happiness flowed through the great ship. We cleaned up the flats, heads and messes, shaved and showered, whistled and hummed. My job that day was to paint those strange naval objects – ringbolts, bollards, fairleads and shackles – which sprouted from the wooden deck of the fo'c'sle. Gulls wheeled and circled overhead as white as washing, and for the first time, with ecstatic disbelieving pleasure, I watched the grinning dolphins romping and plunging in our wake.

Gibraltar is a very British piece of abroad with its Boots and W H Smiths, but for Tom Dash and me it was as foreign as could be. At about 1530hrs on the next afternoon we fell in, eyes shining, to enter harbour. The guns fired a noisy salute and by 1600hrs the great ship was secured alongside the jetty while, in midstream, the *Dido* was moored to a buoy. We both wished we were back aboard her, but at least that night we could go ashore.

Next to us was an American battleship with several variants on our own more traditional Tannoy announcements to laugh at: 'Liberty guys to glamorise' was one such.

We fell on deck at 1800hrs, but before we were allowed to march ashore the RPO read us a bizarre warning from the Admiral commanding the Home Fleet:

There have been of late several incidents in Gibraltar to the discredit of the service. It is up to every man proceeding on shore to behave in an exemplary manner, not only to redeem the Fleet's good name, but also for their own sake.

Actions in Gibraltar are liable to be misinterpreted so the wise man proceeds with circumspection. Alcohol in Gibraltar is liable to be of an explosive nature, so that the wise man is moderate in his intake. The local 'jungle juice' and 'merry-merry' should be avoided. Most of the public houses are in or near Main Street, where public lavatories are few and far between, so the wise man asks for and uses one on the premises before leaving. Urinating ['that means pissing,' interposed the RPO helpfully] in the streets is a very serious offence. Commanding Officers are to see that all Libertymen understand these instructions, which are to be read aloud and explained.

After listening, with ill-concealed hilarity, to this little catechism and delighting in its balanced mixture of officialese and almost Biblical reiteration, we were allowed to go.

We marched through the dockyard. The sunset looked like the disembowelling of a tropical bird. The twilight was both violent and sensual; houses and colonnades swarmed with unseen watchers. Cacti and palms embodied our excitement; even the advertisements for Nestlé's Milk, being in Spanish, read like poetry. In Main Street fat shopkeepers stood at their doorways selling rubbish, but we did find some Edwardian postcards. In one of them a man with a long moustache sat dreaming on a balcony. In the smoke from his cigarette, a young woman, whose dress was covered in tinsel, had materialised.

We went into a café called the Trocadero and ordered vermouths from a Spanish waiter with beautiful eyes but a skin badly disfigured by smallpox. On the stage a fat woman in red and gold net danced for the Fleet. I bought a cake made of cream in the form of a rose. It had no taste. We smoked cigars and moved from bar to bar. We came across one of our Petty Officers alternately embracing a blonde whore and eating cheese sandwiches. On the other side of the room four sailors were beating up a fifth, but were so drunk as to make little progress. Nevertheless, the boy wept bitterly, his hair hanging over his eyes. Various other matelots were dancing together. Others, ignoring the notice 'No men allowed on the stage' were singing 'Maggie May'. Tables were overturned, glasses broken, and the manager, sighing resignedly, charged more and more for his raw alcohol and blackcurrant juice.

'Not only to redeem the Fleet's good name, but also for their own sake . . .'

As we reeled back to the ship, singing 'Nobody knows you when you're down and out' and reciting bits from Stephen Spender's translation of Frederico Garcia Lorca, we could not fail to observe that, on every corner, unwise men were relieving themselves with evident satisfaction.

Next day Tom and I spent the morning on some low rocks from which the British Fleet emptied its gash (rubbish) into that tideless sewer, the Mediterranean. Our job was to burn out paint pots, a very satisfactory occupation, yielding a pleasure not unlike picking one's nose. As we worked, some of the Spanish dockyard maties, admitted daily into Gibraltar to earn their living, turned over the mounds of rubbish in a search for half-eaten sausages or scraps of meat, which they dried on a wooden box and then ate with relish.

Despite the fact that the workmen were on British territory, Tom and I saw this as a symbol of Franco's exploitation of the working class. Spain, being so close and, with the exception of Portugal, the sole remaining bastion of Fascism in Europe, had an almost pornographic effect on us; that is to use the word 'pornographic' in the sense of arousing simultaneously both excitement and revulsion. Spain, we felt, had been the 'pure' war. While secretly disagreeing with the British Anarchists in feeling that the struggle against Hitler was simply one corrupt force opposing another, we still thought of Spain as the great lost cause. There, before it had been crushed by the Stalinists, Anarchism had been a reality and not simply an ideal; had inspired action and fired guns. The death of the Republic had been mourned by a galaxy of talent: Auden and Isherwood, Spender and Connolly, Picasso and Miró. Like many of our generation we were infatuated with Lorca, a poet now seldom mentioned, and whom we believed (for later on the authors of his death were to become much disputed), to have been shot by the Falangists. In retrospect, the Civil War has come to seem more like a vivisection laboratory where two equally cynical and authoritarian powers experimented, under ideal 'field' conditions, with the techniques of sophisticated destruction. Some had already recognised this, but the message had not yet got through to us. Spain was more a state of mind than a place. Among the burning paint pots and scavenging dockyard maties we looked across the Straits to Algeciras and dreamt of freedom.

We couldn't go ashore that evening but there was some very interesting news. On our return from Villefranche, our next port of call, there was to be an expedition to Seville via Jerez on offer to all members of the Fleet, both officers and men, at six pounds per head. Apart from the six pounds there was another condition: we had to wear civilian clothes – no problem for the officers, who went ashore in them anyway, but an obstacle to us. Not an insurmountable one, however. Tom and I immediately put our names down and wrote home; both of us for our civvies and me for money as well.

Next day was a 'make and mend' so, although we were meeting Felix that evening, Tom and I decided to go ashore early and walk up the rock to see the apes. Alone, released from social and class pressures, we were truly happy and at peace. We climbed in brilliant sunshine and showers of rain, through woods smelling of leaf mould and fern, past villas where children in red dresses played with hoops and white doves sat in the branches of olive trees. Cacti threw fantastic shadows across our path. We saw a child's swing hanging in a grove. High up, from the north face of the rock, we could see the bull-ring of Lalinea.

'Oh black bull of sorrow! Oh white wall of Spain!' we quoted simultaneously. We picked narcissi and stuck them in our hats.

At last we found the apes, the responsibility of the Army, guarded by two friendly Tommies almost as agile as their charges. There were four large males in the enclosure, eight smaller and more active females and several babies, like kittens with the faces of sad old men. One of the males sat on an iron bar with a three-hundred-foot drop beneath him and made water.

We'd a quote ready for that too, although not from Lorca: ' "All is not gold that glistens," said the monkey, as he pissed in the sun.'

Towards evening we came down into the town and met Felix, who had the 'orrible Peter Ward with him and we got very drunk. Felix's deep booming voice and magnificent laugh put us all in the best of humours, and the evening turned into a kaleidoscope of full and empty glasses, eyes, paper flowers, breasts, cigars, castanets, nuts, oranges and darkness. The Liberty guys, suitably glamorised, were everywhere but there was no inter-fleet fighting. At one point Tom and one of the American sailors changed hats. We met the Baron, who bought a round of drinks to toast 'all Weymouth whores'. A Yank staggered up to Felix and asked him if he gave head. Felix said he didn't.

'Goddam it,' said the Yank. 'You've lost me two mother-fucking dollars.'

Quite suddenly, with that illusory and inexplicable speed which is a side-effect of drunkenness, Felix and Peter vanished, and Tom and I found ourselves trying to persuade a rather solemn Negro US army officer that the basis of society was criminal.

'I've been in the Pacific,' he told us somewhat irrelevantly, 'but I believe in the good book, the Bible.'

It was pouring with rain and we took a taxi back to the *Duke*. Next day we heard that Felix had been arrested trying to crawl across the Spanish border. Pissed as a newt and covered in mud, he had spent the night roaring out in a police cell that his father was an Admiral; naturally no one believed him and he was returned under escort to the *Dido* next morning to be punished with a few days' stoppage of leave.

We sailed at noon; the *Dido* for Casablanca, the *Duke of York* for Villefranche.

The trouble with being young and trying to write is other writers. Whatever you've been reading last gets between author and object, producing a solemn and ineffective pastiche, and so it was in my case. 'Going abroad' seemed to me so significant that I had begun to keep a journal (which doubled as letters to my mother) and which, however useful to me now as an aid to memory, has caused me, on re-reading, nothing but acute embarrassment and even from time to time a physical blush. The Surrealist declamatory style covered any revolutionary or poetic statements but, when it came to description, my current model was Cyril Connolly's *Unquiet Grave*, a book then recently published, which had impressed me both deeply and disastrously.

We sailed for Villefranche [I wrote]. The blood soon moves with the sea. We arrived in the morning: mountains, the sleeping villas of the rich and the town on the quay. The seduction of colour: violet, white, pink, lemon, blue, green and scarlet. The seduction of heat, the wish to become a plant, to grow roots, vegetate and decay.

Ashore, Tom and I had several adventures. On our first leave, in a little bar as evening was falling, an enormous woman and her seven-year-old daughter came in. The child, who carried a marigold, was affected in the extreme. She told us she was a queen, strutted like a peacock, scratched herself like a monkey, offered us her hand to kiss and stuck her fingers in the air shrieking with manic laughter.

Her mother smiled fondly, showing discoloured teeth. She told us her daughter's name was Monique. Later, after omelettes, Camembert, French bread, red wine and coffee, feeling very much men of the world, smoking Gauloises and trying out our deplorable French on the *patron*, Monique was taken upstairs to be put to bed and immediately the *patron* intimated, a finger laid alongside his tapir-like nose, that if we waited the mother would return. This news froze us with horror but we could think of no way to escape.

The woman came in. Before, she had smelt strongly of sweat. Now it was of sweat and cheap but pungent scent. She was not alone either. With her was another elderly whore, but bony and angular where she was fat and greasy. We bought them drinks, hoping to delay or avoid any further move. They nibbled our ears and ran down the Americans, whom they claimed were not *gentils*. They asked us if the English were as 'cold' as popular French legend maintained. We were in a quandary there: too enthusiastic a denial would only precipitate matters, but national pride demanded some defence. This, mild as it was, brought on the crisis. They led us into a back room where there was a divan, a brass bed and a portable bidet. On the discoloured walls was an Edwardian print of a naked woman with enormous thighs and buttocks. The fat *putain*, not unlike this image if considerably less fetching, reclined on the divan and patted a place for me to sit on it. The skeletal hag began to pull the petrified Tom towards the dubious bed. An inspiration, conceived in panic, struck me. I looked at my watch and clapped my hand against my brow in an exaggeratedly histrionic manner. The charm of their company had made me forget the time. We must catch the last bus back into Villefranche. Both women protested noisily, but I was firm. We would return on Monday. Slightly mollified they insisted on seeing us to our bus. There, under the cynical eye of a Petty Officer from the *Duke*, they embraced us fervently.

The next time Tom and I went ashore we decided to visit Monte Carlo, but before we left the harbour I was arrested by the French Customs. Cigarettes and soap were in very short supply in France that spring of 1947 and, like most of the ship's company, I had thought it worth the risk to smuggle. So carelessly had I planted these commodities about me that, while I was buying a stick of nougat at a stall, a plain-clothed official, after the most casual glance at my bulging person, signalled to a uniformed colleague, tapped me on the shoulder, and told me to accompany them.

In the cool Customs shed I decided the best thing was to come clean. I put everything down on the long trestle table, and they demanded an explanation. I told them they were all for my mistress in Monte Carlo. She smoked like a chimney. And the soap? Very necessary *après l'amour*. They smiled. I took the opportunity to slide two packets of Gold Flakes away from the others and towards them. I carefully didn't look in that direction. The packets vanished. They said I could go, and showed me how to stow away the soap and the rest of the cigarettes more convincingly. The thing was, they told me, that some sailors smuggled things ashore to sell on the black market. '*Déplorable!*' I agreed in my absurd French accent accompanied by exaggerated Gallic gestures. '*Absolument déplorable!*' I think it was my ham acting that made them spare me.

Tom was waiting nervously for me at the bus stop. As the queue was very long and there was no sign of a bus we decided to hitch-hike. Tom was at his worst, bullying me about everything both personal and political until I lost my temper and threw his hat into a public flower bed.

In a café we talked to a boy from Paris. He told me he was an Existentialist, but then most young Frenchmen with any intellectual pretensions claimed to be that in 1947. As Breton and Sartre were at it hammer and tongs I felt obliged, despite my secret admiration for the recently published *Age of Reason*, to defend Surrealism. He brushed this aside with that air of superiority and infallibility of which French youth has always had the secret, dismissing Breton as only interested in external phenomena. If he had been less beautiful, I might well have lost my temper. As it was I asked him to come on board the next day when the *Duke of York* was to be open to visitors.

Leaving him on comparatively amicable terms we set off in the direction of Monte Carlo and eventually we were given a lift by two elderly English ladies who were driving into the principality to shop. They were clearly very rich and told us how relieved they were that the war was over and they could return to live abroad, especially now that the Socialists had taken over and were making life impossible in England. Tom and I knew better than to disagree and anyway, as Anarchists, we felt under no obligation to defend Attlee. I did wonder though what Felix would have done. Probably he would have insisted on getting out and walking, especially if he'd had a few drinks.

Far below us lay the *Duke of York* at anchor. 'A fine life,' said one of the old trouts. They dropped us outside the casino.

I fell immediately and guiltily in love with Monte Carlo. I argued with Tom that if it represented a bad system, it was surely to be superseded by a worse. At least pleasure was involved whereas the grey conformity to come ... I looked at the policemen in their musical-comedy uniforms, the cab horses in their little coats. In the shops were unbelievable luxuries to my war-starved eyes: scent bottles in the shape of medieval towers, lips or stars, orchids streaked with strange colours, huge boxes of chocolates compared with which David Webster's offerings looked like a packet of jelly babies.

Men in uniform were not allowed inside the casino, but we bribed an official with some of the cigarettes I'd brought ashore – for following my arrest I hadn't found the courage to try and sell them in Villefranche – and he showed us round. I was particularly impressed by the little theatre. Its gilt and velvet, cherubs and swags of carved fruit seemed the epitome of Edwardian opulence. I would return here with Edouard, I promised myself. I knew he adored the tables and had, several times in his life, faced ruin through his passion for gambling. He had once shown me a photograph of himself strolling along the seafront with a mistress in the 1920s, very much the *boulevardier* with his Maurice Chevalier straw hat and cane.

Short of funds, I suggested to Tom that we went into the most expensive hotel to see if anyone picked us up for dinner. Surprisingly he agreed, aware no doubt that if there was any carnal price to be paid I would do the paying. At the long white bar of the Hotel de Paris I ordered two martinis. 'They are paid for,' said the barman, sleek as a worldly prelate, but it was no rich queen who sidled up to us. Our benefactor was an ex-naval Captain, a loveable old bore abrim with breezy anecdotes. He invited us to join him for dinner – 'Now I don't want you to refuse, lads. Wouldn't ask you if I couldn't afford it!' – and introduced us to a smart, bored woman in her late thirties – 'Runs one of me businesses.' A little later her mother appeared, a dear old thing whose sole contribution to the conversation was to divide everything – people, objects, dishes, décor, politics, places – into one of two classes: 'nice' or 'not nice'.

The Captain took us to a small but expensive restaurant. Tom clammed up completely, but it didn't really matter as our host ranged the seven seas and some forty years afloat on them, while his business associate contributed a certain amount of contemporary scandal. She told us that in their hotel was an ex-mistress of a French duke who brought back a different impossible man every night, but even the servants treated her with contempt! Her mother didn't think this was at all nice. The Captain offered no comment, but went booming on about destroyers during 'the first show'.

After dinner they went to a boxing match and we to the station, Tom complaining bitterly at the boredom of the meal and attacking me for playing up to them. I found this a bit tough as he hadn't exactly held back on either food or drink and had left me to show interest and gratitude. While waiting for the liberty boat we drank green chartreuse and I sent off a letter to ELT. There was a lot of flirtatious *entente cordiale* on the jetty between some French and British sailors. Next day the French boy came aboard as promised and I showed him over the ship. In the chain-locker flat where I had taken him, not innocently, but without much hope, he suddenly made a pass at me, and for half an hour the disciples of Jean-Paul Sartre and André Breton forgot their differences in each other's arms.

I I

Before returning to Gibraltar we moved out into the Atlantic for some more manoeuvres. Passing another Mess Deck I was unexpectedly seized, debagged and had some jam shoved up my arse to the accompaniment of excited and humourless laughter. As a public schoolboy I took this fairly philosophically, reflecting that after all it could have been boot polish for starters, but it led me to think about what I really felt about the Lower Deck and this was easier to do on the huge impersonal *Duke of York* with its wearying and complicated routine, and its inflexible bullshit. My jam besmearing was fortuitous or, if not so, no more than the result of my advertised effeminacy. I looked coolly that evening at my messmates. There was only Tom I was close to, and our friendship was constantly under strain. For the rest I admired our Leading Seaman, the very funny, astute, humane and well-informed Bill Rainbow. There were three other ratings who seemed to me to have an instinctive grasp of life. They were under-educated, but unblinkered by prejudice or convention. For the rest, I thought, they were all babies, mental age about five and with no curiosity or wish to grow up. The only difference between them was that some were nice babies and some nasty. It was true that most of them were tolerant and easy-going, but there were times, especially when I was over-tired, when the monotony of their conversation, the squabbling over rations, the endless sexual badinage and the senseless and sexless reiteration of rhythmic swear words, drove me almost distraught with irritation. By a chance remark of mine, I discovered that two-thirds of them had never heard of Bernard Shaw. This really surprised me as he was always in the newspapers, frequently to be seen prancing about in his tweeds and bathing-suit on the newsreels, and two of his plays had been made into comparatively successful films. I looked at my mess-mates with almost Fascist contempt that evening. Perhaps the jam had upset me more than I realised. One boy was writing a letter to a girl he'd met in Portsmouth and quite liked, but wished to make it clear that he didn't want her to think he intended to go steady. He asked my advice. Would it be better, with this in mind, to finish up his letter with 'God bless' or 'cheerio'? I said I didn't see it mattered. The mess deck rocked with scorn. 'I thought you were meant to be fucking educated!' said the letter-writer. 'Of course it fucking matters!' The general consensus was that 'cheerio' was less committing and I sulkily slung my hammock.

Arriving back in Gibraltar we discovered that my money for the Spanish trip hadn't arrived and nor had either of our parcels of civilian clothes. We solved the first problem by going on board the *Dido* and, as no one had any money to lend us, cashing a cheque with the Chaplain. The clothes presented a more serious problem as the one condition the Spaniards had made was that nobody, neither officers nor men, was to wear a uniform. I solved it with the aid of a friend in the clothing store. Some time before the Navy had ordered an alternative working rig, but decided against issuing it. It was to have been called 'Number Eights' and consisted of non-bellbottomed canvas trousers and pale blue shirts. In the stores there were also a number of canary yellow ties of unknown significance and some badgeless red parachute berets. Tom and I tried these outfits on, 'borrowing' them in exchange for a ration of tickler and the promise of both our tots before dinner. Personally, I thought we looked rather dashing.

The next morning, when it was still misty, with the promise of heat, we climbed excitedly into the cutter and were rowed across the calm waters of the harbour to where the officers and ratings in their 'civvies' were waiting to board the coaches into Spain. Comparatively few ratings had decided to go but among them were Felix and the 'orrible Peter Ward. Felix was at first effusively friendly to me (less so to Tom whom he had not forgiven for half-accidentally cutting his nose the night we got so drunk in Gibraltar), but suddenly, after a few words from Peter, he became inexplicably cold and distant. When Peter had gone off for a pee, I asked him what it was all about and, rather shamefacedly, he told me. Peter had insisted, and Felix had agreed, that as they were to be in civilian clothes, they must look smarter than any of the officers; a revenge aimed to compensate for Peter's irritation at being ordered about by men he privately considered extremely common but whose uniform entitled them to treat him as an inferior. In consequence, both had gone to immense trouble. Peter was in a very well-cut suit in Prince of Wales check and looked as if he were on his way to a rather smart race meeting. Felix presented an equally impressive if rather more rural image in good but excessively hairy tweeds and shoes heavy enough for rough shooting. The officers in their off-the-pegs, blue blazers and grey flannels were indeed, in the most literal terms, out-classed. Peter's rage and Felix's coldness (for despite his many true qualities he was not entirely displeased to be chosen out of the entire ship's company as the only possible companion by the son of an earl) was due to finding their one-upmanship ruined by having to acknowledge two figures dressed like the opening song-and-dance act on a third-rate music-hall bill.

Two coaches were waiting, but what with all the sulking and furtive explanations going on, we were rather late finding seats. Somehow (I forget if I engineered it or not), I found myself on the same coach as Felix and Peter with Tom sitting by the driver in the other one. Accident or no, I was disgracefully relieved. Without Tom's aggressive intransigence, I could at least bring Peter round to the point of toleration – not, to be fair to myself, that I cared all that much about his good opinion, but I was desperate to regain the right to Felix's company, without whose jokes and cultural cross references I felt the trip would lose much of its zest. As an initial tender of my good intentions I removed my tie and beret and put them in my ditty box, promising to buy a more suitable tie at our first stop. Felix's naturally gregarious and affectionate disposition soon surfaced but Peter still sulked. 'I won't have lunch with you!' he snapped.

The coaches moved across no-man's-land towards the heavily-guarded frontier, containing this microcosm of the great British obsession with class structure. To recap in more general terms: an aristocrat and a member of the upper-middle classes having dressed up in order to demonstrate the social inferiority of their middle-class naval superiors are betrayed by the appearance of a couple, one middle class, the other educated working class, the former of which is prepared to disassociate himself from the latter in order to regain the attention of the member of the upper-middle classes, who is himself unwilling to relinquish the approval of the aristocrat. At the same time I was equally obsessed with Spain, as of course were Felix and the betrayed Tom. Here entirely different cultural criteria were at work: Egalitarianism, Revolution, Anarchy! How the mind is able, admittedly more often when one is young, to accept two simultaneous concepts, which not only bear no relation to each other but furthermore demand totally different responses, has remained a continuous puzzle to me. I glared with loathing at the soldiers at the border in their 'dung-coloured uniforms', shook with fervent indignation as an officer stopped an old peasant with a donkey and, having emptied the panniers full of rags and papers on to the dusty ground, stirred them over with his jack-boot and strode off. I inwardly cursed the policemen in their coal-scuttle hats and cloaks, and blessed the impassive peasantry in whose heart, I was sure, still smouldered that revolutionary spark which would one day burst into glorious flame.

We moved on into Andalusia, Felix and I quoting Auden at each other, and wondering – wrongly as it happens – if Cyril Connolly, Spender or Isherwood had passed along this way a decade earlier. Peter asked who on earth these people were. 'Poets,' we told him. 'Writers,' he snorted with the contemptuous indignation of the confirmed philistine. I'd achieved my object. Felix would never isolate himself for two days with someone who'd never heard of Auden.

In retrospect it is amazing just how much that poet did mean to people of my generation and temperament. He was of course a great poet, but I think there was more to it than that. My own belief is that he was able to express our revolutionary aspirations while at the same time indicating that he shared our background and our guilty love/hate for its way of life and institutions; a spiritual nanny to bandage our knees and warm the milk for our Ovaltine after our imaginary struggles on the barricades. Even when prophesying the collapse of capitalism, he made its decay wistfully attractive and there was, in his stern admonitions, something reassuringly reminiscent of a popular and fair-minded head of the house telling one off for slacking. Even the phrase for which he has been so often and so severely attacked, 'the necessary murder', had no more weight than 'the necessary beating' which would hurt him more than it hurt you, but was essential for the sake of the school.

This is not a recantation. The younger Auden was infinitely superior to the drunken and dribbling reactionary of the later years, and Fascist Spain remained, up to the death of Franco – indeed up to the time of writing – a repressive and brutal régime. Speaking as an Anarchist, I held even then no illusions about Stalinist Communism or indeed any other kind. What I regret though is the way I couldn't look at what I saw without interpreting it through a grid. If one learns anything as one gets older, and sadly one forgets a lot too, it is to objectify.

The trip involved a visit to a sherry factory on the estate of a marquis. By the gates were two wire cages, one containing budgerigars, the other crocodiles. As it was siesta time the tall white buildings were deserted. In the sunny yards were trees of bitter Seville oranges. We walked between the great vats of maturing sherry, past armies of bottles and through the yard where the barrels were made. The guide told us they were made from real American oak, and that it was very expensive. Finally we came to a cleared space at the end of one of the buildings. Here was a long trestle table on which were dishes of stuffed olives, bits of cheese, anchovies and rusks. Girls in Andalusian costumes offered us sherry, glass after glass of it, and pretended that they were unable to understand the word 'no'. We, for our part, pretended that we minded. Swigging it back, I sententiously suggested to Felix that it was clear that the Government wished us to see the country 'through an alcoholic mist'. Equally solemnly he stopped drinking long enough to agree.

On the ends of some huge casks which lined the walls were photographs of previous marquises. In one of them the present owner, as a small boy wearing a straw hat, was playing with a toy sherry barrel. A little later he appeared in person, and stood there, plump, sleek, and smiling blandly, as he watched us lurching about. On leaving we were presented with three sample bottles of sherry and a big bottle of Spanish brandy. If my conjecture as to the intentions of the Spanish Government was in any way justified, we were certainly co-operating most wholeheartedly.

We lunched in Jerez at a hotel where the page-boys insisted on shaking hands. I remember walking about the lobby arm in arm with one, but as everybody was so drunk it seemed in no way indiscreet or even mildly unconventional. Lunch was a disaster. Most of the ratings were 'flakers' in the lavatory and the *Dido*'s Doctor was constantly interrupted. Although by this time I could have joined Felix and Peter, I decided not to, believing it would serve as a mild slap across the wrist to Felix, and sat down with another rating off the *Dido*. It was as well I did so. The rating vanished precipitously between the *hors d'oeuvres* and the two fried eggs which followed it, and simultaneously Tom appeared, roaring drunk and in no mood to avoid a confrontation with the 'orrible Peter Ward, which would have carried us all back to square one.

Tom's bus had visited a different factory, which had given them just as much to drink and nothing at all to eat and, although he carried on from where the other rating had left off, it wasn't enough to settle the sherry and he was violently sick afterwards.

After lunch I wandered through the town like a somnambulist Pied Piper pursued by a great number of children, for I had foolishly given one of them a small coin. They were dressed in rags, pitifully thin, and their hair was shaved close to their skulls, which were covered with scabs and bald patches. On returning to the coaches, Felix took a photograph of Tom and me surrounded by these waifs – all of them, I must admit, grinning like demons.

Between Jerez and Seville we slept. In a letter to my mother I explained that this was because 'the country was flat and dull'. I suspect that even if we had been crossing the most dramatic and romantic terrain in Europe, we would have slept just the same. In the suburbs, passing a San Francisco convent, Peter suddenly and uncharacteristically burst into song:

> San Francisco,
> Open your golden gates,
> Never a stranger waits,
> Outside your door!

I took this to be a sign that he was mellowing. Felix did too. He gave me a conspiratorial wink. I was right, and with Felix and me acting as buffer states, Peter and Tom found it just about possible to co-exist for the rest of the tour.

The Spanish authorities did us pretty well for our six pounds. They put us up in Seville at the Hotel Madrid, which I found enchanting. There was a courtyard full of plants and weathered statues. The floors were tiled. Very old maids tottered about their duties wearing uniforms of an Edwardian formality, and in the corridors, on the darkly papered walls, were huge elaborately framed nineteenth-century academic pictures: lionesses suckled their young, seas of treacle crashed on cardboard rocks, paper flowers burgeoned, wooden parrots preened. Over the reception desk was the official photograph of the Generalissimo, and here and there, about the passages, statues of saints and many examples of what I had learnt to think of as 'cet objet-là' – the crucifix.

The reason I called the crucifix 'cet objet-là' was the result of a story Edouard had told me about a quarrel between Breton and Magritte just before Magritte returned to Brussels from Paris at the beginning of the 1930s. Magritte and his wife Georgette went to a Surrealist séance in a Montmartre café and Georgette (possibly put up to it by René, who was by no means devoid of mischief) was wearing a crucifix which had belonged to her mother. On seeing this, Breton, whose atheism was of a religious intensity, started back like a vampire in the same situation, demanding to know why and by what right Madame Magritte should come to a Surrealist meeting wearing (and he pointed towards it) cet objet-là! Magritte took it very coolly. It was her mother's. What did it matter? She was fond of it. Breton persisted in his indignation. The Magrittes left the café. René's independence of spirit was too real to yield to Breton. He remained a Surrealist certainly, but at a distance.

I loved this story and made Mesens tell me it many times but, as a convinced atheist and having no love for the sadomasochistic symbol of Christianity, I found it very amusing to refer to the crucifix at all times as 'cet objet-là', although not without awareness that there was, within Breton, a certain pedantic exactitude bordering on the absurd, and that this was part of the joke.

Some time before dinner Felix and the mollified Peter came to our room and we drank lots of brandy out of tooth mugs. Things went smoothly enough for us to eat together and we discussed sexual deviation. Tom took no part in the conversation – he was sulking because he'd been forced to wear a tie – but Peter adopted the duty stallion attitude: screwing girls was all right, anything else perfectly disgusting. Felix and I spoke up for inclination. If a man falls in love with a stag that is his (and the stag's) affair; the only wrong was to believe there was anything superior about it. What we were really doing of course was talking about our own feelings under the cover of a theoretical discussion. Not that in my case stags came into it, but the young waiter did.

By the end of the dinner we were quite drunk again and Peter's heterosexuality had won us round sufficiently to produce general enthusiasm at the idea of a visit to a brothel. He had quite a lot of money, he said, and would stake us. We could pay him back later. We looked up the Spanish for brothel in Felix's handy phrasebook where, rather to our surprise, it was listed, and we tumbled out into the street. After asking several men who looked as if they might visit brothels but who in fact rejected our enquiry quite crossly, we got into a taxi. The man, leering at us intermittently, drove dangerously down several tortuous side streets and dropped us outside a considerable house. We were let in by an old woman dressed in rusty black and wearing a silver 'cet objet-là' round her wrinkled neck. She showed us into a room with stuffed bull's heads on the dark green walls. Around the table sat the girls, all quite pretty and chattering away like budgies. With them sat the boss, a mild-looking old man wearing a beret. He greeted us ceremoniously. The old woman quoted her prices, scribbling them down on a piece of paper to make certain we understood. Suddenly Peter announced that, after all, he had no money and the rest of us burst into relieved giggles. I suppose we would have gone through with it, but I remember being secretly delighted we didn't have to. It took some time to convince madame that we were not, after all, punters; she clearly thought we were simply haggling and kept making reductions on her piece of paper; but finally she understood. Everyone took it quite calmly, the girls asked for cigarettes. We sat smiling at them for some time and then, with noisy bravado, left. Out in the street we all turned on Peter, hypocritically pretending to be frightfully disappointed, but soon after we found ourselves in a bar, Peter's money mysteriously rematerialised and we drank ourselves legless on Spanish brandy.

I have no recollection of going back to the hotel but woke, with a monster hangover, to find a basin full of vomit on the surface of which floated a cigar stub and a dead carnation. While I was trying to unblock the sink with the stalk of the flower, the phone rang. 'This is the manager,' it said. 'Your be'aviour last night was hay disgrace. I shall 'ave to hask you to leave the 'otel.' With visions of court martial if this were to become known, I barked back with all the authority I could muster that he must be mistaken, and asked him to come and see me in my room in ten minutes. There was a giggle on the other end of the line. It was Felix. Later he confessed that he, in his turn, had been worried. So convincing was my bluster that he feared he might have got on to a Lieutenant Commander's room by mistake.

The drain unblocked and rinsed, I took a bath and tottered down to breakfast feeling as fragile as a piece of Dresden.

'Is this all we get?' growled a Lieutenant at the next table as they served us coffee and rolls in the pale sunlight of the courtyard. I allowed myself a world-weary smile. The Mesens had taught me to accept the idea of continental breakfast. I didn't even admit to myself that, like the Lieutenant, I'd much sooner have tucked into bacon and eggs.

Two sailors, looking very much the worse for wear, staggered in off the street and sat down. I knew one of them slightly and asked what he'd been up to. He leered triumphantly and slapped the back of his neck several times; a Lower Deck piece of mime representing sexual congress. The surrounding officers glared at him like figures in an H M Bateman cartoon. He suddenly realised where he was and, blushing furiously, mumbled an apology.

Tom hadn't surfaced for breakfast but as I was on my way upstairs to pack, the Lieutenant who had complained about his breakfast called me over. I felt very worried for a moment, believing that perhaps after all Felix's joke had some basis in reality, but it was all right.

'Would you pass it on to the chaps,' he said, 'not to get so drunk today. The point is they think you're all naval officers so don't let the side down. We want to get the most out of it of course and have a jolly good time and all that, but yesterday several people passed out and that's really not on. So pass it on eh, there's a good chap.'

I said I would, having no intention of doing so. I resented his

assumption that, just because I'd been to a public school, I was
prepared to act as prefect to his house master. In the hall, under the
photograph of the Generalissimo, I wrote postcards to Edouard
and Reggie and stuck smaller versions of the same image on each
of them. I've always been puzzled that dictators, or come to that
kings and presidents, choose to have their portrait on stamps to be
licked with the tongues and banged into place with the fists of their
subjects. It doesn't do them any harm of course, but nor is it very
respectful. I gave Franco a good double thumping.

It was time to sight-see. Tom was unwashed, stale-pissed and
very irritating. Peter was at his most affable. It had begun to drizzle.
The orange trees glowed in the damp air. José, the guide, said we
must wait for the Father who was to show us over the cathedral. I
was delighted he was late, plump, and very short of breath. As soon
as he was on the bus Tom announced he had to go for a piss.

'Hurry up,' hissed Peter, seething with irritation. I was disloyally
pleased by Tom's angry discomfiture.

When he did get back the bus wouldn't start anyway, so we had
to walk through the fine rain. Seville seemed more austere than I'd
imagined, but there were statues and fountains, tiled pavements
and palm trees – we were abroad all right.

Given my intransigent atheism it may come as a surprise that I
was prepared to enter a cathedral, but I had rationalised that some
time before, and even tried out my solution on ELT, who had given
me an official (Surrealist) dispensation. Church parades apart, and
I was soon to do something about that, I swore I would never go
into a church for an overt act of worship; a resolution I kept until
my father died in 1961 when, unlike Joyce's Stephen Dedalus, I
broke my vow for my mother's sake and, having done it once
without shaking my non-faith, have been to several weddings and
funerals since. At the time, I argued that churches were also
museums and the repositories of treasure. To treat them as such
and nothing else was no betrayal. One didn't after all concede
anything to their spiritual claims. With this rubric to still my
conscience, I followed the plump little priest into the great early-
Gothic edifice.

No nave leading up to the high altar, I noted with the disapproval
of an ex-Protestant communicant. Private chapels all round the

walls and a great cluster of them in the centre, each with a saint or
'*cet objet-là*' illuminated by a plantation of candles flickering and
guttering. The statues varied a great deal; some were like Victorian
wax dolls, others like Gothic carvings. There was one larger chapel
in High Baroque, marble and gilt with Doric columns.

'Here hall the 'igh class people his married,' said the Father,
showing his bad teeth. 'General Franco's daughter his married here.'

There were pictures in some of the chapels, but coated with heavy
brown varnish and difficult to see through the railings. There was
a Murillo, a painter I've always disliked anyway: a saint rolling up
his eyes to heaven at a cherub as vulgar as Disney. Here and there
were huge pop-eyed figures used in carnivals which secretly, as an
ex-C of E worshipper, I found rather a shocking idea. The same
was true of the information, handed out by the priest in the most
casual way, that on certain feast days the choirboys, dressed in
scarlet surplices, danced, accompanying themselves on castanets,
on the steps of the altars. Nothing like that ever happened in Christ
Church, Linnet Lane, Liverpool 17, or in the chapel at Stowe School,
Bucks. It sounded extremely frivolous.

I was reassured when a bell rang, and the old cleaning women
stopped scrubbing the pavements, crossed themselves and prayed
devoutly until another bell released them to continue their work
with renewed vigour. There was proof of Pavlovian conditioning
and holy brainwashing. Despite the dancing and pop-eyed carnival
grotesques there was power here and religio–political horse trading.
Franco was a devout Catholic and, in exchange, the Church were
good Fascists. It had stopped raining when I came out, with a keen
sense of release, into the Cathedral Square. I asked Felix if I was
right and he reassured me that I was. The Church, he said in his
measured and considered way, was perhaps the strongest factor in
winning the war for the Falangists. Peter looked irritated and
puzzled. Church for him was where you went in the country or, if
in London, for baptisms, weddings, funerals and memorial services.
What were we making such a fuss about?

We went over to the Alcazar, built by the Moorish Emirs and
later taken over by the Spanish king, who added a second storey.
No crisis of conscience here. I walked confidently through the court
and rooms proclaiming it self-evident that such fine proportions,

such restrained and refined intricacy, could only be the fruits of an advanced civilisation. I chose to ignore, or perhaps at that time didn't even know, that the most hideous atrocities of the Spanish Civil War had been perpetrated, admittedly in the service of Christian Franco, by his Moorish troops. The Spanish floor was a splendid junkshop of many periods. The pictures in particular were deliciously bad. There was one enormous painting of a solemn nineteenth-century couple looking at a fountain representing a pissing horse. There was also an ornate billiard room presented by Edward VII and preserved intact.

Franco, the guide told us, had helped with the restoration of the exterior. 'Franco, he come. He say: "What's be'ind this wall?" They say: "Hay Moorish wall, sir." He say: "Take down this wall".' I tried to find something discreditable in the story but failed.

It was nearly lunch time and Felix and I went off together to have an apéritif, This was not difficult as Tom wasn't speaking to anyone, and Peter was still irritated by my hysteria and Felix's don-like analysis of the links between Fascism and Catholicism. We had sat down in a square, sipping white wine, nibbling olives and little bits of raw fish, when some men approached and offered us a shoe-shine. We accepted. The sun shone. We were content. Before we were aware of it, the shoe-shine men had pulled off our heels, replaced them with new ones, and were demanding the equivalent of eight shillings each. How did the Anarchist and Socialist react to this? Did we accept it, even welcome it as a sign of the ability to revolt even under the most oppressive regime? We did not! Pretending that he had to change a note Felix hurried off to look for José. I remained, trying to appear impassive under the suspicious eyes of our opponents. It took Felix twenty long minutes to locate the guide but when he did there was an almighty rumpus, involving not only our assailants and our champion but swelling rapidly to include many passers-by, some of our party, some of theirs. Eventually José reached a compromise. We must pay four shillings each. With bad and blimpish grace we did so. On the way to lunch José launched into another of his worryingly neutral stories.

'These men, they cheat hanyone – even Spanish peoples. A friend hof mine meet a man. He say: "Hi ham the gardener hof the Bishop hof Seville. Hi sell you some seeds hof the most beautiful carnations hin the world." My friend buy them, he plant them and hup come not one carnation! Just hay lot hof dirty grass!!!'

I didn't even try to find an anti-Fascist moral in this one.

After lunch we climbed into the buses for the long drive back. After Jerez it grew darker. We finished the brandy. Felix and I chatted quietly as the bus drove on. The last light died on the hills. We crossed the border and parted on the quay. We swore that if, after our demob, there was an uprising we would go and fight. We were not to be put to the test, of course. Franco died in 1975 in the same hospital as a man dreadfully tortured by his police.

At noon next day I watched the *Dido* steam past with some envy and irritation. It was en route for Casablanca, which to me, as a lover of Bogart films, was sacred ground. We, on the other hand, were bound for Madeira. It took two days and, as the harbour wasn't big enough to accommodate a battleship, we anchored some distance off shore. On arrival little boats, manned by bare-footed Portuguese of piratical appearance, rowed out to barter wicker furniture and needle-boxes, and stalks of green bananas, a fruit unseen in England since the second year of the war. The ship's Tannoy warned us that trading was forbidden, but gazing over the side I could see jerseys and seaboots furtively passing out through the portholes of the Lower Deck. It was a cold day and the boys who dived for pennies hugged their bronzed bodies and shivered.

Tom went ashore the next day but I decided not to. By morning a ground swell had arisen and didn't die down until the day before we left. There was no leave as it was too rough for the liberty boats and so I never got ashore at all, whereas Tom was stranded for three happy days and crowed about it non-stop on his return. Our relationship had by now soured into almost continuous bickering and was never really to recover for more than an hour or two at a time.

We sailed for Portland, the first few days in hot sun with everybody off duty sunbathing on the deck. While we'd been away England had experienced one of the coldest winters of the century and as we approached the Channel it was back to heavy sea jerseys under the cold grey skies. Despite the weather I was in high spirits. In three days Tom and I were to return to the *Dido*. It's true I had fourteen days' stoppage of leave for losing my paybook but, as I'd hoped, when we were transferred the RPO scribbled out the punishment. I rushed happily away to find the Baron, Edward Wood, Felix and the 'orrible Peter Ward, all very friendly and larger than life on the dear little ship. The next day we were sailing back to Chatham and, in a fortnight's time, leave. Nothing could spoil my pleasure, but one unfriendly eye was watching me, determined to do its best. Warrant Officer Perkins was biding his time.

12

Warrant Officer Perkins' first opportunity wasn't long in coming although in the event he muffed it, a setback that made him all the more determined. I had assiduously cultivated an artistic reputation on the *Dido*, sitting on the deck sketching the harbour, or going ashore with sketchbooks and paints to turn out fairly competent if completely unoriginal gouaches of wherever we happened to be. My motivation was not entirely affected, I genuinely enjoyed sketching, but I discovered that there were side-advantages too. Any job which required some painting skill, ship's posters for example, fell my way. There was the time too when the British Council (there was as yet no Arts Council) sent to the *Dido*, for the edification of the boy seamen who were expected to be given a certain amount of general education, a series of large boards on which were photographs and reproductions comparing African sculpture with Cubist painting. There were some notes provided but this somewhat esoteric subject was not part of the Schoolie's armoury and, having satisfied the Commander as to my competence, I spent a pleasant afternoon while everybody else was on deck doing something freezing and boring, explaining to the admittedly indifferent boy seamen (including the one with skin like a ward-room plate) how the masks and fetishes of the Ivory Coast and the French Congo were more important than Cézanne in the development of Braque and Picasso, a theory I had assimilated from ELT Mesens.

When we arrived at Chatham the Captain decided to hold a cocktail party for the senior officers of the Home Fleet on their return from the Mediterranean cruise. The Commander suggested I be commissioned to paint a large mural to hang between the guns on the Quarter Deck and I proposed a mock early sea map, with mermaids and monsters and humorous illustrations of the places we'd visited. This was accepted and for several days I toiled pleasantly at the work. On Gibraltar I placed the three wise monkeys wearing naval officers' caps and at Villefranche sailors and tarts (the Commander asked me to move the position of one of the matelot's hands). It was finished in time and hung in its place looking, I had to admit, quite decorative. It was something of a success, a talking-point, and, when the party had been going on for some time and a great deal of gin been taken, I was sent for by the proud Commander and made much of. I was also given far too much to drink and by the time I staggered down to the Mess Deck, my first optimistic reaction to the alcoholic excess had turned lachrymose and revolutionary. It was past Lights Out but I was determined to persuade my grumbling shipmates that the triumph of Anarchism was overdue. Standing on a mess table and speaking, for some incomprehensible reason, in a strong German accent, I appealed for them to shed their chains. The noise I was making attracted the attention of my enemy and he came below to find out who was responsible. Luckily another stage was imminent. Revolutionary fervour was about to yield to nausea. Hanging on to one of the bars from which we slung our hammocks I was sick mostly over his shoes. He grinned like a wolf; I could see his features clearly in between the waves of approaching unconsciousness.

'Leading Seaman,' he said with deceptive mildness, 'this man is drunk and I hold you responsible. He's on a charge and you too for neglecting your duty. See the mess is cleared up immediately.'

The Leading Seaman said he would do as ordered but, if he might be allowed to say so, he felt it inadvisable. Perkins coloured and told him, with menacing calm, to explain himself. The Leading Seaman did so – undeniably drunk, but made so by the Upper Deck – case likely to be dismissed – mural for cocktail party – hardly likely to make it stick.

The Warrant Officer thought it over, and decided to fight another day. As he left the Mess Deck, I collapsed and was put into my hammock by the Leading Seaman and a very diverted Baron. I woke with no remembrance of any of this but was told about it at breakfast.

'Watch out for that Mongolian shirt Perkins,' advised the Baron.

'He's a right bastard and anyway he's out for your fucking blood now.'

Perkins said nothing more about the incident. I passed him at stand easy in the recreation space and he didn't seem to see me at all. I had no further trouble from him before I went home for Easter leave.

In the middle of my leave the King of Denmark died and we were recalled, as the *Dido* had been chosen to represent the Fleet, and to carry across an elderly Admiral and a marine band which was going to play in the funeral procession. The admiral seemed quite a cheery old gentleman, who promenaded the ship most of the day, acknowledging our salutes with bluff panache. Felix, however (and after all he had an inside knowledge of Admirals), thought he'd be a bit of a bastard if crossed and we were indeed warned to creep about the ship in the early morning for fear of waking him.

We arrived at Copenhagen at dusk and made fast to the jetty, watched by a large crowd. I was very surprised by how alike the Danes looked: to my eyes they seemed almost as interchangeable as a similar gathering of Chinese. Only one young man stuck out from the rest and he turned out to be a Geordie who had settled there and was soon exchanging what were undoubtedly obscene, but to my ears impenetrable, pleasantries with two stokers from his native Newcastle who were leaning on the gang-rail.

Scrubbing decks early next morning (as quietly as possibly for fear of disturbing the Admiral) I could see rather more of the place. We were quite close to that banal little mermaid, but on the quay was a statue of a polar bear with two cubs which had a certain kitsch charm. The Baron however didn't think much of it. 'Fuck a bear with birdshit all over its swede,' he said dismissively, and indeed it was almost white with the droppings of the great flocks of pigeons which, rather than the gulls, seemed to have commandeered the dockyard.

Stand easy produced a surprise. Instead of the usual meagre biscuits or soggy fruit cake, there was tray upon tray of Danish pastries and cakes bursting with real cream. How can this be, I asked myself, as I wolfed down a second plate from the kiosk in the recreation space. Denmark was occupied and we weren't, and yet, only a year after the end of the war, they've got all the cream cakes they want and we've still got butter rationing. It was a question we were to ask ourselves for several years to come.

That afternoon Felix and Edward were on duty and I was so irritated with Tom that I refused to go ashore with him. I asked another rating, an engaging fellow with a weakness for the ballet, and, as he had a date at seven that evening, arranged to meet the Baron at a typical rendezvous – 'Outside the baronial lavatory in the main square at seven o'clock for "big eats".'

The city was cleaner than any I'd encountered before and had dealt with mourning its late King with a certain commercial astuteness. In the window of a parfumerie was a single large white bottle of scent with a black bow round its neck and, in a very chic couturier, a solitary black hat acknowledging the respects of an unaccompanied black shoe.

We went to a modern art show of young Danish painters, very Expressionist, messy and derivative, but I managed to see some paintings by Munch, whom Edouard had described as 'the van Gogh of the North'. Then we drank Schnapps, which I'd never tried before and found quite extraordinary, exploding like a warm but lethal jellyfish at the back of the nose.

At seven the balletomane went to meet his date, and, rather louchely, I took up my station outside the gents. It was indeed baronial by contemporary British standards, clinically clean and extremely large with its own cloakroom and shoe-shine parlour. As the Baron hadn't shown up by 7.30pm I decided to give up and went into one of the smarter restaurants for dinner. I ordered fish with a rich sauce, half a duck, an ice, and cheese and biscuits. Halfway through the Gargantuan meal I saw the Baron wandering past and ran out to fetch him in. Had I known how drunk he was I'd have hesitated and indeed his carry-on over the next hour will explain why Felix and my other friends refused to go ashore with him.

Explaining that he had spent the afternoon asleep in a park, a statement confirmed by the mud and grass all over his person, he yelled 'Shirt' at the waiter and ordered the duck. This was some time coming but it didn't worry the Baron. First he grabbed a piece of fish that someone had left on his plate at the next table and then, realising that his behaviour was causing a bad impression with the solid Danish families around us, aggravated the offence by explaining to me very loudly and at some length that they had all, without exception, played with themselves when young. At last the duck arrived and the Baron, having jabbed at it once or twice with a fork, picked it up in both hands and gnawed at it with uninhibited and noisy satisfaction.

As most of the Danes understand English rather well and the Baron in between his shark-like assaults on the duck's carcass continued to accuse them of 'interfering with themselves', a linguistic variation on his previous assertion but no less insulting, I was very relieved when the 'Shirt' was summoned and the bill assertively demanded and reluctantly settled.

We walked out without any major disaster and were accosted by an extraordinary-looking child with a grotesquely large head covered with thick golden curls, who offered to lead us to a bar, where Bing and Bong provided the music. Here we got stuck into litres of ice-cold lager and I began to catch the Baron up. At his suggestion I bought a rose from an itinerant flower-seller and presented it to a girl on the other side of the room telling her, with tedious and repetitive gallantry, that she was the Mona Lisa of the twentieth century.

Drink had unloosed the Baron's id and that same beast which had thrown the boiling water over my feet came lumbering out. The Baron produced a dagger and said he wanted to stab somebody. He left the café and I nervously followed him, although how I could have frustrated his murderous intentions if he had persisted I can in no way imagine, unless it was by drawing them on myself. Happily his mood changed again and, after eating several sandwiches from a slot machine, a source of nourishment unknown to me until then, we fell into several other bars and, although the Baron got drunker and drunker, there was no recurrence of his psychotic aspect.

Somewhere I conducted a small orchestra with a bread knife. They were playing *The Flower Waltz*. Somewhere I danced with a girl with a most un-Danish-like complaint – BO. The Baron made friends with a very small American sailor with bright red hair and no chin. They sat together with their arms round each other's necks, spilling their beer and moaning about their respective navies. Eventually I found myself drunkenly propositioning the Mona Lisa of the twentieth century, who had mysteriously reappeared – or was it that we had returned to the original bar, the domain of Bing and Bong? She rejected my advances most gently.

'You are reminding me,' she told me in her sing-song Danish accent, 'of a gay rabbit' – a simile rather more accurate than she was perhaps aware.

Earlier that day I had bought a large Danish Blue cheese and, unexpectedly, hadn't left it anywhere. It may seem strange to the contemporary reader that I should have bought it at all; today Danish Blue is a despised comestible, a sure sign of a provincially unimaginative and usually impoverished cheese board, but in war-time Britain and for some years after there was only one kind of cheese, a sweating and flavourless soap known officially as 'Cheddar' and more generally as 'mousetrap'. I knew therefore that there was little I could take home that would please my family more than a large Danish Blue, creamy and veined within its rough-cast protective rind. It was the thought of my father's delight that kept me in possession of the cheese throughout that long, drunken, peripatetic evening, but as the Baron now declared his intention of slinging his mick and crashing the baronial swede, I decided to accompany him back to the ship and leave the cheese in its box on the gangway in charge of the guard.

Both objects I accomplished; the Baron staggered aboard, the watch accepted the cheese and I turned back towards the city in search of further adventure. As I walked across the quay I could hear, through an open porthole, the tones of 'The Well-tempered Keyboard', a proof that the Baron had reached the Mess Deck. As to what I still expected of the night I had no firm idea – perhaps the Mona Lisa of the twentieth century had made some vague promise to fob me off. What I finished up with was a ballet dancer in a white mackintosh, a deceptively young man with remarkably bad teeth. His name was Hans and he invited me back to his flat, where he produced a bottle of Madeira, a coincidence which, in my state of heightened alcoholic consciousness, seemed disproportionately significant. It was clear that he had hoped for rougher trade than I, but we had quite a cosy time and, as the level of the Madeira fell, he became increasingly confidential. He clearly regretted, if for personal reasons, the departure of the occupying forces and he showed me several photographs of handsome young Germans both in and out of uniform affectionately inscribed. I found this perversely fascinating, but was even more intrigued when he searched out several propaganda gramophone records made by a German swing band called Mister Charlie, with the lyrics in English. There was one about Churchill. It went:

> He helps the Jews
> He's a friend of the USSR
> He's here, he's there, he's everywhere,
> The man with the big cigar.

The backing, although a shade ponderous, wasn't too bad; the trumpet player patently influenced by Nat Gonella.

At first light I left Hans, snoring gently, to his dreams of blonde Aryan beasts and caught a tram back to the dockyard. Going back on board I discovered I had precipitated a crisis. The dog watch had forgotten to tell the morning watch about the cheese and they'd been terrified out of their wits, believing it to be a bomb. I apologised, collected it, and went below for breakfast.

After acting out the naval formula for facing the day: a shit, a shower and a shampoo, I changed my socks, pants and nautical tee-shirt, polished my shoes, ironed my silk and went to find Felix and Edward.

We'd put in to see the funeral procession, which meant in effect a day ashore, and off we went. We caught a tram and Felix told us that it was essential we behave. It was, after all, he emphasised, 'a solemn and portenious occasion'. We immediately, including him, began to giggle helplessly. It didn't matter though. Everybody on the train and indeed throughout the city was incredibly cheerful, laughing and joking as though off to a wedding. We passed the Danish Horse Guards on their way to join the procession. In their dusty blue uniforms they looked like the chorus from the touring company of an under-budgeted production of *The Student Prince*.

On reaching the centre of the city we sat down in a café to an enormous second breakfast and almost missed the procession. A slow march in the street reminded us of why we were not aboard.

The coffin was passing on its gun carriage. Our marines, we decided, were as smart and co-ordinated as automatons, the French chic but casual. I hummed a music hall song I'd found on an old 78 record in a junk shop in Weymouth, 'Ain't it grand to be bloomin' well dead!'

Felix admitted, rather shyly, that it was his twenty-first birthday. We went back to the ship. I borrowed some money to take him and Edward out to a celebratory dinner, and we gorged like boa-constrictors and drank like fishes.

The measured strains of Johann Sebastian greeted me as I returned to my Mess Deck. The Baron was back too, and in good spirits. He had spent the evening, he told me, 'hanging out of a fifteen-year-old party in a tent'. She spoke no English but had apparently expressed her enthusiasm by singing throughout the repetitive phrase 'Hey-bob-a-rebob', a rhythmic cry taken from a recording by Cab Calloway which was very popular at the time.

We sailed in the morning. The passage back was rough and Felix's birthday dinner was lost over the side. We docked in Portsmouth on Saturday morning and I resumed my broken leave.

The cheese was a great success. My father's mother, a forceful old lady, came as usual to Sunday lunch and, on seeing the Danish Blue, was beside herself with envy. She had been brought up by her grandmother on the Cheshire marshes and was given to old-fashioned expletives of an eighteenth-century flavour.

'Dash m' wig!' she snorted. 'Where did you get that cheese?'

From that day on, my father always referred to cheese as 'Dash m' wig'.

My leave over, I returned to the *Dido* and we resumed our purpose-less meandering along the south coast until it was time for the summer cruise: a visit to Guernsey followed by a 'goodwill' tour of Scandinavia. It was now spring, and, in recompense for the arctic winter, both warm and beautiful. There was very little to do. We painted ship, skived as much as we could, and envied those who left to be demobbed.

Warrant Officer Perkins decided that it was high time to have another shot at getting me into trouble. As I've mentioned earlier I had stuck on the inside of my locker a reproduction of Magritte's *Le Viol*. Perkins, passing one day when my locker door was open, decided it was obscene and reported me for displaying it. Next day, just before noon, I was sent for by the Commander, who felt obliged to see if the charge was justified. I opened my locker door and, controlling his amusement with some difficulty, he asked me to explain it. I was only too eager to oblige. Did it provoke desire, I asked rhetorically, lust? Surely not. Compared with the pin-ups on my shipmates' locker doors it was infinitely less aphrodisiac. Magritte's purpose in painting *Le Viol* was . . . I was all set to launch into a lengthy analysis of the painter's intentions when the Commander, with the thought of a pink gin in the ward-room rapidly gaining the ascendancy, cut me short.

'I really don't think, Warrant Officer Perkins, that in this case . . .' I stood there, finding it hard not to register my pleasure at my enemy's discomfiture.

'You may go, Able Seaman Melly.'

'Ordinary Seaman, Sir.'

He looked surprised, asked me how long I had been in the Navy and said he would look in to why I hadn't been promoted. As a result, a week later, with the helpful recommendation of the Leading Seaman of F Mess, I was made Able Seaman, and back-dated six months with quite a lot of pay. *Le Viol*, much to the indignation of Warrant Officer Perkins, continued to smile hairily if enigmatically at the ship's company every time I opened my locker door.

Despite this shot across my bows, and its unexpectedly helpful outcome, I in no way kept what is now called a low profile. On the contrary I decided to attempt an extremely provocative and perhaps, up until that time, unprecedented feat: to have the religious denomination on my naval papers altered to 'atheist', and to be given permission not to attend church parade. My reasons for this were part irritation, part genuine conviction, and certainly part exhibitionism. My strategy however was the opposite of Surrealist intransigence. I went to see the Chaplain, a reasonable young Welshman with whom I had a rather friendly relationship. To him I put it that as a sincere Christian it was surely as offensive for him to realise that a non-believer was being forced to pay lip-service to

what he believed in, as it was for me to pretend to worship something I had no faith in whatsoever. He was entirely convinced by
this argument and agreed to be called in my defence when I appeared
in front of the Commander on 'requests and defaulters'. It went
extremely well and the only concession that I was forced to make
was the definition of my non-belief as 'agnostic' rather than 'atheist'
which I'd asked for. My papers were solemnly and officially changed
– 'Religious Denomination: Agnostic' – and I was excused church
parade.

Warrant Officer Perkins, a keen non-conformist, thought to punish me for this impertinence. He told my Chief Petty Officer that,
on his orders, I was to clean out the heads during the service. I
wasn't taking that lying down. I went screaming to the Chaplain –
Wasn't it a further insult to his faith to equate it with cleaning out
latrines? He was nearly as angry as I was and went to see the
Commander. The order was countermanded and I was free to sit, I
must confess smugly, reading the posh papers and listening with
some pleasure to the distant singing of Anglican hymns, for which,
like Sybil, I had always preserved a nostalgic affection.

The reactions of the ship's company were variable. Predictably
the Baron thought it well worthwhile. Despite his love of Johann
Sebastian, he was a true iconoclast and the only religious observation I heard him utter was when the Tannoy, early one Sunday
morning, announced 'Holy Communion on the recreation space',
he asked the mess if 'anyone fancied going up for a wet (drink)'.
Others, either from conviction or convention, were shocked in
varying degrees, the majority were indifferent, but the most surprising reaction came from the ferocious, bearded Master at Arms.
Passing his caboosh (small office), once again crowded with woolly
animals, I was startled to be called by name.

'I hear,' he said, sewing boot-button eyes on a puce duck, 'that
you've had your religious denomination changed to agnostic.'

I explained that I asked to be described as an atheist but had been
forced to accept the less definitive description.

'I didn't know,' he said, biting off the thread, 'that you 'ad the
intelligence to be fuckin' atheist. Now piss off.'

I went away glowing with that special pleasure that comes from
the favourable opinion of someone you fear.

Sex on the *Dido* was comparatively low key but uncensorious. There were a few obvious homosexuals, the doe-eyed writer for one, many total heterosexuals, and a fair number of those who would, on a casual basis, relieve sexual pressure with their own sex. It was accepted, for instance, on my Mess Deck, that on Saturday make and mends (half days off) anyone who fancied some mutual masturbation would crash down in the coat locker, a structure of closely-meshed wire like a medium-sized cage. As an open part-time invert I was often solicited on these occasions and usually accepted. Sometimes my masculine role both surprised and disappointed those who had misread my predilections. Mostly, however, it was no problem, and there was as relaxed and tolerant an atmosphere as any I've encountered. I had a sometime affair with a Corporal of the Marines who shared my watch on the Quarter Deck, but this was only in the middle watch and mostly, from his point of view anyway, to allay boredom. I think he really preferred our other pastime, which was to raid the officers' galley for bacon, eggs and sausages and fry-up on our electric fire laid dangerously on its back. Sex was not really an issue on the *Dido*. There was much the same atmosphere as at a fairly easy-going public school.

On shore of course the Baron, and those like him, picked up women and, being far from discriminating, would return on board most mornings boasting of some fairly grotesque conquest.

I had resumed diplomatic relations with Tom, but mostly only in respect to our jazz sessions, and I seldom went ashore with him. For Felix, on the other hand, my friendship had grown warmer and I was very pleased, while anchored at Weymouth, when he asked me to go home with him. His father lived in a village not far from Dorchester, a suitable place for his retirement as it was near enough to the sea to add a tang of salt to the air. Here, berthed in an early nineteenth-century Gothic rectory with fine no-nonsense Georgian furniture and portraits of earlier nautical Aylmers on the dining room walls, he was in a position to play squire with stick and spaniel.

'Treacle,' he'd shout at the dog: 'Come here! Here, boy! Heel!' and to the farm labourers: 'Pigs all right, John?'

His wife was like a character out of a play by the then popular dramatist, Esther McCracken, slightly eccentric, rather careless in appearance, given to saying the first thing that came into her head, and extremely kind and easy-going.

There were strawberries and Devonshire cream for tea, sea trout for dinner and, on my first visit, another retired sea-dog and his wife were staying in the house.

'My father's last words,' he told us over the brandy, 'were: "for God's sake, m'boy, always dress for dinner" and he was right. It stands for such a lot.'

Felix and I exchanged sardonic glances, resorting to that peculiarly English defence-mechanism by which we can accept what we know to be indefensible. At a village fête the following week our satirical aloofness was put further to the test. Here were feudal privilege, archaic prejudices, forelock tugging, and paternalism rampant, but here too were an organic wholeness, a sense of responsibility and a human scale. Confused by our responses, we concentrated on the more absurd aspects – not that this was difficult.

Through the crackling public address system the local Canon announced the loss of two dogs: 'Such jolly little fellows. One little chap is called Nelson and his brother is Rodney.'

It was evident that Admiral Aylmer was not the only ex-Navy officer to have hove to thereabouts. There were pro-blood sport pamphlets in the temporary lavatory, and almost exaggeratedly Hardyesque rustics in charge of the stalls. Best of all there was a play, acted by the village children with a touching lack of talent and Dorset accents as rich as clotted cream: 'Furry Bluebell, moi dear, oi wonder whurr her Majesty can boie?'

'I find country life a dangerous seduction,' I told Felix on our way back to the *Dido*, and he agreed. Certainly when at home he took on much of the texture of his parents' life, bringing me out what he called 'a stiff whisky to keep the cold out' when I was finishing a sketch in the garden and acknowledging the respectful greetings of the villagers to the manner born. Yet both of us believed in a fairer, more egalitarian society where greetings were an equal acknowledgement of shared humanity and not an outward sign of social status. My own mixed feelings were based on flimsier foundations. My father, despite a lifetime spent of necessity in a Liverpool office, had a yearning for the life of a modest country gentleman, a taste he was only able to fulfil under the aegis of his rich uncles. Most summers they would 'take a place', and round them would gather the more impoverished members of the family to shoot the moors or fish the river. As a child on warm Welsh evenings, beating the pine woods to drive the clattering pigeons towards my father's gun or watching him cast over the river Clwyd, I too fell in love with the idea of such a life. I inwardly envied Admiral Aylmer his ordered life and small domain.

Back aboard, before the summer cruise, there was an audition for a variety concert, one act from each ship, to be given that autumn in front of the King and Queen when they were inspecting the Home Fleet on the Clyde. Sacrificing republican feelings to show-biz I offered 'Frankie and Johnny' and was selected by the Chaplain of the *Duke of York*, the Val Parnell of the project, to represent the *Dido*. I was very pleased and wrote immediately to my mother to suggest she come up to Scotland for the occasion. Later I was told that I was not to appear after all, but this lay ahead, and it was in high spirits that we left Portland for a summer cruise, believed to be to Scandinavia, and my last few months in bellbottoms.

13

Disappointment awaited us. We were told that we were to visit not, as had been rumoured, Norway and Sweden, but Guernsey – and then return to Chatham. I was not at all thrilled about Guernsey, as it was too English to be thought of as being properly abroad. Nor was I forced to reconsider my prejudice on arrival. The island had been occupied by the Germans and there had been some accusations of fairly widespread collaboration. As a result there was a certain strident patriotism, a feeling that the war was only just over, and this manifested itself in thousands of Union jacks of all sizes, photographs of Churchill in most pubs and shop windows, and hundreds of posters showing a bulldog with a swastika between its teeth. The effect of this somewhat ostentatious Anglophilia was undermined by a small boy who approached us as we walked into St Peter Port and told us that he hated the British in general and British sailors in particular, a point he proceeded to amplify with a series of ineffectual but undoubtedly viciously-intended kicks and blows.

It was a Sunday and the pubs were officially shut, but we were told that there was one open on the other side of the island. We found a café serving eggs in any quantity (there was still a severe shortage on the mainland), and I ate eight at a sitting cooked in many different ways: boiled, fried, poached and scrambled. I was to pay for this later with an angry boil on my leg. Towards evening we caught a bus in search of the pub. Felix was worrying about his sex life, attributing his lack of success to his inability to distinguish between girls that might and those that wouldn't. Whenever we passed one he would ask us crossly 'Would she?' or 'What about her?' Edward Wood and I answered with an assumption of libidinous expertise to which we had no right.

The island seemed dull, even on so beautiful an evening. It was flat and littered with greenhouses and, while there were many rather pretty Jersey cows, Felix told me – whether seriously or not I have never been able to decide – that they were 'unfashionably light in colour'. We found the pub, a Thirties half-timbered building with those dispiriting horse-brasses in the saloon bar. It was quite lively however and half the ship's company had homed in on it. After a time Felix went off, with the gloomy air of one who foresees failure, to try and pick up a girl 'who might', but Edward and I stayed put and began to get drunk. As usual the beer acted as a catalyst. There was a faded blonde at the bar asking, from time to time, for a gin and tonic in a painfully refined accent. I said something about the Palladium to Edward and she intervened.

'Aye have sung there,' she told us. 'Aye have sung all over the West End in the old days. The Albert Hall, everywhere.'

She pointed to a variety bill for the local Palace that was pinned up behind the bar. At the bottom in very small letters it said 'Grace Roberts – the Welsh Nightingale'.

'The billing is all wrong,' she said. 'It is meant to include "of wireless, film, and television fame".'

This last surprised me particularly. There had been a little television before the war in London; my father had seen it once and thought there was no future in it, but it had hardly got going again by 1947.

There was a curious noise like a bullfrog. We turned to face a tiny shrivelled man in spectacles who smiled at us, opened his mouth and croaked again even more loudly. I thought he was suffering from some affliction and tried not to smile but when he had croaked twice more I realised he was doing it deliberately. He too pointed to the variety bill and I worked out that he must be 'Mimco – the Australian Mimic'. He treated us to quite a repertoire of imitations, but refused to perform his speciality – someone blowing up a bicycle tyre – on the grounds that it was too noisy.

Another figure, 'the Great Marvo', the top of the bill, executed several conjuring tricks. He had an enormous wart on the side of his nose, but his tricks were extremely boring. We fell into conversation with a separate group who turned out to be a rival concern, the local rep. They were rather pathetic and swanky and being unable to imitate bullfrogs or tell us what card we were holding, launched into elaborate dirty jokes involving a great many 'funny voices' and offered us free tickets to their next production, *Jane Eyre* which, with that irritating habit actors have of shortening the names of plays (*eg* 'As You', 'Much' or 'The Dream'), they referred to as 'Jane'. They did, however, give us a lift back in their taxi to St Peter Port where Edward, who had a weak head, was sick over the seafront.

The next day I had no shore leave but one of my nautical artistic duties to perform. Everywhere we went it was the custom of the *Dido* to hold a children's party and it was my job to make-up the boy seamen as 'pirates', a task I enjoyed possibly overmuch. Later I was on cell duties. Taff had been recaptured for about the fourth time and put behind bars until there was a chance to hand him over to the naval police for yet another spell in the glasshouse. Despite the horrors to come, he seemed as cheerful as ever.

'They'll 'ave to dismiss me from the service sooner or later,' he said in his Cardiff accent. 'Stands to reason, Boyo.'

We were two days on the way to Chatham, the sea broken only by the ship's bows. Gazing over the side at the steady stream of foaming water rushing past the great metal plating, it was possible to believe that it was the ship which was static, the ocean on the move. On the deck, in the hallucinatory clarity of the summer light, two marines, wearing masks, fenced among the stanchards and bollards. Smoking a cigar, contemplating a pleasurable shit, I was visited by the temptation to sign on, to travel the world, to know that whatsoever happened I would be clothed, housed and fed. I rejected it almost immediately: the discipline, the monotony of the Mess Deck, the ship lying, a dispossessed hulk of rusting metal, in the dockyard drizzle. Besides, I had to admit, the Navy might well refuse to have me. Useless at all but the most menial tasks, both rebellious and argumentative, I was more or less tolerated in the comparatively Anarchic gap between war and peace; and while on the subject of Anarchism, it would be impossible to square up my convictions with a career in the Navy. As an infiltrator or saboteur? Not me. Anarchism was too noble a concept to be denied in this way. Its means must be as honourable as its ends. I was an open Anarchist, making no secret of my commitment to anyone who was prepared to listen. In my locker were neat piles of pamphlets by Bakunin, Kropotkin, George Woodcock and Herbert Read which I left systematically about the Mess Deck hoping someone might pick them up and become interested. Somebody had. Warrant Officer Perkins had picked them up and become very interested indeed.

14

There was something afoot. The cancellation of the Scandinavian cruise, the unexpected return to Chatham, were more than just an Admiralty whim. Rumour ran riot, but we were not kept in the dark for long. The morning following our arrival both watches, including watch-keepers, were ordered to fall in on the Quarter Deck – an unprecedented command in my experience. We were, the Commander told us, about to be addressed by the Captain, who had some very sad information to impart.

The Captain was a short, plump man, neither popular nor unpopular, and indeed seldom seen by anyone below decks except for the wardroom stewards and the ratings on the bridge. He told us first that he would shortly be leaving the ship, probably during the Scottish voyage, and that the Commander would be assuming temporary command. If this had been all he had to tell us, we would have felt that, in implying that it was enough to reduce the ship's company to manly tears, the Commander had misinterpreted our feelings towards his rather anonymous superior officer. It was however only coincidental. The reason why the Captain was leaving the ship was because the Admiralty had decided – 'Whether rightly or wrongly', said the Captain in a rare display of feeling – that the *Dido* was for the scrapheap, redundant! This, he added, would not of course affect those due for demob, but he was sure it would be a matter of regret for the regular ship's company, who would shortly have to return to their barracks for reposting. Meanwhile he hoped that the spirit of the ship . . .

Where he was wrong, in my case at any rate, was in believing that only the regular ship's company would be upset. I am by nature sentimental to a fault, and it was all I could do not to sob audibly. It was ironic that the very next day I was to be put on a serious charge which could have given me cause to cry in earnest.

That evening, too short of funds and too despondent to go 'up the Smoke', Felix, Edward and I, all of us due for demob in a few weeks, got maudlin drunk, on the *Dido*'s behalf, in a gloomy Chatham pub. The beer was responsible for a minor disaster that night. In a dockyard they lock up the heads to avoid polluting the harbour and any rating taken short is expected to go ashore and use the latrines on the quay. Sensibly enough nobody does. An empty tickler tin is left by the open porthole, and is baled out into the darkness as many times as it is filled. Rising crossly from my hammock I grabbed the tickler tin and began peeing in it, only to find that despite aiming accurately (a fact I checked) I was soaking my feet. In my fuddled state it took me some time to work out why. An empty tickler tin can be put to several uses, and one of them is for helping to make the washing-up water soapy. To do this all that's necessary is to punch several holes in the bottom, put in some fragments of issue soap and then swish the tin rapidly around in the hot water until it produces sufficient lather. In my haste to relieve myself I had grabbed the wrong tin. Lying in my hammock with damp feet, I began to feel a little less sentimental about the *Dido*.

The next day Warrant Officer Perkins approached me with a look of grim satisfaction on his face. I was to come up to the locker flat and open my locker. Why, I wondered? He surely couldn't have persuaded the Commander that *Le Viol* was obscene after all. The Commander was waiting there looking rather severe. I smiled at him and he didn't smile back, but asked me to open it up. I did so. Warrant Officer Perkins pointed to the Freedom Press pamphlets. The Commander asked me what they were and why I had so many of each. I told him that they were Anarchist literature and whenever possible I distributed them among the sailors. A look of total astonishment passed across the Commander's kindly aquiline features. Did I realise that these were subversive pamphlets aimed at undermining the State, the Armed Forces, the Church, even the Navy itself? I said yes of course I did, but . . .

There was no but. I was on Commander's Defaulters next day and had better recognise the seriousness of the charge. If proven it could lead to a court martial. Shore leave suspended. Warrant

Officer Perkins took the pamphlets, but I asked for an example of each to prepare my defence. The Commander nodded. I took them and went aloft, rather perplexed, to talk to Felix.

Felix was not perplexed at all. Anarchism opposed, both in general and in detail, the whole structure of society from the Head of State down. It was quite specific in declaring that its triumph could only be achieved through revolution. It dismissed all armed forces as the tools of the status quo and elective representation as a sham. I pointed out that so did Bernard Shaw, and yet there was a complete edition of his plays and prefaces in the ship's library. A good point, Felix conceded, and his advice to me was to spend the evening marking suitable passages on such subjects as Royalty, God, the military, politicians and anything else relevant in support of my case. I did what he suggested and, before slinging my hammock, had found a selection of quotes which, taken out of context, made the Anarchist pamphlets sound understated.

Next day I faced the Commander. Perkins made a statement; finding a tract on the table in F Mess, reading it and discovering it to be not only subversive but, and here he coloured, an attack on God, the King and every other institution and standard that decent ordinary people held sacred . . . There was a great deal of feeling and passion in Warrant Officer Perkins. His animosity was not entirely personal. He genuinely loathed everything I subscribed to. The Commander asked me what I had to say. I began by asserting (here again Felix had advised me) that if the recent war stood for anything, it was to ensure freedom of thought and expression to all, including those holding minority views – even those which might appear repulsive to many people. The Commander made vaguely sympathetic noises to all this; Warrant Officer Perkins clearly dismissed it as immaterial. After a short pause the Commander became more specific, opening what he called 'this twopenny-halfpenny subversive rubbish' and asking me, as a member of the armed forces, to justify its dissemination. He then read out certain passages and I retaliated with one of my prepared quotes from Shaw. To begin with he asked if this was relevant. I assured him it was so, and he accepted it. Warrant Officer Perkins made it clear in his cold way that if he were sitting in judgement he'd have thrown the collected works of the Sage of Ayot St Lawrence into the harbour. After we'd covered Royalty, God, the family, universal suffrage, the profession of arms and kindred topics – the Commander reading from the Anarchists in measured tones, me trying to make Shaw sound as inflammatory as possible – he asked me what formed the basis of my quote-for-quote defence. I, in return, asked him if he found the passages from Shaw as subversive as those from Kropotkin, Woodcock and other libertarians. He admitted he did so. I then pointed out that I had borrowed the collected works of Shaw from the ship's library, where they were freely available to the entire ship's company.

The Commander paused. A very slight smile hovered about his face. He suppressed it. Shaw, he said, was after all a famous writer. These chaps, and he gestured dismissively at the pamphlets, well he'd never even heard of them. That was an easy one. In that case Shaw was the more dangerous. A famous writer must surely carry more weight than the authors of 'twopenny-halfpenny pamphlets'.

This was of course untrue and I knew it. Famous writers in general, and Shaw in particular, are licensed. For those seeking a voice to speak up for them, a prophet to translate their discontent into issues and actions, the eloquent unknown subversive carries far more weight than a famous jester of the Establishment. This happily didn't occur to the Commander. He remained silent for some time. Then he gave judgement: I was an educated man. Much as he disapproved of them, it was possible for me to read and even benefit from such writings. The majority of the Lower Deck was not so privileged and might take everything literally. It could be especially dangerous for those who had made the Navy their career. As I was due for demob in a few weeks, he had decided not to proceed with the charge. I daren't look at Warrant Officer Perkins. Any sign from me of triumph or satisfaction might have driven him over the edge. The Commander continued: he was confiscating all my Anarchist literature. It would be returned to my home address after my demobilisation. He understood from Warrant Officer Perkins that I also subscribed to an Anarchist newspaper. I must cancel this or have it sent home. Anything to say?

'Thank you, Sir.'

'That's all right, Melly, but any further infringement of my ruling and you'll be on a very serious charge indeed. Case dismissed.'

'About turn,' shouted the Chief Petty Officer. 'Quick march,' and, into my ear: 'Jammy bastard!'

I'd won! Warrant Officer Perkins had lost his last and most serious bid to undo me. I told Felix that I'd triumphed entirely through his advice and my own eloquence, and I believed it. It seems to me now that the fact the Commander quite liked me and was perfectly well aware that Warrant Officer Perkins had it in for me were equally valid reasons for his decision, and that the knowledge that I'd only a few weeks to go in the service and the sweat involved in setting up a court martial may well have come into it too.

Although I didn't connect the two things at the time, I'm now convinced that my non-appearance at the Royal Naval Command variety performance two weeks later was the work of the Warrant Officer. The chaplain told me the powers that be had decided my act wasn't suitable after all, and the other *Dido* entrant, a writer called Chinnery, a rather humdrum amateur conjuror of the 'take a card' school, appeared instead. I was upset but never for a moment thought that my defence of Anarchism had anything to do with disqualifying me from singing 'Frankie and Johnny' in front of the King.

Freed from the Commander's ban on shore leave I went up to London a couple of times but found it less satisfactory and stimulating than during my distant days on the *Argus*. Many of the people I rang up were either away or engaged or said they were. I'd told most of them I was coming to live and work there after my demob and the prospect of being used as a convenient and regular source of food and drink by a penniless art gallery assistant was obviously less attractive than an occasional visit from a bellbottomed sailor.

The Mesens, of course, were a different matter, but here things were if anything less satisfactory. The gallery was almost ready to open: the coconut matting was down, the bookshelves installed and above the desk behind which I was to sit, a high relief sculpture by F E McWilliam of a vast displaced eye, ear, nose and mouth was already in position. What I found worrying was Edouard's excessively businesslike approach. He dismissed my highly coloured version of my pro-Anarchist stand rather impatiently, concentrating almost entirely on my future duties – the till, the addressing of invitation cards, the telephone switchboard, the invoicing of accounts – and he told me that I must go to nightschool to learn French. He also let out that he had written to my parents suggesting that, after I'd left the Navy, I should return home for three months to master touch-typing and shorthand. Writing to my parents behind my back! Was this the act of a Surrealist poet?

The Surrealist Group had almost entirely disintegrated. Most of the foreigners had returned home and Simon, who had anyway quarrelled again with ELT, had joined BOAC as a steward. Sadi Cherkeshi had gone to train as a naval architect in Istanbul. I visited his ex-landlord, the gruff and humorous WS Meadmore of Margaretta Terrace SW3, and him at least I found totally unchanged. His wife still took lodgers and, although they were full at the moment, it occurred to me that, nearer the time of my coming to live in London, I might write and ask him if they would be prepared to take me on. Meadmore apart, I returned to Chatham wondering if I wouldn't have preferred the life of a cub reporter on a Liverpool paper after all.

We left for Scotland which, like Guernsey, I resented as not being 'really abroad'. After four days at sea we anchored at Rosyth. Felix and I went once to Edinburgh, a city with which I fell instantly in love. It was not so much the old town – despite its twisting, rather sinister medieval juxtaposition of squalor and grandeur and its association with Burke and Hare – which attracted me, nor yet the austere beauty of the Georgian new town. It was the rich absurdity of the Scottish Victoriana.

We dined in what was then called the Caledonian Snack Bar and is now the downstairs bar of the Café Royal but is otherwise mercifully unchanged. Behind the carved mahogany bar several magnificent stained-glass windows of sportsmen in the fashions of the 1870s: a cricketer with his beard and bat, a football player, a fisherman, a clean-shaven huntsman, a bewhiskered deer-stalker. The evening light, streaming through these worthies, cast lozenges of purple and red light on our lobster and schooners of sherry. On the walls were ceramic tiled murals of famous nineteenth-century inventors and scientists.

We steamed up to Nairn, a grey little town where it was drizzling, and Felix thought the moment had come to produce a bottle of schnapps he'd smuggled aboard at Frederikshavn. Edward had bought a little guidebook and, as the level of the schnapps went down, it drove us into increasingly manic hysterics. 'Nairn folk,' it read 'look at you with kind eyes, schoolchildren smile and give you a cheery "hello" and babies in their prams wave fat little hands at you.'

The next day, the three of us walked to look at Cawdor Castle, an expedition that for some reason brought my insane and confused bouillabaisse of snobbery to the boil. 'It has that indefinable feeling of history, of a line of sperm, of continuous possession which no public park or National Trust property can have,' I told Felix. To ease my Anarchist conscience at these crypto-Fascist notions, I added that the only way to defeat 'the aristocratic seduction' was 'a general aristocracy of the spirit'. 'Man,' I told him and Edward, 'must possess the nobility of the lion, the grace of the antelope, the lust of the goat. It is no solution to tear down castles in order to erect grey housing estates or pessary factories.'

Acting on permission from the lodge-keeper, we wandered about the grounds and were rewarded by the sight of the seven-year-old young Laird playing with his nursemaid. 'Fair-haired and sturdy' was how I described him, and I was delighted when he waved to us from his nursery window as we were leaving.

On the walk back to Nairn, I launched into praise of the Pre-Raphaelites. Not of course 'their deplorable religious works', but their veneration for 'the details of a hedgerow, the intricate veining of leaves, the furry underside of nettles, the berries, grasses and bright-eyed birds'. How Edward and Felix let me get away with it speaks more for their tolerance than my oratory – still less my ideology. I do remember thinking that Edward seemed 'rather silent' but put this down of course to his 'dislike of walking'.

That evening in Nairn we went to the cinema to see that excellent American thriller *The Lady in The Lake*, but here too I couldn't resist drawing conclusions afterwards. If the film was accurate, to fight in the defence of 'the American way of life' was absurd. Negroes, bums, outcasts, and rebels were the true heroes of the USA . . . Unlike my earlier eulogy for 'the line of sperm', it was at least a view which would have found favour in the decades to come, but it was just as glib, just as unconnected with any evaluation based on experience. Waiting on the jetty – the water still and milky, the sky primrose yellow, the ship twinkling half a mile out – I finally shut up. A Cornish Able Seaman we all knew slightly and who, sober, had struck us as a rather dour figure behind his formidable black beard, was trying to persuade his equally drunk friend that no good would come of his attempt to approach, with bestial intentions, a small white dog sitting under the marble statue of a Victorian divine holding a Bible.

'Moi old lady,' he said, ''as gart six black cats. They be better for 'un than thart gude darg!'

He kept it up in the liberty boat. After observing the *Dido*'s Medical Officer and Schoolmaster, who had been ashore together and were both very pissed, he concluded that 'the Doc's after the Schoolie's arse, but the Schoolie's so drunk and wet 'e don't know whart 'e's up to'. We could see no basis for this observation but found it amusing enough nevertheless. 'Besoides,' he added as an afterthought, 'Doc's so drunk 'eself 'e couldn't roightly tell if oi 'ad sif or crabs.'

We laughed a lot, while behind us the darkness obscured 'the furry underside of nettles' and 'the bright-eyed birds', and the reels of film proving 'the absurdity of fighting for the American way of life' lay stacked in the projection room of the Nairn Electric Kinema.

'Who'll give me his tot if I tell them where they can find a sheep and lend them my seaboots?' It was the Baron who made this offer as he stared through the Porthole at Loch Ewe, a bleak stretch of water in the North-West Highlands surrounded by featureless hills on which, indeed, a few sheep grazed. Sheep-shagging in sparsely populated areas is a well-established naval myth and there was an apocryphal but much repeated story that at Scapa Flow during the war a rating accused of the practice told his Commander that he had mistaken the sheep for a WREN in a duffle coat.

We didn't go ashore as the weather was foul and there was nothing to do except walk, but this didn't stop me watching, with envious irritation, the First Lieutenant and the Ship's Doctor setting off with their rods, and later feeling equally put out to find five or six freckled brown trout lying on a large white dish in the wardroom

when I and the Marine Corporal were carrying out one of our raids
on the wardroom galley during the middle watch. I had not fished
since before the war, and was not to do so again until the middle
Fifties but, like those diseases which lie dormant for several years
only to break out with renewed vigour, I was still a fisherman
waiting only for the opportunity to start again.

We had joined up with the *Superb*, the *Cleopatra*, the *Diadem*
and the *Sirius* in order to paint ship for the royal inspection. The
prospect was grim and, as always when boredom was unavoidable,
frustration spread through the ship like a virus and tempers became
frayed. Next day there was a fight. Our Mess Deck had just been
painted prior to Admiral's rounds when a Geordie sickberth attendant, who had been circulating round the ship claiming 'sippers' of
rum to celebrate his birthday, staggered in. Now that rum is no
longer issued in the Navy this could not happen but in those days
it was the custom for any sailor who had a birthday to visit every
mess claiming 'sippers' until such time as he collapsed. Admittedly
this practice was officially forbidden ever since, according to legend,
two popular identical twins, taking advantage of the tradition, were
given so much that they both died of alcoholic poisoning, but it
was still observed nevertheless. The Geordie was long past wanting
any more rum anyway; he was simply on the way to his own mess
to collapse, but he was so drunk that he pushed out of his path the
duty cook who was dividing the currant duff. There were general
cries of 'fuck off', but the Baron varied the formula by adding 'four
eyes' to his directive and, as the sickberth attendant wore very
strong pebble glasses, this penetrated his fuddled consciousness,
and breaking into great sobs of rage he shouted out: 'Ah'll rip your
bludy throut out Baron', and flew at him. The Baron behaved with
(for him) remarkable restraint – 'Well, I couldn't go for a man
half-canned', he explained later – and the Geordie was pulled off
him by members of both messes, but so great was his rum-fuelled
rage that he broke loose and went for his opponent again and
again. His shirt was in ribbons, his uniform covered in wet paint
and dirt, his face filthy, tear-stained and horrifying in its
impotent rage. I watched him with appalled fascination. Here was
l'homme moyen sensuel with a vengeance! The climax came when,
swinging round, he knocked a large tray of custard all over the

newly painted hatch-combing. The Baron slid tactfully away and the boy, still shouting threats, allowed himself to be led off to his mess. When he came to several hours later he apologised to the Baron, who said: 'That's all right, mate.' This allowed me to theorise at tedious length to Felix on the merits of instant violence (working class) as opposed to the vice of storing up resentment and listing scores to be settled (bourgeois). The fact was I had been disturbed by the fight and needed to rationalise it in order to find it acceptable.

While the painting was going on we had a small ship's concert on board and Felix and I wrote a sketch for it full of cracks about the various officers. Edward, Felix, John the homosexual writer and I acted in it, and it went down very well. Later that evening, just as I was turning in, a wardroom steward came into the mess and asked me if we could do it again for the officers as they were giving a farewell dinner for the Captain and one of the Lieutenants, who'd been at the concert, thought it might amuse him. It was well if noisily received and we were given a lot of gin afterwards, although this time I was careful to avoid excess and got back to my hammock without delivering a revolutionary diatribe or being sick over anyone's shoes. Next morning the ship, a smart grey from bow to stern, steamed slowly out of Loch Ewe, perhaps to the relief of the sheep, and headed south towards the Clyde.

This, had I still been performing in the Royal Command concert, would have been a time of mounting excitement. As it was I felt pretty sour about the whole thing. On arrival we took up our position, ships of all sizes as far as the eye could see. A useless congress of metal, I thought to myself. 'A magnificent spectacle,' said the commentator over the mess radio. The bullshit was intensified hourly. 'No overalls on the Upper Deck,' barked the Tannoy. 'Collars will be worn until 2000hrs.'

The arrival of the Royal Family sent the press and wireless into that curious state of mind where any sign of normal behaviour on their part was described as if it were a charming form of eccentricity. 'The Queen smiled at Princess Margaret, who ran back to the car to fetch her shoes. She smiled and said "thank you",' explained the *Daily Express*. 'A delightful homely moment there,' said the radio commentator. 'Princess Elizabeth has leant forward and made some adjustment to her mother's veil.'

The inspection went smoothly enough. Three cheers, the guns booming, and a distant glimpse of royalty.

'If the government is preparing for another war,' I asked Felix, 'why aren't we on intensive training? On the other hand, if we're as broke as they tell us, why are we spending money on treating the Navy as an expensive toy for gawping crowds, and a means of livelihood for sparrow-brained radio announcers?'

Edward Wood said: 'You can't dislike the Royal Family. You can only feel sorry for them.'

That evening writer Chinnery performed his royal conjuring tricks and I got sullenly drunk in Glasgow.

We hung about the Clyde for a few days before heading down the west coast – the *Dido* for the knacker's yard and me for demob.

The ship's company was dwindling. The Captain was piped ashore and, later the same day, the Baron left us. His exit was typical, standing on the quay in the pouring rain without an oilskin, shouting obscenities and clutching the recordings of his beloved Johann Sebastian. I never saw nor heard of him again.

We reached Chatham on 8 August and, as there was a bottleneck in the demobilisation program, I was sent home on a fortnight's leave. This meant that I had my twenty-first birthday in Liverpool and I asked Felix and Edward up to celebrate. My father photographed us, surrounded by uncles, aunts and cousins, on the lawn. It was a time of limbo.

I returned, not to the ship but to barracks, and another three weeks passed. I didn't go ashore. I felt a curious numbing apathy, expecting every day to be sent for and handed my railway warrant to York, where there was a depot for civilian clothing. I was given useless but easy jobs. I felt a sentimental regret for the end of the *Dido*, and even for my release from the Navy itself.

One fine September morning I was sweeping the barrack paths with an elderly Leading Seaman. I was wondering how, without offending him, I could avoid the proposition he was working up to – 'I'd sooner 'ave a naughty boy than a naughty girl,' he told me by way of a preliminary come-on – when I saw hurrying along between the neat flower beds and painted ships' figureheads, the same agitated White-Rabbit-like Lieutenant who had sent me to the *Dido* over a year before. He told me I should have been demobbed two weeks earlier and seemed to suggest it was somehow my fault. With some relief I said goodbye to the old salt and followed the Lieutenant to his office. Two hours later I was on my way to York.

In the warehouse I chose a brown herring-bone suit, two shirts, a striped tie, four pairs of socks, four pairs of pants and vests, shoes and a fawn mac. There were also a pair of cuff links, back and front studs, and two collars.

These were packed in a box; we had to travel home in our uniforms, and we were warned that if, in the street outside, we were offered six pounds for our civvies we were to refuse, as they were worth at least twice that much.

Nobody offered me six pounds. I walked to the station. It was almost exactly three years to the day since I'd left Liverpool for Skegness. What had I learnt?

How to pipe a Captain on board. How to make rope-ends 'tiddly' on deck. How to wank in a hammock without waking up the entire mess. It was time to leave the navy-blue womb, the steel-clad egg. Full of confused but passionately-held theories, and unjustified confidence in my ability to win through instantly, I caught the train home. There was a neat parcel waiting for me stamped OHMS. It contained the Anarchist pamphlets.

OWNING UP

I

Filthy Jazz

My prep-school headmaster Mr Twine was a fat bald brute who aimed, in the decade before the war, to turn little Liverpudlians, whose parents could afford the fees, into tiny Tom Browns.

Looking back I believe he must have been mad, or perhaps he drank. In fairness to my mother and father they had no idea what went on. Twine was constantly stressing that a term's notice was required, and we had seen too much of what happened to boys living through that term to complain.

'*Proditor* – masculine – a traitor,' he would mutter as he set about them, for he believed Latin prose to be the foundation of everything.

During the summer term, if a Test Match was taking place, we were expected to eat our bright pink mince and leaden jam roll in attentive silence, and listen, with real or simulated interest, to the BBC commentary. Any whispering, if detected, led to either a slippering or being hauled to our feet by the skin of the cheek and shaken to and fro.

'It's the pestilential day-school system,' Twine would shout as he hammered the side of our skulls with the knuckles of his free hand.

In me he sensed a contrary spirit, and almost every day would fire questions as to who bowled the last over or was fielding at silly mid-off. As I never knew ('give me your slipper, Melly Major'), I was very relieved when rain stopped play, and even now the sentence 'and we return you to the studio' holds an irrational beauty.

Very often the announcer, in a suitably apologetic voice, would introduce a record by Ambrose and his Orchestra or Roy Fox and his Band. At this the headmaster, with the hysterical violence which characterised all his movements, would push back his chair and attempt to silence the ancient set before the first note.

If, as usually happened, the switch came off in his hand, he would drown the music, as he fumbled to replace it on its axle, by shouting 'filthy jazz!' at the top of his voice.

Sitting po-faced under a sepia photograph of giraffes in the East African bush, I would mentally add jazz to Bolshevism and the lower classes ('*Spurni profanum vulgus*') as things I was in favour of.

As a matter of principle I began to listen to Henry Hall instead of 'Children's Hour' when I got home at night. My headmaster and I had one idea in common. We believed jazz and dance music to be interchangeable terms.

After centuries of purgatory those souls which are imperfect but not eternally damned gain the portals of heaven, and, much to the disapproval of my prep-school headmaster, I was sent to Stowe.

The great house in the landscaped park full of flaking temples and mouldering follies, the Voltairean scepticism of J. F. Roxburgh, the tolerant oddness of the wartime staff were a heady mixture. I was, on the whole, very happy there.

One summer evening a friend of mine called Guy Neal, whose opinion I respected, asked me to come and hear a record; it was called 'Eccentric' and was by Muggsy Spanier. Guy explained that the three front-line instruments – trumpet, clarinet and trombone – were all playing different tunes and yet they all fitted together. We listened over and over again until it was dark. I walked across Cobham Court to my dormitory a convert.

Later that term I was passing an open study window and heard the most beautiful sound in the world. It was Louis Armstrong playing 'Drop that Sack'. I didn't know the boy who owned it, but I knocked on his door and asked if he would play it me again. I discovered that throughout the school were little cells of jazz lovers. Slowly I learnt something about the music and its history, most of it inaccurate, all of it romantic. I heard my first Bessie Smith record. It was 'Gimme a Pig-foot and a Bottle of Beer'.

All over wartime Britain, at every class level the same thing was happening. Throughout the thirties a mere handful of people had remained interested in early jazz. They corresponded with each other about the music, published transitory typewritten sheets, and spent their week-ends junk-shopping for rare records among the scratched and dusty piles of Harry Lauders. Suddenly, as if by some form of spontaneous combustion, the music exploded in all our heads.

I left Stowe and went into the Navy as an ordinary seaman. I took my gramophone and records with me, and at training camp, in Chatham Barracks, and on my ship I found two or three people with the same obsession.

In the *Dido*, in the chain locker, I and a few friends gathered like early Christians in the catacombs to listen to our records. One of them told me that he had heard there was a live revivalist jazz band which played in a pub on the outskirts of London. Actually it was the George Webb Dixielanders but I never got to hear them. I didn't really believe it was possible to play this music any more. I imagined that the secret had been lost like early cubism. I knew intellectually that the Spanier ragtime sides had been recorded in the early forties, but I didn't believe it emotionally. All real jazz existed in a golden age before big bands and riffs and saxophones and commercialism had driven the jazzmen out of the garden. Even Louis wasn't the same, not with those slurpy sax sections behind him. I played my records and dreamed of New Orleans, and the river boats, and the beautiful high yellow whores shouting: 'Play it Mr Jelly Lord' to Ferdinand Morton in the brothel parlour.

During this period my other interest was Surrealism. At the Naval camp in Pwllheli an old school friend called Tony Harris Reed and myself wrote poems, made collages and objects, and eventually wrote to E. L. T. Mesens, the leader of the Surrealist movement in England. We got a reply from Simon Watson Taylor, its secretary, inviting us to come and see him in London. Stationed in Chatham I took him at his word, and wasn't at all surprised to find he owned a huge collection of jazz records. Many of these were extremely rare, and the early blues singers were especially well represented. He even had Cleo Gibson's 'I've got Ford Engine Movements in My Hips', a holy grail among collectors, a title to intone over the ritualistic sharpening of the fibre needle, now of course issued like nearly everything else on an LP.

After demob I came to London to work for E. L. T. Mesens at the newly reopened London Gallery. Although by this time there was quite a lot of live jazz to be heard nobody told me about it. In fact Humphrey Lyttelton had formed his own band and the Graeme Bell Australian Jazz Band had arrived via Czechoslovakia to insist in the face of extreme opposition from the rhythm-club purists that the music could be danced to.

It was at a farewell concert for the Graeme Bell Band at the Scala Theatre, Charlotte Street, that I first heard live revivalist jazz (the word 'traditional' was not at that time in use). I saw a poster for it and decided, although extremely sceptical, to risk the disappointment that I believed inevitable.

The theatre was full. The curtain rose. I don't remember who the opening band were. It is very likely they played badly – most of the small bands did. For me that day it didn't matter. They were playing 'real' jazz, and to my cloth ears it sounded just like the records. I came out of that concert a changed person.

I had discovered too that Humphrey Lyttelton played every Saturday in a hall above the offices of the Society for the Prevention of Cruelty to Children, off Leicester Square.

You queued outside and filed slowly past the windows of the society with their big photographs of little bruised backs, beds made of rags and newspapers, the real belts studded with brass studs, and the plump and smiling children 'three months later in the arms of an officer of the society'. With painful slowness you shuffled up the staircase, paid your entrance money to one of the Wilcox brothers at a table by the door, and walked into the crowded and expectant room. It is difficult to imagine now, all these years later, the atmosphere. At last Humph's great foot rose and fell to thump in the first number.

In the intervals we crammed into the big pub across the road. Like gods, Humph and Wally Fawkes drank with their peers. Beryl Bryden, covered then as now in a large floral tent, pushed her way to the bar like a giggling rhinoceros.

I began to buy the *Melody Maker*. From it I discovered there were other jazz clubs on the outskirts of London, and I set off night after night to look for obscure pubs in Clapham, to penetrate ('the 144 bus stops outside the door') that mysterious area of canals and gasworks to the east of Finsbury Park.

I began to know my fellow addicts. My appearance, eccentric

enough in the rather conventional cast-off clothes of a much larger uncle plus a few *objets trouvés* like a knitted Victorian waistcoat made me easy to remember if harder to love. My violent enthusiasm, frequent drunkenness and personal manner of dancing attracted a lot of not entirely kindly amusement. Much later I discovered that Humph had christened me 'Bunny-Bum'.

Above all I had resolved to become an executant. Too lazy to learn an instrument, I had decided to sing.

2

Good Morning, Magnolia

The very first time I had gone to the Leicester Square Jazz Club I asked Beryl Bryden if I could join her in a duet. I had her cornered against the *art nouveau* ironwork of the lift shaft and didn't see how she could refuse. Actually, although I didn't realise it at the time, she used the classic evasion.

'I'd love to,' she said, 'but I'll have to ask Humph.'

My chance came a month or two later.

'Grand Jazz Band Ball', said the *Melody Maker's* advertising column. 'Fully licensed – Cy Laurie's Jazz Band – Eel Pie Island.'

I hadn't heard Cy Laurie at that time, but I liked the sound of Eel Pie Island. It seemed to go with 'Gut Bucket' or 'Honky Tonk'. It had the right feel to it. I found it with some difficulty. It not only sounded right. It looked right too.

Nowadays there is a bridge, but at that time one pulled oneself across in a leaking boat attached to a rope and pulley. The island is on the Thames near Richmond. Among long grass and luxuriant weeds, decaying weather-board bungalows rot silently and in the centre of the island is a large Tennessee Williams hotel. I approached it full of wonder that warm summer evening. The blistering paint-work caught the setting sun and the sound of the band playing 'My Bucket's Got A Hole In It' echoed across the water towards the Surrey shore.

There were about twenty other people at the Grand Jazz Band Ball, in those days a perfectly respectable number. After I had drunk several pints at a bar half painted to look like the window of a Spanish Hacienda, I asked Cy if I could sing. He couldn't think of any excuse so I did 'Careless Love', the Bessie Smith version in a rough approximation of her style. The twenty people clapped, I sang several other songs, and at the end of the evening Cy asked me if I would like to join the band. I went home in a state of hysterical happiness. I was a singer in a jazz band.

Cy Laurie was a fervent admirer of the clarinet style of Johnny Dodds, a far from unique trait. Most clarinet players were influenced by Dodds, but Cy thought he was actually his reincarnation. He had a long, sad, Jewish face which always seemed at odds with the jerky rather convulsive way he swayed his body as he played.

He lived in the East End where his parents had a jewellery business, and we rehearsed on Saturday afternoons in the dusty upper room of a pub in Bow.

After I'd locked up the gallery, I used to get on the 25 bus in Bond Street and sit, going over the words of the blues I hoped to try out, as the bus sped through the empty city towards Whitechapel.

One Saturday there was nobody there. I went round to see Cy and he told me the band had broken up. I was very upset. At Humph's that night I saw Cy's pianist, Norman Day, and he suggested that I formed a trio with him, a drummer and a banjo player. We rehearsed a few times and then he said that he had answered an advertisement to audition for someone called Mick Mulligan who was forming a band. Seeing my downcast face – I cried very easily in those days – he asked me why I didn't come along too. I said I would and we arranged to meet the following Sunday.

That Saturday at Humph's I behaved as badly as usual. Two people were watching with considerable amusement at my expense. One was Bob Dawbarn, an embryonic trombonist, the other his ex-school friend and fellow jazz enthusiast, Mick Mulligan.

Mick lived with his widowed mother in a detached house in Corringway, Ealing. The house was a surprise. I had hopes of squalor on an heroic scale. The reproduction of Cardinals toasting the Chef in the hall was an initial disappointment. Mick, however, had his own room.

It was small and mostly taken up with a piano, a sofa, a large bar and huge unsteady piles of records. There was lots of cigarette smoke, full and empty beer bottles, and a strong smell of old socks. Mick and Bob Dawbarn were listening to an Armstrong Hot Five. It was all very reassuring, although if one looked out of the window the suburban landscape reasserted itself, and when the record was finished you could hear the whirring of a legion of Atcos.

Mick peered at me short-sightedly. He looked like an exhausted faun. I had a bad dose of impetigo contracted by shaving with a very old blade I had found stuck to its own rust on the bathroom mantelpiece, and half my face was unshaven and smeared with bright blue ointment.

'What a lecherous looking bastard,' he said, and offered me a cigarette.

The rest of the band arrived: a clarinettist, a banjo player, and a man called 'The Hermit' who played the tuba, an almost obligatory instrument in the late forties. Norman auditioned and passed. I proposed that I sing 'Darktown Strutters'. Afterwards with no encouragement I sang several other songs.

What I didn't realise was that Mick had no intention of having a singer. I just took it for granted that he wanted one, and he could think of no way of saying he didn't. The rehearsal continued. From time to time the man next door thumped on the wall.

Afterwards Mick, Bob, and I went for a drive along Western Avenue. We passed the Hoover factory, that great 1930 essay in the mock Egyptian ceramic style.

'All that,' I said, 'to suck up shit!'

Mick and Bob enjoyed this remark, and I think it decided Mick to keep me in the band.

Within a week or two we were inseparable. Mick had a car, quite a lot of money and an insatiable appetite for living it up. I, who should have been studying French at the Clapham LCC night school as a help to becoming an art dealer, was only too willing to tag along. Almost every night we went to a jazz club even if it was thirty miles out of London. Afterwards we ate in a late restaurant catering to the music-hall profession, and I remember as though from a delirious dream two dwarfs on the pavement outside, both imitating Frankenstein's monster and pretending to strike each other in slow and clockwork rotation. Then we went back to Mick's place with a bottle and played records into the small hours. I often slept there and caught the tube all pale and shivering among the well-shaved pink business men from Perivale station the next morning.

My work at the Gallery suffered. Even before I met Mick, I had discovered that a love of pictures is not the only thing required of an efficient employee. E. L. T. had, over the years, acquired a fanatical application to the business side of it all, which he relieved by occasional outbursts of dadaistic anti-commercial jokes. I was only too eager to contribute to these. It was the day-to-day routine that defeated me,

Now that I had met Mick, what had been vague inefficiency turned into inspired anti-commercial delirium. To keep awake during the day I discovered that a Benzedrine inhaler broken under the heel yielded a wad of cotton wool which, if cut into little segments and swallowed a piece at a time, opened the eyes and enlivened the brain. What the eyes saw, however, had nothing to do with the dusting of a bookshelf or the switchboard of a telephone, and the brain, although wide awake, was receptive only to the imagery of the pictures on the walls and not to their prices or potential owners. Looking through the invitation cards, the addressing of which was my principal monthly task and the addresses on which were becoming increasingly inventive and unlikely, E. L. T. would shout in exasperation: 'Are you taking drugs?'

I would deny this accusation indignantly and frequently burst into tears. It never occurred to me that I was.

During this period the band was rehearsing for its first public appearance. Mick's neighbours had finally driven us from 90 Corringway, and we used the upper rooms of various pubs. I suppose that most of early British revivalist jazz emerged from the same womb. Rehearsal rooms existed, of course, but we never thought of hiring one at that time. They were part of the professional world of which we knew nothing.

Many of these pub rooms were temples of 'The Ancient Order of Buffaloes', that mysterious proletarian version of the Freemasons, and it was under dusty horns and framed nineteenth-century characters that we struggled through 'Sunset Café Stomp' or 'Miss Henny's Ball'.

Although we had not yet performed we already had a name. The fashion was for something elaborate and nostalgic. Admittedly Humph was satisfied with 'Humphrey Lyttelton and his Band' but he swam in deep water. Among the minnows, names like 'The

Inebriated Seven', 'Denny Coffey and His Red Hot Beans', and 'Mike Daniel's Delta Jazzmen' were more typical. Mick decided on 'Mick Mulligan's Magnolia Jazz Band'.

This particular form of whimsy was to reappear, although for more commercial reasons, during the recent 'trad boom', but we didn't dress up. Following Humph's lead, an extreme sloppiness was *de rigueur* both on stage and off. The duffle coat was a cult object, sandals with socks a popular if repulsive fad, beards common, and bits of battle dress, often dyed navy blue, almost a uniform. The source of this was largely the post-war art schools via Humph and Wally, but there was also a strong, anti-bop element involved. This was because the two schools came at jazz from entirely different angles. The be-boppers were mostly professional musicians who discovered modern jazz by working on the Atlantic liners, and hearing the music live in New York. As trained execu-tants they were able to understand what the great modernists were doing. As artists they were determined to preach the gospel on their return.

The revivalists began with the old records, and only learnt to play because they loved a vanished music, and wished to resurrect it. Depending on their purism, they drew a line at some arbitrary date and claimed that no jazz existed after it. The modernists did this in reverse. Nothing existed pre-Parker. Before that there was only a lot of Uncle Toms sitting on the levée strumming banjos and crying 'yuk, yuk, yuk'.

Very slowly things changed, initially on a personal level. The two schools began to meet socially to argue and listen. Eventually some of the traditionalists became modernists or mainstreamers, and others began to realise that Gillespie and Parker, Monk and Davis were not perverse iconoclasts but in the great tradition, and the modern musicians stopped imagining that bebop had sprung fully armed from the bandstand at Mintons, but had its roots in the early history of the music.

The band's first job was at the Perivale Youth Club. The audience were few in number and very young. There was no microphone, and I tried to amplify my voice by shouting into an empty biscuit tin.

The young lads listened politely. After about half an hour an even smaller boy poked his head round the door of the recreation room and shouted: 'Chocolate biscuits in the canteen.' Points rationing was still in force and the whole room emptied immediately for the rest of the evening.

After a month or two Mick decided that the time had come to ask someone to hear us and give some constructive advice. He approached Jim Godbolt, who had been manager to The George Webb Dixielanders and was therefore, as far as we were concerned, a figure of great authority.

Godbolt, thin and tense, his head with its pointed features crouching between his shoulders as though emerging from its burrow into a dangerous world, his eyes as cold and watchful as those of a pike in the reeds, came and listened.

Actually Mick couldn't have chosen a less sympathetic person. Jim had been watching us for some time in the 'Blue Posts', the pub nearest to the London Jazz Club now that it had moved to 100 Oxford Street, and disliked us very much. Firstly, he had decided we were 'hurrays' – public-school jazz fans – an expression he himself had discovered in a short story of Damon Runyon's one anti-social Christmas – and secondly, being in those days a formidable prude, he was appalled by our language and sexual behaviour. I suspect that his motive in accepting Mick's invitation was not untinged with malice.

At the end of the session Mick and Jim went into conference. They talked for about twenty minutes while the rest of us stood some distance off, waiting for the verdict. Jim left, Mick came over. 'He says we should give up.'

We didn't though. Our belief in the music helped us over this bitter blow; we were all fighting for a despised music we knew to be worthwhile. It may seem incredible but at that time, before I sang, I used to appeal to Bessie Smith to inspire me. Today in the traditional world only Ken Colyer managed to keep this religious fervour burning inside him. The battle has been won and therefore lost. It's in the mainstream bands and among the modernists you still find the true spirit of non-compromise. Of course, they are less naïve about it all, and more able to mask their feelings behind a wisecracking cynicism, but then they are much older than we were. In fact some of them were us.

Musically the greatest drawback to the progress of Mick Mulligan's Magnolia Jazz Band was the amiable Bob Dawbarn. He
played his trombone entirely by ear and found it impossible to learn
chord structure. At the very beginning Mick did the same, but
although a man of a formidable lethargy for ninety per cent of the
time, Mick has always found it possible to apply himself savagely
for short periods and he learnt all about chords in under a week.
This meant that bridge passages and even arranged chori were
now a possibility – or would have been without Bob. Mick tried
everything – sarcasm, threats, pleas – but Bob never learnt about
chords.

Socially though – and the Mulligan band always existed socially
more than musically – Bob was an enormous asset. He had a ragged
moustache, a very old mackintosh, and for no very explicable
reason, for he was Ealing bred, a slight Liverpool accent. He looked
far older than he was and affected the hangdog manner of someone
who sells brushes from door to door. In fact he was a criminal-court
reporter for an agency. He also had a middle-aged mistress. A fact
I found very impressive at that time.

I was equally impressed by Mick's general success with girls. He
would often leave Bob and me in his car while he went into one or
another of an entire round of flats or houses, and we, having no
other means of transport, had to sit there for well over an hour.
Dawbarn's only revenge was to smoke as many of Mick's cigarettes
as possible. Bob had little success with girls apart from his mistress.
Nor did I, but I was still more interested in chaps.

Mick was convinced, and he may well have been right, that this
was because I 'hadn't had enough of the other'. Although by no
means puritanical about homosexuality, he thought there was less
in it for all concerned and a little absurd, and he did what he could
to put me on the right path.

Mick's analysis of my condition may well have been the truth. I
moved slowly from homosexuality to bisexuality and from there
to heterosexuality. No moral decision was involved; in my view
no moral decision is involved, it just happened. I became aware of
this early one Sunday morning in the band-wagon about ten years
ago.

We were travelling back from some job and I woke up as we

drove through the outskirts of London. Through prickling red eyeballs I watched a crowd of young cyclists from the East End pedalling past us for a day in the country. They wore shorts and T-shirts and were clean, very young, and full of energy and high spirits, the reverse in fact of the hung and exhausted group of musicians among which I sat. I looked at them with pleasure and speculative interest. I saw them, but when they had passed I suddenly realised that I had only looked at the girls. It was a moment of revelation.

For six years I lived in the top floor front of a house in Margaretta Terrace SW3. It's a pretty little street with architectural detail slightly too large in scale. It was built in 1851 for prosperous tradesmen, but its elegance and proximity to Westminster made it popular with early Victorian MPs as a suitable place to set up their mistresses.

There are plane trees all the way down one pavement, and the harmony of leaf and peeling plaster, small house and Corinthian pillar is unique and delightful.

My landlord was a man called Bill Meadmore, author and civil servant, expert on the history of the circus, chain-smoker and kind-hearted ogre.

I first met him when I was still in the Navy and used to come up from Chatham to attend the meetings of the Surrealists in the Barcelona Restaurant.

Simon Watson Taylor had first lived in my room and he had made way for Sadi Cherkeshi, a young Turkish poet. When I had neglected to book a bed at the Union Jack Club, he used to let me snooze in a chair until it was time to catch the train back to barracks. In this way I came to meet Bill and his wife, Dumps. If I had a long pass I would sometimes stay there the whole time and eat with the family. I got to know them all well, and when I came to London to work I wrote and asked if they would have me as a PG.

I hung my collection of Surrealist pictures on the walls, discovered what bus would take me to Bond Street, and lay on the bed, a Londoner at last.

There were two beds in my room and one of them had two mattresses on it. In consequence, after the word had spread round the jazz world, my room became a week-end dosshouse for bedless lovers, habitual last-tube-missers, provincial visitors and a hard core of friends.

Sober, I realised the absurdity of the idea, but by the time Humph had played 'Get Out Of Here And Go On Home' every Saturday night, I was convinced that between six and eight people, all of them drunk, could climb three flights of stairs in an old house, undress, descend and ascend past Bill's open door to a lavatory difficult to locate in the dark, and even listen to a gramophone with a sock in the amplifying trumpet, without waking him up.

Bill was a light sleeper and as angry as an old bear if disturbed. On comparatively quiet nights he would wait until breakfast before complaining, but if things were right out of hand he would come up the stairs. He slept in a shirt. His hair was long and white. He would simply fling open the door with dramatic violence and glare. The sight of him standing there was enough to turn us all to stone for most of the night.

One night I heard him coming and we all pretended to be asleep. He came in, switched on the light and went from bed to bed lifting the blankets and examining the bodies feigning unconsciousness beneath. At last he stalked towards the door and turned out the light. 'George,' he said, 'what do these animals eat in the morning? Hay?'

Mick was perhaps my worst risk. In the small room next to mine slept Bill's middle daughter, Janet. She was engaged and very much in love, but always rejected Mick's lunges with tact and charm. One night Mick threw open the door of her room and hurled himself in the dark on to the approximate position of her bed. She'd moved it under the window and he landed with all his weight on the floor. I got him to bed and there was no sound of Bill getting up downstairs. Next morning I told Mick what had happened and pointed out that it might be as well if he could leave the house without actually having to meet Bill face to face. He agreed warmly but unfortunately was bursting for a piss. He crept down the stairs and looking apprehensively over his shoulder towards the door of Bill's room, opened the door of the lavatory. Bill Meadmore, an obsessive non-lavatory-door-locker, was sitting there reading the *Manchester Guardian*.

'Good morning, Magnolia,' he said quietly.

That Bill Meadmore and his wife put up with me for over six
years still surprises me. His general attitude, one of affectionate
exasperation, is best demonstrated by quoting in full a letter he
wrote me after a particularly noisy night. Green as I was I wrote
him a hurt reply. This added to his pleasure. Here is what he wrote:

> 7 Margaretta Terrace,
> Chelsea, SW3
> 9 August 1950

Dear Esq. George Alan Melly,

The last Mick-straw has broken my feeble but patient back.
I have endured your drunken and dissolute ways, your wanton
waste of light, gas fire, hot bath water, horse radish, beans,
lavatory water, your assumption that my library was yours,
and that you had a right to read the *New Statesman* and the
Obituaries in the *World's Fair* before me. I never said an
unkind word when your thick head broke the witch bowl
and Dumps' heart, nor when you, in your efforts to conquer
Everest, pulled down the balcony next door. I tried to grin
when you purloined the money from the telephone box and
used my bath salts. When the house trembles at its foundations
with your coughing, caused by your unchristian way of living, I
do not complain, and have comforted myself with the reflection
that every cough brings nearer the day of your demise.

This letter is not a grumble. I have tried to be patient and
understanding of a character that is a throw-back to the stone
age and who would have been a joy to Freud. Alas, I am not
Freud. I never reproached you when you made this house a
doss for band boys and barrow spivs, nor when you plastered
the walls of a lovely room with obscenities and childish scrawls,
and notwithstanding that you occasionally paid the moderate
rent asked for one room, persistently regarded the whole of
the house, including the two telephones and the two lavatories,
as exclusively your property. And the top landing. The horde
of undesirables whom you have introduced into the house have
pissed over the lavatories (not into) and worn threadbare with
their hobnailed boots the stair carpet. I even have not been

safe from the rest of your family who roost here and make the house smell abominably of Liverpool and gin, and Gibraltar rock.

All these things I have borne with a sickly smile. My simple nature has assumed that it is proper for you to associate with such loose women as the Andys and the Irises, the Beryls, and the other flower girls. I have tried to consider that a certain amount of sexual intercourse was necessary for you, both natural and unnatural intercourse, thinking that otherwise you might find yourself in prison for loitering in public lavatories, or for rape or intercourse with birds, fishes and animals. I gloss over the noises you make, the strange, curious bursts into Zulu war cries, the din of the contrivance which you refer to as a gramophone.

I return to the LAST STRAW. Even I, the most wid-minded, tolerant, generous and gentle of a fair-play cricket race, cannot and will not tolerate this house becoming a common bagnio, a sponge house, a place of assignation, a pimp's brothel, or for Mick the Mulligan to bring his doxies here and perform his strange tribal rites with them in the early hours of the morning. And I strongly object that I have the next morning to straighten every picture in the house. Nor am I interested in his unflowing jabber whilst 'on the job' and his evident determination to propel bed, doxie and himself across the floor of the room. But these are things of the past, they will never happen again. The wheel of the wagon is broken and the time has come, my dear Alan, for us to part and you to find a new dump and Dumps.

We have decided that it is better to have the French girl from the Congo, so therefore, my dear Alan, please take this epistle as notice to quit. To give you plenty of time in your hopeless search for some place in Oakley Street with the same amenities as HAVE obtained here, you have been granted ONE MONTH.

THIS NOTICE IS FINAL AND IRREVOCABLE

W. S. Meadmore

BOSS

Bill's wife, Dumps, gentle and rushed, took it all in her stride. If, after finishing breakfast, I asked for a cup of tea to take upstairs, she would murmur, 'Love on a plate?' On one occasion when, believing the house empty, a girl and I were experimenting in a bath, she knocked gently on the bathroom door and pointed out in her mild way that it was not part of our agreement. Less ferocious than Bill, she was no less original. They gave me something absolutely unique, a room where I could live exactly as I chose, and a home at the same time.

On Sunday mornings in Margaretta Terrace, I made everybody get up and help clean my room. Even Mick was bullied into using a pan and brush. The rag and bone man passed shouting, 'Old lumber'.

At five to twelve we walked round to 'The Cross Keys', a public house which the revivalist jazz world held in reverence because its landlord, Billy Jones, had depped on piano with the Original Dixieland Jazz Band when they were in England in 1920 at the Hammersmith Palais de Danse. With a little persuasion he would sit down and play rags until closing time. Sometimes the musicians or aspiring musicians would bring their instruments and jam, and I would sing.

Our band began to appear in public, inevitably as a supporting group and usually in South London. Chas Wigley, a small and dapper man who wore a bow tie and worked in Covent Garden in the night, was continuously opening clubs. There was one in a garden behind a pub which, on fine summer evenings, worked a little magic, but most of them were in the upper rooms of those huge, characterless boozers in the high streets of the South London boroughs. The opening night was usually quite full, but followed by a rapid decline until the only audience was Chas's own family and our friends.

After the club shut there was a party at Chas's house in Clapham: brown ale, cheese sandwiches and jazz records late into the small hours.

Mick and I would sometimes call on Chas in the Garden, and drink among the porters until the grey dawn broke over the Endell Street clap hospital.

3

An Entrée in the Provinces

Although we had a small public, and although we knew most of the musicians, Mick had not achieved any musical impact. Our first success was in Acton where we played the interval spot at the opening of a new club. The promoter and band leader, Doug Whitton, had gone to a great deal of trouble to make it an important opening in the convention of the day. He had persuaded those jazz critics who had kept the flame alight in the dark days to come and drink at the club's expense, and more importantly, the Marquis of Donegal to come and open it. This ensured that the opening would be covered in the musical press.

Not that the Marquis was a fluent speaker. In fact he usually managed to get the names of the bands wrong and frequently lost his way towards the end of a sentence. It was his presence that counted. The critics were a varied lot with only their interest in jazz in common: Max Jones who wore a beret and dark glasses; the enthusiastic Derrick Stewart Baxter who lived in Brighton and whose passion for the blues could turn his great face red; Rex Harris, saturnine, soft-spoken, elegantly bearded, by profession an optician, by conviction a strict New Orleans man; Jimmy Asman who had come to London from the Midlands full of jovial bonhomie and bluntness; Ernest Borneman, a German-born anthropologist and novelist – and lastly and in a way most memorably, Sinclair Traill with his protruding blue eyes, Air Force moustache, casual throw-away manner and legendary reluctance to stand a round. Sinclair was an early pet of Mick and mine. His seedy but real charm and remarkable way of getting through life in the face of every obstacle reminded us of Waugh's Captain Grimes. He was constantly in Lord Donegal's company at that time.

Later Sinclair became a friend of Gerald Lascelles, first cousin to the Queen. 'Gerald' took the place of 'Don' in Sinclair's anecdotes, and they were always together at jazz functions.

These jazz critics, most of whom hated each other, were treated with enormous respect in the jazz world at that time. No jazz concert was complete without one of them as compère. What they wrote was studied with reverent attention.

I don't remember which of them were at Acton that night, but the band's performance was described in several papers, and a photograph of me singing 'Frankie and Johnny' appeared in a magazine called *Jazz News*.

The editor of *Jazz News* was actually Jim Godbolt, but the comment underneath the photograph was warm and even enthusiastic. Mick was decidedly impressed and even suggested changing the name of the band to 'George Melly's Magnolia Jazz Band'.

'Frankie and Johnny' has always been my most successful number, principally because of its dramatic story line and, as I realise now but would have denied then, what talent I have is dramatic rather than vocal. At this period my version was comparatively uncluttered with special effects. Falling down, simulating two people making love, opening a kimono, standing on tip-toe to look over an imaginary transom, firing the little forty-four, etc.; all these have gradually attached themselves to the song like barnacles to the bottom of an old ship. Even so it was always comparatively elaborate and theatrical.

Because of Acton, Mick felt ready to accept rather ambitious jobs: not Humph's club – this he thought might kill our chances – but Cook's Ferry Inn for example.

Cook's Ferry Inn was one of London's earliest jazz clubs, and was the base of the Freddy Randall band. Freddy played a fiery trumpet, much influenced by Muggsy Spanier, and his band was decidedly 'white'. In consequence the New Orleans purists had little time for him, but he had a large following, especially in North London. He was also one of the first Dixieland bandleaders to turn professional and go 'on the road'.

To reach the Ferry was a considerable labour. You caught the tube to Finsbury Park and then there was a long bus ride through the depressing suburbs with their chain-stores and second-hand car lots on the bomb sites. Finally there were half-hearted fields and factories making utility furniture or art metal work, and then a bridge over the canal in the style of the city of the future in the film *Things to Come*. The Ferry was on the far bank of this canal, a big 1935 pub in Brewers' Georgian with a hall attached. Its isolation had its advantages. The canal tow-path and the surrounding fields were suitable for knee-trembles and yet you could still hear the band.

The journey home was full of problems. For reasons either alcoholic or sexual it was always the *last* bus and its crawling progress put a terrible strain on the beer-filled bladder. On one occasion I had to stand on the bus platform and piss out into the reeling night. The god who looks after drunks stood by me and I was neither caught by the conductor nor fell off into the road.

The central London jazz clubs in those years were all unlicensed. Jazz was the reason the audience were there. At the Ferry the public were mostly locals who liked jazz as a background to drinking and social intercourse.

Early in the band's history 'Hermit', the tuba player, left us and was replaced by a sousaphone player called Owen Maddock, a tall man with a beard and the abrupt manner of a Hebrew prophet who has just handed on the Lord's warning to a sinful generation. He was by profession a racing motor mechanic and designer and his hands, coat, clothes and face were always streaked with oil. His appetite was formidable. Thrusting bread and butter into his mouth with both hands he looked like the Goya of Satan devouring his children. As regards jazz he had a passion for the soprano sax of Sidney Bechet, which was so obsessive as to enter even into his erotic life. In his bedroom was an old-fashioned wind-up gramophone above which was suspended a weight through a pulley so adjusted as to lighten the pressure of the sound-arm on the record. On this antique machine he played Bechet records even while copulating. In fact the rather faded blonde with whom he was having an affair at that time told me she found it very disconcerting that, no matter what point they had reached, if the record finished, Owen would leap off and put on another. Now that there are a great many Bechet LPs available it must make his life easier.

*

Our first job out of town was on the south coast. I remember a castle on a cliff and the late sun going down over the water outside the glass wall of the dance hall. It was a perfectly ordinary job but we, having no truck or knowledge of professional ethics, carried our crates of beer on to the stand before we began to play. The manager was so amazed that he didn't even protest. It was, however, reported in the local newspaper.

Our first real success outside London was in Liverpool, and my mother was the cause.

Mick had been to Liverpool with me some months before on a purely social visit, and it had been fairly disastrous. We had been asked to give a lift to a coloured girl, also from Liverpool, who sang with Mike Daniels. Her name was Phyllis and she wished to visit her child who lived up there with her parents. For us the whole coloured race was sacred, but Phyllis tried our faith severely. The AA had advised us to go via Birkenhead. Our intention was to reach home in time to hear Beryl Bryden singing on 'Radio Rhythm Club'. We had, in the car, a gramophone and a number of records mostly by Jelly Roll Morton. We picked Phyllis up in Piccadilly and set off.

Every time we went over a bridge Phyllis said: 'Eh, me tits.' Every time we saw some cows in a field Phyllis said, 'All that meat and no potatoes!'

We were only on the Chester by-pass when it was time to listen to Beryl and had to go into a pub and ask the landlord to tune in for us.

As we were driving through the Mersey Tunnel Phyllis told us she didn't like New Orleans jazz really. She 'went more for modern like'. Sensibly enough she hadn't told us before. Faced with such blasphemy we might well have made her hitchhike.

We dropped her by the Empire and drove home. My mother and Mick didn't really take to each other, although she thought him 'very attractive'. Both Mick and I have suffered throughout our whole relationship by people thinking that, in his case I was responsible for leading him astray, and that in my case, he was responsible.

My father didn't help by saying the coffee tasted like ferret's piss. Somehow my mother thought that Mick was responsible for him saying this too. My mother was also certain we were having an affair. 'Why didn't you tell me?' she asked. I denied the whole thing, but she was by no means convinced. I can't really blame her for this. Although Mick is physically entirely hetero, he likes his men friends so much that it's an understandable fallacy.

Next morning at breakfast there was one fish-cake left over, and my mother pushed it on to my plate. Mick noticed and never forgot. The fish-cake became symbolic.

That afternoon Phyllis turned up. My mother didn't take to her either, not because she was coloured but because she was so Liverpool. She had her child with her. Both my grandmothers came to tea. They sat on each side of Phyllis as though she was a coloured Alice and they the Red and White Queens. Suddenly her child farted very loudly. Phyllis looked from one grandmother, severe and Jewish, to the other, severe and Christian. 'It wasn't me,' she said.

My mother's whole attitude towards jazz had been ambivalent. She didn't mind jazz concerts, but hated the idea of us playing in dance halls. Whenever we were near Liverpool and I went home to sleep, she would ask how the concert went. When I told her it was a dance, she would always ask, 'Did they all stop and listen when you sang?'

Mick's mother was very much the same. In later years, whenever we were playing in a particularly empty and tatty dance hall, Mick or I would suggest that Maudie and Alice (his mother's name) should really be there to share their sons' triumph.

My father, with his admirable motto, 'as long as they're happy', worried less, although he was convinced the jazz thing wouldn't last. He based this assumption on the fact he had invested in a roller-skating rink during the twenties and, shortly after, the craze had died, and he had lost quite a lot of money. He died during the trad boom in 1961, amazed that it was still going on.

Even so it was my mother who arranged our first appearance in Liverpool. She was involved with a charitable institution and, following my self-interested advice, despite the active opposition of several reactionary members of the committee, she decided to raise funds during their appeals year by organising a jazz concert. This took place at the Stadium, a huge building usually devoted to boxing and all-in wrestling. She contacted the Liverpool jazz promoters of that period, two brothers. They agreed to help and booked Freddy Randall, other name bands, and a few local groups. She insisted we were to appear. They'd never heard of us, and wanted to put us on the side stage with the local groups. She said no. Either we appeared 'in the ring', or the whole thing was off. This is typical of my mother. She might disapprove of what her children do, but if they insist on doing it, she will fight for them like a tiger. My father called it her 'partridge defending its young' act. It is, I suppose, a very Jewish characteristic.

She won, but even so we were booked to appear early on. There was a huge audience – traditional jazz was experiencing its first boom – but no Mick. My father was very worried. 'It's a good crowd,' I told him. 'Yes,' he said, 'but that's no use if Mick doesn't turn up.' We drove to Lime Street Station and found out that the train was late due to fog outside Rugby. At last it arrived. Up the platform strode Mick and the others, Owen's tuba gleaming fitfully through the steam. We were in time to go on in the best spot and went down a bomb. On the strength of it we were booked to do a concert at the Picton Hall. We had achieved an entrée in the provinces.

Manchester was the next step. There jazz was in the hands of a man called Paddy McKeirnan. Unlike most of the promoters in those days he believed in jazz *as a business*. He didn't just run a jazz club. He was the director of 'The Lancashire Society for the Promotion of Jazz Music'. He wrote to Mick offering him a contract to appear at the Grosvenor Hotel, Manchester. It was a real contract with clauses. Mick's acceptance began: 'Dear legal-minded sod . . .'

We went down well in Manchester too. Paddy, in those days a decided puritan, was less happy about us personally. Mick asked him which of the girls fucked.

'In Manchester,' said Paddy, severely, 'we don't discuss things like that.'

Mick had stopped taking an active part in the wine business, and gone to work in a record shop in an arcade off Piccadilly.

This was a curious venture in itself. The boss was called Stephen Appleby. He had an air of languor and called everybody 'my dear', and at first meeting you believed that he must be a homosexual of the kind who, under a vague manner, hides a formidable and ruthless sense of business. In fact he was aggressively hetero and a compulsive husband. He fell in love with girl after girl and, if the affair lasted long enough for the previous divorce to come through, married them one after another. In principle the shop should have proved a gold-mine. It had a recording studio in the basement where it was possible for Colonials to record Christmas and New Year messages on wax (there were then no tape-recorders), or the owners of talking budgies to keep a permanent record of the cleverness of their little pets. Upstairs were the stocks of records. There was, for so small a shop, a considerable staff. A recording engineer, Mick, Sinclair Traill, and a Swedish lesbian as well as Stephen himself. The social atmosphere was lively and varied, very much at the expense of the profits. Mick and Stephen spent a great deal of time in a pub in Jermyn Street, the lesbian was usually too emotionally involved with her difficult friends to pay much attention to invoices and firm orders, the recording engineer was often upstairs with various girls at the very moment he should have been recording the budgies or the Australians.

The firm also recorded revivalist jazz bands for the private label called Tempo. It was in the little studio downstairs that Mick's band and myself first made what the musical press of the time referred to as our 'début on wax'. Full of scotch and surrounded by cardboard egg-boxes nailed to the walls, we produced several lamentable sides. My own contribution was a version of Bessie Smith's 'Take Me For A Buggy Ride'. It is almost unbelievably flat and practically all on one note. It sold quite well, and was solemnly defended and attacked in Sinclair's *Jazz Monthly*. Later, in order to achieve more atmosphere, we recorded in a public hall. The records on this session at least simulated the echoing acoustics on those amateur discs of ancient New Orleans veterans like Bunk Johnson, which had begun to reach this country.

4

We're Getting Paid, You Know

As a band, and much to E. L. T. Mesens' sorrow, we were now solidly established, and worked two or three nights a week in town and quite often played the provincial jazz clubs at weekends. Slowly, almost imperceptibly, revivalist jazz gained ground as a popular music. Humph was undoubtedly the cause, but the rest of us prospered in his shadow. In most of the big provincial cities there were now enough fans to support a local jazz club, and enough casual interest to fill a small concert hall or theatre every now and then.

It was, however, the universities and art schools which provided most of the audiences. We played Cambridge under the aegis of Jimmy Asman who had become that university's jazz critic elect. Due to their National Service, several people I had been at school with were still up. I drank gin at the beginning of the evening with Guy Neal in his rooms, and finished lying on a marble-topped pub table in a yard watching the stars spinning in the cold heavens.

At Oxford we played in a pub too, but without official sanction. The proctors raided it and the bulldogs asked Mick his name and college.

'Who,' he asked the trembling undergraduate organiser, 'are these pricks in bowler hats?'

We carried the drum kit up the marble staircase of the Royal College of Art, South Kensington, under the huge canvases of babies in sinks and kitchen tables covered with cornflake packets and cheese graters that were *de rigueur* at that moment. Johnnie Minton, a regular at Humph's, when not engaged in fisticuffs in some corner of the room, would caper wildly in front of the bandstand, and Lucian Freud, who exhibited at the Gallery, might raise a hand in greeting while staring with obsessive interest in another direction.

The music we played was more or less as before, New Orleans classics in the style of early Armstrong or Morton, and for my part blues from the Bessie Smith repertoire or the lesser singers of her period. The personnel of the band, however, began to change, mostly because the amount of work we were doing bit into working hours, and those of us who worked from nine till six found it harder to meet both our obligations.

Norman Day, the pianist who had first taken me to see Mick, had gone. His place was taken for a time by a lad from the Poly called Brian Burns. I use the word 'lad' advisedly. He was one of the world's eternal students and never to be seen, even on the hottest day, without one of those endless scarves. After he had gone Johnny Parker joined us.

Johnny, younger than Mick or I, had just finished his National Service. We knew him before. He used to appear in jazz clubs smiling shyly in his neat uniform, and would sit in with us or play during the interval. He specialised in rags which he handled, as their composers intended, with delicate precision.

When he left the army, he too went to the Polytechnic in Regent Street to study chemistry. His parents lived in a semi-detached in Beckenham, and he always caught the last train home. He was very small and looked younger than he was.

The jazz atmosphere took Johnny by the collar and shook him roughly. Within the year he was a wild one. Within the year too he had dashed through every sexual stage in record time. He was almost a virgin when he left the army, and despite a rather one-sided affair with a randy NAAFI girl, had never masturbated. This he soon corrected with fanatical zeal, even announcing his intention to indulge on railway trains en route to the provinces. Then he went mad about girls and, being both small and sexually aggressive, became extremely successful.

On drums there was first a young and very respectable boy called Norman Dodsworth, but he didn't stay long, and after him, fresh from Leeds and the Yorkshire Jazz Band, we managed to obtain the services of one of the most quietly eccentric figures of the whole jazz world. His name was Stanley Bellwood.

*

Leeds, that island surrounded by forty-shilling tailors, was the home of the Yorkshire Jazz Band. It was led, during its long and stormy history, by a burly half-coloured Yorkshireman called Bob Barclay. Bob lived in a cellar in a rotting elegant house near the city centre of which he was officially caretaker. The rest of the house was a small garment factory. I used to stay with him, but this had two disadvantages. For one thing you didn't get to bed until about six because Bob insisted on playing every record the YJB had ever made, and for another thing, when you did get to bed, his large boxer dog used to show how fond of you it was by leaving great snail tracks of mucus all over your face and arms.

Stan Bellwood had played for Bob. He came to London to join us bringing with him his girl-friend Doris.

Doris was a big lumbering girl who was almost handsome. Stan was much smaller than her, wore a neat moustache and punctuated every sentence with a nervous little staccato laugh. This pair descended on London in general and on the Mulligan band in particular, determined to wrest a living from jazz alone. We were perhaps averaging six pounds a week each at that time so it was in itself a hopeless proposition. They did their best, though.

For a start they moved in on each of us in turn. Their technique was simple. They pretended to have a flat in some distant part of London, and late at night Stan would ring up (Meadmore in a rage hurling open the bedroom door and shouting: 'Telephone! Blast you!') and say they had missed their train, but happened to be round the corner. Once installed, with Doris's underwear all over the house, they were extremely hard to get rid of. They were with me, under protest, for ten days. After the whole band had shaken them off, they took to spending the night in the Charing Cross Lyons Corner House. At that time you could sit there until six for the price of a cup of tea. The clientele was both seedy and dodgy; male and female prostitutes, layabouts and mysteries, small-time tearaways. When every other door was barred to them, Stan and Doris, their eyes wide open and bright red, would sit nibbling Benzedrine inhalers, for you were not allowed to sleep, until they were turned out into Trafalgar Square just as the starlings were waking up.

Due to their aristocratic disdain for work, we called them Lord and Lady Bellwood, and by extension, the Corner House, still in all its Edwardian Baroque splendour, became known as 'Bellwood Grange'.

Stan was still drummer when the band went professional, and in consequence the money got more reasonable. This did him little good however as Doris was given to the expensive whim. She would demand strawberries out of season (off a barrow), for example, so they were hardly better off.

Later Stan left the jazz world and became a public house manager.

As a band we were now completely established. Mick had lost his initial astonishment at getting into a train for an hour or so, and finding everybody at the end of the journey talking in an entirely different accent, We began to play concerts at the beginning of the fifties, and were a particular success in my native city. On my insistence, the whole band used to come home for a meal. Once I even persuaded my mother to have them to stay. I told her that other band parents did, and that anyway they weren't fussy about where they slept. She found out otherwise. Several of them demanded extra pillows and blankets. I never pressed her again. She didn't really much care for the tea performance. The moment everybody arrived they would start playing *fortissimo*, preferably on each others' instruments. At tea, in the early days of the band's history, we insisted that Owen Maddock sat at the far end of the table so that the rest of us would get a chance to have something to eat. This meant he faced my mother and she was forced to watch plateful after plateful of food vanishing into his bearded jaws. He would eat with one hand, and spread peanut butter on his next slice with the other so as to waste no time.

Our early concerts, held in a Victorian classical building in the civic centre were perhaps, in all the band's long history, our greatest triumph. In the interval the band and my father would dash across Lime Street into 'The Legs of Man' for several quick drinks, but in fact we were intoxicated by the applause. Both my grandmothers insisted on coming. I don't know what they really made of it all. My father's mother would only say: 'I can't think what your Great Aunt Eva would have said.' My mother's mother would suggest, in a comparatively unfriendly way, 'You must hypnotise the audience to make them clap like that.' From this I took it that she, at any rate, remained unhypnotised.

Douglas Byng, an old friend of my mother's, was appearing in pantomime one Christmas and came to tea the day of a concert. As it was Sunday he also came to the concert itself. He seemed to enjoy it.

'It reminded me,' he told my mother afterwards, 'of those dear old days in Harlem.'

It was for me a sharp pleasure to see on the hoardings, in the streets of all my childhood's memories, the posters with my name in big black letters.

It was through jazz, the classless music, that I began to know Liverpudlians outside the middle-class barriers of my parents' world. Girls too. I derived iconoclastic pleasure from having it off in the public parks where fifteen years before my brother and I, neatly dressed and pedalling our tricycles, accompanied our nurse on sunny afternoons.

It was in Paddy McKeirnan's club in Manchester (in those days it was held in a hotel called the Grosvenor) that we first encountered violence. Mick had left the bandstand to go to the gents, and discovered a young thug kicking another one in the face. Mick had stopped him, told him not to be a bastard, and gone back to play. Later on he went for another piss and found him doing exactly the same thing. He'd dragged him off and the boy had pulled a razor on him. Mick relieved him of this and frog-marched him out of the building.

After the session, having no instrument to pack up, I wandered out on to the steps to breathe a little air under the Mancunian stars. The young thug and his mates surrounded me and jostled me into a dark corner. One of them had a bottle, as yet unbroken, but he had begun to tap it against the wall, gradually increasing the strength of the blows. When that breaks, I thought, he's going to push it in my face. They were swearing and lunging round me to work themselves up to what they meant to do. One of them grabbed me by the lapels and gave me the head, that is butted me with his forehead. My nose started bleeding.

I was anaesthetised by fear. I subconsciously did the only thing

that might work and it did. I took out of my pocket a small book
of the sound poems of the dadaist Kurt Schwitters, explained what
they were, and began to read. The book was knocked out of my
hand, but I bent and picked it up again, and read on:

> langerturgle pi pi pi pi pi
> langerturgle pi pi pi pi pi
> Ookar.
> langerturgle pi pi pi pi pi
> Ookar.
> Rackerterpaybee
> Rackerterpaybay
> Ookar.
> langerturgle pi pi pi pi pi
> etc.

Slowly, muttering threats, they moved off. I can't explain why it
worked, but I suspect that it was because they needed a conventional
response in order to give me a going over. If I'd pleaded or attempted
to defend myself, or backed against the wall with my arm over my
face, I think I'd have had it.

We ran into violence on very few occasions. We saw a great many
punch-ups in dance halls, although none in jazz clubs, but they
hardly ever involved the band.

Although it was some time before we thought to turn professional, Mick had begun to think professionally. My first intimation of this came as a great shock. We were playing a concert in
Wimbledon and, prior to our stint, I was loosening my tie, pulling
my shirt half out of my trousers, and messing up my hair. Mick
was watching me with rising irritation.

'Smarten yourself up a bit, cock, before we go on!' he suggested
crossly when I had finished my anti-toilet, 'we're getting paid you
know.'

A month or two later we had another brush. We were playing at
'The Queen Victoria', North Cheam, a regular venue of ours over
the years. Mick asked me what I wanted to sing. I suggested
'Thinking Blues', one of Bessie Smith's most austere numbers. Mick
blew up. 'For Christ's sake, cock,' he shouted, 'we've just got the
audience going a bit.'

I walked off the stage and sulked in the bar. We had a stormy interval during the course of which I told him I'd a good mind to leave the band and join 'The Crane River'. At least Ken cared about jazz, not the bloody audience. We finished several pints later with me weeping into my beer, but won over, as usual, by Mick's charm.

As it happens, the emergence of Ken Colyer had led to a great deal of soul searching throughout the whole revivalist jazz world. I first heard him on a river-boat shuffle some years before. Like most people at that time I thought he was joking.

The early river-boat shuffles bore little relation to the twelve bands, two steamers, Margate and back 'Floating Festivals' of recent years. Everybody knew everybody. We all squeezed on to a little boat which chugged up-river to Chertsey. At the locks there was jiving on the tow-paths. Beryl Bryden swam to enthusiastic cheers. The music and the moving water, the bottled beer and the bare arms, melted into a golden haze. The last defiant chorus from the band as the ship turned in midstream before heading for the pier in the warm dusk sounded really beautiful.

There was no question of us playing that year; Mick had only just formed the band. Even so he had brought his horn, because on the way back we were to tie up for an hour at Eel Pie Island, and there was to be an open-air jam session for the second line. Ken Colyer was on board, and seeing Mick had his trumpet with him, asked if he could borrow it when we went ashore. Mick said yes, imagining that he would blow a couple of numbers and then give it him back. Not a bit of it. After about half an hour Mick asked him for it back, and Ken refused! Mick told me about this and added 'and have you heard him?'

What we expected a trumpet player to aim at was the early Louis Armstrong noise. Ken didn't sound anything like that. His wavery vibrato and basic melodic approach was based on Bunk Johnson. He sounded, and intended to sound, like an old man who had never left New Orleans when they closed Storyville. He played traditional, not revivalist, jazz.

Later on he formed a band, 'The Crane River Jazz Band'. The Crane River is a muddy little stream which trickles past London airport on the road to Staines. The band played in a large hut at the side of the pub. I went to hear them and thought they were dreadful. There were no solos. Every number was ensemble throughout, and to my ears monotonous ensemble at that. The bass drum pounded away, the clarinet ran up and down the scales like a mouse in a wheel, the two cornets (Sonny Morris was Ken's partner) wavered and trembled, the trombone grunted spasmodically. To ears tuned to the Morton Red Hot Peppers it was a horrible noise.

Later, as we heard more of the Bunk Johnson and George Lewis sides, we began, slowly and reluctantly, to appreciate the qualities of Ken's approach. It was primitive but serious. It was also patently sincere. The NO fanatics called Ken 'The Guv'nor'. With satirical intentions so did the rest of us. In time, however, it was no longer a joke. After the Crane River broke up, Ken rejoined the Merchant Navy with the intention of deserting in New Orleans. He succeeded, and got to play with the old veterans who were still alive. He got put in jail too, and came back to England an heroic figure. Chris Barber and Monty Sunshine had a band ready for him, but they had reckoned without his formidable single-mindedness. He rounded on them for attempting to dilute with commercialism the purity of New Orleans music. Chris and Monty left. The Chris Barber Jazz Band, basing its music on a tidied-up version of Ken's, moved into popular favour and sparked off the trad boom of the late fifties. A great many people made a great deal of money out of this, but not Colyer. Awkward as an old bear, often too drunk to blow properly, he played as he wanted to since the very beginning. His band had the first skiffle group. At a recording session Ken went into the box to hear the play-backs and rejected the lot.

'You can't hear the fucking inner rhythms,' he told the astounded engineer.

Even Humph, although he has always denied it, was affected by Ken's ideas. For a month or two he turned to look over his shoulder. The ghost of Mutt Carey whispered in his ear. Then he turned away, and swam slowly and deliberately into the mainstream.

One of Humph's characteristics is to believe that what he plays at any given moment is what he has always wanted to play. He re-writes his musical history like a one-man Ministry of Truth in *Nineteen Eighty-four*, but the files of the musical press remain as they were. Only the other day in an old book of press-cuttings I came across a description of Humph listening to a modern jazz record and then, when it had finished, turning away with the remark: 'Back to sanity and 1926!'

The year of the Festival of Britain, it was decided to hold a concert of British jazz at the newly opened Royal Festival Hall. The body behind this venture was the recently formed and clumsily named National Federation of Jazz Organisations, a non-profit-making body whose committee was made up of a great many jazz critics, a few of the more powerful promoters and a couple of executant players. Its President was, inevitably, the Marquis of Donegal.

At the suggestion of some of the committee, he went along, coronet in hand, to ask Princess Elizabeth if she would come ('honour the occasion by Her Gracious Presence' in more trad terms), and she, or her advisers, said yes. Before the concert started she shook bands with all the bandleaders, and the following week the musical press was full of this or that familiar face grinning ferociously up at her from the slightly winded position, while the rest of the line waited their turn wearing that special expression of jovial despair which surrounds Royalty on every public occasion.

Mick came back-stage in a state of quivering nerves. The two band numbers were ambitious and complicated arrangements, and sounded ragged and unconvincing. My own song was 'Rock Island Line', and according to Lady Donegal 'amused HRH' but didn't mean much to the rest of the audience. The whole concert in fact was dogged by Royal Flu, and the only band which got going at all was 'The Saints' from Manchester.

Their success was, I suspect, due to the fact that the Royal Family is based in London. Like all Mancunians they were in a state of constant irritation that so much went on in the capital, whereas anybody could see that Manchester was in every way superior. They played their stint with dogged unconcern and raised the roof.

Outside the Festival Hall stood the pavilions and domes of the Festival of Britain, that gay and imaginative flyleaf dividing the grey tight-lipped puritanism of the years of austerity from the greedy affluence which was to come.

Mick was tinkering about with the band sound. He always tinkered because he was unable or unwilling to impose a musical style on any other musician. The average bandleader tells his musicians what noise he is after, and, if they refuse to play in that style, they either hand in their notice or get the sack. Mick never did this, or at least only when things got right out of hand. The periods when the band sounded quite reasonable, and the times when it was embarrassing to be connected with it, were dictated by events rather than controlled by musical policy. There were times when a trombonist played modern-tinged mainstream on his left and a traditional clarinettist doodled away on his right, a modern drummer dropped bombs behind him encouraged and supported by a right-handed piano player, while a banjo player, pissed out of his mind, hammered out a dragging two-beat half a bar behind everybody else.

Another factor which held us back was that Mick, after the initial enthusiasm of the early days, developed a pathological hatred of rehearsal. There were times when the rest of us ganged up on him and demanded them. This made him very angry, but he usually gave in, and for two or three weeks we would rehearse. Then, using every possible excuse – lateness of musicians, double booking by the rehearsal rooms, the large number of dates the band had – he would gradually let things slide until the next explosion of musical frustration from the chaps.

When the music has become terrible the obvious thing to do is take the sound to pieces, to strip it down, and then to put it together again checking every stage. What Mick did was to add other instruments. At this time for example we had two banjo players. One was Johnny Lavender, a quiet photographer with a constant smile lurking under a half-hearted moustache. The other was a roly-poly middle-aged man called Bill Cotton who was a kind-hearted formidable piss-artist.

Bill's musical speciality when drunk was to break his strings in the middle of a number. You could tell when this happened without turning round because he played at about twice the volume of Johnny Lavender, and the noise from the rhythm section almost died away. The replacement of a broken string was a comic performance in itself. He would hold the banjo about two inches from his nose and with slow glassy-eyed deliberation fail time and again to thread the new string on to the key. Eventually by the law of averages he succeeded, tuned his instrument with conscientious precision and then, often only a bar or two later, another string would snap.

Conversationally, as an evening wore on, Bill became the victim of a single idea. Cigarettes were still scarce, and he had discovered that you could always get them at an all-night café near Gunnersbury Station. If any of us ran out in a coach or train after a job, it didn't matter where we were, the outskirts of Bedford or the Essex marshes, the plump snoring figure would subconsciously sense our dilemma, jerk upright and mumble 'Gunnershby Schtathun' before collapsing again.

This ability to respond to a situation like a galvanised frog was one of his more extraordinary feats. One night, returning from a jazz club outside London in a fog, we got on to a roundabout and circled it a dozen times trying to find the right exit. Eventually we succeeded. Bill, apparently out to the world, spoke. 'Pity,' he said, 'I was just getting fond of it.'

How he got the sack was absolutely in character. It was shortly before we turned professional, and we were to play a job for an important promoter of that period called Maurice Kinn. The night before Mick had given a party, but warned everybody that they must be on time for the coach meet at 10.00am up the side of Madame Tussaud's. At the end of the party Bill had gone round emptying all the dregs from the glasses and then staggered off home to get a clean shirt. He had, of course, fallen asleep and arrived at the meet an hour after the coach had left. Mick and I were waiting.

'Sorry, cock,' said Bill, and added in a rather pathetic attempt to justify himself, 'I've lost me voice.'

'You've lost your fucking job too,' snapped Mick, and hailed a taxi to take us to the station. Looking out of the rear window I could see Bill swaying slightly in the middle of the pavement using his banjo case to help him keep his balance. Next time I saw him, several months later, he told me that he'd had to leave the band because of his day job.

Sometime before Bill left we'd played a concert in Holland and this brought home to me yet again the difficulty of remaining a junior employee at an art gallery and becoming something of a figure in the revivalist jazz world. I had caught the earliest plane (the others were returning by boat) in the hope of getting to the gallery by ten o'clock, but I realised it was a slender chance. The plane didn't land until 9.10 and although I took a taxi, I didn't turn into Brook Street until 10.45. ELT was away on the Continent, so although nervous – I had sworn I'd be back on time – I had hopes of getting away with it. Nothing doing. His wife, Sybil, who was a buyer in a big Regent Street shop, was waiting for me and *furious*. She was quite right, but I found it very hard, after an evening crowned by a lot of applause, to feel it really mattered. ELT was just as angry when he got back. With the Surrealist reverence for eroticism he told me that the only valid excuse for being late was if I had been making love. Although I was usually a little late for work, it was never the direct reason. There was, however, to use a phrase of Mick's, 'a great deal of it about'.

His determination to wean me from homosexuality gradually succeeded. Perhaps the most traumatic experience was, however, none of his doing. Johnny Parker had found an attractive if rather criminally-minded girl and lumbered her back to Margaretta Terrace for about ten days on the trot.

She was called Pat, but we called her 'Cow-Pat' because she had a distinct Gloucestershire accent, and there were a great many other Pats floating round the jazz world at that time.

I paid her no attention. I was recovering from a dose of clap, and although I had only another four days to go before being given the OK (three months quarantine they give you – surely this errs on the side of caution?), I had no wish to stir it into life again, and return to sitting in the long line of Cypriot waiters in dinner jackets, proud ponces and furtive junior clerks on the hard benches of the special treatment department, Endell Street. She, however, thought otherwise and climbed determinedly into my bed.

This, more than anything else, gave me heterosexual confidence, and Mick too did his best, both deliberately and by accident.

He sometimes arrived in the middle of the night with a girl, usually a night-club hostess, he had picked up, and so drunk he could do nothing about it. I was the gainer here, but usually he didn't mind because by the time I went down to breakfast he was sober enough to perform. Once though he came a cropper. While I was eating my bacon and egg downstairs, she told him primly: 'I don't like it in the morning.'

Quite often he brought back a girl from a jazz club on his way home to Ealing, and left her there afterwards. I would sit and read while he was at it. Once he noticed that my book, a turn-of-the-century edition of *Hard Times*, was upside down.

On another occasion, he was sleeping with a girl when a very jealous girl-friend of his shouted outside in the street that she knew he was up there with somebody and was on her way up. He pushed the girl he was with into my bed, flung himself down on the mattress on the floor (she was at the door) and simulated, without too much difficulty, a drunken stupor. He wasn't best pleased when I took advantage of this situation, but there was nothing he could do about it.

Later on, when we went pro, we began to lose touch with life in London because we were hardly ever there, but at this time we lived a full London life in a dozen different worlds.

Through Sinclair Traill we were asked to the houses of the rich and insecure where the ice tinkled in treble scotches.

In contrast to this uneasy world, we sometimes stayed the night with Jimmy Asman and his wife Dot in their tiny house in Plumstead. Jimmy, bearded and jovial, thought of himself as a no-nonsense Rabelaisian figure, but was at heart something of a prude. Because his house was so small and so full of jazzmen and their girls, he had to allow them to sleep together, but he didn't really like it. In his bedroom there was a small bed which he called 'The Grandstand' because it overlooked his bed, and he would give this to obviously randy couples in the hope that the proximity of him and Dot would restrain them. It never did, of course, and sometimes he got quite angry. He was, however, generous and warm-hearted if overfond of the idea that eight pints of beer and a loud fart were the insignia of the free spirit.

Under the aegis of the NFJO it was decided in 1950 to hold a Jazz Band Ball at the Hammersmith Palais. The excuse for this was that it was exactly thirty years since the Original Dixieland Jazz Band had made their début there. It was in a way the apotheosis of the revivalist jazz movement. The Committee of the NFJO sat at a table in evening dress, and the groups played on alternate sides of the huge pantomime-Baroque bandstand under the revolving multi-faceted mirror-globes, while coloured spotlights combed the enormous crowds.

The size of the audience surprised the press; they had no idea of the popularity of revivalist jazz. *Picture Post*, which covered the event in a long article, was intrigued by the daytime *persona* of the jazzmen.

'Who would believe,' it said, 'that Chris Barber is an out-of-work clerk, Mick Mulligan the Director of a firm of Wine Shippers, and George Melly a frock-coated usher in an art gallery . . .'

The frock coat was a picturesque invention but, in the years that followed, it persisted and grew in absurdity in both press reports and programme notes. I became a 'frock-coated usher at the Tate Gallery', and then 'frock-coated assistant curator at the Tate Gallery', and finally, the frock coat discarded in the face of a larger pretension, 'The Curator of the Tate Gallery'.

The night of the Hammersmith Jazz Band Ball it seemed that the whole world had gone jazz crazy. We believed it anyway, and when E. L. T. Mesens told me a week or so later that the gallery was going to close down, and Mick suggested that we went professional, I agreed with joy and optimism.

But there were other, less idealistic people with their fingers on the jazz fans' pulse who realised that here was a huge audience temporarily excited by revivalist jazz, and a large number of bands willing to appear in front of that audience for the glory of it and very little money. What could be done about it before the moment passed? Logical conclusion: hire the largest halls available all round London, book the maximum number of bands, and run a series of Sunday concerts until the interest falls. For a month or two the huge suburban cinemas were full of jazzmen and jazz fans. Each band played for about five minutes which meant they chose their fastest, loudest numbers – 'rabble rousers' was the trade name – in the hope of making some impact on the audience.

If we'd had any foresight we would have refused to take part in these self-destructive marathons, but like the Gadarene swine we charged over the cliff, and in no time at all revivalist jazz in London was moribund.

Only Humph had the good sense and dignity to abstain. He refused to play unless he was allotted at least twenty minutes. If the rest of us had followed his lead, the slump need never have happened.

The same pattern repeated itself on a much larger scale during the trad boom, but the difference was that at least that time the bands made a lot of money out of it whatever the cost in musical integrity. We, poor fools, made nothing but a little beer money.

It was while the concerts were happening that Mick and I turned pro.

By the time we were completely professional the personnel of the band had changed almost completely.

There was a transitional period when I helped E. L. T. to clear up the gallery, weighing all the waste-paper in the cellar (we got thirty shillings for it), selling the books in lots to invited clients and cataloguing the pictures for an inter-directors' sale. This all took several months, and by the time it was finished the revivalist boom was over, and Mick had had a good long think.

Dawbarn, our first trombonist, had gone some time before. His refusal to learn chords was the reason, and a justifiable one, but Mick had found himself unable to give him the sack quietly and reasonably, and it had all happened on Christmas Eve at Cook's Ferry when he was very drunk. Bob took this badly, and for a long time wouldn't talk to Mick at all.

In his place we had an Australian called Ian Pierce. He had played for a time with the Graeme Bell Band, and was quiet, timorous, literary-minded, an Anglophile, and very highly strung. He had a beautiful ugly face functionally designed to support his huge nose. When amused he spun round and round as though in pain, holding on to his nose with one hand as if afraid suppressed laughter might blow it off. We called him Wyllie because he had been so amused by this story about a great uncle of mine.

My great uncle Bill was physically senile and would sit all day smoking Turkish cigarettes through an ivory holder in front of the fire. Behind him hung a large picture of a river bank painted in the 1870s by an Academician called Wyllie. When we were children, we would always ask my great uncle who the artist was, not because we didn't know, but because we so enjoyed watching him haul himself half out of his chair, swinging his head and shoulders round to face the pictures, before he answered us.

'That one?' he'd gasp.

'Yes, Uncle Bill, the river scene over the carving table.'

'It's by a feller called Wyllie,' he'd say, and fall back into his chair on the point of collapse.

This heartless anecdote so tickled Ian that he spent the whole evening repeating 'a feller called Wyllie' and then going into a nose-holding spin.

Soon after Wyllie joined us Johnny Parker left. Humph offered him a job. At the time I was amazed he accepted. I can't imagine why I was now. The pay was better, the prestige enormous, and the music on a completely different level. It was I suppose because I had a formidable sentimental loyalty towards Mick and the band, and imagined everybody else had too. As a result Wyllie changed from trombone to piano. This was an improvement because, although he had lovely ideas, he was so nervous that he could hardly ever pull them off on trombone, essentially an extrovert instrument, whereas on piano it was just a question of hitting the right notes.

On trombone, a boy called Roy Crimmins took over. He was a brilliant technician influenced at that time by Jack Teagarden. He hated the amateur approach of the revivalist movement, was ashamed of appearing on the same bill as professional musicians, and was very much in cahoots with Stan Bellwood who felt the same way. Between them they produced an atmosphere of near mutiny which led to increasing tension over the next couple of years.

Owen Maddock left. For a time we used Jim Bray, an ex-tuba player who had taken up double bass. Jim has lived through every development in the jazz scene. He left us to join Humph. Later he was with Chris Barber playing traditional jazz, and then joined Bruce Turner and played mainstream. Tall and balding, he is a repository of waspish anecdote, his upper lip curled in permanent amusement, his hands black with the oil of the ancient cars and motor bikes which are his passion.

He was replaced on bass by a professional called Barry Langford.

Moustached and Brylcreemed, he had no particular interest in jazz, but simply played whatever he was paid to play. At one time he had worked for a comedy band and had played a bass which laid an egg and had a telephone in it.

Finally on clarinet there was Paul Simpson.

Paul has been around the jazz scene since the very beginning. He is an incredible mixture of contradictions. He can be very funny and extremely charming. He can be infuriatingly big-headed. He is given to moods of such black despair that anybody seeing him coming remembers urgent appointments and hurries away leaving their unfinished drinks on the counter.

He boasts of his excessive appetites, how much he could eat, how much he could drink, how many orgasms he could achieve in a night. We formalised this later.

'There goes Paul,' we'd say, 'off to eat three separate curries, drink twenty pints of cider, and then run round the room with a girl on the end of his cock with her legs round his shoulders.'

Musically he has some talent on almost every instrument. He can also play approximately in every idiom from New Orleans to modern; but only on piano, despite his limited technique, does he show real feeling.

Paul is tall and heavily built, but not as tall or as heavy as he imagines. He has blond hair and a red face, the traditional cider-drinker's flush, and looks rather like a bull terrier.

Mick, whose ears are as sharp as his eyes are dim, was always hearing Paul running him down as a musician. If somebody came up and requested a particular number, Paul would tell them that of course he knew it but Mick didn't. This didn't endear Paul to Mick. This then was the band at the time we went pro:

Mick Mulligan	Trumpet and leader
Paul Simpson	Clarinet
Roy Crimmins	Trombone
Ian Pierce	Piano
Johnny Lavender	Banjo doubling guitar
Barry Longford	Double bass
Stan Bellwood	Drums
George Melly	Vocals

We had a photograph taken and reproduced for publicity purposes. The photographers lined us up in profile on a series of steps. We looked young and very nervous.

Finally Mick decided we ought to have an agent and Jim Godbolt, despite early destructive advice, agreed to take us on. Jim had worked for a time with the Lyn Dutton–Humphrey Lyttelton Agency, but had decided to set up on his own. We were his first clients. Despite his irascibility – and his tendency, when angry, to hurl the telephone across the room – he became well liked in the sub-world of agents and ballroom managers, concert promoters and jazz club organisers. He and Mick were a great comic turn. There was nothing I enjoyed quite so much as Jim's accounts of Mick's devious excuses for inefficiency, or Mick's accounts of Jim's neurotic explosions. Around this thin heron-like figure a whole comic tradition of disaster has grown up.

The Christie Brothers, Keith and Ian, were an authoritative source. They used to share a room with Jim in Gloucester Place.

One night they both woke up to find Godbolt hanging from a narrow bookshelf high up the wall. He was stark naked.

Keith said, 'Look, Ian. Godbolt's having one of his nightmares.'

Godbolt said, 'Godbolt is not having one of his nightmares.'

Godbolt's own account of his co-habitation with the Christies is tinged with bitterness.

Keith's socks were famous throughout the jazz world. In fact at one time Keith was called 'The Wendigo' after a story by Algernon Blackwood about an elemental of the Canadian back-woods who took possession of trappers and forced them to leap through the wilderness twenty feet at a time shouting: 'Oh, my feet! My burning fiery feet!'

Godbolt has always been fastidious, and used to complain that when he opened the door of their room, Keith's socks would meet him, not so much as a smell, but rather as a bee-like hum.

One night Ian Christie peed in the washbasin where Godbolt, who was on one of his periodic health kicks, had left a lettuce to soak. Godbolt could never decide if he was glad or sorry to have woken up and heard him.

Later Godbolt moved into a single room in Gloucester Place. It was triangular with the bed under the window. It was also on the ground floor at the back of the house. One afternoon Godbolt was having it off with his girl-friend (the early puritanism had largely withered) when he looked up and saw the fat twelve-year-old son of the landlady leaning on the window-sill watching. Godbolt leapt up or off in a spluttering rage, and threw open the window. The landlady's son, who was standing on a dustbin, appeared unmoved. He waited until Godbolt had finished and then said quietly: 'You 'ave your fun, and I'll 'ave mine.'

We had an agent, and Mick bought uniforms, and hired coaches to take us to jobs. As a final break with the semi-pro past he changed the name of the band. 'Mick Mulligan's Magnolia Jazz Band' became 'Mick Mulligan and His Band'.

5

The Dance Halls of Great Britain

I was still living at Margaretta Terrace, the only alteration in my life being not going to the gallery. For a month or two I spent every morning in bed, but realising that I was becoming more and more greedy for sleep, I began to get up between nine and ten.

Mick's life had changed completely. He had left Ealing and set up house with a very pretty blonde girl called Pam Walker whom he had met on a river-boat shuffle.

The first proper tour we went on was organised by Maurice Kinn. It lasted ten days and included Dingwall, a very small town in the far northwest of the Scottish highlands.

Mr Kinn provided a manager and compère, a Jewish comedian called Michael Black. Michael was so Soho in appearance and attitude that it was difficult to imagine him as far north as Camden Town. He wore a camel-hair overcoat with enormous padded shoulders, and had a Don Ameche moustache and a permanent five o'clock shadow. He was very worldly within the confines of his own tiny world.

Michael was exactly the sort of man who is always popping in and out of Wardour Street barbers asking if Harry's been in, or what won the three-thirty or can he be fitted in for a cut and friction in about an hour and a half. He was a compulsive joke teller and kept a little book of esoteric reminders.

'Now what's this one?' he'd say. 'Jewish Bishop and pineapple chunks? Oh, yes. There was this Jewish feller, very sharp dresser, lovely gold watch, cuff-links, the lot, well . . .'

He started telling jokes as the coach drove up Baker Street and didn't run out before we got back.

He also did a short cabaret act on most of the jobs. This was set material, and included imitations of such stereotyped figures as James Cagney, Humphrey Bogart and Peter Lorre.

The first job on the way up was Liverpool where we did our usual concert at the Picton Hall. Michael did his act and was not too well received by the purist jazz fans.

'What about some jazz?' they kept shouting.

They weren't too keen on the new band either.

Michael fixed the digs for us on this tour. His technique, usually unsuccessful, was to introduce himself to the landlady or hotel receptionist by smiling exaggeratedly and then announcing in a posh accent: 'I'm Michael Black of the BBC.'

When he had fixed the digs, he'd come out of the building, lean into the coach and tell us he'd managed to get a concession.

'Knocked her down a tosheroon,' he'd boast. Often he hadn't at all.

As we drove further and further north, Michael seemed a more and more unlikely figure. In the Scottish borders he started an absurd argument that it would only take him about ten minutes to run up and down a very large hill that would patently have taken three quarters of an hour to climb.

In Dingwall he came bursting into the hotel bar in a state of acute shock.

'My life,' he shouted, 'there's only a flock of sheep in the street already.'

When I developed a sore throat in Edinburgh he took me to a doctor. He couldn't resist inventing an elaborate lie.

'This is George Melly, the famous singer,' he told the unimpressed old practitioner. 'His throat's terrible, and he's got three broadcasts with Joe Loss, a big charity cabaret, and then he's got a film to make. Now I want you to really give him something good. No rubbish. There's thousands of pounds at stake.'

'Open your mouth wide,' said the doctor, paying no attention whatsoever.

I enjoyed everything about the tour except the jobs. For the first time we were playing mostly in dance halls. The dancers complained about our tempos, and as they passed the front of the stand would turn and look at us with cold hatred over their shoulders. Mick called them 'swivel-necks'.

The small handful of jazz fans who turned up complained on the other hand about our commercialism.

In Edinburgh we played a very tough hall at Leith. A ferocious looking man beckoned me over as I sat by the piano waiting to sing.

'Will you tell your idjits tae mak less bliddy din,' he growled.

I think we got £15 a week each for this tour, which seemed to me an enormous amount even though I didn't have any left when we got back to London.

We travelled in hired coaches at this period. Mick had bought an old van during the semi-pro days, but it had begun to fall to bits, and although perhaps it could have been repaired, he had parked it on a bomb site when it had broken down one night and never gone back for it.

Coach hire is very expensive, and in the end Mick bought a coach and added a driver to the payroll. We went rapidly through a series of mad old men. There was one who couldn't take any criticism and was always losing his way. 'Right. That settles it, guv,' he would shout at Mick when it was pointed out that, according to a signpost, we were now twenty miles further away from the job than we had been an hour before. 'Give us me cards. I'm off.'

There was another who liked to be called 'Pop', who made a habit of standing in the road by the coach steps, and helping members of the band by patting them lingeringly on the bottom as they struggled aboard with their instruments.

There was a short filthy old thing in a very long overcoat held together with a length of twine. His party trick was taking snuff. Mile after mile he crammed it into his hairy nostrils and sniffed away so juicily and loudly that we could hear him above the noise of the engine.

He had, during many years' driving, worked out an arrangement with almost every transport café in Great Britain: a coach load of people eating in the caff in exchange for a free meal in the kitchen.

We didn't mind this too much in principle. We *had* to eat in transport cafés ourselves most of the time for financial reasons, and furthermore he did know which were better value than others. What we objected to was the way he automatically swung the coach off the road about lunch time and drew up in front of one of his fry-up stations. Sometimes we would tell him that we'd rather drive on into the next town where there was more choice and we could have a beer if we fancied it. This made him very angry. Once he came with us into an AA hotel where we had imagined we'd be safe from his Steptoesque grumbling. When the waiter handed him the menu, he held it for some time between his snuff-stained fingers and then asked bitterly: 'Aven't yer got no working men's dinners?'

In fact, although some transport cafés are disgusting, with congealed sauce round the necks of the bottles and pools of tea on the table with crusts of bread floating in them, some are perfectly reasonable. There are gleaming jukeboxes and pin-tables and fruit-machines, and tables are clean, and the food, although standardised and limited, is at least hot and edible. In the long sour-mouthed nights on the road, where there is nothing to do but try to suffocate yourself to sleep under a blanket or watch the cat's-eyes unwinding monotonously in the headlights, the transport café is actually something to look forward to, a few minutes of light and warmth in the dark cold hours between leaving the dance hall where the old caretaker and his one-eyed dog snooze over a tiny electric fire, and climbing into bed in the London dawn, grey and shivering from lack of sleep.

We still played a few jazz clubs, mostly in the provinces and, due to the fact that several towns still wouldn't license Sunday cinemas, there was the odd concert. Most of our jobs, however, were in dance halls.

The dance halls of Great Britain – the halls, that is, where dances are held – can be subdivided into various groups. Starting at the top are the great Palais, some, like Mecca, part of a nation-wide chain, others individually owned.

The Mecca Halls are standardised so that once you're inside you might be anywhere in the country. They are run like military organisations in which the musicians are privates. The band-rooms are full of printed rules: no alcohol to be brought on to the premises (we were actually frisked in some places), no women allowed behind stage except for band vocalists, no fraternisation with the public.

The décor is usually Moorish in inspiration. There are strange bulbous ashtrays on thick stems, a forest of lights sprouting from the ceiling, bouncers with cauliflower ears circling the dance floor in evening dress, revolving stages and managers with safes in their offices and 1930s moustaches.

We never played Mecca jobs for the company but for organisations like university rag committees who hired the halls for one evening. The management were still inclined to treat us as though we were working for them, and once Mick had gained confidence, this led to innumerable rows.

'We are working for the rag committee of which this is the secretary,' he would explain icily to some officious under-manager who tapped him on the shoulder as he was drinking at the bar. Sex was another bone of contention. Once in Manchester I was caught outside the boiler house by the stoker, in my dressing-room by the manager, and finally in the bicycle shed by the caretaker. The bee-hived girl and I only made it in the end by using the band-wagon while the rest of the chaps waited patiently outside in the frosty night.

The privately-owned halls were on the whole a great improvement. Of course they very much depended on the character of the manager or owner. Some of these suffer from a Napoleon complex. The hall is their Europe, the visiting bandleader an ear which cannot refuse to listen to their grandiose schemes and delusions. Others are friendly and courteous men who ask you in for a drink after the dance and become, over the years, familiar faces in the endless repetitive nomadic round.

The décor of the dance halls outside the big chains was as varied as their owners. Some were luxurious, influenced by the Festival of Britain, given to a wall in a different colour, wallpapers of bamboo poles or grey stones, false ceilings and modern light fittings made of brass rods and candle-bulbs. Others were as bare as aeroplane hangars, or last decorated during the early picture palace era. Mick's inevitable comment as we staggered with our cases and instruments into these was: 'What a shit-house!'

There was also a series of halls over branches of Montague Burtons and Co-ops. There were always a great many very steep steps to drag the drum kit up.

We also played for promoters whose offices were either in London or some large provincial town, but who covered a particular area and hired halls which had other day-time functions.

Territorial Halls where the floor was marked out with white lines and there were posters showing muscular young soldiers giving a thumbs up in a jungle or diagrams of a machine gun with the parts painted different colours.

Corn exchanges, often rather beautiful nineteenth-century buildings with glass roofs and terrible acoustics. Round the walls were little wood-encased partitions with the names of cattle-food firms or grain merchants painted across the back in faded *trompe-l'oeil* Victorian lettering.

Above all the town halls, massive monuments to civic pride in St Pancras Gothic, where we played on stages big enough to seat an entire chorus and orchestra for 'The Messiah', and the young bloods of Huddersfield or Barnsley staggered green-faced from the bar in a vain attempt to make the gents, and were messily sick under a statue of Queen Victoria or the portrait of some bearded mayor hanging above the marble staircase.

The jazz clubs were moments of release and pleasure from this dismal round. We didn't have to change into uniform, we could drink and smoke on the stage, above all we knew the audience would be on our side and that we would only have to play jazz.

In London, too, we made a deliberate effort to go on playing jazz for kicks. At the beginning of the week, unless we were away on a long tour, we were usually in town, and every Tuesday we played in a cellar club which catered for French students and was called 'Le Metro'.

The club had a curved ceiling and did look rather like a tube tunnel. Behind the bandstand was painted an unconvincing metro train. The bar had Lautrec posters in it. The students, like most French students, were conceited and bloody. We did draw a small audience of our own, however. Some of the more middle-aged jazz fans who liked a drink when they were listening used to come. Also a few modernists used to drop in and even sit in, although this had a disastrous effect on Paul Simpson who immediately began to play bebop.

There was also a ballad singer originally from Liverpool. His professional name was Mike Lawrence, and he used to sing an occasional number with the band.

Mike had rather taken up with a young pretty London girl called Doreen Porter. She had one of those sulky little faces, blonde hair, and a stocky peasant's body like a Maillol. Mike wasn't very interested in her but I was, and she used to come back to Margaretta Terrace sometimes and sleep in my bed, but she'd never go any further.

One night I had just finished singing a number when one of the proprietors, a Frenchman who looked like a small hawk wearing glasses, came up and told me that there was a lady and gentleman at the bar who wanted to see me.

I walked towards the bar convinced I was going to be bought a drink on the strength of my singing, and wearing my 'well thank you very much' face. In fact it was Doreen's mum and dad.

Mrs Porter was a small woman with an acid lemon-sucking face and one of those tight smiles which indicate anger rather than amusement. Her husband was a mild and bullied man who seemed very embarrassed.

'Are you George Melly?' said Mrs Porter. It wasn't a question. It was a statement of unsavoury fact.

'You've been knocking around with our Doreen,' she went on, 'and it's going to stop.'

'Now, Ethel,' said her husband nervously, 'don't upset yourself . . .'

'Be quiet,' she snapped at him, and then turned on me again.

'I know your type. Doreen has been well brought up. I don't want her getting mixed up with people like you. She had a very decent boy. Well, she's given him up. Now when she's twenty-one she can do what she wants, but she's only eighteen, and I'm telling you now that . . .'

I'd been getting quite angry during all this. I stopped her and said that if Doreen wanted to do what she wanted that was all right by me, but that if Doreen wanted to go on seeing me, I intended to go on seeing her.

She hadn't expected any answer. Years of bullying her husband had given her the idea that no man ever answered back, She tried another tack.

'I'll have you know that I shall inform the police. I shall find out where you live and . . .'

'Make an idiot of yourself,' I told her. I decided the moment had come to put an end to this conversation so I offered them a drink. Before she could stop him her husband accepted a brown ale.

'There's someone else I want to see. Another one who's been messing about with our Doreen. He's called Mike Lawrence . . .'

I could see Mike in the middle distance. What was more he saw us with drinks in our hands presumably bought by this couple, and thought it was very mean of me, a fellow singer, not to row him in. Smiling fixedly – he had very white teeth and knew it – he weaved through the jiving couples. I tried, without success, to motion him away with a hand behind my back, but he took no notice.

He came and stood by us waiting for an introduction. I didn't make it. Finally he introduced himself.

Mrs Porter turned on him. He couldn't think of anything to say. He just stood there grinning fixedly.

While Mrs Porter was attacking Mike, Mr Porter turned to me and apologised. 'She gets very 'et up does Ethel,' he explained. 'I'm a man,' he went on, 'I know our Doreen is a very attractive girl. I can see your point of view, but you must understand. A mother's feelings, that's what it is, you see . . .'

'Come on, Fred,' said Mrs Porter, 'we're going.'

'At least you've got something to say for yourself,' she snapped at me. 'Not like 'im. Grinning like a great fool.' She swept out. Mr Porter handed me his business card. He was a heating specialist.

Four minutes after they'd gone Doreen came in stoned out of her mind. She walked up to the bandstand and threw her arms round Mick and kissed him. He was obviously surprised at this because Doreen had made it quite clear that she didn't fancy him at all. He also looked very sheepish because Pam was in the bar. She saw what happened and came storming up to him and hit him as hard as she could on the head with her handbag.

'Fuck me,' he said later, 'just my luck. Hit over the head because a girl who doesn't even fancy me kisses me when she's pissed.'

I took Doreen home that night and we did it.

Doreen and I were together for some months. At first she was fascinated by the people I knew in Chelsea, but after a bit she told me that all that arty chat drove her mad.

'I only like you in bed,' she said, 'and I only like you talking when you're saying dirty things when you're coming.'

Eventually I went off for a fortnight's work in Scotland and although Doreen had said that she hoped I'd still want her when I got back, she didn't ring me up again.

*

Mick and Pam had left their old flat and moved into a room in a flat round the corner from me. The owners were a couple called John and Buddy. John was a very sweet shy man with glasses and a moustache who liked to play the trumpet. Buddy was a big positive woman whose charm and personal kindness just about made up for her extreme right-wing views. Even so we were always having terrible shout-ups, especially after several of the huge gin and tonics which were as much part of the ambience as the click of the backgammon counters and the placing of bets over the telephone. Buddy also had two alsatians. Mick loves dogs, especially large dogs, with a passion verging on the unbalanced. He gathers them up in his arms and licks their faces enthusiastically. He calls them 'lovely old mushes'. The near loss of an ear lobe not long ago has made no difference. I don't mind dogs providing I know them well, but I treat them with respect, and will cross the road rather than pass a chow or boxer out on its own. Buddy's dogs were mother and son. The male was a rather soppy old thing, but the mother had been trained as a police dog. She was called Misty Mum, and I was terrified of her. Due to her conditioning, if you shook hands with Buddy or lit a cigarette for her Misty Mum would leap up and seize your wrist between her jaws. She was also a good house-dog as they say.

Mick found it hard to get up in those days, and one of my duties was to come round and tell him it was time for the band meet. I would try and get there early enough for us to catch a bus into town, but usually found that, by the time he was ready to leave, it was necessary to take a taxi. Mick thought I was very mean to only contribute the equivalent of my bus fare towards this.

One morning Pam, Buddy and John all being out, and my knocks and rings producing no signs of life, I pushed open the sitting-room window and threw a leg over the sill. I was there for an hour before the door of the room opened and Mick looked in. Misty Mum's jaws held my calf quite gently, but her low growling and the slight increase in pressure when I tried to move or cry out convinced me that it would be better to remain still and silent.

Mick and Pam weren't at Buddy and John's very long. One night after a concert they had a terrible row, and Mick gave Pam a black eye in the hall and rushed out into the night.

I was just about to eat a delicious plateful of cold roast beef in the kitchen. Buddy comforted Pam, and John asked me to go out and find Mick and tell him he mustn't come back. I put down my knife and fork and walked along the embankment. Mick was leaning on the wall staring at the oily water. I told him and said he could stay the night with me. Then I went back to see what was happening.

Pam had gone to bed. John said he realised it was nothing to do with me, and gave me a large brandy. On the table was my plate of beef, and I was starving. Even so I felt it would be heartless to suggest I eat it, so I drank the brandy and left.

For a few days Pam stayed there and said she would never go back to Mick. She did, of course, and shortly afterwards they found a flat in Lisle Street behind Leicester Square.

This street, with its electrical spare parts shops and very old whores, became so much a part of the Mulligan legend that you couldn't imagine him living anywhere else.

6

Lovely Digs

In the afternoons we used to drink in 'The Mandrake'. It had started as a chess club, but gradually it had absorbed cellar after cellar under the pavement of Meard Street. A good club is its members. The two bosses, Boris, huge and taciturn, and Teddy Turner, volatile and Jewish, accepted jazzmen as contributory. In the evenings, after the pubs were shut, we were encouraged to sit in, but it was the afternoons I liked. Under today's regulations there are far fewer afternoon drinking clubs. This deprives people of a keen anti-social pleasure: the knowledge that you are drinking and getting drunk when everybody else is working. I enjoyed the slow idiotic and repetitive conversations or arguments. The barmaids turning into goddesses, the feeling that time was not a member.

Our other stronghold was the 'A and A Club'. According to the yellowing rules by the entrance, 'A and A' stood for authors and actors, but in fact those who used the premises were mostly taxi-drivers, clip-joint hostesses, waiters, small-time criminals and jazz musicians.

The A and A was housed in a tall ramshackle building tucked away in an alley behind the Charing Cross Road. There were a great many stone stairs up to the club entrance and on one of them slept an old woman under a pile of newspapers. Although there was a door with a spyhole in it, unless the law was putting the pressure on it was usually open and you could walk right in. There were two rooms in use: a restaurant, and above it a billiard hall patronised for the most part by the taxi-drivers.

The restaurant was a long, cheerful, none-too-clean room with a counter at the end and a kitchen off. The food was Greek, very reasonable and surprisingly good. We usually went there when we got back into town after a job, but the atmosphere was so lively that, although we intended leaving in time to catch the next all-night bus, we often sat until the first tube in Leicester Square.

There was a juke box which held an uncharacteristic selection of good jazz and Greek music, and in the entrance to the club there was a football machine usually manipulated by seriously involved Cypriot waiters.

At one table sat an old man with a long white beard. He was an astrologer and, for a small fee, would work out your horoscope with the aid of tattered charts of the heavens. Another regular was Gypsy Larry. Larry was in his sixties but his nut-brown face, vivid black eyes, and very white teeth suggested a much younger man. He wore a brilliant red neckerchief and talked pure old-style cock-ney. One of his stories began: 'So this geezer went for a pony in the carsie . . .'

There was often a live session at the A and A, but as there was no piano, and brass or woodwind instruments were discouraged, this was confined to guitars and banjos. Gypsy Larry could play guitar, and 'Banjo George', a dignified grey-haired man who looked like an accountant down on his luck, usually sat in with him. Among the various jazz musicians who also contributed was Diz Disley.

Diz had come to London from Yorkshire where he had been at Leeds Art School and was also a member of the Yorkshire Jazz Band. He wears a beard and has the face of a satyr *en route* to a cheerful orgy. He is full of talent and a real anarchist with a built-in anti-success mechanism. He sleeps through appointments with edi-tors who would like to employ him as a cartoonist or, if he has the job, doesn't send in his drawings on time. He became a popular compère on a BBC pop programme not long ago and then missed several editions because he was in jail for contempt of an Income Tax court. He is generous with his money, and unscrupulous when he hasn't any. If reproached he simply says: 'Be fair,' and if this doesn't help adds: 'Tarrah then. Fuck off.'

What Diz has is a great feeling for style, an eye for the human comedy, and a tongue to transmit its flavour.

I saw a lot of him at this time. One day we ate in an Indian restaurant in Chelsea. There was an elderly woman at the next table talking about circuses in a loud, slightly dotty, way.

'I will never go to the circus,' she told her companion, 'because of the performing animals. I should only make a scene, and it wouldn't do any good, so I don't go.'

Diz nodded in vigorous approval, his head cocked like a tom-tit on a coconut.

'The whole point is,' she went on, 'that I can't bear animals having to learn tricks. I don't mind if they do tricks naturally. Now my doggie . . .' and she patted the snuffling old hearth-rug at her feet. 'He can do lots of tricks, can't 'oo, darling. 'Es, of course 'oo can, but the point is that the tricks he can do, he's taught himself . . .'

There was a moment's silence in the restaurant while the lady drank some water. Disley completed her sentence for her quietly but clearly.

'Like fuckin' barking,' he explained amiably.

Another A and A *habitué* was a girl called Kinky Mavis. She was not a great beauty, but a serious eroticist with a large assortment of chains, fancy-dress (nun, schoolgirl, police-woman, etc.) and a collection of photographs she liked to spread around her bed. Outside this she seemed a friendly uncomplicated girl.

Mick never went up the A and A much. After a couple of visits, he had decided it wasn't his atmosphere. He only liked talking to people when he was drinking and, in London at any rate, only ate when he was starving. Even then, he would usually settle for five or six pies at a stall. Like a wild animal he had established his chosen tracks through the Soho jungle and seldom deviated. He was a raver of habit.

One afternoon we had stopped for a drink at a small pub in Essex. There was a village green in front of the building, and grazing on it a tethered goat. There is something very un-English about goats. It's not only that there aren't many of them, it's their pagan eyes, either milky-blue or honey-yellow, with their elongated pupils, and their extraordinary smell, and the way their skeletons are so functional, so in evidence, with the flesh draped on the bones like heavy material.

With a glass of beer gleaming and glinting in my hand under the light-splashed East Anglian sky, I walked over the green and patted the animal's taut neck and the bulging flanks supported on the neat splayed legs. Suddenly, without looking up from its grazing, the goat began to shit. Like a speeded-up film of a flower opening, its whole arse split and a formidable number of turds in clusters like black grapes emerged and fell steaming on to the grass.

I was surprised by this rather dramatic event and walked back to the band who were sitting on a long bench outside the low white clap-boarded building and attempted to describe what I had seen.

Mick listened and then asked, as though seeking information, how many points I got for seeing a goat shit. This was how the points game started.

At first it applied simply to animals shitting: two for a dog; five for the more secretive and fastidious cat; only three for a cow but an extra two if it was pissing at the same time.

I don't know at what moment 'the points system' was extended and widened to take in minor accidents and personal disasters, nor how long it was before it crystallised and became exclusively concerned with deformities, dwarfs and cripples, but eventually it did. The awarding of points became a popular band sport. A pre-sick joke.

Mick has always been concerned with the significance of certain numbers. Very soon the comparatively modest 'eighteen' became linked to points.

'At least eighteen,' he would say as we stopped to allow a hunchback with a surgical boot weave across the road in front of the band coach.

'Points' also became a noun as in the sentence: 'He is points.'

And to describe some physical handicap not immediately apparent, such as an expensive artificial leg, the word gained an adjective.

'Have you noticed?' Mick would ask out of the corner of his mouth. 'He's subtle points.'

Descriptions of athletic events on the radio were considerably enriched by the invention of the points system. Sentences like 'He has been awarded the maximum number of points' or 'I'm afraid she has lost several points there' gained a new significance.

There was in the jazz world at that time a man who was worth at least eighteen. His name was 'Little Jeff', and he was a dwarf jazz musician. He played trumpet and sang. Before the war he had worked with Nat Gonella around the music halls – presumably on

the Johnsonian principle that why people want to see a dog walking
on its hind legs or a woman preaching is not because they can do it
well but because they can do it at all. It was his size and not his
musical ability which had won him his livelihood. Even so he could
play the trumpet quite well and was at that time lively and active.

During the bombing God had seen fit to aim a splinter of glass
at little Jeff and paralyse him from the waist down. This just
about doubled his points rating but didn't break his spirit. He now
propelled himself in an invalid car from jazz club to jazz club
and would borrow Mick's trumpet and sing and play a couple of
numbers. One was 'Old Rocking Chair's Got Me' – he was not
unaware of the pathos of his position – the other, 'I'm In the Mood
for Love'.

The only trouble with little Jeff was that he had to be carried
from his invalid car to the bandstand, and he was extremely heavy
for his size.

It was here that Paul Simpson carried little Jeff in by himself.
Although crimson in the face he didn't drop him, but reached the
chair and walked away puffed up with pride. He hadn't gone more
than a few steps when little Jeff began to shout out in pain. In his
relief at being able to put him down, Paul hadn't been careful
enough. Little Jeff was sitting on his balls.

In my view the points game is no worse and no better than the
conventional response to deformity. When we started it may even
have been better because we shocked ourselves into taking deformity into account. In time, however, our attitude hardened into
convention. We simply thought 'eighteen' where most people think
'how tragic' and with as little sense of involvement.

In the early fifties the 'West End Café' in Edinburgh used to book
jazz bands from London for a fortnight at a time, and eventually
they got round to us. I was very excited by this because it was the
band's first long engagement, and I found it possible again to
relate to jazz history. Even the name of the café, in appearance a
conventional Scottish tea-room, was the same as a venue in Chicago
where Armstrong had played in the early twenties. Another advantage was that we could play jazz all evening with no waltzes or
sambas, and that I was sure that Mick would find it essential to

rehearse some new numbers as we would be facing more or less the same audience every night.

We stayed *en pension* in a boarding house. On the table at every meal were huge cake stands loaded with every sort of sconc and roll. I have always been greedy and eat myself to a standstill. Until then I had been thin. Edinburgh was a watershed. I got into the coach at Baker Street a skinny lad and got out three weeks later a fat man. Mick took to calling me 'Fatso' which he shortened to 'Fat'. An incidental effect of my altered metabolism was to stop me drinking beer altogether. Consulting a calorie chart I discovered that gin was the least fattening spirit and for a long time drank it neat at a single swallow, a sight which convinced most people of my depravity.

The Edinburgh jazz musicians were divided into two cliques. There were the purists led by a clarinettist called Sandy Brown and a trumpet player called Al Fairweather. They played at that time Ken Colyer music at its most uncompromising and listened to our brand of Dixieland with glowering disapproval. Al and Sandy have the two Scottish faces: Al's is the craggy one with watch-spring eyebrows, Sandy's the long dour one with the Kilroy nose. He also wears a beard and balded early.

Their rivals played Condon music. Again there were two outstanding personalities, Alex Welsh and Archie Semple, although their band went under Archie's name. Alex was short and jolly. Archie was tall, thin, and charming in a jumpy kind of way.

The Brown–Fairweather axis and the Welsh–Semple clique hardly communicated. We became more friendly with the latter, and after finishing our Edinburgh stint went on a short tour with the Semple band. During the course of this, Archie decided to come down to London and join the Mulligan band on clarinet. Did this mean Paul Simpson left? Of course not. Mick bought him a baritone sax and yet again the band grew bigger and more unwieldy, but Archie's rather Peewee Russell flavoured style was a distinct acquisition. Mick was never against featuring soloists (it gave him time for a quick smoke in the wings), and to listen to Archie was a genuine pleasure.

*

Shortly afterwards two more personnel changes took place, and both replacements were Scottish. Why are there so many Scots jazz musicians, and, come to that, why so many good ones? Sandy Brown, a convinced nationalist, has a theory that it's to do with the fact that Scottish folk music is still a reality.

Johnny Lavender, the chicken-hating banjoist, left to go and practise photography in Canada. In his place, Mick took on Jimmy Currie, a convinced modernist who played amplified guitar.

Jimmy was the antithesis of the rest of us. He was a great dandy, and used to bring away on tour several suits which swayed rhythmically from side to side in their cellophane covers from a rail at the back of the band coach.

Uncomprehending and irritated we asked him why. He explained in his high-pitched Edinburgh accent: 'Well, man, you've got to look sharp for the chicks.'

For the same reason he was very concerned about his thinning hair and, to disguise this, he grew it very long at the back of his head and brushed it forward over his cranium, arranging it in little curls at the front. Although this took a long time and needed constant attention, it worked well enough in the ordinary way but sometimes, when he was carrying his amplifier from the coach to the hall, or walking through the streets looking for somewhere to eat, a sudden gust of wind would blow the whole thing backwards leaving his head bald and a good foot of hair streaming out behind him. Later on, long after he had left the band, he – sensibly – bought an expensive toupee. Only the other day I saw him wearing a new one, completely convincing for anybody who didn't know him, in 'distinguished' grey.

He was also the first person I knew who used 'Old Spice' after-shave lotion, at that time unobtainable in this country. He told us that he 'got the fellers to bring it over on the boats'.

Jimmy worked out a cabaret act which Mick sometimes asked him to perform at concerts, mostly for our pleasure. For no self-evident reason Jimmy's act involved him pretending to be a Mexican. He opened and closed it with a chorus from 'South of the Border', and wore a sombrero liberated, I suspect, from the wardrobe of some Latin–American group he had worked with in the past. I can still remember some of the abysmal patter which he delivered in the conventional sing-song of the Cowboy film peon.

'My girl friend, she's not pretty, but then she's not ugly. She's sort of in between – pretty ugly. When I first saw her she was standing outside a pawn shop picking her teeth, so I went inside the shop and helped her pick the teeth she wanted, etc. . . .'

Our new bass player, Pat Molloy, although of Irish origin, was born in Dunfermline, a small Scottish town on the other side of the Firth of Forth from Edinburgh. He was very small, a practising Roman Catholic, and had a classic Irish face with black curly hair and a complicated mouth full of teeth. It was these which made his Irish–Scottish accent very difficult to understand.

He had been an insurance agent in Dunfermline: 'I was very, very respected in Dunfermline,' he would often tell us, but had left over a muddle with money. He was scrupulously honest, so it had been a genuine muddle mostly due, we gathered, to allowing people who couldn't pay to leave it over to next week, and marking their books as though they had paid, and then forgetting if they had or not. A muddle due to kindness in fact, for he was a very kindhearted little man.

Pat had discovered in the cheerful blasphemy of the Mulligan band, perhaps, the most worrying milieu for him. He took, as they say, 'refuge in drink', in his case Guinness. Sober he was a polite person. When drunk he began to swear, not as most people swear, in order to emphasise what they have to say, or from verbal poverty, but as though possessed. At the same time his face would alter. His eyes rolled, his nostrils distended, and his mouth grinned fixedly revealing his formidable teeth.

Pat was a virgin. He once told me that when he had been working in a sack factory a girl had pushed him back on to a pile of the finished product and 'tried to rape me, but I managed to push her off'!

He owned an enormous collection of the sort of suits you can see on men waiting for the pubs to open on Sunday mornings in Camden Town, bright blue with floppy trouser bottoms. He was also a great runner of mysterious errands involving small brown paper parcels.

Drinking and gambling so complicated his financial life that for quite a long time he was forced to live in the band coach which was parked on a piece of waste ground behind King's Cross. He washed in the nearby public baths and ate in a café. His wardrobe hung across the back of the coach, his belongings along the shelves.

But despite these economies, he was always having to approach Mick for subs and loans. Mick, although prepared to help him out, rather dreaded these moments, not only for the money involved, but because Pat insisted on giving him an hour-long explanation of just why and how his finances were in such a mess. He prefaced these sessions with a sentence that Mick learned to dread. 'I wonder,' he would say, 'if we could have a little chat?'

Pat's real obsession was his instrument. His double bass was an old one and, alone among the instruments in a jazz band, the age of a double bass would appear to add to its standing in the eyes of its owner.

During journeys it lay across the back seat of the coach, and, whenever we passed over a level-crossing or humpbacked bridge, and in consequence bounced into the air, Pat would give a loud anguished cry of 'the bass', and scurry down the coach aisle to make sure it had suffered no damage.

Musicians' reactions to their instruments vary a great deal. Clarinet players, due to the flimsy nature of the clarinet, become hardened to minor disasters, although at the same time given to irritable exasperation. Between overhauls a complicated forest of elastic bands replaces weak springs, little green pads are constantly falling off, and reeds have to be singed with matches in an attempt to harden the blowing edge.

Trombonists are very neurotic about their horns. They're usually fairly neurotic anyway, but it's impossible to say whether they become trombonists *because* they're neurotic or become neurotic *because* they're trombonists. It's easy to see why they worry about their instruments. The long slide, incredibly vulnerable and, if bent only a fraction, completely useless, which must nevertheless be temptingly pushed out over the heads of an audience, is the main cause, but also the fact that many people tend to think of the trombone as a musical joke is a contributing factor. Most trombonists alternate between pushing their technique beyond its limits and angry self-parody.

Trumpet players are musically pretty extrovert on the whole.

Because it is quite hard to damage a trumpet short of jumping on it, they treat their instruments with a certain indifference.

Mick's various trumpets – he had almost as many as he had suits – were always in terrible condition, but even so they had to seize up before he cleaned them. This, in itself a distressing process for a spectator, usually took place in tiny dressing rooms when we were changing into our uniform, and it was difficult to avoid being forced to bear witness. It involved flushing out all the tubing by running hot water through under pressure, and Mick would draw our attention to anything particularly interesting as it slithered down the plug-hole.

Mick always maintained that he found it hard to blow in tune after he'd cleaned out his trumpet because he'd got used to compensating for the distortion produced by the blockages.

Once, when Mick was a member of a band which had formed to welcome Louis Armstrong at London Airport, Louis borrowed his trumpet to blow a few notes with the group for the benefit of the press photographers, and handed it back with the words: 'You want to get the saveloys out of your horn, man!'

During tours a continuous problem was finding somewhere to stay. We had an ideal in our heads; a pub where the bar was still swinging however late the job finished, where the landlady actually preferred us to have breakfast at about 11 a.m., and where a girl with a strong local accent was accepted as your wife when you got back, even though you had booked in as a single before the gig.

Here and there such places actually existed, but usually some compromise was necessary.

Some bands had their accommodation booked through their offices which meant in fact staying at AA hotels, but these were the prosperous organisations like the Lyttelton Band. Others kept a methodical record of everywhere they stayed and wrote off in advance. We did neither. We had a rota and tried to fix ourselves up when we arrived, taking it in turn to actually find the digs.

As we were often late, and might have as little as half an hour to spare before we were due on stage, this was a nightmare.

Of course, as time went on in most of the big towns we knew where to go. In Sheffield it was Mrs Flanagan.

She was a large, kind woman who always wore slippers and an apron. Her house, big and unbelievably shabby, was situated in the seedy area which usually surrounds provincial universities dating from the last century. An area of unlikely dogs copulating in the rain, sad Negroes and Indians, women in curlers going to shop wearing dusty maroon coats over their nightdresses, large Catholic Churches, junk shops full of rags and broken electric fires, pubs standing alone on the corners of bomb sites, bright poster hoardings, graffiti and children's street games chalked all over the pavements.

Mrs Flanagan seldom moved out of her kitchen except to answer the bell or bring in the breakfasts. Her kitchen was not large, but as well as her it contained a very old spaniel, two cats, and a budgie. It was considered advisable to ask for boiled eggs for breakfast.

In the dining-room was an old piano, a sideboard with jumbo-sized cornflakes packets on it, a looking-glass surrounded by photographs of bandleaders who had stayed there and disfigured by musicians who had worked for them. Soon after her accession, somebody stuck up a postcard of the Queen among the other photographs. On it was written: 'Lovely digs, Mrs Flanagan'. It was signed 'Liz and Phil'.

Over the dining-room table with its jug of thin bluish milk, tea-stained sugar, and sliced white bread, was a remarkable lampshade which all of us for many years believed to be made of fur. One day somebody climbed on to a chair to examine it more closely, and in touching it dislodged a thick cloud of brown dust.

The beds were very damp, but once you got warm they were quite comfortable as they exuded a steamy heat due perhaps to the flannel sheets. The banisters, the walls, the handles of the knives, in fact everything in the house, felt both gritty and greasy.

Mrs Flanagan was tolerant of every kind of behaviour except sexual promiscuity.

'If yer want to go wi' a scrubber,' she'd tell us, 'there's plenty of them sort of 'otels, but don't bring 'er 'ere!'

Ken Colyer, the week before he got married, had turned up with his fiancée and persuaded Mrs Flanagan they were already man and wife. Mrs Flanagan always read the *Melody Maker* from cover to cover every Friday in her kitchen, and the following week had come across a photograph of Ken and his bride on the steps of Fulham Town Hall under the legend, 'Married Yesterday'.

She came storming into the dining-room and brought it to our attention. 'Wait till I see that Ken Colyer!' she shouted. 'I'll learn 'im! Coming 'ere for a bloody rehearsal!'

If you asked Mrs Flanagan to lend you anything – cards, dominoes, a clothes brush – she would hand it over with a sweet smile.

'Luke after it luv,' she'd say, and then add, after a long pause, 'It were Flanagan's.'

On the other hand, in Manchester there was never any trouble in finding a hotel where you could lumber back a scrubber. These hotels were usually converted terrace houses in which the original rooms had been split into narrow corridors and minute rooms as though bees had been building a hive in a hollow tree. They were full of half-complete innovations aimed at the American servicemen from the Cheshire airbases who stayed there with their girls on week-end passes.

'Cocktail Lounges', remnants of modern wallpapers which ran out half-way round a room, sixpence-in-the-slot electric shavers usually out of order, loudspeakers in every bedroom with a control switch marked 'Light. Home. Room Service'.

A late-night phone call to book a double room revealed in one sentence the only strict rule: ' 'Ave you got luggage, sir?'

Breakfast in the dining-room on Sunday morning was an unreal and dream-like experience due to the fact that the American servicemen's wives, club hostesses in the main, were wearing cocktail dresses.

It was perhaps because of the number of American servicemen who converged on Manchester every week-end that the city preserved a distinctly wartime atmosphere, wide-open and yet tatty, throughout most of the fifties.

Mick and I, after the jazz club session was over, sometimes went on to 'The Stork Club' which had its premises at the bottom of a dark court off Cross Street, and was run by an ex-wrestler called Billy Benny who looked rather like Henry VIII and had a slight harelip. In exchange for a song or two from me, he was prepared to set them up all night.

'Any time George will thing a thong,' he told us, 'I'll puth up a bottle of whithkey and we'll make some hap!'

He was also a fund of unsolicited but useful information about his hostesses.

'They're no good,' he'd tell us as two of them swayed past on their way to the ladies. 'Strictly platers.'

There was also in Manchester a service which until surprisingly recently existed nowhere else outside London, somewhere to eat in the small hours. All round Piccadilly were pie stalls which sold marvellous hot pies: steak and kidney, meat and potato, cheese and potato. The fierce physical pleasure of biting into one of these, a little drunk in the frosty night, is enough, even in retrospect, to fill the mouth with saliva.

There was also a very disgusting all-night restaurant where, one midnight, a drunk American speared a long thin sausage, a part of the 'Mixed Grill', and shouted at the apathetic waitress who had just banged it down in front of him: 'What do you call this for Chris' sake? A goddam dog's cock?'

But if Manchester kept alive, despite austerity, everything which was raffish and roaring about wartime night life, Birmingham preserved intact the wartime atmosphere of shortages and rudeness, the grey relish of the puritan in control. It seemed to us that the people of Birmingham were forced to bite their tongues in order to stop themselves from countering any request or demand with the whining reiteration of the sentence, 'Don't you know there's a war on?'

Alone of all the big cities, we were never able to discover in Birmingham anywhere reasonable to stay. Most of the boarding houses were run by rat-trap-mouthed women married to Poles. We seldom parted on amicable terms.

Late breakfasts were the main cause. One woman, furious that none of us had come down before half past nine, angrily switched off the wireless which I'd tuned in to 'Housewives' Choice'. When she'd gone out again, I switched it back on.

She came storming into the room.

'Did you sweetch eet on when oi'd turned eet off?' she yelled.

'Yes.'

'Roight. Thet settles eet. Get owt at wonce. All of yow!'

'Not before we've eaten our breakfasts.'

'Roight. Then oi'll ring up Sergeant Green. 'E'll come reound on 'is boike and sort yow lot out! Yow'd better go at once. Are yow going?'

'No.'

'Roight. Oi'll ring up Sergeant Green roight away.'

We finished our breakfasts and left, but Sergeant Green hadn't appeared. Her husband, who took our money, apologised on her behalf. 'My wife,' he told us in his Polish–Birmingham accent, 'she is very highly strung. Very easily upset yow see.'

But on another occasion it was a Polish boarding-house keeper himself who was our protagonist.

Ever since eight o'clock he had come banging into the communal room where we were all sleeping, and shouted and yelled at us to get up. 'I wonder what he'd do,' I asked the chaps, 'if the next time he comes in we all start to imitate dogs?' We decided to find out, and had several rehearsals. Some of us barked. Some growled. Some yapped. It sounded quite impressive.

Five minutes later the man came in again. All of us funked it except Mick. His performance wasn't really up to much. Very quietly and just once he went 'Wuff'.

Why is Birmingham, the town we christened 'The Arsehole of England', so horrible a place? Perhaps it resents its proximity to London. It's never felt far enough away to develop its own personality. Its only defence is a joyless legality, a 'holier than thou' gloom.

Long before it was necessary, Birmingham had developed a complicated one-way system simply, we felt, for the pleasure of allowing you to glimpse at the end of a no-entry street the building you were aiming for, and then forcing you to detour for another three quarters of a mile. Cafés shut earlier in Birmingham than anywhere else. Sundays are deader. The accent more hideous. The pubs more reluctant to sell proprietary brands, more inclined to impose the brewers' filthy substitutes. A bottle of local whisky once rattled about undrunk in the bottom of the band wagon for over a month, and it is not that we were given to scotch advert chichi. It was simply undrinkable even when we were drunk.

The Demon Brum has, to a greater or lesser extent, possessed the whole Midlands. Leicester, Nottingham, Coventry, Wolverhampton, all these towns evoke the figure of a commissionaire exerting his authority. It is not until you reach the Potteries that cities begin to regain their confidence, to become centres, not outer suburbs.

In reaction there is a considerable violence under the surface. The audiences at Birmingham Town Hall, that surprisingly beautiful neo-classic building at the very centre of the city's hideous heart, are famous for their extremes. If they liked you they stamped for over five minutes. If they were against you they threw corporation lavatory rolls and pennies. They were inclined, throughout the whole jazz decade, to extreme revivalist conservatism. When Humph went mainstream and played a concert there with his new line-up, a whole row of the audience raised, during Bruce Turner's first alto chorus, a long banner reading 'GO HOME DIRTY BOPPER'! To execute this project reveals a fanaticism verging on the unbalanced. I can imagine no other city where it could have happened.

Another city where we spent a great deal of time was Newcastle upon Tyne. The City Fathers refused, long after anyone else in England, to allow cinemas to open on Sundays. In consequence jazz concerts, held at the Essoldo, were full every week. Newcastle is the most foreign of our great cities. The Newcastle accent sounds like a Scandinavian language, and indeed there are a great many words of Norwegian origin in the local slang. We stayed at a boarding house which catered for Scandinavian seamen and there was rye bread and a smörgasbord washed down with great jugs of ice-cold milk for breakfast.

As time went on, our touring life took a certain shape. For example, Albert Kinder, a Scouse promoter who intended to tie up jazz in the North, had succeeded in organising a regular week-end for touring bands, culminating in a concert in the 'pool. The jobs on Friday and Saturday were usually a NAAFI dance at a RAF training camp near Warrington, and a public dance held in the Territorial Drill Hall, Widnes.

The RAF job was remarkable for the terrifying appearance of the two coachloads of girls imported by the authorities to dance with the trainee airmen. The whole area was still thick with US air bases, and it was only natural that any fun-loving young woman of normal appearance gravitated towards them. In consequence those left over verged on the grotesque. Their eruption into the canteen where we sat waiting to play never lost its dreadful fascination.

In Widnes we were made honorary members of the Sergeants' Mess which had a bar. It also contained a very ugly but willing woman known to the sergeants as 'the Widnes Bicycle'. One night, when we were drinking after the dance, a member of the band, his judgement clouded by beer, gave her a knee tremble at the back of the building. Although keen enough on the act itself, the Widnes Bicycle was suspicious of the musician's motives.

'I know the only reason you're doing this,' she told him. He imagined that she had guessed, accurately, that it was because he was drunk enough to ignore her repulsive looks, and began to feel rather sorry for her.

He therefore said nothing, hoping she would drop the subject and spare him the necessity of lying reassuringly, but she went on.

'I know. Don't think I don't know! You're only going with me . . .'

He waited hopelessly, staring at the glowing chimneys of the chemical factories along the shores of the Mersey. '. . . so you can go back and swank to the fellers.'

Another regular job was the Gaiety Ballroom, Grimsby. This huge hall was privately owned by an elderly Jewish gentleman of extreme old-world courtesy, two younger Jewish brothers with a new joke each time we came, and a Scottish lady with the appearance and manner of a kindly Lowland Sunday School teacher. There was also a manager called Freddy who had played tuba in the resident band when the Gaiety first opened in 1926. There was a photograph to prove it in the office, and an old night watchman with a small corpulent dog, with one sightless eye like a white grape.

At the end of the dance, Mick and I were invited up to the table at the side of the stand where the owners sat, and the elderly gentleman congratulated us, 'Very nice show, Mick', and asked us into the office for a drink. We discussed the state of the business, listened to the two jokes from the two brothers, and drank large whiskies under the photographs of champion ballroom dancers receiving cups in the decade before the war, and the 1926 band in the evening dress of the period with a sunset painted on the huge bass drum and Freddy holding his tuba in the back row.

Then we left the hall, pausing for a minute or two to chat with the night watchman and pat his dog as they sat side by side with the long night ahead of them under a mural of Cleopatra on her barge.

The nearest pub to the Gaiety was a mile away so we became, as did all the visiting bands, automatic members of the Working Men's Club. The Gaiety, which looked from the outside like an aeroplane hangar, was built on one side of a railway cutting, the Working Men's Club occupied a large loft over some deserted stables on the other side. During the changeover waltzes, when the resident band was taking over from our rhythm section, Mick and I would charge out of the ballroom, down some steep steps to road level, under the railway bridge, and up the dark lane to the club which was a friendly place full of fat women and very old men with watery eyes wearing caps.

In fact we drank a great deal in Working Men's Clubs, Miners' Institutes and the like, especially in the North. The most magnificent of these was in Crewe, a reminder that in the nineteenth century, when it was built, the railwayman was considered the aristocrat of the working class. Marble, glass and heavy mahogany carving were there to prove it, and let into the bar were large reproductions of Pre-Raphaelite ladies.

During the summer in Grimsby, it was the custom of the Management to hire bands not simply for one night, although we often did play these in winter, but for a whole week with Tuesday and Thursday off.

We stayed in a boarding house a quarter of a mile from the Gaiety. It was run by a jolly little woman called Doris who wore spectacles and usually had her hair in curlers. She always left out a huge wedge of cheese, some cream crackers and a pub-sized jar of pickled onions for us when we got in. Her husband was a dental mechanic and made his false teeth somewhere on the premises. He was a little man with a yellowish complexion. If we bumped into him on one of the landings, he would grin, as though to advertise his products, and scurry out of sight. Doris had a daughter who was a schoolgirl when we first stayed there in the very early fifties, and a school teacher when we last saw her in 1960. There was a son too who was always stretched out on the carpet of the front room (although taking up progressively more space over the years) reading comics.

The kitchen was often full of Doris's friends, middle-aged ladies in a state of infectious euphoria. Most of them worked behind the refreshment counters at the Gaiety. One of them told fortunes from tea leaves and made endless jokes about her black underwear, a decidedly unerotic concept. 'She's as nutty as a fruit cake,' Doris would say after every sally.

The first few times we stayed there Doris's father was alive although very old and several points. Even after he died ('It were all for the best,' said Doris next time we arrived. ' 'E were past it'), we were reminded of him because at strategic points throughout the house, at the turn of the stairs, above the bath, by the side of the lavatory, were the aluminium handles which had helped him to haul himself about.

Still alive, although a little stiff in the joints on our last visit, was a large collie dog called Shaun. He was a coat fetishist, and could often be surprised rogering the mackintoshes in the hall.

Being resident at the same hall for a week at a time had its advantages sexually. We got to know a group of girls who used to stand night after night by the side of the stage and were known, according to Freddy, as 'the Grimsby Trawlers'. The bandwagon, parked throughout the week up an alley at the side of the ballroom, was comparatively comfortable.

I once asked one of the Grimsby Trawlers to come out with me on the band's night off. She stood me up, but explained why the following evening, during the interval.

'I couldn't come,' she told me, and added, as though it were a perfectly adequate reason, 'You see I were asked out by . . .' and here her voice became dreamy with the grandeur of it all, 'the Mayor of Cleethorpes' son.'

I became fond of Grimsby over the years. It's a long town, lying close to the miles of fishdocks which are its *raison d'être*. Entirely undistinguished architecturally, it has nevertheless a certain picturesque quality arising from the fishing. Little shops sell ropes and nets, the pubs are full of men wearing blue jerseys with herring scales on the backs of their hands. There was (he no longer exists) a tattooist called Dusty Rhodes near the entrance to the dock. There are marvellous junk shops, and in one of them I bought for five shillings a phrenologist's head. Even in the long streets of mean red-brick terrace houses where a photographer's glass case full of weddings is an event, you can still smell the sea, and the weather too is mercantile: squalls, storms, brilliant sunshine, grey drizzle within the space of a day. Once, walking towards Doris's local with Diz Disley who was depping with us for a month or two, I tried to explain to him why I liked Grimsby. He waited until I'd finished, and then remarked quietly but firmly, 'I prefer fucking Venice.'

In the Scottish border town of Melrose there lived an ex-lawyer called Duncan McInnon. He was short and plump with an untidy off-ginger moustache and protuberant blue eyes. He dressed in wrinkled grey flannels and hairy sports coats (somehow they are always more hairy in Scotland) with large leather-covered buttons. Following his success in running Saturday-night hops all over the borders using local dance bands and small Scottish country groups, he developed larger ambitions, turned himself into a company called 'Border Dances Limited', and appointed Jim Godbolt as his London agent. It was Jim's job to book bands and send them up to play for anything between one week and three on Duncan's circuit, and in consequence from 1953 until the band folded in December 1961 we would find ourselves at least once a year working our way north.

Although several of Duncan's venues were extremely profitable he was always teetering on the edge of disaster because of his obsession with a huge white elephant in the shape of the Market Hall, Carlisle.

In itself, Carlisle is an unpleasant place largely, I suspect, because it cannot decide if it is English or Scottish. It's the only town in England with state pubs, and an evening in one of these is enough to shake the convictions of the most doctrinaire socialist. They're like alcoholic post-offices.

The market hall is enormous with lots of permanent little shops over most of the area. There is a large concrete floor about the size of three football fields, and it was this which Duncan hoped to turn into the centre of the city's night-life. He had taken a long lease from the Council, built a stage, cut off the dance-hall area from the shops by suspending enormous dirty green tarpaulins, installed a great many heaters among the iron girders, and finally, in an attempt to suggest gaiety, had stuck thousands of little mirrors mounted on cloth around the bottom four feet of the supporting columns.

Even before the first time we went to play for Border Dances Ltd we had an idea what to expect because Jim Godbolt had gone up for the opening night. Geraldo was the bandleader and he, Jim and, of course, Duncan had been invited by the Mayor to a dinner preceding the dance. There had been speeches including a very long one from Duncan which made up in fervour and enthusiasm what it lacked in coherence or relevance, and then the whole party made for the hall. There was a gentle incline leading down past a butcher's shop to where a gap in the tarpaulin gave entry to the dance floor. Jim was walking behind Duncan who was holding on to the arms of Geraldo in his immaculate tails. Suddenly Duncan slipped and fell, dragging Geraldo down with him. It was an inauspicious beginning.

That first evening, according to Jim, there was at least a decent crowd, but the night we made our début, even when the dance was at its height, there were only about twenty people. It was a freezing night in early spring, and the heaters, glowing faintly some thirty feet above our heads, did nothing to remedy this.

At about nine o'clock we came back from the state pub, reluctantly removed our overcoats and relieved a band called 'The Mighty Redcoats'. They were a local group and Duncan had chosen their name. He had a very nineteenth-century taste in promotion and publicity. His posters were couched in baroque circus prose, the source of some embarrassment to Mick, and of amusement to the rest of us. Mick has always displayed an almost ostentatious modesty, and one of Duncan's announcements full of ornate superlatives was guaranteed to make his head sink into his shoulders. I doubt 'The Mighty Redcoats' would have chosen their name if left to themselves, but Duncan employed them almost every night, and they had little choice.

As the front line were blowing through their mouth pieces to warm them up sufficiently to play in tune, Duncan himself climbed up on the stage. We had met him only briefly in the pub, where he had bought us a large number of double scotches, and hadn't really taken him in.

He walked to the front of the stage, eyed the tiny audience belligerently, and launched into a speech lasting a good half-hour. The gist of it was that the people of Carlisle didn't deserve the first-rate entertainment that Border Dances were bringing to them, but that Border Dances intended to go on doing so nevertheless; that he, Duncan McInnon, would fight and fight until he had made the Market Hall, Carlisle, into the greatest centre of ballroom entertainment anywhere in the North.

He concluded, as we were to discover he usually concluded his speeches, by reciting in full Kipling's 'If'. He then, with a climatic gesture, ordered Mick to play and, at the first note, jumped off the six-foot stand on to the concrete floor. He fell heavily, but leapt to his feet. The back of his coat and trousers were covered with powdered white chalk strewn there to stop the dancers from slipping. Near at hand was a young soldier with his girl. Duncan seized the girl and danced off with her into the middle distance jigging up and down in a kind of frenzy. With the exception of the pianist, who had his back to this, nobody in the band could play at all. Occasionally Mick or Roy would manage a strangled note but it would immediately degenerate into a fart of laughter.

After the dance was over, Duncan invited Mick and me into a small room where Border Dances stored their mikes and refreshment trestle-tables during market days. He had with him a friend and a bottle of whisky. He locked the door and pocketed the key, explaining that he would refuse to let us out until Mick had agreed to change over from jazz to Irish music. Eventually he fell asleep, and we were able to remove the key and escape.

I have always enjoyed the Border Tours except for the jobs. Carlisle was in a class by itself, but even the other venues were pretty depressing. Hawick Drill Hall; The Corn Exchange, Berwick-upon-Tweed; The Rosewall Institute; The Town Hall, Galashiels: to repeat these names is to visualise bars, comparatively empty Scottish parochial halls with a row of very plain ginger-haired girls dressed in floral prints of unfashionable length sitting along one wall, and a group of raw-boned lads huddled together in the opposite corner. The dances all started late and went on into the small hours.

Dumfries was the only exception. Duncan's dances there were

held on a Saturday, and the huge hall was packed. Furthermore, they finished early on account of the law about no dance continuing into the Sabbath. As a bonus there were always fights breaking out somewhere in the crowd and, as the stand was high, we had an excellent view.

We stayed in hotels in strange little towns with one broad street lined with plaid-obsessed drapers and tobacconists selling Scottish novelties, fishing tackle shops, and butchers who are called 'fleshers'.

We drove past ruined abbeys and over rivers where a salmon fisherman stood waist high.

We drank in the men-only bars, experimenting with malt whisky and chasing it with 'wee heavy' beers.

We ate high tea in the shadow of laden cake stands, and pudding suppers, black, white or haggis, with bread and butter, and cups of tea poured out neat with a jug of milk on the table.

We breathed the marvellous air.

But every night we had to play a Duncan job.

7

King of the Ravers

Between 1951, when the first revivalist boom was over, and 1953, when the scene began to recover, we were on the road all the time. We tried to keep some foothold in London and we ran our own club in a rehearsal room in a Gerrard Street basement and, on the rare occasions we were in town on a Saturday night, organised all-night raves.

The word 'rave', meaning to live it up, was as far as I know a Mulligan–Godbolt invention. It took several forms. The verb as above, 'a rave' meaning a party where you raved, and 'a raver', one who raved as much as possible. An article once described Mick as 'The King of the Ravers'.

During a National Savings Drive in 1952, Mick and Jim derived a great deal of harmless amusement by ringing each other up every time they saw a new poster and reading out its message with the word 'Rave' substituted for the word 'Save' 'HELP BRITAIN THROUGH NATIONAL RAVING', 'WANTED 50,000,000 RAVERS', etc.

Mick and I were the first people to organise all-night raves, and they were an enormous social success, but a financial loss. There were several reasons for this. For one thing the men who owned the rehearsal room insisted on half the take, and the number of tickets we were allowed to sell was limited by the fire regulations. As a result, after paying the band, printing the tickets, putting an advert in the *Melody Maker*, and buying a barrel of cider for the musicians who came along to sit in, the most we could expect was four pounds each and in fact, when it came to the share out, we were usually a pound or two out of pocket.

Anyway we didn't really run the all-nighters to make money. Although today the idea of spending a whole night in a crowded airless basement at a small loss appears extraordinary, it was very exciting then.

Forced as we were by commercial necessity to occupy most of our lives playing strict tempo music for dancing, the all-night sessions were an escape back into the jazz atmosphere of our beginnings. We could dress in shit order, fall about drunk, and tell people who criticised us or our music to get stuffed.

Of course the Mulligan band couldn't play from midnight to seven in the morning. We played three one-hour sessions and relied on musicians who wanted a blow to fill in the gaps.

There was no difficulty here, in fact there was an embarrassment of riches and a confusion of musical idiom which made arranging the groups a question of great tact and firmness if the whole thing wasn't to degenerate into a huge and messy jam session.

Revivalist jazz was in the melting pot at that moment. The majority remained faithful to the Morton–Oliver–Armstrong sound, but others were moving after Humph into the mainstream or beginning to think that Ken Colyer's back-to-the-roots ideas were right. In some circles white Chicago jazz was in the ascendancy, and yet even here there were two schools of thought, the back-to-the-twenties enthusiasts and the more recent Eddie Condon Dixieland fanatics. To confuse things further a few bebop musicians would drop in. Somehow all these had to have a blow and yet be kept out of each other's hair. Mick left this to me – in fact he left most of the organisation to me, and sometimes, if he was drunk enough, would even sneak back to his flat round the corner in Lisle Street and fall asleep so that I had to go and wake him up in time for our next session. He was going through a period of enormous lethargy and had made me band manager at what I now consider the cynically inadequate recompense of one pound a week extra. For this I had to collect the money, pay the salaries, apologise to ballroom managers when we were late, and keep a book in which I wrote down the innumerable subs which everybody in the band seemed to need at the most inconvenient moments.

One of the revelations of our all-night parties was that there was a whole generation of jazz musicians in England who pre-dated the revival and yet played swinging music in the Harlem style of the late thirties. Some were professionals like Lennie Felix, a small elf-like pianist influenced by Fats Waller. He played with tremendous attack, his face and body twitching and jerking in sympathy

with his musical ideas. Others were amateurs, and the most remarkable of these was a timber merchant called Ian 'Spike' Macintosh
who played trumpet in the style of mid-period Louis Armstrong.
Small and neat, a little moustache and horn-rimmed spectacles, he
looked exactly what he was, two sons down for Public School and
a house in Cuffley. But inside him was a wild man in chains. He
played with extreme modesty, his back to the audience, and a
green beret full of holes hanging over the bell of his trumpet. In
conversation he was both courteous and restrained, but he could
become very aggressive if anybody suggested that there was any
other trumpet player than his hero.

At parties there was a psychological moment when he would
lurch towards the gramophone and take off whatever record was
playing if it hadn't got a Louis on it, and substitute one that had.
Another anti-social habit was his reaction when his host turned
down the volume. He'd just wait until he wasn't looking and turn
it up again.

He once offered Mick and me a lift home from a suburban jazz
club in his car, and when we were safely inside, drove all the way
out to Cuffley despite our protests. His wife was away, and he
wanted us to sit up all night listening to Louis and drinking whisky.
It was an enjoyable night, and didn't finish until three the following
afternoon when the local closed. It was just that we hadn't planned
on it. Macintosh's friends were another hazard: huge city men in
waistcoats, and pre-war musicians with patent leather hair. There
was a moment when he started a jazz club in a city public house,
and the guv'nor, an enormous fat man with the sensitivity of a
rhinoceros, took to putting in an appearance at other clubs where
we might happen to be playing. One night he staggered in to Le
Metro while Joe Harriot, the West Indian alto player, was sitting
in with us. As soon as the guv'nor's eyes focused enough for him to
realise that it was a Negro who was taking a chorus, he leapt and
capered across the front of the stand shouting, 'Walla! Walla!
Walla!'

But despite Mac's party tricks and city mates, we all liked him
very much. He was kind, loyal, and generous, and he could, when
on form, play absolutely beautifully.

A regular at our all-night raves was Dill Jones, the Welsh jazz pianist. He would turn up with the rest of his group from the night club where they played, just as the dawn was breaking over Cambridge Circus. Dill was unique in that he could sit in with any band, whatever idiom they favoured. He loved and understood all periods and used to reproach both revivalist and modernist alike for their narrow prejudices.

'If it swings it's jazz,' he used to say, 'and if it's jazz it's all right by me, boy.'

Mick always held it against Dill that he was disinclined to pay for a round of drinks. This has always been one of Mick's real obsessions. It doesn't matter how boring somebody is, as long as they stand their round Mick will describe them enthusiastically as a good nut. Personally I don't mind one way or the other. I like some people who are mean and dislike other people who are generous, but Mick won't have it. At one of our all-nighters we had ordered an extra barrel of cider at Dill's request. 'I'll be bringing down quite a lot of people,' he told us, 'so it's only fair, see. Just let me know how much.' When it came to the crunch, Dill said he didn't have the ready on him, but would pay us next time he saw us. He never did, and Mick never forgave him. Although this happened in 1951, and we bumped into Dill hundreds of times before he emigrated to America in 1961, he always refused to hand over the two pounds, claiming for the first year or two that he was a bit short, and after that insisting that he had paid it. Mick, for his part, never let slip an opportunity of mentioning it, especially when he'd had a few.

'Hello, Dill,' he'd say, 'enjoy that cider, did you?'

At seven a.m. the band played its final number and we'd all crawl up out of the sweat-scented cellar into the empty streets of a Sunday morning in the West End. Hysterical with lack of sleep, accompanied by a plump art student, her pale cheeks smeared with the night's mascara, I'd catch the Chelsea bus and try to read the *Observer* through prickling red eyeballs as we swayed along Piccadilly, down Sloane Street, and into the King's Road. Then a bath, one of those delirious fucks that only happen on the edge of complete fatigue, and a long sleep until it was time to get up and face the journey to Cook's Ferry or whatever jazz club we were playing that evening.

*

But our periods in London were now both spasmodic and brief. The city had become a place to collect clean shirts and socks from. We put into it like sailors into port. Our lives there had lost their centre.

Most of the time we were actually travelling between jobs. We got to know the roads of Britain so well that a glance out of the coach window could tell us where we were.

The flavour of the different regional landscapes alone was enough: the flat featureless Dutch-like farmland of Lincolnshire; the honey-coloured stone and intimate scale of the West Country; the sprawling suburb of the Midlands; the hunting-print look of Cheshire and Shropshire; the kilns of the Potteries and the chimneys of the industrial north; the wild moors along the Pennines where the sheep are always black with the soot of Lancashire and Yorkshire.

Certain strange images remain. On the old A1 (there were no motorways then), thirty miles out of London was a house, the walls of which were covered with cut-out animals and faces: giraffes, seals, bears, cartoon characters. On the road to Barrow-in-Furness, which skirts the Lake District, was a small factory which manufactured something which used a great deal of bright blue dye (possibly it manufactured bright blue dye?) and the whole building, the surrounding grass and vegetation, the boulder-strewn stream which ran between the factory and the road were all bright blue. But most of it is a jogging blur of half-sleep after transport café meals, the jumping print of paperbacks, the dramas of the poker school round a flat-topped tom-tom case.

Although I was interested to know parts of the country where I had never been, what I found absolutely hallucinatory was to return as a jazz singer to places I had known well as a child – Liverpool particularly, of course, but by no means exclusively.

North Wales was such an area. As a very little boy I had spent holidays in the Edwardian resorts of Llandudno and Colwyn Bay, and later, during the thirties, my father rented a farm or cottage in the Clwyd Valley to be near his uncle's fishing, and we had driven in almost every morning to swim in the baths at hideous Rhyl and gimcrack Prestatyn.

Now in my middle twenties I came back several times every

summer. We usually played at Rhyl in a large dance hall, part of the same building as a cinema. One July evening we arrived there in time to see the film before the dance started, and I discovered with pleasure, keen beyond logic, that they were showing a revival of *King Kong* which I had never seen. All through that marvellous film some memory kept nagging me. There was a link between film and place, I couldn't nail it, but at the moment when Kong, mortally wounded by the machine-guns of the circling biplanes, tenderly places Fay Wray in the roof guttering of the Empire State Building before plunging to his death, it came to me. A summer afternoon of 1935. My father driving me into Rhyl from Denbigh, where he had taken a cottage, to see *King Kong*. The discovery that children under sixteen weren't allowed in. Bitter tears on the sea-front. My father telling me I would be able to see it when I was older, and me protesting 'but it won't still be on'. We played at Denbigh too. The ballroom of the County Lunatic Asylum was available for public dances when the patients were in bed, but when we arrived in the late afternoon to leave our instruments they were still wandering about.

'Men! Men!' shouted a middle-aged woman from a window before she was pulled backwards by unseen hands, and one morning walking out of the town to look at the cottage where I had stayed as a child, I was accosted by a respectable middle-aged man who asked me if I realised that Africa used to be Welsh.

'No,' I said, 'I hadn't realised that.'

'It's because she wouldn't wash,' he explained.

I remembered walking past the 'loony bin' with our nurse. If we'd been naughty she threatened to ring up for the van. She used this to frighten us, not only in Wales, but when we got back to Liverpool in late September, and as I lay in bed I could hear the gangs of ragged children from Lark Lane singing in the street:

> They will dress you all in blue
> Just because you've lost a screw.

They meant Rainhill, the Merseyside Asylum, but for me they were singing about the Denbigh Institution.

In Llandudno we played to an audience of perhaps twenty old ladies and gentlemen, most of whom left in the interval. Every time I sang the manager turned off the microphone. Mick controlled himself until after 'The Queen' and then blew up. He shouted that the night before we had played to a packed and enthusiastic dance hall in Prestatyn, and that many of the audience would have come along if the concert had been properly advertised. He said it was an insult to me to turn off the mike every time I sang. He threatened to report the whole thing to the Musicians' Union. Pausing for breath he noted that the manager was smiling delightedly.

'Everybody who appears here loses his temper with me,' the man explained with great satisfaction. 'They all do it. Even the most famous.'

Another Proustian gig was the Civic Hall, Nantwich. We played there fairly regularly right through the fifties.

Outside the Parish Church, not far from the hall, was a billboard painted to resemble bricks in outline. Each brick represented five pounds of the five thousand needed for the restoration fund, and as the money was raised, the bricks were filled in with solid red paint. When we first played Nantwich, Mick and I were in our early twenties and only two or three of the bricks were red. The last time we were there, Mick's hair was grey at the sides, I had a pot belly and a bald patch, and the wall was almost filled in.

We still played concerts in Liverpool during the winter, and my mother didn't mind this. There was something possible for her about a concert. In the summer of 1952, though, we did a job which gave her considerable pain. We played in a tent for a week as part of 'The Liverpool Show' on Wavertree Playing Fields. Our tent was between a display of cage birds and an exhibition of photographs showing the work of the police. We did two shows in the afternoon and three in the evening. My father quite enjoyed coming along after dinner to pick me up and have a beer or two with the band in the bar tent with its smell of crushed grass, but my mother was worried about who would discover I was working in a side-show. As it happened, the only time she did come she met the ex-chauffeur and ladies' maid of a late cousin of my grandfather, their faces grim with disapproval.

'Good evening Aimie. Good evening, Stanley.'

'Good evening Mrs Tom,' said Aimie, and then added, 'I can't think what Miss 'Olt would have thought about Master George singing in a tent.'

In the same year, 1952, Mick's passion for dogs found practical expression. In one week he bought an alsatian puppy when he was drunk in London, and a bull terrier puppy in Doncaster. The bull terrier was one of a litter belonging to a fan. Its mother had whelped in a pigsty on an allotment. Mick bought it one afternoon after a lunchtime session in 'The George'.

For some weeks this animal travelled in the coach. It was Mick's intention to train it to guard the instruments and uniforms, but because it smelt so strongly of its birthplace, pissed and shitted all over everything, and revealed, even that early in its life, an aggressive and hysterical personality, we raised a corporate objection, and Mick agreed to leave it behind in town.

Doncaster was a town we never played at, but in which we quite frequently stayed. The landlord of The George, a large pub in the market square, had been a pro musician in the thirties and in consequence gave bands special terms and sympathetic treatment. On the debit side he was inclined to go on about the profession and to wake you up by shouting,

'Come on't, lad. You're due on't bandstand.'

The puppy's original owner was one of a little gang of staunch fans who used to turn up wherever we played in Yorkshire. He was a cobbler and had a skin curiously like leather of an unpleasing yellow colour. His mates were a varied lot. One was an attractive young man with a cast in one eye whose ambition was to achieve at least three knee-trembles during the course of an evening at the Palais. He usually managed at least two. I once asked him, not how he made the first girl – there is a strong tradition of promiscuity in Yorkshire – but how he got rid of her prior to chatting up the next one. He looked at me incredulously, and then told me, his voice full of 'ask a silly question' implications: 'Aye tells 'er to fook off.'

The jovial leader of this gang was a rotund man with a nervous and continuous laugh. He lived in a caravan with his pretty, gypsy-like wife, and was a legitimate photographer with pornography as a side-line. As models he used local girls who wished to supplement their earnings in the mills, and some of his friends whom I imagine didn't get paid at all. He was always showing us his new sets, presumably with an eye to flogging them, but we never bit.

In the jazz world there are one or two people who have a passion for dirty snaps and collect them, but these are specialists. Mick and I were perfectly prepared to 'have a bird's eye' or 'a squint' as Mick put it, but not to actually pay out money. Besides, although these rather amateur efforts had a certain naïve charm, and suggested, which is unusual in this context, that the participants were actually enjoying themselves, they lacked the precision which is surely the essence of pornography. When Mick looked at them he demonstrated a delusion of his which he never lost. He would tilt the print at an angle as though this made it possible to see more of what was going on.

The pornographer was also something of a pimp – the two professions are often allied. He once told me that there was a female crane driver of his acquaintance who had told him that she was willing to pay 'twenty pounds for a night wi' George Melly'. The tart in me was impressed at such a generous offer; the feminine at such a masculine approach; the masochist at the idea of a female crane driver. I asked her pander what she was like.

'She's all right,' he told me. 'She's not a beauty like, but she's got a fair pair of bristols and muscles like an Irish bluddy navvy. By gum she can go and all.' To emphasise this he raised an arm in phallic imitation and clapped the back of his neck rapidly with his other hand. I declared myself agreeable but we never met.

One morning in the Market Hall, Doncaster, I saw an image so extraordinary and dreadful that I have never forgotten it. Mick and I had crossed the road from The George to buy him a pair of socks. Mick never washed socks on tour. He'd wait until the pair he was wearing became too stiff for comfort and then buy some more. Besides, we both liked covered markets; the mounds of glowing fruit, the carcasses of animals, the fat women holding up cheap underwear in front of their bodies to see if it was 'them'.

There was a fishing stall and, on a table in front of it, a large tin basin in which thousands of maggots, many of them dyed pink or green, writhed and boiled in the bran.

Standing with his face a few inches from this erupting mass was a child with a huge head. He was wearing a cap as Mongol children often do, and was staring at the maggots with an almost hungry intensity.

8

And So the Band Folded

Commercial stability, a constant struggle during the first three lean years of the fifties, led Mick during 1952 to a further expansion of the personnel. Not content with a four-piece front line, a four-piece rhythm section, and a blues singer, he decided that what the band needed was some glamour, and began to look around for a female vocalist. It was Archie Semple who found her, a London girl of Italian origin called Olga Bagnaro, stage name Jo Lennard, who had begun to sing around a few of the clubs. Jo's style was simple but her pitch was good and above all she could swing like the clappers not only on up-tempo numbers but on slow ballads as well. She was a pretty girl with big brown eyes, 'well-stacked' as they say in American gangster novels, and with an insatiable appetite for carbohydrates, particularly in the form of chips, spaghetti, and cream cakes. She spoke with the soft mid-Atlantic accent of most London girls in show biz, but sometimes reverted deliberately into broad cockney when angry or happy. She lived with her parents in a tenement flat in the Elephant and Castle district, and was a strong local patriot, and proud of her working-class origin. She took me once to her local, and introduced me to a gang of tearaways of her acquaintance. They were real tearaways, nothing to do with the teddy boys who were beginning to emerge at that time. These gentlemen, most of them about thirty, wore expensive, rather conservative, suits and large hats. They managed to look both relaxed and tense. They all drank brown ale.

There was a talent competition on that night, first prize five pounds, and we both decided to enter. Mick wouldn't have been too pleased if he'd known, but we weren't earning so much that we could ignore the chance to make some extra money. She sang 'Them There Eyes' beautifully, and I sang 'Frankie and Johnny' not so well. At the end of the evening the winners were announced. Jo had won first prize and me second. This was in fact as it should have been, but even so I was rather surprised at the result because although she'd sung much better, 'Frankie and Johnny' was a showy and eccentric number and I had won the most applause. One of the tearaways explained.

'Jo 'ad to win, you see, she's a local girl, like. 'Ope you don't mind.' I assured him I was delighted.

Although at first Jo was perfectly friendly to me, she paid me no particular attention, but after a month or two she began to sit by me in the coach, eat with me in cafés and restaurants, and drink with me in pubs. From then on we were a couple.

For some months we hesitated on the edge of marriage. I used to go and eat at her parents', huge and delicious dishes of chickens in spaghetti. I was taken to meet her rich uncle, a bookie with a flat in Kensington, all lilac wallpapers and Hollywood bed-ends, and a pretty blonde wife with a surprisingly dirty laugh. I met her grannie too – she called her Nanna – a tiny, old lady in a dark kitchen who showed me family records out of a mother-of-pearl box.

Jo's father, a hairdresser with a hairline moustache, said to me one day: 'We don't mind Olga being with a band. She enjoys it and she likes you.' He paused and then added, slowly: 'But if anything happened to her, I'd be round.' I looked at the budgerigar climbing its ladder and, as they say in Yorkshire, thought on.

Jo and I didn't get married for a number of reasons. A considerable barrier for me was the fact that she was a Roman Catholic. I was, after all, a militant atheist and the idea of marriage in the vestry of a Catholic church with a promise to bring up our children in the faith would have been a lot for me to swallow. The main reason, however, and it is, after all, a valid one, was that we were not really in love. We liked each other very much indeed, but we weren't in love.

Eight musicians and two vocalists was a large personnel for a touring band, but one day Mick announced that we were to have another addition. This was Mike Lawrence, the singer who had been given such a bollocking by Doreen Porter's mum down the Metro Club. Mick had, of course, tried to justify this – as a commercial band we needed a male commercial singer to handle ballads and waltzes, etc. – but the fact was Mike had asked Mick for a job one night when Mick was stoned.

He joined us three weeks early. We were on a short tour of Ireland, and he turned up, without any explanation, in a small market town in the west. This was a real lumber. The promoter of the tour, a young Dubliner, believed it was possible to fit eight musicians, their instruments, two vocalists, and himself at the wheel into a Volkswagen. It was *just* possible, but extremely uncomfortable. After Mike's unexpected arrival it was three vocalists and this *was* impossible. Luckily most of the time we were unconscious from lack of sleep and draught Guinness.

At the beginning of the tour Mick tried to protest to the promoter about our travelling conditions and indeed much else, but he took no notice at all. He just smiled politely as though Mick was discussing the weather. On the very first day, driving out of Dublin to a job a hundred miles away, he suddenly stopped the wagon and disappeared for over half an hour without any prior explanation. When he got back Mick asked him where he'd got to go. 'To Mass,' he said and drove on. As it was the week after Easter this happened fairly often, but in a short time the agnostic section of the band learnt to head for the nearest bar which was usually the nearest building, and often – another thing that surprised us – a grocer's shop.

Most of the jobs we played were in small places, and indeed the first night we drew up in front of the hall to find the caretaker driving out some chickens with his broom. The MC wore evening dress which had gone green with age and was so rotted it could scarcely support the row of medals he had won in the revolution. We had, of course, rehearsed the Irish National Anthem, 'The Soldier's Song', a stirring tune of great length which, unlike 'God Save the Queen', it is impossible to cut, but this was the first time we had played it in public. Irish dances go on even longer than Scottish dances, often until three or four in the morning, but at last it was time. The MC announced the National Anthem and stood stiffly to attention. We began. But in the middle a patriotic but very drunk young man climbed up on the stage. We were a bit nervous. Did he consider our version lacked sufficient fervour? Did he consider it an insult that we, bloody Saxons, should play it at all? But in fact he only wished to sing the words. He started out of key, and then fell down still singing. Our first Irish dance was over.

That night we had been surprised to find a couple of crates of Guinness on the stand for the musicians. We put it down to the size and rural character of the village, but even in the larger towns it was the rule and, after the dance was over, we usually found ourselves drinking Irish whiskey with the manager until broad daylight. Throughout the tour Mick spent quite a lot of time indignantly telling people he was English, but his Irish blood, however much he denied it, showed itself in the way he launched into ferocious arguments during these drinking sessions. There was one row about birth control which would have ended in blows if everybody hadn't been too drunk. Mick raved on in defence of Durex Limited while the manager and his friend shouted him down with cries of ' 'Tis worse than murder so it is!'

After an hour or two of this, the sessions were inclined to turn sentimental and maudlin, and various Irish gentlemen would oblige with patriotic songs, many of them starting with the word 'Sure'.

In Donegal, at eleven o'clock one morning, we were stopped by a drunken policeman who leant against the car door for three-quarters of an hour expounding, while the growing line of cars honked behind us, on the beauties of the country.

In a cottage where we changed, I bought for five shillings a beautiful and old china hen which I spotted on the window ledge. The owner was delighted with the transaction, and told me that he had something I would really want although he wouldn't let it go under the pound. He disappeared leaving me to speculate on what it could be. Some treasure from the great house acquired during the troubles? It was a calendar of the Taj Mahal and the water changed colour to show the weather.

On that tour we didn't only drink too much, we ate like pigs too. It was still the austere time when the greedy English rich would cross to Dublin for a week-end to gorge on steak and salmon, butter and double cream, all unobtainable in rationed Britain. We weren't rich but we were English, and even Mick stuffed himself at every opportunity.

Our last date was in 'The Four Provinces Ballroom', Dublin, a comparatively sophisticated venue. We went down well, but there were no Guinness crates on the stand. After it was over we hurried into taxis and were driven through the wet streets of the city to catch the night boat to Liverpool. It was a stormy passage, and we played cards and drank rum while Irish labourers fell about to the rhythm of the ship, using the moment's pause between the rolls to lift a bottle to their mouths, and the potential chambermaids and hospital cleaners snored chastely by their suitcases in the saloon.

Grey with lack of sleep we docked in Liverpool in the wet, windy dawn, and I went home for breakfast. That night in Nantwich, I pulled the towel out of my case to wipe the soap out of my eyes, and the china hen fell to the floor and was smashed to bits.

Mike Lawrence, who enjoyed singing, got very little satisfaction out of his association with us. He didn't sing at all in jazz clubs and very infrequently at concerts, while even at dances, Mick's hatred of rehearsing new numbers meant that once the band had mastered about six songs from Mike's repertoire it never learnt any more – and besides, with three vocalists, none of us got an opportunity to sing much. Mick, however, insisted that we all sit together at the side of the stand during the entire evening – this was part of his 'professional' mystique – and furthermore smile broadly but remain silent. Whenever we did talk, he would turn and hiss at us: 'Will the vocalists stop rabbiting?' The rest of the band called us the choir. Also, at the time Mike joined us, interest in traditional jazz was just beginning to revive. We began to play more straight jazz dates, and even appeared at the London Palladium in a guest spot at one of Ted Heath's sell-out Sunday Night Concerts. We had only twenty minutes, and Mick worked out this could include two vocals at most. Poor Mike, who was very show-biz minded, and for whom the London Palladium was holy ground, was yet again rowed out. If I'd been him, I couldn't have remained as good-tempered as he did, but even so he was by nature a tense and highly-strung person, and it began to tell on him. He would get into terrible silent rages during the course of which he would flush a dark red, and then pale to an almost greenish white. He had a certain type of Liverpool face, large in area, but with small, almost feminine features arranged closely around a little nose like a parrot's beak. At the height of one of his crises his lips would compress so tightly that the mouth seemed to disappear altogether.

But although at the beginning we had several brushes – if Mick wasn't there, Mike would try and take over who sang what and when, and I wasn't having any – we got on very well. Our shared Liverpool background gave us a lot in common, and Mike had an inventive and very personal sense of humour. Together we fathered an imaginary Scouse Catholic family, and improvised incidents and conversations round them when the mood took us:

'You know our Bernadette? 'Er fairst Mass and she's sick right down the front of 'er lovely white frock just as she's going up to the altar,' I might start. It was Mike, however, who added the touches of wild inspiration.

'It come of 'er eating no breakfast,' he would go on, 'she's so pious like, you know. I said to 'er: "Go on. Eat your kipper. Father Riley won't know." But not 'er.'

He was a fund of Liverpool children's street songs and catches:

> Father cut the whiskers off the bread.
> There's a woman in the shit-'ouse 'alf dead!
> There's a cat upon the wall, And it's only got one ball.
> And it's looking for the other on the shed.

An extraordinary adventure we shared together happened in Glasgow. After a concert in the St Andrews Hall the band was invited by a butch young man in jeans and a polo-neck sweater to be his guests at a restaurant. He didn't look as if he had a penny but it turned out that his father owned a fleet of fishing boats. Furthermore, the restaurant was, for those still frugal days, exceptional. Candles shone on greedy faces, huge steaks followed the scampi and our host had ordered a whole bottle of whisky to be placed in front of each of his guests. We'd already had quite a few in the nearest bar to St Andrews Hall, so by the time we'd finished our coffees we were all very drunk, had done nothing about finding digs, and it was two o'clock on a cold Glaswegian night.

Mick, Mike and I found ourselves reeling through the streets together. We decided to start at the top and fell into the hall of the Central Hotel. We were told by a brusque night porter that there were no rooms vacant. The same happened at the North British, St Enoch's and the Ivanhoe.

Finally we hailed a taxi, and asked the man to take us round places to stay. Down and down we went. Small hotels, boarding-houses, transport digs, doss-houses. At last we were directed into a tenement building and told there was a place which might take us 'up the stair'. Mike and I went to investigate. Mick remained in the taxi rigid with whisky.

We staggered up two flights of tiled steps and rang a bell. A young queer in the filthiest white steward coat I've ever seen came to the door, and we asked if he had a room. Drunk as I was, I could see a compliant gleam in his eye as he said yes. He showed us into a double room squalid to the point of disbelief. Two rusty bedsteads, an old sink, peeling green walls, a broken window pane mended with cardboard. I pulled back the blankets on one of the beds and pointed out that the sheets looked very much used.

'Oh, dearie me,' said the young man, 'it must have been over-looked. I'll see what I can do.'

At this point Mick, pale green in the face, loomed up in front of us and asked what the fucking hell we'd been doing and did we realise he'd been sitting in the fucking taxi freezing to fucking death for half a fucking hour. We said we'd only been up there for five minutes, but he may well have been right. The time sense – as he too has proved over and over again – entirely disappears when you're very drunk. Anyway, despite the fact that there was a bed for him, he was too angry with us to stay and stumbled down the stairs again and out into the night.

Mike and I ordered breakfast in bed in the morning, and climbed between the filthy bed clothes. A dreadful night of dreams! Huge insects marching in procession along the floor. Groping awake just in time to find the sink and be violently sick. More dreams of pustules and crab-lice, and at last a desperate awakening, eyeballs throbbing in the harsh winter light shining through the filthy window, and an old woman smelling of rotted knickers standing at the foot of the bed with a breakfast tray. Cracked cup, bread and marge, a pullet's egg. We thanked her through cracked lips. She leant towards us and whispered:

'Ye can trust me. I'm only the working lassie, but if any o' the gairls come in tae ye, luke tae your wallets.' It was obvious, and if we'd been less paralytic the night before we'd have cottoned on at once. We had slept in a brothel.

I got up and took my wallet out of my coat pocket and hid it under my mattress. Mike did the same. Then we got back into bed. A few minutes later the door opened and a quite young but hideous whore came in wearing a filthy street coat over a creased nightdress.

'I heard you come in last night,' she said, 'and I heard Maggie bringing in your breakfast the noo. Can you spare a cup of tea?'

She sat on the end of the bed to drink it. She made no pass at us so I presume she thought we were lovers.

'That Jeanie across the stair,' she complained, 'she took a mon all night for ten bob. It's no' right. It's letting the rest of the lassies doon. Och, last night I was doon tae my last poond. I bought a half bottle of whisky. I were coming up the stair and I dropped it. It ran doon the stair sae I sat doon and keened over it. A polis-man stopped. There I was sitting on the stair, the gude whisky running down in a stream between ma legs and making a wee pool on the street.

' "Hae you pussed ye'sel?" he asks.

'Och, I'm that unlucky if I went tae the Sahara for sand I'd no find any.'

She talked for over an hour, and all the other girls came in and sat on the beds. I was beginning to feel better, even hysterically well with the false health of a bad hangover, and about eleven o'clock sent one of the whores out for some scotch.

At last Mike and I got dressed, and went straight to the nearest public baths before rejoining the band.

Mick, cheerful and friendly, had forgotten what had happened. He'd woken up in some respectable digs on the outskirts of the city.

A band on the road, tolerant to each other's major faults and shortcomings, are inclined to develop almost paranoiac feelings of hatred about small habits and mannerisms. For example my obsessional custom of arranging the contents of my pockets – money, keys, wallet, cheque-book – in a kind of neat collage on the top of a chest-of-drawers used to drive Mick, if he was sharing a room with me, into a state of irritation so intense that it could only be relieved by messing it up again.

A great deal of conversation, which would appear almost insane to an outsider, is taken up with describing and reiterating the faults, irritating verbal or physical peculiarities, small vanities and pretensions of any member or members of the band who aren't present. Furthermore a musician who is a friend can become an enemy, someone to be avoided at all costs, and then, a week or two later, become a friend again. As in medieval Europe the pattern of alliances is always changing.

'When the coach gets there,' whispers A to B, 'try and slip off before C notices us and tags on.'

Mick and I both liked Mike Lawrence, but we would do anything to avoid eating with him. It was not that his manners were particularly bad, although he shared with most musicians a habit which offended our middle-class prejudices, he buttered his rolls with his soup. It was simply that he based his behaviour in restaurants on a mid-Atlantic conception, complete with accent, and at the end of a meal would inevitably say to the waitress: 'Could I have the check, honey?'

He also used a great deal of tomato sauce. Not that this in itself irritated us – most of the food needed tomato sauce to make it edible – but if the bottle wasn't on the table, and in some extraordinary way it never was when we ate with Mike, he would call over the waitress and say: 'Could I have the ketchup, honey?'

Was it really because of these two sentences, one inevitable, the other well on the cards, that Mick and I would pretend we didn't want to eat and then belt off in the other direction in search of another restaurant as soon as Mike was out of sight? It seems mad, but if you ask any musician who has been on the road he tells you stories like this.

After Mike Lawrence had been with us about a year, he got an offer to sing with an All Girls Orchestra and decided to accept. It would mean after all that he got a chance to sing a bit more, to learn a few more numbers, and perhaps to get the break he was counting on. I met him a month or two later and asked him how he was getting on.

'Not too bad, Georgie,' he told me, 'but I can't bear the way their lipstick comes off on their mouth-pieces.'

He never did get his break. I don't know why. He'd a good voice in the Billy Daniels spirit, he could swing, and he knew how to project. Perhaps he wanted that break too much. Anyway after a couple of years he retired from the business altogether.

In the spring of 1953 boredom and frustration within the band produced some radical changes. Mike Lawrence had already left, now Jimmy Currie, the guitar player, followed him. He went to join a vocal group which achieved some commercial success. The night before he actually departed, Jo Lennard was made sufficiently angry by something he said to throw a cream bun at him across the dressing-room. Tension was on the increase all round.

Next Archie Semple, the clarinettist, left to join Freddy Randall. Mick knew about this offer because Freddy had, quite correctly, rung him up to warn him he was going to make it. He therefore asked Archie what he intended to do, and Archie denied he had any intention of taking it up. I suspect a certain Scottish caution lay behind this denial. He wanted it all sewn up and sealed before committing himself. Then one night, only an hour after he had yet again told Mick he definitely wasn't leaving, we heard him talking to Freddy in what he imagined was a soundproof telephone kiosk in our hotel. He was confirming the date he was to join. I had an unpleasant quarrel with him over this, not because he was going, but because he had lied.

'I suppose you think I'm a shit?' he asked me.

'Yes,' I said.

It nearly came to blows, and it was Mick who calmed us both down. Actually I suspect Mick derived some satisfaction from this shout-up.

A month or two before, Archie had come to me to say that if something wasn't done to improve the musical side of the band he was going to leave. He was entirely fed up with Mick's lack of interest. He'd tried talking to him, but all that happened was that Mick offered him a drink and changed the conversation. Could I do anything? What did I suggest?

He was perfectly right. Mick at that moment was sunk in one of his periods during which you would imagine that to play jazz was exactly the thing he disliked doing more than anything else in the world. We limped through the same programme night after night, and his only concern seemed to be drinking with the promoter during the intervals, in order to win a few minutes off our playing time.

I suggested to Archie that we approach Jim Godbolt who, as band agent, was naturally concerned with the quality of what he had to try to sell, and see what we would work out. The outcome was that Jim asked Mick to come round to the office, and when he arrived, he found the three of us sitting like an inquisition under the map of the British Isles with its coloured flags showing all possible venues, and determined to obtain sonic satisfaction. We failed. Mick lost his temper and accused us of conspiracy and blackmail. He told us he intended to pay no attention to what we had to say under these conditions, and we could all get fucked. He stormed out of the office leaving us sitting there. Later he attacked Jim on his own for going behind his back, and me, on my own, for betraying our friendship. What was extraordinary was that he made us both feel real shits, and yet our intention had been to *improve his band*. This was all we wanted to do – to make the band better.

He was therefore not displeased to find Archie and me on the edge of a punch-up. He felt it proved some point.

So Archie left too.

Finally Jo Lennard got an offer to join the Ronnie Scott Big Band, and she accepted. Musically she had become very frustrated with singing the same three or four numbers night after night. Financially Ronnie's offer was an extremely tempting one, and emotionally she and I had reached a certain impasse. She told Mick of her decision and was to leave in the middle of March.

The band was again contracting.

A few days before Jo was to leave, we were playing a gig in Eastbourne and ran into real trouble. Half-way through the second set a group of yobs came in led by a tall psychopath looking for trouble. They marched up to the stand and began to pull at Jo's dress. Mick attempted to reason with them, and the leader jumped up on the stage followed by his gang and started a punch-up. In the middle of this the police burst into the hall. The gang-leader shouted a warning and the rumble stopped. Mick jumped off the stand, told the gang-leader he thought he was a bloody fool but wasn't going to take it any further, shook his hand, told the angry police sergeant he didn't intend to lodge a complaint, climbed back on the stage, announced the next number, and carried on playing. The police, after circling the hall a few times, left.

A few sets later I was singing a number called 'Send Me to the 'lectric Chair'. I was accompanied only by the rhythm section. The front line were having a quick smoke-up in the wings. I became aware that the gang-leader had climbed back on the stage and was advancing on my left. I carried on singing. When he reached me, he grabbed hold of the microphone lead and jerked it so violently that he broke the connection. There was complete silence. He then pulled a chiv out of his pocket and was holding it so that it just touched the side of my throat. He began to mutter threats in a low voice, gradually working himself up to violence. I didn't move an inch. I felt like a rabbit mesmerised by a stoat. Beyond fear. Somewhere else.

Behind him, out of the corner of my eye, I could see Mick creeping out of the wings, and after what seemed like a very long time indeed he sprang and pinioned the yob from behind. Then it all happened. The rest of the gang broke over the edge of the stage like a wave. Pat Molloy put his bass out of danger, and raised a chair. I saw Stan Bellwood bring down the edge of his largest cymbal which luckily just missed the head of one of the enemy. Jo had her shoe off and was using the heel. Everything was confusion, kicking, breaking chairs, shouted insults, blurred faces. Then it was all over. The gang vanished. The police were back, and the gang-leader, his arm bent behind him, was taken away. The manager told Mick to play 'The Queen'. His reaction was typical.

'We've won half an hour off our time,' he whispered triumphantly as Stan led in with the drum roll.

The police told Mick and me that we had to appear in court in a week's time to give evidence against the ringleader. Mick said that it would mean coming all the way down from the north and then travelling back again the same day. Surely there were plenty of witnesses in the audience who saw exactly what had happened and actually lived in Eastbourne? The Inspector looked severe. We were subpoenaed to appear. They'd been after this man for a long time. They needed us. There could be no excuse.

As we walked back to the digs Mick said that as we were lumbered he could at least get his coat replaced. The sleeve had been torn in the fight, and it was a Corporation dance. It would happen in Eastbourne, of course. We'd played some of the toughest towns in the British Isles, and it had to go and happen in Eastbourne where the old come to die. The next day we drove up to Grimsby to play a couple of nights at the Gaiety, followed by an American camp somewhere in Lincolnshire on the Sunday, a job in Chester on Tuesday, a day off on Wednesday (Mick and I would have to travel overnight to give our evidence), and the Denbigh Asylum job on the Thursday.

Diz had replaced Jimmy Currie on a temporary basis. Nobody, especially him, ever thought of him as a permanent replacement. His temperament was too mercurial to allow him to keep a job for long. He was with us until either we found somebody else or he got fed up.

Jo's last official job was the final night at Grimsby, but as she wasn't joining Ronnie Scott until Wednesday she decided to do the American camp as well. We were driving back to Doris's afterwards.

We did the jobs in Grimsby ('Very nice, Mick. Good show, George') and on a cold March evening drove off into Lincolnshire to find the US base.

Most travelling bands at that time played a lot of bases all over the country. They were indistinguishable; a huge gum-chewing sergeant in charge of us, a sergeants' mess in a modified Hilton Hotel style, an audience which didn't want to know, a drunk who kept on asking for 'Deep in the Heart of Texas', very long hours, one-armed bandits to tempt us to throw away more than we were earning, the provoking sight of huge steaks with French fries disappearing into the faces of the crew-cutted elephantine-arsed army of occupation.

I can't remember anything special about that evening except for a notice which read: 'No lady guest will be permitted to attend open night in the Sergeants' Club with more than one member of same during any one month.'

At last we finished, and after a few drinks climbed wearily into the coach. It was freezing cold, and Jo and I sat next to each other under a rug. We felt a bit drunk and sentimental. It was our last night together. The driver climbed in and started the engine. We drove off. Soon the heater began to work, and Jo fell asleep on my shoulder.

It was about four o'clock and only twenty-five miles from Grimsby. In relation to the job in Chester the next day, Grimsby was in the wrong direction, but we'd decided to go back there because we could leave all our things, and besides it would have been hard to find digs in the middle of Lincolnshire to take us at that hour.

At six o'clock, as the first cold grey streaks of dawn were smearing the eastern sky, we were still careering through the flat countryside. Mick emerged from under a coat, and having peered at his watch asked the driver where the fuck we were.

'Och, I got a wee bit lost,' came the answer, 'but we're nearly there noo.' Grumbling but reassured, Mick crawled back under his coat. I was awake, Jo's head on my shoulder. I lit a cigarette and stared out of the window. We seemed to be approaching a town of some size. It must be Grimsby. The driver seeing a town on the flat horizon, and an apparently straight road ahead of him, put his foot down; but the town was not Grimsby, and the road was not straight.

We were on the outskirts of Boston fifty miles from our destination. We knew the town well as we had often played at a hall called 'The Gliderdrome', famous for its white-hot stoves, a unique and dangerous method of heating which effectually prevented brawling, and also for an eccentric member of the public, a young man who appeared in full evening dress, stood in front of the bandstand, bowed to the audience and then raised a baton he had been presented with by Joe Loss, and conducted us throughout the evening.

We had even considered staying in Boston that night, but had decided against it because it was a hard place to find digs. We had memories of a night when we had been forced, by lack of accommodation at any price, to sleep in the coach, taking occasional little walks through the freezing streets to try to get warm.

If all had gone well, in a few minutes we would have drawn up in the main street, recognised the 'Stump', the famous church spire so popular with suicides, and rounded on the driver, but the road was not straight.

Three quarters of a mile out of Boston it suddenly bent, and at the same time crossed a bridge over one of those canals which irrigate the flat fields of Lincolnshire and are called 'ditches'. The driver had his foot down. He didn't see the bend in the road until it was too late. He braked. We skidded across the road towards the low stone wall of the bridge. I was awake and saw it happening. I felt entirely detached, almost a spectator. I seemed to see it all from outside and from various angles, as if I were watching a film.

We crashed through the side of the bridge and out into the void beyond. The coach turned over in the air. Splinters of glass, luggage, instruments and bodies obeyed the law of gravity, but almost indolently, almost outside time. I remember shouting, 'Here we go', and thinking 'this is probably my lot'. Then the coach hit the water twenty feet below.

In the ordinary way, they told us later, the ditch would have been twelve foot deep so we would have drowned. Later in the year, they pointed out, it often became little more than a trickle so we would have been smashed to pieces. As it was, after a moment or two watching myself struggling under water, I was able to stand up in four feet of water and look about.

The coach was on its side, so that above us through the broken windows we could see the cold grey sky. We counted each other and we were all there. Paul Simpson had a badly cut hand, and I had a cut under one eye and a bleeding finger. Everybody else seemed all right. I began to shiver.

Jo was crying and we all patted her on the back to cheer her up. This was the worst thing we could have done, because several long splinters of glass had punctured her back and lung cavity.

Diz Disley climbed out through the emergency door and waded ashore. He came back in a few minutes with a ladder. 'Me bling ladder,' he explained in a Chinese accent. He used it to make a bridge between bank and coach and some of us climbed across it. The others waded to the opposite bank and scrambled up it. In two small parties we advanced on the two houses at each end of the bridge. The noise of the crash had woken them and their lights were on.

The house which Disley, Jo, Paul and I were soon to disrupt was a villa belonging to the local photographer. It was of modernistic tendency and had petrol blue tiles. The photographer's wife seemed very kind. She put Jo, who by this time was feeling very ill, to lie down on the sofa in the lounge, and rang up for an ambulance. She showed the rest of us up to her bathroom and went to make some tea. Diz and I shared a steaming hot bath giggling with hysteria. As my finger was still bleeding badly, I decided to go to the hospital in the ambulance. Jo was on a stretcher. Paul had convinced himself that he had cut a tendon in his hand and would never be able to play again.

When we got to the hospital they rushed Jo in for an examination and left Paul and me sitting on a bench in the emergency waiting-room. I had got the chats, and made lots of jokes while they were stitching up my finger. The sister didn't smile. When she'd finished she said that she was surprised I could make jokes when the girl who was with me was quite likely to die. They were going to operate immediately, but there wasn't much hope. I hadn't realised she was even seriously hurt, and asked if I could wait while they operated.

While I was sitting there, a priest hurried past into the theatre. He had come to hear Jo's confession and give her the sacraments.

They took two hours operating. When they'd finished, the sister, who by now could see how upset I was, came and told me that, as she was a strong girl, the surgeons thought she had a fifty-fifty chance. They wheeled Jo past on a trolley. She had no colour at all. I took a taxi and went back to the band.

By this time the photographer's wife had largely recovered from her attack of warm-heartedness. You couldn't exactly blame her. Half the mud from the ditch was all over her fitted carpets, and her lounge was full of jazzmen dropping ash all over everything and making a terrible noise. Mick was in the hall on the phone to Godbolt, and it was all getting too much for her.

Even so the couple in the small house on the other side of the bridge, although they had no bathroom and no telephone and he was a farm labourer, couldn't do too much for their contingent.

Mick saw me come in ('Would you mind wiping your feet?' asked the photographer's wife) and asked me how Jo was. He asked, of course, quite casually, imagining as I had that she was suffering from shock. I told him they thought she had a fifty-fifty chance. He put the phone down on the table – I could hear Godbolt's voice barking irritably – and I told him what I knew. He picked up the phone again and told Jim to let her parents know.

He finished talking to Jim and rang the hospital ('I hope you're keeping an account of all those phone calls,' said the photographer's wife) and asked how Jo was. No worse, they told him, but of course it was too early to say anything definite.

Mick sent the rest of the band home by train, and he and I moved into a pub in the town. We drank about a bottle of rum a day for the next two days and never got drunk. We had settled on rum as 'comforting'.

We salvaged what we could from the coach. The instruments were all right although of course they had to be dried and greased to stop them rusting. We took the uniforms to a cleaners. They would be needed again in three days, the longest Jim thought we could cancel our engagements.

Jo's parents arrived and with them her Uncle George. When we were getting the stuff out of the coach, the two men were measuring the skidmarks on the bridge above us. They looked stern and speculative.

I spent a lot of time at the hospital and was allowed to see Jo. She was on the mend. My mother sent her freesias. I'd rung her immediately after the accident as I guessed it would be in the papers.

Finally Mick and I sent the uniforms and instruments by train to Denbigh for our next date, and travelled down over-night to give our evidence at the trial of the psychopathic yob in Eastbourne.

We broke the journey in London and rushed home to change into suits. We met at Victoria Station at 8.30. Mick had his Uncle Jim with him who had insisted on coming along to 'lend moral support' as he put it.

Mick's Uncle Jim wore a beard and a beret and looked rather like an artist in a cartoon in *Punch circa* 1903. He was not an unkind man, but very reactionary and given to great self-dramatisation. We could have done without him that day.

We gave our evidence. The magistrate, once he had understood that we were jazz musicians, seemed inclined to treat us as if we were the accused. Admittedly, my appearance didn't help. The unhealed cut under my eye give me a very villainous appearance, but even so I feel it was our profession which made him so unpleasant. He was particularly incensed over the fact that Mick had shaken hands with the yob after the first fracas.

'You shook hands with this man?' he queried in a voice like a creaking gate. 'Now why did you do this?' Mick explained that he wished to show he had no ill feelings, and had imagined that the whole incident was closed.

'And yet it was not,' said the magistrate. 'It does appear to me the most extraordinary behaviour.'

When it came to my turn – 'Is this man also a jazz musician?' – it was explained to the bench that I had cut my eye in an accident and not during the fight.

The yob had a long list of convictions for causing or attempting to cause bodily harm and was sent down for six months.

We walked out of court to be met by Uncle Jim in a state of near hysteria. He had been sitting in the public gallery and had overheard the yob's mates muttering threats and writing down our home addresses.

'Officer,' shouted Uncle Jim at the policeman on duty, 'get these men out of town.'

Mick and I refused to take any notice of him, and went into the local for a much needed drink before catching the train.

Later Mick wrote to the town clerk to ask if the Municipal Authorities would pay for his coat. He got a brusque refusal citing that the coat had been torn *after* he had shaken hands with the man, and that therefore it was his responsibility.

That night we played the first job since the crash.

I went up to Boston to see Jo while she was getting better. Her back looked like a railway junction. Eventually she sued Mick and won. The Corporation also sued for the repairs to their bridge, and they won too.

This shouldn't have mattered in the ordinary way as Mick's Insurance Company would have paid, but it was discovered that the driver had lied in filling in his qualifications, and had claimed to hold a licence which he hadn't got. What was so aggravating was that there was no need for him to have this licence anyway – it was for something like driving public transport – but because he'd claimed he'd got it, the Insurance Company didn't have to cough up a penny.

Afterwards, whenever we crossed that bridge, we would ask Mick if it belonged to him. He never really liked that joke. 'Very fucking amusing,' he would mutter.

When Jo was all right again she joined Harry Gold's Pieces of Eight (Ronnie Scott had found another vocalist), but after a bit she got married and left the business.

A month or two later Mick, who was fed up with everything anyway, decided to give up the band altogether.

He put it to me that I could go solo. Jazz was on the up again, and there was plenty of club work. He would be my manager, and I ought to be able to make out pretty well.

He told the rest of the band one night when we were playing a South London jazz club. Nobody seemed either upset or surprised. During the interval I heard Stan Bellwood and Roy Crimmins making plans to form a band of their own.

'And I've got a great gimmick,' said Stan, 'we'll call it, well it doesn't matter, "The Crimmins–Bellwood Allstars", something like that, and then, on the posters, under the name, in big letters in Day-Glo, we'll 'ave the words "SELLING EXCITEMENT"!'

And so the band folded. Wyllie took his wife and child back to Australia and a job in a Melbourne bookshop. The others gigged around or joined other bands, and Stan, despite his ambition to sell excitement, sold his drums instead and became, as I said earlier, a publican.

9

The Real Reason Is I Love Him

Towards the end of 1953 and during the opening months of 1954, there was indeed a great deal happening in the jazz world. I refer here to our jazz world. The modernists lived their own life which touched on ours as little as if they had been vets or haberdashers.

Ken Colyer came back from New Orleans like Moses coming down from Mount Sinai with the Tablets of the Law. Chris Barber and Monty Sunshine had a band waiting for him. To the growing number of New Orleans purists he trailed clouds of glory, and every note he blew was sacred.

Humph was in full revolt against his revivalist past. For some time he experimented wildly, dropping the trombone altogether and trying such far-out combinations as a West Indian rhythm section. His monthly newsletter was a masterpiece of dialectical justification.

Finally he settled for mainstream, the small-band jazz of the late thirties and early forties, the music to which he has remained faithful ever since.

Alex Welsh decided to come down from Scotland and form a band to play white Dixieland jazz, similar in character to the music produced by various American groups under the direction of the guitar-playing professional whisky-drinker, Eddie Condon.

The great success of that time, however, was the band which had attracted and held all Humph's disappointed revivalist fans, and which won the adherence of the recently self-styled Beatniks (until that year they had called themselves existentialists), Soho layabouts and the art-school students, and was led by my first boss, Cy Laurie.

His cellar-club, an enormous basement in Windmill Street just off Piccadilly, was jammed, and his all-night raves, based very much on our earlier efforts but financially tenable, in his larger premises, merited a shocked article in the *People* with photographs of necking couples lying on the floor and a wealth of salacious moralising.

It was at Cy's that I first got to know David Litvinoff, an extraordinary person on the fringe of a dozen worlds. The fastest talker I have ever met, full of outrageous stories, at least half of which turn out to be true, a dandy of squalor, a face either beautiful or ugly, I could never decide which, but certainly one hundred per cent Jewish, a self-propelled catalyst who didn't mind getting hurt as long as he made something happen, a sacred monster, first class.

David can only breathe in London. We once went to the country to deliver some furniture to somebody's mother. He was appalled at the waste, at the lack of human activity. 'All that grass. All those trees . . .' he speculated irritably. 'They must be worth something to somebody.'

His hatred of nature is so intense that he refuses to acknowledge that there are any separate species of bird. He calls them all – even sparrows – ducks.

Cy Laurie's success was very largely due to his manager, a plump, middle-aged man with grey, hair brushed back over his head in wirelike strands. He realised that national, as opposed to local, fame was the product of publicity, and to this end employed a publicity agent called Les Perrin. At this time such tactics were unheard of in the jazz world, and they certainly paid off.

Les Perrin, a tiny cockney sparrow, was a dynamo of ideas. He would distribute pamphlets from a helicopter, fire bullets through a band coach window and, in Cy's case, build up a fanatical following whose identification with the band was hysterical rather than musical.

A little later, with the ascent of Chris Barber, Cy's star began to wane. Always a prey to self-doubt, and given to fanatical solutions and mystical enthusiasm, Cy broke up the band and went to India to study, so it was said, under a guru.

The National Federation of Jazz Organisations was attempting during this period to keep the growing enthusiasm for the music under some kind of control. This was to avoid the over-exposure which had all but killed off the interest during the earlier boom in

1950. The only trouble was that the elected committee was so divided by differences of opinion as to what jazz was, and so split by personal animosities, that it had a difficult job keeping itself under control. During the year 1953–4 I served on this committee. I had been proposed as a kind of joke at the General Meeting but somebody seconded me and I was elected. While the band was still in existence I had never been able to attend a meeting, but after it broke up I used to go along every other Tuesday to The Three Brewers, Seven Dials, and put in what Mick would call my 'two penn'orth'. It was during my term of office that Big Bill Broonzy came over under the auspices of the NFJO to do a series of concerts. This was a very big deal indeed. He was the first American jazzman to play in England since the war. The Musicians' Union, in a hopelessly parochial way, refused to allow Americans in although it was obvious that in fact the interest they would arouse would *create* work for British musicians on the same bill. They only let Broonzy in because he was a folk singer.

For me the idea of hearing an American Negro singing the blues was almost unbearably exciting. I went along to his first concert at the Conway Hall in a state of tense anticipation. Alan Lomax introduced him at great length while Bill stood patiently at his side. I found Lomax extremely paternalistic. I knew he'd done a great deal for the blues, got Leadbelly out of prison, recorded work songs in prison camps, and rediscovered many forgotten and obscure artists – for all this we owe him a great deal – but I got the impression that he felt he owned them. The southern voice droned on and on. Finally it got too much even for Bill, an extremely well-mannered and equable man.

'. . . and ah am sho,' said Lomax, 'that when yo' heah Big Bill . . .' 'If they ever gets the chance,' said Broonzy resignedly and the round of applause had the effect of hurrying up the introduction.

I won't describe how I felt listening to Bill that summer evening. This was the first live blues I'd ever heard in my life, the music I loved, and love above any other, sung by a great artist.

His whole visit was a splendour. There were sessions that lasted all night long, the most memorable at Jimmy Asman's tiny house in Plumstead, where Bill would drink a whole bottle of whisky and talk over quiet chords on his guitar, lie outrageously about things he had seen and done, and sing the blues until the dawn broke over Woolwich.

The NFJO promoted a series of concerts in the provinces for Bill, but delegated the responsibility to various promoters. We decided that it would be as well to appoint some representative of the federation to watch our interests in each town and for the Liverpool concert I proposed my father. He was delighted, took his duties very seriously, and wrote us a long report which ended: 'Mr Broonzy was received with prolonged and enthusiastic applause, and declared himself willing, if only it were possible, to continue to sing all night, a statement I am prepared to believe.'

Bill stayed with my parents and told my mother that this was the first place he had stayed in England where you didn't have to put money in a meter for the gas fire. He ate an enormous breakfast: two plates of corn flakes, two helpings of bacon and eggs, and about a loaf and a half of toast. My father was so fascinated he was very late for the office.

Broonzy came over four or five times before he died. I got to know him well and loved him very much. He helped to create the taste for Mississippi-style blues, and opened the way for all the singers who came here later.

Dressed in a black shirt, black trousers, black socks, black shoes, a very expensive black sweater from Simpsons, and a white silk tie, I embarked on my solo career.

Mick managed to arrange several little tours of the provincial jazz clubs at a fee of ten pounds a night. As I'd only been getting three with the band this seemed an enormous amount. What I failed to take into account was that I had travelled free in the coach, and now I had to pay my own train fares. Also I had to pay Mick commission so I was in fact no better off.

I would have been actually worse off if it hadn't been for Alex Welsh coming down to London from Edinburgh to form a band. Alex realised that, whereas he was still comparatively unknown outside Scotland, I had a certain reputation. He therefore used me a great deal, encouraged by Mick who was for a short time his manager as well, and could draw commission from both of us. Then Mick began to itch to get back in the business. There were several reasons for this. The improvement of the situation financially was certainly one, not to mention the fact that a bandleader earns considerably more than an agent to a modestly-paid singer and a newly-formed band; but it was not only this. He was after all only twenty-six, and had known applause and enthusiasm. You don't go into the jazz business simply to earn money. There is a wish to play in front of an audience. There is some element, although Mick hid it better than anyone I have ever met, of exhibitionism. At all events slowly, so slowly you could hardly see it happen, Mick began to play again.

At first he didn't even form a band of his own. He just used Alex's. While Alex was still finding his feet this suited him too, but as he became better known the situation got impossible. The promoter of a jazz club could not be expected to be best pleased if he booked Mick Mulligan one week and Alex Welsh the next and found himself landed with virtually the same group plus or minus Mick. Furthermore, Alex became established in his own right, was approached by a serious agent and saw no reason to spend his evenings blowing away for Mick's benefit when he could be doing it for his own. There came a time early in 1955 when Mick had to re-form a band. He asked me to join it and, despite an offer from Alex, I did.

Many people would have said I was mad. Alex took his responsibilities very seriously. He rehearsed. He was determined to succeed. Mick, as I well knew, alternated between bursts of enthusiasm and complete apathy from which nothing could shift him. He drank a great deal in those days and in consequence often played extremely badly, whereas Alex was still a teetotaller – a failing he made ample amends for later – and was known, in a not entirely kindly spirit, as The Lemonade King.

Of course I also drank and quite often sang disgracefully because of it, but I never took that into account when thinking of Mick's lapses. In fact Mick and I discovered later that whenever one of us was describing to the other some drunken shout-up with a third party, we inevitably made our enemy talk in the slurred voice of the Music Hall inebriate whereas we, in retelling our triumphant and cutting role in the argument, always assumed a sober and rational voice.

Furthermore, my own status had improved out of recognition. An appearance with Alex at the Festival Hall in one of the NJF's Festivals of British Jazz had been recorded, and my version of 'Frankie and Johnny' was actually selling quite well. I had been cheered for three minutes, and about thirty seconds of this intoxicating noise is at the end of the record to prove it. Fame, that dangerous bird, brushed my cheek. Several offers came from agents to manage me as a solo artist, and then I joined Mick, a bandleader without a band.

The real reason is I love him. Two stories to show why. One night we played an RAF camp and, unable to find digs, were kindly offered a billet by the Wing Commander. His only condition was that we were quiet, a not unreasonable request as it was by this time two o'clock in the morning and we were next door to airmen who had to be up at six. Mick stayed behind for a final drink, and the rest of us, stoned out of our heads, staggered along the neat paths to find our hut.

After crashing, despite detailed instructions, into several sock-scented billets full of sleepily angry personnel, we eventually found our own quarters and began to shout, scream, pillow-fight, fall about, and finally managed to push over a wardrobe. At this moment the door burst open and there stood Mick absolutely livid with rage. For three minutes he gave us a perfectly justifiable bollocking. We took it with the masochistic repentance of the very drunk. We were ashamed of ourselves. Mick was perfectly right. We hung our heads. Then, in full spate, he stopped and looked at the flimsy wardrobe at his feet.

'What the fuck,' he shouted joyfully, and jumping into the air landed on top of it, splintering it to match-wood.

The other story I heard only the other day from Ian Christie. Mick was very drunk and playing a solo. His control was minimal, his head entirely empty of any constructive musical ideas. His timing gone. All he could do was blow unbearably loudly, his neck swollen, his eyeballs popping with effort. Ian listened with embarrassed irritation. When somebody is playing as badly as that it reflects on everybody in the band. Finally Mick finished his thirty-two bars of nothing, and waved his bell in the direction of the trombonist to tell him to take the next chorus. He turned to Ian, his face running with sweat:

'All the noise and vulgarity of Freddy Randall,' he said, 'with none of the technique.'

I stayed with Mick, despite periods of exasperation and occasional tempting offers, for the next seven years.

10

A Good Conductor

Most people who decide to form a band go about it like this: they approach any musicians they want and, if they are already with another group, make a financial offer. They advertise in the musical press and hold auditions. They get around the smaller clubs to see if there is any potential talent in the semi-pro bands. They brief spies to keep their ears open in the provinces.

Mick did none of these things. He let it get about he was re-forming and then sat on his arse. Being Mick he was about twice as lucky as anyone else would have been. For a start disagreements within the newly formed Alex Welsh Band shot three musicians into his lap: they were Ian Christie (clarinet), Pete Appleby (drums), and Frank Thompson (double bass).

Ian Christie was already well known in revivalist circles before he joined Mick. He had played second clarinet with Humph, and had co-led, with his brother Keith on trombone, a band called 'The Christie Brothers Stompers'. This had two distinct periods: the first when Ken Colyer on trumpet had a decidedly purist flavour, the second with Dickie Hawdon, basically and progressively modern. Ian, unlike his brother, was the opposite of eclectic, and the band broke up.

Keith's modernist tendencies led him into the Ted Heath Band. Ian's musical conservatism held him faithful to revivalist jazz. Even within this field he was extremely dogmatic. All he really liked at that time were the late Louis Armstrong, Condon music and, outside this pattern but with extreme fervour, the Mississippi blues singers like Broonzy.

His own playing was accomplished but limited. His principal influences were the New Orleans clarinettists, Edmond Hall and Albert Nicholas. Neither are dramatic players. They are both lyricists. Their effect on Ian was to lead him to play a continuous string of notes at approximately the same volume from the first bar of a number to the coda. As a result his solos, when he was on form, were often beautiful in an unpretentious and restrained way, but in ensemble, because he didn't listen to what the rest of the front line was up to, had no give and take. He just played, as if he were taking a solo. Furthermore he had a bad memory for arrangements. This suited Mick very well, as it gave him a perfect excuse not to hold rehearsals.

'What's the use, cock?' he would ask. 'Ian can never remember new numbers.'

It was this difficulty which had led to his departure from the Alex Welsh Band. Alex and Roy Crimmins were after an arranged sound, and Ian was continuously holding them up. I attended several rehearsals, and could see that the extreme politeness with which Roy and Ian treated each other, masked exasperation and near enmity. When Archie Semple left Freddy Randall and offered to rejoin his old Edinburgh friend and musical sidekick, it was a foregone conclusion that Ian would go.

Ian is small, almost mouse-like in appearance, and wears horn-rimmed spectacles. His movements are neat and precise, his vocabulary enormous, his accent Lancastrian. His father, a piano tuner by profession, was Scottish, but his mother came from Blackpool where Ian and Keith were brought up.

Ian had qualified as a photographer before coming south, and until it became possible for him to earn his living as a full-time musician, had worked in the photography department of Harrods. The idea of him asking debs to smile was not without irony, as his considerable talent for hatred, his powers of invective, his whole reserve of malice were directed night and day, drunk or sober, at the upper classes (short 'a'). The word 'hurray', Jim Godbolt's happy synonym, became in Ian's mouth a deadly insult. Collectively he referred to Hurrays as 'the enemy', and to a typically hurray face, either of the chinless, slack-mouthed variety, or of the florid small-eyed strain, as 'an enemy face'.

To work himself up yet further he had only to say the words 'public school'. The phrase 'public-school hurray' was enough to produce a psychosomatic state not far removed from apoplexy.

One fine winter morning at about eleven o'clock we were driving through the West Country, and were forced to stop by a hunt crossing the road. It was a pretty, if absurd, spectacle, and the rest of us were inclined to watch it pass with tolerant pleasure. Not so Ian. He lowered his window and subjected the entire charade, from the leading hound to the last velvet-capped child on a pony, to a blistering stream of insults. Mick was amazed. 'I thought he was going to pass out,' he told me later.

Ian and I frequently engaged in violent political rows. Most of these took place late at night in the wagon when we were both rather drunk and, whatever the subject, followed an identical course. Ian was on the extreme left bordering – although he never joined the party – on the edge of official Communism. I took the anarchist position, holding that ends never justify means, and that authority, whether on the left or right, is always wrong. Ian usually finished up by accusing me of talking a load of liberal humanist shit. There was one memorable incident in these otherwise identical and fruitless arguments, and this was due to a misunderstanding. Ian had been stressing that all my thought patterns were the result of my middle-class background. I agreed that this might be true but that it was after all an accident where any of us were *dropped from the womb*.

'Don't try and confuse the issue with that Surrealist bollocks,' shouted Ian. I was puzzled, and asked what he found Surrealist in what I'd been saying. It turned out he'd thought I'd said *lopped off the moon*.

In general the rest of the band ignored these shout-ups, preferring to sleep unless there was a bottle circulating, but Mick would occasionally enter the lists only to find himself, like a passer-by intervening in a fight between man and wife, turned on by the pair of us. Mick's political ideas are extremely reactionary although he is the opposite of pragmatic in day-to-day life.

Ian's political viewpoint forced him to consider Mick, in his role as bandleader, as a representative of the boss class. He was always pressing for a change of structure. He wanted the band put on a cooperative basis with Mick taking a double share. Mick refused to countenance this idea. He *liked* being band-leader, and besides it was probably true that he did make, when things were going well, considerably more money than a double share. I was against it because I preferred a straight screw with none of the responsibility for breakdowns and broken contracts, and the rest of the band didn't want to know either.

Until he got married Ian was usually involved in some intense affair. It was only occasionally he was able to treat sex on a light level, and he was not very adept at the quick chat-up followed by a knee tremble. He had a habit if he saw one of us getting on well with a girl he fancied of sailing in with a cry of 'Is this man annoying you?', but it never worked. Besides, if it had, he wouldn't really have enjoyed it much. He was an extreme romantic. Just by chance most of his premarital affairs were with upper-class girls.

Some days before his wedding, Ian's father gave him as a joke a vulgar rubber toy. It was about six inches long and turned one way represented a girl wearing a shawl over her head, but turned the other way it became an erect penis. The next evening during the interval of a seaside dance I was leaning on the esplanade and became aware of Ian standing below on the shingle at the edge of the incoming sea. Suddenly he raised his arm and threw the phallic pun as far as he could. Being rubber it floated, and the waves deposited it again at his feet. It was a very Freudian moment for a Marxist.

Some time ago a dreadful game went the rounds. All it consisted of was deciding who among your friends and acquaintances were 'winners' and who were 'losers'. Likeable characteristics had nothing to do with the decision – many losers are extremely likeable – but neither did material success guarantee you to be a winner. Paul Getty for example is a prototype loser. The distinction, and it is a very hard one to make in a great many cases, is that the loser gives off an aura of defeat and possible disaster, whereas the winner emanates a justified confidence in the inability of things to go wrong. It was no less shaming to be judged a winner than a loser. Only the players derive any satisfaction from it, and that based on extremely suspect motives. One thing is certain, however, and that is that if the game had been invented at the time everybody in the band would have judged the drummer, Pete Appleby, a one hundred per cent winner.

Pete Appleby, small but wiry, is one of those people who seem to have no past history. His childhood, a period of which even the most non-Proustian is unable to prevent some impression forming over a period of years, remained a complete mystery to us. We did meet his father once for a few moments, because the band-wagon was passing his house and Pete had something to tell him, but apart from the fact he looked exactly like a slightly older version of Pete and wore a bow tie, we learned little from this encounter. His mother, whom we gathered was separated from his father, we never saw. The only concrete fact I can recall about Pete's early years was that during the war he had been evacuated to Bedford and gone to school there.

His later career was equally sketchy, although it was certain that he was in the Navy. Pete was even prepared to talk about this period of his life occasionally, but the trouble was that, being one of nature's Walter Mittys, he frequently promoted himself. If any of the band pointed out that he appeared to have risen in rank since the last time he told us a particular story, he would give the answer with which he always refuted any accusation of inconsistency. Moving his padded shoulders rapidly about, his inevitable response to emotional stimuli, he would tell us with emphatic confidence: 'I never said that.'

Most of Pete's naval stories were to remind us of the fact that he had served under Prince Philip, and that they were like 'that'. In the course of these stories Philip would call Pete 'Pete' and Pete would call Philip 'Phil'. Actually if they were like 'that' it is on the cards that Pete did call Philip 'Phil' because he had a horror of calling anybody by their full name and would shorten it if possible. If it was a two-syllable name like 'Gerry' there was no problem. Pete could call its owner 'Ger', but if it was a name of only one syllable like 'Mick', Pete would prefer to shorten the surname, and usually called Mick 'Mul'. He invariably referred to himself as 'Apps'.

For a long time none of us could decide why Pete was so different from the rest of its, almost as if he belonged to a different species. I forget the exact moment of revelation, but after it the problem no longer existed. What made Pete so different was simply the fact that he came from, lived in, and was loyal to, South London.

The problem no longer existed, but there was still a linguistic block. We had for some time no adjective to describe South London in general and Pete Appleby in particular. We could and did say that Pete's clothes, for example, were typical of South London, or that he had a very South London approach to driving the band-wagon, but we knew there must be a word for it, and at last I found it.

I was reading Mayhew's *The London Underworld* in the wagon and came upon a description of a gentleman who had crossed Waterloo Bridge and entered 'a transpontine brothel'. From then on Pete's clothes were transpontine clothes. Pete's driving was transpontine. Pete himself was transpontine.

Of course he had a come-back. Once he had understood that the word meant nothing more than 'across the bridge' (and yet for the rest of us how much more) he pointed out that to him 'All you cunts is transpontine.' He had logic on his side, but he knew it didn't work.

Pete didn't drink and had a fantastic reserve of energy. It was natural, therefore, that during the five years he was with the band, he put in most of the driving. He was paid for it at so much a mile, but although this certainly influenced him, it wasn't the only reason he drove so much. He genuinely had a feeling for driving, and also enjoyed the power it gave him over the rest of the band. The times he liked best were when he was the only driver in the band. Very often the bass player was also a driver, and towards the end Mick raised the energy to reapply for his own licence but there was a year or two when Pete alone was legally entitled to take the wheel.

During this period, if he was angry with the rest of us for hanging on at the end of a dance or jazz club to drink when he wanted to drive home, he would wait until we were on the outskirts of London and then pull into a layby for an hour's sleep. On two occasions during rows with Mick he found himself in the happy position of handing in his notice, and then giving Mick the keys to the wagon knowing full well that he would have to be placated, persuaded to take them back, and drive on. To remember his cry of ''oo's the driver then?' is still sufficient to stimulate my adrenalin.

As a driver he was a natural, although given to taking consider-able liberties. He was always very polite to lorries, making the accepted signals, and flicking his lights on and off, but he couldn't bear being overtaken by a private car and when this happened would chase it mile after mile. If anybody irritated him he would lean out of his window and shout: 'Where did you learn to drive?' or, if there wasn't time for the whole sentence, he would make do with 'Cunt!'

There were times when a gentleman so addressed would take advantage of the traffic lights burning red at the next intersection to jump out of his car and threaten Pete with physical violence. When this happened Pete would point over his shoulder with his thumb to where the rest of us sat unaggressively in the back of the wagon and explain laconically: 'There's seven of us.'

Cars were Pete's god, and the garage, pronounced 'garidge' in the accepted transpontine manner, his church. He was always driving up to the meet in a new second-hand model, and spent a lot of time on long journeys explaining the complicated deals he was engaged on with various used-car firms. Needless to say he was always the winner in these transactions.

Pete, despite this one extravagance, always seemed to have plenty of money. As I said he didn't drink. 'Don't see no point in it,' he explained. 'Pissing all you get up against a wall and making cunts of yourselves.' On the other hand he gambled, but unlike the rest of us, won consistently. Here his non-drinking certainly helped. During the long smoky nights in hotel lounges or boarding-house bedrooms, while the rest of us became more and more befuddled as the bottle passed, Pete, clear-eyed and obsessed with the will to win, played us like a matador plays a bull. He was a brilliant bluffer, and knew how to needle us into exasperating raising and frighten us into throwing in good hands when he had nothing. When he pulled off a coup, 'Packed 'ave yer? Beaten a Queen 'igh could yer? Thought so,' his shoulders would gyrate in such an ecstasy of glee as to suggest that he might at any moment leave the ground. As well as being a good player, he was also diabolically lucky.

Drummers have an enormous sexual potential for a certain type of girl, and Pete, although small and no beauty, had considerable charm. He looked not unlike Frank Sinatra. His reaction to being told this was in fact typical of his own special line of mock-modesty. 'Funny you should say that,' he would tell the girl as he packed up his drum kit at the end of a dance with a special puzzled frown on his face. 'Several girls 'ave said it. Don't see it meself though.'

What is perhaps missing from this description is how likeable Pete was. His very outrageousness worked in his favour. His self-dependence and absence of self-pity commanded a certain respect. He had one very comical delusion, namely that everybody was blind outside the band. Time after time he would be caught pulling faces, and if anybody struck him as particularly ridiculous, he would hold up his open palm and jab at them from behind it with the forefinger of the other hand convinced that they wouldn't see what he was doing.

I was glad to hear recently that his cheek, his outrageous poise, remains unimpaired. Not long ago the Chris Barber Band booked in at an hotel and saw in the register that the Donegan group were staying there too, and that Mr and Mrs Appleby were in room eight. They crept up in a body and threw open the door hoping to catch Pete in some embarrassing situation or at least to discomfort him.

''Ullo boys,' he said getting out of bed in his immaculate pale blue silk pyjamas. A mound of bedclothes showed where 'Mrs Appleby' lay concealed. Pete grinned and with a quick movement whisked the clothes off the bed revealing a naked young lady looking none too pleased. ' 'Ow bad!' said Pete Appleby.

Like Ian Christie and Pete Appleby, Frank Thompson joined us from Alex Welsh. He had from Mick's point of view a great advantage. He owned a station wagon and was prepared to rent it to the band for a very modest sum per week. This seemed to solve the transport problem. With Pete and Frank both able to drive, we could travel overnight, and accept bookings hundreds of miles apart on consecutive dates, a necessary lumber while we were re-establishing ourselves. Furthermore, the cheapness of the wagon meant that Mick could take jobs at a much lower rate than was possible in the grandiose days of coach hire. However, as with so much to do with Frank Thompson, it only seemed to solve it. His station wagon was so old, and broke down so often, that Mick was always having to hire fleets of taxis or take the whole band by train, so that in the end it worked out as a very expensive form of economy.

Inside Frank Thompson's head a permanent fairy godmother waved her wand. All pumpkins were coaches. All rats were coachmen. His wagon was a case in point. Whatever went wrong with it, as far as he was concerned it remained a new and efficient machine.

Frank's appearance was against him. He was short and yet gangling. His hair, although heavily Brylcreemed, fell down in a lank cow's lick over his forehead, and stuck up in spikes on the crown. His complexion was yellow, his skin rough and engrained with grease from repairing his vehicle, and his teeth were green and furry. His most memorable feature was his nose, a Cyrano-type organ, enormous and snub.

He didn't drink alcohol, but in pubs would order a pint of orange squash. This going down was an unattractive sight. The same applied to his consumption on every possible occasion of large and squashy cream cakes.

Perhaps his best cabaret, and it lost nothing from daily repetition, happened when the van stalled. There was no question of a self-starter, and Frank had to get out and crank it into life with the starting handle. This seldom took less than nine or ten attempts, but it was his timing which, if he had been a comedian, gave the performance its distinction. He was out of sight behind the bonnet for a count of nine, and then on the ten his face in agonised profile would shoot up in front of us to an accompanying lifeless cough from the engine. Very often the handle kicked back, and Frank would stagger about the road in a dramatic fashion clasping his wrist.

I believe it was Ian who first pointed out that this scene had very much the flavour of *Monsieur Hulot's Holiday*, a film most of us had seen, and we took to chanting the name 'Hulot' every time Frank cranked up the handle. We prolonged the first syllable on a rising note while he remained invisible and then shouted the second syllable as loudly as we could as he sprang into view. By about the sixth repetition he very often lost his temper and used to pace off and sulk round a corner for a minute or two.

We also called him 'Hulot' as a nickname, although after a time this got to be pronounced 'Youlow' in imitation of Pete Appleby. Pete, of course, hadn't the faintest idea who the original Monsieur

Hulot was. He never took in anything outside his own interests however much it was talked about in the wagon, but he was delighted with the name, and was even willing to overlook that it contained two syllables.

Frank Thompson's delusions extended far outside the confines of his van, but what was so extraordinary about him was that he never seemed to mind our being able to compare what he said with the reality. He told us for instance that he had a flat in town and a house in the country and this turned out to be a single room with a sink and the use of the bathroom m a small terrace house in Clapham, and his mother's identical house three miles further out into the suburbs.

Like the rest of us he was frequently in a financial mess but he found it necessary to tell us: 'You know it's an extraordinary thing. Whenever I get into money difficulties another legacy falls into my lap.'

He was not a bad-hearted person at all but, like the boy at school who is always bullied, he managed to bring out the worst in us all.

He eventually got engaged and on tour he used to put a large photograph of his fiancée by his bedside. In Scotland Paul Simpson, who was with us during one of our tromboneless moments, pencilled in a moustache on the young lady's upper lip. Frank was furious, although he couldn't find out who'd done it, and actually suspected his main persecutors, Ian Christie or Pete. It wasn't of course a kind thing to do, but then Frank's reaction was so typical as to alienate any potential sympathy.

'I've rubbed out the moustache,' he told us as we loaded up the wagon next morning, 'and I forgive whoever did it, but . . .' he paused to give what he had to say its full weight, 'if they'd have drawn in breasts I'd have killed them.'

Mick had decided to make it a small band this time, so with clarinet, drums and bass fixed up, he'd only a piano player and trombonist to find. Our first pianist – they were always changing – was a tall Glaswegian called Angus Bell.

The first time I met Angus 'Miff' Bell we nearly had a fight. It was several years before he joined the band and just after he'd come down to London to earn his living as a pianist. It took place in

Henekey's Cider Bar in Kingly Street, a favourite fall-about station for the musical profession at that time.

We were introduced by a mutual acquaintance. I was at my fattest and was wearing, Miff told me later, a red waistcoat obviously dating from my slimmer days. He took an instant dislike to me, and I to him.

After some minutes' conversation I began to realise from certain remarks of his that he was a Scottish nationalist, and I had the audacity to disagree with him . . . I knew, of course, that Scottish nationalists existed but never imagined that I might meet one, particularly in the jazz world, and thought that a few words would convert this tall dour Scot from his convictions. Miff, much to my surprise, told me to get stuffed.

By the time he joined the band he'd turned against these ideas and indeed like all 'ex-people' – ex-Catholics, ex-Communists, etc. – had turned against his previous convictions with a special violence. What he hadn't lost, indeed what had probably attracted him to fascism in the first place, was a constant manic rage, only now it's found outlet, to my continued pleasure over six years, in ferocious black humour.

Miff's daemon demanded a considerable quantity of drink in order to materialise. He remained faithful to malt whisky, a taste acquired in his Scottish nationalist days, and he became very anti-Sassenach when he couldn't get it. Although he no longer rooted actively for The King over the water, he remained in this, and much else, a convinced patriot. Every time we crossed the border into Scotland he would sing 'Speed Bonny Boat' in that curiously exaggerated 'rrrolling' tenor deriving from the late Sir Harry Lauder. When he was really raving Miff would begin to caper around doing what he called his 'bits and pieces'.

'Finger in bum. Finger in mouth,' he would shout in his distinct brogue, suiting the action to the words, and then, after a few more seconds of 'leaping aboot', he would yell, 'CHANGE FINGERS!'

His imitation of the Pope was another speciality. As this had to be performed sitting down it was usually given in the wagon. It was a generalised picture of the head of Christendom rather than a portrait of any particular pontiff. I deduce this because it didn't alter at the death of Pius and the election of John. It consisted of pulling out his thin face until it turned crimson from lack of breath and at the same time squinting at his nose. Then, raising two fingers in benediction, he would slowly lean backwards on his seat until his legs, bent at the knee, rose into the air presenting his bottom to the spectators.

Miff's mother-in-law – she was a lowlander and very anglicised so he called her 'Mummy' – gave him an old fur coat to wear in the wagon on cold winter nights. This did him good service for some years, although the sight of his ginger hair and freckled snub nose emerging from the shabby but feminine collar was a distinctly comic sight. At length he decided that the coat had to go and waited for a suitably symbolic occasion.

This materialised in Scotland while we were touring the Highlands. Although Miff had been brought up in Glasgow he had in fact been born in a market town in the Western Highlands, and one morning as we passed very near it, Miff asked Pete to stop the wagon. There was a signpost pointing down the road towards the village. On it was written: 'To the Free Kirk. One mile.' The 'Wee Free', that most narrow of all churches, still dominates large stretches of the Highlands with its joyless hellfire puritanism. Miff hung his coat on the signpost and pinned a note saying: 'A present from Angus Bell to his native village.' At his suggestion Mick got out his trumpet and blew the 'Last Post' while the rest of us stood in a circle at the base of the signpost and pissed on the coat in the cold bright morning light.

For six months we had no permanent trombonist and Mick's block against doing anything until the last possible moment meant that he never tried to fix a temporary until the morning of a job. When, as quite often happened, he couldn't find one at all, he substituted a different front-line instrument, usually Paul Simpson on baritone sax.

He did try out two trombone players as possible fixtures but neither stayed very long.

The first was Harry Brown who, although ex-Lyttelton band, was a convinced modernist by this time and very unhappy playing Dixieland so eventually he had to go.

It was Harry, however, who found Mick his nickname. Apparently, he had been waiting for the last tube one night, and had been drawn into conversation by one of those near-tramps who haunt platforms and bus-shelters late at night. He asked Harry what he did. Harry admitted he was a musician. The man said that was a very rewarding profession as long as you had a good conductor. That was what made all the difference, a good conductor. He asked Harry what his conductor was like. Harry told him he was all right. Next day he told us about this encounter, and the name stuck. From then on Mick was 'the conductor'.

The other try-out was another Scotsman called Davie Keir. Like Pat Malloy, the Irish–Scottish bass player, he too came from Dunfermline. He shared with Miff an interest in Scottish nationalism which he tried to synthesise with certain Communist ideas. He was also drawn towards fascism, but as he was a kind person whom I cannot imagine performing a physical act of cruelty, the attraction was based on naïve and credulous premises. In fact, Davie's fascism had a Nietzschean origin. He believed in the superman and he believed he was a superman.

He could believe anything, and the more impossible the easier he found it. He reminded me of the White Queen who told Alice that she could sometimes believe as many as six impossible things before breakfast. The last time I saw him he was on the edge of a conversion to Catholicism based, as far as I could make out, on a book by Group Captain Cheshire about Christ's shroud.

When Davie had saved up a few pounds he left us, as he left every band he played with, to form a band of his own.

Eventually Mick found his trombonist. He came from Liverpool and his name was Frank Parr. We had known him for a long time. He had played for many years with his local, semi-pro band, the Merseysippi, and used to come round the back of the Picton Hall to see us in the days when we'd played concerts there.

He was a professional cricketer, and although this meant nothing to me – I have had a block against all team games since my preparatory school – Mick was very impressed.

The summer before he joined us, Frank kept wicket for Lancashire and quite often going round to Lisle Street I would find Mick slumped immovably in a chair in front of his newly acquired television set, watching a tiny grey Frank crouched behind the stumps. Mick told me he was brilliant and would probably play for England the next season.

It might therefore appear extraordinary that, far from playing cricket for England, the following summer found Frank touring with a jazz band. The reason had nothing to do with Frank's wicket-keeping, but it had a lot to do with Frank. From what I can gather, although the 'gentlemen' and 'players' labels have disappeared, the attitude of the cricketing establishment remains firmly entrenched. The professional cricketer is not just a man who plays cricket for money. He has a social role. He is expected to behave within certain defined limits. He can be a 'rough diamond', even 'a bit of a character', but he must know his place. If he smells of sweat, it must be fresh sweat. He must dress neatly and acceptably. His drinking habits must be under control. He must know when to say 'sir'.

Frank, we were soon to discover, had none of these qualifications. He was an extreme social risk, a complicated rebel whose world swarmed with demons and Jack O'Lanterns, and was treacherous with bogs and quicksands. He concealed a formidable and well-read intelligence behind a stylised oafishness. He used every weapon to alienate acceptance. Even within the jazz world, that natural refuge for the anti-social, Frank stood out as an exception. We never knew the reason for his quarrel with the Captain of Lancashire, but after a month or two in his company we realised it must have been inevitable.

Frank had a rather fine head set on a long but muscular neck. In repose his face resembled one of Nevinson's pastels of gallant NCOs which achieved such popularity during the last war, but it was seldom in repose. A family of grimaces and ticks were usually in residence, the most spectacular of which was a gum-baring similar to the rictus of a sudden and painful death.

Frank used to go through his repertoire of 'mushes' as Mick called them at any time, but it was catching the sight of himself in a mirror which inevitably provoked the whole series. Dressing-room, boarding-house bedroom, Victorian public house, the staircases of dance halls, wherever a sheet of glass threw back his image, Frank's urge to play Caliban took over.

He had the hard, spare, useful body of the professional athlete.

Its only failing proportionately was that the legs were a little short in relation to the length of the waist. This would have been unnotice-able if he'd had his clothes made or even altered, but what clothes he did buy were off the peg; the legs of the trousers were an inch too long, and the excess material gathered below the buttocks in a series of sagging folds like the backside of an elephant.

Frank's attitude to clothes, like his attitude to so much else, was to use them to make his personality less easy to accept, as yet another barrier between himself and the others. He would, of course, deny this, and make out that he didn't care, but this simply wasn't true. His clothes were not just shabby or old – they were anti-clothes.

His mac was famous, but personally I always found his sweaters more extraordinary. Under the arms, the perspiration had eaten into the dye in such a way as to produce a series of rainbow-like rings, the darker colours at the centre nearest the glands. Frank's sweat was in any case unique and he was very proud of it. It didn't smell of sweat at all for a start. The nearest I can get to it is the smell in the hallway of a cat-infested slum. Somebody once discovered written in the lavatory of a Soho drinking club the words, 'It's always summer under the armpits', and Frank, whose obsession with formalised linguistic concepts remained constant, always used the word 'summer' to describe the state of his armpits. Several times a day, with the stylised gestures of a Japanese actor, Frank would lean slightly backwards, bring his arm round in a wide curve in front of his body, and plunge the hand through his shirt opening and under his arm. There would then be a pause during which you could count four slowly. Then the hand was withdrawn with the same hieratic deliberation, and carried up to the nose where Frank would sniff it, emit an 'ah' of great satisfaction, and announce 'Going a bit!' in the voice of a man at peace.

The same phrase he applied to his socks on hot days, but there was nothing unique about the smell of his feet, and in this depart-ment Mick ran him close. To be fair Mick wasn't very keen on washing either in those days and, in justification, used to say that too much soap and water destroyed the natural juices, but the point was that Mick didn't bath much out of indolence, Frank *because* it made him smell.

Frank never washed any of his clothing. He used to save it up, wearing anything in rotation, until we did a job in Liverpool when he took it all home for his mother. This was not laziness. It was part of his Liverpool mania. Liverpool was for Frank the Golden City and the Good Place. Towards the end of the band's history he began to accept London as a possible town to live, but for the first few years he went about as though he had just been expelled from the Garden of Eden. If we drove along behind a lorry with the word 'Liverpool' written on its tailboard, Frank would shout it aloud. The sight of a Liverpool face galvanised him as though he had touched a live wire. Everything in London – tea, people, the air itself – was compared to its detriment with the Liverpool equivalent. It's true that all ex-Liverpudlians are hysterical patriots – one day I found myself calling the town 'home' and I hadn't lived there for seventeen years – but Frank was exceptional in his fervour.

Food and drink were the other weapons in Frank's armoury. He was extremely limited in what he would eat for a start. Fried food, especially bacon and eggs, headed the list; then came cold meat and salad, and that was about the lot. Any other food, soup for instance or cheese, came under the heading of 'pretentious bollocks', but even in the case of the food he *did* like, his attitude was decidedly odd. He would crouch over his plate, knife and fork at the ready in his clenched fists, and glare down at the harmless egg and inoffensive bacon enunciating, as though it were part of some barbarous and sadistic ritual, the words 'I'll murder it.' What followed, a mixture of jabbing, tearing, stuffing, grinding and gulping, was a distressing spectacle.

In relation to drink he was more victim than murderer. He drank either gin and tonic or whisky and, once past the point of no return, would throw doubles into himself with astonishing rapidity, banging the empty glass down on the counter and immediately ordering another with a prolonged hiss on the word 'please'. He passed through the classic stages of drunkenness in record time, wild humour, self-pity, and unconsciousness, all well-seasoned with the famous Parr grimaces. His actual fall had a monumental simplicity. One moment he was perpendicular, the next horizontal. The only warning we had of his collapse was that, just before it happened, Frank announced that he was 'only fit for the human scrap heap' and this allowed us time to move any glasses, tables, chairs or instruments out of the way.

Frank's spectacular raves didn't stop him looking censorious when anyone else was 'going a bit' – he used the same phrase for socks or drunkenness – but then we were all like that.

If I think of him I can see certain gestures; his habit of rapidly shifting his cigarette around between his fingers, his slow tiger-like pacing, his manner of playing feet apart, body leaning stiffly backwards to balance the weight of his instrument.

His music was aimed beyond his technique. Sometimes a very beautiful idea came off, more often you were aware of a beautiful idea which existed in Frank's head. In an article on Mick in the *Sunday Times*, Frank was quoted as saying: 'All jazzmen are kicking against something, and it comes out when they blow.'

This was a remarkably open statement for Frank who, during a wagon discussion on our personal mental quirks and peculiarities, had once told us that he was the only normal person in the band.

This gained him his nickname, 'Mr Norm', and any exceptionally Parr-like behaviour would provoke the conductor into saying: 'Hello Frank. Feeling normal then?'

11

He'll Have Us All in the Bread Line

Once the band had re-formed, once the days of deps and fill-ins were behind us, touring continued much as before. Such changes as took place in the kind of jobs available or the popularity of the music were due to other, more ambitious spirits than the conductor's. In one way, it was more difficult for a band on the road to know what was going on than for the most cloth-eared member of a provincial jazz club who could at least hear a different group each week. Except for the occasional big concert or jazz festival we hardly got a chance to listen to other bands, and only Frank Parr, who neither knew nor wished to know anybody outside the jazz world, was prepared to spend a rare night off cruising round the London clubs to remedy this. Even so we were aware of the radical change taking place. It was just that Mick, the least commercial of men if it meant hard work, had decided to ignore it.

He theorised that it was better to stay in the second rank. You could be sure then, he argued, of a modest but steady living. You didn't price yourself out of the clubs and smaller dance halls during your hey-day only to discover that during your decline you could get no work at all. You went on, fatter in the booms, leaner in the slumps, but at least available for what jobs there were. In consequence the rise of Chris Barber during 1954–5, and the resulting swing away from revivalist jazz towards traditional, made no difference to the Mulligan band whatsoever.

Mick was not alone in his failure or refusal to jump on this particular band-wagon. Humph played mainstream from reasons of conviction. Alex Welsh remained faithful to Dixieland. Sandy Brown and Al Fairweather, both recently down from Edinburgh, moved against the current with strict historical logic, from their early championship of the most uncompromising traditionalism

towards a brilliant and individual paraphrase of the Armstrong Hot
Five.

Mick continued to play a loose approximation to the later Arm-
strong-cum-Condon sound, not from any burning integrity,
although it is certainly true that he preferred this sort of music, but
because to have changed would have meant a lot of sweat and many
hours of rehearsal.

What was the difference between revivalist and traditional jazz?
Revivalist jazz was based on the Negro jazz of the twenties as it can
be heard on recordings of that period. It was played (the original,
not the revival) by musicians who, for the most part, had come
from New Orleans and had been in at the birth of jazz in the
brothels and cabarets, in the street parades and funerals during the
early years of the century; they had moved north after the naval
authorities closed down Storyville in 1917, and had developed the
music further (ruined it according to the traditionalists) during the
next decade.

What the revivalists thought of as 'New Orleans Jazz' was the
music of Armstrong, Morton and Oliver – New Orleans musicians
but based on, and recorded in, Chicago during the Prohibition era.

What the traditionalists meant by New Orleans Jazz – for both
schools claimed the same name – was the music played by musicians
who had never left the city, and whose style was presumed to have
remained unaltered since the first decade of the century. The basic
difference between the two sounds is that revivalist jazz includes
arranged passages, solos, and considerable emphasis on the individual musician, whereas traditional jazz is all ensemble. There are
of course many other differences, but this is the most obvious.

The revivalists accused the traditionalists of sentimentality, of
basing their music on the recordings of very old men past their
prime, for it was not until the early forties that the surviving veterans
were rediscovered and recorded, and they claimed furthermore that
those musicians who *had* stayed in New Orleans had done so only
because they were inferior in the first place, and that the music had
reached its golden age in the hands of those who had been good
enough to go to Chicago, and inventive enough to take the music a
step further.

The traditionalists put forward no such reasoned arguments.

Like most fundamentalists they just knew they were right. Real New Orleans Jazz had never left New Orleans. Everything which had followed was less pure, less moving. The very genius of men like Armstrong had betrayed and ruined the music from which they sprang. 'Back,' as Ken Colyer put it, 'to the roots.'

Modern jazz was of course outside this dispute. Modern jazz was like the Roman Catholic Church at the time of the Reformation. It had developed historically from the origins of jazz but had, in the eyes of the early revivalists, become decadent and it was time to return to the source. The revivalists represent in this parallel the Church of England. Later the traditionalists arose, like the non-conformist sects, to accuse the revivalists themselves of decadence, of meaningless ritual, of elaboration. Back to the Bible – jazz from New Orleans; Away with Cope and Mitre – solos and arrangements; Down with the Bishops – Armstrong and Oliver.

Ken Colyer was initially responsible for this revolution. It was he who established the totems and taboos of traditional jazz, the pianoless rhythm section, the relentless four-to-the-bar banjo, the loud but soggy thump of the bass drum. Even so Ken by himself would never have effected the trad boom. He was too uncompromising, too much a purist. Picasso, accused of ugliness, pointed out that the inventor is always ugly because he has had to make something which wasn't there before, but that afterwards others can come along and make what he had invented beautiful. It was rather like this. Ken invented British traditional jazz. It wasn't exactly ugly – on the contrary, it was quite often touchingly beautiful – but it was clumsy. It needed prettifying before it could catch on. Chris Barber was there to perform this function.

Chris Barber had been around for a long time. He had a great love of jazz, but towards it as towards everything else, his approach was pedantic in the older and less critical meaning of the word. He was a record collector who knew the matrix number, personnel, and date of recording of every record in his immaculately filed collection. He had studied trombone at the Royal College of Music. His other interest was fast cars, and he carried over into jazz a somewhat mechanistic approach to the music. He also possessed a formidable will to succeed, and a complete belief in his ability to do so.

During the early days of the revival, Chris had a band which was based exactly, even to the presence of two cornets, on the King Oliver sound. He was converted to fundamentalism by Ken Colyer, and when that holy fool returned from New Orleans in 1953, it was Chris Barber who had a band ready for him. Within a month or two Ken sacked the whole band, or the whole band resigned – both versions were about, depending on who was telling the story – and Chris added Pat Halcox on trumpet and became, for the second time, a bandleader in his own right. The formation of the Barber Band in 1954 seemed to us at that time of purely parochial interest. Later it was proved to have been a watershed.

It is a temptation to look backwards, to select those events which showed the way things were going, and imagine that they appeared significant at the time. This is just not true. During the same months in which the Colyer–Barber schism was taking place, a whole new world was in the process of being born, and we were entirely unaware of it. I can't remember the first time I heard the word 'teenager'. I don't know at what point I began to take in the teenage thing. I doubt many other people can either.

It was certainly through its musical aspect that we did begin to realise what was happening. We had heard the Bill Haley record of 'Rock Around the Clock', and decided that it was a drag. I can remember asking who was the white blues singer somebody had put on the gramophone at a party, and learning with some surprise that it was Elvis Presley. When Haley's film was shown, we read in the papers about fans rioting, and had taken in that the ten records which were selling best in any one week were being printed in the *Melody Maker* in order of popularity. But at first none of these things seemed very different from what we were used to. Fans were nothing new. Dickie Valentine for example had a fan club which held an annual reunion at the Hammersmith Palais. Hit records were a fact. We never bought them, but we knew they existed. What we failed to understand was the age of the new audience. Dickie Valentine's fans were between eighteen and twenty-five. The records of Donald Peers or 'Winnie' Atwell were bought by Mums and Dads, but the new audience, the multitude outside, the secret society preparing a revolution in 'the Two Is', Old Compton Street, were sixteen or less. There had, of course, always been young jazz fans, but they'd just liked jazz and happened to be young. What was different about the teenagers was that they were young first and foremost, and everything they did and said, everything they liked or rejected, was useful in that it identified them *as a group*. At that time the boys were faced with conscription. This meant that they knew their 'real life' as adults was not in question. Between leaving school and going into the army, they could live out a fantasy life, their pockets full of money from a dead-end job. Circling round them and quick to move in were various interested adults – agents, record companies, clothing manufacturers, concert promoters – but the invention of the teenage thing was initially the work of the teenagers themselves. It was they who chose Haley and Presley as their heroes, and it was from their ranks that they threw up and deified their first British idol, Tommy Steele, *né* Hicks.

It was through Tommy that I first began to understand it all. Following the modest success of my recording of 'Frankie and Johnny', I had been put under contract by Decca. As whatever fans I did have were jazz fans and had presumably bought my record for that reason, I suppose it was inevitable that the company decided I should record more commercial material. My first attempt to conquer the pop market was a Dixieland version of 'Kingdom Coming', the American civil war song. I substituted the word 'Brothers' for the word 'Darkies' throughout, and Mick added a tuba and flute to the instrumentation, but despite our efforts to compromise it only sold about a hundred copies. My next shot was a comic song of the twenties called 'My Canary's Got Circles Under His Eyes', and this too was a complete failure. It was due to its release that I came to meet Tommy Steele.

Television, still confined to one channel and furthermore considered an essentially working-class entertainment, provided the occasion. The Birmingham studio, in advance of its time, had a weekly programme featuring the new releases and illustrating them visually by what was then an unheard of innovation; the artists themselves miming to their own records. The week that 'Canary' was issued, Tommy Steele had a new one out too. It was called, as far as I can remember, 'Rock with the Cavemen' and wasn't to become one of his great hits, but he'd already recorded 'Singing the Blues' and was a very big deal indeed. The only thing was I'd never

heard of him. I didn't listen to pop music at all in those days except
by accident, and although I'm sure there must have been a lot about
him in the *Melody Maker*, I didn't read the pop pages there either.
He, in his turn, hadn't heard of me. I don't know which of us was
the more surprised to discover that neither of us was aware of the
other's existence.

After we'd finished the first run-through, I thought it would be
friendly to ask this fresh-faced lad across the road for a drink. His
manager, a very astute young man called John Kennedy, came with
us. Tommy drank orangeade. John Kennedy said he'd have a beer.
'Pint?' I asked. He accepted, and was told off by Tommy whose
Dad had told him it was common to drink pints. Tommy asked me
if it was my first record. I said it wasn't, and asked him if it was
his. He told me it wasn't either. He then suggested that if I was to
be a success in show biz it would be as well to dress a bit more
sharp. He put this to me with such charm that I couldn't take
offence. He asked me what sort of car I had. I told him I hadn't got
one. He looked at me with the sort of pity usually reserved for the
badly deformed and offered to run me back to town after the show.
We were at the Ferry that night, and I accepted immediately. We
did the transmission and were back in London in just over two
hours, a rather terrifying experience in those pre-M1 days.

Sitting next to Tommy in his powerful open car, aware of his
heavy gold watch, his strange but immaculate clothing, his complete
confidence in himself, his cocky innocence, I found myself puzzled
and fascinated by him. When I got to the Ferry, I tried to explain
about him to the rest of the band, but they hadn't heard of him
either. It was a good session. The place was full and enthusiastic.
We all drank quite a lot, and in the second interval I had a knee
tremble under the canal bridge. By the end of the evening I had
forgotten about Tommy Steele.

But not for long. During the next few weeks I saw his name
everywhere. This always seems to happen. You hear of somebody
for the first time, and from then on can't open a newspaper without
seeing their name. It's a kind of magic.

A month later we shared a concert bill with Tommy in a cinema
somewhere on the southern outskirts of London. We did the first
half, and nothing happened at all, even Pete's drum solo won no

more than token applause. The audience was not hostile. It was just that we didn't seem to be there. We were rather puzzled and a bit hurt. I saw Tommy in the interval. He was very friendly.

''Ow's "Canary" going then?' he asked.

One of the band knew the alto player in his group. He was a modernist playing rock and roll for the money. This he felt entitled him to a good moan-up.

'I used to be a musician,' he told us in the pub, 'but now I'm just a fucking acrobat!'

I was curious enough to go back behind stage to watch the opening of the second half. I saw that the ex-musical acrobat stepped, by mistake, on the plug connecting Tommy's guitar with the amplifier. He didn't own up, and when Tommy switched on his instrument, it didn't work.

''Ere, me guitar's broke!' he cried in anguish.

The interval was extended a further five minutes while it was mended. During this delay a low continuous hum began to rise from the auditorium. It was like a hive of bees getting ready to swarm. I looked through the peep-hole and saw with some surprise how young the audience were. Furthermore most of them were girls.

The moment the curtain went up a high-pitched squeaking and shrieking started. I was absolutely amazed. After a couple of numbers I left and went back to the pub. The band was playing darts and Frank Parr was getting quite drunk. The orgiastic cries of worship inside the cinema were perfectly audible, and this moved him to prophesy.

'You hear that!' he announced as he swayed about, 'that's the death of jazz. We've had it. In six months we'll all be in the bread line!'

When the concert finished, thousands of girls streamed out of the cinema and clustered round the stage door. Frank leaned against the door of the saloon bar and watched this spectacle.

'The death of jazz,' he reiterated, 'rock and roll, the beginning of the end, and he'll have us all in the bread line!'

Frank's pessimism was exaggerated, but there was no doubt that rock and roll did give traditional jazz a hammering from which it took a year to recover. The big Festival Hall concerts came to an end, and so did the fortnightly concerts in the smaller recital hall in the same building. These, held under the auspices of the NJF, came under various headings based on the musical style of the groups involved. 'Back to New Orleans' featured either Ken or Chris; 'Dixieland Revisited' either Alex or ourselves, and there was also a less well patronised 'Modern Jazz Workshop'. Rock and roll put an end to all this. Modern jazz had a small, if perceptive and faithful, audience anyway, and its exponents were resentfully accustomed to neglect. It was the rest of us who felt betrayed, and the Mulligan band began to suspect, as they copied down in their diaries the increasingly empty date-sheet for those months, that perhaps Frank had been right after all.

But we didn't starve, and we didn't have to give up. The jazz-club audiences, older at that time than during the trad boom of the early sixties, remained faithful enough to give us some work in town, and we found ourselves booked in again at some of the venues we used to play in our very early days. Furthermore, the north of England, always resistant to fads which they thought of as originating in the south, continued to support jazz on a comparatively generous scale. We still played The Bodega regularly for Paddy, and sometimes the whole band, sometimes Mick and me as guest artists, were featured on the bill of some extremely successful concerts which he promoted in Manchester and elsewhere under the all-embracing title of 'Jazz Unlimited'. Finally most of the dance halls found it uneconomic to employ rock groups except as an occasional gimmick. They could only play for twenty minutes at a time, and they drew in a young audience who alienated the regular ballroom dancers, so we won out there.

A sign of the times were the large notices: 'NO JIVING. NO ROCK AND ROLL.' which appeared prominently displayed in the various dance-halls up and down the country.

Even at the height of its popularity, rock and roll was not unchallenged. There was also skiffle, a bastardised rather folksy music with a strong country and western flavour and a preference for the material of the great Negro folk singer, Huddie Ledbetter.

Its history is typical of the kind of *accident* that seems to operate in the popular field, and is the opposite of the imaginary Machiavellian manipulation of taste which most people think of as the way it works. Of course when something does become popular there is any amount of exploitation, but that is rather different.

Skiffle: first the word. Originally it was used to describe a kind of sub-jazz in which kazoos, tea-chest and broom-handle basses, seven-gallon jugs, and empty suitcases replaced the more conventional musical instruments. Presumably in the first place these improvised instruments were the invention of poor Negroes unable to afford the proper thing, but during twenties skiffle music caught on as a novelty, and in particular a white group called 'The Mound City Blue Blowers' achieved considerable vogue. By 1953 the public had naturally enough forgotten about skiffle, and only the serious jazz-record collector knew what the word meant.

Like so much else, the skiffle boom originated with Ken Colyer. In order to provide a contrast to an evening's diet of undiluted New Orleans ensemble, he introduced a short vocal session of Negro folk music with himself and his banjo player, Lonnie Donegan on guitars, and Chris Barber on bass. Ken himself sang most of the numbers, helped out from time to time by Lonnie. He called these interludes 'Skiffle Sessions', to differentiate them from the more serious activity of playing blues, rags, stomps and marches, and they achieved great, if localised, popularity among the band's followers. In choosing the word skiffle, Ken was, of course, consciously misapplying it. It was as a trumpet player that he would wish to be judged; skiffle had a light-weight almost flippant sound to it, but I feel that his version of these old songs was surprisingly moving and authentic, a case of what the folknics would call 'identification'.

When Ken's band broke up and Chris picked up the pieces, he naturally retained the skiffle-session idea. Lonnie Donegan took over the singing and became very popular round the clubs, although personally I always found his country and western nasal whine rather unpleasant. His version of 'Rock Island Line' originally part of a Chris Barber in Concert LP, was requested so often on the radio that it was put out as a single and rose to be top of the Hit Parade. Lonnie left Chris and formed his own group. He became a big star, the first member of the jazz world to do so, and was widely imitated.

By historical irony some of the smaller groups, unable to afford proper instruments over and above the leader's guitar, began to use washboards and kazoos and especially tea-chest basses with broomstick handles. Gypsy Larry owned one of these and could produce from it a remarkably accomplished noise.

The skiffle craze had its own radio programme on Saturday mornings. It was called 'Skiffle Club' and was the direct forerunner of 'Saturday Club' even to the extent of having Brian Matthew as compère. I was invited to appear occasionally on this show and formed within the Mulligan Band a group I called 'The Bubbling Over Five' after an obscure band on a record from the collection of Simon Watson Taylor. There was Miff, Appleby, Diz on guitar, and on bass a newcomer called Alan Duddington. We always seemed to be having new bass players. Unlike other musicians connected with the band, they had a high turnover.

Alan came from Lancaster. He was younger than the rest of us, still in his early twenties, a neat precise person, a bit of an old maid, with a very slight Lancashire accent. His features were a little on the weak side, but redeemed from mediocrity by a large and noble nose similar in character to that of the first Duke of Wellington.

He was proud to be a musician, but not proud to be in the Mulligan Band. Everything about it distressed him – the music, our attitudes, the way we dressed – and it was very surprising how long he stayed, especially as he was teased unmercifully and without a moment's respite.

Why did we tease him? There were in fact two reasons. For one thing he reacted so splendidly, concealing his mounting exasperation under a tight-mouthed, straight-backed indifference with only an occasional low sigh, or at most, a quiet if terse 'very amusing' to show we were getting through, but the real reason was that he *knew* he was right about everything. There was no question of doubt. There was no possibility that any alternatives existed, or that some things were a matter of personal taste. On every subject, at every level, Alan Duddington was right. If anyone disagreed with him, he didn't shout or even try to argue. He just repeated his own opinion in a quiet but firm voice until whoever was trying to contradict him gave up.

Alan was a perfectionist. He had certain standards, certain things he expected to happen. However far short reality fell from his expectations, it never affected his optimism. However often he didn't get what he wanted, it never occurred to him to lower his sights.

Opposite the Town Hall, Huddersfield, is a small public house called 'The County'. It's a friendly little pub, but as regards food anybody could tell at a glance what you could expect: crisps, nuts, possibly a pie or a sandwich. One evening we arrived in Huddersfield rather late and Mick told us we hadn't got time to go and eat, but perhaps we could grab a sandwich in the nearest boozer. Duddington looked at him coolly; 'I presume there's no objection if I have a crab salad instead?' he asked.

'No, cock,' said Mick, 'but where?'

'In the public house,' explained Duddington as though to an idiot child. We took it for granted that he didn't know the pub, and that once he saw it, he would realise there wasn't a chance, but that wasn't Alan. He marched in, and ordered a small strong ale and a crab salad. The old girl said they didn't do a crab salad. Alan looked hurt and surprised.

He was very fussy about his small strong ales too. He would first look along the bottles of beer until he had spotted what he wanted – barley wine, Stingo, whatever the local brewery supplied – and then order it by name. Very few people drink these small and potent ales, and quite often the barmaid would spend a long time searching the shelves for it, and even come back to Alan to tell him she didn't think they had any. She would find him standing up as stiff as a ramrod and pointing at the bottle he'd asked for.

It was his nose and personal fads which provided us with most of our ammunition, and the wagon was our usual theatre of cruelty.

His nose. How we went on about it! If he fell asleep, somebody, usually Frank Parr, would trace out a tiny head with a huge hooter on the steamed-up window so that it was the first thing he saw when he woke up. ('Very amusing.') Whatever came up in conversation was, if it was in any way possible, altered to include a reference to noses, e.g. 'Cat on a hot tin nose', ('Very fucking amusing.')

His habit of opening his suitcase at frequent intervals and producing a bar of chocolate which he unwrapped and ate with the formality which characterised all his movements was another moment in the day we never allowed to pass unremarked. There was an obscene limerick we all knew about an old girl of Silesia. Its last line was: 'If Jimmy the tapeworm don't seize yer!', and we pretended to believe that Alan's perpetual chocolate eating was because he had a tapeworm.

'Jimmy-time, Alan?' Frank would ask politely every time Alan opened his suitcase.

He tried to defeat us by forestalling this question.

'What time is it, Frank?' he'd ask as he reached for his suitcase.

'Jimmy-time,' said Frank in a matter-of-fact voice.

Even when he had left us, we didn't allow him to escape. We discovered that he was appearing at the Metropolitan Music Hall in the Edgware Road with a country and western group and hatched a plan.

We all of us went to a joke shop one afternoon and bought enormous false noses. That evening we took a box at the Met as near as possible to the stage. We had previously got in touch with another member of the group whom we knew, and put him up to telling Duddington that he had met a beautiful girl who had told him that she was mad about Alan, and would be sitting in a box that evening hoping that he would smile at her.

Just before Alan's turn was due, we hid below the level of the front of the box and put on our noses. As the curtains drew we slowly rose to our feet. Alan was staring at the box. Instead of a girl, there was the whole Mulligan band in their false noses.

What was nice about Alan was that he never bore any grudges. Despite our rotten teasing, despite even this final malevolent prank, he has always, on the few occasions we have met since, greeted me in an open and warm way. I doubt the rest of us could have claimed as much.

Skiffle was never a real threat to jazz, but even rock provided us with occasional employment. From tune to time we appeared on 'Six Five Special', the prototype teenage show. It had a live audience, and two compères, Pete Murray and Jo Douglas, while outside the Riverside Studios in Hammersmith a little group of young girls used to cluster and shriek their love. At the time it appeared madness, but I imagine a re-showing of a programme picked at random would seem both staid and droll.

During one appearance on this show we met Wee Willie Harris, a small and frantic rock singer and piano player who, lacking the sex-appeal of Tommy or Terry Dene, dyed his hair pink or green. We discovered that he was already known to us. As 'Fingers' Harris, he used to play interval piano at the Wimbledon Jazz Club. We bumped into him again a little later at Mrs Flanagan's for, unlike most of the artists who 'made it', he had the foresight to avoid big hotel suites and save against his decline. One morning, looking out of the window of Mrs Flanagan's dining-room, I watched him setting off for some appointment in the pouring rain, the collar of his raincoat stained pink from dye which had run from his hair.

Tommy Steele grew too old for his audience and became what all rock singers claimed they wished to become, 'an all-round entertainer'. Poor Terry Dene went into the army, an event which the authorities attempted to use, *vide* Presley, as a boost for that increasingly unpopular interruption to civilian life, and was straightway released on psychological grounds, a circumstance which gave rise to an outcry of rage from filthy Blimps of both sexes and the newspaper you'd expect. The rock and roll stars themselves became younger and younger until it came to an end due to the difficulty of recording while still in the womb. Before this happened there were two tiny ones who achieved success: Laurie London who, it was reported in an interview, wrote his God-bothering hit, 'He's Got the Whole World in His Hands', while sitting on the lavatory, and Jackie Dennis who gyrated in a kilt. At a large charity dance where the band appeared, I had the pleasure of watching with Mick a screaming row between these two mites because only one of them, Jackie Dennis as far as I can remember, was included in that part of the evening which was to be broadcast. 'I'm a bigger star than you, and if I'm not on I won't appear at all,' piped one. 'I'm higher up the Hit Parade than you anyway.' squeaked the other. Above their heads, their managerial fathers were engaged in similar, if less high-pitched, argument.

Skiffle faded, rock and roll eroded, and Chris Barber, his band now including a remarkable Northern Irish ex-art teacher called Ottilie Patterson who sang in uncanny resemblance to Bessie Smith, began to attract a larger and larger audience. Although a few purists, faithful to the Ken Colyer line, found Chris's music over-commercial, it was fresh and well played. Chris, convinced of his own worth, brought a serious, rather dignified approach to his music and presentation. His audience likewise was appreciative but unhysterical. It is hard to remember that out of these gay if formal occasions was to sprout the grotesque and funny-hatted excesses of the Trad Fad.

12

Done, Been Here and Gone

In 1955 I'd got married. This took place in Scotland because my wife's parents were Roman Catholic converts and, as she was under twenty-one, we were forced to elope. Our decision dovetailed in with a Duncan tour of the Borders, and a guest appearance with Freddy Randall at Birmingham Town Hall on the way up, allowed us to feel justified in travelling by train instead of squashing into the band-wagon.

We registered for the obligatory period into a small hotel in Leith Walk, Edinburgh. Every day I set off for the job but getting back in the small hours was more of a problem. Later I discovered that I needn't have been quite so conscientious. Most people simply booked in, informed the Lord Provost of their intentions, left a suitcase and a few clothes to imply residency, and came back in time for the ceremony. As it was, obsessed by the idea of something going wrong, I somehow or other struggled through the Scottish night and into my pyjamas before it was time to get up for breakfast. Quite often it was necessary to leave almost immediately for the next gig. I can still hear through waves of sleep the elderly waitress asking in her precise Edinburgh accent if I would prefer 'porridge or fruit-juice?' The name of the town 'Berwick-upon-Tweed' evokes a rainstorm of some five hours' duration during which I huddled in a shop doorway until they opened the station for the first train. When the job was nearer Edinburgh the problem was less acute. Frank Thompson was still with us on bass at that time, and for a small bribe and a bed booked into our hotel was willing to drive me back. Furthermore the whole project appealed to his romantic nature.

'I'll get you married if it's the last thing I do!' he would mutter through clenched teeth as we tore along the dark country roads with unnecessary urgency. What made this odd was that like my future in-laws, Frank Thompson was a Roman Catholic.

These drives through the small hours were not without other manifestations of his imaginative temperament. Sometimes when we were so nearly there that the lights of Auld Reekie glowed tantalisingly in the sky, Frank would start swerving about, shouting that he could see lorries bearing down on us. He would draw into the side of the road, cradle his head in his arms on the steering wheel and, for a good three quarters of an hour, complain of hallucinatory fatigue. There was nothing I could do about it. I had to pretend to believe every word he said.

During an elopement, once your three weeks' Scottish residency is established, you are allowed to go away for a week, the banns yellowing in the window of the Registrar the while, and return on the morning of the actual ceremony. At the end of the tour I travelled back to London in the band-wagon to do some jobs, and Victoria went to stay with my mother in Liverpool.

The convenient way the Scottish tour coincided with our elope-ment may suggest a bit of luck bordering on the uncanny. In fact the truth is more prosaic. Victoria and I had known each other for some time, and were able to arrange our elopement to fit in with the Scottish tour, although the Randall concert in Birmingham did appear as a last-minute bonus.

Before our marriage we'd found a flat. The room in Margaretta Terrace was too small and I'd discovered that an old school friend of mine, the painter Tim Whidbourne, had bought a large house down the unfashionable end of Cheyne Walk, and sub-divided it. In the rather damp basement was a young man called Andy Garnett who was a business-efficiency expert. He told Tim that he found the rent rather too high and would be willing to share the place with us. We'd have our own bedroom, and he'd sleep in the communal sitting-room. There was a bathroom and a kitchen adjoining the Thames. The half-share of the rent was within my means, and despite objections from Victoria I took it.

Andy was one of the original members of the Chelsea Set. He was hysterically inventive, curious about everything, mercurial, sensitive, an obsessive raconteur with an especially rich vein in frantic obscenity. Despite the fact he had been to Eton, even Ian

Christie took an immediate liking to him, although he compensated by calling him 'My favourite hurray', to Andy's slight irritation. Victoria on the other hand didn't get on with him a bit.

She would lie in bed keeping up a stream of whispered rage while the unsuspecting Andy had a rather noisy shit in the bathroom and blundered about the sitting-room. After years of band life, I couldn't see why she minded us sharing our first flat with somebody else.

It was Andy, yet another RC, who was responsible for me getting to the Register Office in Edinburgh on time. The night before I was married I was to give a lecture at the Institute of Contemporary Arts in Dover Street on the subject of 'Erotic Imagery in the Blues', and then catch the midnight up from King's Cross. Using Simon's collection of early blues records as a basis, I had prepared a serious theme dividing my subject under various headings: 'The Machine as a Sexual Image', 'Animal Symbolism in Erotic Blues', 'Sexual Metaphors in Rural and Urban Blues', etc. In the Chair were two jazz critics, Vic Bellerby and Charles Fox. Quite a large number of ICA regulars turned up and so did a great many of my friends. What divided the Chair and the ICA regulars from my friends was that the former had no idea I was getting married the next morning, while the latter knew it very well. While the Chairmen were introducing me, Mick Mulligan came up and handed me a glass. I nervously swallowed it in one. It contained four neat gins.

When the Chair had finished David Litvinoff rose with a question. Was it, he asked politely, permitted for the audience to wank during the recital? There was a pained silence from the bulk of the audience and an ominous shriek of laughter from my contingent. I began my talk.

At the beginning I stuck to my text although, under the effect of Mick's perpetually renewed gins, I understand I threw back my head and joined in several of the records. Ian Christie snored quietly in the front row, but woke up to ask when he was going to hear some jazz. As there was a Bessie Smith record playing at the time, I took this very badly and threatened to throw him down the stairs.

After the interval I put aside my subject altogether, and delivered a comparatively incoherent attack on the ICA itself referring to it throughout, with a certain lack of originality, as 'The Institute of Contemporary Farts', occasionally relieving the tedium even I felt arising from constant repetition by offering an alternative version, 'The Institute of Contemporary Arseholes'. When the Chairmen attempted to close down the meeting David Litvinoff pushed them both off the platform and took over. During this struggle he apparently sang his own version of Bessie's 'You've Been a Good Old Wagon, But You Done Broke Down' with the word 'Chairman' substituted for 'Wagon'.

The evening finished badly with the staff of the ICA stacking up the chairs and the friends of the bridegroom unstacking them. A sculpture in sponge and burnt cork by Dubuffet was destroyed. I was insensible.

Andy Garnett got me down the stairs, into a sports car, and on to the train at King's Cross. I didn't wake until we crossed the border. I was in clean blankets but with a terrible head and a mouth like a gym mistress's armpits. 'Thank God I wasn't sick,' I told my companion, a Scottish merchant seaman. 'You weren't sick!' he said. 'You was sick three times, Jock! Your mate told the guard you were getting married and slipped him a quid when he got youse on the train. You've had three sets of blankets. I'd slip him another quid if I was you.'

I got up and shaved. I looked dreadful, and my appearance wasn't helped by the rather bright blue ill-fitting suit I'd bought at a second-hand outfitters ('Entire Wardrobes purchased. West End Misfits, etc.') in the Charing Cross Road, or by the pink carnation I bought on the way to pick up Victoria from our hotel in Edinburgh. At the Register Office she was handed a large bouquet from the Glasgow Jazz Club. It was of daffodils and iris.

The aftermath of the ICA lecture filled the correspondence columns of the *Melody Maker* for several weeks. One ICA member said that he would have left 'except I was frightened to pass the group of teddy boys near the door'. Mick Mulligan was one of them as it happened.

I wrote in defence citing Dada and Rimbaud, but leaving out Messrs Gordon and Booth which was perhaps unfair. Simon also wrote:

Bessie Smith – and Clara and Trixie too – would have been on the side of the 'riotous' element among which I am glad to include myself . . .

But the masterpiece was a dead pan 'attack' on the whole evening by Chas Robson, a regular from Cook's Ferry with an impenetrable Geordie accent and a compensatory obsession with Wittgenstein. A typical paragraph read:

The unfortunate young man who gave the lecture, and the 'despicable minority' appeared, quite happily and sincerely to accept and proclaim a gutter morality based on sex and jazz – a case of 'publish and be damned' – but if Mr Wheeler [my principal critic – GM] wishes to retain his responsibility then I beg of him to heed the dangers of accidental contamination inherent in his asymptotic approach to the heart of jazz by eschewing all further contacts with the music . . .

Actually Chas had been involved with the ICA before. He had brought to the attention of the staff at a Jazz Social that a young man was removing some of the huge photographs by Cartier-Bresson which were on exhibition at the time with the words: 'Eh, Mister, someone's pinching your fucking snaps!'

After our marriage Victoria and I returned to Cheyne Walk. We wrote to her parents who were very angry but soon forgave us. They were pleased, when they came to see us, to discover that Andy was a descendant of Blessed Saint Adrian Fortescu, an Elizabethan Catholic Martyr. They admired English Catholic Martyrs.

In under a year our marriage was in a very bad way. It's difficult to say now whose fault it was – if indeed it was anybody's – but I was certainly as unhappy as she was, and when Simon Watson Taylor offered me a room in his flat, I accepted and moved out. Victoria was away for the week-end so I pedantically divided our wedding presents and Pete Appleby came over in the band-wagon one afternoon and, for a quid or two, helped me to move. There were a few things that wouldn't fit into the wagon in one load, and these I wheeled over later in a handcart belonging to 'orace. It wasn't too far – up Blantyre Street, across the King's Road, up Park Walk, right along the Fulham Road, up Redcliffe Gardens and into Tregunter Road. Simon, who works for BOAC, was in America the day I arrived. By the time he got back, I'd all my pictures hung, my books and clothes put away, my furniture and objects arranged.

Victoria became a model and sometime later she went to Rome on spec and stayed there, working for the fashion houses for over three years. We wrote each other chatty and friendly letters and I sent her my new records.

Although a lot of people in the jazz world knew our marriage was breaking up – for one thing Monty Sunshine's girl friend had a room in Tim's house – nobody said anything. This was always a sympathetic part of our code. In relation to personal troubles we never interfered unless the person involved wished to discuss it. Behind his back, my back in this case, there was undoubtedly a great deal of highly enjoyable speculation and gossip, but while I was actually present it was taken for granted that I would prefer to be treated as if everything was OK. In the ordinary way Mick was as punctilious as anybody in observing this civilised relic, but one evening, very drunk, circumstances forced him into such a corner that his only defence was to be as unpleasant as possible. This was by no means a unique instance but it was the most extreme.

After a pub crawl, we had finished up in a cellar club in the Fulham Road. It was called 'La Fiesta' and was run by a small ginger-haired anarchist called Gus. In its favour was an open fire, cheap food and wine. Against it, bullfighting posters, a Spanish guitarist, and cries of 'Olé' from some of the clientele. But it was open late and we often used it if we'd been drinking in Finch's and got 'the taste'.

Sitting there that night, Mick discovered that he had no cigarettes and called over the waitress, an elderly, amiable woman dressed as an Andalusian peasant. She told him they'd run out, but that there was a machine over the road, and that if he gave her a florin she'd go and get him some. Mick had no change and gave her a pound. She took it without any objection and a few minutes later came back with the cigarettes and the change. Mick, without thanking her, picked up both the change and the cigarettes and put them in his coat pocket.

Sometime later as she was passing, Mick asked her in a sarcastic voice if she had got his snout yet. She didn't hear, imagined he was thanking her for her help, smiled, and hurried past with her order. On her way back he said he hoped she'd enjoy spending the pound. She looked puzzled. I told him that she had in fact brought him both the cigarettes and the change. He gave me a look to suggest I was somehow in on the racket. For the next twenty minutes or so he subjected the poor woman to unpleasant remarks every time she came within earshot, and at last I could stand it no longer. I leant over, took the cigarettes and the change out of his pocket, and put them in front of him on the table.

He looked at them for some time, checked the change twice, and put it in his trouser pocket. Then he looked for a long time at me, his eyes swimming about like goldfish. Finally he spoke. 'How's your married life going, cock?' he asked me.

While I was still at Cheyne Walk, at the very moment I was at my most miserable, a marvellous thing happened. The Musicians' Union finally reached an exchange agreement with its American counterpart and the Louis Armstrong All-Stars came over to this country.

They played for ten nights in London on a revolving stage at the Empress Hall, Earl's Court, an absurd choice in every way, far too big and acoustically lamentable.

Furthermore, somebody at the American end, unaware that it was an interest in jazz which would make people want to go and hear Louis, and that if a whole evening's blowing was too much for the old man, there were plenty of other jazzmen, many of them far from overworked, we'd have been delighted to hear too, filled up the first half of the bill with a series of vaudeville acts including a Mr Peg-Leg Bates who danced in a surprisingly agile manner on his single artificial limb, and of course scored a great many points but was not exactly full of high jazz content.

In consequence, during the first half of every evening, the bar became a 'Who's Who' of British jazz, and the critics – whose enthusiasm for the local product had rather naturally cooled over the years – reappeared, their mutual enmity in no way impaired by the passage of time.

Among the musicians, Humph's great height emerged from the surrounding animation, while from the general hubbub, the voice of Diz Disley, a fanatical Louis enthusiast, could be heard peppering his lyrical monologue with his favourite adjective.

We were out of town for the opening and it was several evenings later before I was able to leave the dusty and empty flat, and walk up Blantyre Street in the direction of Earl's Court. It was very sunny, and even the railings of the Gents at the World's End seemed made of gold. I walked all the way to the Empress Hall repeating to myself, over and over again, 'I'm going to hear Louis Armstrong.' That extraordinary hunger in the pit of the stomach, a sensation which even the idea of jazz had been able to induce in me in the early days, came back again. Louis Armstrong, who had been brought up in New Orleans, played with Oliver, accompanied Bessie Smith.

Jazz is an impure art. There's a great deal of romantic nostalgia involved. Even the early British bop musicians who used to sneer at our sentimentality have fallen into the trap. Minton's has become their Storyville, Parker their Buddy Bolden.

After the interval the All-Stars, each to his own round of applause, climbed on to the platform and tuned up. The crackling American voice over the amplifying system requested our attention. The house lights died. A spotlight picked out the curtained entrance from which the boxers usually emerge on their way to the ring, and out stepped a small, surprisingly plump, Negro in evening dress who, accompanied by discreet chording from the distant band, advanced slowly down the gangway playing the opening chorus from 'Sleepy Time Down South'. It was the most moving sound I ever heard in my life.

Later, of course, after I'd heard Armstrong several times both in London and the provinces, it was possible to make several criticisms: a very limited repertoire, too many vocals from Velma Middleton, a singer who made up in bulk what she lacked in swing, the 'show-biz' insincerity of some of Louis' mugging, but nothing could destroy the magic of those first few phrases. How after all those years a man of his age could blow with such freshness, excitement and invention, and at the same time impose on every note his own inimitable stamp is beyond explanation. Furthermore, the fact that for at least thirty years he had had no real life, no centre, only a series of hotel rooms, planes, ships, concert halls, recording studios, and yet could evoke, night after night, a whole way of life that vanished before the end of the First World War seemed little short of miraculous – unless, as André Breton suggested, music is the most stupid of the arts.

I wasn't at the London Jazz Club the night Louis sat in with whatever band was playing, but somebody who was there stood next to Ken Colyer during the session and was naturally interested to hear what Ken, for whom Louis Armstrong was *the* enemy, the traitor who had left New Orleans and changed the course of the music, would have to say when he'd finished.

Armstrong blew his final coda, and stepped off the stage to a roar of applause and a flutter of autograph hunters. Ken turned to make his way back to the 'Blue Posts'.

'He'll do,' Colyer said laconically.

One of the band myths, relating in this case to Ian Christie, was that if at a party he asked: 'Who's that hurray cunt by the mantelpiece?' and then discovered it was a literary or artistic figure of some eminence, he would scarcely allow time to mutter 'Oh, really?' before scampering across the room to engage him in conversation. This story which Ian always emphatically denied, and which in consequence the rest of us produced at every possible occasion, may have been true or untrue, or as is most likely, a gross exaggeration of the truth, but Ian was no more a lion hunter than the rest of us. Like most people, we were all keen to meet someone we admired for one reason or another. It was just that most of the band only wanted to meet jazzmen, who were seldom if ever hurrays. We were all inclined to concentrate on approaching those who played the same instrument, or in my case, sang. This was natural enough, as not only were we most likely to admire someone who could do magnificently what we did less well, but also we had a ready-made subject for conversation. It was therefore quite understandable that Mick should have gone to some trouble to meet Louis Armstrong, the man he had most admired since his adolescence, and during Louis' London engagement, he spent a fair amount of time in his hotel suite. There he had the childish but none the less real satisfaction of answering, at Louis' request, the telephone, and recognising the excited stutter of Chris Barber, already the most successful British bandleader and well aware of it too, asking deferentially if he might speak to Mr Armstrong.

'Oh, hello, Chris,' said Mick, 'Mick Mulligan here. I'll just ask Louis. Hang on, cock.'

The rest of the band followed the pattern. Ian saw most of Edmond Hall, Frank of Trummy Young, and as for Pete, he actually moved in on Barrett Deems for a day or two, where, drummers being what they are the whole world over, I've no doubt that they enjoyed an entirely satisfactory relationship based on the technical intricacies of the drum kit and a willingness to listen to each other boasting about their percussive abilities. When Louis went on tour in the provinces, the organisers sent the rest of the bill home and employed local jazz bands. This, although by no means an ideal solution, was certainly an improvement and no doubt helped to draw in, on the grounds of local patriotism, many of the audience who might otherwise have been put off by the exorbitant, but no doubt necessary, price of seats,

Having a night off in Grimsby when Louis was playing in New-castle upon Tyne, we drove up to hear him, and went to both concerts. Between the shows, using Mick's prior acquaintanceship, Ian, Frank and I accompanied him back stage and spent a long time in Louis' dressing-room. He was kind and friendly and accepted a token whisky from the bottle we'd taken round, but I felt we weren't really there. This is by no means a criticism; travelling year in and year out all over the world and meeting hundreds of admirers daily how could it be otherwise? What was so surprising was the number of people here he *did* remember, but what was significant was that he had known them all before the war when interest in jazz was still a comparatively minority affair. Sinclair, for instance – 'my man, Sinclair' as he called him – and Nat Gonella. From his post-war visits I wonder if he remembered more than a handful of people – Humph and Chris certainly, Mick perhaps, and almost without doubt due to their continuous attendance on the band, Diz and Beryl Bryden. Beryl in fact was so devoted in her pursuit that she would be there to wave off the coach when it left London for the provinces and be waiting to welcome it when it arrived at the other end.

Louis' dressing-room manner was an extension of his stage per-sonality. He was willing to talk about the early days – 'King Oliver, he was my man' – and more than keen to impress on us, as he did on everybody, the importance of inner cleanliness, and the efficaciousness to this end of a product called 'Swiss Kriss'. It was all, however, in my view, on the surface, and it was only when he discovered that one of his entourage had neglected to book a seat on a plane for his wife, Lucille, to go to London to get her hair 'fixed', and for a moment lost his temper, that the real man showed through. Within a few seconds he had recovered himself, the 'red beans and rice' mask was back in place, and he was telling Mick, as he rubbed white ointment all over his astounding lips, pitted and cratered like a photograph of the moon, how essential it was for him, as a trumpet player, to 'look after your chops heh heh heh!' I met Louis several times over the next six years, but never tried to remind him that we'd met before.

In the years that followed most of the great American bands and a great many solo performers came over under the new arrangement. We met those of them we particularly wanted to, worked with some of them, listened to most of them. After a time, although we admired their work and envied their ability much as ever, we gradually lost that sense of awe, the feeling that the gods had come down to walk the earth. Respect replaced idolatry, and in the case of the Condon band visit in 1956, imitation resulted in temporary disaster.

The Condon band were famous for their tough, hot jazz, and equally for the amount they drank. It was, I suppose, natural that Mick should be over-excited by their visit. Not only did he admire their music but, in Eddie Condon's ability to swallow the hard stuff and yet continue to run a band over so many years, he saw the justification of his own periodic excesses.

The day these drunken, middle-aged delinquents arrived, Eddie's first official engagement was to sign copies of his famous autobiography and drinking-primer *We Called It Music* at a jazz book and record shop in Charing Cross Road. A great deal of whisky was provided by the thoughtful management. Mick, Ian and Frank were among the guests. After the official junketing, during the course of which Mr Condon signed such copies of his memoirs as was necessary with a wide selection of names including on occasion his own, the whole party moved to a nearby drinking club called 'The Cottage'.

Here the photographer from the *Melody Maker* took several shots of Mick and Eddie with their arms round each other's shoulders, a gesture which could be interpreted as affectionate respect or mutual physical support. An article in the same paper had recently crowned Mick 'King of the Ravers', and it was felt that a record of this, his first meeting with his American counterpart, was worthy of publication. Eventually Condon, Wild Bill Davison, George Wettling and company retired to their hotel, and Mick, Frank and Ian, far too late to arrive in time, set out for Barnet where the band had an evening engagement.

I forget now why I hadn't been at the afternoon's séance; perhaps I hadn't been asked, but I was in consequence completely sober. This meant I had the difficult and indeed hopeless job of attempting to divert the promoter's attention from how late it was getting before they arrived, and the painful recognition, acquired from a single glance at Mick's swimming eyeballs, Frank's manic grin, and Ian's puppet-like animation, that it was going to be a bumpy evening.

Barnet Jazz Club, which held its weekly meetings in a Trade Union hut, was typical of the suburban and dormitory town clubs which had begun to open within a thirty-mile radius of the Charing Cross Road, in order to cater for the growing interest in traditional jazz, which the success of the Chris Barber band had sparked off. What usually happened was that a promoter would examine a map, settle for an area as yet virgin territory, and open two or three clubs with common membership on different nights of the week about ten miles apart. During the height of the trad boom in 1960–61 these clubs sprang up and proliferated like weeds on a bomb site, but Barnet, and its sister club in St Albans, were in advance of the trend. They were founded by Ken Lindsay, an old-time jazz enthusiast from the Asman–George Webb era.

It was the Alex Welsh band who christened these new-style clubs 'The Milk Round'. Although they didn't pay very well they provided regular work during the early part of the week. The official definition of 'The Milk Round' was, that to qualify, a club had to be near enough for the band to get back in time for a drink at The Cottage which closed at midnight.

The difference between these clubs and the older places like Cook's Ferry and Wood Green, was that the audience were not jazz fans who liked a drink and a little live jazz. They were much younger, knew nothing about the history of jazz, wanted 'the trad sound' as a background to jiving and that was all.

The Mulligan band was not very popular on this circuit. It had no banjo for a start, and was inclined to stretch its intervals. Its appearance on the stand that evening, three quarters of an hour late and with the whole front line obviously extremely drunk, was calculated to displease the new puritans who had paid to come in. Their irritation mounted when Ian fell asleep on a chair during a trombone solo, nor were they in any way placated when Mick launched into a long apology, almost incomprehensible even to me, who at least knew what he was on about, but pure gibberish to the audience who had certainly never heard of Eddie Condon, the main justification of his argument. There were a great many complaints, several demands for money back and, despite Ken Lindsay's affection for Mick, it was some time before we worked for him again.

There were several equal disasters during the Condon Band's British stay. Quite often the conductor didn't appear at all, and in some ways this was better as we could tell the promoter that we knew he'd been complaining of imminent 'flu, but more often he *did* appear, late and drunk, with no greater excuse than a favourite sentence of his in these circumstances:

'There comes a time when you say "fuck it".'

A lunch-time drink with Wild Bill Davison, Condon's trumpet player, was where the eggs of these dreadful evenings were laid, and the Cottage Club the incubator in which they were hatched. The Cottage had taken over from The Mandrake as the trad-world club. It justified its name by a thatched roof over the bar, a false window on one of the walls, through which a naïve but sentimental picture of a country lane failed to achieve the intended *trompe l'oeil*, and a large number of horse brasses. The afternoon clientele was made up of those jazzmen who had got 'the taste', in Mick's phrase, in a lunch-time pub, and a small but regular coterie of elderly music-hall artistes who appeared to be permanently 'resting', but at night it was entirely taken over by trad-jazz musicians, and to burst in there just before midnight after a milk-round job was to discover our whole world crammed into one room.

In the basement, for the main bar was on street level, there was a piano available for rehearsal during the day, much to the rage of the music hall clique, and for impromptu sessions at night. The manager we called 'Cottage Al', and there were, among the regulars, several of those kind, plump, promiscuous girls who occupy an underrated and therapeutic position in this frequently lonely and often desperate life.

During the visit of the Condon Band, 'The Cottage' really came into its own as a falling-about centre. Professionally, however, the tour was not a success. Like Mick, Eddie was inclined to launch into the stream of consciousness in front of an audience, a large proportion of which would have preferred to hear more music. I only saw them perform once, a late-night concert at the Festival Hall. The organiser had conceived the idea of arranging a series of tables round the edge of the platform to produce an intimate club atmosphere. I was amused to see the conductor as one of the extras. Although I was sitting in the circle, I could tell without any bother at all that he was in the same condition as the band.

Finally the Condon mob, to the grief of 'Cottage Al', returned to the States, and Mick to comparative sobriety. Wild Bill and Condon from their end and Mick from his took to ringing each other up in the small hours when the mood took them, an operation complicated by the difference in time between the two continents. The telephone has always proved a temptation to Mick in his cups. He once took a great liking to the bandleader Joe Loss, when we played a dance with him at Leeds University. After it was over, and we'd travelled back to London in the band-wagon, I went up to Mick's flat to finish off a bottle of whisky. He was going on about what a 'good nut' Joe Loss was, and it was all I could do to prevent him ringing him up for a chat there and then at five fifteen in the morning.

The Kansas City Blues singer Jimmy Rushing became my own particular mate among the regular visitors. Jimmy, the original 'Mr Five by Five', had influenced my style for some time before he actually came over to sing with Humph, and I very much wanted to meet him. When I did we became immediate friends. He was, as the song says, 'five foot high and five feet wide', but Jimmy's bulk, and its attendant problems – getting in and out of cars for example – appeared irrelevant except to give his movements a deliberation, an almost balletic adjustment of weight in relation to gravity, which suggested his inner calm. His slow smile, the controlled lyricism of his singing, his anecdotal ability, every story built like a blues with repeated lines, are all more evocative of Jimmy Rushing than his twenty stone.

Jimmy doesn't drink much, but he loves parties, and it was a pleasure to watch him sitting there taking in, with sardonic yet kindly amusement, the mounting absurdity washing up against him like the sea against a rock. At one party I gave for him at Tregunter Road I'd asked all the band except for Frank Parr, not out of nastiness but because Simon, who was in town, had just bought a new carpet, and it is Frank's habit when drunk to stub out his cigarettes under foot. In the end, of course, I relented, but warned him about the new carpet. Inevitably he forgot and Simon threw him out. Half an hour later he was back to apologise. Simon declared himself bored and indifferent to what he had to say, but was on the point of giving in when Frank, in the very middle of his tearful repentance, took the cigarette out of his mouth and ground it into the carpet with his heel. I shall never forget the expression of mock pain which spread over the face of Jimmy Rushing at that moment.

Jimmy saw me perform on several occasions and was very complimentary, not about my voice, but about my showmanship. This was reassuring. The general feeling in the band was that my poncing about had become a bit much. Ian Christie, for example, while acknowledging that whatever popularity we retained with the public was due to me, resented the way this allowed Mick to pay the minimum attention to the musical side.

'It's not very bringing up,' said Ian, 'for a musician to feel he only gets work because you can imitate a monkey.'

He was referring in particular to my practice on 'Organ Grinder' of swinging about the stage, scratching myself and examining the conductor for fleas during the band chori, but his criticism was intended generally, and I did to some extent share it.

Jimmy wouldn't have any of it. 'We're entertainers,' he insisted, and told me by way of practical emphasis about a producer of 'them big Harlem shows I was in during the thirties'. It was this gentleman's custom to line up the chorus, 'Them beautiful high yellow girls', at the front of the stage on the first day of rehearsal and tell them: 'I don't care if you've been fucking all night, when the show starts, I want you to get out there and *show them teeth*.'

Jimmy had one small and rather endearing vanity. He liked to hear his own records. His way of achieving this, for most people imagine that the last thing an artist wants is to hear himself, was to ask if you had such and such a record of his because 'the arrangement is so pretty and I haven't heard it for some time'.

I was always sad to see him go, and sometimes went to Waterloo Station to wave good-bye when he caught the train to Southampton, for he refused to fly anywhere. He would walk a little down the platform and then swing round on one foot to wave, holding his grey trilby in place with his other hand, his brilliant red shirt catching the light. I would always remember his adaptation of the traditional way the old itinerant blues singers finished their songs:

'If anybody asked you who done sung this song,
Just tell 'em little Jimmy Rushing done been here and gone.'

The practice of using a British group on the same bill as a visiting American band became, after the Armstrong All-Stars' provincial tour, pretty widespread. In the case of solo artists the accompanying group was selected if possible because they played in the same idiom. Jimmy Rushing naturally sang with Humph whose brand of mainstream was approximately the same vintage as pre-war Basie with whom Jimmy had made his name. The New Orleans veterans on the other hand usually played with Ken Colyer.

Chris Barber carried this a stage farther by actually importing, for admirably altruistic reasons, as his own band at that time could fill the largest concert halls in the country, a series of old and forgotten blues singers.

Some of these have since achieved international stature through the present boom in rhythm and blues; others, kindly old gentlemen who had been working in obscurity since the early twenties and beyond, enjoyed their temporary share of the limelight and retired again into the shadows. I am thinking in particular of 'Speckled Red', an elderly piano player and blues singer of great charm who was so delighted with his reception here that he contemplated staying and opening a school of ragtime.

He was an Albino Negro with just a few spots of pigmentation, hence his name. He was also very short-sighted and between numbers would remove a list from his breast pocket, peer at it closely and, having reached a decision, announce with great courtesy: 'My next selection is a song called "You Got the Right String But You're Playing with the Wrong Yo-Yo". I thank you for your attention.'

He dressed like a Southern Colonel in a rye whisky ad, and his life, which had been hard, had failed to embitter his patiently sweet character.

The Mulligan band, never an automatic choice to accompany American visitors, did occasionally get in on the act. This only happened when the bigger names weren't available, but was none the less rewarding for that.

We did one tour with Big Bill Broonzy and a younger Gospel singer called Brother John Sellers. Apart from the pleasure of hearing and being with Bill for a week, there was the additional if less kindly interest of watching the interplay of two entirely dissimilar characters.

Brother John obviously considered Bill as something of a has-been. He was furious when Max Jones, reviewing their first London concert together, made it clear that he found Broonzy the finer artist. Not that Max was particularly strong in what he had to say; he simply suggested that, although Brother John could swing adequately enough, for those who preferred a more authentic blues style, Broonzy was of greater interest. This however was quite sufficient to infuriate Sellers. He slammed down the *Melody Maker* and hissed through his teeth: 'Why! That lil' bol' head man!'

His habit of shaving with depilatory wax, a painful and lengthy process, was another facet of his behaviour which Bill found endlessly amusing, and he would mime the operation with surprising accuracy for a man so different in build and temperament. It's true that superficially Broonzy appeared a far more naïve character, almost illiterate and, due to his age and background, a walking compendium of stock 'Uncle Tom' mannerisms, even going so far as scratching his head forward from the back, but it was all on the surface. As Mick said so often. 'There's a lot going on in that old nut.'

When Bill died we were sent some rather harrowing photographs of his funeral. Brother John officiated in religious drag, and Broonzy lay in the open casket – the excuse for what was clearly a big emotional deal.

We could imagine what he would have said.

The other major tour we did was with Sister Rosetta Tharp, another Gospel singer. I was rather nervous about this. I admired her as an artist, but had always understood that the Gospel singers, although full of jazz feeling, were an ostentatiously pious lot. The blues singers certainly did nothing to dispel this idea. Broonzy was once booked to appear at the Albert Hall on the same bill as the magnificent Mahalia Jackson, and was terribly worried about what the Baptists would have to say about it when he got back to the States.

'They think the blues is sinful music,' he told us.

He was also inclined to believe it himself. His criticism of Ray Charles – 'He's singing the blues sanctified, and that ain't right' (a reference to the obvious gospel-influence on Charles's style) – showed that he accepted the moral superiority of the hot gospeller.

I wasn't, of course, over-concerned about the Baptists back in the Stares, but I thought we might be in for a tiresome and God-bothering ten days.

In fact it was a rave. It's true that Sister Rosetta, who could, as we discovered at a private session, belt out a marvellous blues, would never do so in public, but that was about her only strict rule. One of her numbers was called 'God don't like it', and the words were aimed at most pleasurable human activities. It became clear to us within the first two days that if she believed in what she was singing, she must realise that she was causing the Almighty almost non-stop displeasure, but that there was no sign it bothered her at all.

On stage her performance was splendid, although we all found her introductions a bit strong. The sentimental piety of these was, however, in part relieved by the outrageous way she managed to plug her recordings in the same breath as the love of Jesus. When she actually started singing though, her formidable bottom swinging like a metronome in time to her wailing voice and emphatic guitar, it was pure delight. She wore on stage a series of brilliant dresses with plunging necklines, and a great deal of chunky jewellery.

She asked me whether I approved of these and I told her yes, emphatically. They reflected the larger-than-life theatricality of her personality to perfection. She seemed pleased.

'Lots of people has criticised me because I don't wear robes like Mahalia do!' she explained. 'Well what I says is robes suits Mahalia and they don't suit me. The Lord is beautiful, and I dress pretty to praise the Lord.'

The only member of the band who couldn't take Sister was Miff Bell. This dated from our very first concert with her. During the course of one number she decided to play a few chori at the piano, and not only failed to signal her intention, but simply backed towards the instrument still singing and smiling at the audience with her usual manic expression of piety, but having made contact with the piano stool, she gave a kind of controlled twitch with her monumental backside and shot Miff into the outer darkness. She did the same every night.

'The old black coo!' Miff used to mutter with rage, as she sat hammering the keyboard.

The day she left England, Mick and I went round to say good-bye to her at her hotel off the Edgware Road. She flung her arms round us and tried hard, although obviously feeling no pain at all, to make herself weep.

13

An Increasingly Dull Noise

Several years before Ian Christie joined the band, Mick and I bumped into him one Monday evening in a pub in South Kensington called 'The Hoop and Toy'. We drank together until closing time and enjoyed each other's company very much. As we swayed about on the pavement outside before going our separate ways, Mick, with the serious optimism of the convivial drunk, suggested that we made it a regular Monday date.

Needless to say neither Ian, Mick nor I ever looked in at The Hoop and Toy again, not even the following Monday, and when Ian finally joined the band we often referred to the incident; if we had a job on a Monday, Mick would apologise to Ian for having to forego the pleasure of our weekly reunion. The satisfactory element in this simple joke was that it somehow exemplified a general truth. It was rare, once the days of semi-pro enthusiasm were over, for a musician to form a proper friendship outside the confines of his own band. We all knew each other, but it was very much on the 'Hello, man. How's it going?' level. The reason for this was that, being on the road most of the time, it was difficult to meet except on a casual or accidental basis. It was almost like being a member of a ship's company. It was therefore with some surprise that, answering the telephone quite early one morning shortly after I had moved to Tregunter Road, I discovered it was Wally Fawkes.

I'd known Wally for a long time, but very much on the Hoop and Toy level, first as a hero of my early Humph club days, later as someone I was always happy to see at a party or in a pub. Several years before I'd done a gig for him, a twenty-first birthday in the Home Counties where I'd nearly had a fight with the burly bearded academician, Ruskin Spear, who was attacking Max Ernst, and whose own paintings I described in my rage at this blasphemy, as

'Sickert's wet dreams'. What I remembered best about that evening was the presence, for want of a revivalist, of a bomb-dropping bop drummer called Dave Smallman whose only vocal contribution was the phrase 'Crazy shit, man!'

I'd also been round to Wally's place a couple of times, but none of this was enough to suggest that his telephone call that Thursday morning in 1956 was purely social. In fact what he wanted to ask me was, would I be interested in writing the dialogue for 'Flook' in the *Daily Mail*, and if so could I come round and discuss it in the office that afternoon. I said yes to both questions, put the phone down, picked it up again and rang up my father in Liverpool because he was a great Flook fan and I knew he'd be knocked out.

At the *Mail* that afternoon I wished I'd waited a bit before telling him. The art editor, Julian Phipps, warned me I mightn't make the grade, or that if I did, it might be necessary to use me as one of a team. However, with a lot of initial help from Wal, I managed to coast over the first few weeks and, almost a decide later, was still writing 'Flook' under his critical but entirely constructive surveillance.

In retrospect that telephone call entirely changed the direction of my life, and yet, if I'd been on tour or even out shopping, Wally would have had to ring up somebody else. The stock-pile was only three days ahead of the paper instead of the statutory three weeks, and Humph, who was scriptwriter at that time, was out on the road. Wally had recently left the Lyttelton band whose increasing professional commitments had led to this decision, and Humph was, in his fashion, returning the compliment. That morning Wal and Julian, faced with the strip grinding to a halt, had reached the conclusion that a new scriptwriter had to be found at once. I found out later it was Jim Godbolt who had suggested me.

The immediate effect of writing Flook was financial – even at the comparatively modest salary of my trial period it more than doubled my income – but it also had a disastrous effect on my ego. Here the deflationary tradition of the Mulligan band came in useful. On the first tour following my change of fortune Mick, irritated by my pseudo-casual proffering of the *Daily Mail* every morning, and my anxious hovering about until I was sure that he had read my contribution, remarked quietly but acidly that it was very good of me to let Wally draw my strip. This was the opening shot in the campaign to cut me down to size, but it was only a beginning. The band never let anything go if they could avoid it. An early and shame-making attempt to hammer out some script in the Cottage Club one quiet afternoon was frequently resurrected. My newspaper order to night porters in hotels, my pre-breakfast expeditions to newsagents when in digs, seldom passed without comment, and none of this did me any harm at all, but I was not going to be laughed out of actually getting my script written. I brought my typewriter (it became known as the 'Flook machine') away with me on tour, and if at dances there was a suitable room near the bandstand I would sit and work between songs. 'Office satisfactory?' the conductor would inquire with sardonic politeness as he passed on his way to play the opening number.

Inside the band the Flook money altered my life very little. I was able to buy more whisky and ate better on the road, and I took to travelling up to the first job of a tour by rail, but that was about all. Mick usually came with me on the train. It meant we could leave London much later than the wagon, and of course it was also more comfortable. Only Frank Parr, to whom the wagon was a holy place, seemed to resent our defection to British Railways. With typical verbal ingenuity he took to calling us the BTCs, initials standing for both British Transport Commission and Big Time Cunts.

It was in London that my life changed and I very quickly found the way to jack up my standard of living a little above my new-won prosperity. There were drinking sessions with Wally and a circle of Fleet Street acquaintances in El Vino's after our weekly conference at the *Mail*. A girl-friend of sophisticated appetites told me she saw no reason, with what I was earning, to continue eating in cheap cafés, and made me take her to Wheelers, the Ivy, and the new and expensive little restaurants that were beginning to spring up round the King's Road, a habit which, even after our affair was over, I saw no reason to drop. I began to go to the theatre too. *Look Back in Anger* coincided with my apprenticeship to Flook, and from then on I saw almost every production at the Court and The Arts. It was Ian Christie who first persuaded me to go. 'It's a play about the chaps,' he told me enthusiastically. I began to buy pictures again, and less constructively was for a short but disastrous period involved in the private chemmy parties which were held each night in a different studio or flat somewhere in SW1 or 3. On the credit side all this experience came in useful in keeping the strip topical – 'Flook meat' was Wally's phrase for it – but then so did my other life with the band.

From 1955 until the band folded at the end of 1961, there was very little change professionally. The music remained static and so for the most part did the personnel. We played fewer concerts and more jazz clubs. We covered and re-covered the roads of Britain from Wick, a few miles south of John o' Groats, to Redruth, a similar distance from Land's End.

Except for the occasional evening when one or more of us was too drunk, we usually gave satisfaction. It was an increasingly dull noise we made but comparatively professional, and during the last twenty minutes or so we pulled out all the stops and for the most part succeeded in stirring up the audience to some effect. This last burst had become, like everything else to do with the music, completely predictable. It was known as 'the show', and during the second half Mick would keep us informed with increasing satisfaction of how long there was to go before it was time for it. 'Bracket of waltzes, bracket of slows, and then the show,' he would mutter out of the corner of his mouth after an elaborately sly glance at his watch.

The show consisted of three numbers. First Pete's drum solo which was set into the framework of 'Didn't He Ramble', an old New Orleans funeral march. During the opening bars, which were at a very slow tempo, I used to walk on carrying a trombone case as though it were a coffin, a piece of 'business' originally conceived in high spirits which had become a fixture. Then, after two vocal and two instrumental chori, I would pick up the 'coffin' again and march slowly off stage followed by all the band except Pete. At the last moment the front line would turn and blow three introductory chords before diving into the wings to light up, and Pete would then hammer away for a variable but always satisfactory length of time. At the beginning it had been necessary for Mick to listen throughout as the brief prearranged patterns of thumps and crashes which told him it was time to lead the band back on for the final chords was dependent on Pete's whim. Later Pete incorporated a quiet passage, in imitation of Cozy Cole, to provide a contrast to his atomic finale, and this helped considerably. 'It's all right,' Mick would say, puffing away in the darkness, 'he hasn't reached the quiet bit yet. Inspiration has descended, thank Christ.'

At concerts in theatres I had an additional job during 'Didn't He Ramble'. After walking off stage with my coffin, I had to climb hurriedly up the wall ladder to the electrician's platform and signal to him the exact beat on which to extinguish all the lights except for a spot on Pete. I used to enjoy this, but then I enjoyed everything to do with concerts.

After 'Didn't He Ramble' it was time for 'Frankie and Johnny', or 'Harry Fallers' as Mick called it with reference to my trick of falling down at the point when Frankie shoots Johnny. I had learned to do this with some expertise, and if the mood took me would hurl myself off quite a high bandstand. Although this looked rather dangerous, the only real hazard was that I was less adept at climbing back on to the stage, and if there were no convenient steps, I was sometimes reduced to running round through the pass-door and coming in half a chorus later.

If I chanced to land on the dance floor in such a position that it seemed possible to look up a girl's skirt, Mick would raise an inquiring eyebrow requiring either a thumbs up or down. We all have our obsessions, and Mick's was what he called 'a flash', a view of thigh and knicker. In the early days the wide skirts and top-like style of jiving were very productive of flashes, but during the trad boom female jeans became *de rigueur* and a heavy elephantine jumping from foot to foot swept the jazz clubs. Flashes became very rare, and the conductor correspondingly desperate like a drug addict cut off from his supply. Due to his short sight, it was possible to tease him by pretending to see entirely imaginary flashes in the middle-distance. If we kept this up long enough he would finally ask Ian to lend him his glasses. That Mick was a genuine flash addict was reinforced by the fact that he didn't care what the girl looked like.

After 'Frankie and Johnny' we finished off the show with a boring old tear-arse rabble rouser called 'Momma Don't Allow' in which vocal chori forbidding, on Momma's behalf, every instrument in turn alternated with solo chori from the instrument in question.

At the end of 'Momma Don't Allow' it was Mick's custom in dance halls to play an abbreviated version of 'The Queen', less to prove his conformism – although naturally most dance-hall managers insisted on the convention – more to convince the audience it was all over. Sometimes when in his Condonesque mood, the conductor would announce the anthem as 'Corky's Tune'. Corky was our name for the Queen. It dated back to my naval days. A friend of mine, a staunch republican, had always referred to the reigning Monarch as 'Korky the King'. He had chosen this name in imitation of 'Corky the Cat', an animal who appeared in a strip cartoon on the front of the *Dandy*. Early in the band's history I had told Mick about the King being called Korky, and the name had stuck. When the Queen succeeded she also inherited this derisive pseudonym, but we dropped the 'K' in favour of a 'C' because alliteration no longer applied.

One Christmas the *New Statesman* published a satire on the *Radio Times* Christmas Day programme page. At three p.m. I was surprised to see 'Corky and her German Band', and at midnight 'Corky's Tune'. A footnote explained that 'Corky' was 'Jazz slang for HM', a rather wide attribution as, despite some general favour, the name was more or less confined to the Mulligan band. How the *Statesman* discovered about 'Corky' I never found out, unless Simon Watson Taylor had told John Raymond, then literary editor, in Finch's in the Fulham Road.

When I was in the Navy I found it strange and marvellous that whatever lay outside the portholes – foggy British dockyard, Norwegian fiord under a midnight sun, the Cap d'Azur at night – everything on the ship stayed exactly the same. In the Mulligan band the Volkswagen worked in the same way. Inside it we became a hydra. We worked on 'the myth'. We recreated the past and earmarked the present for future use.

The wagon itself contributed a great deal. To close the double door required calm and expertise in turning the handle. Otherwise one of the two rods which moved upwards to engage the inner rim of the frame failed to connect. Miff Bell had a tendency to lose his temper if anything mechanical didn't work immediately, and it was he who most often fell foul of the doors. Cursing and swearing he would bang them open and shut, yanking the handle up and down, and eventually, led by Frank Parr, the most observant and priest-like of all the wagon *habitués*, a slow chant of 'normal doors' would begin, adding if anything to Miff's manic hysteria.

The interior of the wagon was of tin, and the heating only worked in the front. It had its own smell, difficult to define, but based on old newspaper and dog-ends. Frank's love of disorder and my neurotic neatness clashed spasmodically over the inside of the wagon. Driven mad by the knee-deep accumulation of rubbish, I would gather up armfuls of old Sunday papers, sandwich crusts, empty quart-bottles, dog-ends and cigarette packets and ram them into dustbins at the back of pubs or dance halls. I even bought a little dustpan and brush and several ashtrays with rubber suckers. When I'd got the wagon basically tidy, I would fold the blankets and 'Mummy's' fur coat along the back seat and stack the paperbacks in one corner. I even, although this was not a popular move, sprayed the interior with a scented atomiser. The rest of the band, although uncooperative, were amused and indifferent to my efforts, but Frank would eye them with aggressive distaste. Not only did he refuse to use the ashtrays; he worked on the suckers until they refused to grip, so that the ashtrays fell to the floor and were eventually lost.

The band instruments were for the most part tied on the roof rack. On a long journey an end of the rope inevitably worked loose and began to beat a syncopated, curiously regular, rhythm on the tin roof. This was known as 'the spade bongo player'. He became one of the phantoms who attended us at all times. Other demons lay dormant in the wagon itself. 'Maggie May', a Liverpool prostitute of violent erotic appetite and a gift for lyrical obscenity, occasionally possessed me. Miff Bell was an admirer of 'Maggie May'. He himself had been known to receive a 'Message for the Day' from God. God was sparing with His messages however, although He was seldom ignored for long on our side. During violent storms Ian Christie spent a great deal of time banging on the tin roof and demanding to be struck dead. On the other hand, faced with an exceptionally beautiful view or even a striking effect of light, we would, after due consultation, give God a polite round of applause. He was not unique, however. Pretty girls passing in front of the wagon at traffic lights or, in later days, zebra crossings, received the same accolade, and would blush, glare, or smile according to their nature.

Although Ian was the first to join in if God was in question, his hatred of cliché made him rather impatient at certain repetitive aspects of the myth. The ceremony of chanting the Jewish shop names while driving through Whitechapel – 'Jacobs, Cohen, Isaacs, Cohen, Fishberg, etc.' – used to provoke an exasperated groan of 'how fucking boring', and the same was true of our passage through the first Welsh town after crossing the border – 'Evans, Jones, Jones, Davis, Evans, Morgan, etc.'.

He also attempted to impose a personal censorship on stories or anecdotes which he felt had been repeated too often or too recently. 'Forbidden,' he would cry, and this gained him the nickname 'the Pope of the forbidden' although it did nothing to check our love of reiteration.

Ian was only referred to as 'The Pope' while actually in the act of forbidding, but his usual nickname, 'Bird', also evolved in the wagon. It had nothing to do with the late Charlie Parker, an artist whom at that time he rejected. It arose during a session of one of those games where you invent animals or birds which seem to fit the personality of different people. We were playing round the band and when it came to Ian somebody said he was definitely a bird, and added as a more exact description: 'A four-eyed Short-arse, which makes its nest in old *New Statesman*s and flies through the air crying: "It's the system".' This produced general laughter, although Ian's own response had the staccato machine-gun corps quality with which he acknowledged jokes at his own expense, but typically it was the name 'Bird' which stuck.

Linguistic selection in the band always seemed to work on a haphazard basis. At the same session I was described as a toad, and for a time too this looked like replacing 'Fat' as my nickname, but it didn't. Ian on the other hand was always called 'Bird', despite the conductor's attempt to change it to 'The Shrike' in acknowledgement of the thorny impaling of Ian's verbal attacks.

14

A Bit of Fun

Jobs and towns melted into each other. There was no way of placing events chronologically and the regularity of certain gigs helped to destroy our sense of time. The annual engineers' ball at Leeds University with its obligatory dinner jackets and acres of chiffon and goose-flesh; the monthly appearance at 'The Bodega', Manchester, on Saturday night followed on Sunday by 'The Cavern', Liverpool; the eternal suburban 'milk round' at the beginning of each week; an event had to appear pretty weird to secure a place in our corporate memory for more than a day or two. Furthermore, even when an incident earned its niche in the myth, it became increasingly hard to place it. Sometimes there was a clue. One night, for example, a young girl and her brother at Leicester Jazz Club asked us back to a party, but failed to prepare us for the adult set-up. Their mother, a hard and desperate woman of a ravaged beauty, sat by the fire talking to her lover who leant against the mantelshelf. He was a swarthy man of extraordinary good looks but so short that their faces were almost on a level. Meanwhile their father, a doctor it would seem, roamed from room to room knocking back glass after glass of neat gin and roaring with laughter. When he appeared dressed in a white coat and brandishing a hypodermic syringe, Mick and I decided the time had come to go to bed and lock our doors – a precaution which proved justifiable as throughout the night he rattled the handles at regular intervals, muttering and chuckling. We would, of course, have remembered that night, but almost certainly forgotten when it happened. What enables me to date it within a month was that we had with us a boy called Johnnie, a regular at Cook's Ferry who happened to be in Leicester that night on business, had seen our name on a poster, come to the jazz club and rowed himself in on the party. When we entered the house, which was furnished in a style of opulent vulgarity based on Knole sofas and huge Chinese vases turned into lamp standards, he remarked that it was all very *Room at the Top*. I didn't know what he meant, and he explained that it was a new book about the rich in the north. As this was first published in March 1957, made a great stir, and would certainly have been brought to our attention by the Press within a day or two of the party at most, it's possible to say that we were threatened by the mad doctor in March 1957, but such clues are rare.

Of all the provincial cities we visited regularly it was Manchester which continued to supply forbidden stories on a lavish scale. It was here for example that Ian and Mick discovered the Caterers' Club, and full of enthusiasm took me there one grey afternoon after the pubs shut. It was a small room with a bar, originally a shop but with the window boarded up. It was lit by naked bulbs, the floor was bare boards, and on the wall was a hand-made poster which said 'Try our cocktail, 1s. 6d.' The object of the club, according to the yellowing rules, was recreational and social, and designed to appeal to people in the small hotel and boarding-house business. In fact, the clientele were low-grade villains of a Dickensian aspect and the oldest whores in the world. We spent several happy hours listening to one of these: a toothless but cheerful lady called Margaret. She thought we were 'college students' and was proud to introduce us as such to her sisters in vice although we discovered that students, while respectable enough, occupied a comparatively humble position in her scale of social values.

'I've been with all sorts,' she told us. 'When I've got me teeth in and me make-up on like, well, you could take me anywhere. I've been to posh restaurants and clubs, with, well, you know – business people.'

Every time another old bag came in, Margaret greeted her warmly, but as soon as she was out of earshot told us, grinning and waving every time she saw her acquaintance looking in our direction, that she didn't keep herself clean and went with 'the lowest of the low for a dollar'. Margaret herself, she told us, only went with respectable people, sea captains and the like. She liked the club because they didn't let the blacks in. Now the Paramount Club, she told us, she wouldn't go there any more. They let them in there. Not long before she *had* gone in for a drink with a Polish seaman and he'd brought out a great wad of notes to pay. Well, that was foolish of him she agreed. Then he'd gone into the gents and not come out. Well, after a bit she'd asked the owner if he'd been in his gents lately. No, he'd said, why? Had she?

'Cheeky monkey,' said Margaret and went on with her story. She'd explained to the owner that her 'friend' had gone into the gents twenty minutes before and not come out. He'd gone to look and found him lying face down on the floor.

' 'Is wad of notes 'ad gone, of course,' said Margaret, and was about to drink when a new thought occurred to her.

' 'E were dead,' she added in a thrilling if unconvincing whisper.

Towards the end of the afternoon we were joined by a friend of Margaret's, an enormous man of formidable griminess wearing a neck scarf. Whether to take the piss out of us, or because he thought it genuinely funny, he pretended to be a homosexual. His imitation was of music-hall origin and consisted for the most part of wetting an extremely dirty finger every few seconds and applying it to his eyebrows while holding an imaginary mirror with his other hand.

He was obsessed with the meanness of the woman who lived in the room above him and to whom he had frequently lent 'cupfuls of shugger' and other household essentials, and to whom that morning he had applied for a 'bit of bacon fat'. What was extraordinary was the way he said 'bacon fat'. You could almost see a dirty frying pan with the fat in it. It was almost hallucinatory. Furthermore, he managed to introduce the phrase a surprising number of times into his recital.

'I said: "Luke, all I'm asking for is a bit o' bacon fat." She said: "I've got no bacon fat." Well, I could see 'er frying-pan on't gas cukor full o' bacon fat. I said: "What's that in't pan? 'Appen it's bacon fat." She said: "Aye, but that's all t' bacon fat I've got so fook off." I said, "I will an all and you can stuff yer bacon fat . . .".'

Round the corner from the Caterers' Club was an Indian restaurant where Mick and I often went for a meal. One evening, prior to our appearance at The Bodega, we were just finishing enormous platefuls of fried rice, Madras curry, chicken biriani, chutney, lime pickle and chapatis, when a Mancunian funeral party came in and occupied a large reserved table in the middle of the room. There was a nice old mum, obviously distressed by the loss of her husband, a burly middle-aged son and his wife who had a mouth like a contracted sphincter muscle, an unsympathetic daughter and her hen-pecked husband, a porcine grandson. They were served soup and halfway through a family row broke out. It began when the daughter-in-law asked the daughter to tell her husband to hold his knife properly. Within a moment there was a full-scale shout-up. Cries of: 'You always thought you were too good for him. Well you're nothing,' and 'Why don't you say something? After all you're meant to be my husband,' were audible among the general confusion. At intervals the poor old mother tried to calm everybody down by pointing out that 'Dad's still warm in 'is grave', but nobody took any notice. There were too many old scores to settle, too many slights and insults to rake over. Finally both couples and the grandson rose and left at the same time, neither willing to acknowledge that it wasn't they who'd been insulted, and a minute or two later an Indian waiter came in, cleared away the soup plates and replaced them with enormous helpings of steak and chips. The old lady asked for the manager who turned out to be Irish and refused to refund the price of the steaks although he declared himself willing to let her off the peaches and custard which were to follow. She sat for a moment and then came over to our table.

'Would you fancy a couple of steaks each?' she asked us sadly. 'They're all paid for and it's a shame to let them go to waste.' After our huge meal, we were forced to refuse although, as Mick said, 'I'd have noshed the lot if I could have done, the poor old cow.' She quite understood, ate her own steak, paid and left.

Neither of these stories can be dated with any certainty. All I know is that they happened sometime between 1954 when the second band formed and 1958 because after that we left the rather squalid digs we had patronised in that area since we first played for Paddy and began to stay in an hotel the other end of town, an institution not noticeably more luxurious, but with several compensating features. We called it 'El Sordid's'.

It was quite a large hotel in an area on its way down. It had a reception desk, a dining-room with separate tables and a lounge with a television set. The proprietor was an elderly sad-faced man with the look of a Lancashire music-hall comedian. In homage to the US airmen who were his main clientele, he wore a shirt outside his baggy grey trousers. On it was a sunset going down behind some palm trees.

You were allowed to lumber back a scrubber, but you were charged for it. If you were alone the bill was a pound for bed and breakfast. If you were with a girl it was twenty-five shillings each, in effect a twenty-five per cent sin charge. There was, furthermore, no truck with the usual polite fiction of Mr and Mrs. Your bill was made out for 'one couple: B & B . . . £2 10s.'

In Liverpool I stayed at home, but the band used a shabby lodging house on Mount Pleasant. It was run by a family of Liverpudlian Chinese and was later shut down after police observation. I went back there one night after The Cavern for a drink with Mick, and found an excited family row in progress. Two Chinese men were carrying out a radiogram they claimed belonged to them. Several fights broke out in the hall with some risk to a number of toddlers who were wandering about between the legs of the various factions, eating crisps. A woman kept yelling: 'You've got a lovely wife and kiddies in a flat in Birken'ead and you live over 'ere wid a prostitute!', but the remark which knocked us out was when one of the Chinese men shouted at another in a strong Scouse accent, 'Der trouble wid youse is you're yeller!'

The Cavern, where we played on Sunday nights, has become world famous as the womb of the Liverpool sound, but in those days it was staunchly trad although just as packed and steamy. The audience sat in front of the small stage on about twenty rows of seats or jived at the back and sides of the long low cellar under the sweating brick arches. When we came back from the pub after the interval we could see clouds of steam billowing out from the door at the top of the steep stone steps which led down to the Cavern. It looked as if it must be on fire.

The girls in the audience had that dreamy, rather sad, slightly scruffy look that Liverpool girls have. They were a decided contrast to the Manchester girls of the previous night, who were much smarter, more brisk and matter-of-fact, and tended to have good if stereotyped legs and, less sympathetically, a special mouth with thin lips curving tautly down at the edges. I called this 'the Manchester mouth' and it was surprising how often it reoccurred.

My father used to come to The Cavern after dinner with my Uncle Alan. He was usually a little high after his evening session in The Albert, and used to flirt mildly with the girls in the band-room. He called them 'the band mice'. 'Mouse' as an expression for a girl had been widespread in the mid-fifties. Bruce Turner had been responsible for its popularity. 'Must have that mouse, Dad,' he used to say, but later it had given way to the word 'chick' which, in its turn, had been superseded by the still prevalent 'bird'. My father however remained faithful to 'mouse' until his death. He was very popular with the Liverpool mice because he was affectionate without being at all lecherous. A few weeks after he died we played Liverpool and a girl to whom he had always been warm and friendly asked me where he was. I told her, and her eyes filled with tears. Very sadly she said she could hardly believe it.

'Last time you were here,' she said quietly, 'it was raining, and I come in all wet, and he said me tits was smaller and must have got shrunk in the rain. I'm very sorry to think he's gone.'

My father didn't like The Cavern because it was so hot and crowded. About 1959 we moved to a much larger club, The Mardi Gras on Mount Pleasant, a few doors away from the Chinese Hotel. This was much bigger and quite plushy, and he liked it better, but I always preferred The Cavern. It had far more atmosphere.

Just before we transferred the management had begun to use a Beat group sometimes, instead of a local trad band during the intervals. In 1963 when the trad boom began to fade a little these took over the whole session. Among the other groups were 'The Beatles'.

The word 'scrubber' has cropped up quite frequently in this story, and perhaps the time has come to attempt a precise definition of what it means, or rather meant, for I understand that in the Beat world it has become debased and now means a prostitute. In our day this was not the case. A scrubber was a girl who slept with a jazzman but for her own satisfaction as much as his. Each scrubber had her own area, would turn up at the band's first job within her boundaries, sleep with the musician of her choice that night, travel on to the next job with him, and such jobs after that as lay within her province, and leave the band when it crossed the border into the next scrubber's territory. I don't mean to suggest that there was only one scrubber in each area, in fact many of them travelled in pairs, but that each individual was faithful in her fashion to one member in any given band. In her fashion, because many of them were very experimental sexually and would take part in gang bangs but only with the permission and participation of her regular partner.

Most scrubbers specialised in men who played a particular instrument. There were scrubbers for bass players, drummers, clarinettists, bandleaders, singers, and so on. Scrubbers were not distributed over the whole of the British Isles. In London and the towns within an eighty-mile radius there were lots of girls who did a turn, but no scrubbers in the full sense of the word because the bands usually travelled back to London the same night. Other areas, Scotland for example, were too imbued with the puritan tradition to tolerate the scrubber. In fact, scrubbers were mostly to be found in an area stretching from the West Coast to the East, but ending at a line drawn through the Potteries to the south and Newcastle upon Tyne in the north. It was the Alex Welsh Band who invented the name for this area. They called it 'The Scrubber Belt'.

Once in Barrow-in-Furness, Pete Appleby and I picked up two scrubbers and, at their suggestion, drove out of town to a field above the sea. While on the job I heard Pete shriek with laughter and lifting my head discovered that a nearby furnace was blasting and the landscape for a moment or two was as bright as day. ''Ow bad,' Pete told the rest of the band later. 'I'm lying there feeling up this chick when it all 'appens, and suddenly I can see old Fat's arse going up and down like the clappers!'

The two most famous scrubbers of my time, who invariably cropped up in any conversation between jazzmen whenever they met, both came from Yorkshire. From Leeds, Jean Patterson set out each week-end in search of pleasure. In Bradford, Mucky Alice studied her *Melody Maker* to decide where to aim for after work on Fridays.

Jean Patterson, a big bonny girl with a friendly warm smile, was famous for her experimental temperament and her formidable breasts and was equally popular with both British and visiting American bands. Once she came round to pay us a social call in the band-room at Sheffield City Hall. She had with her another girl, older than herself and very anonymous in appearance.

'Be careful what you say in front of my friend,' warned Jean. 'She's not like me. She doesn't like a bit of fun.'

A friend of mine on a recent trip to America wandered straight off the boat into a bar where a coloured trio were playing. Just after he'd bought his first beer, the leader made an announcement: 'Our next selection,' he said, 'is an original by our bass player. He entitles it "Theme for Jean Patterson".'

A month or two ago I invited an American blues singer to come and spend the day with us. As we live rather far out, I arranged that we should pick him up at his hotel, and at the agreed time knocked on his door. 'Come on in,' he said, 'I'm just up.' He was pulling on his undervest. Through the gap between his extended arm and torso I saw Jean Patterson zipping up her skirt. 'It's fucking Melly,' she said.

She looked marvellous, brown, relaxed and happy. She came to lunch and stayed until it was time for her to catch her train north. She radiated contentment and reaffirmed me in my belief that what you really want to do, provided it respects the identities of other people, is the basis of a workable morality.

Mucky Alice was not, as her name might suggest, unclean in her person. In fact, like most scrubbers, she took some care and pride in how she looked, although an ambition to startle led to some rather strange ensembles. In fact the 'Mucky' came from two other young ladies from Bradford who, lips tight with disapproval, once spat out that they didn't know how 'you can go with Mucky Alice', and the adjective, like the 'dirty' in 'dirty week-end', had a moral rather than sanitary application. Alice had rather curious tastes. She was a masochist and liked being tied up. I usually had my fishing reel in the wagon so the tying-up was no problem. As a sadist, however, I'm afraid I was found wanting, and she complained that my bites and smacks erred towards the tentative. On the other hand we both liked fucking in difficult or bizarre circumstances. Top of the list came about during the interval in a small northern town hall. While I was working, Alice discovered a door which led through into the magistrates' court, and we did it in the dusty dark in front of the bench.

Alice and I had a fairly steady relationship over several years. The good thing about a proper scrubber, as opposed to a local one-night-stand, was that they never asked you what you did in the day; an infuriating question after a two-hundred-mile trip in the wagon, a three-hour session and the same distance to cover the next morning. Nor did they counter almost every remark with the phrase 'yer wah?' to indicate bored incomprehension. In fact they could talk our language. Alice was sexy and enjoyed sex. She was generous too and would stand her round or even lend me money if I was broke. I had heard recently that she was married and asked Jean Patterson the day she came to lunch if this was in fact true.

'Married?' she said, 'she's always married. Now who is it she's married to this week?'

15

An Unlikely Totem

I'd known Edward Montagu since my naval days when he'd been in the Irish Guards with Tim Whidborne. One morning in the winter of 1955 he rang me up with a request. He'd seen the band were giving a concert in Bournemouth the following Sunday. Would we like to look in at Beaulieu afterwards and play an hour or two for his house-party? He offered drinks and something to eat, and I said I'd put it to the band and see what they thought. Although it meant going ten miles out of our way, they said yes.

When we arrived at the palace, we were shown up to the drawing room in Edward's flat. There were about a dozen people including Ken Tynan, and I believe this was the occasion on which the Ian Christie 'Who's that hurray cunt over there?' myth originated. There was a table with every sort of drink on it near the fireplace, but this was for the guests. For the band there was a crate of brown ale and two plates of sandwiches. There was a certain amount of chuntering over this, but nothing was said at the time. We played for about an hour and a half and then drove home. Ken Tynan asked if he could have a lift, and managed to find room at the conductor's feet in the front of the wagon. No sooner had we driven off than Ian began a furious attack on Edward's meanness and bad manners in only offering the band beer when his guests could have what they wanted. Mick took the view that this was perfectly justifiable, and the resulting shout-up extended its territory to include all our usual political disagreements.

Mick was put down by the ferocity and logic of Bird's argument, but a week later he was to have his revenge. We were in Blackpool, and after the dance were invited as usual for a splendid meal of home-made cheese and potato pie at Ian's parents. His father had spent the evening at the local and was in an amiable if repetitive condition.

'My son,' he kept telling us, 'has been entertained by Lord Montagu in his own house.'

Ian, who had obviously told his dad because, like most of us, he told his parents anything he thought might interest them, was extremely put out. Mick was merciless. Assuming a bland and interested expression he turned round in his chair and said to old man Christie: 'Lord Montagu? Ian?'

'Yes,' said Ian's dad. 'My son. He's been as a guest in Lord Montagu's own place.'

He needed very little encouragement to repeat this information several times during the course of the evening.

Mick always used this devastating trick whenever a girlfriend or parent let drop, in innocent pride, that a member of the band had been swanking about anything. None of us was able to discover a counter-ploy, nor did we ever have an opportunity to repay him in kind – his pathological modesty and indeed constant self-deprecation saw to that.

It was because of our evening at Beaulieu that Lord Montagu asked us to appear at the first jazz festival he promoted in the summer of 1956. This was a comparatively small-scale venture: two local bands, the Dill Jones trio and us, providing an afternoon and evening session on the palace lawn. Several hundred people turned up and behaved with enthusiastic decorum. At the end of the last number Edward climbed up on the rostrum and promised, to ironic but friendly cries of 'Good old Monty', to hold a bigger and better festival the following year. There was no local opposition; on the contrary the pub and village shop were delighted with the extra business. We got to know Beaulieu pretty well over the next six years. For old times' sake we were booked every year, although in a justifiably and increasingly modest position on the bill. We watched the whole thing grow. The one day became two days. The low platform gave way to a huge antique roundabout with the musicians replacing the horses – 'Harmless amusement for all classes' read the refurbished circus baroque lettering round the perimeter of the awning.

A camping ground was available for those who brought their own tents. Beer and hot dog stalls sprang up around the edges of the great lawns. By night the palace was floodlit. Extra-festival attractions were tried out: a cricket match between musicians and Lord Montagu's eleven, a church service with music by members of the Dankworth band.

The success of Beaulieu pupped other jazz festivals and Montagu himself presented 'All-Night Carnivals of Jazz from Beaulieu' at large venues in the far north, but none of them managed to project the magic of the original, and from all over the country at first hundreds, later thousands, of people drove or hitch-hiked to listen to two days of jazz in this comparatively inaccessible corner of Hampshire.

Until 1960 there was never any trouble. Through Chris Barber the audience for traditional jazz was expanding steadily, and although perhaps its appreciation grew increasingly superficial, it was still based on the music. Beaulieu certainly had other facets, the mellow charm of its setting and a strong permissive atmosphere. In the late evening the extensive and well-shrubbed estate was athrob, and a policeman with fully developed voyeur tendencies, whose actual job was to see that no trouble developed at the festival, once told Mick that he found nothing in his whole life as rewarding as a discreet patrol round the grounds while the last band of the night was stomping it out under the stars.

But all this did nobody any harm, and for the first four years, although the increasing number of visitors, unable to leave until the festival was over, certainly put some strain on the small village at the palace gates, Beaulieu was for us something to look forward to as we travelled through cold foggy nights in the grim provinces.

In 1960, however, the trad boom was under way.

The reasons for the trad boom, indeed for any fad in pop music, are finally unsolvable. Trad had been around for some years, and Chris had won it a large audience and could, at that time, fill any concert hall in the country, but it was not a pop music exactly. Its audiences were young, but not particularly young. The majority were in their late teens, but many were in their early twenties. There was a proportion of art-school students, and a larger proportion who hoped to be taken for art-school students. These were inclined to dress rather beat and dance with no shoes on, and however rural a job, there was sure to be at least one such couple leaping about in front of the bandstand. They were known among the band as 'the local weirdies', but apart from them there was no trad uniform. It was the emergence of Acker Bilk which changed the whole scene.

Acker was born in a Somerset village, but had cut his jazz teeth in Bristol. He'd started to play clarinet in an Army detention cell in Egypt while serving a sentence for falling asleep on watch – a story which must have appeared in print as often as how Louis Armstrong learnt to play cornet in the Waifs' Home, New Orleans, or how Humphrey Lyttelton sneaked off from the Eton and Harrow Match at Lord's to buy his first trumpet in the Charing Cross Road.

In the mid-fifties Acker had run a band in Bristol, and I'd guested with him one cider-ridden evening. His music was very much based on Ken Colyer, and had the clumsiness and honesty which marked the genuine disciple.

Towards the end of the fifties, Acker had built up a solid following in Bristol, and thought the time had come to try his luck in London. He formed a band and then almost starved. Eventually, when the record companies, impressed by the success of the Sunshine–Barber recording of 'Petit Fleur', were recording every trad band in sight, he got his chance. This might well have come to nothing had he not been placed in the hands of a Mr Peter Leslie, a smooth and amusing PRO who conceived the idea of promoting Bilk with a great deal of Victorian camp. It was he who decided on the 'Mr', on the heavy music-hall chairman prose on the record sleeves, on the striped waistcoats, and, above all, on the bowler hat. That this whole concept ran against Acker's rather earthy and rural personality may well be the reason it succeeded. 'The Alberts' and 'The Temperance Seven' had been pushing Victoriana for many years with only a limited impact, but when Mr Acker Bilk was created, his success was instantaneous.

At first sight he was an unlikely totem for a teenage religion. With his little beard and balding head, twinkling eyes and decided waddle, he looked more like a retired pirate than anything else. He revealed a basic if sympathetic sense of humour based on sending up his West Country burr, the catch phrase 'watch out', and the frequent interjection into his public pronouncements of a noise which can only be described as sounding like a vigorous yet watery fart. But none of this can explain his deification in the early months of 1960. As it was, Acker became a password among the young, and the bowler hat, usually with his name daubed round the crown in whitewash, a cult object.

His more extreme followers wore, not only the bowler, but army boots, potato sacks, old fur coats cut down to look like stone-age waistcoats. This outfit became known as 'Rave Gear', an expression first coined by an eccentric jazz promoter called 'Uncle Bonny' who encouraged the wearing of it in his chain of southern clubs. On the whole, however, 'Rave Gear' was rare in clubs, and only came into its own at the festivals or at the gargantuan all-night raves which were held under the echoing dome of the Albert Hall or among the icy wastes of the Alexandra Palace.

Another mark of the raver was the CND symbol. Among the musicians there were some, myself among them, who were actively committed to the cause of nuclear disarmament, and the same was certainly true of a proportion of the trad fans, but I rather felt that for most of them the symbol was anti-authoritarian rather than anti-nuclear – not that I found this in any way unsympathetic.

What was infuriating about the trad fans *en masse* was their complete intolerance of any form of jazz which fell outside their own narrow predilection. Of course it can be argued that we too had been pretty biased in our early days, but in our favour we were fighting for a neglected music in the face of indifference and ridicule, and furthermore our idols were the great originals. The trad fans neither knew nor cared about Morton and Oliver, Bessie Smith or Bunk Johnson. It was exclusively British trad they raved about, and although it was the better bands who went to the top, any group, however abysmal, was sure of a respectful hearing as long as the overall sound was right. The basis of that sound, the instrument which provided the heartbeat of the trad Frankenstein monster, was that dullest and most constricting of all noises, a banjo played chung, chung, chung, chung, smack on the beat.

Some bands held out obstinately against banjo-mania. Humph, Al and Sandy, and later Bruce Turner, ploughed a lonely mainstream furrow. Alex Welsh, although he capitulated enough to use a banjo on the occasional number, remained faithful to the noise he wanted to make, a fierce but disciplined amalgamation of Condon-music and arranged Dixieland. They worked because there were enough clubs to give them a certain amount of work, but they had a harder struggle than a great number of vastly inferior bands. Not that the whole of British trad was rubbish. There were some fine musicians in the better bands, but by reducing the music to a formula, by breaking through into the pop world, by over-exposure and repetitive gimmicks, trad signed its own death warrant. What seems odd in retrospect was that many of the musicians involved had been prepared to all but starve for the music in the days before the break-through and yet, once the boom came, were willing to do anything however idiotic in the name of commercialism.

It is, however, tempting but inaccurate to imagine that every British trad band sounded identical, and that all of them wore funny uniforms. There was certainly a basic trad noise and several of the bands not only reproduced it exactly, but dressed up as Confederate troops or Mississippi gamblers in order to do so. There were exceptions however. Kenny Ball for example dressed his band in ordinary suits, and although the recordings which brought him fame were very pretty-pretty – 'traddy-pop' was the word invented to describe this noise by its denigrators – at clubs and concerts Kenny could blow some exciting jazz. He himself had a formidable technique acquired during his many years as a travelling dance-band musician, and while far from contemptuous of money, he knew and loved early Armstrong.

Chris Barber too scorned fancy dress, and though he may be considered as playing John the Baptist to Acker's Saviour, while the trad boom was actually at its height he was experimenting with rhythm and blues, and playing a fair amount of arranged Ellington as well as his usual material.

Still it was a monotonous and dreary time. The airwaves were turgid with banjos, programmes like 'Easy Beat' and 'Saturday Club' were clogged with trad, but at least these were only intended to reflect popular taste, not to direct it. More lamentably, and much to the impotent chagrin of its producer, Terry Henebery, 'Jazz Club' itself, until then a genuine platform for every kind of jazz, received orders from above to limit itself exclusively to trad.

In fairness, I myself had nothing to complain about financially during the slow ascension of trad and its three-year omnipotence. The discovery by the BBC that I could compère led initially to an occasional appearance on Jazz Club in this capacity and eventually to a more or less resident post. Furthermore as a trad band became obligatory on every pop programme, I was booked to compère a lunchtime potpourri called 'Bandbox' which lasted for well over a year, and later, after the Mulligan band had actually folded but before the trad bubble burst, a similar rush-hour mic-mac called 'Pop-along'. There were also occasional plum engagements for the Corporation like compèring a big jazz festival at the Albert Hall, and as a direct result of working regularly for the BBC, I was offered a fair amount of work as MC for commercial promoters both at jazz festivals and concerts. Whenever possible, Mick arranged it so that I was able to take advantage of these offers, which anyway frequently worked both ways. If a promoter wanted me as compère, he was often prepared to take Mick and the band on as part of the bill.

Considering that the Mulligan band played a long way outside the accepted trad idiom, they did a lot of broadcasts. Mick's personality was the reason for this. He remained modest and helpful without in any way crawling, and the producers, fed up with bandleaders on the make who were willing if necessary to kiss their rings and bandleaders who *had* made it doing the big-time, enjoyed working with him. He also thought to buy them a drink in the break between rehearsal and transmission, a social gesture which never seemed to occur to most of his colleagues.

Jimmy Grant, the producer of 'Saturday Club', was a great favourite of Mick's and mine. He cottoned on so completely to the Appleby legend. At broadcasts only Mick and I were handed scripts, and Pete, giving the excuse that he needed one to remember the order of the programme, but in fact because not to have a script of his own was an affront to his ego, used to ask if there was a spare one. Jimmy, Mick and I used to have a giggle about this, and eventually Jimmy arranged that when his secretary came down from the control box at the beginning of rehearsal with a script for Mick and me, she also gave one to Pete with his name written across the top. Jimmy's expression of blissful mischief as he watched, from behind the glass panel, Pete's pseudo-casual acceptance of this proof of his importance endeared him to us for ever.

We also continued to record. In 1958, for instance, Decca, finally convinced that my commercials were uncommercial, allowed me to make an LP of jazz and blues material. This was recorded live in the upper room of a public house called 'The Railway Arms' in West Hampstead in front of an invited audience. It was a very enjoyable evening, and some of the tracks, those recorded early on, were not too bad. Towards the end of the session everything got rather out of control. Among the public was a contingent from Finch's in the Fulham Road including a small blonde lady of indeterminate age who became extremely drunk. For one thing she demanded to sing. 'When can I do my song, Micky-Mick-Mick?' she kept on shouting in between takes. 'Micky-Mick-Mick' told her to shut her hole but to no effect. During the interval she invaded the band-room where the company had provided a few bottles of the hard stuff for the Mulligan band and guests. Here the blonde lady decided to take her clothes off. While this was taking place, the man who had brought her was roaming the public rooms looking for her, and chanced to land up outside the door to the musicians' bar at the same moment that I was unsuccessfully trying to effect an entrance. I'd been for a pee, but didn't see why this should bar me from the free drinks, and yet, although I banged and shouted, it was evident that someone was leaning against the door on the inside to stop me getting in. I walked across to the opposite wall and charged, but even though the door gave a little, it slammed shut again before I could take advantage of it. At this point the man, suspicious and rightly so that his girlfriend was somehow the cause of my difficulty, came to my assistance in what I imagined was a purely altruistic spirit. We charged together, the door flew open and there was the blonde lady flashing her tits. Mick somehow managed to blame me. 'Typical,' he said – he was on the verge of the 'how's your married life going' cycle. The girl, seeing her boyfriend, covered her breasts with her hands in the 'September Morn' position.

'You always spoil everything,' she told him petulantly.

He told her he was going home at once and was she coming? She said no, and on one of the tracks of the LP, a song called 'Farewell to Storyville' which was recorded towards the end of the evening, and unwisely included audience participation, she can be heard joining in the chori half a tone sharp and half a beat in arrears.

We had to re-record several of the numbers we'd done in the

latter half of the evening. We did this in the Decca studio proper and they dubbed in the atmosphere and applause later, but due to the difficulty of reassembling an actual audience, 'Farewell to Storyville' had to stand. It's a pretty rough old noise.

I made several EPs too during the late fifties, and the band recorded several LPs and EPs also, some with me on the vocals, some purely instrumental. My own records never sold very well, in fact I was usually a little in debt to the companies because my royalties never quite covered my advances. Recently however the issue of an LP called 'British Jazz in the Fifties', an anthology which included a couple of tracks by me, did surprisingly well, and clear of debt at last, I received a cheque the other day for three pounds fifteen.

As well as recording and broadcasting, I occasionally appeared on the box; in fact about once a year somebody would decide I was to become a television personality on one level or another. Unfortunately, or possibly fortunately, I come over on the telly as camp as Chloë and look drugged up to the eyeballs to boot, and after a single appearance I'd be dropped until I was rediscovered twelve months later. Still Mick and I had really little cause to complain at the way things went for us. We never really made the big time, but then to have done so, or even tried to do so, would have meant changing the whole band sound, which from Mick's point of view would have meant far too much work. He was lucky here to be able to count on unexpected support from Frank and Ian, not because they were afraid of rehearsal – quite the reverse – but because they detested the trad noise.

Once, during a sticky period financially which happened to corre-spond with the time Chris Barber had begun to make it, Mick actually flirted with the idea of seeking the flesh-pots. This came out during one of the drunken band discussions in the wagon on the way back to London. Everybody was putting forward different ways of increasing the band's earning power, solutions like more rehearsals, individual practising, new numbers, in fact all the suggestions guaranteed to put the conductor into a filthy temper. He was sitting in the front seat next to Appleby, saying nothing, but with his head sunk into the nylon fur collar of his pale grey shortie quilted mac, an unlikely garment he had bought because it was the first thing he'd been shown in a shop in Charing Cross Road when he'd been caught out in a cloud burst. Everybody's remarks were of course aimed at Mick although delivered in a rather serious detached way as though part of an abstract discussion. Eventually Mick got the needle.

'Only one way to make it these days,' he growled. 'That's to get a banjo. If you've got a banjo you're unassailable. Unassailable.'

A great cry of protest arose from the back of the wagon, but Mick wouldn't budge. As always when he was drunk and angry, a single idea took over. Whatever anybody else said, he countered it with the unassailability of the banjo. Furthermore, he finally insisted, he was going to get a banjo player. Of course none of us took him seriously, but Mick actually did get a banjo player, or at least a guitar player who said he was willing to play banjo.

His name was Bill Bramwell, and he was well known as a bass player too, and had played jazz all over the world since 1945, and had composed several TV jingles, but work was rather thin at that moment, and as he could manage to play with us and fit in most of his outside jobs as well, he decided to join us for a bit. He also looked on it as an opportunity to play some jazz. For the first week or two Bill did actually bring along the banjo he'd bought as his passport into the band, and even played it on a few numbers, but he soon dropped it, and later even took to amplifying his guitar. Mick didn't mind. His honour had been satisfied, and like the rest of us he much preferred guitar anyway.

Bill was a bit older than the rest of us. He came from the same generation of jazzmen as Lennie Felix and Dill Jones. He was less blasé then we were, and had managed to retain much more enthusiasm for playing. On listening to himself on playback he would sometimes say how good he was. This, of course, was a great source of malicious delight to the conductor.

The very first week after he'd joined us we pulled up at a garage somewhere in South London on the way home from a job in Gillingham, and Bill told us that he'd thoroughly enjoyed the evening's session. 'You all love each other,' he explained, 'that's why you swing. You can't play jazz unless you love each other.' It was remarks like this which convinced Ian Christie that he and Bill were on different wavelengths and as time went on a considerable and mutual antipathy built up. Bill had recently married. He was Welsh working class himself, but his wife came from a county family in Devon who were also Roman Catholic and there'd been a grand wedding with Bill in a grey topper. Bill was rather impressed with his new relations and was always telling stories of what a marvellous old gentleman his father-in-law was. Squire of the manor and so on, but completely natural. Conservative and a bit crusty but very kind at heart. This also used to drive Ian mad.

Usually however they treated each other politely but distantly; but one night in the wagon a splendid explosion took place. Ian was in the back seat, Bill in the middle seat. Ian had said that what was really important was to be yourself. Whether the remark was aimed at Bill or not I can't remember, but Bill thought it was, and turning round mimicked Ian's accent.

'Be yourself,' he said, 'you've got to be yourself.'

Ian took no notice and went on talking, but every time he paused to draw breath, which was admittedly not often, Bill would say it again. Eventually Ian got the pin, and remembering that Bill had once told us that he had been to a psychoanalyst who used to knit while he was in session, began to reply in kind. Whenever Bill said anything Ian would mutter 'knit, knit, knit' in a manic frenzy. Eventually Bill and Ian faced each other over the back of the seat, and crimson with rage shouted in each other's face:

'Be yourself! Be yourself!'

'Knit, knit! Knit, knit, knit! Knit, knit, knit, knit!'

For Frank Parr on the other hand Bill Bramwell appeared to be a figure of fun. Because of the existence of an old blues singer called 'Bumble Bee Slim', he called Bill 'Bumble Bee Fat'. This name took into account not only Bill's comparative rotundity, but his habit of humming loudly to himself when taking a solo. Frank also removed any photograph of bald, plump, bespectacled men from the pages of the newspaper to take them home where he claimed to stick them in his 'Bill Bramwell Book'. Bill of course was bald, plump and bespectacled, and did bear a remarkable resemblance to most of the judges, business men, criminals, or anonymous figures Frank tore out for his collection. I've never actually examined 'The Bill Bramwell Book' but knowing Frank I dare say it existed.

Bill was the only member of the band to outwit the conductor's financial one-upmanship. We were meant to be paid weekly, but as this meant sitting down during drinking and dart-playing time, and working out what we were owed in relation to what we'd had in subs, Mick did everything he could to avoid settling up, preferring to peel off a tenner from the wad of crumpled notes he kept stuffed in his back pocket with the inevitable query: 'Will this do for the mo, cock?'

As a result none of us knew exactly where we stood, and when eventually we did bully him into settling up, were likely to forget the five we'd had in the Working Men's Club during the interval at St Albans three weeks before, or the fifteen we'd taken on the way back from Nottingham. The conductor, with his photographic memory, never forgot and alleviated the boredom of paying out by making us feel guilty and dishonest. In my case he would rub more salt in the wound by calling me Maudie, a habit dating back to the extra fishcake, and implying that my mother's spirit watched over me at all times.

'Forgotten about the fistful when we stopped at that boozer outside Leicester, Maudie?' he'd say coldly. Maudie was also meant to be behind it when I had a good night at poker.

Bill Bramwell's counter-ploy was to never ask for settlement. On the contrary he made a point of accepting subs at all times, but deliberately confused the issue by asking for odd sums like three pounds ten, or twelve pounds and a cheque for another eight. In the end it was Mick who had to ask Bill if he'd like to straighten out and, as he said later, 'I can't remember what the bugger's had. I'm sure I was done'.

Getting paid was known as the eagle shitting. 'Can the eagle shit tonight?' somebody, usually Frank Parr, would ask. It was a great satisfaction to us all when Mick noticed that the little street off Piccadilly where his bank was situated was called Eagle Place.

Mick and I liked Bill Bramwell very much. He was kind and funny. His humour depended on an exploitation of childishness which seemed very droll in relation to his rather adult and serious appearance. He was good at the sustained anecdote too, piling absurdity on absurdity until it was quite painful to go on laughing. To his disadvantage he snored very loudly. When in the Middlesbrough area we used to stay with a clergyman and his wife. He was a nice and funny man with a wooden hand – or rather two: one for weekdays and a smarter one for Sundays – and he was, as he put it, 'Resident Rev' at a reform school. He had run the jazz club in Newmarket before taking this post and that's how we'd got to know him. When we stayed with him in the small modern house provided by the detention school for its incumbent, there was plenty to drink, his wife cooked an enormous amount to eat, and we had a ball. During one of our visits we didn't go to bed until it was time for the Resident Rev to conduct Holy Communion. When he came back for breakfast he was met by one of his children in a state of panic. 'Daddy,' said the little girl, 'there's a lion in one of the bedrooms!' It was Bill Bramwell snoring.

Bill left after a year or so to join an advertising firm on the musical side, but he still played occasionally with us – broadcasts, recording sessions and so on – when Mick felt we needed a fuller sound. He rowed me in on several commercials too, mostly advertising film designed for the African market, and we also did occasional prison concerts.

Mick was right about the unassailability of the banjo; without one we only got the crumbs that fell from the traddies' table. There was, however, one moment when we nearly made a film. In 1957 Ealing decided. that a jazz band on the road would make a good subject for a picaresque comedy, and somebody had recommended the Mulligan band as a source on which to draw. As a result a director and a producer spent some time travelling about with us in the wagon. They were both called Mike.

The producing Mike was only with us for one tour, and managed to get his face slapped in Swansea by telling a young lady he could get her into pictures. He was rather drunk at the time. The directing Mike came with us on several tours. He was a nice, tall, curly-haired, enthusiastic, clumsy man, and afflicted with a bad stammer when excited. This usually happened when he recognised the potential of some northern scene, a shabby dance hall backed by slag heaps or a fish and chip shop reflected in a dirty canal. He'd never been north of Golders Green before, and these images had yet to be turned into clichés.

'T-t-t-t-terr-terribly visually exciting d-d-d-dear boy,' he would shout as he leapt about looking at such vistas through framing fingers.

We were all very impressed by the thought of being used as the basis for characters and camped it up like mad. As the film company provided a great deal of whisky this was even easier than it would otherwise have been. Staying in one hotel, Frank drank himself into being fit only for the human scrap heap in under five minutes and on to the floor in ten. Next morning we were all in the bar and he did it again. The fat bespectacled landlord came in at this point, stepped carefully over Parr's body and, without registering any surprise, wished him good morning.

That night we were booked to appear at a Lancashire seaside resort only thirty miles away. We not only contrived to be late, but indeed Frank didn't appear at all until the second half. There was a revolving stage and the conductor, who was at his most waggish, waited until Pete had begun his drum solo and then set it in motion. Pete was, of course, sober, and every time he appeared behind stage, would shout 'Drunken cunts!' at us before disappearing again into the light.

After the producer had seen enough, it was the turn of the writer, a Scottish novelist called James Kennaway. He had written a book about officers in a Highland regiment, but we were initially outside his terms of reference. To start with he hated us very much. In The Bodega, at the end of his first night with us on the road, he stood, his eyes full of angry tears, and beat his clenched fists against the wall.

'You're all shits!' he shouted. 'I hate you. I hate you.'

We didn't think he blew up a storm either to begin with, but by the time he left us to write his script, we were entirely reconciled. Actually it wasn't us that changed but him. He turned into a real raver.

James wasn't starry-eyed about us though, even by the end. He recognised our defensive cliquishness, our tendency to 'put it on' to impress him and others, the way we used funny voices for weeks at a time. Whether any of this would have got into the film I don't know. The company folded and it was never made.

We'd been offered fifty pounds each initially for allowing ourselves to be used as a basis for fiction. When we heard the film was off all of us, with one exception, took it for granted that we could kiss the money good-bye. The exception was Alan Duddington.

'Mick,' he suddenly announced in the wagon a good few months after most of us had forgotten the film had ever existed as a possibility. 'Could you ask if we could have the fifty pounds before Christmas? I'll need it to buy presents for my folk.' Shortly after this Alan left us and Gerry Salisbury replaced him.

Everybody in the band loved Gerry. He had married into the budgie and garden gnome belt, but his origins were Cockney–Italian, and he was in fact a cousin of Jo Lennard. He had been brought up in Covent Garden, and told some marvellous stories of his childhood. In particular I remember an incident in which a policeman, with whom the entire Salisbury family had been on bad terms for a whole year, was invited in at Christmas for what he imagined to be a peace-offering in the form of a seasonable drink. It had been well-laced with 'Jollops', a very strong laxative which, according to Jerry, worked instantly.

'He goes running down the stairs holding on to 'is ring to get to the outside toilet in time,' explained Gerry in his slow deep voice. 'And when 'e gets there, 'e discovers that the old man's been and gone and nailed up the door!'

But for Gerry his Chaucerian world was in the past, and by the time he joined the band he was living with his wife and baby daughter in his in-laws' semi out at Mill Hill.

Gerry's mind worked all right, but rather slowly, like a record player at the wrong speed. He realised this, and had developed a set of mannerisms to go with it. If asked a question he would stand absolutely still for a moment, and then he would turn his whole body towards his interrogator as though it were on a revolving platform for displaying sculpture, and subject him to a long and searching stare. Finally, when Gerry was ready, he would give a slight jerk, lift his eyebrows, and deliver his answer which was always pertinent and usually humorous.

Gerry's features were rather beautiful, and he had very long eyelashes, but his movements, and in particular the impression he gave that his head, neck and torso were not articulated, made him add up to a comic figure. With his completely deadpan face he reminded me of Buster Keaton, and indeed he had a real passion for early film comedies.

He used to share the driving with Apps, and when that gentleman decided he would like a break – this didn't happen very often as he was paid by the mile – an amusing little scene took place.

Pete would draw up in a layby and on the cue: 'Like ter drive for a bit, Ger?' both of them would throw open the two front doors of the van, and climb out. They would meet directly in front of the bonnet, small animated Apps and the slow-moving and stolid Gerry, and exchange a few words. These were, of course, inaudible for the rest of us in the back of the Volkswagen, but somehow the contrast between them suggested a music-hall exchange, and we called it their 'Wheeler and Woolsey Act'. Having finished what they had to say to each other, they completed their little walk. Pete would climb into the passenger seat and go to sleep, Gerry into the driving seat and start up the engine. It was a perfectly reasonable way of changing over, and much more sensible than clambering across each other's knees, but it always seemed faintly ridiculous.

Gerry's passion was coarse fishing, and he managed to interest Pete in this too. It made a change from their continuous rabbiting about second-hand cars on long journeys, although Pete soon reduced it, as he reduced everything else, to a formula. Every time we passed over or near a stretch of water, whether canal, river, pond, lake or reservoir, he would turn to Gerry and say: 'Must be a few in there, Ger.'

I confessed to Gerry that as a child I had been a keen trout fisherman, and he did his best to hook me on coarse fishing. We did spend several freezing days off on the banks of a small and muddy pond near Stanmore live-baiting for pike. I quite enjoyed these Spartan expeditions, but the final result of Gerry's propaganda was to rekindle my passion for trout. He refused to have anything to do with it, even in Scotland where it's very cheap.

'It's not a working man's sport,' he explained. He had retained from his Cockney childhood a fierce sense of class loyalty.

More than anyone else in the band, Gerry was a real musician. His thinking, so slow and earthbound in everyday life, became charged with originality once it turned to music. He was a good bass player, but what he should have been was a trumpet player.

He used to play if Mick was ill, or would occasionally take a number if we had an especially long session, and his phrasing and the construction of his chori were absolutely delicious. The only trouble, the only tragedy really, was that he had no lip. Lip in a trumpet-player is the ability to go on playing without your mouth starting to jelly-up on you so that you can't blow. A lot of it, of course, comes from playing continuously; you develop a hard lip in the end as you can see from examining the extraordinary cushion of leather in photographs of Louis Armstrong, but Gerry had played a lot at one time and another, and it just didn't happen. After a couple of numbers he couldn't blow any more. Mick on the other hand had a lip of iron, and some ability to swing, but compared with Gerry he was very uninventive. It was very sad.

Gerry was not really so much an active figure in the band; he was more of a spectator, but his originality of vision, his stolid refusal to be shaken by anything, his eye for the absurd, provoked the rest of us into every form of mania and excess.

The abortive film project was the only chance we had of becoming national figures although we had a certain reputation as good copy. Patrick Campbell, the humorist, came with us to Oxford one night in 1957 and wrote a very funny piece about us in his column in the now defunct *Sunday Dispatch*. What especially pleased us about this was that he got several points poetically wrong. For example he misheard our expression, 'Put me in a snout' (i.e. Give me a cigarette) as 'Cut me in the snuff'. Also that particular night, the wagon picked up Gerry Salisbury and me at a pub called 'The Target' on Western Avenue. The reason for this was that we had been fishing unsuccessfully for pike in the pond in Stanmore. Gerry told the band that there was meant to be a huge pike in that pond which could take even full grown ducks. Frank Parr interjected at this point with a quote from some obscure poem. 'The wolf-jawed pike,' he intoned solemnly.

In Patrick Campbell's piece this came out as: '. . . to pick up George Melly . . . He told us that he had been fishing for Wolf Jaw, the monster pike in Stanmore Pond.'

From that day, 'Cut me in the snuff' became the way we did ask for a cigarette, at first humorously, but eventually as a matter of course, while Wolf Jaw, the monster pike of Stanmore Pond, joined the spade bongo player as one of our permanent phantoms.

I myself began, as the years went by, to appear quite frequently outside the band, not only on the radio, but as a solo compère and performer. One of the most profitable and enjoyable of these extra-Mulligan jobs was for Paddy McKiernan who organised for three years a show called 'Rhythm with the Stars', designed to expand the sales of the *Daily Express* in the north. The first year I compèred and sang a spot with Chris Barber. The second I just sang with Mick, but in my own spot and billed as a solo artist; the third year I compèred again and sang with Mick, but what seemed to me absolutely fabulous was what I got paid. A hundred pounds! I had never earned so much in my life in such a short period.

I discovered how to get rid of it, however. We played a different town every evening, and as I was usually in Paddy's company, I stayed at the same four-star hotels, ate at the best restaurants, and stood a great many very expensive rounds into the night.

The show consisted of a mixed bill, part jazz, part pop. The first year the star was Eddie Calvert. We opened in Manchester, the hall was packed with Chris Barber fans, and Eddie got the bird. He came down to the dressing room in a very bad temper and began to bawl out Paddy while he changed. Every time he swore, his father, who was sitting there in a cap, said: 'Now, now, Eddie,' in a mild voice.

In the middle of his diatribe he suddenly turned on me. 'It's all right for you,' he shouted, 'you're only an amateur.' After so long on the road I took exception to this, and told him I had been singing 'Frankie and Johnny' – the number had gone down particularly well – for over eight years almost every night.

'Was that you falling down?' snapped Eddie. I said it was.

'You'll get cancer, you know,' he spat out, and returned to the attack.

But solo jobs were rare. For the most part we completed the fifties like somnambulists, always tired from the all-night poker sessions, often drunk, doing something we had once done for love out of habit. Jazz and the Mulligan band had a relationship like a failed marriage. We stuck together because we could see no alternative.

In Cleethorpes, on the way up to a Scottish tour, we chanced upon a figure who seemed to symbolise our condition. She was called 'Musical Marie' and was attempting, in a tent on the front, to beat the world record for non-stop piano playing. Before it was time for our first session we paid our sixpences and went in to see her. She'd been at it fifteen hours and had almost three more days to go.

She was a fat lady dressed in a powder-blue gown. She sat at the piano listlessly tinkling away. Her manager, a flamboyant middle-aged man, told us that she was in ordinary life a Manchester housewife.

'Every tune she plays,' he kept emphasising, 'is a real melody.'

'What happens when she wants to piss?' Mick asked.

'She continues playing,' explained the manager, 'a screen is brought on to the stage, and she uses an Elsan behind it. She never stops playing for one moment. All recognisable tunes.'

The Elsan, he explained, was brought on and removed by a lady in Red Cross uniform. The manager himself fed her on glucose.

When the dance was over we passed the tent on the deserted front. Through the loud speakers we could hear Musical Marie playing her hesitant and stumbling notes into the small hours. She was still at it when we left next morning. I was interested enough to ring up Cleethorpes Town Hall from Scotland a few days later. I spoke to the Town Clerk.

'Oh, yes, she broke the record,' he told me, 'played for a further 'alf 'our so there'd be no argument, and was then carried into t' Dolphin 'otel in a state of collapse.'

In 1960 the trad boom was at its height, and a riot occurred at Beaulieu. It wasn't a vicious riot. It was stupid. The traddies in rave gear booing the Dankworth Band. A young man climbing up the outside of the palace in the floodlights waving a bowler hat from the battlements. Cheers and scuffles. Then, when the television transmission was going on and Acker playing, the crowd surged forward and began to climb the scaffolding supporting the arc-lights. The few police and the official stewards struggled with them, and the BBC went off the air.

Gerald Lascelles shouted at a young man to climb down.

'Say please,' said the young man.

'Please,' said Gerald.

'No,' said the young man.

Somewhere in the audience was a boy who'd killed a taxi-driver and come to Beaulieu on the money. The papers, of course, had a field day.

The next year there wasn't a riot. Inside the grounds there were lots of police with dogs but there was no need for them. Modern jazz and traditional took place at different sessions. Anita O'Day, in a lace dress so tight she had difficulty climbing up the steps to the roundabout, sang 'Sweet Georgia Brown' while the dancers silhouetted against the floodlit wall jumped for joy in the warm night. It was very beautiful.

The trouble was that there were too many people for the village to absorb, not enough lavatories, too few litter bins, Local feeling rose high, and at midnight Edward Montagu told the Press that this was the last festival he would hold at Beaulieu. Trad jazz had outgrown its most typical and happiest occasion.

16

What Has Happened to the Chaps?

During my first year and a half at Tregunter Road I was sexually a freewheeler. One night in a club I watched a coloured girl doing a snake-charming act. When she'd finished and had dressed, and was on her way out of the place, I left the girl I'd brought with me, rushed up to her and kissed her on the mouth. I persuaded her to come over to the bar, bought her a drink and she gave me her telephone number. The girl I'd left so abruptly didn't say anything but a few days later, following another act of aggressive and quite unnecessary sexual insult on my part, we broke up.

I didn't do anything about the snake charmer for some time, but one evening I found her name, Cerise Johnson, and her telephone number in my wallet. I rang her up and asked her over. We went out to dinner, back to Tregunter Road, and eventually to bed. I liked her very much – she had an extraordinary line in hot chat – but the next day we went away on tour.

A week or two later it was Christmas and I felt I'd had the whole Christmas thing, so on the way home from a family supper at my sister's flat I rang Cerise up again, picked her up from the Bayswater Hotel she had a room in, and took her home in a taxi. This time she stayed two days. We saw each other regularly after that and gradually slipped into an affair.

The first intimation of trouble happened the first time I took her to Cook's Ferry Inn. She had a row with a band – I didn't hear it actually happen – and threw her shoe in the canal. I put this down to having drunk too many whiskies, bought a new pair of shoes and made Cerise apologise. But it was only the beginning. Cerise was often violent and for the next two years I was seldom without scratches on my face. Before one lot had healed properly there was a new display.

At the beginning of our relationship I was frequently in the wrong. I tried to treat her in the casual way I'd treated my other girl friends and she wouldn't have it, but later on her attacks were without any basis in reality. It was usually somebody else she went for – a girl she imagined had tried to date me, someone she claimed had insulted her on the grounds of colour. She was extremely strong, and I felt it necessary to intervene, thereby adding fuel to her obsessive suspicions. After the initial outbreak she could usually be persuaded to leave, but once home she'd work herself up into a rage again. This time it was me she went for. She fought like a tiger and was far stronger than I am. Although we usually finished with Cerise riding me, bleeding and bruised, in bed, there was nothing much in it for anybody else. The jazz world is prejudiced to a fault in favour of the coloured race, but they found Cerise a bit much. She'd soon had rows with most of my men friends – girls were of course out of the question – and as Simon refused for a time to allow her in the flat (she'd threatened him with a broken milk bottle and tried to set some spades on us in the middle of Notting Vale during the riots) we found ourselves living more or less in isolation in a flat she'd taken in West Kensington. We went to the theatre and to night clubs, we saw her friends, mostly coloured cabaret artistes, but apart from the band and Wally, the whole of my social life went by the board.

Why didn't I leave her? Fear mostly, but also I felt a great affection for her. She could be wounded as well as wound. Although even in the flat, and with no outside stimuli to provoke her, she could suddenly appear possessed and, screaming hysterical nonsense, attack me with such violence that on several occasions I was frightened for my life, ninety per cent of the time she was gentle, loving, erotic and protective. To leave the flat, however, was to court almost certain disaster.

One night we went to a party at the Fawkes' in Swiss Cottage: a big house, lots to eat and drink; Jimmy Rushing was the guest of honour. Mick was there. So was Pam. Although Wally had seen Cerise in action several times, he knew how much I admired and liked Jimmy and decided to risk it. Within half an hour it had started. I'd gone to the lavatory and when I came back I found Cerise screaming at the foot of the stairs. She claimed that the

French *au pair* girl – a plain girl who had by this time fled prudently up to her room – had been making eyes at me.

'Anaemic white shit!' Cerise was yelling. Wally was blocking the staircase. Sandy Fawkes and several other guests were trying to persuade her she'd been mistaken. This she managed to twist so as to accuse them of colour prejudice. What made this especially absurd in retrospect was that one of the people so accused was Max Jones, the jazz critic, who if he believed in God, which he doesn't, would be convinced He was black.

After some minutes, still screaming with rage, she threw open the door of the sitting-room and rushed full-tilt into the rock-like figure of Jimmy Rushing who was sitting playing the piano. He immediately played the opening phrase of 'Shoo fly don't bother me'. She called him a white man's nigger. He took no notice at all.

There was one man at the party who had never met Cerise before, and seeing her surrounded by a large group of Caucasians, he waded in on her side. This was all she needed. Her fantasy had a believer. She went outside into the front garden and began to collect a pile of stones and rocks which she intended to throw at the windows. Pam Mulligan went out after her to try and talk her out of it. I'd had enough and decided to opt out. She'd promised not to make a scene. I'd told Sandy and Wally I'd guarantee this time it would be all right. I felt absolutely miserable. I poured myself out a tumbler of gin and drank it down neat in one swallow. Then I went over to Jimmy Rushing at the piano and asked him to play a blues. He did and I began to sing with the tears streaming down my face. As the gin hit me I slid, still singing, towards the floor and passed out. Mick Mulligan picked me up, according to Wally, as tenderly as if I'd been a sick child, carried me through into the kitchen and put me on the couch. He was arranging a blanket over me when Pam came in from the garden.

'I've managed to calm her down,' she said, 'she wants to take George home.'

The next moment personified, according to Wally again, the whole difference between Mick's attitude to men and women. After all the tender care he'd displayed towards me, he turned to Pam and said: 'Why don't you keep your fucking hooter out of it?'

But Pam had succeeded in calming Cerise, who came back into

the house, picked me up off the sofa, threw me over her shoulder like a sack, and marched out.

The strange thing about Cerise was that she took it for granted that I fucked in the provinces. She didn't seem to care either. Once I caught crabs – she spotted one when she was going down – but she didn't seem a bit put out. I nervously insisted that you could catch them off a lavatory seat or from dirty sheets. She just smiled and said I shouldn't go with such dirty girls. I said I hoped she hadn't caught them from me.

'Crabs don't bite me never. Me blood too rich,' she explained. Furthermore, she wouldn't let me buy any ointment. She insisted on searching them out herself.

'I likes to crack 'em between me nails,' she told me.

It was only in London she expected complete fidelity. She once did a week's cabaret in Manchester and told me she'd be back on the Monday. On the Sunday night I went out with my sister Andrée. She drove me back and said she'd come in for a drink. The door to Simon's basement flat is round the side of the house in a dark dustbin-haunted alley down some steep steps. As Andrée and I were walking down this passage laughing and chatting, and I was feeling for my key, Cerise spoke from the shadows.

'Who's that white pussy you got there?' I told her it was Andrée whom she knew well. 'That's OK then,' she said. 'You in luck it weren't no white pussy you tipping home with,' and she replaced the heavy iron dustbin lid she'd been holding at the ready.

Simon didn't bar Cerise from the flat for long and we sometimes stayed at her place, sometimes mine. One afternoon Cerise was cleaning the flat as I was expected back that evening. Simon was putting on his BOAC uniform to go to London airport. The bell rang. It was Victoria back from Rome with nowhere to stay. She asked Simon if she could stay there.

Simon told me later that he drove his scooter out to the airport trembling with nerves. He was convinced Cerise would murder Victoria. She didn't though. When I came in after the job she told me coldly that my wife was asleep on the divan in the sitting-room. I went in to say hello, and Victoria kissed me affectionately. Cerise and I went to bed.

'She must go in the morning,' she said not unreasonably, 'I'm your woman. How she think she tip in here after three year and give you tongue sandwich?'

Next morning I told Victoria she'd have to find somewhere else. Cerise was quite calm if unfriendly until she'd gone. Then she let fly.

I didn't contradict her. I was so relieved that nothing terrible had happened. Victoria found a modelling job and a basement flat in Chelsea. Cerise and I lived together much as before for another five months.

Then suddenly she told me she'd decided to go and work on the Continent. She'd been offered a job in Paris, fares paid, and decided to take it. I went to the airport to see her off. I stood on the roof of the new Queen's Building and watched her walk – she walked beautifully – towards the plane. I couldn't believe she was going. After two years I was sad, but my strongest feeling was relief.

I went over to spend a week with her in Paris shortly afterwards. I'd promised. It was all right, but we both knew it was over.

I came back to London and within the month Victoria and I said, well, it might work this time.

It didn't work at all. Within a month of being together again we both knew it. There were concrete reasons of course, things either of us could point to as to why it didn't work, but the real reason was that we didn't add up. We weren't a couple.

We moved first to a basement flat in Swan Walk. Here we got on very badly. Then, both of us imagining that if we had something solid there was a chance to build up a relationship again, we bought a house on Hampstead Heath. It didn't do any good either, but as it was bigger, we got on better. There were even days when it all looked possible. We'd go to the pictures and come back arm in arm, we'd have a nice dinner together at Wheelers, but nothing came of it. We started to lead our own lives. It wasn't hell or anything like it. More a cushioned limbo.

Appleby had left the band to join Donegan and was replaced, after a week or two, by a plump funny manic-depressive from Bristol called Fat John Cox. He was a dandy with little feet for whom nothing ever went right. He was married to a beautiful German wife he'd met in Cologne. He called her 'Missus'. He called the conductor 'Leader'. He moaned and complained about everything in his strong Bristol accent. He looked, like a lot of fat men, rather lesbian. He was interested in sadomasochistic fetishism and eating. He sometimes tried to go on a diet, would hold out for a day, and then go to a pie stall and eat six pies.

We ran through an exceptional number of bass players in 1960–61. The most memorable was called Cliff – small, bespectacled, with a fine crop of acne. We nicknamed him 'Weasel'. He was much younger than us and got everything wrong. He was Ian's particular *bête noire* on two counts. The first day he joined the band, he observed in his whiny transpontine voice that it was surprising there should be three public school boys in the band. Mick – Merchant Taylors', me – Stowe, himself – Alleyn's. The Bird's face was a real joy at that moment. On the other hand he offended Ian's feeling for the good life by getting everything wrong. Favourite fish – cod; in a restaurant he'd order a drambuie with his soup.

Ian and I went fishing whenever we had a chance. I got better at it, much to Frank Parr's annoyance. He used to enjoy it when I came back in the evening with nothing to show for it. 'Caught anything?' he'd ask with an infuriating smile on his face. The first time I was able to say yes and produce a pound grayling was a sweet moment. I began to welcome Scottish tours.

Mick and Frank played golf together. Mick usually won and Frank would lose his temper and attack the putting green. This very much offended Mick's sense of propriety as did Frank's habit of playing stripped to the waist on fine days so as to expose himself to 'the currant bun' or 'big fellow' as he called the sun. Eventually, despite his pleasure both at winning from Frank and making him lose his temper into the bargain, Mick wouldn't play with him any more.

We did a tour of Ireland in 1961. I neglected to do any Flook strip and got back to find an angry Wally biting his nails and five days backlog. This was the only time this happened.

That Easter my father died. He was sixty-one. His funeral was the last occasion Victoria put in an official appearance as my wife.

Later that summer the editress of *Queen* magazine sent for me and said that Colin McInnes had suggested that I might write something for them. Colin was a keen Flook fan and I had written a laudatory article in the *Twentieth Century*. I did a piece for them called 'A Week-end in the Jazz World'. In it I wrote: 'On the road. Ten years of it. I seem to have spent a lifetime looking out of grimy windows in digs at backyards in the rain. Weeds, rotting iron, collapsing outhouses.'

That article was in fact the key to my release. Out of it came other reviews and pieces, my Flook money had gone up and Wally and I were doing a weekly cartoon for the *Spectator*. I was also compèring 'Jazz Club' regularly, and I suddenly realised I could make enough to pack it in. It took me a week or two to raise the courage to tell Mick. I did it one evening in a pub.

'I was thinking of doing the same,' he said.

He had recently bought a house on the Sussex coast. Pam and the children were down there the whole time. He kept on the flat in Lisle Street as a *pied-à-terre*, but most nights he used to drive the extra eighty miles home. He was thinking, he told me, of buying an off-licence in that part of the world. He had begun to yearn for a home life, regular hours, fewer hangovers. We decided that 1 January 1962 would be the day to disband.

The band were divided. Ian had begun to write a jazz column in the *Sunday Telegraph*. He thought he might make out as a writer too. Miff could always get along. Fat John decided to form his own band. Frank was the most pessimistic. In July of that year, the last Beaulieu.

On the river-boat shuffle, or 'Floating Festival' as it was called in the high noon of the trad boom, I sang, as had become accepted custom, an obscene Liverpool ballad called 'The Lobster Song'. In Margate we went to the flea circus: 'This little lady is Madame Frou Frou. And this is Hercules, the strongest flea in the world.'

Steaming slowly back through the pool of London in the dusk, I reflected nostalgically on other years. The time Simon Watson Taylor brought John Raymond and he, charmed by the high spirits and physical beauty of all the young people, said that for the first time he understood the point of the Welfare State.

The band's last autumn. In the Colony Room early in October I met Diana; she was also married. We spent the afternoon together, I was meant to be taking Victoria to the newly opened 'Establishment Club'. I rang her up and she said did I mind but she'd been asked out by somebody else. I said no. I took Diana. Afterwards we went and made love on the heath. We knew that day we were going to get married.

Three days later I went in to Victoria's bedroom to tell her. Before I'd got it out, she told me she was leaving. She'd fallen in love with somebody else. I gave her my reciprocal piece of information. She asked who it was. I told her.

'But she's quite pretty!' she said.

A few weeks later Victoria left in her Floride and Diana moved in with her two children and a Victorian bassinette.

Many people think it was Diana who persuaded me to stop touring. I had in fact decided three months before I'd met her. Diana came to all the jobs we could manage during the band's last three months. At the Anarchists' Ball at Fulham Town Hall, Mick said to me while we were going out of a pub together: 'You've got yourself a good one there, cock.' I thought he was being sarcastic on the 'another good chap lost' level. 'No, cock,' he said, 'I mean it.'

That Christmas Eve we played The Bodega. Frank Parr fell off the stage and pulled down a huge Christmas tree on top of him. That was the last real moment in the official history of the band. The final job, a BBC show called 'Trad Tavern', proved to be a remarkably unemotional evening.

Actually, although the band no longer existed, we played together a lot over the next year. The trad boom was still on and I agreed with Mick to do a weekend a month and the odd job near town. Indeed so elastically did the conductor interpret his terms of reference that at one moment it was like being on the road and I had to put my foot down.

Diana and I bought a mini-van and she learnt to drive. I loved that year. She'd hardly been out of London, and it was all new for her. She turned it on for me too.

As well as band work I compèred a big festival for Paddy in Blackpool, and a three-day stint in Cleethorpes.

At the Albert Hall around Easter 1963, Diz Disley, Rolf Harris and I were linkmen for a BBC spectacular of 'Jazz 'n' Pop'. The jazz bands got a lot of applause, but the stars of the evening were 'The Beatles', a group I'd only just heard of. The bell had begun to toll for trad.

Over the next two years trad died. Clubs closed. Managements turned over to Beat groups. Only the toughest bands survived. The Mulligan band, unaware of it at the time, did its last job. In '64 I hardly sang at all – a few cabarets, the festivals at Redcar and Cleethorpes were about my lot. We loved these jazz festivals. It's great to see the old faces milling about in the private bar tent. Humph, Sandy and Al, Jim Bray and Alex Welsh. It's like the instant vision of a whole life which is meant to flash before the eyes of the drowning.

At the time of writing rhythm and blues is taking over from Beat. This is nearer allied to trad and several of the bands have made the jump. What is good about rhythm and blues is that it has meant that almost every month one or more Negro blues singers come over on tour. We went to Croydon recently. A young, serious audience, and several figures from the past: Jimmy Asman and Derrick Stewart-Baxter.

Lately there have been some signs too of trad reviving on a small scale. I have sung recently in a South London pub and a rugger club out at Osterley. The audiences were enthusiastic. The atmosphere fresh again. It seemed to be for love not money.

Do I regret anything? Only this. I'm vain enough to find it hard to walk up the queue outside the Marquee on my way to listen to Howling Wolf, and to be completely unrecognised by several hundred blues fans. Wally Fawkes went through the same thing some time before me. He was a great figure in the revivalist days, second only to Humph. You get over it, he told me. I'm beginning to already.

When I started this book the trad boom was still on. Certain statements at the beginning are now inaccurate, but I'll let them rest. In the middle there are one or two references to the beat boom. That too is dying. If I was to aim at up-to-the-minute accuracy I should have to correct the proofs right up to publication date.

What has happened to the chaps?

Mick has his off-licence and grocery. He comes up to see me once a month with a booze order. He is still my manager. His character too has altered. He washes and shaves every morning. He works long hours to make his business a success. He has decided the time has come to 'pull his finger out', and yet his charm is as irresistible as ever. Under his white coat beats the same anarchic heart.

Ian, after a period as a photographer and a stint in a PRO office, is now a feature writer on the *Express*.

Fat John is doing lounge work. He has a trio in various clubs.

Appleby is still with Donegan. He turned up to see me not long ago in an American car that filled the street.

Frank is general manager for the Acker Bilk organisation.

Gerry Salisbury plays on Sunday mornings at a jam session in a pub in Kentish Town. He also works for a car firm.

What is marvellous is that once again I can listen to jazz. Sinclair Traill asked me if I would like to review blues records for him. 'We pay, of course,' he told me. Needless to say, he doesn't, but it's very exciting to get a packet of records every month.

But what about the raving and the birds? Don't I miss that bit, some people ask and more people think.

No. I read a book recently by a man now dead called Verrier Elwin. He was a marvellous old man who spent most of his life in India. He wrote this:

Today, and for many years past, my old loves have been concentrated on my beloved wife, in whom I have found the essence of them all. I am a better lover now for those experiences.

AFTERWORD

... and so I left the jazz world and became a journalist. That was forty years ago. It wasn't such an abrupt transition as you might think, though. Wally 'Trog' Fawkes and I usually dropped in to El Vino's, Fleet Street's famous fall-about station, after our weekly Flook conference at the *Daily Mail*.

My gamble paid off. Quite soon I had a TV column in the *Observer* and was appearing regularly on *The Critics*. My mother *was* pleased.

Diana and I had bought a large house in Gloucester Crescent surrounded by the trendy media. We lived a full social life, gave and went to dinner parties; I'd inherited a much-loved step-daughter, Candida, and we made a lovely son called Tom; we owned a cottage in Wales ... but by the end of the decade things weren't going so well between us and we nearly, but didn't quite, split up. We were still sometimes happy but more often sad.

On top of that, I felt there was something missing. Film scripts, books, an award for my *Observer* column; nothing seemed to lay this as-yet-unidentified ghost. Then Wally told me that on Sunday mornings several pro (or ex-pro) jazz musicians met to play for fun in a pub in Islington called New Merlin's Cave – and why didn't I drop in? So I did and found out what it was that had been haunting me – I was desperate to sing again.

Soon we were being offered jobs elsewhere. The Beatles' ex-PR Derek Taylor of Warner Brothers took us up. We made an LP and were invited to play, much to our surprise, at Ronnie Scott's (and we're still there every Christmas twenty-seven years later).

The work just escalated and something had to give. It did – I resigned from the *Observer* and John Chilton and I, with three other regulars from Merlin's, were back on the road. People thought we'd gone mad.

In the early 'Feetwarmers' days we were as wild as ever, probably wilder, as it all felt like playing hookey from the adult world. We toured the US several times, Asia and the Antipodes. We all came on as thirties' gangsters (now it's only me who wears fancy dress, although John remains a dandy). Gradually we got the act together – or at least John did. Not only a fine trumpet-player, he selects the material, arranges it, and watches my performance with a beneficent but constructive eye.

Jazz is not our whole life, though. Both of us, aware of Time's Winged Chariot, have other irons in the fire (I can mix a metaphor as well as the next man). John writes his meticulously researched jazz biographies. I write books too, lecture on modern art and broadcast quite a lot.

Yet jazz is mainly where we're at. We're drawing full and appreciative houses, and will continue as long as we can. We went pro again in '73 but these days, after the final number, I go no more a-roaming by the light of the moon. Diana and I, becalmed at times or driven before the storm, seem to have made harbour.

Yes, I have heard the chimes at midnight but now prefer to listen to them from a Queen-sized bed, in a comfortable hotel, sipping drinking chocolate and dunking digestive biscuits while wondering if I can quite be bothered to watch an 'adult' movie . . .

George Melly
April 2000

READ MORE IN PENGUIN

PENGUIN CLASSIC BIOGRAPHY

 Highly readable and enjoyable biographies and autobiographies from leading biographers and autobiographers. The series provides a vital background to the increasing interest in history, historical subjects and people who mattered. The periods and subjects covered include the Roman Empire, Tudor England, the English Civil Wars, the Victorian Era, and characters as diverse Joan of Arc, Jane Austen, Robert Burns and George Melly. Essential reading for everyone interested in the great figures of the past.

Published or forthcoming:

E. F. Benson	**As We Were**
Ernle Bradford	**Cleopatra**
David Cecil	**A Portrait of Jane Austen**
Roger Fulford	**Royal Dukes**
Christopher Hibbert	**Charles I**
	The Making of Charles Dickens
Christopher Hill	**God's Englishman: Oliver Cromwell**
Marion Johnson	**The Borgias**
James Lees-Milne	**Earls of Creation**
Edward Lucie-Smith	**Joan of Arc**
Philip Magnus	**Gladstone**
John Masters	**Casanova**
Elizabeth Mavor	**The Ladies of Llangollen**
Ian McIntyre	**Robert Burns**
George Melly	**Owning Up: The Trilogy**
Raymond Postgate	**That Devil Wilkes**
Peter Quennell	**Byron: The Years of Fame**
Lytton Strachey	**Queen Victoria**
	Elizabeth and Essex
Gaius Suetonius	**Lives of the Twelve Caesars**
	translated by Robert Graves
Alan Villiers	**Captain Cook**

READ MORE IN PENGUIN

In every corner of the world, on every subject under the sun, Penguin represents quality and variety – the very best in publishing today.

For complete information about books available from Penguin – including Puffins, Penguin Classics and Arkana – and how to order them, write to us at the appropriate address below. Please note that for copyright reasons the selection of books varies from country to country.

In the United Kingdom: Please write to *Dept. EP, Penguin Books Ltd, Bath Road, Harmondsworth, West Drayton, Middlesex UB7 0DA*

In the United States: Please write to *Consumer Services, Penguin Putnam Inc., 405 Murray Hill Parkway, East Rutherford, New Jersey 07073-2136.* VISA and MasterCard holders call 1-800-631-8571 to order Penguin titles

In Canada: Please write to *Penguin Books Canada Ltd, 10 Alcorn Avenue, Suite 300, Toronto, Ontario M4V 3B2*

In Australia: Please write to *Penguin Books Australia Ltd, 487 Maroondah Highway, Ringwood, Victoria 3134*

In New Zealand: Please write to *Penguin Books (NZ) Ltd, Private Bag 102902, North Shore Mail Centre, Auckland 10*

In India: Please write to *Penguin Books India Pvt Ltd, 11 Community Centre, Panchsheel Park, New Delhi 110017*

In the Netherlands: Please write to *Penguin Books Netherlands bv, Postbus 3507, NL-1001 AH Amsterdam*

In Germany: Please write to *Penguin Books Deutschland GmbH, Metzlerstrasse 26, 60594 Frankfurt am Main*

In Spain: Please write to *Penguin Books S. A., Bravo Murillo 19, 1°B, 28015 Madrid*

In Italy: Please write to *Penguin Italia s.r.l., Via Vittorio Emanuele 45/a, 20094 Corsico, Milano*

In France: Please write to *Penguin France, 12, Rue Prosper Ferradou, 31700 Blagnac*

In Japan: Please write to *Penguin Books Japan Ltd, Iidabashi KM-Bldg, 2-23-9 Koraku, Bunkyo-Ku, Tokyo 112-0004*

In South Africa: Please write to *Penguin Books South Africa (Pty) Ltd, P.O. Box 751093, Gardenview, 2047 Johannesburg*